This newly comprehensive and detailed exploration of the African past, reaching from prehistory to approximately 1870, is intended to provide a fully up-to-date textbook, thematically organized, for undergraduate students of African history.

Reflecting several emphases in recent scholarship, Professor Isichei focuses on the changing modes of production, on gender relations and on ecology, laying particular stress on viewing history 'from below'. A distinctive theme is to be found in her analyses of cognitive history.

The work falls into three sections. The first comprises a historiographic analysis, covering the period from the dawn of prehistory to the end of the Early Iron Age. The second and third sections are, for the most part, organised on regional lines; the second section ends in the sixteenth century; the third carries the story on to 1870. Explaining each facet of the continent's history with exceptional erudition, balance and sympathy, Professor Isichei displays both an immense learning and a thorough command of the literature.

A second volume, now in preparation, will cover the period from 1870 to 1995.

A history of African societies to 1870

A history of African societies
to 1870

ELIZABETH ISICHEI

University of Otago

CAMBRIDGE
UNIVERSITY PRESS

Published by the Press Syndicate of the University of Cambridge
The Pitt Building, Trumpington Street, Cambridge CB2 1RP
40 West 20th Street, New York, NY 10011–4211, USA
10 Stamford Road, Oakleigh, Melbourne 3166, Australia

© Cambridge University Press 1997

First published 1997

Printed in Great Britain at the University Press, Cambridge

A catalogue record for this book is available from the British Library

A catalogue record for this book is available from the Library of Congress

ISBN 0 521 45444 1 hardback
ISBN 0 521 45599 5 paperback

Contents

Contents

Illustrations

Figures

Maps

Acknowledgements

This book was begun at Cambridge in 1991 and so it seems particularly appropriate that it is published by Cambridge University Press. I am deeply indebted to Jessica Kuper, for her patience in waiting for the manuscript, and her flexibility about its length. I am also profoundly grateful to the book's three anonymous readers, whose assessments were enormously encouraging and helpful.

I visited Cambridge during a seven-month sabbatical leave. I am most grateful to the Fellows of Clare Hall, Cambridge, who elected me first to a Visiting Fellowship, and later to a Life Membership. During my sabbatical I also visited the University of Washington at Seattle, where I have the warmest memories of the kindness of Simon Ottenberg. I acknowledge, with gratitude, research funding from the University of Otago Division of Humanities Research Grants Committee, and a most timely grant from the University Research Grants Committee towards the costs of maps and indexing. I am grateful to my invisible friends of the Internet, especially the members of Nuafrica.

Much of this book has been written while I have been running a university department and carrying a heavy teaching load. I am greatly indebted to the helpfulness and efficiency of the Religious Studies Secretary, Sandra Lindsay, and of the staff of the University Library, particularly the Reference Department, for whom no interloan request was too obscure.

My beloved youngest son, Frank, was my companion during my sabbatical, as he is now, in Dunedin. It is dedicated to him.

Part I

Continental perspectives

Perimeters

The lyf so short, the craft so long to lerne,
Th'assay so hard . . .
                    Chaucer, *The Parlement of Foules*, I

I began original research into the African past in 1967, and taught history in African universities, first in Tanzania, and then in Nigeria, for sixteen years. My research led me to fieldwork in remote villages, and to both European and local archives. I was the first historian of the Igbo people of south-eastern Nigeria – whose population is greater than that of many independent nations – and of Plateau State. Now that I am much closer to the end of my career than its beginning, I felt drawn to attempt the history of the continent to which I devoted the best energies of my adult life.

A legend recorded among a small people in central Nigeria tells of a hero who plucks a blade of grass and through the hole reveals a whole new world.[1] He is then empowered by its discovery. Something of this magical transformation is experienced both by the westerner who embarks on a voyage to the cultures of other peoples and by the African who explores her own past.

And the end of all our exploring
Will be to arrive where we started
And know the place for the first time.[2]

The difficulty, of course, is that there is an infinite number of possible African histories. Our choices are limited by the available source materials, and also, to an extent greater than we might care to admit, by convention – the paths trodden by our predecessors. A historian who confined himself to a single region and a single theme reported, 'Scholars who attempt to synthesise a wide range of material quickly discover that they have a limited number of tools and an infinite array of intractable difficulties.'[3]

I have spoken of directions chosen by other historians, but there are many such paths. At one level, this book is a series of conversations with alternative views of the African past – particularly, though not exclusively, those most conveniently called Africanist and radical – categories explored in the pages which follow. These are debates to which my own earlier writings have contributed; my own voice in the past is one of those with which I engage.

No single model does justice to the complexity of a multidimensional past. This book is organised around a number of interlocking themes. Perhaps the most important is ecology, the interaction between African communities and their very different environments. Consciously or unconsciously, historians reflect the preoccupations of the present in their interpretation of the past. For obvious reasons, contemporary historians pay considerable attention to famines, epidemics and droughts, and these are themes which recur in the pages which follow. But a model based on scarcity does not do full justice to economies which often produced a surplus both of food and treasure. 'Here hunger is not known,' said the nineteenth-century Lozi on the Zambezi flood-plain.[4] Scarcity is a powerful explanatory tool for exploring the African past; but West and West Central Africa had some of the most varied currencies of the pre-industrial world. Like Africa's art treasures, they do not reflect want.

At the heart of all African history is the productive base – agriculture, pastoralism, crafts, mineral extraction, fishing, hunting and gathering. A true integration of gender into historical writing is to be attained not by concentrating on real or imaginary queens – though both find a place in this history – but by analysing production. Women often did the farming, and always processed and cooked food; they were often the potters, the spinners and weavers; in some societies they processed salt, and panned alluvial gold. Off the coast of Angola, they dived for shells used as currency. In West Africa, women usually controlled trade in foodstuffs in local markets; men traded in slaves, ivory or gold.[5]

The relations of production are central to an understanding of the political process. Radical history, however, has sometimes been criticised for concentrating on structures to a point where the particularity of the local community, or the life of the individual, becomes invisible.

This book is an essay in history from below. It required no conscious effort to populate it with people – they found their way into the narrative naturally and those who found no space fought for inclusion. History from below assumes a knowledge of the political superstructure; a study of the Crowd in the French Revolution presupposes some knowledge of a particular sequence of events in time. The historian of Africa cannot ignore the rise and fall of empires, which provide a much-needed chronological structure, and which impinged, of course, in varying ways and to varying degrees, on the life of the poor. African history has moved beyond an exclusive preoccupation with Great States and Big Men, but the study of the past, at least on a continental scale, can find no intelligible shape without them. And when we focus on individual experience, we find, inevitably, that it is the captains and the kings who are most fully documented.

Cognitive history is a central theme of this study; some African societies, especially in the Islamic world, have left a legacy of written texts, and much can be gleaned from oral literature. But many cognitive maps are represented in non-verbal forms, such as sculpture, body painting or textile designs. These are often difficult or impossible to locate in time, and when we interpret them in written texts there is a danger that we are in fact inventing something new. In a sense, of course, the whole business of writing about Africa is an invention, and much has been written in recent years on the artificiality of the enterprise.

A fundamental insight of much writing on Africa is the paramount importance of people (rather than land, or possessions). This is abundantly documented in oral sources, and is often adduced to explain domestic slavery. This leaves us with a problem – why were people sold abroad in the Atlantic or Indian Ocean slave trades, or killed in religious rituals? (Neither phenomenon, of course, was universal.) There seems to have been, in the thought of many African societies, a profound tension between different loci of value – the need to share and the need to accumulate, the desire for followers and the retention of treasures. Kings accumulated treasures – regalia, valuable cloth, sculptures in ivory, copper or gold. But in the nineteenth century, the home of an Igbo villager was also likely to include a sealed room for the family's wealth, often in cowries or manillas. It is a profound irony that these currencies, introduced by Europeans, became worthless in the colonial period.

African peoples tended to view the world as a zero sum game, where the prosperity of one is obtained at the expense of another. Witchcraft stereotypes grow out of this tension; it has been called the dark side of kinship.[6]

This book falls into three sections. The first deals with questions of historiography and interpretation, and with prehistory, ending with the Early Iron Age. The second and third sections are organised on a regional basis – the dividing line between them lies, very approximately, in the sixteenth century. History, of course, refuses to fit neatly into chronological or regional divisions. Zwangendaba's career began in Natal and ended in Tanzania. To reflect this extreme artificiality, I have deliberately used different geographic units of analysis in successive sections.

The sixteenth century can be taken as a dividing line between 'states based on local resources' and 'political structures heavily reliant on outside sources'[7] – largely through the impact of merchant capitalism. This period has been called an age of commercial elites and warlords – African, Muslim and European.[8] But many peoples were little affected by the outer world until well into the twentieth century; the states of the Western Sudan or the Swahili coast were involved in it long before 1600.

This book ends in 1870; a second volume is planned, to cover the period 1870–1995. I am mindful, however, of the Igbo proverb that no one is certain of his meal until he has eaten it!

It is very fully documented, and I have sometimes thought uneasily of the Moroccan scholar of the early eighteenth century, who gave 2,100 lectures on the particle 'b-'.[9] Data about sources are located primarily in notes, to integrate them closely with the text and thus enable the student to explore the literature on which a particular interpretation is based. I have tried to provide, within the covers of a single book, materials with which to explore themes as diverse as whether the Almoravids conquered ancient Ghana, and the impact of international capitalism on the San.

The great weakness of general histories of Africa is reductionism; because they cover vast expanses of space and time, they move at a very high level of generality, and the variety and multiplicity of African realities become invisible. Reductionism is not necessarily avoided by writing at considerable length, but it is certainly not avoided without it. I have endeavoured to write, not only history from below but a history in the round, a history which finds a place for art on the rocks, witchcraft beliefs, masking and spirit possession cults, as well as for cooking and the kitchen garden.

The modern study of Africa began in a state of euphoria; scholars believed, with Nkrumah, that if the political kingdom was attained, everything else would follow. The rapid collapse of parliamentary democracy and an ever spiralling external indebtedness soon undermined this optimism, which a partial return to democracy has done little to restore. The hopes of the optimists now focus on tiny Eritrea, and on the fragile balance of Mandela's South Africa.

Africanists sometimes fail to realise how little is known about Africa in the world around them. They would do well to reflect on the extent of their own ignorance of the history of Melanesia, or of Siberia. They are fond of affirming that it is no longer necessary to defend the existence of African history as a discipline. But, engaged in intricate debates among themselves, they often fail to realise how narrow is the beam of light all their industry sheds.

The general reader's image of Africa is derived from television and the press – a melancholy composite of Aids, famine, coups and civil war. Racial prejudice feeds on ignorance, as do political misjudgements. In contemporary Africa, hard-pressed governments sometimes question the utility of academic history. But both coups and corruption spring from despair – a despair which in its turn is rooted in a lack of historical perspective. A knowledge of the past is a necessary dimension of African self-esteem and sense of identity.

None of this, of course, means that the African past should be idealised, or romanticised.

> Speak of me as I am; nothing extenuate,
> Nor set down aught in malice.

Othello's words are an excellent guideline for the historian of Africa. The crisis of Africa has become a truism, not only among journalists but in the scholarly community. Many believe that there is indeed a crisis without precedent, attributed variously to exploitation by the so-called developed countries, ecological catastrophe, African misgovernment – or a combination of all three. African scholars have been particularly resolute in their analysis of the last variable. Others believe that the crisis lies less in objective reality than in our perceptions of it,[10] that it is one more in a long series of distortions in foreigners' perceptions of Africa. Undoubtedly, exploring Africa's past sheds light on the dilemmas of the present.

I would not wish to begin this study, or end it, on a note of gloom. Instead, I would like to borrow the words of a much earlier expatriate in Africa, which were substantially true of my own long stay. (I cannot, in all honesty, endorse his praises of the water supplies!) They come from the *Kebre Negast*, the national epic of Ethiopia, finally committed to writing in 1320. In it, Azariah, the Jewish priest who accompanies Menelik to Ethiopia, has this to say: 'And from the time that we have arrived in your country everything that we have seen hath appeared good to us. ... And as for what we have seen there is nothing detestable, and there is nothing malign in what we hear.'[11]

1

Prelude: Africa and the historians

> After a while the truth of the old tales changed. What was true before,
> became false afterwards.
>
> A Kuba elder[1]

Written sources

All history is ideological, because all history reflects the concerns of the
individuals and societies which produce it. What is remembered, and, where
possible, recorded is what is felt to be of enduring importance. Because of this,
we continue rewriting history – not because new facts come to light (though they
often do) but because we have learned to understand them in new ways.

A general work of synthesis is the visible apex of a pyramid, based sometimes
on original research, but more often on specialised studies written by others.
These rest in their turn on many different kinds of evidence. 'African history' is a
shorthand for many very different specialisations. The historian of medieval
Ethiopia works from manuscripts in Ge'ez – which few non-Ethiopians read –
and only Egyptologists (who do not consider themselves historians of Africa) can
understand the original records of ancient Egypt. The historian of Benin (the
Edo kingdom, not the modern nation) studied records in Portuguese, Italian,
French and Dutch, as well as English.[2] There is a vast body of material on the
African past in Arabic, much of it written by Africans, and also a corpus of work
in African languages, such as Fulfulde, Hausa and Swahili, transcribed in Arabic
script.[3] A history written in Arabic by a scholar of Timbuktu in *c.* 1665 is called
Kitab al Fettash, The Book of the Seeker; it would in many ways be appropriate for
the present volume.

Language skills are only part of the expertise required of the historian of
Africa; some studies have led their authors into subjects as arcane as the
properties of copper oxides and sulphates, or the different 'races' of sorghum.
Historians of Africa are perhaps unique in their readiness to absorb the findings
of other disciplines – archaeology, linguistics, human palaeontology, botany,
animal genetics, and geology – the list is far from complete.

In European sources, we perceive the African past through a glass, darkly. Its
authors rarely spoke the languages of the peoples they described (this is also true
of many modern academics) and they have always, inevitably, seen Africa
through the 'I-glasses'[4] of their own culture. A nineteenth-century English visitor
sketched the bronze pectoral mask which forms part of the regalia of the king of
Igala, in central Nigeria. He called it 'not unlike "the man in the moon"' and

drew it accordingly.[5] Because this sculpture still survives, we know his drawing is a travesty. But what if the original did not survive? Some of the source material in European languages was written by Africans; much of this, but not all, dates from the nineteenth and twentieth centuries. The autobiography of the Igbo, Olaudah Equiano (1745–97), is a justly celebrated example. He fell victim to the Atlantic slave trade as a child, but won his freedom and settled in England. Narratives from within, of course, are not immune from their own distortions. His account contains a number of literary echoes; his childhood home cannot be identified and its inconsistencies suggest it is a palimpsest of his own memories and those of other Igbo victims of the slave trade.[6]

Oral literature

There is a sense in which African studies are somewhat marginal, in universities outside Africa. And yet it has been claimed that African historians have been at the cutting edge of research methodology; those who suggest this are thinking, above all, of oral history.[7] The collection and analysis of oral literature – not only material of an overtly historical character – is of crucial importance in the study of the African past. Many African societies kept no written records, and because the spoken word is more difficult to preserve than the written one, oral traditions are rigorously selected. What is omitted is as revealing as what is preserved, and traditions sometimes speak most eloquently through their silences.

Certain patterns tend to recur. Traditions of origin are preserved as the founding charter of a state's identity. They are often symbolically rather than literally true; their interpretation tends to be obscure and disputed. The Mbundu of Angola have at least three different traditions of origin, and the Kuba of Zaire have no less than seven alternative creation myths. The question we must ask is not 'Which is true?' but 'What kind of truth do these embody?'

In kingdoms, traditions often have a court bias, the justification of a dynasty's right to rule. This often means that facts which run counter to this claim are elided or reinterpreted – a successful usurper becomes a younger son. Whole historical epochs were personalised, and their innovations attributed to a culture hero who is often a king. Shyaam, magician and first king, is such a figure among the Kuba. In the colonial period, traditions were often changed or even invented, to support one or the other claimant to political office, and the process continues. The spread of western education has led to the publication of oral histories, a task pioneered by western-educated Africans in the nineteenth and early twentieth centuries. This has preserved information which might otherwise have been lost, but books of this kind – Johnson's history of the (Oyo) Yoruba, Egharevba on Benin – tend to become an Authorised Version, making the collection of alternative traditions impossible. For, in only too common a paradox, informants trust the printed word rather than the continuation of that oral tradition on which the book was based in the first place.

Historians have tended to concentrate on centralised kingdoms rather than on peoples who lived in small autonomous villages. There are obvious practical reasons for this – it is much easier to write a history of a unified state than of, for instance, the 2,240 village groups of the eastern Igbo! But sometimes they have implied that centralised kingdoms were in some way more advanced than miniature polities – though those who think so would not consider Zaire more developed than Monaco.[8] Historical research tends to focus on large states and major ethnic groups, and the study of small peoples, such as the Yako or Rukuba, is generally left to the anthropologist.[9]

The *History of West Africa to 1800*, edited by Ajayi and Crowder, is a justly celebrated work which has been through three editions, in each of which chapters felt to be out of date have been replaced. But the chapter on 'stateless societies', written by an anthropologist, continues to appear in it – and to be very widely cited – though the approach is ethnographic rather than historic, and it concludes with a discussion of the growth of states. Great States re-emerge, even in a chapter devoted supposedly to the so-called 'stateless' polities.[10] And sadly, papers which set out to make a case for the study of small-scale states sometimes ignore the growing corpus of work in this field, in a most determined fashion.[11] Oral history has often been unconsciously elitist, because it has been collected from professionals, such as griots, who looked to a court patron. A recent valuable paper pointed out that a kingdom consisted of a number of social groups, each with its own oral history. The kingdom of Jaara, in modern Mali, was overthrown by al-Hajj Umar in 1862. Almost half the people in the region where it was located are of slave descent, and women of slave ancestry are the custodians of their oral tradition. It is a profound irony that those who were abruptly cut off from their history by enslavement join the custodians of the history of the captor society.[12] There is a further paradox: the African scholar who drew attention to these traditions does not, as a male, have access to them.

Oral tradition proper refers to testimonies which have been passed down, as distinct from reminiscence. But the latter is a precious source for the history of our own times, recording voices which are otherwise silenced.

Historians who collect oral traditions must also do archival research, but the reverse is not always true. Archival research and fieldwork require different skills and, to some extent, different temperaments. Archival research is solitary; some of its most gifted practitioners feel ill at ease with the constant encounters with strangers which oral history requires. Whatever the reason, an otherwise excellent book such as Freund's *Capital and Labour in the Nigerian Tin Mines* (1981) is marred by his inexplicable failure to interview living tin miners. Some historians obtain a comparable insight into individual experience by studying sources such as the popular press – but only a tiny minority of the African population was literate. Popular songs, folk tales and proverbs speak from the heart; they are a valuable source for cognitive history – the problem is that they are often undatable.

African historians collecting oral history among their own people have great advantages in fieldwork, especially in their command of the appropriate language. They may well not have the language skills or opportunity for research in widely scattered European archives. For most European historians, a facility in different European languages is more readily acquired than competence in a tonal and perhaps little-studied African language. This became evident to me in my years in Africa, in the course of innumerable encounters with historians from abroad grappling with what was then the obligatory *rite de passage* of fieldwork.[13]

In the case of some historians, this was a brief sojourn in the field, using interpreters, providing what was essentially a cosmetic veneer for a history in fact based on archival materials.[14] I made attempts to bridge this gap, first in *Igbo Worlds*, an anthology of both oral and archival sources, and later in the series Jos Oral History and Literature Texts.[15]

Some excellent works published in recent years have been based on archival sources alone. The author of one of them suggests an informal division of labour, European historians concentrating on the archives and African historians on fieldwork.[16] Scholars are coming to realise that the polarity between written and oral sources is itself an artificial one. The European authors of published and unpublished accounts of African history or ethnography relied on local informants, whose words are the submerged subtexts of their narratives.[17]

History and anthropology

Both oral historians and anthropologists do fieldwork in Africa, and the relationship between the two is a complex and changing one. In the past, historians were often critical of anthropological writing which was frequently – but not invariably – located in a timeless and imaginary ethnographic present. But anthropologists came much closer than historians to an understanding of African societies in their total complexity, studying variables such as kinship, ritual and culture. The divorce between the two was due less perhaps to doctrinaire considerations than to the impossibility of doing justice simultaneously to both structure and process.

Meanwhile, anthropologists have become increasingly sensitive to the variable of historical change. Some of the finest studies of the African past are the work of anthropologists – Peel's history of Ilesa, Horton's accounts of cognitive change among the Kalabari, Janzen's study of Lemba.[18] Historical writing has become richer and more densely textured, concerned with ecological factors including climate, famine and disease, religion and kinship.

Anthropological analysis has undergone an intensive rethinking from within; much of this has been the work of African specialists, such as Fabian.[19] Hard questions have been asked about fieldwork and it is realised that much anthropological enquiry has been formulaic – a classic instance of an invention of Africa. Vansina points out, with characteristic insight, the remarkable degree of similarity in the vast corpus of published and unpublished ethnographic writing on the Zaire basin. This undoubtedly reflects stereotyping in the questions asked.[20]

Functionalists and structuralists

Different schools of anthropology have mounted significant challenges to the methodology of the oral historian. The first form this took was functionalist – oral traditions were interpreted as a 'mythical charter' for present social realities. They often undoubtedly do work in this way, but this does not, in itself, invalidate them as a record of past events. Claude Lévi-Strauss is the founding father of structuralist anthropology, a school which was, for a time, immensely influential. He interpreted oral traditions not as more or less accurate mirrors of past events but as statements which embody a different kind of symbolic truth. The mind, he believes, tends universally to perceive reality in terms of paired opposites – such as Nature and Culture (symbolically expressed as the Raw and the Cooked, the title of one of his most famous books), or Life and Death. Legends which apparently tell of the foundation of states, for instance, are really essays in cosmic speculation, and belong rather to the history of ideas (which is not in itself to diminish them – rather the reverse).

Lévi-Strauss worked on Native American mythologies; his ideas were applied to central Africa in an enormously influential study by the Belgian anthropologist Luc de Heusch (see p. 112 below).

Some historians of Africa, notably Christopher Wrigley, absorbed the structuralist viewpoint to a degree which cast doubt on the literal veracity of virtually all historical traditions.[21] J. B. Webster and his collaborators were at the other end of the ideological spectrum, extrapolating the reigns of precisely dated kings far into the past, in a way most of their colleagues found unconvincing.[22]

Some historians are moving towards a more sophisticated synthesis in response to structuralism, where traditions are seen as neither entirely symbolic nor wholly true, but rather as a composite of myth and real event.[23] To disentangle the two is a task requiring great skill and subtlety. It was once assumed that oral traditions comprise a core of truth and a penumbra of myth. But it has been suggested that the core is a cliché, and the accretions mirror real events. But of course the symbols and clichés are also 'real', mirroring landscapes of the mind. Historians' increasing agnosticism about the literal truth of the traditions they collect is mirrored in a recent dictum by the scholar who pioneered the critical use of oral testimonies: 'For the most part [traditions of origin] represent cosmological speculation.'[24] These clichés, or recurrent core symbols, pose many problems of interpretation. Sometimes they are clearly part of a single far-flung complex: the myth of the immigrant hunter-king found throughout Africa's southern savannas is an example. But essentially the same myth is found far away, among various peoples in Nigeria. Woot, the Kuba culture hero, is a Drunken King, insulted by his sons, defended by his daughter. His wife discovers salt when she is a fugitive. Does this story embody echoes of missionary stories which gradually penetrated the Zaire basin from the Atlantic coast or are such stories the great archetypes of the mind which Jungian analysis attributes to the collective unconscious?

Historians are increasingly conscious of the way in which oral traditions are shaped both by the way in which human memory operates and by the fact that they are always related for an audience. The tendency for the concrete rather than the abstract to be remembered contributes to the crystallising of events and processes as clichés. Feedback from an audience helps make the testimony a collective product.

The basic tool of historical research is the quest for independent confirmation from different sources. This is a complex task, for sources are often not truly independent. The king lists of Bunyoro and Buganda, in Uganda, largely confirm each other; a chronology based on them, and other evidence, was hailed as a triumphant step towards locating the African past in a firm temporal context. Later critiques showed first that the Bunyoro list was not truly independent, but was consciously constructed to fit the Buganda data – which itself has come under increasingly critical scrutiny.[25] More profoundly, it has been suggested that the very making of lists is the product of a literate culture.[26] The distortion in the Buganda and Bunyoro king lists seems to be that of lengthening. But the limitations of human memory more commonly result in the telescoping of history. The process of settling in an area and the formation of large political units are entirely distinct phenomena, and the former is undoubtedly in most cases far more ancient. But even remembering this caveat, it is clear that the available evidence leads us to place the origins of many states far too late, and events which really belong to the Early Iron Age are transposed to the fifteenth or sixteenth centuries or even later. This is true of the interlacustrine kingdoms, and of much of Central Africa. It is also demonstrably true of some West African polities. All available evidence suggests that the Igbo have lived in much their present homes since the dawn of human history. But a dense network of mutually consistent family genealogies places the formation of many settlements in the sixteenth or seventeenth centuries.[27]

Where written sources extend far into the past, they provide a precious resource against which oral testimonies can be checked. Where they are lacking, until the nineteenth or even twentieth century, historians tend to rely on linguistic and ethnographic data, as well as a sensitive awareness of the dynamics of the traditions themselves. Where written evidence exists, it sometimes suggests that oral testimonies have a truly astonishing reliability.[28]

It has been suggested that both oral histories and traditional written chronicles focus on political events to the neglect of socio-economic change.[29] Vansina says of the Kuba, in words which are applicable to many other societies as well, 'For the most part, political events dealing with succession, war, law, administration, and the royal personality were remembered.'[30] Yet they do, in fact, preserve much socio-economic data, and these data are particularly valuable because they are not the primary focus. At the present time, the interpretation of oral tradition is at least as individualistic as art criticism. A highly regarded and sophisticated study of the Mbundu of Angola and their neighbours suggests that the people mentioned in historical traditions represent titles in the possession of particular lineages.[31] There is evidence to support it, but it cannot be conclusively proved, and the postulate is the basis on which the whole book rests.

The scholarly community tends to see the oral traditions of any given people through the eyes of its specialists – literally for much of Nigeria (but not Igala), symbolically in Central Africa.

Despite these caveats, oral history is often both remarkably accurate and strikingly truthful. Buganda, at the apogee of its power and influence, preserved traditions, both of its humble origins and of defeats at the hands of Bunyoro.[32]

Africa's historians

We have seen how both the written and oral sources for African history are shaped by the conscious or unconscious aims of their authors. This is, of course, equally true of modern historians. Nothing shows the way in which historical and ethnographic literature is shaped by one's preconceptions more clearly than the history and ethnography produced during the colonial period. Its authors were naturally preconditioned to be aware of the creative role of white invaders from the north. It was initially assumed that the stone structures of ruined Great Zimbabwe were the work of Phoenicians or built for the Queen of Sheba. Cecil Rhodes welcomed the theory of its exotic origins as it offered a positive precedent for intruders from afar.[33] Frobenius saw the corpus of Ife sculpture, the relics of its glass industry, as proof that it was the site of an ancient colony of Etruscans, the reality underlying Atlantis. Colonial ethnographers saw traces of Egyptian influence everywhere, bolstering their theories with amateur etymology.[34] The belief that sacred kingship and iron smelting diffused into black Africa from Egypt and Meroe respectively was to have a long history, surviving well into the period of modern scholarship. There were other versions of the so-called Hamitic hypothesis,[35] which attributed the foundation of states in the Western Sudan to a Berber or Arab *héros civilisateur*.[36] Sadly, some African writers welcomed such theories – sadly, because they had internalised the assumption that Egyptian civilisation was superior to that of black Africa.[37] European writers tended to glorify the achievement of ancient Egypt, while they marginalised not only black Africa but also the Maghrib, which a French author called 'one of those rare Mediterranean countries which made no original contribution to civilisation'.[38]

We should not, of course, dismiss the work of colonial ethnographers. The writings of colonial officials such as R. S. Rattray or C. K. Meek contain much of enduring value, and it is a sign of a maturing discipline that historians of Africa are increasingly willing to acknowledge this. A natural reaction against the Hamitic hypothesis led a generation of scholars to emphasise the indigenous roots of everything. Now they are more open to an understanding of black Africa's many linkages with the ecumene. Jan Vansina says – in this case, probably wrongly – of a distinctive theme in Nupe, Benin and Yoruba art, 'The whole motif derives from the Hellenistic Mediterranean.'[39]

It is no coincidence that the study of African history took shape as a serious field of academic endeavour at the time when many African states gained their independence. Both African and expatriate historians shared in the hopes those years engendered. Those historians who chose African history as a research field[40] did so out of a generous sympathy for African aspirations.

The dominant impulse in the 1960s – which I shared – was to prove that black Africa had a history at all, a history as worthy of study as any other. This was a salutary reaction to a historiography which saw Africans as the passive backdrop to the deeds of white proconsuls and missionaries. Not only the ignorant believed that black Africa had no history worthy of study: it was an Oxford historian justly famed for his scholarship who described the discipline as the study of the unrewarding gyrations of barbarous tribes,[41] thus drawing on his head the obloquy of a generation of Africanists. Max Weber, one of the founding fathers of sociology, had made much the same point earlier; he was 'indignant that the history of the Bantus could be studied as much as that of the Greeks'.[42] The great art critic Roger Fry, admiring African sculpture, reflected: 'It is curious that a people who produced such great artists did not produce also a culture in our sense of the word.'[43]

Historians of Africa were critical of colonialism, stressing the violence with which it was imposed, its often unconscious racism, its *immobilisme*. They laid great stress on resistance to its imposition, which was seen, both by scholars and by African politicians, as a prelude to the triumphs of political nationalism.[44] The first generation of politicians in independent Tanzania were the conscious heirs of Maji Maji, the great anti-German uprising in the early years of this century. Historians focussed primarily on political and economic history, studying great states partly to show that Africans were capable of creating and maintaining them. They wrote about long-distance trade, successful entrepreneurs, the rationality of African economic choices, in a conscious corrective to stereotypes of African inertia and backwardness.[45] For similar reasons, they devoted considerable attention to indigenous forms of literacy.

By the late 1970s, something of a crisis had developed in African historical writing.[46] The optimism which had heralded African independence became increasingly difficult to sustain. Civil wars, military coups, a cycle of impoverishment and indebtedness and recurrent famines, had a traumatic impact on a discipline which had been shaped by the exigencies of the present. Many historians – myself among them – interpreted these various afflictions as the (presumably temporary) consequences of particular historical circumstances. Thus political instability could be explained in terms of colonialism's divisive and artificial boundaries, and ethnic conflicts through its invention of ethnicity (pp. 97, 106, 123 below).

The historiography of the 1960s and early 1970s had undoubted weaknesses, including a reluctance to confront the deficiencies of African societies, past and present. However well-intentioned, this produced many imbalances of historical judgement. We have noted one example – the tendency to regard state formation, whatever the cost, as a Good Thing. Nowhere was this more glaring than in studies of the transatlantic slave trade, where the desire to depict the African as *homo economicus* rather than as victim or comprador led to an undoubted tendency to minimise its evils, and stress its positive by-products.[47] Shaka and the marauding captains of the Mfecane were depicted as creative state founders, with minimal emphasis on the enormous misery and loss of life for which they were responsible.[48] There was a tendency to ignore the exploitative aspects of pre-colonial states, and to idealise the traditional rulers who led resistance to colonialism, assuming that their interests were identical to those of the ruled. There was a marked tendency to eulogise African entrepreneurs of all varieties; gradually, the shortcomings of at least some of them became evident, and 'kleptocracy' became part of the vocabulary of academic discourse.

Reductionism was a weakness as fundamental as elitism. The initial focus of Africanist history was political; within this, it tended towards the analysis of Great States, and, in the words of a seventeenth-century visitor to West Africa, to the study of 'Kings, rich men, and prime merchants, exclusive of the inferior sort of *Blacks*'.[49] Peoples organised in small-scale states tended to be overlooked; here my own work, first on the Igbo and later on the Jos plateau, was a corrective.[50]

The Africanists of the 1960s and 1970s were attempting to demolish the mistaken stereotypes on which racism rests. They were also, in a sense, engaged in a conversation which may have been the wrong one to choose. In a partly unconscious endeavour to prove to critics like Trevor-Roper that Africa indeed had a history, they cast their own work in a quasi-European framework. Wilks' vast study of nineteenth-century Asante is a classic example. He was reacting against stereotypes, in early European accounts, which depicted Asante as bloodthirsty and barbaric. He constantly uses words such as bureaucratisation, and the less acceptable face of Asante life – human sacrifice – is interpreted as judicial execution.[51] The work is meticulously documented and researched; it has been criticised[52] on the grounds that by assimilating Asante life to western models, it diminishes and impoverishes it. Looking back on my own 'Africanist' years, I can see that I too was involved in a perpetual dialogue, both with the biases implicit in my sources and with the assumptions of other historians of Africa, who tended to define the African past in terms of Great States. I began *The Ibo People and the Europeans* with a quotation from Margery Perham: 'the groups of the south-east have no history before the coming of the Europeans'.[53] I felt that I needed to prove that the study of Igbo history itself was a valid enterprise. It seems to me now that this essentially defensive attitude was unnecessarily restricting.

The largest single cluster of African historians in the 1960s and 1970s was associated in various ways with the University of Ibadan. All were agreed in denouncing the shortcomings of missionaries and colonial governments. But there were considerable areas of ambiguity. Ajaye and Ayandele wrote books covering a quite similar area, concentrating on Nigeria's early educated Christians, the predecessors and in many cases the ancestors of the nation's later elite.[54] But in a later study, Ayandele denounced them furiously; significantly, it was not for any shortcomings in their social vision, but for their cultural ambiguity, their distance from their African roots.[55] Traditional rulers were sometimes idealised for their opposition to colonialism, sometimes, in a proliferation of studies of Indirect Rule, critiqued for their opposition to the modernisers. To a striking extent, the Ibadan school focussed either on resistance to colonial conquest or on aspects of government; many Nigerian historians came to take an active role in government, often as state commissioners in military regimes. Surprisingly little attention was paid to social history.[56]

The Marxist perspective

The most sustained and trenchant attack on 'Africanist' historiography came from Marxists (who often called themselves neo-Marxist, materialist or radical). At their most doctrinaire, they compressed all other historical writing about Africa into a single school, variously termed liberal, bourgeois, nationalist, historicist or Africanist. How sad and inexplicable it would once have seemed that 'Africanist' should become a term of condemnation, or empiricism be rejected as 'nihilism'.[57]

'Liberal' historians of Africa (to use the least pejorative term) do not form and have never formed a single united school. They have often been, very properly, enthusiastically at variance with each other. We have noted Wrigley's critique of

Fage; one might equally well note a myriad other controversies, including a famous exchange about the so-called Dar es Salaam school.[58]

Materialist historians, of course, do not form a united school either and beyond the core of those who consider themselves Marxists or neo-Marxists there is a large circle of scholarship, bearing the clear imprint of Marxist insights – as, indeed, the present work does. Iliffe's study, *The Emergence of African Capitalism*, takes Marx as its starting point.[59] Marxist writing on Africa has sometimes been barren and doctrinaire; there was once a sterile quest to accommodate African history to the writings of the Master, whose reflections were based on the experiences of industrial Europe. This led to unpromising lines of enquiry: in the 1960s there was much unprofitable debate concerning whether the African experience was an example of Marx's Asiatic mode of production. In 1972, the French Marxist Coquery-Vidrovich made an interesting attempt to define an African mode of production in terms of the way in which rulers reaped a profit from long-distance trade. This was widely criticised, not least because it emphasised exchange rather than production.[60] The rejection of experience in favour of dogma, somewhat in the style of a medieval theologian, is not entirely dead. In words which became, perhaps, for the historians of the 1980s what Trevor-Roper's sentiments on barbarian tribes were for their predecessors, two Marxists wrote: 'We reject the notion of history as a coherent and worthwhile object for study.'[61] This approach, especially associated with the French Marxist Althusser, provoked in one of Britain's most celebrated Marxist historians a furiously indignant polemic.[62] The forms which the rejection of experience can take are many and strange. A writer on the medical history of Tanzania is an example. 'In a Marxist construction of social reality ... only human agency is causal ... If only human action has causal efficacy, then germs cannot be said to cause disease.'[63]

And yet Marxist insights have inspired some of the most perceptive writing on the African past. A group of French Marxist anthropologists working in West Africa, and especially Claude Meillassoux, have had a great impact on African historical writing. Meillassoux made a plea for a more complex and nuanced study of modes of production, reacting against the (western) stereotypes of classical economics.[64] He focusses on what has been called the politics of reproduction, and in particular on the conflict between village elders and youths over the control of resources in general and wives in particular. Marxist and feminist analysis has shed much light on the division of labour by gender, and created a new awareness of women's role in production. Some have criticised Meillassoux on the grounds that the polarities he describes are not peculiar to Africa. This does not in itself invalidate his insights. Inevitably, he stresses structure rather than process; in a sense he extrapolates the experience of a few West African societies into a generally applicable model.[65] But he has had a transforming effect on historical writing – nowhere more than in South Africa, where, because of both its industrialisation and its class structure, Marxist concepts are most readily applied.

Marxist history has led to a more holistic approach to the African past, a greater awareness of material culture. It is a great strength of 'mode of produc- tion' theory that it concentrates attention both on the actual process of wealth creation and on its distribution in society.[66] It is a weakness that the application of the theory over vast areas may lead us to underestimate their differences, the particularities of local historical experience. Different scholars define and locate modes of production somewhat differently. A widely accepted sequence runs as follows: lineage mode of production, tributary mode of production, slave mode of production, merchant and then industrial capitalism. It tends to impose a false sense of a linear and inevitable development.

It is by no means always self-evident who is, and who is not, a Marxist – and it should be noted that *marxisant* is not a term of approval. (I was startled but not displeased, years ago, when a reviewer called me a disciple of Frantz Fanon, something of which I was hitherto unaware!) Wilks described his history of Asante as Marxist. Terray, whose Marxist credentials are indisputable, endorses Wilks' Marxist approach, but a critic pointed out that Marxism first appears on page 700![67] Even Coquery-Vidrovitch, a central figure in French Marxist writing on Africa, refers to her own intellectual preferences as 'supposedly Marxist'.[68] Klein says of himself, in words many historians of Africa would echo: 'my Marxism is rather diluted. I have difficulty accepting the labour theory of value and find it impossible to reduce all history to class struggle. Nevertheless, I find that the concept of a mode of production is a very powerful tool for historical analysis.'[69]

Another historian endearingly compared his own studies of French Marxist literature with the adventures of Winnie the Pooh in pursuit of a Woozle![70]

A mode of production has two parts: the *forces* of production (ecology, labour, technology, raw materials) and the *relations* of production (the extraction and distribution of a surplus). Clarence-Smith suggests some detailed questions:

Who controlled (not owned) the means of production and how? If . . . a restricted group, what right of access did the majority of the population have, and in return for what kinds of payment? Was the extracted surplus redistributed, or was it wholly, or partially retained by the restricted group? If it was retained, how was it realised, in economic investment, leisure activities, conspicuous consumption, or the mainte-nance of repressive political and ideological apparatuses? . . . Did the dominant group interfere directly in the process of production?[71]

An awareness of the changing relations of production informs some of the best writing on archaeology.[72] It shapes some outstanding historical monographs: Kea's densely textured work on the seventeenth-century Gold Coast is enor-mously richer than its 'Trade and Politics' predecessors.[73] The difficulty is that the study of a large number of variables tends to obscure the chronology of events. It is a central problem in multidimensional history. And the model, while shedding light on reality, should not be confused with reality itself. 'Modes of production do not exist.'[74]

Some exponents of Marxism have written as if the world of culture and ideas was simply the reflection of the material base. There are, of course, passages in Marx which say just this: 'The mode of production of material life conditions the social, political and intellectual life process in general. It is not the consciousness of men that determines their being, but, on the contrary, their social being that determines their consciousness.'[75] Marx, however, did say that he was not a

Marxist![76] One of the most important differences between palaeo – and neo-Marxists is the latter's increasingly sophisticated awareness of the autonomy of cognitive history.[77]

Dependency theory

There is a fundamental division in radical thought about the merits of dependency theory.[78] It draws its inspiration from the writings of André Gunder Frank, who was concerned with 'the development of underdevelopment' in Latin America. Frank regarded the impoverishment of the Third World as an ongoing process, the result of the exploitation of the metropolitan countries. The late Walter Rodney and Samir Amin were influential proponents of this viewpoint in the African context. The title of the former's most widely read book, *How Europe Underdeveloped Africa*, still worth reading for all its polemicism and oversimplifications, encapsulates the theory.[79]

Orthodox Marxists are critical of dependency theory on several grounds: that it emphasises trade rather than production, and that it negates Marx's emphasis on the positive aspects of capitalism. They also point out that it tends to replace class with regional conflict.

I was greatly influenced by dependency theory when I worked on the impact of the Atlantic slave trade on the Igbo, since it seemed to cast much light on this encounter. Dependency theory critiques the comprador, the local collaborator who makes external exploitation possible, whether the king who sells slaves, or the modern politician or military ruler who enriches himself by collaboration with the big multinationals. But dependency theory has its limitations. It reduces Africans to the helpless victims of international market forces and sheds no light on the long periods of time when external exploitation was unimportant. International capitalism had no impact at all on the Anaguta of Jos plateau in central Nigeria until the early twentieth century. As late as the 1950s, its impact was insignificant, in part through the conscious choices of the Anaguta themselves.[80] Dependency theory ignores the enormous differences between the different peoples who experienced the impact of international economic forces and responded to them in one of a wide variety of ways. It is profoundly pessimistic about their capacity to transform their own lives. Perhaps, in its own way, it is just as Eurocentric as the Hamitic hypothesis.

The basic inspiration of both Marxists and dependency theorists is concern for the poor. But this has, increasingly, become a central preoccupation of African historical writing in general. It derives, in part, from a tradition of 'history from below'[81] in English scholarship. Often specific insights from historical research elsewhere have fed into African studies; Hobsbawm wrote a famous book on bandits, and in due course, a collection of essays on banditry in Africa appeared.[82] Possibly bandits have replaced Improvers as the historian's romantic heroes. But many historians of Africa who do not consider themselves particularly radical are concerned with the poor and obscure. That monument of scholarship and humanity, Iliffe's *The African Poor: A History*, is a particularly distinguished example of History from Below.

The least satisfactory aspect of some – not all – radical writing was its intolerance of alternative views, its tendency to regard all non-Marxist writing as a 'school' to be condemned. I pointed out long ago that a belief in the verbal inspiration of sacred texts, intolerance of alternative views and conviction of one's own infallibility have long since been unacceptable in theology. Should it be otherwise in African history?[83] But having said this, it is important to acknowledge that some of the most original writing in African history is the result of materialist insights, and its influence is writ large on the pages which follow.

All research is in some sense ideological; facts neither select nor explain themselves. What is important, is that theory should illumine historical research, and never replace it.

Goethe said, 'Grey is every theory, and green and gold is the tree of life.'

Alternative models: Braudel and *la longue durée*

Fernand Braudel, who died in 1985, was one of Europe's most celebrated historians. His masterpiece was his two-volume study of the Mediterranean in the age of Philip II,[84] a work of great erudition, full of finely observed social detail – the walnut trees which shade villages in the High Atlas, fuel shortages in Cairo. It was immensely influential, not least as an example of history in the round.

Braudel was impatient with sociologists, feeling that they paid too little attention to social change.[85] But he was also critical of 'the history of events: surface disturbances, crests of foam ... surface manifestations of these large movements and explicable only in terms of them'.[86] He stressed the importance of social processes occurring over centuries – *la longue durée*. The expression threads its way through his writings, and is echoed in much historical literature which appears to owe little else to his work. It has become part of the baggage of historical writing. There has been a reaction; some notable modern scholars have written in defence of narrative history.[87] Dates and 'events' are necessary points of reference in an otherwise unnavigable sea – and it is notable that part of Braudel's great work was in fact concerned with 'events'.

Braudel paid much attention to the physical environment; scholarship has moved beyond his rather simplistic and static geographical determinism. His book is full of pictures of Mediterranean ships but he does not reflect on the consequences of the timber cut to build them.[88]

Braudel's impact on African studies has been limited.[89] This is partly because he began his research in 1923, and published the first edition of *The Mediterranean* in 1946, relying, therefore, for his North African material on French ethnographers writing in the inter-war period whose work has long since been overtaken by more recent scholarship. Not surprisingly, his influence has been greatest on those working in related fields, that is, on historians of the Maghrib.[90]

Landscapes

In *The Ibo People and the Europeans*, published over twenty years ago, I wrote of 'a people in a landscape', a theme to which I reverted in my *History of Nigeria*. This emphasis grew, not from Braudel, whom I had not at the time read, but from the experience of living successively in very different African environments. The importance of ecology is one of the key insights of contemporary writing on Africa. Book titles and subtitles reflect this – *The Ecology of Survival*[91] or *The Historical Anthropology of an African Landscape.*[92] It grows out of the too evident impact of a deteriorating environment on contemporary human lives. A treatise al-Maghili wrote in the late fifteenth century for the benefit of a king of Kano has a curiously contemporary resonance: 'Cherish the land from the spoiling drought, from the raging wind, the dust-laden storm . . . and the beating rain.'[93]

Sometimes a failure to locate historical writing firmly in a changing landscape reflects an inadequate familiarity with it; southern Nigeria is often described in books and atlases as located in a belt of 'rainforest'; there is indeed a substantial area of which this is true – the Benin forest – but most of southern Nigeria has been transformed for many generations by human industry. It was said of Yorubaland, in 1891: 'Far and wide, the land has for generations, and indeed for centuries, been cultivated by these industrious natives. The hatchet, the fire and the hoe have removed all traces of the original forest.'[94]

Famine and disease, for obvious reasons, loom large in modern historical writing. Ford's pioneering study of the impact of tsetse fly, published in 1971, was a precursor.[95]

Alternative models: the frontier

Interesting attempts have been made to adapt Jackson's concept of the frontier, which has been so seminal in American historical writing.[96] In an African context, this becomes less a tide sweeping across a continent than an infinite series of internal frontiers, a recurrent pattern of pioneer settlers who then become 'owners of the land' in relation to later immigrants. Often this movement is essentially conservative – the migrants endeavour to recreate the social structures of the society they have left, but with a more favourable position within it. Like the white settlers of America, the frontierspeople very often moved into areas which were already inhabited.

One strength of this approach is that it moves beyond the invention of watertight and monolithic 'tribes' and finds room for the – often multilingual – people of the borderlands. An alternative, independent form of the model focusses on the Islamic frontier.[97]

The problem of gender

Half Africa's people are women. They are responsible for virtually all food preparation and child rearing, and often play a dominant role in agriculture. Crafts are gender-specific, and in many areas women control trade (specific commodities are often sold only by men or only by women). But in much historical writing women are invisible, except for the rare, and sometimes legendary, queen. This is equally true of some of my own earlier work. I felt alienated from the feminist writing of the 1960s and early 1970s because of its white middle-class character – limitations which mainstream western feminism has long since recognised and reacted against. I felt that it was self-indulgent to agitate about matters such as inclusive language in liturgy when millions were threatened by famine. Partly because of the admiration I felt for the vitality and achievements of the Nigerian professional and market women with whom I was in daily contact, I did not sufficiently recognise the way in which colonialism eroded the position of women, or the fact that they are often the poorest of the poor. Women's invisibility in academic writing in the colonial period and later did much to cause their neglect in many development projects, which too often left women both poorer and more burdened than before. This distortion was recognised and in part corrected, largely through the writings of feminist scholars.

Feminist, like radical, scholarship has fed important insights into African studies as a whole, inspiring, for instance, some notable studies of the history of the family. But studies of women and the family have often been compartmentalised – books and papers are either totally concerned with women, or not at all.

There is an increasing awareness of gender in work which is not specifically feminist. The anthropologist van Binsbergen studied the Nkoya, a Zambia people also known as the Mbelwa, and while doing so translated a traditional history by a local pastor, assuming that rulers whose gender was unstated were male. It ws only when he was asked to contribute to a conference on the Position of Women in the Early State that he read the text with new eyes, and came to understand it as describing a transition, from 'a peaceful stateless situation when ... women were politically and ritually dominant to male-headed systems in which violence predominated'.[98]

Conventional histories concentrate on political and economic change, and many fine studies focus exclusively on men in positions of authority, the Captains and the Kings. The balance is not to be redressed by concentrating on the rare historical instances of women in authority, such as Nzinga (p. 399 below), but by directing our attention, as Marxist historians urge us to, to the forces of production.

Cultural expression tends to be gender-specific too: men are metal workers, wood carvers or masked dancers; women have their own outlets which vary from culture to culture but may include particular genres of oral art (like the grinding songs of northern Nigeria) or textile design or body painting. These have often been little studied; if they change at all, the process is difficult to document. Much of their communication is non-verbal. Can these unheard voices and unseen symbols find a place in a general study? I grapple with this problem in the pages which follow.

Whose discourse?

African history has been written either by westerners, or by Africans trained in western traditions. It has been suggested that 'the study of Africa, more than of any other continent, has been dominated by aliens and their theories'.[99] A recent pamphlet by a group of eight church leaders in South Africa, six of whom were women, and most of whom were illiterate, made the same point.

Until now all the research and all the literature about the so-called 'African Independent Churches' has been the work of outsiders. Anthropologists, sociologists

and theologians from foreign Churches have been studying us for many years and
they have published a whole library of books and articles about us. Each of them has
had his or her own motives for studying us. Generally, their motives have been purely
academic. We have become a fertile field for the kind of research that will enable a
person to write an 'interesting' thesis and obtain an academic degree . . . It is therefore
not surprising that we do not recognise ourselves in their writings. We find them
seriously misleading and often far from the truth. They are full of misunderstandings,
misconceptions and falsehood. In trying to understand us outsiders suffer serious
handicaps. They have their own frame of reference, the assumptions of anthropology
or sociology or a Western theology. We find ourselves judged in terms of these
norms.[100]

These words make sobering reading for a historian of Africa.

Scholars have become aware that all ethnographic description is, in a very real
sense, an Invention of Africa.[101] Some peoples – the British, French and
Americans among them – conduct ethnographic studies, and others are perpetually studied. Those studied would not recognise themselves in the accounts
which are written of them, to which they tend not to have access anyway. The
problem is not solved by learning an African language, or entering with great
empathy into the world of the Other. We are prisoners of the rationalism taken
for granted in the western world. An example makes this clearer. In 1873–4,
British forces defeated the Asante. The western historian will explain it in various
ways: the disparity in armaments and resources, or various factors which
weakened the Asante. Asante tradition has a different explanation: it was caused
by the loss of the Asantehene's war charm in the Pra river.[102]

The concept of academic history, its diverse subdivisions – political, economic,
social, religious – grew up in the western world. Those who study the African
past, myself included, are the prisoners of intellectual categories which did not
develop in Africa. The alternative is not to invent a system of 'African thought'
and work within its categories. Such endeavours have been made and found
wanting.[103] A facile solution is to place everything in inverted commas – 'slaves',
'Nguni' – but this becomes little more than a stylistic affectation.

Anthropologists of Africa, rather than its historians,[104] have been influenced
by thinkers conveniently called postmodernists or poststructuralists. Some of the
best known names are those of Foucault, Derrida, Ricœur and Toulmain, and
the semiotician (and novelist) Eco. They are, in many respects, at variance with
each other, but they share certain basic assumptions. A key word in their writing
is 'discourse', by which they mean the total system of language and meaning in a
given society, which, unconsciously, shapes our thinking from the cradle to the
grave. Foucault regarded it as an instrument of coercion, and in studies of the
European past used the approach of the 'archaeologist' to resurrect forms of
discourse which have been forgotten or marginalised.[105] Foucault was oblivious
to the Third World: his vision was not only Eurocentric but francophone, but his
insights have been applied to other parts of the world in a number of thought-
provoking studies. Edward Said wrote of 'orientalism' as the creation of
European thought.[106] Its implications for anthropology were explored in a series
of important books, where specialists in Africa made major contributions.[107]

The problem is perhaps most acute in the case of symbolism. A symbol, by its very nature, has many dimensions of meaning. What is the relationship between the symbolic universe the scholar analyses in an African people and their own perceptions? The late Victor Turner described the extremely rich symbolic universe he found among the Ndembu. If the Ndembu themselves did not – could not – analyse their own rituals in the same way, does this kind of description truly mirror their own cognitive world? In Mary Douglas' fine study, *Purity and Danger*, she states explicitly, with reference to her account of the Lele pangolin cult: 'The metaphysical implications have not been expressed to me in so many words by Lele ... No one member of the society is necessarily aware of the whole pattern.'[108] In other words, she discerns patterns in the Lele experience which are not apparent to the Lele themselves.

We have referred to the increasing readiness of materialist historians to accept the validity of African cognitive maps. An important collection of essays on South African history is subtitled 'African class formation, culture *and consciousness*'.[109] A valuable study of a Zionist church in South Africa describes its thought, often expressed in non-verbal ways, as *appropriate* for its members' life situation.[110]

Religion is often of great importance in African cognitive maps, past and present, though in the holistic universe of the 'traditional' way there was no word for religion, and no concept of it as a distinctive mode of being. 'If a people's behaviour is in part shaped by their own images and concepts, to the degree that these images and concepts are ignored and alien ones imposed or applied, that behaviour will be misunderstood and faultily explained.'[111]

An influential book published in 1980 was called *The Invention of Culture*. It was echoed in the title of a study by a brilliant Zairois scholar, V. Mudimbe, *The Invention of Africa*.[112] Historians and anthropologists have come to realise that we invent cultures, rather than describing them, that their books are 'true fictions'. The anthropologist's field notes describe one social fact but not another. She attends one ceremony but not another held at the same time – or, of course, those held before her arrival or after her departure. Her informants have their own silences: some are intended, and some reflect the fact that people describe what they think of, what seems important at a particular time. The historian does the same: she takes notes on a tiny fraction of what she reads, selecting those passages which seem significant at that particular time. Studies have been made of the silences in famous texts: the invisibility of Nuer and Dinka women in Evans-Pritchard's writing on the Nuer, Lienhardt's *Divinity and Experience* (on the Dinka).[113]

We have learned to look askance at the academic conventions which once ruled unquestioned. The poststructuralists have not created a new paradigm but have taught us to see the limitations of old ones. They have reminded us of the artificiality of the various academic disciplines into which we divide our interpretation of reality. Neo-Marxists have long symbolised their critique of these divisions by their adoption of the term 'political economy'. Poststructuralists tend to opt for 'ethnography'.

Points are easily scored off the poststructuralists, who sometimes write as if they alone stood outside the discourse of their time. No one does. One may catch glimpses of another cognitive world in a society like nineteenth-century Asante, where the primary documentation is abundant and the secondary literature perhaps uniquely rich. Nothing more.

Societies, like individuals, make a series of decisions, which are often subconscious, about what is important to them; these decisions are reflected in their lives more than in their words. It has been said that the Australian Aborigines have chosen not to accumulate possessions, in order to be free to elaborate complex worlds of religion and art. In Africa, much of the most advanced technology went into bronze sculpture. Iron, smelted at great cost in fuel and labour, was used in sculpture, as well as for utilitarian purposes. Wood carving (with built-in obsolescence in a tropical environment), the energy expended in dance, masking cults, religious rituals, all embody cultural choices. It is difficult to reflect them in a book of this size, but I have attempted to do so, in so far as the existing literature allows. The study that follows is a theme in counterpoint which concentrates, above all, on three variables – the ecological factor, the economic base, which made everything else possible, and the cognitive maps Africans constructed to make their world intelligible.

Silences

Oral and written sources sometimes speak most eloquently in their silences. These silences are deafening, but it is not always easy to know what they mean. Historians are becoming aware of the importance of 'listening for silences', aware, too, of a 'past containing many voices, often discordant ones'.[114] The difficulty is that many of these voices can no longer be heard.

Historical texts reflect, not the totality of historical experience, but that small fraction of it which is preserved in various kinds of source material. These sources themselves are often explicit about their silences. In the words of one version of the Sundiata epic:

> If you ask whether in that intervening period [between two
> famous kings] there were other kings,
> Of course there were,
> But their names are not known.[115]

In the 1820s, it was said of the Akan, 'Little kingdoms have been ... annihilated ... whose names have almost become obsolete.'[116] In the words of a modern historian, summarising one dimension of the work of a generation of French poststructuralists: 'The historian is never a specialist of past events ... He [*sic*] is ... a specialist of past signs [sources]. More accurately, he is a specialist of those past signs which have survived into the present.'[117]

We construct our own maps to make sense of both familiar and unfamiliar landscapes. But 'map is not territory'.[118] Of this, we must continue to remind ourselves.

2

Out of Africa: the precursors[1]

> All interest in the past is a dialogue ... The more precisely we listen,
> and the more we become aware of its pastness, even of its near-
> inaccessibility, the more meaningful the dialogue becomes. In the
> end, it can only be a dialogue in the present, about the present.
>
> M. I. Finley[2]

Where should a history of Africa begin? Any answer is essentially arbitrary. I have
opted for an extreme form of *la longue durée*, and begin at the very dawn of
human history. Lévi-Strauss once pointed out that history consists of 'areas each
of which is defined by a frequency of its own ... Dates do not form a series, they
belong to different species. Coded in the system of prehistory, the most famous
episodes of modern history would cease to be relevant.'[3] Here we deal with
millions of years; as we come closer to the present, the entire time frame alters.
Contemporary Africa, as presented in the media, often appears as a chaotic
backwater. But if we enlarge our time frame sufficiently, we find that humanity
began in Africa. The earliest fossil remains of proto-humans, or hominids, have
been found there, and also the earliest examples of anatomically modern man.
Archaic forms of *Homo* migrated out of Africa, and colonised the Asian land
mass. From there, humanity was to spread to Europe, the New World, and
Australia.

Our knowledge of prehistory has been transformed over the past three decades
or so, and continues to develop by leaps and bounds. The first hominid fossil in
the Olduvai Gorge, in modern Tanzania (Map 1), was found by Mary Leakey in
1959, and the partial skeleton which became internationally celebrated as Lucy
in 1974. An article by molecular biologists, published in 1987, claimed that we
are all descended from an African Eve; this research has now been very seriously
questioned. New hominoid species were discovered in Kenya in 1985–6, and in
Namibia in 1992.[4] As research continues, the frontier of knowledge advances
rapidly, and out-datedness is a standard complaint which recurs in reviews by
archaeologists of general books in their own discipline. The interest of all this is
not purely antiquarian. In what other branch of study do the latest discoveries
figure prominently in *Time*? The findings of prehistory shed a most fundamental
light on the human condition. The debate between 'Out of Africa' and 'Regional
Continuity' theorists (p. 36 below) has momentous implications, because it is
basically about whether ethnic differences are relatively recent, or go back to the
dawn of humanity. Studies of our earliest ancestors, like those of our closest

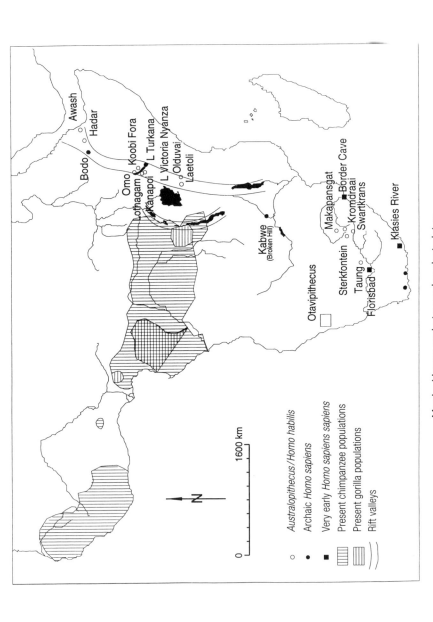

Map I Human evolution: archaeological sites

Awash
Hadar
Bodo
Omo Koobi Fora
Lothagam L Turkana
Kanapoi
L Victoria Nyanza
Olduvai
Laetoli
Kabwe
(Broken Hill)

Otavipithecus

Makapansgat
Border Cave
Sterkfontein Kromdraai
Taung Swartkrans
Florisbad
Klasies River

1600 km

N

0

○ *Australopithecus / Homo habilis*
● Archaic *Homo sapiens*
■ Very early *Homo sapiens sapiens*
▦ Present chimpanzee populations
▥ Present gorilla populations
))) Rift valleys

relatives, shed much light on the human condition. Jane Goodall, who studied chimpanzees in their natural state for decades, was disconcerted to find that they are not always vegetarians, and sometimes made lethal war on each other.

Nearly all hominid fossils survive in fragments only. A whole new genus was identified on the basis of nothing more than part of a jawbone (p. 29 below). Largely because of this, there is much controversy about the relationship between various proto-human and archaic *Homo* remains. It has been jocularly said that human palaeontology, like theology and extraterrestrial biology, contains more practitioners than objects of study!

The archaeologist of Africa inhabits a very different mental world from that of the historian. Prehistory spans whole geological and climatic epochs and its dates are often given as so many million years ago (mya).[5] Its evidence is derived from excavations, the study of ancient stones and bones. Inevitably, it lacks the human interest and individual detail which give warmth and life to history books. (In a sense the popular names which tend to be given to fossils – 'Zinj',[6] Lucy, Twiggy, the First Family – reflect this.) But it sheds light on a past far too distant to be reflected in oral histories or written records, and yields solid quantifiable data about economic life and technological change which often cannot be obtained so satisfactorily in any other way. The analysis of the animal bones at butchery sites, for instance, provides detailed information about diet. But just because our understanding of these vast expanses of time rests largely on stone tools and fossil bones, there is scope for radical differences of opinion, on both chronology and interpretation. When was speech introduced, or the controlled use of fire? Did Europe's Neanderthals die out, or have they contributed to the gene pool of modern humanity? Was early *Homo* a hunter or a scavenger? 'Ardrey believes in the "killer-apes", Isaac in a kind of middle-class genteel protohuman who shared his food . . .; for [Richard] Leakey and Lewin, hominid life was an impoverished projection into the past of Richard Lee's ideas about the !Kung Bushmen.'[7]

There has often been difficulty in reconciling the evidence of ancient bones and ancient stones. Bones shed light on biological change; stone tools and other artefacts, on culture. The Neanderthals – often marginalised as 'cavemen' in popular consciousness – were physically different from *Homo sapiens sapiens*, but had a very similar culture.

There is a considerable element of geological and human chance in the preservation of the archaeological record. The distinctive central Nigerian terracottas associated with the Nok culture[8] were discovered in the course of opencast tin mining. Had tin not been present, quite fortuitously, in the same soil, their presence would remain unsuspected. In great expanses of Africa, no excavation has been done at all.

There is a lively debate on the whole Darwinian concept of evolution. One problem is that the transition from one species to another is seldom documented in the fossil record.[9] This can be explained by its incompleteness – very few bones survive to become fossils. ('Even the best fossil beds preserve evidence of about one skeleton per million.')[10] But there are other difficulties. What kind of transition is possible, for instance, between vertebrate and invertebrate, or jawed and jawless? An alternative model is that of 'punctuated equilibrium, of rapid (in geological terms) change between long periods of stasis'. This is popular today, but is scarcely new. T. H. Huxley wrote in 1870. 'Mr Darwin's position might, we think, have been stronger than it is if he had not embarrassed himself with the aphorism, *"Natura non fecit saltum"* ... We believe ... that Nature does make jumps now and then.'[11]

An allied problem is that of why species – whether australopithecines or dinosaurs – which have lasted successfully for millions of years, disappear. Dinosaurs vanished abruptly 65 million years ago, apparently because the earth collided with a giant comet, and the consequent dust clouds occluded the sun, so that many plant and animal species died. The reasons for the much more recent disappearance of australopithecines and archaic humans are far from clear.

Chronology provides the basic structure which makes historical understanding possible. The dating of archaeological remains is an extremely complex and technical procedure, which has advanced very rapidly over the last twenty years. A relative chronology can be ascertained from stratigraphy – the study of the layers in which bones or artefacts are found in the soil. If they have remained undisturbed, older items should lie under more recent ones, but the layers may well be disturbed, by earthquakes, volcanic action, erosion, or human agency. A valuable application of this principle is biostratigraphy – dating hominid remains by studying the other faunal remains in the same strata (fossil pigs, elephants, antelopes and so on) and comparing them with sequences and dates elsewhere.

A number of scientific techniques have been developed to establish an absolute chronology.

- Radiocarbon dating is by far the most important technique for the time span with which historians – as distinct from prehistorians – are concerned. It can be applied only to materials of organic origin, and has a maximum time depth of some 40,000 years. The principle on which it works is that the carbon-14 isotope decays at a constant rate from the moment of death of an organism. It has a half-life of about 5,700 years.

- Potassium-argon (K /Ar) dating relies on the fact that potassium-40 gradually changes into argon-40, with a half-life of 1.3 billion years. It is invaluable for earlier periods but it can only be applied to rocks of volcanic origin. (That is, it dates not bones but the rocks in which they are embedded, which in itself opens the way to many possibilities for error.) This technique was first used in the 1960s, when it showed that 'Zinj' lived 1.75 mya (now recalculated to 1.79).

- Fission-track dating relies on the fact that uranium-238 atoms fission spontaneously at a regular rate.

- Accelerator Mass Spectrometry has improved both uranium and C-14 dating. AMS requires much smaller quantities of sample material than conventional radiocarbon dating and provides results much more rapidly. It 'has an application in a wide range of isotope-based dating techniques used in a number of different sciences'.[12] 'Java Man' was discovered last century; a recent redating resulted, not from the discovery of new fossils, but from the application of new technology.

- Fluorine analysis measures the amount of fluorine absorbed from ground water by buried bones; it was this technique which proved in the 1950s that the Piltdown skull was a hoax.[13]

- Palaeomagnetism – used to date the oldest stone tools – is based on shifts in the earth's magnetic pole, which has not always been in the north but has reversed itself at 0.7 mya, 2.5 mya and 3.4 mya.[14]
- Dendrochronology, the study of tree rings, has been used mainly in the American north-west.
- Thermoluminescence is a dating technique which was originally applied to pottery, and electron spin resonance is usually applied to teeth. Both estimate the effect of natural radiation.

Some of these techniques – and there are others[15] – are still experimental; the data on which they rely can be influenced by many different factors. To take just one example, the Oldowan event was a period of 160,000 years when the earth's magnetic field was reversed – a reversal within a much longer epoch of reversal. Usually, several of these techniques are applied simultaneously: the earliest stone tools from Olduvai have been palaeomagnetically dated; the rock in which they and early fossils were found has been dated by the potassium-argon method.

The beginnings

It was during the Miocene, which began 22.5 mya and ended 5 mya, that the ancestors of humanity diverged from our closest relatives, the African large-bodied hominoids, the gorilla and the chimpanzee.[16] The DNA of humans and chimpanzees differs by only 1.6 per cent and they seem to have diverged 5–6 million years ago. It is now thought that humanity evolved from a chimpanzee-like creature, and the gorilla was 'an evolutionary specialist'.[17]

The remains of many fossil apes from the Early and Middle Miocene have been found, both in Africa and Asia, among them *Sivapithecus*,[18] *Dryopithecus* and *Kenyapithecus*, but their relationship to later human evolution is obscure and disputed. One dramatic but not widely accepted theory was that humanity had a phase as an aquatic mammal, so that the missing fossils should be found in areas once covered with water![19] In recent years, some important early Miocene fossils have been found in Africa. Homin*oid* remains found in northern Kenya, in 1985–6, are thought to belong to new genera, *Afropithecus*, and *Turkanapithecus*, and dated 17–18 mya. Part of the jaw of another new genus, *Otavipithecus*, was found in the Namibian mountains in mid-1991, and dated to 13 mya.[20] These fossils had aspects which seemed to be transitional between ape and man. It is debated whether either was ancestral to humanity, or belonged to a related clade (evolutionary lineage) (that is, the great-aunt, rather than grandparent, of modern humanity). The Namibian fossil was acclaimed as 'the missing link'.[21] But there are huge gaps in our knowledge of human evolution in the Early and Middle Miocene, in striking contrast with our ever more detailed knowledge of the last 3 million years, with which the rest of this chapter is concerned. These early hominoids are much smaller than protohumans, let alone modern humans: *Otavipithecus* weighed between 14 and 20 kg, as did *Dryopithecus*.[22]

Protohumans

In 1924, at a time when all known early hominid fossils came from Europe or Asia, a skull was found in South Africa, which Raymond Dart, an anatomist, identified, with great insight, as intermediate between ape and man. He named it *Australopithecus*, or southern ape (Figure 1). From 1931 on, Louis and Mary Leakey searched for protohuman ('hominid') remains in the Olduvai Gorge, in northern Tanzania. The Olduvai Gorge is part of the Rift Valley, which runs 1,200 miles from the Red Sea to Tanzania, and cuts so deep a channel in the earth's surface that it can be seen from space. For decades, they found stone tools, but no hominid fossils. Their long search was rewarded when Mary found 'Zinj' in 1959. The shores of Lake Turkana, in northern Kenya, and the Omo river which flows into it, have also yielded important hominid remains, as has the Hadar, in the arid Afar Triangle in northern Ethiopia. It was here that Donald Johanson found 40 per cent of the skeleton of 'Lucy' in 1974. She lived 3.5 million years ago, and was 1.07 metres tall, with an ape-like facial structure, and a brain a little larger than that of a chimpanzee.[23] But the structure of her knee showed that she walked upright.

The evolution of bipedalism was an immensely complex process which may never be fully understood, and to which many factors contributed. It has been suggested on physiological grounds that *A. afarensis*, the species to which Lucy belonged, while predominantly bipedal, may have spent part of the time in trees. Bipedalism freed the hands for other activities; and protohumans developed a more precise grip, made possible by the opposable thumb, which lies, in a sense, at the heart of all our achievements. An upright stance preceded the growth in brain size. It has been suggested that when, during the course of long-term climate changes, much of the forest in Africa gave way to savanna, bipedalism gave our ancestors a decisive advantage. They could travel long distances, and could survive outside a forest environment.

In 1975 Johanson's team found the 'First Family', the bones of at least thirteen individuals. At Laetoli, thirty miles from Olduvai, there was a dramatic find of a different kind (again, by Mary Leakey's team) – the footprints of two hominids from 3.5 million years ago, embedded in mud and preserved by volcanic ash, as were the prints of other animals. The discovery of hominid remains continues, and at least sixty individuals, perhaps as many as a hundred, have been found in Laetoli and the Hadar.[24]

Lucy and the First Family are examples of *A. afarensis*, which lived between 3.5 and 2.8 mya and perhaps even earlier and until recently was regarded as the earliest and most 'primitive' form of australopithecine.[25] No early hominid remains have been found in West or North Africa. It is possible that they have not survived, or that they await discovery. It is generally thought, however, that the latter is unlikely. In 1993, a still earlier specimen was found in Ethiopia, to the west of the Awash – it was named *Australopithecus ramidus*.[26] *Ramidus* lived 4.4 million years ago and was the size of a pygmy chimpanzee. Its teeth were larger than a chimpanzee's, smaller than Lucy's, and the surviving fragments suggested a posture more upright than the former.[27]

Older books divided the australopithecines into two genera, the slender

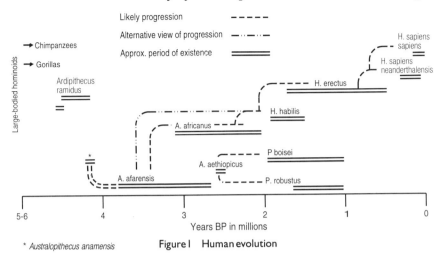

Figure I   Human evolution

* *Australopithecus anamensis*

'gracile' *Australopithecus* called *A. africanus*, found only in South Africa, and the 'robust' form, now often called *Paranthropus*. It is now generally accepted that the weight range of both 'gracile' and 'robust' forms was much the same, between 33 and 57 kg, hence the conventional use of inverted commas. All australopithecines were much smaller than modern humans. The real distinguishing mark of the 'robust' form was a massive jaw and a crest of bone on the skull (needed to support the jaw), which is also found in the male gorilla. The form now called *Paranthropus robustus* in South Africa and *Paranthropus boisei* in East Africa is first attested 2 million years ago and was extinct a million years later. The small-brained *A. aethiopicus* is known from a single skull ('the black skull'), thought to be 2.5 million years old, discovered west of Lake Turkana in 1988. The South African species cannot be dated directly, and we rely on analogies with their East African counterparts, dated by the potassium-argon method.

It was once assumed that *Homo* developed out of the gracile australopithecines, because we resemble them more closely than we do the robust form. It is now generally accepted that *A. afarensis* is ancestral to all later hominids, and *A. aethiopicus* to the robust forms. Some believe that *A. afarensis* was the direct ancestor of the earliest form of *Homo* (*A. africanus*, like the robust forms, dying out) and others that *A. africanus* was an intermediate form. It is clear that different genera of hominids lived at the same time, and sometimes in close proximity to each other.

The dating of protohumans, and the relationship of different forms to each other, has been much revised in recent years; as new discoveries are made, the process will continue. Problems of classification are due largely to the fact that most of these fossils survive in fragmentary form. A further difficulty is that we do not know how much variation existed within a species (all forms of modern man belong to a single species) or between male and female (the sex of these fossil bones is seldom ascertainable). An armbone found in the Hadar was much larger than Lucy's, and the footprints at Laetoli were those of individuals of different height, the taller being five feet. (The male mountain gorilla is much larger than the female, apparently because he must fight with other males.) A considerable difference in size between male and female australopithecines is now widely accepted.

We know little about the australopithecines' way of life. It seems unlikely that they made stone tools, though the matter is debated, or that they could speak, though all the evidence is necessarily indirect. A study of teeth suggests that *A. africanus* was an omnivore, like modern man. *P. robustus* lived on a vegetarian diet in which nuts and seeds predominated – hence a massive jaw and very thick dental enamel. Vegetable food probably predominated in the diet of *A. africanus* as well, as among most – but not all – modern hunter-gatherers, but it usually leaves no trace in the fossil record.[28] Studies of their life expectancy have been made,[29] based on dental evidence. One suggests that 36 per cent of australopithecines died before they reached their teens, and that far more gracile than robust individuals reached childbearing age. In a South African study, none of those examined had lived beyond forty. To see these figures in perspective we must realise that they could be paralleled from many fully modern pre-industrial populations.

Homo habilis

One of the most interesting implications of the discoveries of recent years is that the genus *Homo* (man) is far older than anyone had surmised, and first appeared 2.4 million years ago, and perhaps earlier.[30] It has been surmised that this development was linked with global cooling at that time.[31] There is considerable variation within the earliest form, *H. habilis*, and it may comprise more than one species.[32] *Homo habilis* had a brain of, on average, 630 cubic centimetres (a 'robust' australopithecine brain was on average 520 cm, a 'gracile' one 442).[33] It is noteworthy that although an increasing brain size is invariably taken as an index of hominid evolution, modern human brain sizes vary greatly and bear no relation to intelligence.

Homo habilis means handy man and s/he was probably the first tool *maker*. Earlier hominids had *used* ready-made tools of various descriptions, just as modern chimpanzees use straws to extract termites. *H. habilis* deliberately fashioned pieces of stone into useful shapes.

Older books divide prehistory into the Early Stone Age, the Middle Stone Age, and the Late Stone Age. Despite their inadequacy, these labels are occasionally used in this book, for clarity's sake. Each tended to be identified with a particular artefact – the handaxe (now called biface), the Levallois core, the microlith. Like most oversimplifications, this contains an element of truth, but it is now realised that it is not possible to identify a technology with a chronological period, and that conventional distinctions between the Middle and Late Stone Ages in particular leave much to be desired. It is also recognised that the same peoples made different types of tool in different contexts, and that many artefacts of wood or bone have not been preserved at all. (Often, stone tools are found some distance away from the place of origin of the raw material; their transport, and that of fruit, vegetables and nuts, probably implies the existence of some kind of bag.)

The earliest stone tools – called Oldowan, from the type site, the Olduvai Gorge – were crude flakes and choppers made from modified pebbles. It is generally thought that *H. habilis* made and used these tools. (The pebble minus the flake was originally thought to be the tool; now it is thought that it was simply a by-product of flake manufacture.)[34] The earliest stone tools in the entire world which have been identified with certainty are stone flakes from the Omo valley, dated to 2.5 mya.

It was once the fashion to study the lifestyle of modern hunter-gatherers such as the Hadza of Tanzania or the San ('Bushmen') of South Africa, and extrapolate it back to the remote past – 'Man the Hunter'. This stereotype was based partly on the large numbers of fragmented animal bones found in caves throughout Africa. (These are now largely attributed to animal – including leopard and porcupine – agency.)[35] Many now think that, since *H. habilis* weighed under 45 kg and was less than 1.52 m tall, it is likely that s/he was not a hunter but a scavenger.[36] *H. habilis* was still mainly vegetarian, but competed with hyenas, jackals and vultures for the carcasses left by lions and leopards (or of beasts which died a natural death). These hominids used Oldowan tools (which would have been useless for hunting) to break bones and extract the marrow.[37] It seems likely that they turned to this additional source of calories as a means of surviving in the dry season, when there is little vegetable food available.

Homo erectus

Homo erectus developed some 1.8 mya, and survived until 200,000 ya. *H. erectus* was larger and more intelligent than his predecessor – about 5 feet 6 inches tall, with an average brain size of 1,000 cm. From the neck down, *H. erectus* was much like a modern human, but s/he lacked a chin, and had the flattened brow of a chimpanzee.[38] The only relatively complete[39] skeleton discovered to date was that of a 12-year-old boy who would have grown to be 185 cm tall and to weigh 68 kg[40] (males were probably still larger than females). It was found in 1984 by the outstanding Kenyan fossil hunter, Kamoya Kimeu, at Nariokotome; its recovery took five seasons. It is thought to be 1.6 million years old, and is the most complete fossil hominid yet found which is older than 100,000 years. *H. erectus* fossils have been found not only in East Africa and Ethiopia but also in Algeria and Morocco, where they have been dated to 700,000 and 500,000 ya respectively. A specimen found in South Africa may belong to *H. erectus*, and so may *Tchadanthropus*, found in Chad.[41]

It was *H. erectus* who made Acheulian tools, which are found from Spain in the west to India in the east, as well as in much of Africa.[42] The name comes from the type site, the town of St Acheul in France. Binford rejected historico-cultural explanations and saw the making of Acheulian tools as a biological response of the species, like the migration of birds.[43]

The intercontinental distribution of a distinctive artefact is one of the mysteries of prehistory, as is the fact that handaxes have not been found in Java, though both Java Man and Peking (i.e. Beijing) Man are examples of *H. erectus*. The absence of Acheulian tools in Java has been attributed to an environment where they were unnecessary or to the construction of versatile – but not durable – tools from bamboo. It was, until recently, generally accepted that *H. erectus* migrated from Africa, where the earliest specimens are found, into Europe and Asia, some 700,000 ya, bringing Acheulian tools with him, and establishing himself rapidly in new environments with their help. Recent research has suggested that *H. erectus* in Java may date from 1.8 mya,[11] as old as the oldest African exemplar. If the very early dates for *H. erectus* in Asia are confirmed, it means that *Homo* left Africa before the invention of Acheulian tools. 'Elephants left Africa several times during their history ... No other animal needed stone tools to get out of Africa.'[45] The oldest human remains in Europe are about half a million years old, with the exception of a mandible from the Republic of Georgia, claimed to date from 1.5 mya. (If this is confirmed, it will be the earliest hominid found outside Africa.)

The most characteristic Acheulian tool is the tear-shaped biface, so carefully shaped that it seems to reflect aesthetic as well as practical imperatives. A few stone tools have been found *in situ* at butchery sites, but with these exceptions, we do not know their functions with any certainty. Without the cutting surface they offered, to cut through tough hides, it would have been difficult to consume game. The earliest known Acheulian tools date from 1.5 mya, the most recent, from around 100,000 ya. The Acheulian biface has been called the first distinctive product of human intelligence.[46]

It is possible that it was during this period that speech evolved, though some scholars place it much later. The sites where Acheulian artefacts are found are much larger than those which preceded them, reflecting settled communities rather than butchery sites, and perhaps this implies verbal communication. Since two particular areas of the left hemisphere of the brain produce speech, attempts have been made to shed light on the question by the study of ancient skulls. Broca's area, which co-ordinates the muscles producing verbal sounds, seems to have existed in the earliest forms of *Homo* and even australopithecines, but few believe that speech developed so long ago. The larynx of an australopithecine was like that of apes and monkeys, that of *H. erectus* on the way to that of modern humans.[47] Attempts have been made to teach chimpanzees to communicate; since they are physiologically unsuited for speech, they have been taught sign language, or one of a variety of artificial symbolic languages. But the interpretation of the results is disputed.

Myths from Africa, the Pacific and ancient Greece describe the controlled use of fire as one of the great watersheds in the human past. The controlled use of fire, and the ability to make fire,[48] provided warmth, light and protection from predators and made cooking possible. There is evidence that *H. erectus* made use of fire, although some scholars attribute this development to archaic *Homo sapiens*.

While the hominid brain grew steadily larger, the size of the pelvis remained much the same.[49] This had important consequences; human young are born with an undeveloped brain, and are virtually helpless. The brain grows rapidly in the first year of life and the dependent human infant needs constant care; many of the calories it consumes go to neurological development. The young of the baboon or chimpanzee are born with their brains almost fully developed, which explains their earlier mobility. *H. erectus* babies, like their modern counterparts, were totally dependent on the warmth, care and food provided by their parents. The heat and protection provided by fire may well have played an important role. *H. erectus* lived in caves in China half a million years ago; without fire, this would be disagreeable or impossible. *H. erectus* was triumphantly successful; s/he survived for a million and a half years, and colonised half the world.

One tends to write of a succession of protohumans and forms of *Homo*, each larger and cleverer than an immediate predecessor, and this is, very broadly, true. But it is clear that it is a series of oversimplifications, a kind of shorthand for a wide variety of archaic populations, often living at the same time, who have not been, and cannot be, fully categorised because of the incompleteness of the fossil evidence. Many skeletal remains are intermediate forms, showing, for instance, elements characteristic of *H. erectus*, and elements which belong to archaic *H. sapiens* – the classification of particular bones is a matter of fine judgement. If we add to this the difficulty of establishing an absolute chronology, it is not surprising that experts in this field are so often in profound disagreement.

Archaic *Homo sapiens*

There were a number of distinct forms of archaic *Homo sapiens*, and the labels we use bear little relationship to their real complexity. The famous skeleton found in Broken Hill mine at Kabwe, in Zambia, differs markedly from the Neanderthals, but is similar not only to specimens found elsewhere in Africa, but also to some non-Neanderthal remains in Europe.[50] Its cranial capacity is 1,280 cm, significantly larger than that of *H. erectus*. A skull, found in north-eastern Ethiopia (Bodo), was, like the Kabwe skull, intermediate between *H. erectus* and archaic *H. sapiens*. So are specimens found at Laetoli, West Turkana and in South Africa.

The best known and most studied populations of archaic *Homo sapiens* were the Neanderthals of Europe and the Near East, who died out 30,000 years ago. (The first specimen was found in the Neander valley in Dusseldorf in 1856, hence the name.)[51] Their physiology embodied a very effective adaptation to the last Ice Age, their culture was in many ways indistinguishable from that of early modern humans – they used tools, controlled fire, wore body ornaments and probably clothes, and buried their dead. Their brain was larger than that of modern humans.[52] Why did they disappear, 'snatching evolutionary defeat from the jaws of adaptive victory'?[53] Were they among the ancestors of modern Europeans, or did they die out, supplanted by invading *H. sapiens sapiens*? Specialists debate every aspect of their life, including the extent of their command of language. But there were no Neanderthals in Africa, and their fascinating history lies outside the scope of this study.

Homo sapiens sapiens

It is generally agreed that *Homo* first evolved in Africa, and from there colonised first the Near East and later West Asia and Europe. Until recently, this process was associated with *H. erectus* and Acheulian tools; the redating of ancient Asian skeletal remains suggests it may be earlier, perhaps with the earliest *H. habilis*.[54]

This problem should not be confused with the Out of Africa controversy, which is concerned with a much later period, and the evolution of anatomically modern humanity, *Homo sapiens sapiens*. The Out of Africa controversy began in 1987, when a group of molecular biologists published a paper based on the study of mitochondrial DNA (mtDNA).[55] They used mtDNA from 147 individuals of differing ethnic origins to construct an evolutionary 'tree'.[56] The results suggested that they all 'stem from one woman who is postulated to have lived about 200,000 years ago'.[57] This gave *H. sapiens sapiens* an age up to twice that of the earliest known fossil, but there is no reason why genetic and anatomical differentiation should have evolved at the same time. These findings seemed the more convincing because of fossil finds, which, if not as old as 'mitochondrial Eve' were much older than earlier views of the emergence of *H. sapiens sapiens* (previously estimated at 30,000 to 40,000 ya) had suggested. Skeletal evidence from South Africa Klasies River Mouth in the southern Cape, Border Cave in Natal, and Florisbad in Orange Free State – suggest an antiquity of between 80,000 and 110,000 years, as did two sites in Israel (which was, of course, compatible with the Out of Africa theory). A site in the Omo valley was older (perhaps 130 kya).[58] Because of the significance of the finds, the dates of each excavation are hotly debated, but they are mutually confirming, and the great antiquity of the fossils seems clear.[59] They were much older than fossils of *Homo sapiens sapiens* elsewhere. Of equal significance is the fact that some of these specimens seem clearly intermediary between archaic and fully modern man.

The Rapid Replacement ('Out of Africa') model, whose leading advocate was Stringer, claimed that anatomically modern humans first evolved in Africa, and then displaced all archaic populations elsewhere, including the Neanderthals. There was no admixture because they belonged to different species and hence could not mate and produce fertile offspring.[60]

The Regional Continuity model, whose foremost advocate was Wolpoff, postulated an independent parallel evolution from distinct archaic populations, whose *H. erectus* ancestors did, he agrees, come from Africa.[61] This parallel evolution occurred in Europe, China and Java, as well as Africa. He and other regional specialists claimed that there were, for instance, considerable similarities between ancient human fossils in China and the facial structure of modern Chinese.[62] The great difficulty with this model is the improbability of an independent evolution into the same species in four separate regions, though Wolpoff argues that this could have resulted from genetic drift. Both scenarios seemed equally unlikely – that a new species from Africa replaced all the archaic humans in the world, without admixture, or that archaic humans developed independently into a single species in China and Europe.

It was not long before the Eve theory came under attack.[63] Even those who accepted the African origins of *H. sapiens sapiens* had difficulty with the postulate of a single 'Eve'.[64] Questions were asked about the sample of 147 individuals on which the study was based: eighteen of the twenty 'Africans' were black Americans. And it was pointed out that the methodology was faulty. It was possible to use the same data and construct 'trees' in which Africa does not appear at all.[65] It is also clear that the range of possible dates for a putative Eve was very wide indeed.[66]

But if 'Eve' is defunct, there is still evidence pointing to an African origin for *H. sapiens sapiens*. All researchers agree that different genetic indices show greater variation in Africa than elsewhere; like variation in language, this is taken to represent a greater time depth.[67] Studies of mitochondrial DNA from a truly African population also pointed in this direction.[68] A study of *nuclear* DNA suggested a high degree of genetic variation within populations, and a strong differentiation between African populations and all others.[69] The structure of the limbs of modern humans (which are longer than those of Neanderthals) has been interpreted as a specifically equatorial adaptation.[70]

Interpretations of all this are sometimes complicated by patriotism. Chinese palaeontologists have a strong proclivity for stressing the antiquity of their own archaic human fossils. The French acclaimed Tautavel Man (450,000 years old, discovered in 1974) as 'the oldest European'. When a hominid tibia 550,000 years old was found in West Sussex, '*The Times* said that every Englishman could feel proud to have descended from such a remarkable creature'.[71]

The very rapid development of modern humans is a good example of punctuated equilibrium. The model often used to explain this is bottlenecking: a small founder population, whose genes are thus of disproportionate later importance. One form of porphyria is hundreds of times more common in white South Africans than in other populations, because of the genes of one of the partners in a settler marriage of 1688.

Physical types

In the mid-sixteenth century, a visitor wrote of the Senegal river: 'on the one side thereof, the inhabitants are of high stature and black, and on the other side, of browne or tawnie colour'.[72] Egyptian engravings of the Land of Punt (thought to be the northern coast of Somalia), from *c.* 1500 BCE show both black and caucasoid people and so does Saharan rock art.

Several distinct physical types are indigenous to Africa, in addition to the black populations which comprise the vast majority of its people. The so-called caucasoid peoples of northern Africa – the 'tawny Moors' of earlier accounts – include the Berbers of the High Atlas, the Tuareg of the desert, and the ancient Egyptians. The modern population of northern Africa is a mosaic of different genetic elements; culturally, dialects of Arabic speech are dominant. This kind of admixture goes back thousands of years; the Predynastic population of Upper Egypt was brown-skinned, fine-boned, with wavy hair; in the words of a fourth-century (CE) historian, 'somewhat swarthy ... slender and wiry',[73] but some portraits, including portraits of royalty, show women and men who are clearly black.[74]

The speakers of Khoisan languages in southern Africa, the Khoikhoi and the San, were once known as Hottentots and Bushmen. They are distinguished by their yellowish complexion, 'peppercorn' hair, eye creases, and, in the case of the San, small stature. Genetic research suggests that their separate identity is a very ancient one, 'the dispersal south of populations that gave rise to the living San, most probably by 70/60 ky [thousand years] ago' – that is, before the first aborigines reached Australia, or fully modern humans, Europe.[75]

In Equatorial Africa and elsewhere there are a number of small-statured populations sometimes collectively grouped as 'Pygmies' – the word goes back to classical Greece. Studies of two separate Pygmy populations in Central African Republic and Zaire also suggested that they differentiated 119 kya.[76] These groups have much in common: they do not smelt iron or work stone; they are hunter-gatherers, using the bow; they appear to speak the same languages as their farming neighbours, with whom they have a symbiotic relationship. They include the Baka of Cameroun, the Twa of Rwanda, the Mbiti of the Ituri forest of north-eastern Zaire. There is a vast literature on the 'Pygmies', but their history is unknown, and 'there are no pygmy authors'.[77] Scholars now question whether they should be grouped together at all. 'In truth, Pygmies do not exist. The peoples who exist are called ... Aka and so on.'[78] Genetic research also shows us the superficiality of 'racial' differences. Variations in matters such as skin colour reflect genetic differences of as few as three to four loci. Studies have been made of scores of loci, including enzymes and blood groups, which show that 84 per cent of all genetic difference is *within* ethnic and national groups, and only 10 per cent *between* them.[79] The geneticist who described this concluded: 'The idea of racial type ... is no longer a very useful one in human biology' – or, indeed, anywhere else. A pioneering study made some years ago[80] showed that the Fulbe, despite their light complexions, straight hair and aquiline features, are much closer to black Africans than to caucasoids in other genetic indices, and their language, Fulfulde, is related to West Atlantic languages spoken in Senegal.

New industrial complexes

The many local technologies which came to replace the uniform and beautiful Acheulian complex reflect local inventiveness and the desire to meet local needs. The Levallois core, carefully prepared so that a single blow would produce a flake of designated shape, saved labour, and produced more cutting edge per kilogram of stone, a major consideration when it was brought from a distance. Like the Acheulian biface or the microlith, it is found internationally. In Europe, the associated industrial complex is called Mousterian. Over sixty different tools are associated with it, and it is attributed both to Neanderthals and fully modern man. (It has, however, been suggested that the divergencies in size and form were the chance by-products of continued resharpening.)[81] A very similar Mousterian culture is found in Egypt and Nubia. Further west, in the Maghrib and Sahara, the Aterian industrial complex is readily recognisable by its triangular hafted artefacts, apparently spear points. The Sangoan complex in Central and West Africa was characterised by heavy picks and cleavers; these have been interpreted in terms of a forest environment as having been used for woodworking and the collection of wild tubers, though there is no direct evidence. Like the Acheulian complex, it is astonishingly widespread – there are many sites in West and middle Africa, perhaps representing independent responses to similar environments. In Central Africa, it developed into the Lupemban complex, where beautifully crafted slender artefacts known as lanceolate points preserved an earlier tradition of artistry in stone.

Some surmise that this proliferation of technologies went with the introduction of language, others that this evolved with *Homo sapiens sapiens*, but studies of actual languages have a far shallower time depth. The microlith, a tiny stone flake used in making composite tools, was once held to be the hallmark of the Late Stone Age. It is now recognised that microliths were introduced in different places at different times, and cannot be equated with a particular era. They were fastened with mastic to a wooden handle to form spear heads, arrow barbs, knives, and perhaps sickles. In themselves, they are far less impressive than the Acheulian biface, but composite tools could be mended rather than discarded, and altered to meet particular needs. Only metal was to be more flexible.

The introduction of the bow was a technological revolution. 'Killing at a distance' had far-reaching socio-economic implications, and the flowering of rock art has been linked to it. 'Just as innovation often generates new ritual, so technological advances in hunting techniques ... may have been directly associated with the efflorescence of ritual art.'[82]

Sometimes, but not always, food production, ground stone axes and pottery were added to this industrial complex. The resultant culture is called Neolithic, paralleling usage in Europe and the Near East, though the word is often used imprecisely, and many scholars avoid it for that reason. Ground-stone axes are still used in West Africa in ritual contexts – the priests of the Yoruba lightning god, Sango, extract a lightning bolt which is in fact a ground-stone axe from a house which has been struck by lightning, and sacred groves on the Jos plateau in central Nigeria can only be felled with a stone axe.

Attempts have been made to link artefacts such as sickles and ground-stone weights for digging sticks to the development of agriculture. The difficulty is that these implements could equally well have been used to collect wild food.

Stone tools were only part of a total cultural complex. It may well be that wooden digging sticks and bags were the oldest artefacts of all, but have not survived. Occasionally, as at Gwisho hot springs in Zambia, artefacts in non-lithic materials have been preserved. Wood was used for spear and knife handles and arrow shafts, leather for bags and garments, and so on.

The peoples of the Late Stone Age created glorious rock art, which is discussed in the chapter which follows. Some of it clearly reflects religious practices. The dead were buried with care, and often with grave goods. Like the common practice of interring the dead in a foetal position, it reflects the belief in a life to come.

3

Environment, language and art c. 10,000 – c. 500 BCE

> The Lwena have it that their ancestor was Ndalumuhitanganyi . . . He
> found a primitive people who lived on water lilies and fish and did not
> know how to till the soil.[1]

The pace of change in Africa quickened in the last millennium BCE. Often,
though not always, hunting and gathering were supplemented by regular cultivation and/or pastoralism. The invention of pottery transformed both cooking and
water storage. The next great watershed was to be the introduction of iron
working, the earliest African evidence of which dates from c. 600 BCE. Iron
cutlasses and hoes transformed the tasks of forest clearing and cultivation, and
iron weapons made a great difference in hunting and war, as did the introduction
of the bow at a much earlier stage. It forms the subject of a later chapter. All
these developments were the result of conscious experiments and choices. Their
total impact was a radical transformation of the lives of those concerned.

The differentiation of African languages had long since begun[2] and continued.
Technological and other innovations left 'linguistic footprints' and the historical
study of this period revolves largely round the attempt to understand the sometimes conflicting evidence provided by archaeology and linguistics.

Climate changes

The background to all this lies in world climatic changes. Long-term variations
seem to be caused by alterations in the earth's orbit. In temperate zones, the
most significant change is in temperature – the ice ages – and in the tropics, in
rainfall.[3] It was until recently believed that Europe's glacials and Africa's pluvials
were connected, but this has now been disproved.[4] The technical innovation and
artistic creativity described in this chapter should probably be understood in the
context of the wetter climate of the early Holocene.

The aquatic civilisations of Middle Africa[5]

The Olduvai Gorge, Hadar and the shores of Lake Turkana and the Omo river,
which loomed large in the previous chapter, are now virtually desert. It was not
always so. Millions of years ago, the Olduvai Gorge was a pleasant lake, full of
catfish and tilapia, where birds and animals clustered to drink.

Partly in response to catastrophic drought in recent years, prehistorians have

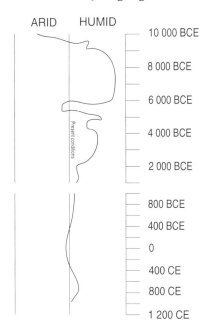

Figure 2   Long-term climate change (after McIntosh and McIntosh, 1981) (break represents a different timescale)

paid considerable attention to long-term climate fluctuation, and few lines of enquiry have shed more light on the African past (Figure 2). These fluctuations must be studied regionally, but certain continent-wide patterns are clear.

The Aterian culture in the Sahara came to an end about 38,000 years ago, as a result of catastrophic and long-continued aridity which made human or animal habitation impossible. Lake Chad was completely dry, and has become so again, with crops planted on the lake bed. The Sahara extended as far south as the latitude of modern Kano, where fossil dunes can still be seen.[6] There are fossil dunes from the same period at Qoz in the Central Sudan, and low lake levels in Uganda, Kenya and Ethiopia. For a time, before 10,000 BCE, Lake Victoria Nyanza had no outlet and the Kavirondo Gulf was dry.[7] The swamps of the Sudd were probably open savanna.

From about 10,000 BCE, rainfall increased, with dramatic consequences. Lake Chad became a vast inland sea, fed by rivers rising in what is now the Sahara desert, and flowing through the Benue to the sea. The Rift Valley lakes expanded, and Lake Turkana flowed through the Pibor river into the Nile.

There was a second, less extreme period of aridity later, which has usually been placed about 6000 BCE, though recent research suggests a later date (4400–3400 BCE) .[8]

Along the ancient shorelines of once enlarged lakes many relics of past aquatic civilisations have been found – bone harpoons,[9] stone weights for fishing nets (or lines), and pottery decorated with catfish spines. Bone harpoons and 'wavy line' pottery have been found near Khartoum and Lakes Victoria Nyanza, Nakuru and Chad, as well as in many parts of the Sahara.

Right in the heart of one of the *ergs* (sand dunes) . . . I have come across the remains of fishers' encampments marked by formidable collections of fish bones (enough to fill several farm carts), of hippopotamus and elephant bones . . . Over three hundred miles farther south I discovered in more than ten camp sites, fish bones, tortoise shells, and those of molluscs, bones of hippopotamus, giraffe and antelope amid which lay human skeletons . . . delicate arrow-heads in flint, gauges for fishing nets and also superb bone harpoons.[10]

In 1942, the great prehistorian Gordon Childe published a book entitled *What Happened in History*. Its very title reflects the importance given to what Europeans, with forgivable ethnocentricity, call the Near East. Childe believed that pottery and agriculture were invented only once, in the 'neolithic revolution' in the Fertile Crescent, and that the latter generated the surplus needed for literacy and urban growth, which he equated with 'civilisation'. In a sense, much archaeological research in Africa has been devoted to disproving him. It is now clear that there were a number of cradles of agriculture, both in Africa and elsewhere in the world. This forms the theme of the chapter which follows. The same is true of pottery. The Sahara's abundant pottery fragments date from as long ago as the eighth millennium BCE,[11] and it is virtually certain that they represent an independent invention.

All over Africa, main meals tend to follow a very similar pattern – a pounded or mashed grain or tuber, accompanied by a 'soup', combining a number of different ingredients. An acceptable 'soup' among the Igbo includes at least six ingredients, some of which are indigenous, such as *egusi* or *ogbono*, and some of which are not, such as stockfish from the North Sea. 'Soup' could not be cooked without a pot.[12] Perhaps few innovations have affected African lives more profoundly.

The distribution of harpoons and wavy line pottery is strikingly similar to that of Nilo-Saharan, one of Africa's four great language families, discussed later in this chapter, but speakers of unrelated languages were clearly part of the aquatic complex as well.[13] Fishing, like agriculture, sustained substantial settled populations, and in some ways these aquatic cultures were intermediate between hunting and gathering, and agriculture.

We have already noted the mid-Holocene dry phase, which was, some believe, severe enough to make the Sahara uninhabitable.[14] In about 2500 BCE, a final period of desiccation began, which may well be still continuing. The great lakes shrank, and many of the connecting water courses disappeared. The sequel has been called 'the balkanisation of a once prestigious self-assured Pan African civilisation', though these words suggest a unity which was probably never there. The suddenness of the change is reflected by 'shoals of dead fish found in former lake beds'.[15] It is not easy to imagine the human anguish which accompanied it all – perhaps similar to that caused by recent droughts and famines.

Fishermen may have turned to pastoralism as the waters receded, a step made both easier and more necessary by the fact that they were already used to a settled existence. As the lakes shrank, new pastures were uncovered and, in East Africa, pastoralists migrated south to exploit them. The fish taboo, found in much of Ethiopia, the Horn, Kenya and northern Tanzania, may have developed in a context of culturally dominant pastoralists, and a fishing culture in decline. But it is also found far to the south, among the 'Nguni' of modern South Africa. Insofar as it precludes the consumption of nutritious foods by the hungry, it is, like other dietary taboos, a classic instance of religion as false consciousness.

The peoples who live on the shores of Lake Victoria Nyanza worship its divinity, the great Mukasa. 'The spirits of all departed fishermen go to live with Mugasha ... Late at night they can be heard singing their canoe songs ... These spirits use the "spirits" of canoes that have been lost in the lake, and fish for spirit fish.'[16]

The beach rangers

Along the lagoons of West Africa, and the coasts of southern Africa, a different kind of aquatic civilisation flourished, and both fishing and shellfish collection were important. South African rock paintings depict both line and spear fishing, and over a thousand miles of coastline great fish traps were made of boulders. They are thought to date from between 5,000 and 3,300 years ago, and are so efficient that some are still in use. In one case, over 2,000 kg of fish were taken in a three-month period.[17]

Local Khoi were still collecting shellfish at the Cape when the Dutch settled there. The Strandlopers (beach rangers), as they were called, were marginalised as poor, and perhaps they perceived themselves as such in comparison with cattle-owning Khoi. But they represented a lifestyle which had endured successfully for thousands of years. Claudius Ptolemy's *Geography*, written in Alexandria in *c*. 150 CE, refers to 'the fish-eating Ethiopians' of southern Africa. Were these the beach rangers? Does the expression imply knowledge of the fish taboo which prevailed among many African peoples?

Saharan art

Rock paintings and engravings give us unique windows through which to see the Sahara in the Late Stone Age. The Tassili is now a virtually uninhabited wilderness, but many of its rock faces carry an extraordinary profusion of magnificent art, which bears poignant witness to a world which is lost.

Rock art is difficult to date. Henri Lhote, who rendered a great service to scholarship by copying many of the Tassili frescoes, divided them into four main phases. The first is the phase of the Hunter, often called Bubalian, after the extinct giant buffalo which figures in it prominently.[18] This was followed by the phase of the Herdsman (Bovidian), of the Horse (Equidian) and of the Camel. The mysterious Round Heads, of which more later, were placed in the earliest period, in the sixth millennium BCE. Mori, who conducted independent research in the Acacus, some 100 kilometres away, followed a similar sequence, but placed it earlier, with the Bubalian phase in 8000 BCE, followed by the Round Heads and then the Bovidian. Muzzolini has argued convincingly that the so-called Bubalian and Bovidian art was in fact contemporaneous with the Round Heads; he believes that all postdate the period of mid-Holocene aridity (which he places, however, in *c*. 6000 BCE).

European prehistoric rock art focusses mainly on the natural world. It is one of the great strengths of its Saharan counterpart that it also depicts men and women. It is clear that 'white' and 'black' peoples lived side by side, along with aquiline-featured dark people whom scholars have often identified – too facilely – with the Fulani. Presumably the 'white' Saharans spoke proto-Berber, the 'black' proto-Mande or proto-Chadic. Saharan art reflects the vitality and variety of their lifestyles, their jewellery and elaborately coiffed hair. The timeless elegance of some of the Saharan women would not look out of place in a modern glossy magazine. Some wore robes and cloaks, others were adorned with body painting. Some figures are strikingly similar to modern West African masks, reflecting the antiquity of this still flourishing cultural tradition. Several show sexual organs and intercourse.

All art filters reality through the perceptions, in part culturally determined, of the observer. Many questions can be asked about Saharan art. Why did these paintings concentrate on giraffes, rhinos, hippos rather than on the fish and rabbits which middens show were more important in their diet? Did they paint 'for art's sake', or to snatch something which endures from the relentless passage of time, or did they paint in the hope that by making an image of a living being they obtained control over it (and hence success in the hunt)? Recent sophisticated analyses of rock art in South Africa explain it in terms of San religious concepts and ritual. Such analysis is possible in a relatively recent tradition – the last San artists died last century. Parallel attempts to interpret Saharan art in terms of modern Fulbe culture are more speculative. These modes of explanation are not mutually exclusive; each, perhaps, is in some sense true. Some paintings show round featureless heads; Lhote called them Martians, and the term has entered the literature. (His frivolous and misleading captioning is a weakness in his work – 'Little Devils', 'the White Lady' so called, not because she was white, but by analogy with the White Lady of Brandberg (Namibia), who is actually a black male!)[19]

Some of the Round Head paintings seem to show religious worship. They are not an early and primitive form, but rather reflect particular religious insights. The Round Heads reflect a reluctance to mirror the human form and thus, perhaps, to control it which has a number of parallels in later African artistic traditions. Some human figures are shown with projecting ears ('feline') or horns ('little devils'), presumably with the same intention. 'Despite the empty faces and frozen attitudes, something emerges, like an interior fire – faith, perhaps.'[20]

Inexorably, the rainfall diminished, and the Sahara became steppe. (It had never been covered with lush vegetation – people and animals clustered round the watercourses and marshes.) One painting shows cattle being watered from a deep well. Horses appear in rock art from the second millennium BCE, ironically just as the environment became unsuitable for them.

Herodotus tells of Libyan noblemen, who crossed the Sahara (presumably in horsedrawn chariots) for a dare.[21] Such chariots are a common theme in Saharan rock art and engraving. They were once thought to reflect trade routes, but these light structures were unsuited for the transport of goods. Other evidence suggests that the Berbers appeared in the southern Sahara to raid, at least in the era of desiccation.

Saharan civilisation seems to have developed in isolation. Its achievements – its art, its pottery, its developments in farming – owed nothing to external influences. Ironically, just as the Maghrib became a hothouse of international cultures, the Saharan environment deteriorated so disastrously that most of its people and animals died or departed.

In the fourth phase of Saharan art, the camel supplants the horse. But significantly, this last phase is degenerate – 'bordering on graffiti' – perhaps reflecting the exigencies of a society where it had become increasingly difficult to survive.

The proto-Berbers, it is assumed, migrated north, the black populations south. Some from each group remained, radically adapting their lifestyle to the demands of a desert environment – the Tuareg, close kin to the Berber, the black *harratin* who cultivated the desert oases under Tuareg hegemony, and the black nomads of the central Sahara, linguistically and culturally kin to the Kanembu and Kanuri. Art on the rocks is not, of course, peculiar to the Sahara. Hunter-gatherers, having no home and few possessions to decorate, often choose to paint on rock, or on the human body. Stone slabs in a cave in Namibia, with naturalistic animal paintings, yielded an extraordinary date of 28,000 BP. Southern rock art is, however, a continuing tradition, and much of it is clearly far more recent. It is analysed, accordingly, later in this study.

It seems to be universally assumed that the rock artists were men, and perhaps this was the case. (On one occasion Lhote suggests that a hand imprint on rock is a woman's, because the fingers are slender!) A San legend recorded in the 1870s, suggests another possibility: 'Little girls they said, one of them said, "It is //*hara* (black specularite), and therefore I think I shall draw a gemsbok with it." Another said, "It is *to* (red haematite), therefore I think I will draw a springbok with it." '[22]

Disease

Africa is a particularly hostile environment as far as disease is concerned. 'African children are more likely to die before maturity than those from any other region ... Nor do the higher risks of death end at puberty ... Africans face some of the world's shortest life expectancies.'[23] Africans have always known this. Igbo parents called their children by names such as Onwubiko, Please, Death, or Nkemdilim, May My Own One Stay with Me. The Yoruba have a proverb that twenty children will not play together for twenty years. The Lozi gave babies temporary names such as Filth or Sorrow, to make them less attractive to a malicious spirit.[24]

Africa has been called 'the home of the most dangerous of man's diseases'.[25] Sixty of the world's 200 species of anopheles mosquito live in West Africa. Malaria was not peculiar to Africa – Oliver Cromwell died of it – but it harboured a deadly variety called falciparum. One of its complications is blackwater fever. Africans acquired partial immunity to it, in part through various blood haemoglobins, including the sickle-cell trait.[26] Another West African insect is the vector of yellow fever, which proved deadly to Europeans, but to which Africans had a high degree of immunity. The tsetse fly transmits a deadly disease to both people and cattle; in modern times it has rendered some beautiful regions uninhabitable. Yaws was a painful (non-venereal) affliction related to syphilis. The two are difficult for a layman to distinguish, and both are called by the same name in French. (Syphilis was a New World disease, which reached Europe, and thence Africa, after Columbus.) River blindness, and a virulent skin inflamma- tion which has driven some to suicide, are both caused by a filarial worm transmitted by a fly aptly named *Similium damnosum*. It infects a tenth of the inhabitants of the Volta basin and has caused whole populations to migrate away from fertile and well-watered river valleys.[27]

Monuments of stone

Colonial observers were fascinated by stone monuments in Africa, often choosing to see them as remains of lost great (probably Hamitic) civilisations. This has bred something of a reaction; it has been pointed out, for instance, that the stone walls and irrigation channels of Engaruka, in northern Tanzania, proved a less successful adaptation to the environment than shifting cultivation. But rock art is not the only evidence of the religious life of Late Stone Age peoples. In some parts of Africa megaliths survive which are somewhat reminiscent of Stonehenge. Hundreds of them are to be found in the borderland between Cameroon and Central African Republic. They are thought to be memorials, but contain no human remains, and were made by cultivators during the first millennium BCE. That they had energy and resources to cut, transport and erect stones so large that they posed a danger to modern excavators, shows the strength of the religious or other beliefs which inspired them. It also reflects a culture which could afford this kind of extravagance.[28] Many megaliths were erected in the Maghrib at the same time, but are clearly part of a Mediterranean cultural complex, and apparently unrelated to their Central African counterparts.

Language and history

We cannot know how many people lived in Africa in, say, 10,000 BCE but the numbers were certainly low – thousands, rather than millions. (There are a number of informed guesses. One, perhaps with spurious precision, puts the population of *West* Africa in 500 BCE at 1,814,000.) Modern hunter-gatherer bands average 20–30 members, and 500 has been suggested as a plausible size for an ethno-linguistic group. Linguistic and archaeological evidence are the two main sources from which we reconstruct the history of Africa for the millennia which begin and end at the beginning of the Christian era. The account which follows describes the main pattern of African languages as they are at present understood. It should be noted that a few radical thinkers have come to reject the concept of language families altogether. The antiquity of various languages and the locations in which they developed are of crucial importance, the base on which the whole structure of interpretation rests. The original cradle of a language is determined by several factors, including the geographic location of its closest relatives. The 'least travels' principle suggests that a language first developed where its branches show the greatest diversity, because it would have had the longest time to develop there. It was once thought that languages changed at a constant rate – the foundation of glottochronology. For some years this approach fell out of favour; the model was based on research in Indo-European languages, and there was no evidence that it was universally applicable. Linguists continued to estimate the age of languages, and historians to quote these estimates, and base much interpretation on them. Glottochronology is now returning to favour.[29] The basic estimation it uses is that after a thousand years of divergence, 74 per cent of common vocabulary will be retained.

The phyla

Giant language families, or phyla, and the problems of historical interpretation they pose, are not peculiar to Africa. Austronesian languages are spoken in south-east Asia and in much of the Pacific (but not in Australia and most of New Guinea). This phylum's interest to Africanists lies in the fact that Malagasy belongs to it, the original settlers of Madagascar having migrated from south-east Asia before the seventh century CE.

Difficulties of interpretation are compounded by the fact that some African languages have been studied inadequately, or not at all, and linguistics specialists differ on some aspects of classification. Moreover, there are problems in historians' eagerness to use data from other disciplines. With very rare exceptions, they lack the training to be able to evaluate, for instance, linguistics data for themselves. Necessarily, we oversimplify when we discuss linguistic evidence in brief compass. Scholars write, for instance, of 'proto-Bantu', and reconstruct roots thought to belong to it, as starred forms such as *-*gunda*, garden. But it is important to realise that these were not specific words from a spoken language. Proto-Bantu is 'a moment of the mind'; it 'cannot be said to reflect the speech of a single community but rather of a congeries of communities interacting with each other'.[30] It is also important not to confuse linguistic with other categories – the basic error of the Hamitic hypothesis, which identified language with race. For this reason, some scholars object to referring to Khoisan-speaking peoples as 'Khoisan'. Similarly, historians have often described the spread of Bantu languages, of pottery styles and of iron working, as a single complex, but each is a quite distinct phenomenon.

Peoples can and do change their languages, as the contemporary spread of Swahili and Hausa remind us. Nineteenth-century observers described the spread of Fante on the Gold Coast. It was said of Winneba, in 1816, 'The Fante language is used here ... The primitive language here is called Afoetu ... the natives on some occasions use it.'[31] The 'Pygmies' of the Zaire forest have totally lost their own language, but retain their culture and lifestyle. The historical evidence provided by linguistic data is often ambiguous and confused. Nevertheless, we must make the fullest possible use of it, because in many cases there is no other evidence to be found.

Afroasiatic[32]

It seems likely that proto-Afroasiatic (Figure 3) was first spoken between the Nile and the Red Sea 15,000 or more years ago. It has six main branches – Semitic,

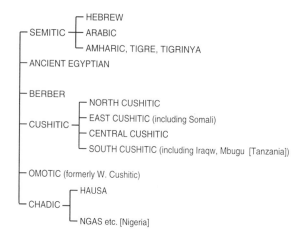

Figure 3   African language families: Afroasiatic

Ancient Egyptian (and Coptic), Cushitic, Omotic, Berber and Chadic (Map 2). It has been suggested that Old Kingdom Egyptian and Akkadian are rather more divergent than Romanian and Portuguese, the implication being that the Afroasiatic branches separated in c. 6000–5500 BCE.[33] In the Maghrib, Berber has been largely supplanted by Arabic. It survives in twenty widely separated locations between the Siwa Oasis, west of the Nile, the Atlantic coast of Morocco, the Senegal, and Zinder.[34]

Semitic includes not only Hebrew and Arabic, but also Amharic, Tigre and Tigrinya, spoken in Ethiopia. These languages are descended from the language of immigrants from south-east Arabia before 500 BCE. Arabic is now spoken as a first language in Egypt and much of the Maghrib, but is not, of course, indigenous there.

Berber is spoken in the Maghrib, where it has not been supplanted by Arabic (for instance in the High Atlas). The language of the Tuareg, Tamasheq, belongs to this family.

The third branch of Afroasiatic, Ancient Egyptian, is extinct. Long since supplanted by Arabic, it is known only from written sources, but a form of it survives as Coptic, used for liturgical purposes by Egyptian Christians, who have spoken Arabic for a millennium.

The Cushitic language family has four branches; they are nearly all found in Ethiopia or the Horn of Africa, and include Somali. There are some 14 million Cushitic speakers, and over forty living Cushitic languages.[35]

Southern Cushitic is now spoken only by tiny relict groups in East Africa, but despite this is of great historical interest.

Omotic – formerly considered West Cushitic – is found only in southern Ethiopia; it has some 1,300,000 speakers, whose history and culture are as yet relatively little studied.[36]

It has even been suggested that Afroasiatic divides into two sections – Omotic, and all the rest.

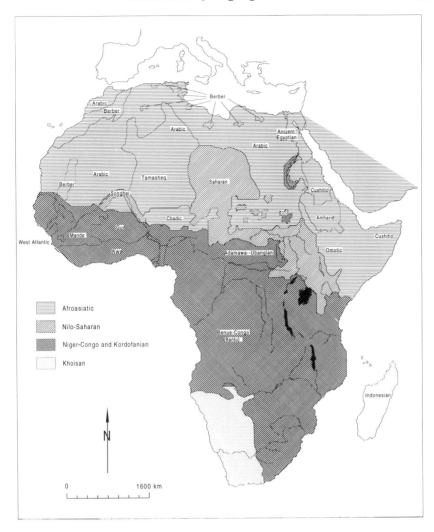

Map 2   African language families

The Chadic branch has the largest number of component languages, variously assessed at between 100 and 200 (depending on whether a given language is listed separately or as part of a dialect cluster). From a numerical point of view, it is overwhelmingly dominated by Hausa speakers. The first language of millions in northern Nigeria and Niger, it has spread still more widely as a lingua franca for trade and as a second language. Chadic languages are also spoken by small peoples to the east and south of Hausaland, which implies that Hausa spread from east to west. It seems clear that there was once a great continuum of Afroasiatic speakers who became isolated from each other as the Sahara became desert.

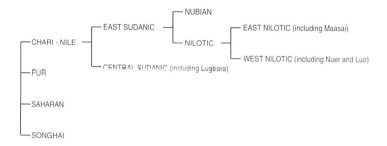

Figure 4   African language families: Nilo-Saharan

Khoisan

This phylum is distinguished by its click sounds, some of which have been absorbed by neighbouring Bantu languages. The Khoisan languages are spoken by Khoikhoi ('Hottentots') and San ('Bushmen') who now live in or near the Kalahari desert. It should be noted that 'San' is a Khoi ethonym. Khoikhoi divides into two major languages, one of which, Cape Khoikhoi, is now extinct. The languages of the San are numerous and deeply differentiated, reflecting the independence of small hunter-gatherer bands. The Sandawe and possibly the Hadza in Tanzania also speak Khoisan languages (the former closely, the latter more distantly related), tiny relict groups long since surrounded by Bantu speakers. Dahalo, spoken in Kenya, has some Khoisan vocabulary and click sounds,[37] and a single Khoisan word has been identified in the speech of a small remote people in the mountains of northern Uganda.[38]

Nilo-Saharan (Figure 4)

This is the most scattered and least studied of the phyla, and some of its component families are likely to be re-evaluated in future. 'Nilo-Saharan is at least as deep in time and as diverse as Indo-European.'[39]

In particular, the presence of Songhai has been questioned, and it is likely that Chari-Nile will be subdivided further: 'Chari-Nile does not seem to stand up as a legitimate family of Nilo-Saharan ... Central Sudanic is especially weak as a sub-family.'[40] Speakers of Nilo-Saharan languages spread across a great tract of Middle Africa – we have noted their putative identification, in the remote past, with a lost aquatic culture. To the west they include the Songhai, watermen of the middle Niger, and architects of a great empire. The black nomads of the central Sahara speak Nilo-Saharan languages, as do the Kanuri, whose historical origins lie there, although they have lived in what is now northern Nigeria for six hundred years.

Chari-Nile, as at present constituted, includes Nubian and the many Nilotic languages, all of which are part of the Eastern Sudanic sub-branch. The first Nilotic speakers are thought to have lived near Lake Turkana. There are two major branches, the Eastern Nilotes, who include the Maasai, and the Western Nilotes, who include the Nuer and Dinka of the Republic of Sudan and their

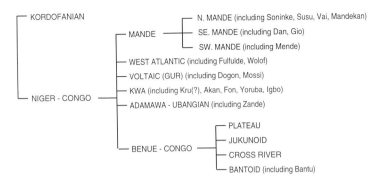

Figure 5   African language families: Kordofanian and Niger-Congo

Luo cousins, whose great migration to the south is analysed later in this book. Alternatively, these families are called Nilotic and Paranilotic, respectively. Some five hundred years ago, Nilotic speakers covered a vast swathe of East Africa. The Southern Nilotes – the Tatoga in Tanzania and the Kalenjin cluster in Kenya – are relict groups, whose survival bears witness to this. Kondoa district in central Tanzania is unique in Africa, because languages from all four phyla are spoken there.

Congo-Kordofanian (Figure 5)

Kordofanian languages are spoken in a small area in the Nuba hills, in the Republic of Sudan. The rest of the phylum, Niger-Congo, covers much of West Africa and all of Bantu Africa. If the link between Kordofanian and Niger-Congo is sustained by further research, it is likely that the phylum evolved in the Central Sudan. This would mean that, quite remarkably, three of Africa's four giant language families (excluding Khoisan) first developed in the same general area.

Niger-Congo

Niger-Congo has six branches, of which we have already had occasion to refer to West Atlantic. The most clearly distinct and hence possibly the oldest is the Mande family, which may well prove not to be part of this phylum at all. It includes the languages of the northern Mande, the Soninke, who were the architects of ancient Ghana, of the southern Mande, the Malinke, who governed ancient Mali, and of the Muslim traders, Dyula or Wangara, who spread Islamic influences through much of West Africa.

The Kwa language family, another branch of Niger-Congo, stretches along the coast of West Africa from eastern Nigeria to Liberia. Some consider Kru part of Kwa, others regard it as a separate language family. Many doubt the distinction between Kwa and Benue-Congo, and they are sometimes grouped together.

The Bantu family is unique (Map 3). Although linguistically it is a sub-branch of a sub-branch, Benue-Congo, its languages cover a huge geographical area and

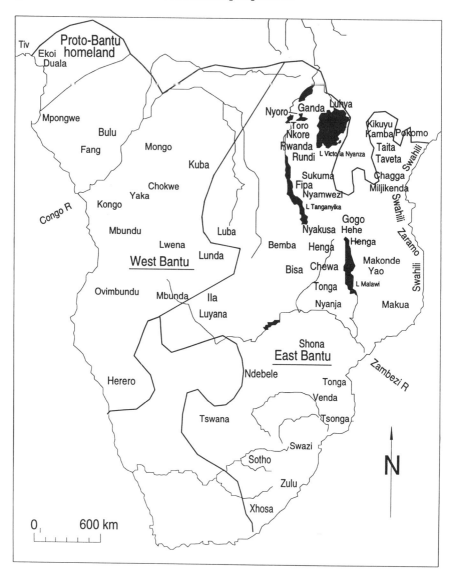

Map 3   Bantu languages

are spoken by some 130 million people, including the Tiv and Jarawa of Nigeria, the Kikuyu of Kenya, and the Zulu and Xhosa of South Africa. Except for the Khoisan, all Africans living south of a line drawn from the headwaters of the Benue to Lake Victoria Nyanza speak one of approximately four hundred Bantu languages. They are so closely related that it has often been assumed that they spread relatively recently. This closeness can be illustrated from the word 'Bantu' itself, which means people, a composite of the root *ntu*, person, and the prefix *ba- – bantu* in Bemba, *abantu* in Zulu, *watu* in Swahili, *antu* in Chewa, and so on. It should be noted that Bantu prefixes distinguish the *people* (waSwahili) from the *language* (kiSwahili). English lacks this distinction, and accordingly writers in English tend too readily to confuse linguistic affiliation with a sense of ethnic identity.

Bantu languages and history[41]

There is an enormous literature on the history – and, increasingly, the historiography – of 'Bantu expansion'. Since the closest linguistic relatives of Bantu are in Nigeria it is virtually certain that the original proto-Bantu homeland and centre of dispersal was in eastern Nigeria, or Cameroon. (An alternative theory was put forward by the late Malcolm Guthrie, placing it in the Shaba area of Central Africa; since this view is now universally abandoned, it need not detain us here, except as an example of the pitfalls which await historians using data from other disciplines.)[42] As one would expect, the Bantu languages spoken to the north-west are the most deeply differentiated.

There was once a debate as to whether the proto-Bantu went through the forests of Equatorial Africa or skirted them. It was, indeed, long believed that they found the forest uninhabitable. ('Impenetrable forest' has often been a misleading stereotype in African studies.) It is now realised, on linguistic grounds, that these forests must have been their first area of settlement after they left their original homeland. Proto-Bantu seems to have included words for yam but not grain, and possibly oil palm and palm wine, as well as a number of words related to fishing.[43] They were also familiar with cattle and goats, but not with iron.[44] Had the Bantu gone no further, we would have a clearly attested pattern of migration, comparable to that of the Luo or of the Fulbe. The difficulty in the Bantu case is the enormous area covered, and the closeness of the relevant languages. There is also the problem of the relationship between the spread of Bantu languages and other important changes which are mirrored in the archaeological record. At much the same time, in areas where Bantu speakers now live, a cultural complex generally known as the Early Iron Age was spreading rapidly from north to south. It was characterised by its iron working, by the fact that its people lived from agriculture rather than hunting and gathering,[45] and by the larger size of settlements. It is known above all by its pottery, made of thick pale red or orange clay, freely decorated with bold incisions, and often with an indented base. The pottery which succeeded it is quite different – grey, sometimes very dark, and thinner; it is sometimes burnished, and sometimes has red or black colouring applied. Some scholars believe that the early potters were men; the change in style reflects the intrusion of a culture where pottery was the work of women.[46]

It was once taken for granted that Bantu speech, agriculture, metallurgy and Early Iron Age pottery were part of a single cultural entity. The tendency of recent scholarship is to separate the components. 'There seems to have been a *necessary* connection between agriculture and metallurgy ... There is *no* necessary connection between farming technology and the other components of the old Iron Age package ... There is no necessary connection between the spread of farming and styles of pottery manufacture and decoration.'[47] It is noteworthy that the Bantu languages east and south of the forest divide into two sections: a smaller and more deeply differentiated western stream, found mainly in Angola and Namibia, and an eastern stream which covers much of the rest of the subcontinent, and includes Ganda, Kikuyu, Chewa, Shona, Venda, Sotho and Zulu.[48] It is thought that they diverged in *c.* 3000 BCE.[49] The pottery also divides into an eastern and western stream but the line of demarcation is much further east.[50] The Eastern Stream first appears in coastal Mozambique and Natal in *c.* 200 CE.

What special strengths enabled the Bantu to spread so dramatically over a subcontinent? Their advance was once attributed to the advantages they obtained by the use of iron but the proto-Bantu were a Late Stone Age people with no obvious technical advantages. An alternative suggestion, now generally abandoned, is that they were propelled by banana power. Bananas, as we shall see, offer many advantages to their cultivators, but as an Asian foodplant they diffused from east to west, the Bantu from west to east.[51] The word 'expansion' also begs a further question: did the *people* expand, or did the *languages* diffuse?

If the former, why did the proto-Bantu leave their homeland in the first place? Overpopulation is the conventional suggestion, but contemporary Bantu speakers live in underpopulated central Nigeria; in recent times at least it has been the Igbo (Kwa family) who have suffered from overcrowding. Why did they continue to expand? Shifting cultivation is the usual answer, but this does not usually have the effect of a steady advance in a particular direction. If the latter, what were the social mechanisms behind this change? Older stereotypes of conquest are now generally, and doubtless rightly, rejected in favour of a model of drift. It is, however, worth remembering that during the Mfecane (pp. 412ff. below) 'Nguni' culture and language did spread in a situation of conquest, and that the spread of the Romance languages in Europe was a concomitant of Roman imperialism.

Khoisan hunter-gatherer communities were probably few in numbers. Agriculture supported denser populations, so they were soon outnumbered. They may sometimes have become Bantu-ised by entering a client relationship, either in time of famine, or through cultural attraction. The process of 'becoming Hausa' in central Nigeria at the present time – the attraction of Hausa language and dress, and sometimes of Islam – offers a parallel to the latter possibility. The continuing process of 'becoming Bantu' is on record in eighteenth-century South Africa, where it was said of a Khoi community that 'they were certainly a mixture of Hottentots and Caffers [Xhosa], as their language had an affinity with both these nations; [physically] they bore a greater resemblance to the caffers, several of whom they likewise had at that time among them'. They were 'in some sort tillers of the ground'.[52] The process of 'becoming Bantu' is still going on in East Africa, with some Southern Cushitic languages such as Dahalo near extinction. It is noteworthy that the primary thrust of Bantu expansion was to the south among hunter-gatherers, and that they could not penetrate more densely settled agricultural populations to the north. It has been suggested that in East Africa they were able to occupy 'wetter wooded ecological niches' which did not attract herders or grain cultivators.[53]

The theory that Bantu and Early Iron Age expansion are different facets of the same phenomenon is still generally accepted. Some radical critics in a number of different disciplines have challenged it. Some linguists have come to doubt the whole concept of language families. Others have questioned whether the Bantu spread was really recent and rapid, suggesting that the strong similarities of language could be due to mutual borrowing, or convergence. This would mean that iron working and agriculture spread among Bantu populations already *in situ*. Ehret suggests that the original spread of Bantu speakers from their homeland was at least 4,000 and perhaps 5,000 years ago; the eastern and southern expansion he dates to the last millennium BCE.[54] What is clear, however, is that linguistic and technological change are separate phenomena, even if in this case the same people were involved. It is clear too that language change is only part of a total complex of cultural exchange, which may express itself in many different ways. The Maasai borrowed Bantu words for items associated with agriculture, but their Bantu neighbours absorbed some of their cultural concepts, such as the taboo on eating game.

A study of 'becoming Swazi' in the nineteenth century sheds light on the evolution of ethno-linguistic identities at much earlier periods. In *c.* 1818, the Ngwane (an 'Nguni' people) fled to what later became Swaziland. The royal clan expanded, because its men had numerous wives and its prestige led others to imitate both their siSwati speech and their rituals, laws and customs. In modern times, 70 per cent of the Swazi were of 'Nguni' descent. There were seventy clans, of greatly differing sizes, and rules of clan exogamy meant that they were linked by an intricate web of marriages. All had become siSwati speakers, and members of the Swazi nation.[55]

Current debates on Bantu expansion, and its relationship with other variables, are closely paralleled by controversies on the spread of Indo-European, and its link with the spread of farming. Some scholars have queried the postulate of a single original language, the stem and branches model, and the whole concept of a 'wave of advance'.[56]

4

Producing more food c. 10,000–c. 500 BCE

> Of every two problems that are discussed
> The first must be on the subject of subsistence.
> Somali poem by Salaan Arabay[1]

A Yao traditional history gives a vivid account of the many different sources of village food supply, and the ways in which the different foods were obtained. Farming was the most important of these.

Among others hardly less important, however, was hunting, the capture of something tasty – birds, game, grass-hoppers, field-mice, fish, crabs and honey. Their weapon was the bow for shooting the cane-rat, the rock rabbit, guinea-fowl and other birds and the mongoose; they set traps for small game, and dug game-pits for the larger kinds; hunting with dogs and with nets was in full swing. All this was the work of the men so that their children and womenfolk could have dainties to eat.

The women did the village work, pounding and grinding corn, making porridge and doing the cooking; cutting firewood, steeping grain, catching crabs and grasshoppers, and gathering vegetables.[2]

All this is much closer to the realities of African life than academic monographs which study a single crop, such as sorghum, and which focus on the growing of food but neglect its culinary preparation. Travellers' accounts, on the other hand, are full of descriptions of African cuisine. The widely travelled ibn Battuta visited Mogadishu in 1331:

The food of these people is rice cooked with butter, served on a large wooden dish. With it they serve side-dishes, stews of chicken, meat, fish and vegetables. They cook unripe bananas in fresh milk, and serve them as a sauce. They put curdled milk in another vessel with pepper-corns, vinegar and saffron, green ginger and mangoes ... When the Mogadishu people have taken a mouthful of rice, they take some of these pickles. One of them eats as much as several of us.[3]

Contemporary Somalia is a land of famine.[4]

In general, meals centred round a carbohydrate staple, which was shared at a communal meal, where everyone present rolled each mouthful into a ball and dipped it in a sauce before swallowing it. The Igbo ate pounded yam in this way, and the peoples of the Maghrib, couscous (made from pulverised grain). The communal dish was a symbol of trust and solidarity and the staple, both in its cultivation and its consumption, was the focus of strong cultural values.

Couscous was called the perfect food, and women prayed aloud during the grinding operation.[5]

Prosperity determined diet almost as much as geography – in differential access to meat, salt and sometimes preferred carbohydrate staples. It is important to realise that farming and hunting/gathering were not mutually exclusive, and that wild fruit, vegetables and fungi, and in many cases, fish and game, often remain important elements in the diet of modern African peoples who have practised agriculture, very expertly, for hundreds, if not thousands, of years. 'Diet' is a more meaningful category than 'agriculture'; it includes items such as forest snails in West Africa, or *ishami*, the water flies of Lake Victoria, both of which added valuable protein to soup. (Modern scientists are currently exploring the protein potential of insects as a contribution to world hunger.) Trees such as the oil palm, the baobab and the shea butter tree were protected and exploited, but not planted. The date palm, oil palm and shea butter tree frontiers are at least as important as political or religious ones in our study of the African past. The date palm transformed life on the northern edge of the Sahara. In the words of an eighteenth century botanist: 'This strip bordering on the great desert and Atlas Mountains, virtually the only inhabited area in the region, is very poor in the fruits of Ceres ... The [date] palm tree, all by itself, abundantly, and as it were, openheartedly, replaces them and provides the basic foodstuffs as well as other commodities necessary for life'.[6]

Generally speaking, land was abundant, and rights in land were rights in cleared land. In Futa, on the Senegal, the one who cleared it, and his heirs, were called master by right of fire, or master by right of the axe. Large areas of Africa are unsuitable, or only marginally suitable, for agriculture, because of inadequate rainfall or poor soils. In Bundu, 88.9 per cent of the land area is unsuited for cultivation, because of the hardness of the laterite; only 1.6 per cent has ever been cultivated, and 0.9 per cent was being cultivated at the time of a survey in the 1950s.[7]

The heart of historical study is the analysis of change. But this should not blind us to the fact that apparent immutability often reflects the fact that a people evolved a lifestyle so satisfactory that they felt no need to effect major alterations in it. If the life of the hunter-gatherer is as agreeable as Lee and others suggest,[8] one may well wonder why anyone opted for the constraints and labour of agriculture. Prehistorians once assumed that the advantages of the latter were so self-evident that it would have been adopted as soon as the possibility occurred to some great innovator. Now we ask not only how and when agriculture was introduced, but why?

Mark Nathan Cohen, in a thought-provoking attempt to answer the question at a global level, attributes it to the pressures of an increasing population.[9] The environment can support only a few hunter-gatherers per square mile: Lee studied 466 Dobe !Kung, and there are about 750 Hadza. The need for a greater supply of calories per head of population also explains the concentration on carbohydrate staples. Other studies have stressed the effects of climate change, and especially of increasing desiccation.

Whether it was adopted because of environmental or demographical stress, or other factors as yet unsuspected, for most African peoples agriculture or pastoralism was to become the economic basis of their lives, and the focus of many of their most cherished values.

The pastoral revolution

The general thrust of research is to place the development of both pastoralism and farming ever further back in the past, and to lay ever more emphasis on independent local initiatives.

In Africa as elsewhere, the spectrum of possible domesticates far exceeded that of actual ones. One may well regret the failure to domesticate the cane rat (grass cutter) and bush fowl, and the extinction of the giant buffalo was an economic catastrophe. Egyptian art shows cranes, gazelles, antelopes, moufflon sheep and even hyenas kept in captivity; this reflects the fact that wild animals were preferred as sacrifices.

Pastoralism remains the major form of subsistence in that vast expanse of Africa which receives less than 1,000 mm of rain a year, an adaptation of crucial importance, 'extracting protein from otherwise unpalatable cellulose of grass and shrubs through the secondary use of the products of domestic ruminants'.[10] There are far more academic studies of cattle herding in Africa than there are of sheep or of goats, which are far more common. The ubiquitous poultry, characteristically owned by women, are curiously ignored. In Ganda tradition, the first man, Kintu, brought a cow, while his wife brought bananas, small stock and a fowl.[11]

Many African peoples have a strong ideological commitment to 'pure pastoralism', but most are to varying degrees agro-pastoralists, and even the most specialised pastoralists depend on other forms of food acquired through trade. Specialists such as the Maasai or Fulbe average some ten to twenty head of cattle per person; most agro-pastoralists – the Nuer among them – average one. Fish and grain are far more important than pastoral products in the diet of the Nuer and related peoples such as the Dinka. It is not for nothing that the latter's priests are called the Masters of the Fishing Spear.[12]

We have seen that art is filtered through the artist's cultural concepts. Historical writing is shaped not only by such determinants but by the availability of evidence. Pastoral and agrarian history is known from a number of different sources – linguistic evidence, actual bones, seeds and pollen grains, rock art, grain imprints on pottery. The study of all these types of evidence is fraught with difficulties: it is virtually impossible to distinguish sheep from goat bones, or to differentiate pollen grains, other than those of maize, at all.[13] Pastoralism seems often to have preceded agriculture, but this may simply reflect the fact that bones are more durable and visible than seeds. The difficulties can be illustrated from within the covers of a single book, where a remarkable discovery of barley in Nubia from 15,000–16,000 BCE was both acclaimed and retracted.[14] And of course all our generalisations are based on what has been discovered by excavation, a minute fraction of what has survived, in itself an infinitesimal fraction of what existed at any given time.

The so-called 'neolithic revolution' in Mesopotamia dates from the ninth and eighth millennia BCE. The first African evidence for pastoralism, cultivation and pottery dates from approximately 7000 BCE. It is particularly striking that this was not in Egypt, the gateway to the Near East, where farming and pastoralism are first attested from *c.* 5000 BCE, but in the region Egyptians called the Western Desert. At Nabta Playa, pottery, cattle, sorghum and barley from about 7000 BCE have been identified. Pottery, sheep and goats are attested in Cyrenaica (in modern Libya) and the Maghrib, from the sixth millennium BCE. Kadero was a neolithic settlement on an alluvial mound near modern Khartoum which flourished some five thousand years ago. Domestic stock – mainly cattle, with some sheep and goats – provided most of the meat component of its people's diet, though they also consumed game, aquatic snails and other molluscs, and wild fruit. There were many deeply eroded grinding stones, evidence of sorghum and millet, and large quantities of pottery and stone tools.[15] A roughly contemporary site on the opposite bank of the Nile, not far away, was inhabited by hunter-gatherers – a good example of the variety and complexity of economic life, both then and later.

The first direct evidence of pastoralism in the Sahara dates from perhaps 5000 BCE. As we have seen, it is difficult to date Saharan rock art, but it depicts a fully developed pastoralism, with large herds, used for milking (the earliest evidence of milking in the world)[16] and as beasts of burden. It depicts multi-coloured cattle, unknown in a wild state. As if to mock the later earnest historian, the occasional otherwise realistic beast in an otherwise realistic herd is painted green. Pastoralism in the modern world is nomadic, probably because it is found in the main in marginal habitats. The Sahara seems to have supported a sedentary pastoralism – reflected in grinding querns and pottery – which has no modern counterpart.[17]

The earliest domesticated cattle in Africa may have been of local origin. North African wild cattle were large with long curving horns. Rock art depicts long-horned cattle, but all actual physical remains so far found in the Sahara are small and short-horned. Egyptian bas-reliefs from the fifteenth century BCE record an expedition to Punt, possibly the Horn of Africa. They show both long- and short-horned cattle, but not zebu.[18] Humped zebu cattle, destined to be so important in African life, came from India, and were known, though not important, in Egypt from 2000 BCE. The date of their introduction in black Africa is obscure and disputed, but was clearly much later. Like their hybrid descendants, sanga cattle, they were hardier and more drought resistant than the local species.

When the Sahara became drier, some of its pastoralists moved south. They reached the West African forest zone in the middle of the second millennium BCE, where they were confronted by the lethal affliction of trypanosomiasis. Some cattle acquired immunity and survived – the *ndama* cattle of Futa Jalon, and the dwarf shorthorn. Dwarfing is a common response to the West African environment, seen also in ponies. African goats and sheep are certainly of Asian origin, since they have no possible local forebears.[19]

In East Africa, from 3000 BP on, and perhaps much earlier,[20] there was a complex of Late Stone Age pottery-making cultures, heavily reliant on cattle and smaller stock, often called the Pastoral Neolithic. They were once called the Stone Bowl people, because of their finely crafted stone platters. They are now separated into four distinct cultures, which some have attempted to identify with

Southern Nilotes and Southern Cushites, though the whole process of equating archaeological complexes and linguistic groups is fraught with difficulties.[21] It is interesting that their cattle were much larger than their modern East African counterparts, closer to the size of buffalo.

Pastoralism and milking were distinct developments. The phrase 'the secondary products revolution' has been used of the plough and milking,[22] and it also applies to the consumption of blood products. People who keep animals suitable for milking often do not in fact make use of their milk, a choice variously explained by cultural preference or the prevalence of lactose intolerance. In West Africa, the importance of milk products to the Fulbe contrasts with the non-milking cattle keeping of many West African peoples.[23] Saharan art, as we have seen, provides the first evidence of milking in the world. Milk and blood were much more economically efficient to consume than meat. A ninth-century account from distant China refers to blood consumption in eastern Africa: 'The land of Po-pa-li is in the south-western Ocean. The people ... prick a vein of one of their oxen, mix the blood with milk, and eat it raw.'[24] Linguistic evidence suggests that Bantu speakers in northern Tanganyika learnt milking from southern Cushites, and that it diffused from there through the southern and eastern Bantu.[25]

Cultivated plants

It is important to realise that a wide range of vegetables were cultivated as well as the carbohydrate staple. The ancient Egyptians grew leeks, onions, cucumbers, peas, beans, radishes, melons, dates, grapes and figs, as well as the carbohydrate staples, barley and emmer wheat.[26] The peoples of West Africa's yam belt cultivated a variety of soup ingredients, such as the fluted pumpkin, with its edible seeds and leaves.

A remarkable number of cereals and other crops (Map 4) were domesticated in the Western and Central Sudan, perhaps by Saharan peoples responding to increasing desiccation. Sorghum,[27] Africa's most important indigenous cereal, produces an extraordinary biomass, all of which is utilised, from a tiny seed. There are five 'races', of which the first was domesticated in the Central Sudan, somewhere between Lake Chad and the Nile. It spread to West Africa, southern Africa and India, where further races were developed, and, in the last instance, reintroduced to Africa. Other African plants and trees, which also became very important in India, include the kapok and baobab trees, cowpeas, and possibly cotton.

Indian sorghum, *S. durra*, is the dominant strain in North Africa, Ethiopia and the Sahel, and, in an age when African and Asian nations are thought of as the recipients of technical aid, it is salutary to remember the diet of countless Indian villagers transformed by the innovations of African farmers, and vice versa.

Pearl millet (*Pennisetum*) is the most drought resistant of African cereals, and was apparently domesticated on the southern edge of the Sahara, during its desiccation. Finger millet (*Eleusine*) is another African domesticate which was established in India in ancient times, as was pearl millet. It is grown mainly in eastern and southern Africa; grains 5,000 years old have been identified at

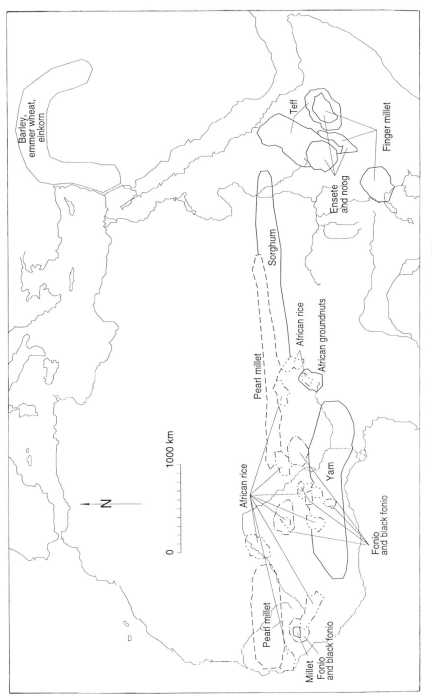

Map 4   Cradles of domestication (after Harlan 1971)

Barley, emmer wheat, einkorn

Teff

Finger millet

Ensete and noog

Sorghum

Pearl millet

African rice

African groundnuts

African rice

Yam

Fonio and black fonio

Pearl millet

Millet

Fonio and black fonio

N

1000 km

0

Aksum, in Ethiopia. In the Sudan, the Arabic word for life, *'aish*, refers to sorghum; in the Sahel, it refers to pearl millet. A clan in Bukoba have a tradition that during their migration to their present home they exchanged the drums of political authority for millet.

African rice, *Oryza glaberrima*, now largely supplanted by Asian rice, was domesticated in the inland delta of the Niger by Mande-speaking peoples. There are other local cereal domesticates in West Africa, including various forms of fonio, such as acha, the tiny grained staple of the Jos plateau in central Nigeria. A field of acha looks much like grass, but the antiquity of its cultivation is reflected in the myths and rituals which surround it.

The West African yam belt is virtually identical with the geographic extent of the Kwa language family. In Ivory Coast, it ends sharply at the Bandama river, beyond which rice is the staple. The two main cultivated species, yellow guinea yam (*Dioscorea cayensis*) and white guinea yam (*D. rotundata*) are closely related to each other; the latter can still be found in a wild state, while the former is a cultigen.[28] Wild yams are often thorny or toxic; the strong and universal preference for eating yam in a pounded form (fufu) may have originated in attempts to reduce toxicity. And still the Igbo pray at New Yam festivals:

> ... remove
> the poison, and the charm in it.

Although it is, in a sense, artificial to concentrate on the carbohydrate staple, such as teff, sorghum or yam, rather than the total diet, it could be said that African societies had a similar emphasis, surrounding the staple – and only the staple – with a complex of cultural values and ritual. The Igbo called the successful yam farmer Yam King, and in the ancient ritual centre of Nri, the priest-king is said to have sacrificed his son and his daughter. Their buried bodies produced, respectively, yams and cocoyams.[29] Rituals often have a clear ecological function – thus, the prohibition on yam consumption before the New Yam festival prevents the consumption of partly grown tubers.

The detailed vocabularies which surround staples reflect a people's expert knowledge of them. The Chagga have twenty words for banana, and the Mijikenda of the Kenya coast an equally detailed vocabulary for coconut palms. It is said, with some exaggeration, that the Igbo have a hundred words for yam. The Djerid, in Tunisia, takes its name from the date palm; a seventeenth-century visitor stated that thirty-nine distinct varieties were recognised there.[30]

Ethiopia is particularly rich in locally domesticated plants, and the variety and antiquity of its staples contrast sadly with its present image as a land of famine. Ensete or false banana is grown for its edible stem and shoots, which require long and laborious preparation. It is the staple of the (Cushitic) Sidama people of the southern Ethiopian plateau. Some believe it was used in early Egypt, but Egyptologists reject the suggestion. Noog, an oil plant, is an Ethiopian domesticate, as is teff, a tiny nutritious grain not found elsewhere. It was once claimed that wheat and barley were domesticated in Ethiopia, because of the great number of varieties found there, but it is now realised this diversity was caused by other factors, especially the altitude. Were wheat, barley and the plough brought by Semitic immigrants from south-east Arabia? If this was so, it seems strange that the immigrants adopted Cushitic terms for all three.[31] The probability seems that hard wheat (which overwhelmingly dominates Ethiopian production) was, like barley and the plough, developed by Cushites in pre-Semitic times. It is hard wheat which is used for couscous in North Africa and for pasta in Italy.[32]

Egyptian agriculture seems to have developed relatively late, though it is possible that earlier evidence lies buried under the Nile silt. By 5000 BCE, Egyptian villages were cultivating emmer wheat, barley and flax, and keeping livestock. Since wheat and barley have been found in wild forms in the Nile valley, it is possible that this was a further indigenous development.

The southern edge of the Sahara

The antiquity of pastoralism and pottery in the Sahara is certain. The history of agriculture there is more doubtful, because it is difficult to distinguish wild from cultivated seeds, and rock paintings of cereal collection from those of its cultivation. Some consider the Sahara one of Africa's ancient centres of plant domestication. The alternative view is that stock herding developed some two thousand years before agriculture, a sedentary pastoralism which has, as we have seen, no parallel in the modern world.[33]

Cereals were apparently domesticated in Tichitt, in Mauretania, early in the first millennium BCE (p. 216 below) But the diversity of millet and sorghum varieties, and the vast extent over which they are now found, suggest a much earlier date. Ancient grinding querns and other evidence point in the same direction. But grinding equipment may have been used for gathered cereals, and the relatively 'late' date for Tichitt is paralleled by still later dates for the Niger Inland Delta and Daima in north-eastern Nigeria (500–700 CE). It is striking that in each case a different staple was involved – bulrush millet at Tichitt, African rice at Jenne-jeno in the Niger's inland delta, sorghum at Daima in north-eastern Nigeria.[34] What we are looking at is by world standards a period of rich cultural innovation. It seems that cereal cultivation in the Western Sudan was a late and very rapid development, a response to environmental stress, and especially increasing desiccation.[35] The great variety of domesticates in the area contrasts strikingly with the small number in the Near East.[36]

Imports from Asia

Bananas/plantains, Asian rice and cocoyam (colocasia) reached the African continent from Asia in ancient times. It was long assumed that they were brought by the first settlers of Madagascar, and it is indeed possible that they did bring Asian food crops with them which later reached the mainland and spread across the African continent. It now seems more likely that these foods moved gradually around the shores of the Indian Ocean over a very long period. Ibn Battuta was ill for two months after eating what seems to have been colocasia in Mali in the fourteenth century.[37] Colocasia is ancient enough among the Igbo to be central in a legend about the First Things.

Citrus cultivation also began in Asia and seems to have spread westward through Arab intermediaries. Early European visitors found oranges in both West and East Africa in the sixteenth century.[38] Bananas are the main staple of a number of peoples in the interlacustrine area, the Ganda, Haya and Soga among them. They make a distinction between bananas which are cooked, roasted, made into beer or eaten raw. Ganda tradition claims that they were brought by Nandi, the wife of Kintu, the first man.[39] Cultivated bananas do not produce viable seeds, and are propagated by suckers, which reduces genetic variation to somatic mutation. Despite this, thirty-one varieties were distinguished in Buganda in 1902, an undoubtedly incomplete list, reflecting the antiquity of their cultivation there. The Asian yam, on the other hand, may have been introduced in colonial times. Watermelons are indigenous to Africa, but the original form was the size of a grapefruit, with bitter flesh, and the large sweet watermelon was ennobled in India. Sugar cane is of Asian origin, though it has been so transformed by cultivation that its wild ancestor is not known with certainty. It spread in the wake of Islam: the first reference to it in Egypt dates from the eighth century, and in East Africa from the tenth; by the twelfth, it was widespread in North Africa.[40] The origins of Old World cotton are disputed – some apparently 'wild' examples are escapes from cultivated cotton – but are probably to be found in India. There was cotton cloth in Egypt, Nubia and Ethiopia in the early Christian era, though it is not certain whether it was locally grown or imported from India. It was grown in Egypt by the tenth century, and spread very widely in Africa in the wake of Islam. The mangoes ibn Battuta enjoyed so much at Mogadishu are also of Indian origin.[41] Coconuts originated in south-east Asia or Oceania. They were well established in East Africa by the time of al-Masudi's visit early in the tenth century. 'They have many islands where the coconut grows; its nuts are used as fruit by all the Zanj peoples.'[42]

Rulers are sometimes credited with the introduction of new plants, the earliest recorded instance being Hatshepsut's expedition to the Land of Punt, which returned with incense trees.[43] Ibn Said, who wrote in *c.* 1286/7, tells of a king of Kanem who experimented with the cultivation of vines, wheat and sugar cane.[44] There may well have been rulers with a taste for experimental agriculture: there were several cases of this in nineteenth-century Ibadan.[45] But most of the innovators were undoubtedly humble women and men, in rural areas. Both the ennoblement of plants through generations of local experiment and the enthusiastic adoption of a large number of unfamiliar cereals and fruit trees reflect their skill and adaptability.

Sugar and other crops of Asian origin were grown by Muslims in Sicily, Spain and the Near East. When Christians conquered these areas, sugar production died out. The kings of Aragon and Sicily tried unsuccessfully to revive it.[46]

From the sixteenth century on, a number of foods of New World provenance were introduced, some of which, such as cassava and maize, have been of the greatest historical importance. They are discussed later in this study.

Khoikoi pastoralists

The Khoikhoi adopted pastoralism at the beginning of the Christian era. They herded first sheep and later cattle, and made pottery which, because of its distinctive style (marked by pointed bases, spouts and lugs), may be an independent invention. Its manufacture began at least two thousand years ago. This is a classic instance of selective change, because they did not adopt agriculture and are one of a small number of African peoples who never worked iron. It would seem obvious that they acquired livestock from the southern Bantu. It is believed, however, that the Khoi word for cow, *kxomo*, comes from the Central Sudanic *ngombe*, and that sheep herding *preceded* the Bantu advent.[47] It is important to remember that the adoption of a word does not always indicate the borrowing of what is signified – the Xhosa word for grass is Khoi in origin.[48]

Cultural changes

Archaeology sheds light on changes in subsistence and trade, but we must look to oral tradition for insights into associated cultural and social changes. The Nuer have a myth about cattle domestication which is full of insight:

Man slew the mother of Cow and Buffalo. Buffalo said she would avenge her mother by attacking men in the bush, but Cow said that she would remain in the habitations of men and avenge her mother by causing endless disputes about debts, bride-wealth and adultery, which would lead to fighting and deaths among the people.[49]

The accumulation of wealth, whether in goods or cattle, led to incipient social differentiation. At Kadero, the burial of a wealthy man was marked by his porphyry mace and carnelian necklace; others had few grave goods, and some none at all.

It was once common to ridicule African pastoralists for their large herds, and their sentimental attachment to their cattle. But in recent times those cattle have probably proved a better investment than the share market. Herds were quickly built up, but easily destroyed by disease or scarcity. Cattle are more vulnerable than people because their diet is so much narrower, but since their life cycle is shorter they rebuild their numbers more rapidly.

Many movements of peoples, and notably the expansion of the Luo and the Maasai, can be explained in economic terms, the need to find new pastures for expanding herds.

The cultivation of major staples made a denser population possible; outnumbered, surviving hunter-gatherers were often marginalised. In theory, well-stocked granaries or yam barns were a safeguard against famine. In practice, dependence on a single staple was often perilous, and hunter-gatherers, with a larger range of hardier food plants to choose from, sometimes fared better. Hunger is a persistent motif in oral testimonies. It is often the hidden dynamic behind migrations, wars, and the rise and fall of kings.

One of the little Bukoba kingdoms on the western shore of Lake Victoria Nyanza has a tradition about a king called Rugomora Mahe. He was exiled, and spent a period as a fisherman, a lowly occupation in Bukoba. When he claimed his inheritance, the lord of the lake, Mugasha, told his wife

to prepare medicines for Mahe so that he could grow crops in his kingdom – where there wasn't any food ... Nyakalembe then gave Mahe every medicine for growing crops, such as cooking bananas, sweet potatoes, *enkuku* (like beans . . .) finger millet and everything else grown today in Buhaya. The women in Buhaya praise Nyaka-lembe as the goddess of agriculture.[50]

This text reflects the links both between wealth (the ability to distribute food) and kingship, and between agriculture and gender. Because they are the plant collectors in all known foraging societies, it seems probable that it was very often women who conducted the experiments which led to plant domestication.[51] Paradoxically, by doing so, they created greater burdens for themselves. The division of agricultural labour by gender varied from one society to another, but to women's tasks were added child care, care of the home, and the laborious processes of food preparation, which involved much pounding or grinding.

Pastoralism tends to be associated with strictly delineated gender roles. Among the Nuer and Dinka, women provided most of the food consumed – grain and fish – while men herded the cattle. Male anthropologists' romantic fascination with pastoralism obscured this until recently.[52] Often, strict prohibitions separated the women from the herds. The Gogo of central Tanzania respond to cattle sickness or drought by having women play the herders' role, so that this signal reversal of the natural order can also reverse unpropitious circumstances.[53] What is significant here is that the association of women with the herds is felt to be unnatural.

For the purposes of academic analysis, we distinguish between animal husbandry, agriculture and hunting and gathering. But most if not all farming peoples supplemented their diet with game and wild fruit, vegetables and fungi. It was usual for them to keep small stock, and in many cases cattle. Many caught fish, often using poison or fish traps. The peoples of southern Nigeria were farmers *par excellence*, but kept, on a small scale, the dwarf cattle the Igbo called *efi*. East Africa's mountain hunter-gatherers kept cattle too. The Maasai had a strong ideological commitment to pastoralism, and despised both farming and hunting, but disaster could and did force them into both activities and there are a number of Maa-speaking agricultural communities, such as the Arusha. In marginal lands, in particular, peoples were flexible, experimenting with a changing mix of animal husbandry, farming, and hunting, gathering and fishing.

The expansion of particular ethno-linguistic groups is often explained in economic terms – Luo and Maasai expansion by the special strengths of humped cattle, the expansion of proto-Afroasiatic speakers by intensive grass seed cultivation, of Chadic speakers by mixed farming, and of Chari-Nile speakers by sorghum. This identification of major staples with linguistic groups is undoubtedly an oversimplification. At this distance in time, given the paucity of the evidence, basically true oversimplifications are perhaps as much as we can hope for.

A continuing tradition of hunting and gathering

For most of human history, people have relied on hunting and gathering, and allied activities such as scavenging. Hunting and fishing remain important male cultural values in the industrialised western world. 'Of the estimated

80,000,000,000 men [*sic*] who have ever lived out a life span on earth, over 90 per cent have lived as hunters and gatherers ... To date the hunting way of life has been the most successful and persistent adaptation man [*sic*] has ever achieved.'[54]

It was once generally accepted that the introduction of agriculture was a decisive step forward which made almost all other advances possible. Hobbes described life in a state of nature as 'solitary, poor, nasty, brutish and short' and the life of the hunter-gatherer was once seen in very much these terms. Over the last twenty years, it has been dramatically reinterpreted.

Richard Lee's extremely influential studies of the !Kung San of the Kalahari desert[55] are exactly paralleled by modern accounts of the Australian Aborigine. Both emphasise the shortness of the hunter-gatherer's working week and a resultant freedom for artistic and cultural pursuits, the varied and nutritious diet, the economic importance of women's activities.

Lee's data are particularly interesting because they describe a people now forced into a particularly harsh environment; many hunter-gatherers, including the San themselves in the past, lived in much more propitious surroundings. Vegetables, fruit and nuts collected by women comprised 60–80 per cent of all food by weight (there are very similar statistics for the Australian Aborigines). They are familiar with 105 edible food plants, the most important of which is the mongongo nut. One San described the perfect diet as honey, oranges, meat and mongongo nuts. Another asked, 'Why should we plant, when there are so many mongongos in the world?' They spent between twelve and nineteen hours per week obtaining food, devoting their ample leisure to social interaction, ritual dancing and the creation of glorious rock art. Studies of hunter-gatherer societies bring out the gregarious nature of food collecting, the element of 'play'.

Partly because of their need for mobility, the San amassed neither possessions nor food. This lack of anxiety about the future led one analyst to call hunter-gatherer communities 'the original affluent society'.[56]

Clearly, we should not idealise hunter-gatherer societies, past or present. It has been shown that the concept of a short working week is based on calculations which exclude the time spent on food processing and cooking. Mongongo nuts are very hard and are laborious and time-consuming to crack.[57] The exigencies of their lifestyle have sometimes forced modern hunter-gatherers to abandon the aged, or practise infanticide. A medical study of the Hadza, a small hunter-gatherer people in Tanzania, gives a grim picture of injuries and disease.[58] Skeletons tend to tell us less about mortality than about such painful but non-lethal afflictions as arthritis and dental decay. 'Lucy' was only twenty when she died, but she already suffered from arthritis of the spine. In pre-industrial societies, many people lived much of their lives in pain. It is one of the many factors which are invisible in conventional history but constant in the African past. It is noteworthy, too, that African specialists constantly cite Lee's study of the San, but seldom Turnbull's study of the Ik of the Ugandan–Sudan border. If the ethnography is accurate, the latter's lives have been so distorted by want that they have largely lost the values, usually so typical of African societies, of hospitality, generosity and family devotion.[59] Because we know so little about prehistoric hunters and gatherers, scholars tend to interpret their lives in the light of modern anthropological studies of contemporary hunter-gatherers. In a sense this is legitimate, but one must be cautious in extrapolating present-day data into the remote past. Hunter-gatherers have their own continuing history – a theme to which we return later in this study. Work patterns were determined by gender, and women's work was not only more productive but more laborious. Saharan rock art shows women bent low over their digging sticks, the male herder leaning on his staff. In a San rock painting, the man is much larger than the woman (size, in African art, is often an index of social importance) but she is carrying the burdens.

5

Copper and iron c. 600 BCE to c. 1000 CE

They own and exploit iron mines: for them iron is an article of trade
and the source of their largest profits.
al-Idrisi (1100–66), on the East African coast[1]

In the perspectives of *la longue durée*, the pace of change in Africa gradually
intensifies. We have seen how in the millennium before the beginning of the
Common Era, three great innovations spread slowly over most of Africa –
pastoralism, agriculture and pottery. The next great milestone, often chosen as a
point of departure by historians, as distinct from prehistorians, was the development of metal working. The age of metals began in about 8000 BCE, probably in
West Asia. Originally gold, copper and iron were used for decorative purposes in
their natural state: 'aesthetic curiosity, not necessity was the mother of invention'.[2] The next step was the discovery of metal working: first annealing (heating
and hammering) and then smelting, which requires a much higher temperature,
but which produces copper from its various alloys. Copper (but not gold or
silver) was hard enough to make into tools. Pharaonic Egypt, for much of its
history, relied on copper implements, and the great pre-Columbian civilisations
of the Andes worked copper, gold, silver and tin, but not iron.[3]

Bronze is an alloy of copper and tin, and brass an alloy of copper and zinc. In
Europe and western Asia, there was a progression from the Copper to the Bronze
to the Iron Age. In general, bronze is much harder than copper, but the copper
used in the Middle East and Mediterranean was arsenical, which has the properties of bronze.[4] The art of forging iron, which is harder still, was discovered in
c. 1500 BCE by the Hittites in what is now eastern Turkey.

The Saharan Copper Age

It was long believed that sub-Saharan Africa went straight from the Stone Age to
the Iron Age, without an intervening copper or bronze age. This is true of most
of the continent, and it is significant that copper is often called red iron. Modern
research has, however, discovered two very significant exceptions – evidence of
ancient copper workings in the Sahara, at two widely separated sites: in modern
Mauritania, near Akjoujt and in modern Niger, near Agades.[5] Both date from
c. 2000 BCE, long before the earliest African evidence of iron working. Once
again, the Sahara turns out to be a centre of innovation. At these sites, natural
copper was worked by annealing, which lends some support to the idea that it

was an independent invention. It was produced on a very limited scale, and artefacts were small in size. In the same region of Niger, iron working seems to have begun in the middle of the first millennium BCE. By this time, the desiccation of the Sahara was far advanced, and since metal working requires abundant water and wood, this is something of a mystery.[6]

Copper mining continued in the Sahara for millennia, both at Akjoujt and in the Agades area, where, in the mid-fifteenth century ibn Battuta visited the copper mines of Takedda (modern Azelik). They were finally abandoned soon afterwards, because of the depletion of both ore and fuel. There were also copper mines far to the east, in the Bahr al-Ghazal, the River of Gazelles, a tributary of the Nile, where a thousand copper shafts have been identified.[7]

The beginnings of iron working

The most puzzling aspect of the history of iron working in Africa is the fact that it seems to have begun in northern Africa and south of the Sahara at about the same time.

Iron first became important in Egypt under the Saite kings (663–525 BCE). The first evidence of iron smelting in Meroe (on the Nile, north of modern Khartoum) dates from the sixth century BCE, but the great slag heaps which led to the misleading epithet 'the Birmingham of Africa' were produced early in the Christian era. Iron working in Aksum, in northern Ethiopia, is thought to date from much the same time.[8] There is no direct, but much indirect, evidence for iron smelting in Carthage (another mystery), but since the Phoenicians came from the heartland of ancient metallurgy, it is generally assumed that it was present from the city's foundation, traditionally 813.[9]

Remarkably, the earliest attested instances of iron working in sub-Saharan Africa are contemporary with those in northern Africa, or even earlier. Most of the evidence clusters around the sixth century BCE, though some studies suggest dates as much as three centuries earlier. The beginning of iron working at Taruga, in central Nigeria, is firmly dated to the sixth century BCE. At Katsina-Ala, which, like Taruga, is part of the Nok cultural complex, iron working began in the fourth century BCE.[10] For a long time, these central Nigerian dates stood in puzzling isolation, but there is now increasing evidence of the spread of iron in modern Ghana towards the end of the first millennium BCE. There is also a seventh-century BCE date for iron working in Niger.[11] It is increasingly clear that Nok iron working was not a mysterious unique phenomenon, but one manifestation among many of a widely diffused Early Iron Age from *c.* 600 BCE on.

Schmidt's research in Buhaya in East Africa revealed a sophisticated iron technology flourishing from *c.* 500 BCE on, and perhaps earlier, associated with the fine pottery, with incised decoration, known as Urewe ware.[12] At first, the scholarly community hesitated to accept this,[13] but it appears to be confirmed by similar dates from Rwanda and Burundi.[14] There is evidence of iron working in Cameroun from the fourth century BCE, and in Gabon at the same time, if not earlier.[15]

Iron working reached southern Africa with great rapidity, and was established in Natal by *c.* 300 CE – a phenomenon which, as we have seen, is often associated with 'Bantu expansion'.

With its associated and distinct but related pottery, the complex described above is generally called the Early Iron Age. It bypassed western Kenya altogether, probably because prospective Bantu settlers were discouraged by the arid zones to the west and south, so that this region went straight from the Pastoral Neolithic to the Later Iron Age. In the history of pyrotechnology, as in the history of pastoralism and agriculture, researchers struggle to fit together the sometimes apparently mutually inconsistent evidence of archaeology and language. The ever earlier dates suggested for metal working are consistent with the fact that proto-Southern Nilotic, dated at least two thousand years ago, includes words for iron and forging.[16] Proto-Bantu lacked words for iron working, but both Eastern and Western Bantu languages share a common vocabulary for metal working – 'ore', 'anvil', 'hammer', 'forging', 'charcoal' – which has been taken to imply diffusion from a single centre.[17]

By the time that the first Europeans reached sub-Saharan Africa, in the late fifteenth century, the Age of Metals was almost universal, and peoples who lacked ore or other requisite resources for iron working bought iron tools and weapons from elsewhere. A few African peoples remained in the Stone Age: the hunter-gatherers,[18] including the 'Pygmies' of Central Africa, such as the Baka, and the San of southern Africa. The lifestyle of the Khoi, as we have seen, exemplified the Pastoral Neolithic; they herded stock and made pottery, but did not practise agriculture or smelt iron. The Bubi of Bioko (formerly Fernando Po) are a particularly interesting case. The island was invaded in the fourteenth century CE; the conquerors had a knowledge of metallurgy, but gradually lost it. Living in isolation, the Bubi developed their own distinctive culture, incorporating elements which have no parallel on the mainland.[19] Their experience reminds us that technological advances can be lost as well as gained. Some 3,500 years ago, the people of the Lapita culture, who lived on a number of Pacific islands, including Tonga and Samoa, made fine pottery, but the people of Tonga and Samoa gave up making pottery about 2,000 years ago, and more recently settled parts of Polynesia, such as Hawaii and New Zealand, had no ceramic tradition at all.[20]

Patterns of diffusion

Not surprisingly, the question of how iron working spread in Africa has attracted a vast amount of attention. Trade in iron objects is, of course, quite distinct from the transfer of technology, and iron smelting, in particular, has often been surrounded by a secrecy which makes its rapid diffusion all the more striking. It was once thought that iron working diffused throughout sub-Saharan Africa from Meroe, but it has long been realised that this is improbable, since smelting in sub-Saharan Africa was roughly contemporaneous.[21] Archaeological work in the Southern Sudan, [22] which has yielded no evidence of iron working before 500 CE, confirms this.[23]

Did iron working spread from Carthage, via Libyan intermediaries? Was it independently invented in Africa? Scholars have been, on the whole, resistant to the latter idea, partly because the extremely high temperatures required make a chance discovery unlikely, and partly because until recently there was thought to be no intermediate copper/bronze age. I originally supported it, on the grounds that meticulous excavations in Borno and Hausaland, which are both north or north-east of the Nok culture, suggest that iron smelting developed there as much as a thousand years later. This seems inconsistent with the advent of iron technology from the vicinity of the Nile or from the Mediterranean world. New evidence about the Saharan Copper Age makes it seem more probable that pyrotechnology did indeed reach West Africa from the north. It is likely that knowledge of iron smelting travelled along a variety of routes. Some believe that it reached the interlacustrine area from West Africa, and others, despite the problems of dating, from Meroe.[24] An independent invention there is a real possibility. The mapping of furnace types might be expected to provide a clue to the pattern of pyrotechnology's diffusion, but they often survive only in fragments, and there is no general agreement on their categorisation.[25]

Iron technology

The most interesting recent research has focussed on two themes: the specific technologies of different iron-working traditions, and their social, economic and political contexts.

There are many technical problems in iron smelting. If the carbon content is too high, the iron is brittle and shatters, but if it is too low, it is soft and useless. Africa has the greatest variety of iron-smelting furnace designs in world history. The most efficient of these, the tall shaft type, makes bellows unnecessary, and was, with one exception (an independent invention in Burma), unique to Africa. The use of preheated air, documented in Buhaya, is another African invention, effecting savings in labour, as the shaft furnace did in fuel. The key African innovation was the production of carbonised steel direct from the furnace.[26]

The quality and quantity of iron production varied greatly. Often, the supply was insufficient to meet local needs. Early in the Common Era, Aksum was importing iron objects from India, despite its own smelting tradition, and East Africa is on record both as exporting iron to India, and as importing it. Good quality and accessible iron ores were widespread, but not universal: they were lacking, for instance, in Buganda.

Iron and the environment

Since the ore was usually abundant, the true cost of iron working lay in the human energy expended and the wood needed for the smelting process. It has been estimated that to smelt a given quantity of iron requires four times its volume in charcoal [27] and some put the figure much higher.[28] Such estimates are necessarily only very approximate, but it has been claimed that the slag heaps of Mema in ancient Ghana, dated to c. 800–1100 CE, represent the consumption of 480,000 cubic metres of wood.[29] A different study suggests that iron smelting at Dapaa, between 1400 and 1700, consumed over 300,000 trees, largely slow-growing hardwoods.[30] The ecological impact was the greater because smelting was often concentrated in a few locations, perhaps to facilitate political control. Vast areas of derived savanna in West Africa were probably the result of hundreds of years of charcoal production. Deforestation as a consequence of iron smelting may have contributed to the desertification of the Sahel, and the decline of ancient Ghana. There was massive forest clearance west of Lake Victoria Nyanza from the middle of the first millennium BCE, which may well have been caused in the same way.

Ruhe, the Lake Victoria Nyanza fishman who became a king in Bukoba, is said to have attempted to build an iron tower to the sky. It collapsed, and henceforth he built in brick. The similarities with the Tower of Babel are astonishing: as with the story of the Drunken King, one does not know whether it is a great universal myth, found in quite unrelated cultures, or whether it reflects missionary teachings. At one level it is a parable about the Otherness of God, the infinite nature of human aspirations, the limitations of our achievements. Schmidt interpreted it as an ecological parable: iron working creates prosperity in the short term, but in the long run leads to disaster, creating a dangerous imbalance between population and resources. Improbably enough, the myth led him to the discovery of hitherto unsuspected iron-working sites.

It is likely that pyrotechnology, like the control of scarce resources such as salt, contributed to the enlargement of political scale and the growth of social stratification. The paradox here, is that the inputs – iron ore, charcoal and clay for furnace construction – were so widely available. The craft of smelting was usually a secret, passed on from father to son. If it was practised in the dry season, and the smelters farmed during the rains, they were likely to become richer than their neighbours. In some cases, control of iron technology may have led to the creation of states, or to the seizing of power by blacksmiths within them. This is a theme developed in the next chapter.

The crucial innovation was iron smelting, not blacksmithing, for the production of steel from the furnace meant that the latter, crucially significant in Asian and European pyrotechnology, was relatively unimportant in Africa.[31] Yet it is blacksmithing which is the primary source of political symbolism. Smelting, conducted in secret, was often symbolically identified with gestation and birth;[32] smithing was part of the public domain.

The uses of iron

A song in honour of Ogun, the Yoruba god of iron, runs:

> Ogun is the chief of all the deities
> Ogun has two iron cutlasses
> He uses one to clear the bush
> He uses one to clear the road [i. e. in war].[33]

Sometimes the adoption of iron has been seen as the fulcrum which transformed the technology of agriculture and war. Clearly, its impact varied from place to place. Poisoned arrows and various forms of traps and snares were probably more important than metal weapons in hunting, though iron knives were invaluable in butchering game. Fire, preceded by ring-barking, was the main way of clearing the land.[34] The Anaguta of central Nigeria had their own smelters and blacksmiths, but the hoes they produced were small and heavy, and in living memory some preferred to use ones made from a hard wood, *tugopi*. The Lango and Teso of Uganda were still using wooden hoes in the nineteenth century.[35] At the end of the nineteenth century, colonial invaders found poisoned arrows more alarming than other weaponry, including firearms, and African peoples fought against them with a great variety of means, including magic and beehives.[36] Nevertheless, both oral traditions and mythology suggest that the introduction of iron working did indeed have a transforming effect on both production and social relations. In the chapter which follows, we elaborate the socio-political implications, in terms of the Blacksmith King and the casted blacksmith. Yoruba myths describe these transitions in powerful symbolic terms. One legend says that the bat was a blacksmith who created human mouths, so that people who had hitherto lived on wood and water could eat food.[37] The mysteries of Ogun, god of iron, still haunt Yoruba imaginations. He is the patron of lorry drivers, and a core symbol in the poetry of the Nobel Prize winner, Wole Soyinka. In one myth, the creator god, Obatala, 'gave people the tools they needed to perform their work. As yet there was no iron in the world, and so each man received a wooden hoe and a copper knife.' Ogun was made a king in return for the gift of iron: 'Give us iron so that we too can be great in hunting and war.'[38]

It would be broadly true to say that iron was used for weapons and tools, copper and its alloys for jewellery and sculpture, and for currencies and other forms of wealth accumulation. But their functions overlapped. There is some superb sculpture in iron, such as the diviner's staff, found among both the Yoruba and the Edo, surmounted by abstract clusters of birds. Sometimes a currency was made of iron. In the seventeenth century the people of 'Moko', – near Okrika in the Niger Delta, made iron coins shaped like a stingray, the size of the palm of the hand. In the nineteenth, the people of the Igbo interior used iron currency half an inch long, shaped like a tiny arrowhead.[39] These particular currencies may well have developed in the era of Atlantic trade, when iron became relatively abundant. The gradual shrinking of monetary symbols is an interesting phenomenon, with parallels elsewhere. Both copper and iron, whether in the form of bars or of currency, provided a way of accumulating wealth, and a form of protection against famine. Cattle filled this role in pastoral societies.

A continuing tradition of copper working[40]

Early Iron Age copper mining was on a small scale, and the hoards of copper ingots belong to a later period. But it expanded greatly – this was the time when the exploitation of the copper of Shaba and Zambia began. Copper was mined at Phalaborwa, in the Transvaal, from towards the end of the first millennium CE, and early Portuguese visitors to the Limpopo called it River of Copper. A hundred and forty-eight ancient copper mines have been located in Zimbabwe, Botswana and the Transvaal.

Some of the most remarkable achievements in the African past are to be found in the field of metallurgy. European copper prospectors were guided by the sites of ancient mine workings. Their African predecessors were often guided by the influence of copper compounds on the vegetation. In Zambia, copper ores were identified by outcrops of green malachite: a modern geologist noted that there were few sites African miners had not located and tested.[41]

Europeans in colonial Central Africa found it difficult to believe that the ancient prospectors were Africans, and postulated the presence of Arabs or Phoenicians.[42] One wonders how they recognised that copper oxides and sulphates of many different colours were all forms of the same metal. African metal casters prevented the copper or bronze from bubbling by including a small amount of organic matter. To transform one of copper's many compounds into usable metal, or red laterite into usable iron, seemed like alchemy.

Natural copper was rare in West Africa.[43] The major known deposits were in or near the desert in (modern) Mali and Niger. At Marandet, in Air, over 30,000 copper-working crucibles were found, dating from the sixth and seventh centuries CE. The scarcity of the raw material makes West Africa's great corpus of bronze sculpture all the more striking. Excavations at Igbo-Ukwu, in Igboland, yielded a large corpus of stylistically distinctive sculpture in leaded bronze, and bracelets of copper, all of which are thought to date from the ninth century CE. These treasures reflect an expert knowledge of metallurgy, since copper alloys are suitable for casting, and the pure metal is more malleable. At Ife, in Yorubaland, a glorious bronze age flowered briefly in the twelfth and thirteenth centuries CE, and then died, perhaps because of shortage of copper. At Benin, the bronze-casting tradition survived into the period of Atlantic trade, when the relative abundance of the metal led to a great efflorescence of artistic expression.[44] Scholarly attention has focussed on these great traditions, but a considerable body of bronze sculpture was produced elsewhere in West Africa as well. Copper bars, manillas and wires became, as we have seen, major currencies in some parts of West Africa. In *nsibidi*, an indigenous script used in the Cross River area, semi-circles represent wealth; they may well depict copper currency.

Africa's main copper resources were in Central Africa, and especially in Shaba, formerly known as Katanga (in modern south-eastern Zaire), and Zambia. The name Katanga first appears in 1806, and may mean 'smelted copper'. The first European miners found a hundred ancient mines there, one of which was three-quarters of a mile long and between 600 and 1,000 feet wide. One has yielded radiocarbon dates from the ninth to the fourteenth centuries CE. We have mentioned the ancient mines of Zambia, most of which were outside the Copperbelt proper. There were other sources of copper in Central Africa. In the early stages of Atlantic trade, the Kongo kingdom exported copper from north of the Zaire river – the Mindouli and M'Boko Songho field (*nsongo* means copper).[45] Vili from the Loango coast travelled inland to this region in large caravans, mined the ore, had it smelted, and brought it back to the coast, where, from the early seventeenth century, it was sold to European merchants. In 1642 a Dutch agent found 22,050 pounds of copper awaiting shipment.[46] Here, too, the wood needed for smelting had a great impact on the environment. In the late nineteenth century, it was said, 'I believe that the total deforestation of this region [Mindouli/Mboko Songho] may be due in part to the centuries-old metallurgical operations, for they must be very ancient.'[47] The social identity of both copper and gold[48] miners varied. At the time ibn Battuta visited the desert town of Takedda, the copper ore was excavated and smelted by male and female slaves.[49] There is a debate as to whether the Akan gold fields were worked by slaves or by free labour.[50] The evidence for Shaba is contradictory.[51] At Messina in the Transvaal, copper was mined and smelted throughout the year by the Musina, specialists who did not farm – a good example of the occupational definition of ethnicity.

Although some copper was sold to European merchants, much more was imported, either during the course of Atlantic trade or across the Sahara. Herbert suggests that at a conservative estimate, 50,000 tons of copper were produced in Africa or imported, up to the end of the nineteenth century.[52]

The uses of copper

In many African cultures, copper was treasured in the way in which Europe and the Arab world valued gold. Copper, typically, has a whole gamut of mystical meanings, some of which our own society shares (the copper bracelet as a folk remedy for arthritis). Kings of Asante, the kingdom of gold *par excellence*, were buried in a copper coffin, and one of the state's key symbols, the *kuduo*, was of brass. Lunda kings wore a bracelet called *lukano*, to symbolise their authority. It was made of copper and of human and elephant sinew. Among the Tuareg, 'A sword without copper on the hilt is destined for the demons of solitude.'[53] The sacred icons of the Yoruba Ogboni society, an immensely powerful secret cult dedicated to the sacred Earth, were made of bronze. Wealth could be accumulated in copper or gold; grave goods made out of them were taken into the life to come.

The mines of Shaba provided the raw material for copper ingots, usually shaped in a Saint Andrew's cross or H-shape, and exported far afield.[54] Over 1,200 were discovered in graves at Sanga on the shores of Lake Kisale, in the Upemba depression; they dated from the tenth to the eighteenth centuries. The nearest source of copper was 300 kilometres away. In the earlier graves (up to the fourteenth century) there are many copper objects, but no standardised ingots. The crosses appear from the fourteenth century on; as time goes on, they become smaller and more standardised, reflecting a process of monetarisation. The same shrinkage is found in the brass rods used in the commerce of the Zaire and elsewhere.[55] Finally, they disappear from graves, copper having become so common that it had lost the rarity and prestige which made it appropriate for burials.

By the nineteenth century, Shaba copper was cast and traded in diverse forms, including the large cross or *handa*, used in the Kasai and even Angola. In the late nineteenth century, the Yeke used copper ingots of 2–3 kg as units of account, and bracelets of copper wire, animal hair and vegetable fibre as currency. These have not been found south of the Limpopo, where Transvaal copper was cast into two distinctive currencies: *musuku* (which had both commercial and ceremonial forms) and *marale*. The two forms have been compared with a top hat and a golf club, respectively. They date back at least to the middle of the nineteenth century. How much older they are is unknown.

The Later Iron Age

The Later Iron Age was sometimes marked by an improved metallurgy. But the decisive line of demarcation in the archaeological record is to be found in changes in pottery styles, which puzzlingly occurred throughout Bantu Africa. A considerable number of regional styles have been distinguished, some of which can be plausibly correlated with known ethno-linguistic groupings. In general, the new pottery was an inferior ware, decorated with knotted grass or cord roulettes. One explanation which has been suggested is that women had taken over pot making, but this does not explain why such a change occurred over such a vast area. In northern East Africa, at least, it seems to reflect the immigration of Southern Nilotes (whose original vocabulary, according to Ehret, included words for iron working).[56]

The interpretation of changes in pottery styles is a complex matter. Often, the ceramic record is virtually all the evidence we have. Nineteenth-century migrations, which are well documented, suggest interesting comparative data. The Ngoni invasion left no mark on the ceramic record in Zambia, whereas Kololo pottery styles became an enduring part of material culture there, although the latter were overthrown in 1864. The explanation seems to lie in the fact that pottery was made by women, in each case, but the Ngoni warriors married locals, whereas the Kololo migrated as families.[57]

Ritual exchanges were an important form of insurance against famine. Grain could only be stored for a few years, and the droughts which endangered the lives of people were still more fatal to cattle. An important source of security lay in formalised gift exchanges. It has been suggested that the uniformity of Early Iron Age pottery styles over vast areas reflected the fact that the ceramic containers holding grain to be exchanged were deliberately decorated in the same way as a symbolic statement of unity. Later, when cattle became the standard form of ritual exchange, regional ceramic variations proliferated.[58]

The general trend is to place the beginning of the Iron Age ever earlier, and the same is true of the Later Iron Age, which seems to have begun in the eighth century CE in southern Rwanda.[59] It was often marked by an enlargement of political scale (though I shall argue that these developments often had earlier roots), and an intensification of socio-economic differentiation. There was an increase in the volume of trade exchanges, and long-distance trade routes developed. Agricultural settlements came to cover a much wider area; Early Iron Age communities had tended to cluster in favourable locations, by lakes and rivers. The Later Iron Age saw an expansion of pastoralism – cattle, for all their susceptibility to disease and drought, were still a convenient way of accumulating wealth, and, unlike precious metals, they multiplied.

6

Models: production, power and gender

Such men are not lords by virtue of treasure or money, for they
possess neither ... but on account of ceremonies and the following of
people they may truly be called lords.
Alouise da Cadamosto (d. 1483)[1]

Introduction

This chapter is a bridge between the historiographic discussion in Chapter 1,
where we briefly introduced the concept of the mode of production and the
relations of production, and the detailed regional histories which follow. Historical writing is specific and contextualised; but facts, as we have seen, do not
explain themselves. From the vast welter of detail in hundreds of monographs
and articles, certain patterns tend to emerge. This chapter is like a landscape
seen from a high mountain top. One will get to know the area better by walking
there. But one will understand it better if one has a bird's-eye view as well.

Village society and the lineage mode of production

'Village' is a kind of shorthand in African studies for any one of a multitude of
small communities. Some are nucleated settlements, surrounded by miles of
uninhabited bush. Others consist of widely scattered hamlets or single homesteads, which are a 'village' or 'town' essentially because of linkages in the mind
and, specifically, the ideology of the shared lineage. In the second part of this
chapter we shall analyse the growth of larger political units; but even in Great
States, most people lived in villages or scattered hamlets, and usually central
government impinged very little on their obscure lives. A mid-nineteenth-
century Hausa poet warned the mighty:

> Do not despise the people of this world,
> People of the bush and of the scattered villages.[2]

Some villages changed their location every few years, in response to the
exigencies of shifting cultivation; others stayed in much the same spot for
decades, or, indeed, centuries, sustained by permanent banana groves, or other
resources.[3]

In a seventeenth-century Kongo village there were about 150–300 people in 30
to 50 homesteads. Lele villages, in the 1950s, averaged 160 people in 45
homesteads. In Tanzania in 1966 Fipa villages had an average population of

270.[4] In West Africa, they were often much larger: in Igboland, in 1950, the average size of a 'self-conscious local community' was put at 4,500.[5]

In a sense it is bizarre to make generalisations about 'the village' on a continent-wide scale, or to extrapolate contemporary realities far into a remote past. But for some parts of sub-Saharan Africa we have abundant eyewitness accounts from the sixteenth and seventeenth centuries, and it also seems that particular social inventions were sometimes so successful that they remained essentially unchanged. A fourteenth-century skeleton was found on the shores of a Rwanda lake. Curled in a foetal position, the grave 'evokes those of rainmakers in present-day fishing groups',[6] a symbol of Africa's continuities during *la longue durée*.

The lineage

The basic ideology of the village was that of the lineage. Sometimes all those born there were seen as the descendants of a real or putative ancestor. A cluster of villages traced their origins to the children of one founder, often, but not always, seen as male.

Asaba is an Igbo town, comprising five quarters or villages, on the west bank of the Niger. Almost all its people trace their ancestry through the male line to Nnebisi, who is thought to have lived some twelve generations ago, was of humble ancestry – the son of a slave and a pawn (human security for a debt, giving service to the creditor until the debt is paid) – who enriched himself by slave trading and elephant hunting. Paradoxically, his name may well mean Mother is Head.[7] Often widely scattered and quite independent communities are bonded by the same, probably fictitious, link – such as the widely separated western Igbo communities collectively known as the Children of King Chima. That Chima, Igbo by name, was thought to have come from Benin reflects the way in which communities readily lay claim to ancestors from prestigious and powerful states.

In this case – and there are many others – rules of exogamy meant that localities were crisscrossed with intricate webs of relationships, derived from innumerable inter-village marriages. Igbo women, living, as they did, in their husbands' villages, often played a major role in resolving local conflicts. Wives 'from outside' were perpetual strangers. This is imaged in the recurrent folk tale where a woman marries a handsome stranger and follows him home, only to find that he turns into a monster. When a wife died, her relations came to carry her 'home', showing very clearly where home was felt to be.

Most societies had a number of different types of conjugal arrangement: exchange marriage, marriage with bridewealth, and marriage by capture or elopement among them. The Anaguta of central Nigeria practised all three, and women were able to move from one partner to the next, in what has been called serial polyandry. Rattray distinguished six types of marriage among the Asante.[8] Matrilineal societies traced descent through the female line, and a man's heirs were his sister's children, but decision making and resources were still controlled by men. It has been described as the concomitant of relatively poor and egalitarian societies, and has declined greatly in twentieth-century Africa.[9] They were often characterised by instability of settlement: women lived with their husbands in their childbearing years, and then settled near their brothers with their grown sons. Female pawnship was common in matrilineal societies; this meant that, in return for payment, a woman's lineage affiliation – and that of her children – became that of her husband. Historians and ethnographers are increasingly hesitant to apply labels such as 'matrilineal'; it is now widely accepted that many societies incorporate both matrilineal and patrilineal elements, and that the scope of matriliny, where it exists, is limited to descent and inheritance.

The ideology of the lineage was necessarily fluid. Immigrants were incorporated into its structure after several generations had passed. The idiom of kinship gradually became a reality, and as generations passed, those who joined a settlement, whether by enslavement or choice, tended to become part of the genealogical calculus. An Asante elder from Mampong explained to Busia, 'Because . . . he came to settle on your land, he became your kinsman.'[10]

The corporate responsibilities of the lineage endured into the life to come. The LoDagaa of northern Ghana were unusual in their belief that the soul, after death, enters a world of rewards and punishments; families were judged collectively. 'The children of one woman and all their progeny will sit together. They'll count how many bad people there are in each group.'[11]

Many villages had a floating community of clients and 'slaves'. One of the most widespread characteristics of African cultures was the use of the language of kinship to represent relations both of ruler and ruled, and of 'owner' and 'slave'. This may well have affected the reality of power relations for the better. It softened the reality of enslavement, and disguised its reality even from those most directly affected. When the Bobangi sold slaves on the Zaire river, they told them that they were paying a visit. Gradually they realised that they had been sold.[12] The language of kinship is probably part of the ideology of sovereignty rather than an explanation of its rise. The title of the Tio king is derived from the word for a village or lineage elder,[13] and the Aja word for king, *ahosu*, originally meant clan head.[14] But in a more profound sense, the ruler stood above all lineages. The Kuba king was told at his accession:

> Let go of your kin.
> You belonged to your mother's clan.
> Now you are your own clan.
> Kill [renounce] your father,
> Kill [renounce] your mother,
> What is forbidden is a female king.[15]

In nineteenth-century Dahomey, Forbes described the language of kinship in the army of that highly militarised state: 'These relationships in military rank are called father and mother; and, as will appear, the male soldier, when accused, appeals to his "mother" to speak for him. Besides this military balance of power, all strangers visiting Abomey have "mothers".'[16]

The language of kinship had built into it a sense of hierarchy, and deference for both age and generational seniority. (These were not, of course, the same thing, and societies which institutionalised generational rather than age grades invariably experienced difficulties.)

The clan

'Clan' is, of course, an English word, which has been applied to very different African realities. A clan traced its descent to a common apical ancestor, and often avoided/respected a common totemic animal. In Igboland, the clan consists of a cluster of village groups, and residence mirrors the genealogical calculus. But in many African societies, members of different clans live intermingled. Often the royal lineage is particularly large, because its members tended to have numerous wives. Among the Igala, the royal clan comprised a quarter of the population.

Like the lineage, the clan is a shorthand representing a wide range of different historic experiences. Sometimes clans fossilise the waves of successive immigrants to settle an area. But they do not necessarily reflect historic patterns at all, and the clan, like the lineage, is often a useful fiction, a way of imposing social boundaries.[17] Several major studies of the history of the lacustrine area of East Africa concentrate on totemic clans. The difficulty is that totemic affiliation can be readily adopted or discarded. There are dramatic instances in Niger Delta history of the rejection of a totemic animal, and several important studies suggest that clans might be more recent than kingdoms. The great matriclans of Asante, now in decline, seem to have developed in the fifteenth and sixteenth centuries as a way of mobilising labour to clear the forest. The clans of the Anlo evolved as a way of protecting the original settlers' rights *vis-à-vis* new arrivals, in a sandy coastal area where cultivable land was limited.[18]

Work and gender

A great variety of ethnographic studies in different parts of Africa point to the same general conclusion: that women bore the heavier work load, and that older men controlled the lion's share of power and resources. A modern study of the Beti of central Cameroun suggests that women work 46 hours a week, dependent men 20, and male elders 5.[19] In most Bantu societies, men did the initial clearing of the forest, while women tended and harvested the crops, prepared food, cared for the homestead, and fetched firewood and water. They collected wild foods and sometimes fished. Pottery making was usually in women's hands, and so, often, was salt processing. Hunting and blacksmithing – both prestigious activities – were always men's work. In some cultures women did the spinning and men the weaving; in others, women did both. Among the modern Shambaa of northern Tanzania, women produce the family's food, while the men concentrate on generating 'wealth', mainly in livestock, for bridewealth, fines and other social purposes, often by selling tobacco.[20]

Because work was gender-specific, a solitary individual could not survive. This is why the household was the basic unit of production. Separation from her own kin, and the burden of work which awaited brides, meant that women's wedding songs often express grief, rather than rejoicing.

> The mortar is worn through
> Because of so much pounding.
> Tomorrow I will go home.[21]

Among the Kuba, masks representing women are distinguished by their tears.[22] Boddy's account of a village on the Nile rings true of many other African societies as well: 'the most notable feature of village life is the polarisation of the sexes ... To the outsider it almost appears as though there are two virtually separate coexisting societies that only occasionally overlap.'[23]

Occasionally, historic women played a dominant role in the world of political and military affairs: Hatshepsut ruled Egypt with her brother for twenty-two years in the fifteenth century BCE, but her monuments were defaced after her death, perhaps because her reign was felt to be contrary to right order.[24] Nzinga founded a kingdom in what is now Angola some three thousand years later.[25] Mythical queens also figure prominently in oral tradition, a phenomenon which we explore later in this study. The central contribution of women to African history lies not in real or imaginary queens, but in production. This can only be discerned on the small stage of local history, which is not easy to integrate with the broader perspectives of the history of a continent, and most existing studies deal with the last eighty years or so. Nevertheless, some nineteenth-century case studies are illuminating. Among the Baoulé of Ivory Coast, women grew cotton and produced thread; their husbands did the weaving, but women controlled the distribution of the cloth. In Maradi, men grew cotton and women spun it, and hired male dyers and weavers to produce cloth. The families of women potters in southern Mali located their homes near clay supplies.[26]

Older men's control of wealth meant that they also controlled the resources necessary to obtain brides. Young men tolerated the situation in the expectation of becoming elders themselves, and because they had little alternative. The ambiguities of the situation were intensified by the fact that it was the young men who did most of the productive farm work, but elders controlled the consumption of grain, preserving the seeds needed for the next planting.

It is likely that inter-generational conflict was the most important form of polarisation at the village level. In some societies, age grades solemnly handed power over to their successors in a ritual resolution of this fundamental antagonism. The age grade of young unmarried Bambara men symbolised their hostility to the elders by their conspicuous consumption, feasting and drinking millet beer: 'being much given to idleness, the kamalenw [bachelors]are trouble-makers and rebels who seek all material pleasure and devote their talents to opposing the [elders] and those who as masters of the community impose on young people the whole weight of an authority that is often absolute and often niggling.'[27]

In the absence of complex technologies, human labour was all-important, in the lineage, the village, and the kingdom. In the words of an Idoma song:

> The king rejoices!
> God gives to those who have people.
> God gives the kingship to the man
> Who has people.[28]

Meillassoux and his school explain the paramount importance of lineage ideology in these terms: survival depends on the continuation of the family group. Moreover, lineage provides an adaptive mechanism when social structures break down – the 'client' or 'slave' is gradually absorbed in the family.[29]

The economic power of older men, their power over women and the young, their control of bridewealth, often in the form of cattle, has been called the lineage mode of production, a concept which has fed many insights into African studies. It undoubtedly has its limitations. Political power was not always monopolised by the lineage elders. The lineage was a cognitive map, locating the individual in the worlds of the living and of the ancestors.

The family was not the most efficient way of dealing with the imperatives of the African farmer's year, with its need for intense labour at the beginning of the rains, and its enforced relative idleness in the long dry season. The work party, concluding, in grain-producing areas, with consumption of 'beer' (which has been aptly described as mildly alcoholic porridge!), was an effective response to seasonal labour needs, and lightened drudgery with companionship. It had the effect of enriching the prosperous (who were the only ones with grain to spare at the end of the dry season). An Akan funeral song runs:

> I ask you to help me in clearing the forest
> Then I ask you to help me in felling the trees on the farm
> Then I ask you to help me in making mounds for the yam seeds.
> But for harvesting the yams, I do not need your help,
> Your subjects, male and female alike, are terrible suckers.[30]

Vertical and horizontal linkages

The vertical bonds of lineage were always potentially divisive. They reinforced the corporate self-image of the village, but also the separate identities of its component families. Several characteristic institutions worked in a contrary, unifying, direction.

One of the most common of these was the male age grade. In societies as different as those of the agricultural Nyakusa and the pastoral Maasai, they were the basic building block of social relations. The former took the institution to an extreme, and male age-grade members and their families lived together in villages.

Different age grades had their appropriate duties, which included public works and defence. All this cemented a sense of corporate identity. The Lele tell a story about the age mates, Eagle and Tortoise, to illustrate the strength of these loyalties. Tortoise asked Eagle for his feathers and was given them. Eagle asked Tortoise for his shell, and received it. Eagle's feathers grew again, but Tortoise died, having chosen death rather than refuse a request from an age mate.[31] In the Mande heartland, there was a perpetual cycle of seven named age grades, and a new one was created every seven years.[32] The Oromo of Ethiopia had a system of eleven named generational – not age – grades in a forty-year cycle, a system called Gada.[33]

Secret cults were an important agency of social control. In some cults all adults were members, and in others selected initiates only. Their characteristic public manifestation was that of masked figures, or disembodied and disguised voices. Typically, youths were initiated in adolescence, in a rite of passage which often inflicted much suffering and deprivation. Initation rituals were full of birth symbolism, and represented a breaking away from the bonds of the natal family, an acceptance of the pleasures and responsibilities of adult life.

> On the day that you die
> your mother won't know
> your father won't know.[34]

Further west, in Sierra Leone and Liberia, there were parallel male and female cults, Poro and Sande.[35] The crucial difference was that Sande dealt only with women's affairs, whereas male cults played a major role in society as a whole.

In Nigeria, all masking societies were male cults (though some included a single elderly woman); one of their explicit functions was the subordination of women, children, strangers and slaves. An account collected early this century among the Kagoma of central Nigeria states: 'the idea of forming a "Dodo" [masked spirit] society started in the village of Agabi a number of years ago. Two men were bewailing the fact that their wives were constantly running away from them and that their children were getting out of hand. They put their heads together to seek a remedy.'[36]

Masking cults acted as agents of law and order, and their anonymity and supernatural aura meant that they could do so without inviting retribution. 'It stops boys from throwing stones at mango trees, and children from taking groundnuts from the farm.'[37] In some societies they stood in ritual hostility to kings, and in others they were a bastion of royal power. These cults often extended over wide areas, and embraced a number of ethno-linguistic groups. Ekpe, in the Cross River area, and Jankai, in central Nigeria, are examples.

The religion of the local community

The ideology of the lineage was reinforced by a cult of ancestors. The role played by nature spirits reflected both the uncontrollable and unpredictable elements in life, and the way in which our lot is largely determined by the environment. In the mountains of Upare, in northern Tanzania, people prayed:

> All our enemies, which are epidemics, wild animals and the witches
> Let them be blind and
> Let them come not to us.[38]

The rivers of southern Nigeria are inhabited by goddesses; their cults are local, and in most cases, unknown outside the vicinity, but the Yoruba river spirit, Oshun the Dancer, is also worshipped in Cuba and Brazil. In modern West Africa, these water goddesses have taken a syncretistic more generalised form – Mammy Wata.[39]

The fear of witchcraft was extremely widespread. Often, but not always, witchcraft accusations were directed towards older women, and they were some-times associated with an ambivalent attitude towards mothers. Gelede is a masking cult of the western Yoruba, where male dancers, dressed as women, dance to appease witches. 'Gelede is the secret of women ... We dance to appease our mothers.'[40] 'God made things double,' say the Ebirra, 'masquerading for men and witchcraft for women.'[41]

Among the Zande, royals were immune from witchcraft accusations, but in the village world these stereotypes were often directed at those who appeared to be a little more successful and prosperous than their fellows. Where all appeared to have access to much the same resources in land and labour, differentials in wealth needed explaining. In a sense, witchcraft beliefs were sometimes egalitarian, but often they punished those who were already poor and in some, though not all, African societies, the typical witch, in Africa as in Tudor and Stuart England, was an old woman, with a reputation for being eccentric or anti-social. There was often a narrow dividing line between the necessary supernatural powers of kings (and leaders generally) and witchcraft. The Tiv of central Nigeria lived in dispersed homesteads and had no kings. *Tsav* was a quality of personality, necessarily possessed by war leaders. But it was readily perverted, and seen as a physical deformation, an internal excrescence, which people of Tsav nurtured by nocturnal cannibalism. These nightly feasts were astral, existing only in the mind, as District Officers discovered when they tried to find actual human remains.

Functionalist anthropologists have often pointed out that witchcraft stereotypes served some useful purposes. They discouraged anti-social behaviour: the witch was characterised by malice and a refusal to share. Witchcraft beliefs defined the normal by inversion – witches walk on their hands, soil the compound, prefer the night, and so on. Like Africanist history, functionalism is an attempt to defend the rationality of African institutions against the prejudices of racism.

Witchcraft accusations reflect the intensity of the resentments which could build up in the little village world. In our own society, hostilities are defused by distance. One can move away from an aggressive neighbour. The interactions of village society were lifelong. But the tortures inflicted on purported witches vastly outweighed whatever useful functions witchcraft beliefs filled. The agonies they endured, subjected to poison trials or beaten to death with thorn branches, were horrific. Most of those who suffered in this way are long forgotten. Zenobia, who died of burns early this century near Yola, in north-eastern Nigeria, speaks for them all.

I saw her bound with string in the midst of a crowd who were saying to her, 'release the spell'. She was shrieking and answering 'I set no spell'. She kept up a continual shrieking as they were burning her. When she first came I said to deceased: 'Would it not have been better to have taken the spell off rather than suffer this?' She replied, 'If I were a witch would I not have done so long since rather than suffer so?'[42]

There were other dimensions of local religion; some societies had a cult of the sacred Earth; this was central, both to the Yoruba Ogboni cult and to the ancient Igbo ritual centre of Nri. Many peoples acknowledged a supreme – and generally remote – High God; since both missionaries and African Christians readily identified this with the God of Christianity, the concept has gone through many changes in the last hundred years. It has been suggested that a supreme God was first introduced into Nyakusa religion between the 1930s and 1950s.[43] In a famous essay, Horton suggested that local divinities were appropriate to the small world of village life, and that as communities became increasingly involved in a wider world, the High God gained in importance.[44] The theory fits some of the relevant facts but not all of them. The great gods of the Yoruba pantheon clearly reflect the majesty of Yoruba kings; some traditions link the two. Sango was an early Alafin of Oyo, and Ogun ruled the town of Ire until he destroyed it in a fit of rage.

Local trade

Long-distance trade figures more prominently in academic literature than local markets. The dramatic exchange of Sudanese gold for Saharan salt captures the imagination but throughout Africa's history small-scale local trade was of much greater total importance. In some cases, villages producing much the same items exchanged them with each other to foster inter-group relations,[45] but more usually, like trade everywhere, it rested on a complementarity of needs and resources. It tended to reflect the productive capacity of different ecological zones: worked iron from the Jos plateau was exchanged for salt from the brine springs of the Benue valley. Great canoes transported fish and salt from the Niger Delta to the interior, bringing back meat and yams. Regional specialisations were supplemented by occupational ones – hunter-gatherers and farmers exchanged honey and game for grain and iron and Fulbe pastoralists had a comparable symbiotic relationship with those who tilled the land.

Salt was produced in the north-eastern corner of Lake Victoria Nyanza, and exchanged for grain from Ukerewe Island, dried bananas from Buganda, and iron in the form of standardised hoes from a variety of producers to the east and south. Other food imports included dried fish and hippo meat. All this is well attested for the nineteenth century, and is probably much older. Goods were transported in sewn canoes, made from a wood which grew only in Busoga. Salt, iron and the rain needed to produce surplus crops were found in some areas but not others. The resources of the lake itself were available to all, but in practice extracted by fishermen and aquatic hunters.[46]

Currencies

We have had occasion to mention iron and copper currencies, and cakes of salt used in this way are discussed later in this chapter. There were many other forms of money. At the time when the first Europeans arrived, the Kongo kingdom was a fully monetarised economy: *nzimbu* shells from Luanda Island and raffia squares filled this role in the west and east respectively. Cowries and manillas were imported in vast quantities in the years of Atlantic trade, and in many ways shell money was closest to the currencies of the modern western world. Money of copper, iron, cloth or salt was both a commodity and a unit of value; this is equally true of gold and silver coins. African currencies were often used for restricted purposes – the accumulation of wealth, tribute, grave goods and bridewealth – rather than for day-to-day transactions. Any standard item of value could and did function as a unit of account, to facilitate transactions, providing a standard by which the relative price of different commodities could be measured. Iron hoes, iron bars, measures of cloth and salt cakes were all used in this way, in different areas and at different times. The great proliferation of currencies in western and central Africa reflected the great vitality of economic life. 'The bewildering "jungle of currencies" . . . fabricated out of iron, copper, raphia cloth, beads and shells . . . constitutes one of the most complex examples of non-capitalist monies in the world.'[47]

The growth of social stratification

Big Men

In his brilliant reconstruction of the early history of Equatorial Africa, Vansina uses linguistic evidence to reconstruct society as it existed in perhaps 1000 CE. There were local leaders, whose status was achieved rather than inherited. The word for these leaders is linked to others meaning fame, honour and wealth, and their authority was symbolised by the leopard, fish eagle and python. The basic unit of social organisation was a food-producing unit whose members were linked by real or fictive kinship ties and were resident in one place. (Vansina calls this a House; it corresponds to what I have called the lineage.) An aggregate of such Houses formed a village. He quotes from a modern source a ceremony of the Djue of Cameroon, which reflects these values:

This elephant [ivory bracelet] which I put on your arm, become a man of crowds,
a hero in war, a man with women
rich in children, and in many objects of wealth
prosper within the family, and be famous throughout the villages.[48]

In the nineteenth century, on the other side of Africa, on the extreme north-eastern frontier of Bantu speech, a missionary described the same values: 'Wealth, a ready flow of language, an imposing personal appearance, and above all the reputation of being a magician and rain-maker, are the surest means by which a Mkamba can attain power and importance, and secure the obedience of his countrymen.'[49] The Igbo shared these values, which are reflected in *ikenga*, the male cult of one's own right hand; personal titles were achieved, not inherited, and involved considerable expenditure. In some circumstances these Big Men may have developed into kings, but the Igbo, like the Kamba and the Djue, continued to live in small-scale polities.

Sacred kings

One of the most characteristic institutions in the Great State was sacred kingship. The king lived in seclusion, and was never seen to eat and drink. An account of the ruler of Kanem, written in 1337–8, would be true of many other sacred kings as well: 'He is veiled from his people. None sees him save at the two festivals, when he is seen at dawn and in the afternoon. During the rest of the year nobody . . . speaks to him, except from behind a screen.'[50] In many societies it was essential for him to be without blemish, strong and healthy. In these cultures it was his duty not so much to rule as to mediate between humanity and the forces of nature, and especially to ensure rain, and the fertility both of the land and of its inhabitants. Sometimes he willingly embraced his death when sickness or old age affected him. A Luba king had his hand shattered by an exploding gun in the nineteenth century, and was put to death by his followers.[51] Sacred kings were found in villages as well as kingdoms. The similarities are obscured by a tendency in the literature to call them priests, or priest-chiefs. They were surrounded by the same ritual restrictions. Among the Dinka, transhumant pastoralists living in small units, the Master of the Fishing Spear went willingly into his own grave when he felt his powers failing. The king of Onitsha, a Niger Igbo town of perhaps five thousand people, lived in seclusion, emerging to dance before his people once a year. He was forbidden to see the Niger, or the ancestral masks. Often, such sacred figures antedated the formation of a larger state, but continued to play a role, on a small stage, within it. The *kitome* of Kongo are an example.

The enlargement of scale

Archaeological evidence from sites as different and far apart as Jenne-Jeno and Igbo-Ukwu suggests that in many cases state formation and social differentiation in sub-Saharan Africa began in the Early Iron Age. By the time the first European visitors reached West and West Central Africa, in the late fifteenth century, there were a number of major states there, among them the Jolof, Benin and Kongo kingdoms. Two traditional histories of Kano suggest different interpretations of its origins. One emphasises the role of food production in famine time; the other concentrates on the religious dimension, focussing on conflicts between the guardians of rival shrines. This reminds us that no monocausal explanation of the rise of the state is likely to do justice to the complexities of African realities.

Centralised states developed where a concentration of resources – often, but not always, iron and salt – produced a surplus which sustained a ruling class. But, even where there was a surplus, people frequently made other cultural choices, and lived in small-scale communities. We must not only ask ourselves by what resources was a court sustained, but in what social, economic and political conditions a particular individual or clan was enabled to acquire control over the lives and resources of others.

European feudalism rested essentially on control of land. Only in Ethiopia was there a comparable development. In most of Africa, as myths and proverbs remind us insistently, land was abundant, and what was in short supply was labour. Every family produced its own food and had access to the basic weapons of war – the spear, or knife, or bow. If there was ample land, how did some individuals and clans acquire political control over others? There is no single or simple answer.

In some contexts, a purely ritual pre-eminence – as in rain-making – was gradually transmuted into political pre-eminence. Sometimes strong government was welcomed as an escape from internal dissension, or as a way of coordinating activity in a time of crisis. The nineteenth century is full of examples of New

Men, who seized power through personal charisma and military abilities. They undoubtedly had their counterparts in the more distant past.

The major theories (which are not mutually exclusive) stress production (whether of food, iron or salt), trade, and the technology of warfare. The Hausa poem known as the 'Song of Bagauda' interprets the rise of Kano in terms of food in time of famine; Bagauda, the hunter, was joined by farmers:

> Then came a killing famine
> And there was no corn to be had; only by coming to them
> Could it be had, and they doled it out in small quantities.
> They became well off in slaves and horses too . . .
> The people were living widely dispersed over the open country, not
>   subject to any authority.
> There was no chief, no protecting town wall.
> The elders said: let a chieftaincy be established.
> They appointed Bagauda.[52]

Mbegha, who founded a kingdom in Shambaa in northern Tanzania, was a hunter who distributed meat. The same pattern is found in Busoga: 'When he said that he wanted to return to his homeland, people prevented him from going and said, stay and judge us when we fight because you are a good man and you give us meat freely.'[53]

Miller explains the evolution of political hegemonies in West Central Africa in terms of scarcity. As populations became denser in the fertile river valleys, people were forced to settle on marginal land. They could support themelves when the rains were reliable, but were threatened by famine in time of drought. They then became refugees, willing to become slaves or pawns in return for food.[54] There are many cases elsewhere in Africa of the exchange of liberty – sometimes, that of a family member – for food. In the 1860s, a missionary on the lower Niger described 'the painful sight of infants and sucklings, children and young men, passing by our gate as slaves, to be sold in order to procure food to support the rest of their family'.[55] The relationship with the refugee did not need to take the extreme form of slavery or pawnship. Often immigrants were allowed to live in a more favoured area, recognising the overlordship of the first settlers as Owners of the Land.

In some societies – Rwanda, Bunyoro – cattle herders became a ruling aristocracy. The Cwezi, semi-legendary fifteenth-century lords in the inter-lacustrine area, were pastoralists. But many of Africa's most famous pastoralists, such as the Maasai, the Nuer, and the Dinka, did not live in centralised states. The Fulbe lived for centuries in small transhumant bands, but in the nineteenth century Fulbe clerics founded the caliphates of Massina and Sokoto. Scholars disagree about the relative importance of trade and pastoralism in the history of Great Zimbabwe.

The Blacksmith King

A very interesting complex of traditions and rituals associates kingship with iron working. When did this develop? It has been pointed out that Early Iron Age smelting sites are not secluded but are in the centre of a community; it is possible that this reflects the iron worker's political dominance. Traditions about the Blacksmith King do not necessarily explain how the state developed. They may well encapsulate a meaning of another kind (as does, indeed, the true fiction of the Bagauda story). Blacksmith, hunter and king bridge the natural and the cultural order. Each has magical powers, which can sometimes be used to ensure rain. The Sacred Blacksmith and the Blacksmith King are international stereotypes, like the Drunken King or the Tower of Babel.[56]

Some traditions describe how those with access to iron seized political power. In ancient Mali, the Kante, a blacksmith clan, overthrew the Soso. A nineteenth-century source suggests that the Cwezi were blacksmiths.[57] On the Tshuapa, a tributary of the Zaire river, immigrants replaced their iron-tipped spears with horn-tipped ones, and thus, appearing harmless, won permission to settle. Then they replaced the iron tips and slew their hosts.[58] A Rwanda traditional historian stated that 'the king of Rwanda himself is the country's supreme blacksmith', and an eighteenth-century *mwami* was buried with two anvils at his head.[59] In Burundi, a smith is always a Hutu, never a Tutsi. But tradition states that the art of working copper and iron was introduced by the first king, Ntare Rushatsi.[60] The interesting example of Ufipa is discussed later in this study.[61]

At the enthronement of a Luba king, his knees are struck, as the hammer strikes the anvil, and he is told: 'I do this to remind you that your forefather Kalala introduced iron working to this land ... Whether for weapons of war or tools of peace ... the anvil is the secret of power and progress.' The distinctive hammer-anvil (*★-jundo*) is a common symbol of kingship in central Africa.[62]

The Blacksmith King is often conceptualised as a benign conciliator. But Kuba traditions tell of a prince called Myeel who was a superb metal worker but never became king because of his severity in fining a village which inadvertently disturbed his ore, an episode in which one can perhaps discern the impatient perfectionism of a historical artist.[63] But while some societies were ruled by Blacksmith Kings, in others, both in Ethiopia and the Western Sudan, smiths and other craft workers formed marginalised castes (pp. 956, 207 and 236–8 below).

Salt

Salt is found in traditions of political genesis as often as iron working, and it is no coincidence that some states, such as the Luba kingdom, grew up in close proximity both to good iron ore and to salt pans. Salt of good quality was rare, and salt hunger is writ large in African history, a concomitant of hard physical work in a tropical climate, and of a largely vegetable and sometimes monotonous diet. 'He who has salt never starves,' say the Sukuma.[64] The fine rock salt of Kisama, south of Luanda, was exported far afield; when the Portuguese briefly seized it in the late sixteenth century, it was said: 'This loss the King of Angola and all enemies felt and still feel today more than anything else we have inflicted upon them. The silver mines mean little to them, but the salt mines are their most valued possession.'[65] (The silver mines did indeed mean little: as the Portuguese discovered in the end, they did not, in fact, exist!)

Often, the salt processors were women – as many as a hundred worked together in one area on the Kongo coast.[66] In some places salt was a currency, despite its solubility.[67] Some traditions state that Great Zimbabwe was abandoned because of the need for more salt for the expanding royal herds.

Salt did not always lead to state formation, of course: the Ijo communities of the Niger Delta exported sea salt to the hinterland, but remained small fishing villages until the advent of Atlantic trade.

The technology of war and state growth

A famous study by Goody drew attention to the forces of destruction rather than production – though the expression is misleading, since war was essentially a means of appropriating production.[68] In particular, war was often a means of acquiring resources through the capture of slaves.

The whole question of the relationship between the technology of war and state formation is a complex one, and there are few generalisations to which one cannot readily find an exception. There was sometimes a connection between archery and small-scale states: among the LoDagaa, a bow and quiver represented the dead man at his funeral ceremonies,[69] but there were many permutations. Egypt's Mamluks were mounted archers, a combination not found in black Africa. In the seventh century, the skill of Nubian archers prevented the Arabs from conquering their homeland. Arabic sources describe how they would aim at the eye – and not miss.[70] African bows had a much shorter range than their Turkish or English equivalents, but this was often counterbalanced by the use of arrow poison (a commodity which, like salt or copper, was traded over great distances).

The horse originated in Asia:[71] paintings of horses and skeletal remains have been found in Egypt from the Eighteenth Dynasty (1580–1350 BCE) onwards; the skeleton of a horse from 1675 BCE was found at a fort at Buhen, near the Second Cataract.[72] At first horses were used to draw chariots, and the practice of riding developed later. The first reference to cavalry in the Maghrib dates from 262 BCE. Horse-drawn chariots are a common motif in Saharan rock art. In the West African environment, horses became smaller.[73] On the Jos plateau, these ponies survived into modern times, and would respond to their master's call, like a dog. They were ridden bareback, with only a bridle. It would be difficult to find a more moving description of the bonds between rider and horse than the words of a Berom in 1950:

You give it water to drink, you walk miles to find it grass to eat, it carries you to hunt and to war, when it is tired you dismount and carry your loads on your own head. When you die and they lead it towards your grave, its spirit may fly out of its body in its anxiety to find you.[74]

From the fourteenth century onwards, cavalry became of central importance in the states of the Western Sudan.[75]

Trade and state growth

In 1375, a Majorcan cartographer drew a map which has often been reproduced in Africanist histories. It shows a man riding a camel and wearing the veil characteristic of the Sanhaja of the western Sahara.[76] He is moving towards the king of Mali, who sits enthroned, a nugget of gold in his hand. The history of the great states which grew up in the Sahel or Western Sudan seemed to be a dramatic example of the way in which long-distance trade contributed to the growth of states. Rulers were able to levy customs duties, and exotic imports from afar augmented the resources with which they rewarded their supporters. They or their representatives spoke for the community in dealings with foreign merchants.

There were undoubted linkages between long-distance trade and the growth of states. But scholars are now more inclined to emphasise production, recognising that the emphasis on trade in Arabic accounts of the Western Sudan springs at least in part from the fact that their authors, or their informants, were merchants. Many peoples involved in long-distance trade, such as the Yao, the Bisa and the Kamba, lived in small-scale polities.[77]

The rise of states is sometimes associated with religious institutions. The cities of Hausaland grew up near the inselbergs which are the haunts of spirits (*iskoki*): Kano near Dala Hill, Zaria near Kufena. In the 'Kano Chronicle', Bagauda is preceded by a hunter and magician called Barbushe: 'By his wonders and sorceries and the power he gained over his brethren he became chief and lord over them.'[78]

None of these factors provides an entirely convincing explanation of why large states developed in some areas and not in others. The Igbo, who lived in over 2,000 separate small-scale polities, and the Bini, who founded a great kingdom, lived in the same natural environment. Some Yoruba lived in kingdoms and others did not. Political institutions reflect cultural choices, made at a level often much deeper than that of the conscious mind.

Traditional histories personalise the growth of states, which they tend to attribute to a great magician and warrior. If we look at events for which there is ample documentation, such as the history of southern Africa at the time of the Mfecane, we find that individuals – a Shaka or a Moshoeshoe – do indeed play a major role.

It is important to remember, too, that kingdoms did not only rise; they also declined and disappeared; oral history, inevitably, reflects the perceptions of the survivors. The 'Song of Bagauda' reminds us:

> Look at the kings who have flourished in the past,
> Their story is near to being obliterated.[79]

A recurrent theme in oral tradition is the rejection of the tyrannical ruler. There are many cases of this in the pages which follow. The Nyoro word for government means heavy or oppressive, and in Morocco the word for government, *makhzen*, means treasure. In Yawuri, in Nigeria, 'There are varying versions of this founding of the royal house but all agree upon one point, that the people did not want a king (*sarki*) but were quite content to jog along in their own democratic way'.[80] The traditions of the Soninke-speaking Kusa tell how they rebelled against an oppressive king, led by Maren Jagen Dukure. But Dukure became a tyrant in his turn, and kept the crops of the state fields for himself. The people covered them with gravel, and moved away.[81] Many others, in the thinly populated savannas, have moved in protest against an unpopular government.

The limitations of the state

Reflecting the political realities of the present, scholars tend to emphasise the essential fragility of pre-colonial states, their limited ability to shape social realities. Conventional historical maps show ancient African polities, like modern nation states, demarcated by precise boundaries. The location of these boundaries is in fact often problematic, and they were always fluid. More fundamentally, African states did not, like modern industrialised nations, form a block of territory within which the impact of government was equally felt. A kingdom characteristically had a central core, where its government impinged most; in outlying provinces, subjection was in many ways nominal and tribute essentially symbolic. The king of Benin sent a party once a year to collect water from the Niger; the alafin of Oyo was given grass to thatch the palace roof. The Lozi royal barge was constructed from materials collected all over the country.[82] Miller, reflecting on this phenomenon in West Central Africa, suggests:

What ambitious men struggled to achieve was … not direct supervision over others, and still less stocks of the physical products of their labour beyond immediate needs, since both people and their fabrications were all too perishable, but rather a general claim to unspecified future labor and its product at whatever moment need for them might arise.[83]

There was a limit to the territory which could be absorbed by an expanding state. The tension between the urge to conquer and the difficulty of administering an ever greater state is evident in the history of Asante. It has been said, in a different context, 'Too few successes cast doubt on the legitimacy of state power in its present form. Too many successes expanded the state beyond the limits effectively controlled by existing forms of rule.'[84]

Tribute

There is a sense in which tribute was the political arrangement of regional trade. Much of what was given as tribute, reflecting the skills and resources of a particular area, was redistributed elsewhere. The kings of Kongo were given salt and currency shells from the coastal provinces, which they distributed inland in return for cloth. Much revenue, of course, was retained as well as redistributed;[85] when a ruler and his retinue travelled in the provinces, the impact could be disastrous. In 1872, the Emir of Gwandu visited Bida, the capital of Nupe. 'After the Sultan's departure, Bida was left as bare as a large green and flourishing plantation of wheat or rye would be after a swarm of locusts had alighted upon it for one day.'[86]

Cities

Urbanisation was sometimes, but not always, a concomitant of the growth of the state. A book by a Dutch geographer of the seventeenth century, Dapper's *Description of Africa*, includes three famous drawings of African cities – Benin, Loango and São Salvador. Some had thought them idealised, but the drawing of

Benin, which includes the palace, its towers surmounted by giant birds, has received extraordinary corroboration from the corpus of Benin art, which includes a model of the palace and a claw from one of the great birds. To a Dutch visitor, seventeenth-century Benin was comparable with Amsterdam.

> The towne seemeth to be very great, when you enter into it, you goe into a great broad street, not paved, which seemeth to be seven or eight times broader than the Warmoes street in Amsterdam ... The Houses in this Towne stand in good order, one close and even with the other, as the Houses in Holland stand.[87]

But some major states had no capital built in permanent materials. In the late ninth century, al-Yaqubi wrote of Kanem, 'Their dwellings are huts made of reeds and they have no towns.'[88] Significantly, the capital of Kanem, Njimi, has never been located. One of the earliest European visitors to West Africa said of the Wolof rulers in 1454: 'though these pass as lords, it must not be thought that they have castles or cities, as I have already explained. The King of this realm had nothing save villages of grass huts, and Budomel was lord only of a part of this realm.'[89]

'Slavery'

Domestic slavery was already well established in West and West Central Africa when the first European visitors arrived, in the late fifteenth and early sixteenth centuries.[90]

In an earlier chapter we described the debates between 'Africanist' and materialist or Marxist historians. An influential collection of essays published in 1977 is an excellent example of an Africanist perspective.[91] Its editors were quite rightly anxious to distinguish slavery in Africa from the very different institution of plantation slavery. The word 'slavery' was placed in inverted commas, or referred to by its local African name. It was seen as one form of marginality among many, part of a continuum of subordination which included debt pawns and wives. Others, more plausibly, say that the difference was one of degree, not kind.[92] The study of slavery in Africa is inseparable from that of Atlantic and Saharan slave exports, which undoubtedly encouraged the growth of domestic slavery. To some, this expansion was so great that it effected a social transformation best described as a new mode of production.[93]

The slave had no lineage (in the sense of a social identity in the captor state). In some societies, this meant that slave status was positively desirable for wives, including royal wives. Individuals were enslaved by violence; some court slaves enjoyed great power and luxury, but the slave, rich or poor, was always at the mercy of his master. In many societies, he was subject to the extreme form of oppression, human sacrifice. The pawn endured a brief and conditional servitude, which ended when the debt was paid.

The realities of African slavery were enormously nuanced, variable and complex. In general, slaves carried out much the same duties as the free population, but they tended to work harder and have a lower standard of living. Park noted that slave traders preferred to buy those born into slavery, 'well knowing that these have been accustomed to hunger and fatigue'.[94] They were often subject to the ultimate form of oppression – sacrifice in religious rituals.

All observers confirm the point which Mungo Park noted among the Bambara in the late eighteenth century, the difference between first-generation slaves and their descendants, who often could not be sold: 'The slaves which are thus brought from the interior may be divided into two distinct classes – first, such as were slaves from their birth, having been born of enslaved mothers; secondly such as were born free, but who afterwards, by whatever means, became slaves. Those of the first description are by far the most numerous.'[95]

Women were particularly prized as slaves; they often became wives or concubines, and were virtually indistinguishable from their free counterparts, especially when they had borne children. All but one of the Askias of Songhai had slave mothers, and so, in the nineteenth century, did some Fulbe emirs, since a youth's first partner tended to be a concubine. Most women slaves, like their free sisters, led laborious lives working in agriculture or crafts. Sometimes there was a division of labour by gender: men picked cloves on nineteenth-century Zanzibar, and women not only picked them, but also separated and dried them. One of the characteristics of a male slave was that 'women's work' could be demanded of him. Muslim women in seclusion relied on slaves to trade on their behalf; after emancipation they depended on their children.[96] The picture of slavery in Africa is complicated by categories of slaves who were privileged and often powerful. The Tyeddo of Senegal were slave soldiers[97] who in effect formed an aristocracy. In some kingdoms, high offices were held by slaves; from the viewpoint of the king, they were more likely to be loyal. This was not always the case: Diara, a first-generation slave, founded a new dynasty of kings in eighteenth-century Segu. The Kaigama, who led the Borno army, was usually a slave and there were great slave officials at the courts of the Alafin of Oyo, some of whom died with their master. Bruce said of the Funj court in the eighteenth century, 'Slavery in Sennar is the only true nobility.'[98] Some slave officials were eunuchs, who were thought to lack both the supporters and the motivation for independent political aspirations. But a black eunuch nicknamed Dusky Camphor ruled Egypt from 946 until his death in 968.

Castes

A system of endogamous craft castes was found both in a large area of the Western Sudan and in Ethiopia. The men were often blacksmiths, married to potters, but other occupations, especially tanning, were casted as well. So were the griots, the praise singers who often played a major role in diplomacy. Often, the casted were thought to have magical and healing powers.

We have devoted considerable attention to the importance of pyrotechnology in African history, and the concept of the Blacksmith King. It seems an extraordinary paradox that smiths and potters, whose work was of such great economic importance, and griots, who were the custodians of their people's cultural inheritance, should be casted.

Some of the most extreme forms of marginalisation are found in Ethiopia.

Among the Gurage, smiths and tanners cannot own herds or cultivate the soil. Like craft castes elsewhere, they cannot marry non-members, or even eat with them. In Darfur, blacksmiths and their potter wives form a comparable despised endogamous caste.[99] But supernatural powers are attributed to them, not unlike those of the Blacksmith King – smiths can control lightning, and their wives are healers. Although marginalised, smiths are often prosperous, especially when there are no restrictions on other economic activities such as farming. Their potential political power was neutralised by the caste system, and their extreme isolation made them easier to control. The marginalisation of craft groups, despite their economic rewards, prevents both the overcrowding of these specialities, and their usurpation of political power. It reflects a world view where the cultivation of land is more highly valued than craft specialisation.[100]

But perhaps castes originate less in the *realpolitik* of kings or the self-assurance of farmers than in awe before the blacksmith's magical powers. He transmutes ordinary earth into valuable metal, and does so by his control of fire. A particularly perceptive study[101] showed the close similarity between *osu* and the sacred king of Onitsha. *Osu* is often translated 'cult slave', dedicated to a divinity, 'horrible and holy' and shunned by all others.

The blacksmith's powers are magical; he is 'other', and can be shunned or revered. Camera Laye is the son of a casted Malinke smith; his childhood memoir, *L'enfant noir*, describes how his father worked gold to the songs of praise singers, and how both his parents had supernatural powers.

Not all smiths, of course, were caste members or kings, and iron working did not always foster the growth of state structures. Among the Igbo, iron working was an elite occupation, the craft a carefully guarded secret, practised by itinerant experts with a high degree of professional organisation.

More on gender roles

There is a sense in which men rather than women were involved in the exosphere: long-distance trade, war and diplomacy. There are many exceptions to this: Yoruba and Nupe women engaged in long-distance trade, and Queen Nzinga represented Ndongo before the governor of Angola, and later founded a state of her own. But there was often a gender-based perception of who should sell what, and it was generally men who embarked on long-distance trade, and trade with Europeans. The Akan have a proverb, 'It is the business of a woman to sell garden eggs and not gunpowder.'[102]

It was not unknown for women to take part in war – the women soldiers of Dahomey are the most famous example – but in general 'it was through war that the "differential relation" between men and women was most clearly demonstrated'.[103]

One of the most interesting dimensions of cultural encounter in the period of colonial conquest and rule was parody. The Asante built imitation telegraph lines in the 1870s, and the Beni dance societies which developed on the Kenya coast in the 1890s included suitably attired Kingi and Scotchi.[104] In southern Ghana, in time of war, women might wear men's clothes or carry 'knives, old flint-locks, imitation weapons carved out of wood'.[105] West African women sometimes reacted to a crisis by going naked or by wearing or carrying green leaves, perhaps in a symbolic identification with the wild.

Ethnic identity

Historians are agreed on the artificiality of ethnic labels. They tend to write of the 'invention' of ethnic stereotypes, referring especially to the colonial period when colonial administrators, seeking to understand and group the peoples they dealt with, tended to rely on 'tribal' categories. What constitutes an ethnic group? Language is an obvious starting point, but both Tutsi and Hutu speak kinyaRwanda and both Fulbe and Tukulor speak Fulfulde. Many families in northern Nigeria now speak only Hausa but still consider themselves Fulbe. The difference between Onitsha and Owerri Igbo is greater than that between Dutch and German; the difference between Ika and Ohafia Igbo is much greater. 'Ethnic' identity was shaped partly by occupational factors (the Bozo were fishermen, the Fulbe pastoralists) and partly by a sense of identification with a particular geographic area (among the Igbo, Enugu, 'upland', or Anaocha, 'white' land).

Largely unconsciously, historians tend to write as if linguistic groups were also social and political entities, distinguished by a large complex of specific attitudes and practices. There are great difficulties in this. 'You ask a Nupe man what all Nupe have in common ... All Nupe, he will say, have the age grade associations, all Nupe have the *gunnu* cult.' As Nadel went on to point out, these and other cultural traits were shared by their neighbours.[106] It is customary to contrast 'Sotho' and 'Nguni', though the opposition is recent and is rooted in language rather than the perceptions of the peoples themselves. But there are exceptions to the conventional generalisations (such as the fact that the Nguni lineage is exogamous, while the Sotho prefer – or insist on – cousin marriage).[107] Polyandry, in some circumstances, is cited as typical of the Lele of Kasai. But some of their eastern and western neighbours, the Kuba and Pende, share this characteristic, and one Lele section, the Njembe, do not.[108] If we extrapolate modern ethnic labels into the past, we are in danger of forgetting earlier ethnic identities which have ceased to exist, like the 'Tebou' brought by Muslim traders to Whydah in the eighteenth century.[109] At the beginning of the sixteenth century, a Portuguese visitor to West Africa drew attention to these silences: 'These merchants belong to various tribes [a list follows] and many others which I omit for the sake of brevity.'[110] But whatever the inadequacies of ethnic labels, it is impossible to write intelligibly about the African past without them.

There is a sense, moreover, in which at least some of these labels reflect dimensions of African thought. Oral cultures preserve what their members consider to be of core importance, and traditions of origin are statements about identity. Often, a sense of unity is symbolised by a myth of descent from a single named ancestor. Thus the Kikuyu tell how God created Gikuyu and his wife Mumbi, and gave them livestock and land, and how their nine daughters are the forebears of the modern Kikuyu clans. The myth is a statement about Kikuyu identity and about rights in land. The Mau Mau insurgents, looking for an ideology, found it here. It was inadequate for their purposes, not least because it excluded non-Kikuyu, but it reflected the continuing meaning of these concepts in their lives.

Cultural complexes

Ethnic groups cannot be identified with cultural complexes. But is it possible to study such complexes and see what light they shed on, for instance, traditions of migration? This kind of study has been discredited by the errors of diffusionism. Its basic methodological weakness was to take a single variable in isolation from its cultural context. In a famous instance, similar rituals in Egypt and Buganda were compared to show that sacred kingship diffused from the one to the other, a comparison which overlooks a multitude of other differences. The mapping of distinctive artefacts is full of interest. Vansina, a pioneer here as so often, has mapped the spread of the clapperless flange-welded double bell from West Africa through much of Central Africa. An important symbol of authority, it is imaged in a terracotta from the classic age of Ife art. Vansina has also mapped the diffusion of the iron throwing-knife in Central Africa.[111] But the distribution of distinctive artefacts does not necessarily mirror areas of social contact; ideas and designs were transmitted from one people to the next, and in most instances the original source and final recipient had no contact with each other.

Where an artefact is unique, its diffusion from a single source is indisputable (the chess set is a classic example). If we study the mythical systems of widely scattered peoples, we find legends which seem as distinctive as the double bell. The occurrence of identical myths in regions of Africa many thousands of kilometres apart – the distancing of the sky, which was once close to earth, or the cosmic race between two representatives of the animal world, which determined human mortality – is one of the many mysteries of the African past. As we have seen, various culture traits – sacred kingship, age grades, masking cults, the use of the metaphor of kinship for political and servile relations – are very widespread in Africa. They have not all necessarily diffused from a single source; there is a limit to the possible ritual expressions of sacred kingship, and there are masking cults in Melanesia and North America. Lonsdale suggests that 'If African kingdoms did share a common fund of political ideas, that was because there is a limited stock of symbols and justifications of authority anyway. If there was a movement of ideas, it was by exchange, by "saturation", rather than diffusion.'[112]

The existence of far-flung networks of culture traits or mythemes is not a problem where they exist at a regional level, even where the region is a large one. The recognition that cults were often regional rather than ethnic was an important step in the understanding of traditional religion in Africa,[113] and one of the finest studies of African religion focusses on such a cult.[114] It is where the same mytheme or culture trait appears on a continent-wide scale that historical understanding becomes so difficult. Having discarded the oversimplifications of diffusionism we are left with something of a vacuum. In the words of one of the few scholars to confront the problem:

The answer must go beyond both the mechanistic assumptions of continent-wide diffusionism and the nearsighted vision of parochial functionalism. The similarities across Africa are too complex to have simply arisen from direct diffusion, yet they are too great to have developed through repeated coincidence. We must see the societies in question ... as having been *constructed* ... from a cultural inventory of symbols and practices that ... predate any particular society being observed.[115]

Myths offer one window into the cognitive universe of the past. The design of settlements and of individual houses and compounds suggests another. One of the most striking changes, as one moves north in West Africa, is the transition from rectangular to circular houses. The latter are the norm in much of sub-Saharan Africa; one of the oddities of the nineteenth-century missionary enterprise was the hostility of European missionaries to circular houses.[116] Africans consciously invested house design with symbolic meaning: 'he sees the circularity of seasons in Nature, or the day and night cycle of sleeping and waking ... A chief argued with me ... that by making a square house I had, at once created four points of near or remote breakage – a circle has no weak point.'[117]

Recent valuable studies have explored the symbolic meaning of the layout of southern Bantu homes around a cattle byre which contains burials and grain storage pits (p. 115 below). There is a paradox in African cognitive history; certain myths and symbols are found over enormous areas, but within any given microcosm there will be great differences of interpretation. Later researchers have been unable to find independent confirmation of the elaborate symbolic universe described among the Dogon, by Griaule and his associates, which depended largely on a single remarkable informant.[118] The Kuba disagree about the meaning of sacred kingship in their own culture.

There is a dispute which may be quite old. The Kuba skeptics claimed that it stemmed from the fact that the king as the richest person commanded the best charms, while the more mystically inclined attributed it to a quality inherent in kingship ... the king also claimed to be polluted, and the Bushoong took him to be an archsorcerer.[119]

People and wealth: the contradictions

Earlier in this chapter, we discussed the importance of kinship and the importance placed on people. A basic premise of modern African studies is that in much of the continent land was abundant but people in short supply, which explains the prevalence both of domestic slavery and of pawning. Another basic insight, which threads its way through the pages which follow, concerns the struggle to wrest a living from an often adverse environment, the recurrence of famine, drought and epidemics.

There are, however, problems with this model. Why, if people were all-important, were they exported as slaves in Atlantic trade, or, in some societies, killed in religious sacrifices? The second phenomenon is less of a problem. As in cultures which cherish cattle but offer an ox in sacrifice, or as in Abraham's willingness to slaughter Isaac, it reflects a decision to offer to divinity what is most highly valued. But why were they sold?

Various answers have been suggested: it is a theme to which we return in the appropriate section of this study (see pp. 334ff.). I believe that the answer lies encoded at the deepest levels in a conflict about the relative value of wealth and people. This contradiction recurs constantly. The Big Man, or king, is expected to be wealthy, but largesse depletes his resources. If he becomes poorer than his subjects or followers, his role is threatened. But an avaricious king may lose his throne.

Harms has written with great insight of the clash between health and wealth on the middle Zaire; in an analysis which is redolent with echoes from other African cultures, he describes the Bobangi entrepreneurs who offered human sacrifices to river whirlpools, and made pacts with crocodile familiars. He interprets the underlying world view as a zero sum game: the total amount of wealth is limited, so one who becomes very rich impoverishes others.[120] Among the LoDagaa of northern Ghana, the witch and the rich man both suffer in burning heat in the life to come for the same time (three years). The thief suffers for five months.[121] Witchcraft beliefs often involve the idea of wealth obtained through an astral or actual human sacrifice – stereotypes which are still flourishing today.

For these societies, of course, were not indifferent to wealth. In the years of Atlantic trade, coastal brokers imported houses from Europe and filled them with valuables, while burying hoards of currency in the ground. West and Central African peoples, in particular, created a vast number of works of art: sculptures in gold, ivory, bronze and wood, elaborate textiles, masking costumes, personal jewellery. Because the western world fully accepts the value of these treasures, they are now, very often, owned by (western) museums, or the enormously wealthy. In 1992, a single Fang ancestral sculpture sold for $550,000.[122] There was an inherent and endemic contradiction between social values which emphasised sharing and generosity and the natural desire for individual security and prosperity. This was not peculiar to Africa (in Europe, medieval moralists agonised over these very issues) but these dilemmas lie at the very heart of much African history.

The chapters which follow analyse a period for which there is some external evidence, but where scholars rely very heavily on oral tradition. No field of African history is more debated or more complex. The father of structuralism, Lévi-Strauss, called myth making *bricolage*, meaning that myths are created from the debris of historical facts. We must now attempt to reconstruct the past from these fragments.

Part II

Regional histories to the sixteenth century

7

Central Africa[1]

The hippopotamus is child of the herd. He dives to the deepest
waters, [because] the white sands [of the shallows] betray him.

Lozi proverb[2]

Environments

The popular perception of Africa is one of equatorial rainforest – Conrad's *Heart
of Darkness* – though savanna, steppe and desert cover much greater areas. Even
in Central Africa, the forest of the Zaire basin is confined to the area between 5
degrees north and 5 degrees south. It is interlaced with innumerable rivers, and
includes many different human habitats, among them vast areas of inundated
forest, particularly valued by fishermen.

Between Malebo Pool and the sea, there are thirty-two cataracts on the Zaire
river (Map 5). Above the Pool, it is navigable for 1,734 kilometres and, together
with its great tributaries, has provided a historic highway for trade. Bonga, at the
confluence of three rivers, was 'the Venice of Africa', built on artificial mounds.[3]

The population of the forest zone is and always has been low, since dense
farming populations tend to destroy the forest cover. Agriculturalists were
attracted to breaks in the dense vegetation, often created by rivers. Rights in land
are rights in cleared land or secondary bush, because of the immense difficulty of
clearing the original vegetation. The forest, as we shall see, was a true home to
the Mbuti of the Ituri forest, but to farmers it was a perennial threat, and a place
of natural and supernatural peril. This perception is expressed in many different
ways, including the hunter's reliance on charms, and his heroic stature in myth.

South of the equatorial rainforest lie great expanses of savanna. Here, the
rainfall was lower, and famine and drought are often the hidden dynamic
underlying political events, re-enacted, in miniature, in the passage of the
seasons. 'There in that fructifying, sterilising sun their hard history is epitomised.'[4] To the south-west, the savanna merges into steppe and barren scrub,
and then into the Kalahari desert. South of the Kwanza, agriculture was only
possible in river valleys, and salt mines were a precious resource in a barren
land.[5] Soil types affected food production as well as climate: parts of central
Africa have poor soils – 'Kalahari sands' – which retain neither moisture nor
nutrients. The Lele and Chokwe lived in such an environment.

North of the forest, there is another belt of savanna, changing imperceptibly
into steppe and desert. A region relatively little studied by historians,[6] it forms
the subject of a later chapter.

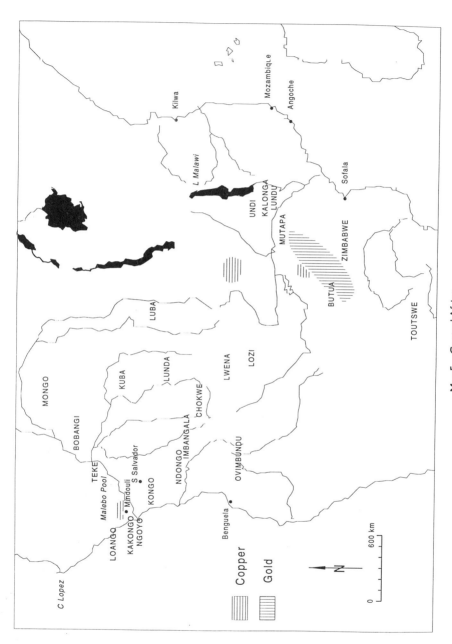

Map 5 Central Africa

Scarcity and survival

Much of the history of the region can best be understood in terms of a quest for security, especially against famine. Authorities differ greatly in their estimates of how long grain could be stored – some suggest two, others as much as seven years.[7] Rain-making was a key attribute of kings, and drought could lead to their overthrow. Famine may well have been the driving force behind the mysterious marauding armies which appear suddenly in the historical record – Jaga, Imbangala and Zimba.

The Atlantic slave trade is best understood in terms of the competition for resources, which was in itself rooted in endemic scarcity.[8] Drought, famine and the fear of social chaos are the dynamic behind the cruel and oppressive aspects of some African kingdoms. The Luba put many royal baby boys to death to obviate the greater destructiveness of fratricidal wars of succession. (Medieval Ethiopia dealt with the same problem by imprisoning princes on a mountain top.) This is not peculiar to Africa. For a time, an Ottoman sultan, on coming to the throne, was obliged by decree to kill his brothers. In the nineteenth century, the Luba went to war with mutilated captives in the front line of battle to terrify their opponents. The myth of the harsh Kinguri who was finally put to death (see pp. 112, 398–9 below) may be an implicit critique of the cruelty of kings. A different myth, which tells of a lost princely child rejected by his father and sought for when the heir died, is an explicit critique of royal infanticide.[9]

To Thornton, the most significant socio-economic division in the (seventeenth-century) Kongo kingdom was between the towns – especially the capital, where the nobility clustered – and the countryside. Some village production was sent as tribute to the capital, but partly because of transport problems, this was insufficient for its needs, which were also supplied by a growing class of 'slaves'. Some of these were officials, messengers and so on and probably had a more agreeable and affluent lifestyle than many villagers.

Vansina described the same basic polarity in the Kuba kingdom, between the villages and the capital, where the royal family and office holders lived, and which had a population of 5,000 to 10,000 in the late nineteenth century. There were 2,000 members of the royal family and office holders in the 1920s – and more in the nineteenth century – and court patronage underpinned the glories of Kuba art. Most Kuba were village farmers (who were, however, eligible to become office holders) and there was a smaller class of the unfree – 'slaves' and pawns.[10]

Production

The details of production varied, but in Central Africa, as elsewhere, work was always gender-specific. It has been studied in considerable detail among the Kongo, where men were responsible for the initial clearing of the ground, for the collection of tree products and for house construction, while women planted, tended and reaped the crops, ground grain for meals, and made pottery. In the words of a late seventeenth-century Capuchin: 'the man is obliged to build a house, to clothe his wife according to her status, to care for the trees, to help pull up roots in the fields when needed, and to bring the wine which he gets every day from the palm trees ... The woman is supposed to provide food for her husband and children.'[11]

Hunters and smiths were always men, and it was men who made both bark and raffia cloth. The quality of the latter was superb, and European observers compared the various weaves with damask, taffeta and brocade.[12] On the coast, women manufactured salt and dived for the *nzimbu* shells used as currency.[13] 'Along its shores women dive under water, a depth of two yards and more, and, filling their baskets with sand they sift out certain small shellfish.'[14]

The details of the division of labour varied. On the eastern side of the continent, Mang'anja women and men were both committed to agriculture, but the long journeys of Yao male traders were possible only because Yao women (and slaves) grew their food.[15]

Vansina says of the Kuba, 'Within every class women were inferior to men. ... During the Age of Kings ... monogamy and the fact that some men worked in the fields beside their wives ... lessened the inequalities. But in the end it was the men who regulated social and political life and the women who endured it.'[16]

Tradition and identity

In the chapters which follow we shall make recurrent use of ethnic labels. It is impossible to write intelligibly about the African past without them. Often they were invented by neighbouring peoples. Mbundu and Ovimbundu are Kongo names for the peoples concerned. Such names are often of considerable antiquity. In a letter of 1535, Afonso I of Kongo described himself as 'Lord of the Mbundu of the Ngola of the Samba, of Musuri of Matamba, ... of the Tyo'.[17]

African languages have become more uniform in this century, and regional dialects have been breaking down. In the fifteenth century, one must envisage clusters of deeply differentiated dialects, making corporate identities less evident.

Ethnic groups understood their own identity very largely in terms of their response to a particular landscape. The symbol of the Kuba state was a canoeist's paddle, marked with the facial scarifications of its various peoples. Communities developed a very high level of expertise in exploiting a particular local environment, often symbolising their dependence on it by an earth shrine or river divinity. When the attachment to a locality was so great, it required strong motivation and courage to move away. But migrate they sometimes did – in a process of gradual drift, or a response to a new frontier of opportunity, or in a desire to escape an intolerable ruler or over-powerful neighbour. Migration is often at the heart of a state's traditions of origin. But paradoxically, a gradual drift over centuries was often not perceived by those involved. (This is an important limitation of the oral historian – oral testimonies can only be expected to encapsulate trends discernible in a single lifetime.) The migration of oral tradition is, very often, primarily a symbolic charter of identity. Thus the Kuba have a tradition of migration from 'downstream', which is not incompatible with other evidence. But linguistic data make it almost certain that they drifted to their present home from north of the Sankuru river – 'downstream' has a symbolic and not literal meaning.[18] Kongo traditions, taken literally, suggest a migration from the east – but 'movement from east to west is a cosmographic universal' and the meaning of these traditions, similarly, is metaphysical.[19]

Over the last twenty years, the history of Equatorial Africa has been the focus of a strikingly rich and sophisticated literature reflecting, to a large extent, the impact of de Heusch's structuralist critique of traditions of origin. Until recently, like historical writing elsewhere in Africa, it has focussed on kingdoms, but many of Central Africa's peoples have opted for small-scale political structures.[20] This choice, too, becomes fundamental to perceptions of ethnic identity. 'Kuba' is a Luba ethonym for a people who call themselves the people of the king. The Kuba speak the same language as the Lele, who are, nonetheless, perceived as a separate people – largely because the Kuba created an extremely complex kingdom, while the Lele had no political organisation larger than the village. This was due partly to the exigencies of the Lele environment, partly to cultural choices no less real for being unconscious.[21] These choices had other consequences: the larger political unit attracted more extensive trade and produced a surplus which sustained the Kuba's celebrated specialist craftsmen and sculptors. Significantly, the classic studies of the Lele are by an anthropologist, of the Kuba by a historian.[22]

Many of the peoples of the southern savannas are 'matrilineal';[23] this creates tensions because residence is usually virilocal and power and resources are dominated by men. The Kuba, it seems, were originally patrilineal and adopted matriliny in the context of intermarriage with the matrilineal Kete (marriages which cross the matri–patrilineal boundary always have problems of descent identification and of inheritance). The Kongo were matrilineal; in the late sixteenth century, the descendants of Afonso were able to monopolise the throne because the princes who succeeded were the sons of slave mothers.[24] The Luba and related peoples form a patrilineal enclave in a predominantly matrilineal belt; linguistic and other evidence suggests that they were originally matrilineal and gradually absorbed the ideas of patrilineal neighbours, seemingly well before 1600.[25]

Dawnings: the evidence of language

Linguistic analysis suggests that when the Western Bantu first reached Central Africa, the village was the largest political unit, and leadership roles were linked with wealth. Surprisingly, there is no linguistic evidence of a link between chieftaincy and the sacred, though this connection was invariable by the nineteenth century. Words for witch, charm, ritual specialist and ritual avoidance existed in proto-Western Bantu.[26] The western Bantu root for 'chief' is *kumu, in Eastern Bantu, *fumu (an Arabic source recorded *mfalme*, king, in Swahili in the tenth century).[27] In parts of East Africa, *fumu* means ritual specialist. The Western Bantu root *banja is found in the north-west, where it means a lodge for a male cult, but south of the Ogowe it refers to the village assembly house and shrine. Among the Kongo it is a capital – Mbanza Kongo. These changes seem to mirror an enlargement of political scale as one moves south.

Dawnings: the evidence of archaeology

Earlier in this book we noted the prevalence of telescoping in oral tradition. This has the effect of placing in the fourteenth century or later developments which may well go back to the Early Iron Age.[28] Archaeology is a precious source of supplementary data for this early period. Excavations of the vast cemetery at Sanga shed light on the otherwise obscure growth of social differentiation.[29] Corpses were buried with rich grave goods – distinctive pottery, and jewellery of iron, copper and ivory. The first burials date from the ninth century, but the majority are later – from between the eleventh and the thirteenth. By the end of this period cruciform copper ingots are abundant. The graves contained double axes and small bells – though not the double bell which is a widespread symbol of political authority.[30] Children were buried with rich grave goods, which suggests that differences of wealth were inherited. One tradition states that the Luba culture hero, Chibunda Ilunga, came from Lake Kisale, though this is not to be taken literally.[31] The most recent graves were distinctively Luba, with pottery of a new style and a general absence of grave goods.

On myth and gender

The traditions of Central Africa's peoples tend to cluster round stereotypes or clichés such as that of the *héros civilisateur* from the east, who is typically both a hunter and a prince. A whole family of stereotypes, which have precise parallels in West Africa, cluster around regnant queens. Were these historical figures? The case of the redoubtable and undoubtedly historic Nzinga of Matamba (d. 1663) cautions us against rejecting these traditions uncritically. Nevertheless, most of these figures have a symbolic rather than literal significance. Stereotypes of a regnant queen sometimes belong to that cluster of images which, like popular images of the witch, affirm the opposite of what they describe.[32] Lueji inherits a kingdom, but political power is wielded first by her brothers and later by her husband (p. 112 below). Some versions of the tradition state that she could not touch the bracelet, *lukano*, the central item of royal regalia, when she was menstruating.[33] The Kanyok have a tradition concerning a queen called Citend, who was forced to surrender power to her infant son when menstruation prevented her from holding an obligatory feast. The Kuba have an almost identical tradition, the story of a regnant queen forced to resign because of menstrual blood.[34] Do these myths justify male domination by describing queens who lost the throne for a reason intrinsic to their very existence?

What is forbidden is a female king.[35]

On the dynamics of change

We are attempting to recover the outlines of a past which is in large part irrevocably forgotten, and which, for the rest, must be recovered from sources which, as so often, focus on the winners, on the states which survived. States of varying sizes rose and fell. Some are forgotten, some survive in the cryptic coding of oral testimonies or equally obscure references in Portuguese sources. Keta, east of Luanda, is an example. Often, older forms of government survive like fossils in the structures of later political forms. The ancient Lunda *tubungu* chiefs still play a key role at the king's installation, and an official called the Nsangyi represents the people who lived near the source of the Zambezi before the Ndembu arrived.[36] The long process of experimentation which later made the successive adoption of foreign food crops possible underlay changes in social, political and economic life. Religion, above all, was a sphere where innovations were tried out and often discarded. African religions promised this-worldly benefits – good harvests, health, fertility, longevity. They could be tried in the balance and found wanting.[37] We shall see later in this chapter how dearth drove the Imbangala to dreadful parodies of life-giving rituals. Insofar as sacred kings were expected to ensure rain, drought and hunger could lead to their overthrow. The myth of the Kinguri – the king who starves to death – may hint at this. The sacred king who willingly chose his death when his physical powers began to fail is well attested, in Central Africa as elsewhere. Because his function was a ritual one, he could be found in a great state or in a tiny hamlet.

Priests and princes

Outstanding studies of the early history of the Kongo and the Mbundu give strikingly similar pictures of their political evolution. These peoples are admittedly neighbours and related, but there is evidence that the pattern delineated is much more extensive.

The basic building block of social organisation in both societies was the matrilineage. Each had its head, who was sometimes a woman among the Kongo. Religion, in Hilton's analysis of the Kongo,[38] has two dimensions. One, called *mbumba*, is the cult of land and water spirits, associated with fertility and the relationship between people and the environment. These spirits were sometimes manifested in female or male mediums, and sometimes incarnated in human form as albinos, dwarfs and so on. (The sacralisation and hence protection of the differently enabled is an attractive feature of many African societies.) The second, called *nkadi mpemba* and linked with sky spirits, was a male preserve. It dealt with society and human achievement – it could be negative, as in witchcraft, or beneficial, as in the powers of the king or of the religious specialists, *nganga*.

Kitome were ancient Kongo priest-kings, concerned with the fertility of the land. (The title is also found among the Luba and Yaka.) The most common *kitome* title was *kalunga*, referring to both water and the frontier between this life and the spirit world, which was conceptualised as water. Some had titles referring to smithing. The Mbundu had the precise equivalent: the shrine guardians of spirits living in water, called *lunga*, and of spirits living in iron icons, *ngola* – whose guardians sometimes became kings. The former word may well be embodied in the names of the Luba culture heroes, Kalala Ilunga and Chibinda Ilunga. A second form of sacred authority was the secret cult, whose initiates among the Kongo included both women and men.

Regional principalities developed later – their rulers were exclusively male. They built up power in various ways: by attracting clients in time of famine or by controlling scarce resources such as copper, good iron ore (or improved pyrotechnology) and salt, using the various forms of sacred authority to enhance their power. The civilisation of I ake Kisale, based on aquatic resources, reminds us that other forms of wealth could also be involved.

Salt, iron and copper are often referred to explicitly in traditions of political genesis. Citend was first recognised as royal by a woman salt maker. The crucial event in the evolution of Kuba kingship is remembered as a contest in making plates (or axes) of copper (or iron). Mbundu traditions, recorded in the seventeenth century, describe an '*ngola* king' who brought 'axes, hatchets, knives and arrows',[39] that is, a more advanced metallurgy. A kingdom which may have been called Vungu developed near the copper mines north of the Zaire; the Kongo kingdom was founded in the fifteenth century, either in imitation of it or by a breakaway regional governor.[40]

One can only surmise the processes which took place. Did these resources produce a surplus which financed an incipient court? Did the number of the strangers they attracted create a need for centralised authority and make the ideology of the lineage seem less appropriate? Charismatic individuals seem often to have transformed a variety of traditional titles into kingship. Echoes of this charisma survive in the recurrent paradigm of the culture hero, credited with a whole array of probable and improbable innovations.

There seems to have been an important centre of early political development among the proto-Mongo, who lived between the Zaire river and Lakes Tumba and Mayi Ndombe. By perhaps 1400, there were hereditary princes called *nkum*, distinguished by their wealth and magical powers. This may have been a nucleus from which certain basic notions spread further – hereditary titles, the territorial state with its own capital, influencing, among other peoples, the Kuba and the Tio. It is possible that the ritual use of white clay and leopard skins diffused as well, but it is unlikely.[41]

In Central Africa, as elsewhere, the collection and redistribution of revenue in the form of tribute was of central importance.[42] It worked best when a state produced widely differing products in different zones, as was the case in Kongo. The court retained a surplus for its own maintenance, which was often supplemented by crops grown by royal slaves. Titled courtiers were entrusted with tribute collection in particular provinces, retaining part for their own use. The symbolic importance of tribute was as great as its economic, and refusal to pay was often the prelude to war. The functions of central government, other than this economic redistribution, were limited – the resolution of internal disputes too intractable or extensive to be dealt with by lineage heads, and external relations.

A king over people

Oral literature is perfused with the insight that a king is a king, not over forests and hills, but over people. Much of Central Africa is very sparsely populated, and its villages were almost lost in the wild. The central question is this: how was one man's rule accepted, when everyone was at much the same technological level, and when people could and did protest against an unpopular king by moving away? There is no one answer. We have noted the power which came from the redistribution of tribute. Kings rewarded their supporters with honours as well as goods. In the Kuba state, this produced a proliferation of personal titles, each with complex insignia, to which all freeborn could aspire.

The need for people underlay their compulsory acquisition as slaves or pawns. Some famous kings, notably Shyaam, the architect of the Kuba kingdom, were sons of slave mothers. The Lunda compulsorily resettled peoples from their frontiers near their capital, to work on the farms which supported it, and much the same seems to have happened in the Kongo kingdom.[43] Slaves who were not sold abroad were gradually absorbed in the societies which acquired them. The lifestyle of the slave and villager may not have been too different – the former contributed labour; the villager paid tribute in kind. A text in a Lele collection crystallises the paradoxes of the slave's existence – his incorporation in his owner's lineage on the one hand, his liability to execution on the other. 'A slave is a man who will do as he is told. If you send him to draw palm wine in the rain, he goes. You call him brother, age-mate, put your arm round his neck, give him palm wine and meat, so that he is happy ... Then when your mother's brother dies, you kill him.'[44]

The Kongo kingdom seems to have been founded shortly before the arrival of the Portuguese; its history is inextricably interwoven with Atlantic trade, and it is discussed, accordingly, later in this study. Further south, among the Mbundu, states developed round traditional religious leaders – the custodians of the *lunga* and *ngola* icons. A number of *lunga* kingdoms were founded, but they were small and often ephemeral. *Ngola* were of iron; they were more flexible as symbols of power than *lunga*, since they were not linked to a specific area, and subordinate titles could be produced freely. A number of powerful *ngola* kingdoms developed, apparently in the fifteenth and sixteenth centuries. That of the *ngola a kiluanje*, 'conquering ngola', developed in the sixteenth century, largely on the basis of its resources of salt and iron, but also through the export of war victims to slavers from São Thomé (it gave its name to Portuguese Angola). But the kingdom soon fell victim to a strange alliance between the Portuguese of Luanda and desperate immigrants, the Imbangala. The latter's role must be understood in terms of events far to the east, in the Lunda heartland, which are themselves linked with a corpus of Luba traditions.

Secret societies

Almost automatically, the historian focusses on the kingdom or the ethnolinguistic group. But secret societies are at least equally ancient. They were powerful instruments of social control, and often cut across ethnic groups. The Butwa society grew up in modern Zambia, between Lake Bangweulu and the Luapala river; its name may come from the Twa of the Lake area who were among its members in the nineteenth century. Women joined it as well as men, and rulers sometimes regarded it as an alternative locus of power.[45]

The rainbow and the kings

The Luba empire reached its greatest extent in the late eighteenth and early nineteenth centuries, but the state at its heart, in northern Shaba, near the Lomani river, was much older. It was rich in salt and iron, whose importance is affirmed in ancient myths and rituals. The fire on which the king's food was prepared rested on three cones of salt, and Nkongolo's adventures included an unsuccessful attempt to develop a salt marsh.[46]

The events – or mythical constructs – to which we now turn are enormously older than the Luba empire, perhaps as old as the civilisation which created the cemetery at Lake Kisale.

Tradition tells of a barbaric king, Nkongolo, who was dated to *c.* 1500, when these traditions were taken literally.[47] A 'conqueror' (not a sacred ruler, *mulopwe*), he was incestuous, sterile, loudmouthed and drunken (one of the two stereotypes which underlie the title of de Heusch's *The Drunken King*). A cultured hunter prince from the east, Mbili Kiluwe (Mbili the Hunter), who had all the royal qualities Nkongolo so signally lacked, married the king's two sisters and fathered a son, Kalala Ilunga (Ilunga the Warrior), who ultimately slew his uncle and seized the crown, founding a royal lineage whose members are *bulopwe*. Nkongolo was 'red', Mbili and his offspring black.

The Lunda myth of origin, in de Heusch's interpretation, is the precise counterpart of this story. A ruler, Yala Mwaku,[48] has a daughter and two sons. The sons kill their father in a dispute over palm wine; he bequeaths the throne to his daughter, Lueji, who marries a noble immigrant hunter, the Luba *mulopwe* Chibinda Ilunga. Her brothers, Kinguri and Kinyama, leave the kingdom in chagrin. Lueji (like Nkongolo) is sterile, but she gives Chibinda Ilunga an additional wife, and her son becomes the progenitor of the historic Mwaant Yaav dynasty.

To de Heusch all this belongs to intellectual history. Nkongolo means rainbow. The rainbow is associated with the deadly serpent in Luba thought, as it is in many of the world's cosmologies. It is fire in the heavens, inimical to life-giving rain. The immigrant prince stands for culture and fertility. This interpretation is supported not only by the meaning of Nkongolo's name but by the fact that Mwaant Yaav, the title of the Luba king, means Lord of the Vipers. The notable English historian Christopher Wrigley endorsed this with enthusiasm, suggesting that such myths are diminished when we restrict them to temporal events. 'The chaos of human experience is transformed into an immense but orderly design, in which kings and planets, storms and sisters' sons, civet-cats and birds of dawning all have their significant movements to perform.'[49] But as de Heusch himself points out, his interpretation does not preclude different, historical ones. A widely acclaimed model suggests that Lueji, Kinguri and so on are really perpetual titles, at the heads of particular lineages. These titled aristocrats, *tubungu*, dominated Lunda political life until the formation of a unified kingdom on the Luba model (symbolised by Chibinda Ilunga). Relationships between these titles are expressed in family terms – as marriages, parents and children, and so on.[50] Palm wine is a symbol for political power, river crossings for phases of transition.

When did all this occur? There are hints that the events mirrored in the

Nkongolo and Lueji myths belong to the Early Iron Age. Yala Mwaku was killed with a wooden club, and his name means 'thrower of rocks'.[51] Chibinda Ilunga has a superior arsenal of both iron weapons and charms. Nkongolo's people could not work iron and obtained iron artefacts by purchase (he was also, as we have seen, unable to manufacture salt). Kalala Ilunga defeated him at a symbolic game by means of an iron ball.[52]

In some African societies, kings and secret societies are fundamentally opposed, but in the Luba state the secret cult was an important adjunct to the king's power, and its initiates shared many of his sacred qualities. The founding myths of the state were remembered with the aid of a mnemonic board (where Nkongolo, for instance, was represented by a red shell). This was one of many indigenous approaches to literacy in the African past.[53] The board was backed with a tortoise shell, and the design of the royal court was symbolically equated with a tortoise. When a king died, his remains were preserved at a sacred memorial village and his spirit spoke through a woman medium.

In the seventeenth century, an elaborately structured kingdom developed in the Lunda heartland, which outstripped its Kuba and Luba neighbours. Several major titles were held by women – *swana mulunda*, mother of the people, and *lukonkeshia*, mother of the king.

Kingdoms of fire

The modern nation of Malawi derives its name from Maravi; the word refers to an interrelated cluster of kingdoms which grew up among speakers of ciChewa in the region between the upper Zambezi, the Luangwa, and Lake Malawi. In modern times, 77 per cent of the speakers of ciChewa live in Malawi, 14 per cent in Zambia, and 9 per cent in Mozambique, but their cultural and linguistic unity is obscured by the fact that they are known by different ethonyms in different places – Chewa, Mang'anja, Nyanja, Cipeta and Zimba.[54] They are often called the Maravi. By the late sixteenth century, there were three Maravi kingdoms, known by the titles of their rulers – the Kalonga, the Undi and the Lundu. According to a widely accepted interpretation, the oldest of these states, that of the Kalonga, south of Lake Malawi, was founded in perhaps 1400 by 'Luba' immigrants, the Phiri, who intermarried with the local Banda clan. Whether these traditions reflect real movements of individuals or the migration of ideas of kingship across the southern savannas remains obscure. Later, two further kingdoms were established, the Lundu's in the Shire valley, and the Undi's east of the Zambezi.[55] 'Phiri' means hills – as we shall see, there is a widespread symbolic connection, in East Central Africa, between hills and kings.

In a remote past, the proto-Chewa and their northern neighbours, the proto-Tumbuka,[56] seem to have had very similar religious concepts. Among the latter, the supreme God was manifested in the spirit Chikang'ombe, who took the form of a great snake and visited his wives – woman mediums – at hilltop shrines. The proto-Chewa also had a great serpent spirit (called Tunga), women mediums and hill shrines. Some at least of the women mediums seem to have possessed territorial authority. Under the Maravi kings this was eroded by male political authority and a cult of royal graves.[57]

Mbona was originally a Chewa spirit wife of Tunga. Later he metamorphosed into a male prophet, beheaded by the Lundu in a time of drought, after a conflict over rain-making. One version states that Mbona was asked to undergo the poison ordeal, on the grounds that he had withheld rain. He refused, and fled with his followers to the south, but was pursued and executed as a witch. Wells, and the sacred imprint of his feet, mark the route he took, and in modern times, when afflicted by drought, people have rebuilt his shrine.[58] The myth embodied an implicit critique of royal tyranny (which was also evident in the Nyau mask societies) and a condemnation of witchcraft accusations.

Fire was so sacred to the Maravi kings that the word *maravi* itself means fire. They lived in seclusion, tending a sacred flame which was fed with the mats used in girls' initiation rituals. Its black smoke was thought to turn into clouds and then rain. When the king died, the fire was extinguished and a period of lawlessness followed[59] (the symbol is a common one, and found far from Malawi). The ritual importance of fire is also reflected in a myth which tells of an age of primeval harmony between God, spirits, humanity and the animals. But man accidentally invented fire and set the grasslands ablaze. God, spirits and animals fled, and God punished man with mortality.[60] In *The Raw and the Cooked*, Lévi-Strauss suggests that fire is a symbol of the transition between Nature and the world of human Culture.

In the sixteenth century, the Maravi kingdoms were involved in wars which may well have been occasioned by Portuguese penetration of the Zambezi and a desire to control the river's trade, particularly in ivory. Newitt, indeed, has argued that the kingdoms were first founded at this time.[61]

Ferocious soldiers called the Zimba slew the Swahili traders on the Zambezi in 1572, and attacked the Portuguese in the same area twenty-one years later. They are said to have invaded the Kenya coast but it is most improbable that those involved here were the Zimba of distant Zambezia. It is just possible that they had no objective existence and are simply a projection of fears of the Other,[62] but this is, perhaps, unlikely. Contemporary sources ascribe the expansion of the Zimba to the ambitions of a chief 'who was lord of a little kraal . . . but who was most ambitious of human honour'.[63] The Portuguese called the Zimba cannibals (sometimes an epiphenomenon of famine). The Zimba leader was Tundu; there is still a cult of a violent spirit called Chitunda in the Shire valley, and there are hills there called Matundu, Tundu's people.[64]

It is generally accepted that the Zimba served the Lundu, lord of the lower Shire valley: contemporary accounts stress their devotion to a sacred king, and the latter's powers as a rain-maker. The lower Shire valley was strategically sited for trade and had the great advantage of combining wetland cultivation (rice) and dryland cultivation (cotton). It was able to feed starving immigrants in time of drought and exported local cloth (*machika*) to the coast as well as importing textiles.[65] The Zimba seem to have been refugees, perhaps from famine, who sought security in plunder and the powers of a rain-maker king.

In the early seventeenth century, a powerful ruler, Muzora the Uprooter,[66] established an empire which stretched from Lake Malawi to the sea, but did not long survive his death. He defeated the Lundu, and in 1631 formed an alliance with the Mwene Mutapa, intended to expel the Portuguese from Zambezia.[67]

After he died, his kingdom disintegrated into smaller principalities, and the Yao took over control of the ivory trade, which had been one of the bastions of his power.

Ivory and gold

Ivory and gold were of minor importance in Central African societies as items of domestic consumption. Craftsmen made them into treasures for aristocrats, but for ordinary villagers they offered a way of supplementing the household income in the dry season when farming was impossible. Ivory and gold were valued mainly as export commodities: Muzora's state exported ivory via the Zambezi, and so, probably, did his predecessors. Gold was an important export in the Shona kingdoms, and treasures from Asia were found in the ruins of Great Zimbabwe.

In return they obtained cloth and beads, which provided a way of storing wealth, and a safety net in time of famine. But they were obtained at a price. Elephant hunting was as dangerous to the hunter as the hunted. Some of the gold of the Zimbabwe plateau was alluvial but there were also gold mines, narrow shafts up to 90 metres deep. Skeletons – often those of slender girls – are sometimes found at the bottom, together with iron bracelets worn only by women.[68] Gold mining was dangerous and immensely laborious; perhaps as much as 50 per cent of the profit was siphoned off by kings.[69]

In modern times, the importation of the products of industrial capitalism has often destroyed indigenous industries. In the period we are now considering, imports may well have acted as a positive stimulus to local textile production. Eastern Africa both imported and exported cloth and iron, and spindle whorls abound – the earliest known examples are from Kilwa and Mapungubwe, and numerous instances have been found in Great Zimbabwe.

The iconography of rule: hills and stone walls – the first phase

Do the ruins of long-abandoned settlements provide us with cognitive maps to guide us through forgotten landscapes of the mind? A remarkable attempt has been made to extrapolate modern ethnographic data back to the Early Iron Age. Among the modern 'Nguni' and Sotho-Tswana of South Africa dwellings are arranged in a distinctive symbolic manner which has been called the Southern Bantu Cattle Culture. Roundhouses are grouped round a cattle byre, in an order which reflects seniority; in the central area, where grain is also stored, senior men are buried, and men's meetings held. Within a house, the right side is associated with men, the left side with women. The front is appropriate for the secular discourse of public life and private religious rituals are held in the back yard.[70] This pattern is found in large numbers of archaeological sites in Zimbabwe, the Transvaal and Botswana.[71] As in the interpretation of San or Saharan art, there are problems in extrapolating modern ethnographic data into the remote past, but despite this, these insights have been used to good effect in interpreting sites going back to the Early Iron Age.[72]

Near the headwaters of the Limpopo, on the borders of the Kalahari, in what is now eastern Botswana, there are the remains of many hilltop settlements dating from *c.* AD 700 which seem to follow this layout, and which are known as the Toutswe culture. They were abandoned in the late thirteenth century, apparently for ecological reasons. There are four times as many sites from the six centuries of the Toutswe culture as from the six which followed. The Toutswe people kept cattle and cultivated millet and sorghum; the elite lived on the hilltops. Their wealth was clearly derived from pastoralism.[73]

Mapungubwe ('the hill of the jackals') is further east, near a ford on the Limpopo, on the northern edge of the Transvaal. The valuable items found here contrast oddly with the desolate environment and reflect a wealth obtained in Indian Ocean trade, presumably via Sofala, a southern outpost of Kilwa. Cowries and glass beads from India have been found there. The capital, on Mapungubwe Hill, was settled in the eleventh century, though some of its satellite towns are several centuries older, and was abruptly abandoned in the twelfth. The rich lived on the hill and were buried there; excavations uncovered ivory and bone carvings, copper artefacts and the earliest gold objects found in southern Africa – a sceptre and a gold rhino. Again, there seems to have been little settlement in the area for a considerable time afterwards. It seems likely that here, as in the Toutswe complex, the herds caused the environment to degenerate to a point where it could no longer sustain a substantial settlement. Perhaps, too, it lost its role as Kilwa's trading partner to Great Zimbabwe.[74]

Ingombe Ilede, in modern Zambia, lies at the confluence of the Zambezi and Kafue rivers. It was another prosperous market town, founded and abandoned in the fifteenth century, probably because its trade and copper mines were taken over by the new state of the Mwene Mutapa, lower on the Zambezi. Fragments of Indian textiles attest to its involvement in international trade, but the most dramatic finds were large ingots of copper from the Urungwe hills, destined for an African market.

These various sites bore clear evidence of social stratification. An elite gained wealth and power, in part by appropriating the profits of regional and international trade. Foreign imports and the products of local goldsmiths and ivory carvers delineated elite status and gave rulers considerable patronage. But pastoralism was also a source of social differentiation; cattle made it possible to store and multiply wealth, and were another source of patronage. The modern name of Ingombe Ilede means 'where the cows lie'. As we shall see in the case of Great Zimbabwe, it is possible to explain the growth of centralised states through foreign trade and through pastoralism. The two are not, of course, mutually exclusive.

Zimbabwe

Zimbabwe is a Shona word, meaning 'building in stone'. Dry-stone walling was common in southern Africa, but Great Zimbabwe was unique in the size and grandeur of its stone structures. When Carl Mauch came upon its overgrown ruins in 1871, he thought they had been built at the orders of the Queen of Sheba. Zimbabwe is known to us only from its archaeological remains, sadly much disturbed by white treasure hunters. It seems to have been resettled several times, from the eleventh century on, and finally abandoned in the late fifteenth century.[75] There were many exotic imports, among them Indian glass beads, and pottery from China and elsewhere. Clearly it exported gold and ivory to the merchants of Kilwa who came to trade at Sofala. The ruins of Zimbabwe include a granite outcrop with stone walls and terracing, and what is called the Great Enclosure, where stone walls 10 metres high surround a number of other stone structures including a conical tower. It is universally agreed that the walls were symbolic, not defensive, in their purpose.

Great Zimbabwe is known only from the archaeological record, and in recent years scholars have made striking – though necessarily inconclusive – contributions to understanding the cognitive map which underlies its structures. Huffman believes that Great Zimbabwe was constructed on the same lines as Mapungubwe; neither follow the layout of the Southern Bantu Cattle Pattern. In both, the aloofness of a ruling group is symbolised by residence on a hill and by stone walls. The king lived on the rocky outcrop, a symbol of male power. In modern times, when a Shona king dies, it is said, 'The mountain has fallen'. Huffman believes that external trade – not pastoralism – made the decisive contribution to the political transformations these capitals represent, and that different sections of the Great Enclosure were used for male and female initiations. The Shona no longer hold group initiations, but they have survived among the related Venda and a praise song for a Shona king's senior sister tells of them:

> you have done a kindness, one on whom everyone relies; . . .
> A service has been rendered, Lady Moyo,
> soothing shade to the weanling;
> where you are the girls gather to play.[76]

Eight birds of grey-green soapstone were found in the ruins; each is perched on a pillar and incorporates human elements (such as toes or fingers rather than talons). It is thought they represent royal ancestors.[77] Estimates of the population of Zimbabwe vary enormously. Huffman suggests 11,000–30,000, others put it lower. Most people lived in roundhouses outside the monumental stone structures.

There were at least fifty smaller *madzimbabwe*, mainly located along the southern edge of the plateau. Garlake has argued that their location was chosen because they were strategic points on the routes of transhumant pastoralists and thus reflect the basic dominance of cattle in the economy.[78] They clearly reflect the diffusion of political symbolism and were doubtless the capitals of regional rulers. Finds of finely burnished pottery on the hilltops reflect an elite lifestyle. Commoners lived, not in the stone structures on the hilltops, but in surrounding villages on the plains.

We can read ruins, like myths, in many different ways. In a sense one proceeds by the kind of intuitive leap one makes when reading poetry. Huffman and Garlake disagree with each other; possibly, both are in some sense right.

Was Zimbabwe abandoned because trade moved to the Zambezi, where Swahili merchants founded settlements at Tete and Sena in the late fifteenth century? Was gold exhausted in its vicinity? (Great Zimbabwe was located to the south and east of the gold-producing areas.) Did the pressure of its inhabitants and their herds deplete the ability of their environment to support them? Perhaps all these things played a part. Oral tradition suggests that ecological factors were decisive: a son of the last Zimbabwe king travelled north, seeking salt for the royal herds, and founded the kingdom of Mutapa, north of modern Harare.

Stone structures did not always reflect the pomp and circumstance of kings. The Zambezi Tonga also built elaborate terraces and protected their cattle in heavily fortified enclosures. But in their case, they built in stone to protect the meagre resources of their poverty, in a desperate attempt to defend their stock in a world of warring war lords.[79]

An alternative lifestyle: the Mbuti of the Iteso forest[80]

The Twa of Rwanda, the Baka of Cameroun, the Mbuti of north-eastern Zaire, and the Aka of Central African Republic have often been grouped together as 'Pygmies', because they share a forest hunter-gatherer lifestyle, and a similar physical appearance. They stand about four and a half feet (132 cm) tall, widely but not universally interpreted as a response to a forest environment,[81] and when they leave the forest they sometimes suffer from sunstroke. Some communities have been absorbed by their agriculturalist neighbours. All have lost their original languages, though they give their own distinctive tonal imprint to the Bantu or Sudanic languages of their neighbours. The appropriateness of grouping them together has, as we saw in an earlier chapter, been energetically challenged. 'Pygmies do not exist.'[82]

Those who still live as hunter-gatherers have developed a symbiotic relationship with farming communities. To farmers the forest is hostile, the abode of dangerous animals and fearsome spirits; they struggle to prevent its encroachment on their clearings. To the Mbuti, the forest is a loved friend. They lack elaborate rituals – though they have absorbed initiation *rites de passage*, but not witchcraft beliefs – from the Bantu. Their main religious form of expression is a long festival of dance, song and trumpet music, in which they create closer links with the forest. Women build their temporary houses and collect much of the food, but seem to have more freedom than in farming societies. An Mbuti tradition states that it was women who first controlled the sacred trumpets now played by men. Another myth explains the supreme importance of song. It tells of a boy who found the Bird with the Most Beautiful Song, and brought it to his camp. But his father begrudged the food given to the Bird, and killed it: 'and with the Bird he killed the Song, and with the Song he killed himself'. An Mbuti elder told a sympathetic observer about their understanding of God: 'We can't see him, perhaps only when we die will we know and then we can't tell anyone … But he must be good to give us so many things. He must be of the forest. So when we sing, we sing to the Forest.' Vansina writes profoundly about the ambiguity of Bantu-speaking agriculturalists to the 'Pygmy' hunter-gatherers, citing the way in which myths of origin describe how they taught the newcomers to understand various forest environments:

By the nineteenth century, all surviving bands of pygmy hunters and gatherers were serfs for the villagers, who held profoundly ambivalent views about them. They were a despised, uncivilized, subhuman race, unfit for sexual congress with any farming woman. Yet they were the fountain of civilization: the first in the land; the inventors of fire; the teachers about habitats; the wise healers with medicinal plants; sometimes even the first metallurgists; and on occasion, the first farmers.[83]

8

Eastern Africa

Peasants are like cockroaches, which settle on cultivated land.
The high flyer is caught on the ground: the eagle does not eat clouds.
To give is to lay up for oneself.

Ganda proverbs[1]

Landscapes

The perimeters of East Africa are defined, to some extent, by water: the Indian Ocean, a chain of inland lakes (Map 6). But the major determinant of the lifestyle of many of its peoples has been aridity. Much of northern Kenya and Uganda is close to desert, as is inland Tanzania. Their peoples live on the margins of want even in good years, and are never far from famine, as the events of recent years have reminded us. Even where conditions are less extreme, there is often a chronic shortage of water, and the land is covered with the barren thorny scrub called *nyika*.

> I hunt
> in the waterless *nyika*
> and cook game
> in juice wrung from wild sisal leaves.[2]

The Yao remember an ancient dispersal, caused by the fact that 'they did not have enough land for gardens'.[3]

Altitude attracted higher rainfall, as it does on the Ethiopian plateau. On the slopes of Kilimanjaro, for instance, banana plantations flourished. Lake Victoria Nyanza had the same effect on lands to the north and west and on Ukerewe Island, but not on its drier eastern shores. The better favoured areas attracted refugees in time of famine and, in some but not all cases, created the surplus which financed the courts of kings. The kings of Ukerewe were noted rain-makers, because their efforts were clearly successful.[4] The coast had a relatively high rainfall, but its soils were poor and unproductive.

People dealt with the problem of aridity in different ways: by growing low-rainfall staples such as millet, by supplementing their diet with game and wild plants, or by establishing farms in different ecological zones. Sometimes they practised irrigation – Engaruka, in northern Tanzania, with its elaborate stone terracing and water channels, is a famous example, and the Sonjo still practise irrigation in the vicinity. But it often led to as many problems as it solved;

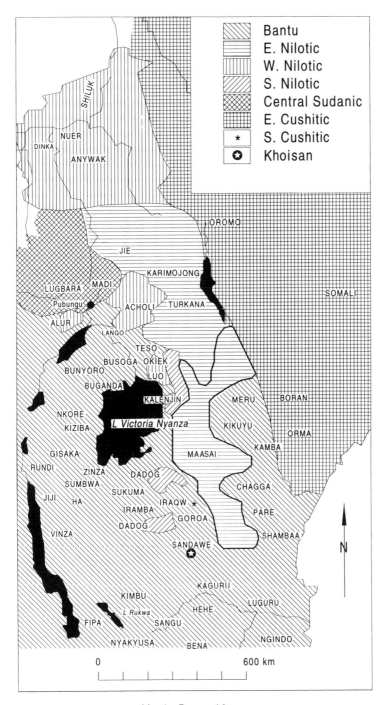

Map 6   Eastern Africa

Engaruka was abandoned in the seventeenth century, after several hundred years of settlement, apparently because of soil salinity or failing water supplies. Paradoxically, oasis communities depending on irrigation were often inhabited by Maa speakers, pastoralists from preference. The Il Chamus, a tiny group of Maa speakers at Lake Baringo, had a 'wonderfully ingenious' irrigation system in the late nineteenth century. By the early twentieth century it was in a state of decay and they had reverted to pastoralism.[5]

Hunger shortly before the harvest was commonplace. A relatively slight fluctuation could create a catastrophic famine, against which the community's own efforts could not avail. Their basic powerlessness was reflected in the prevalence of rain-making specialists and shrines. In Tanzania, many of the former seem to have been of Dadog origin.[6] The impact of disaster was often localised – the droughts and pandemics of the 1890s devastated the Maasai and Karagwe but left other peoples unscathed. In this situation, the cultivation of inter-group linkages was an important safeguard. 'Food is friendship,' say the Maasai. Friendship was not always sufficient; a mid-nineteenth-century famine in Usukuma is remembered as 'the famine of the profiteers'.[7] Because kings were sources of rain and protection, a famine or epidemic could lead to their overthrow. Two successive kings of Ukerewe were deposed in 1830 and 1835, one because the rain was too heavy, and one because of a drought.[8]

In some areas, tsetse fly added to the perils of the wilderness, though the zones where it is prevalent expanded in the late nineteenth and early twentieth centuries and the exact pattern of its earlier incidence is often uncertain. Tsetse is fatal to most domestic stock, and several species cause deadly sleeping sickness. The Shambaa avoided the *nyika* because they recognised that it harboured another peril – malaria. The population of East and East Central Africa was densest on the coast, in the more favoured areas such as the slopes of Kilimanjaro, or in the vicinity of the great inland lakes or the Zambezi valley. Few people lived in the barren scrub inland from the coast. One of the most important differences between East and West Africa is demographic. Southern Nigeria or Ghana is full of teeming towns and villages; the modern population of Nigeria was conservatively estimated at 95.7 million in 1985; that of Tanzania at the same time, with a slightly larger land area, was 21.1 million.[9]

In much of East Africa, ecological constraints have meant that political units have remained small. Characteristically, their traditions have a shallow time depth, which creates many problems for the historian. This is evident in two well-known collections of essays dealing with the pre-colonial history of specific ethnic groups in Kenya and Tanzania.[10] In some cases this may reflect relatively recent settlement, but the evidence of archaeology and language suggests that in many cases the land has been long settled; it is the oral traditions which have been telescoped.

Much more is known about the coast than the interior. The first extant account of the former[11] was written at Alexandria in *c.* AD 100 and archaeological fieldwork has shown that the first Swahili polities were founded some eight hundred years later. Are they more ancient than settlements in the interior, or is it just that more is known about their past?

The coastal settlements north of Kilwa had strikingly little to do with the interior until the beginning of the nineteenth century. The Zaramo live in the immediate hinterland of what is now Dar es Salaam, but a title holder was called 'the chief who does not see the water'.[12] The symbolic importance of shells reflects the otherness of the sea to inland peoples. The Kimbu and Nyamwezi adopted the *Conus* shell (or rather, a disc cut from the shell's base) from the early eighteenth century on, as part of the regalia of aristocrats. Its spiral form is an international symbol of eternity. A myth which recalls the iron Tower of Babel, referred to in an earlier chapter, tells of a chief who tried to build a tower to the moon, hoping to wear it as a *Conus* shell disc. The *idea* of the discs spread before the reality – the Sukuma wore fibre imitations until 'Arabs' brought the real thing in the nineteenth century.[13]

Ethnicity and identity

In East Africa, many ethnic labels – and the sense of corporate identity they indicate – are of recent vintage. 'Hehe' dates back to the nineteenth century and comes from the war cry 'Hee, hee', but in the 1930s, asked for their 'tribe', many of them gave the name of their small ancestral community.[14] 'Nyamwezi' means 'people of the moon' (that is, the west, where the new moon is first seen), a name given by coastal peoples to adventurous traders reaching the coast in the early nineteenth century.[15]

Ethnic identities, in East Africa as elsewhere, were in constant flux. The 'Maasai' were very different in 1500 and in 1900. To use the same label for each is to suggest a continuity and uniformity which never existed. To speak constantly of 'proto-Maasai' or 'proto-Kikuyu' is not only stylistically wearisome, but simply replaces one static ethnym with two. All this is not peculiar to historians of Africa: historians of the British Isles refer without hesitation to Tudor and modern 'parliaments'.

What were the perimeters of Africans' perception of their own identity? The task of definition was perhaps the central function of oral tradition. Language is a dimension of ethnicity but the two are not identical. The Taita, just north of the Kenya–Tanzania frontier, have a strong sense of identity, but speak two different Bantu languages, Dawida and Saghala. They live on three fertile mountains in the Taru desert which have attracted a constant stream of refugees from famine and war. Further north, the Embu and Mbeere live side by side, speaking the same Bantu language and with a common tradition of origin. But they regard themselves as distinct peoples, a perception based on distinct lifestyles which are rooted in ecology – the Embu live on the slopes of Mount Kenya, and the Mbeere in the dry savanna.[16]

Many East African ethnic groups are composites of peoples who came to the area at different times and gradually adopted a common language and forged a common identity. Often, they preserved the memory of their earlier identity as a 'clan', its unity symbolised by something from the natural world such as the Grasshopper Clan. The history of Busoga, for instance, has been written in terms of clan movements. 'The basic units of aggregation are described as clans: though what "clan" means in any given context is itself a puzzle – the idea of clanship itself may be no more than a useful fiction, a way of arranging groups and of establishing their boundaries.'[17]

Ecology and livelihood were important dimensions of ethnic identity. Honey was a core cultural symbol for the forest-dwelling Okiek, as cattle were for the Maasai. Both the Fipa and the Shambaa derived their names from their physical environment. 'Fipa' means plateau, another nineteenth-century ethonym, attributed to 'Arab' traders from the coast. 'Shambaai' is the place where bananas thrive – the slopes of the Usambara mountains. Nyika is a recurrent ethonym.[18]

Myths emphasise the role of livelihood in defining the boundaries of identity. A man from Mbeere is said to have had four sons, to whom at his death he bequeathed a pastoralist's staff, a bow and quiver, a spear and a digging stick. The recipients became respectively the ancestors of the Maasai, Kamba, Athi (Okiek) and Kikuyu.[19] Peoples could and did change both language and lifestyle: Maasai lost their herds and became Dorobo; the latter acquired them and became Maasai. It was this very flexibility which gave an element of choice to ethnic affiliation, as its ambiguities provided an area of freedom. All this has been lost in modern times, and ethnic labels have too often become a prison.

Migration looms large in oral testimonies, and is often at the very core of a people's perception of their own identity. 'We are they who sprang from the hill "yao" ... From that hill the Yao tribe originated, and it is the birth-place of all the Yaos.'[20] Despite this, most people lived and died within a radius of ten miles of where they were born. Since their lives depended on it, they came to have an immensely detailed knowledge of local resources. In the western world, skills are transferable. 'The botanist does not study a forest, he studies forests.' Africans survived by mastering a particular environment. 'The Taveta ... were the people who adapted themselves to life at the side of one river.'[21]

In the last chapter, we concentrated on peoples who shared a Western Bantu linguistic and perhaps cultural heritage. In East Africa, Southern and Eastern Cushites, Southern and Eastern Nilotes and Bantu met in a long-continued and immensely complex series of encounters. These categories are linguistic; but the peoples concerned constructed symbolic fences to define their separate existences. The Kenya Luo, like all modern Nilotes but unlike their Bantu neighbours the Gusii, practised dental evulsion. The latter practised circumcision and clitoridectomy but the Luo did not. The Gusii had totemic clans, unlike their Nyanza Bantu neighbours, the Luhyia.[22] Ethno-linguistic perimeters are not meaningless. They are central to African thought, as reflected in traditions of ethno-genesis.

The north-east frontier

For millennia, East Africa has been a place of encounter for different ethno-linguistic groups. Their history is largely one of creative exchanges, of socio-political, economic, and religious ideas, mirrored in vocabulary borrowing and language change.

The first inhabitants of East Africa seem to have been Khoisan-speaking hunter-gatherers, their presence attested not only by the survival of tiny relict groups – the Sandawe, and perhaps the Hadza – but by the retention of Khoisan click sounds and vocabulary in other ancient languages such as Dahalo. Rock art, so typical of the San, is found in great abundance in Tanzania, and over a thousand rock paintings survive in the area where the Hadza lived as hunter-gatherers until recently. This art, moreover, is similar in style and content to that of South Africa – for instance, in the popularity of the eland motif. In the course of the first millennium BCE or soon afterwards, three completely unrelated groups drifted gradually into East Africa – the Southern Cushites, followed by the Southern Nilotes and the Bantu. The original homeland of the Southern Cushitic language family lies in south-west Ethiopia.[23] Today, like the Khoisan speakers, they form tiny relict enclaves in north central Tanzania, which are, in most but not all cases, well on the way to linguistic absorption by their larger neighbours. These peoples are, or have been until recently, hunter-gatherers, but are, paradoxically, credited with the introduction of agriculture, pastoralism and pottery, and have been plausibly identified with two pastoral Neolithic industrial complexes. They once covered a much larger area, as is attested by the many words of Southern Cushitic origin in contemporary East African languages, but the majority were gradually absorbed by other linguistic groups. Southern Cushites are thought to be the source of the practice of circumcision, and the fish taboo. (A case has also been made for age-grade organisation, but this is too common to be attributed with certainty in this way.)

The Southern Nilotes came from the vicinity of Lake Turkana and were, like the Southern Cushites, potters and pastoralists. The Nilotic community may have broken up in the third millennium BCE, and proto-Southern Nilotic seems to have developed perhaps two thousand years ago. A much more ancient date seems precluded by the fact that proto-Southern Nilotic includes words for iron and forging.[24] Where Early Iron Age people selected the best sites – often by lakes or rivers – the Southern Nilotic immigrants settled in the drier areas, practising both pastoralism and agriculture.[25] Their main modern representatives are the Dadog of northern Tanzania and the Kalenjin of Kenya. Kalenjin is a very recent ethonym, coined when Kenya was near independence, and embraces ten different ethnic groups. Together, they have perhaps a million members, half of whom are Kipsigis or Nandi. The hunter-gatherer Okiek speak a distinct Kalenjin language. For a time the Kalenjin, like the Southern Cushites before them, occupied a great swathe of territory in central Kenya and Tanzania, despite the influx of Bantu speakers and Luo. By 1600 CE, their territory was shrinking, and the Maasai had begun the dramatic process of expansion which led their historian to call them the Lords of East Africa. The Kalenjin have eight revolving age grades, which always have the same names. Like all social structures, these make an oblique statement of values – in this case, affirming the continuity of past and present, the desirability of walking in the paths of the ancestors. Like many other peoples who lacked centralised political institutions, including the Maasai, they had charismatic religious leaders (*orkoiyot*, prophets, or seers). The Kuria and other related Bantu peoples in Tanzania have eight age grades, some of which have the same names as their Kalenjin counterparts. These seem to mirror encounters in the past, now forgotten.

A modern language map of East Africa is dominated, not by Southern Cushites or Southern Nilotes, but by Eastern Nilotes, Eastern Cushites and, above all, Bantu. But often, in language or culture, they carry the imprint of their now obscure predecessors.

The hunter-gatherers

Modern hunter-gatherers are not necessarily the physical descendants of those of the remote past – though they may be in some instances.[26] One response to famine was migration, but another was to revert to hunting and gathering, at least for a time.

East Africa's hunter-gatherers have often been called Dorobo, a Maasai term meaning cattle-less, hence poor. But its ultimate source is a Southern Nilotic word for 'forest'. It is an inaccurate blanket term for a variety of communities, speaking different languages and practising different lifestyles.

Hunter-gatherers are relatively few in numbers (there were some 50,000 Okiek in 1970) but have a strong sense of cultural identity. Some modern observers, seeing them through Maasai eyes, have described them as marginal (again, the western romantic identification with the values of male pastoralism – *cherchez la vache*). The reality is more complex, symbolised in the paradoxical Maasai myths, which claim both that Dorobo do not value cattle and that they were the source from which the Maasai themselves obtained them.[27]

Hunter-gatherers are often bilingual, and their experience over the last two centuries provides well-documented instances of the language change which was clearly so important in the past. The Okiek have spoken a Kalenjin language for at least a millennium; some are adopting Maa, and some a pastoral lifestyle. The El Molo, a tiny group of desert fisherfolk at Lake Turkana, adopted Samburu (a form of Maa) at the turn of the century, as a result of a Samburu influx among them caused by cattle disease and drought. Many became pastoralists too, effectively 'becoming Samburu'. These modern examples give us precious insights into language and culture change in the remote past.[28] The Yaaku, who live north of Mount Kenya, spoke an Eastern Cushitic language with Khoisan loan-words; now they too are adopting Maa.

Hunter-gatherers do not perceive themselves as marginal. They have a strong sense of cultural identity. Like the Mbiti of the Ituri forest in Equatorial Africa, they have lost their language while retaining their preferred way of life. Ceramics are seldom associated with hunter-gatherers, but the Okiek made, and have long made, distinctive decorated pottery, and often keep cattle. Hunter-gatherers survive, occupying different ecological niches from those of farmers and pastoralists, to whom they are linked by ritual and economic exchanges.

Ethonyms change, and it is not easy to decode traditions of these early encounters in the twilight zone where myth and history mingle. Many of East Africa's agricultural peoples have detailed traditions of encounters with hunter-gatherers. The Kikuyu, Maasai, Taita and others have traditions of the 'Gumba' – short in stature, expert bee keepers, potters and iron workers, dwellers in roofed excavations in the ground. The association of technical innovation with an ancient autochthonous people, here and elsewhere, may simply mean that the former is perceived as very old.[29] The attribution to them of short stature is a very widespread stereotype, and probably symbolic – as is its opposite – 'there were giants in those days'.[30] Taita and Kikuyu traditions speak of the Asi or Athi (which means hunter). The Kikuyu acquired land from the Athi, going through ceremonies of mutual adoption; gradually the latter 'became Kikuyu', as the Asi 'became Taita'. Taita traditions also tell of a quite distinct people, cattle owners and farmers who built in stone, whose stone artefacts survive, and whom it is tempting to identify with Southern Cushites.

The Kalenjin tell of a vanished people called the Sirikwa; excavations attributed to them are very common – the 'Sirikwa holes'. Who were the Sirikwa? Sutton believes that in the past they were the Kalenjin themselves. Okiek traditions describe them as Maasai.[31] There is clearly a connection between the Sirikwa holes (? cattle kraals) and the cave-dwelling Gumba.

The Singwaya connection

The study of the African past is a theme in counterpoint, between a people's perceptions of their past and objective reality, although we should not forget that tradition itself is part of that 'reality', shaping behaviour and events. Where our only evidence is tradition itself, supplemented by linguistic and archaeological evidence, interpretations are often in dispute – the case of the Cwezi, discussed later in this chapter, is a classic instance.

But on the East African coast, oral testimonies can be collated with classical sources from late antiquity, and with records in Arabic, Portuguese and Swahili.

The Swahili, Mijikenda, Pokomo and Taita have a tradition that they once lived on the coast of southern Somalia. The first to leave were the Swahili, who founded a number of small coastal states in Kenya and Tanzania. The others moved a shorter distance south and lived in 'Singwaya' until a further diaspora was caused by Oromo aggression in the sixteenth century.[32] The Taita moved to the Taita Hills, the Pokomo to the Tana river valley, the Mijikenda (Nine Towns) to hilltop sites on the modern Kenya–Tanzania frontier.

The languages of all these peoples but the Taita belong to the Sabaki subgroup of North-east Coastal Bantu. There are still Bantu place-names, and a few Bantu speakers, near modern Mogadishu, and sixteenth- and seventeenth-century maps show Singwaya between the Tana and Juba rivers. In 1331 ibn Battuta described the coast between Mogadishu and Mombasa as Swahilini, the first known instance of this word. Oromo expansion can be securely dated to the sixteenth century from Ethiopian and Portuguese written sources, and the chronology of Mijikenda age sets fits in well with this. If this – and other – evidence was not available, historians would debate as to whether Singwaya really existed, or was a purely mythological construct.

But there is a sense in which Singwaya is precisely this. Large sections of the peoples who relate the story did not in fact come from Singwaya. The Taita, as we have seen, speak a different Bantu language and if actual migrants from Singwaya joined them their language was absorbed. Mijikenda traditions are explicit that the Nine Towns assimilated many from other ethno-linguistic groups. Migration from Singwaya became a core symbol of Mijikenda identity, underpinning both ritual and the socio-political organisation of their hilltop settlements, built around charms 'from Singwaya', so potent that when their bearers set them down during a journey, they died.

The Swahili[33]

Today, Swahili is spoken as a first language over hundreds of miles of coast, from southern Somalia in the north to northern Mozambique in the south, and on islands which include Zanzibar, Pemba, and the distant Comoros. The name Mozambique comes from a Swahili town, Msumbiji. Standard Swahili, originally the dialect of Zanzibar, is the official language of Kenya and Tanzania, spoken as a second language by many millions. The word, Arabic in origin, is cognate with Sahel, and means shore.

The first Swahili polities were founded in the ninth century, in the Lamu archipelago and in Kilwa. They were always small, often covering less than 40 acres. Shanga, an ancient state which ceased to exist in the early fifteenth century, had 139 coral houses on 14 acres. It is noteworthy that the sites of the first settlements were not chosen for their suitability for international trade, and often were not on good harbours. The first Swahili settlers were farmers, fishermen and iron workers rather than merchants.

Swahili history and linguistic analysis have been greatly revised in recent years. The Swahili and their language have often been perceived as an exotic presence – Arabic culture in exile, whose indigenous African nature – always obvious in that the Swahili are black Africans – is central in recent studies. (Ibn Battuta, in 1331, described the people of Kilwa as 'Zanj of very black complexion'.)[34] Swahili is a Bantu language with Arabic loan-words, many of which date only from the nineteenth century.

The core symbols of Swahili identity – houses built from coral, literacy in Arabic or Swahili, imported Islamic pottery and Chinese porcelain – were always the preserve of an elite. Most homes were built in adobe and thatch, and a study of potsherds in one Swahili polity showed that when foreign trade was at its height, only 1 per cent of its pottery was imported. Most Swahili villages were not involved in international trade, and continued to rely on fishing and farming.

Each Swahili state has its own tradition of a Shirazi founder who married a local woman – intermarriage is also attested in the *Periplus*, which mentions 'ships with captains and agents who are mostly Arabs, and are familiar through residence and intermarriage with the nature of the places and their language'.[35] The immediate difficulty – that the Shiraz is a Persian port, and that the loan-words and inscriptions are Arabic – is more apparent than real, as most of the sailors were Arabs. It is now thought that many of the immigrants came from the ports of the Somali coast. As in the Western Sudan, elite families claimed Arab ancestry and developed elaborate genealogies as a symbol of identity. Foreign visitors came to trade, and lists of trade goods figure prominently in their writings. The efficiencies of water-borne transport were such that bulky commodities such as ivory could be transported across the Indian Ocean with ease. A dhow crossed the Indian Ocean in a third of the time it took a camel to cross the Sahara, and carried as much as a thousand camels.[36] In classical times, ivory, tortoise-shell and rhino horn were exported, in return for spears, axes, swords, awls and glass dishes.[37] Al-Masudi visited the East African coast in 916 and described the purchase of ivory, ambergris and tortoise-shell.[38] The geographer al-Idrisi (d. 1166), stated that 'They own and exploit iron mines: for them iron is an article of trade and the source of their largest profit.'[39] In other words, East Africa had become an exporter, rather than an importer of iron.

Kilwa became rich through the export of ivory and gold from the Zimbabwe plateau; it was the most distant point that could be visited if traders returned home the same year. Ibn Battuta went there in 1331 and called it 'One of the most beautiful and well-constructed towns in the world'.[40]

In Chapter 6, we noted the theory that the divinities of traditional religion are local ones and give way to Islam or Christianity when a community becomes part of a wider world. Islam was to become a core symbol of Swahili identity. It had not yet been adopted when al-Masudi visited the region, though there were clear Islamic influences: 'The Zanj have an eloquent language and men who preach in it. One of their holy men will often gather a crowd and exhort his hearers to please God in their lives and to be obedient to him.'[41] The first transcription of a Bantu word is found here – *mufalume* (modern Swahili, *mfalme*), king. By the time of ibn Battuta's visit Islam had been long established. He said of Kilwa, 'The chief qualities are devotion and piety.'[42]

The first written literature from the Swahili coast was in Arabic. The earliest surviving Swahili manuscripts are from the eighteenth, perhaps the seventeenth, century. They were not, of course, the first to exist. Much African literature, being oral, is anonymous, but we know the men and women who wrote Swahili poetry by name. Saada Taji li Arifina, the first known woman Swahili poet, wrote in the late eighteenth century, lamenting her husband's neglect. Muyaka of Mombasa (d. 1837) wrote poems on many subjects, including a hungry cat. None is more moving than his lament for a wife who died young

> I would rather have the small boat
> my first little vessel
> although it was unsteady and shaky
> the waves never rose above her head
> but she drowned near Ngozoa
> on a dark night.[43]

One of the best known and most haunting Swahili poems is a lament for Pate, destroyed by civil war. By Sayid Abudallah, who died in 1820, it is both a moralist's reflection on the vanity of this world's treasures, and an elegy for the glories of the Swahili past.

> How many rich men have you seen
> who shone like the sun?
> Their dwellings brightly illumined
> with lamps of crystal shell and copper;
> the nights stayed as light as the days,
> beauty and fortune surrounded them . . .
> Now they occupy the city of bitterness . . .
> and the pressure of the grave meets them.[44]

This is poetry, not history, though how people understand their past (and present) is an important dimension of reality. Fourteenth-century Kilwa was 'one of the most beautifully and well constructed towns in the world'. The Portuguese sacked Kilwa and Mombasa repeatedly, and by establishing trading posts on the Zambezi cut the former off from its traditional sources of gold and ivory. A visitor in 1819 called Kilwa ' a miserable village'.[45]

It would be an oversimplification to say that the advent of the Portuguese ruined the Swahili coast. Kilwa developed new trade contacts in its immediate hinterland, and Mombasa, despite repeated attacks, sustained a vibrant commercial life.[46] The lives of the northernmost Swahili were disrupted less by the Portuguese than by Somali and Oromo expansion. All this passed. No alien hegemony has ever endured on the Swahili coast.

The Fipa

Ufipa is the plateau between Lakes Tanganyika and Rukwa, a bridge between East and Central Africa. There were about 134,000 Fipa in 1967, and undoubtedly fewer in pre-colonial times. They formed stable nucleated villages, enriching the soil by composting. The first Fipa political centre was at the Eternal Village, Milansi, whose king has a continuing connection with blacksmithing. The symbolic role of iron suggests the Milansi kingdom was founded in the Early Iron Age. The important salt pans at Ivuna, south-east of Ufipa, were worked from the early thirteenth century on, and dried fish from Lake Rukwa was a further important resource. Later immigrants, the Twa, founded two rival kingdoms, though Milansi survived as a tiny independent enclave. The Twa had to avoid iron-working locations and to retain strong links with pastoralism, still practising a milk-drinking ceremony. It is possible that they were connected with the pastoralist royal families of Rwanda or Nkore.[47]

At one level, these are seen as real political transformations – the Twa arriving in the seventeenth century, the kingdoms dividing in the eighteenth. But the *form* of the myth deals with cosmic opposites. The first Twa are women – named, suggestively, Womb Person, Earth Person and Child of Stone. Two later marry Nyika hunters, and their children found the royal dynasty. At one level, this is the classic encounter of indigene and immigrant. At a profounder level, the women represent energy, wealth, the earth and productivity; the mountain Milansi kingdom, the intellect and spirituality.

As in many African kingdoms, the Queen Mother was virtually co-regent with the king, with her own court, officials and estates.[48] She named the dead king's successor and could dethrone an unacceptable ruler. A woman magistrate decided a range of sex-related offences and imposed fines – which seem to have been the only obligatory imposts in Ufipa. We have spoken of the harshness of some kingdoms; Willis stresses the voluntary nature of tribute in Ufipa, the consensual quality of government. If severity is linked wih scarcity, this quality in Fipa life may be linked with abundance, and especially with the efficiency of their compost based agriculture.

A small number of high offices were reserved for Twa, most others for commoners. Whereas royal lineages tend to expand, the Twa have almost vanished; this probably reflects the opportunities open to commoners, and choices of identification made accordingly.

The *ntemi* complex [49]

By the nineteenth century the western half of modern Tanzania was covered with a network of small principalities. Their traditions tend to have a relatively short time depth. Their institutions were patrilineal, in contrast with the great belt of matrilineal peoples further south, though succession to kingship was sometimes matrilineal. Their sacred kings were often called *ntemi*, the cutter, probably a reference not to warfare but to the original clearing of the bush. Three Chagga principalities – in the Kilimanjaro area far to the north – claim an ancestor with the same name.[50]

The *ntemi* complex includes the people who were later called the Nyamwezi, and who now number a third of a million; in the nineteenth century they lived in some 150 small polities. A Nyamwezi *ntemi* lived in seclusion, and was put to death when his health failed. The culture of the Nyamwezi is virtually indistinguishable from that of their more numerous northern neighbours, the Sukuma, whose ethonym means 'north', a good example of the artificiality of ethnic labels.

In the nineteenth century, a number of warlords arose in the region, who in some cases created larger political units.

The Kimbu

The Kimbu lived in thirty-eight principalities; they originally called their sacred rulers *umwani*. This has now changed to *mutemi* [51] through the influence of the Nyamwezi, the people to whom they feel themselves closest. There are some 50,000 Kimbu, sparsely scattered over many square miles of barren mountain woodland, and the small size of their polities reflects both demographic factors and scarce resources. They shifted their settlements frequently. In the words of a Kimbu schoolboy: 'If you walk upon the hills which stand in Ukimbu you will see old settlements on their summits, broken pots, and house-posts for the houses they built, and stones for grinding their millet ... Even today Kimbu move house when their fields are no longer fertile.'[52]

Like many other African peoples, the Kimbu relied on a mixture of farming (millet and sorghum being the traditional staples), hunting and the collecting of a great range of wild fruits, vegetables and fungi. Like the Okiek, they had a passion for honey, and some individuals had as many as a thousand hives. The threat of famine was never very far away. A myth tells of a leader who introduced pumpkins, telling the people to harvest and eat them but leave the seeds. The starving people ate the seeds as well. He would take no payment but a handful of earth – the founding charter of his principality.

Like other sacred rulers in tiny states, the Kimbu kings claimed the full range of spiritual powers of the royal rainmaker. These powers are encapsulated in stories told of Ipupi, 'Terror of those who wake'. He lived on a mountain, like the king of Milansi, and attacked his enemies with drought and plagues of rats which consumed the harvest. He did not die in the normal way, but entered the earth voluntarily with his principal wife – another widespread stereotype.[53] Like so many other myths, it embodies the stereotypes of Earth and Mountain, Rain and Drought, Nature (the rats) and Culture (the harvest). A woman became chief if there was no suitable male, and her husband would receive the title of 'queen'.

Whereas settled farming peoples saw the forest as perilous and menacing, the attitude of the Kimbu was ambivalent. The Kimbu hunter sings:

> The lion is my father,
> And you, elephant, are my kinsman.[54]

The secret society, to which both women and men belonged, had a name which meant wild animal, and was conceptualised as a lion spirit.

The highland oases

In northern Tanzania and southern Kenya, mountains rise above the dusty plains like Pilgrim's Delectable Mountains. Not only do they attract a relatively abundant rainfall but they are often blessed with rich volcanic soil. Historically they have been like oases, attracting desperate refugees from drought and famine. Peoples such as the Shambaa, Kikuyu and Chagga live on the mountain slopes, at an altitude of some 3,500 feet. Most of their oral traditions have a time depth of some 300 years and do not reflect the true antiquity of settlement.

The oldest oral traditions are found in the Upare mountains, which lie between Usambara and Kilimanjaro. Even here, there is a considerable gap between the time depth of the oldest oral testimonies and archaeological finds of pottery dating from late in the first millennium CE.[55] Traditions tell of an ancient ruling blacksmith clan, of refugees from famine, of principalities founded on the basis of rain-making powers. The association of smithing and political power, and the usurping of authority by immigrant dynasts, exactly parallel the history of Ufipa, far to the south.

Similar events occurred in Shambaa, where the Kilindi dynasty gained power in response to the challenge posed by immigrants. There were some 272,000 Shambaa in 1967. They originally lived in independent ridge-top settlements, and their first king is remembered as a hunter from the south called Mbegha – again, the paradigm of the immigrant hunter-king who won support by sharing meat generously. The historic background to the growth of kingship seems to have been the crisis created by the immigration of a cohesive and linguistically unrelated group – the Southern Cushitic Mbugu. Some became linguistically absorbed by the Shambaa; others retained their own language, settling in a different ecological niche higher up the mountain.

The tradition is codified in the language of myth, and embodies the same metaphysical polarities we have observed in other contexts. Mbegha begins as an outcast who cut his upper teeth first. He hunted first pigs and later a lion, and in the end became a king – isolated, as in his beginnings. The wilderness is dangerous, as is the one who even unwittingly breaches major taboos. Mbegha makes a gradual transition to full humanity, and his political relationship with the

Shambaa is symbolised by their exchange of game for the carbohydrate staple.[56] Nkanda, who founded principalities in Usukuma, left his home in Uzinza because he cut his upper teeth first.[57]

The reign of the last king of a unified Shambaai is remembered as a golden age. Kimweri reigned from *c.* 1815 to 1862. A great rain-maker, he dealt with his enemies by his control of the elements, and relied on the (commoner) maternal uncles of his sons to restrain them when they were provincial governors: 'Not all kings had peaceful reigns but peace was the characteristic of Kimweri's years . . . An elder would say, "My lord, my son is about to lose his wife." Kimweri would say, "Go to such and such a place. I have a cow being kept there, take it." '[58]

The Meru live on the northern slopes of Mount Kenya, the Kikuyu on its southern slopes and in the Nyandarua Range, and the Kamba in another mountain environment further south. Both Kikuyu and Kamba traditions claim they were hunters and pastoralists before settling in their present homes. Above them, the mountain is too cold for comfort; below is dry savanna.

All speak closely related languages of the Thagicu subgroup of Eastern Bantu, which began to differentiate a thousand years ago. All have traditions which suggest migration from different directions and relatively recent arrival. The historian of the Kikuyu believes, on the evidence of age sets, that the Kikuyu reached their present home in the seventeenth century, after a migration from northern Meru. The peoples of the Meru cluster have a detailed tradition of flight from an island on the coast, in escape from tyrannical strangers, which their historian accepts as true and places in the eighteenth century. The Kamba tell of complex migrations from an original home in Kilimanjaro via Mbooni. Their historian again accepts this, placing their arrival in Mbooni in the seventeenth century.[59] But the archaeological evidence suggests Iron Age (apparently Bantu) settlement since the twelfth century; the linguistic evidence suggests that Thagicu speakers have lived in close proximity to each other for at least a thousand years. The Kikuyu may well have come from Meru, but much longer ago than surviving age-grade data suggest. As we have seen, the time depth which can be preserved in the human memory is limited, and in its perspectives the past is truncated. It is most unlikely that the Kamba came from Kilimanjaro, let alone the Meru from the sea. The island of Mbwa is as mythical as Avalon, and elements in the story are clearly mythemes which are very widespread indeed. (The people escape from Mbwa when a diviner parts the sea; this is a common symbol of the emergence of a people's identity, as in the Israelites and the Red Sea. The Fipa have a comparable myth about the parting of the waters of Lake Rukwa.) Islands readily acquire symbolic meanings, perhaps because their boundaries are precisely known. Meru age sets take it in turns to play the roles of 'insider' and 'foreigner'. Their migration story is probably to be located in this symbolic idiom.[60]

The Kikuyu comprised ten clans, nine of which traced their descent to the daughters of Gikuyu and Mumbi. Rapid rivers divide the mountain slopes into many ridges; the Kikuyu, like the other highlanders, were divided into many ridge settlements, *mbari*. Unity, as so often in African societies, was maintained by a system of male and female age sets: '*riika* [age set] mates looked upon each other as actual blood brothers or sisters'.[61] The Kikuyu are a good example of ethnic identity as process. We have noted their ceremonies of mutual adoption with the Athi, who often 'became Kikuyu'. Their relationship with the Maasai was extremely complex. They were linked by trade, marriages and blood brotherhood pacts; though the Maasai sometimes raided them, the impact of the raids was minimal. Kikuyu society absorbed a number of Maasai elements, especially in the sphere of war. Some individuals acquired cattle and 'became Maasai'. During the famine of the 1890s, a Kikuyu who had lived as a Maasai herder saved Maasai children by placing them with Kikuyu families.[62]

In a sense, it was only necessary – or possible – to define ethnic identity in a frontier situation. But it was precisely in this situation that identities were most ambiguous and most flexible.

Kitara and the Cwezi

The oral traditions of centralised kingdoms tend always to have a greater time depth than those of small-scale polities. Their greater resources often sustain professional remembrancers, and dynastic history is clearly perceived as encapsulating the charter of a clan's right to rule. Sometimes its history is preserved by royal women. The great kingdoms of the interlacustrine area – Buganda, Nkore, Bunyoro – and their smaller neighbours in Busoga and Buhaya have long seemed to provide the firm chronology which is the essential context of historical understanding. Their traditions were written down at an early date by the first generation of the western-educated. They make many references to relationships with their neighbours – 'tie-ins'. They also referred to eclipses – which could be, and were, dated. An article published in 1972, outlining a chronology for the interlacustrine area, was seen as a landmark in the evolution of the discipline.[63] No sooner had it appeared than it was challenged. David Henige, in an influential book and a series of important articles, applied the canons of textual criticism to interlacustrine – and much other – chronology and found it wanting.[64] In particular, the texts by early Ugandan intellectuals were not independent and were shaped by political considerations, and the eclipses were symbolic rather than astronomical.

Bunyoro traditions tell of three successive dynasties of kings – the Tembuzi (whom most historians regard as mythical), the Cwezi, and the firmly historical Bito, of Luo extraction, whose last ruling representative was deposed by Obote in 1967. Those who accept the Cwezi as historical place them in the late fourteenth and fifteenth centuries, which accords well with the dating of the major earthworks, made by a cattle-owning people in Bunyoro, called Bigo bya Mugenyi, Forts of the Stranger.

Bunyoro traditions, confirmed in essence by those of the Ganda themselves, claim that Kimera, twin brother of Rukidi, the first Bito king, founded a kingdom in Buganda. The many Hinda dynasties of Buhaya and Buzinza trace their origin to an eponymous ancestor who was a son of the last Cwezi ruler, and Nkore (Ankole) to Ruhinda's son. This dense network of mutually consistent dynastic histories carries its own conviction.

A major debate centres round the historicity of the Cwezi. At the two opposing poles are J. Bertin Webster and Christopher Wrigley. Euhemerus was a figure in the ancient world who believed that the gods were originally historic kings; Webster is his modern counterpart. His work has many strengths – he has done more fieldwork than most of his critics and he has a particular gift for collaborative ventures, of which *Chronology, Migration and Drought* is one. It is one of a number of studies which, with great humanity, extrapolate famine as a major historical variable from present catastrophes far into the past. But he takes tradition with a literalness and imbues it with a chronological precision which virtually all other historians of Africa find unacceptable. Even the Tembuzi become historical kings.[65]

Christopher Wrigley was deeply influenced by the Belgian anthropologist de Heusch; his review of the latter's seminal work, *Le roi ivre*, in the *Journal of African History* influenced a generation of historians. To Wrigley, the Cwezi saga is pure myth, comparable with *The Lord of the Rings*. It is, he believes, concerned, at the profoundest level, with the central issues of human existence, and to see it as history is to trivialise it. This kind of debate is not peculiar to African studies. Scholars have long discussed what kernel of truth, if any, lies at the heart of the Arthurian legends. But is it not possible to read a world of deeper meanings into historic experience?

It is impossible, in a work of this kind, to do justice to the richness of the Cwezi saga and its many regional variants.[66] In barest outline, the Bunyoro version runs like this. The last of the Tembuzi was Isaza, who offended the lord of the underworld. The latter gave him beautiful cattle which he valued above all else. The cattle wandered away into the realm of the underworld, and Isaza followed them, only to become a perpetual prisoner there. The next kings were the Bacwezi. There were only two of this line: Ndahura, who was the grandson of Isaza, and Wamara. As an infant, the former was rescued from the riverside by a potter – the baby in the bullrushes mytheme. Soon, things began to fall apart. The favourite cow of the crown prince Mugenyi died, and he was with difficulty restrained from suicide. A cow was slain for divination but the omens were so bad that the king and his followers vanished beneath the waters of the lake. If they were historical figures, they were unable, by some psychological quirk, to withstand adversity. The Cwezi are remembered as white. Where black is the normal colour of mankind, white becomes characteristic of the spirit world. Rukidi, who succeeded them, is remembered as a hirsute uncouth stranger from the north, although of Cwezi descent. Bunyoro tradition identifies him with Winyi Isingoma, the founder of the Bito dynasty.

There are problems here. There was nothing particularly uncouth about the Luo, nor did they share Rukidi's unfamiliarity with pastoralism. Why should the Babito kings, for eighteen generations, preserve the memory of this unprepossessing ancestor? To Wrigley, the answer is obvious. The whole saga is a commentary on the human situation – the universal lordship of death, the origins of human government.[67] By the time the first eyewitness accounts of Bunyoro were written, in the 1860s, the Cwezi were the mediums – usually women – of a pantheon of spirits such as Wamara, Lord of Death, and Ndahuru, God of Smallpox. We have already had occasion to mention Mugasa/Mukasa, divinity of Lake Victoria Nyanza. There was a tradition that the Cwezi were former inhabitants, who had vanished, and that they had been blacksmiths.[68] Were the

Cwezi, like so many other African rulers, connected in symbol or actuality with iron working? Were their nineteenth-century mediums, as Berger suggests, the heirs of pre-Bito rulers, and is the hairy Rukidi a piece of anti-royal propaganda? Their image undoubtedly mutated in colonial times: white administrators saw them as creative white invaders, a precedent for what they perceived their own role to be. Bunyoro writers could only gain by exaggerating their empire, and had every reason to do so in a colonial situation dominated by the Ganda.

From the date of its foundation until the early eighteenth century, Bunyoro was the uncontested giant of the interlacustrine area. In Buganda, dynastic history begins with an Adamic figure, Kintu, first man and first king, though tradition also speaks of autochthenes, and of later migrants from Bunyoro, led by Kimera. Kintu means 'man' and is undoubtedly symbolic. If the Cwezi were historic figures, Kimera lived at the end of the fifteenth century.

It is likely, however, that the Buganda state is much more ancient. It began as a small principality, to the north of Lake Victoria Nyanza, in what is now Busiro County.

A political structure of some sort, small in scale and mainly ritual in function, may be taken to have existed in northern Busiro, where the ancient shrines are clustered, at a time far beyond the reach of historical tradition . . . the rituals of Ganda kingship are both too elaborate and too archaic in character to have been evolved within the past few centuries.[69]

The shrine of Mugasa/Mukasa is on the Ssese islands. It has been suggested that the core of the ancient state was in *both* the islands and Busiro, 'and that this fact was represented by a ritual division of power between king and god'.[70]

Kingship in Buganda was not integrated with the Cwezi legend, and the spirits at the heart of Ganda religion had no links with royalty.[71] 'Ndaula, the nineteenth Kabaka, "stipulated on ascending the throne that he should not be made the medium of the God Mukasa."'[72] It is possible that the guardians of the spirits were an incipient focus of opposition to an unusually absolute sovereign.

Buganda had no counterpart to Bunyoro's powerful royal clan. Successive kings adopted the clan affiliation of their mothers and there were bitter wars of succession as rival clans fought for the throne. Princes were excluded from power and some kings executed large numbers of potential rivals. In the mid-seventeenth century, Buganda began to expand, in a dramatic recovery after a Bunyoro invasion. This new kingdom may have had little connection with the ancient principality. It was at its most powerful in the nineteenth century – a situation reflected in the colonial situation, which, here as elsewhere, perpetuated power structures as they were encountered (or, more correctly, perceived). The cruelty which often characterised it is succinctly reflected in a Ganda proverb: 'The king is the lake, which kills those who fish, and those who do not fish alike.'[73]

After the disaster of Bunyoro invasion in the early eighteenth century, the Baganda regained their independence, creating a new state and acknowledging what was probably a new dynasty.

The divinity Mukasa and the proverb which tells of powerful and capricious kings both image, in different ways, the overwhelming presence of Lake Victoria Nyanza. This great inland sea dominates the traditional history of the peoples who live nearby. The Suba, who live on its Kenya shores, tell of an ancestor who was brought ashore on a floating island of reeds. There is a whole genre of myths of this kind concerning the stranger from the water who becomes a king. The Kwaya take their name from the fish-eagle (whose feathers, in parts of Africa far from Lake Nyanza, are a symbol of priest or prince).[74] Their eastern neighbours, the Zanaki, believe that their first rainmaker was a woman from the lake, and that all future rainmakers must be the children of stranger women.[75]

East of Buganda lie the sixty-eight small polities of Busoga. Their historian believes that some clan genealogies have a time depth of twenty to thirty generations (going back to 1250, with an error margin of 150 years).[76]

Busoga traditions feature two clearly mythical culture heroes, Kintu and Mukama. As in Buganda, Kintu is both a leader of an immigrant people and a culture hero who brings bananas, millet, cattle, clans or totems. Sometimes he is God, or the son of God. One Ganda legend describes how death came into the world because of an act of disobedience on the part of Kintu's wife.[77] These traditions say more about theology than history, but they do encapsulate a real historical memory of ancient population movements.

We are on surer ground with 'Mukama', symbolic shorthand for Luo-speaking immigrants between the sixteenth and eighteenth centuries who established themselves as ruling elites.

The legend which describes the uncouth Rukidi may be a subtle form of anti-royal propaganda. The Nyoro word for government, *bulemi*, is associated with weight, *bulemezi*, something oppressive – which is, it seems, how it is perceived.[78] Royal chronicles sometimes describe the nemesis of oppressors: Kagulu, a mid-eighteenth-century Kabaka of Buganda, made visitors kneel on iron spikes and lost his throne and his life. (The story of the spikes is a widespread symbol of wanton cruelty.) Traditions do not only speak of kings and wars. In Busoga, 'Bandha was a doctor and he cured people, blind people, and deaf people, and he cured war wounds'.[79] The catastrophe of famine, and the wars and migrations to which it led, shout through the oral histories, where changes of dynasty sometimes only whisper. There seems to have been a period of drought and famine in the interlacustrine area from the 1580s to the 1620s. Herring made a bold and imaginative attempt to correlate traditions of famine with the records of Nile floods made at Cairo from the seventh century CE on. His conclusions were vitiated by a defective database,[80] but this would clearly repay more study.

Some oral histories speak of cannibalism at this time – a stark index of starvation.[81] Ganda traditions relate that people at first had neither food nor stomachs. God supplied both when asked, but warned that the stomach would 'cause pain, labour, and theft'. But Nkya replied, 'Nay my brother, but it is only hunger that has ears; apart from it there would be no submission among men, for man will only obey him who provides him with food.'[82]

The Luo diaspora

The Luo diaspora is one of the most dramatic and fascinating themes in East African history. Their homeland lies in the southern Republic of Sudan. Luo belongs ultimately to the same Western Nilotic language family as Nuer and

Dinka, whose history is considered elsewhere in this study, but is deeply differentiated from both, which suggests that a long time has elapsed since their separation. The various Luo languages, spoken over a vast terrain in the Republic of Sudan, Uganda and Kenya, are still closely related, a dialect cluster. The Nuer and Dinka are surrounded by Luo speakers – the Shilluk, speakers of an archaic dialect, to the north, the Bor to the west, the Anywak ('Anuak') to the south-east. Our concern here, however, is with the Luo who migrated much further south, to Uganda and Kenya. We have already noted the Luo dynasts of Bunyoro and Busoga, now long Bantuised in speech and culture. The Jo-la-Lwo (Palwo) survive as a Luo-speaking section in Bunyoro. The Alur, Acholi and Lango are other Luo-speaking peoples in northern Uganda; by far the largest Luo group is in Kenya, where they number over a million. The Padhola are a Luo-speaking enclave in south-east Uganda.

How, when and why did this diaspora occur, and in what way did the Luo, stateless in their homeland, become the ruling elite in many of the societies they joined? Ehret believes that the proto-Dinka/Nuer split from the proto-Luo early in the first millennium BCE.[83] Webster, collating oral traditions with data on Nile levels, suggests that the 'Nilotic cradleland' broke up in the first half of the eleventh century, as a consequence of drought.

The various Luo-speaking peoples have a tradition that they lived for a time at Pubungu on the White Nile north of Bunyoro, and scattered because of a quarrel. The story of the Spear and the Bead is a classic Nilotic myth, told with many variants by many different peoples, and analysed elsewhere in this study (see pp. 210–12). This dispersal is often dated to the fifteenth century, though, as we have seen, linguistic and other evidence suggests that this is too recent. An alternative scenario, persuasively argued, suggests that the Luo migrated to the Bunyoro region much earlier, before the rise of the interlacustrine kingdoms, and that their subsequent migration to the east *and northern Uganda* was caused by upheavals in the Bantu world.[84]

If this suggestion is correct, it was the Luo who acquired the idea and trappings of kingship from the Bantu. The Bunyoro origins of kingship are explicit in the traditions of Acholi ruling families, and the name of the Soga culture hero, Mukama, is the Nyoro word for their king. The Bito royal name Winyi may be cognate with Bantu words for a ruler, such as *mwene*. The first Bito ruler (equated with Rukidi) was Winyi Isingoma. The second word is also Bantu – master of the drum. So, it seems, is Pubungu.[85]

Why did Luo succeed in becoming a ruling aristocracy among so many non-Luo peoples? Among the Alur, it has been suggested that they had the habit of authority – which is simply to locate the problem some generations further back. Wrigley suggested that some form of centralised authority was necessary to establish viable agricultural communities (for instance, to build up grain reserves) and that this is symbolised by the tradition that Acholi and Alur founding princes brought rainstones.

The actual process is well documented. The royal clan always tends to expand more rapidly than the rest of society, since princes acquire more than their fair share of wives. Its scions move away in search of a kingdom of their own. Cohen has studied the process in detail in Busoga. Karuoth (Luo) princes grew up, not with their fathers, but in their mothers' homes, establishing there a new nucleus of power with the support of their maternal kin.[86] Although some Big Men are described in their history, the much more numerous Kenya Luo opted on the whole for more egalitarian institutions.[87]

Pastoralists and the premise of inequality

Nothing emerges from the Cwezi legends more clearly than a pastoral people's passion for their cattle – the king who follows his herd to the land of the dead, the prince who contemplates suicide when his favourite cow dies.

The history of Bunyoro, and, still more, of Nkore and Rwanda, was once seen in terms of an invading pastoral aristocracy, imposing its rule over local cultivators, a picture now sharply modified. In modern Bunyoro there are few cattle, for the herds have fallen victim to disease or war, so the distinction between pastoralists and farmers has come to have little meaning. Nkore, the largest of the kingdoms whose dynasties claimed descent from Ruhinda, was indeed dominated by pastoralists. Cattle were taken in war and had to be defended by force of arms, so herdsmen tended to be warriors. But the distinction between farmers (*iru*) and pastoralists (*hima*) was not immutable. Tradition also remembers notable farmer warriors. Rich farmers could become pastoralists and poor pastoralists farmers, and it was the cultivators who worked iron and made weapons. Nkore clans included members of both.[88]

The Eastern Nilotes

In an earlier chapter, we noted the presence of Late Stone Age pottery-making pastoralists in the Rift Valley area, some five thousand years ago. Attempts have been made to correlate the various ceramic traditions with major linguistic and cultural groupings.[89] The validity of this has been questioned[90] but it is clear that for many centuries pastoral peoples, sharing some cultural attitudes but speaking different languages, have lived there.

The Eastern Nilotic language family is dominated, in demographic terms, by the Maasai and other Maa speakers. In the 1970s, the Maasai were thought to number over 226,000; other Maa speakers included the Arusha (97,000), Baraguyu (29,000), Samburu (58,000) and smaller communities such as the Il Chamus.[91] The languages most closely related to Maa are Jie and Karimojong, spoken in northernmost Uganda, and Turkana, spoken across the border in Kenya.[92] This makes it overwhelmingly probable that the original Eastern Nilotic homeland was west of Lake Turkana. The influence of Eastern Cushitic neighbours – Somali, Oromo and Rendille – is mirrored in loan-words and cultural traits, most notably the taboo on consuming fish, fowl and game. Maa speakers now occupy a vast swathe of territory in central Kenya and Tanzania, but differences in dialect are minor, reflecting the great rapidity of their expansion from the seventeenth century on.[93] What made this rapid expansion and the comparable but less extensive expansion of the Turkana possible? An interesting analysis suggests that the crucial factor was cow power – the superiority of zebu cattle over sanga. But expansion was also built into Maasai social structures. Adult males were divided between *murran* (warriors) and elders. The latter controlled both cattle and wives. The former had their own sphere of power in raiding and war, often under the leadership of hereditary prophetic figures, and this enabled them to build up further herds of their own.

The Maasai have a cultural attachment to pastoralism so strong that ideally they live exclusively on its products – mainly fresh or curdled milk, occasionally supplemented by steers' blood or meat. It has been suggested that this is an extreme and recent adaptation, but despite a diet high in cholesterol, they have low levels of it in their blood and a low incidence of heart disease – the result of a unique genetic adaptation which reflects centuries, if not millennia, of a largely milk diet.[94] The Maasai, like other pastoral groups, have often been called egalitarian, but since their way of life required substantial herds, it was, in a sense, an equality which excluded the poor altogether.[95] In practice, pure pastoralism was an unattainable ideal, and the Maasai have always obtained additional food and other items by trade with hunter-gatherers and farmers. From the Dorobo they obtained honey, buffalo hides for shields, kudu horn trumpets and other commodities, in exchange for sheep, goats, meat, milk and, very rarely, a cow.[96] In a reaction against an older literature which depicted the Maasai as marauding warriors, recent studies emphasise the economic and social ties which bound them to their neighbours. They undoubtedly preferred to raid pastoralists, if necessary other Maasai, rather than farmers, who lacked the cattle which made warfare worth while. A Maasai who lost his cattle could only survive by turning to hunting or farming. Sometimes he was able to build up his herds again, but not always. During the disasters of the late nineteenth century, Maa-speaking Samburu overcame their dislike of fish consumption and took refuge with Eastern Cushitic El Molo, fisherfolk of Lake Turkana. In time, the latter willingly adopted both the Maa language and pastoralism.[97]

Pagasi is on the escarpment of the Rift Valley, between the Maasai and the Sonjo, Bantu farmers who live in fortified villages among them. Since the first recorded Maasai age set, in the late seventeenth century, it has served as a place of refuge for Maasai in trouble, and of acculturation for farmers 'becoming Maasai'. Some recruits were formally adopted by Maasai families, thus joining a Maasai clan. The central institution of Maasai life was the age set, and some whole communities adopted identical or similar age sets, building inter-ethnic bridges in this way.[98]

9

Africa south of the Limpopo

[Those] whom we met on the way, did not know of what nation they
were, they merely called themselves by the names of the rivers along
which the same resided and also at times land Khoi.

A visitor to the Eastern Cape, in 1752[1]

The environment

It was, above all else, rainfall which determined the pattern of settlement and the
shape of individual lives in Africa south of the Limpopo (Map 7). Communities
defined their rights to water precisely, but away from it boundaries were vague
and ill defined. Nearly all Xhosa place-names refer to rivers and lakes,[2] and, as
the epigraph of this chapter suggests, many Khoi communities defined their
identity in this way.

The climate of the Cape is Mediterranean, with winter rainfall, and hence
unsuited to African cereals such as millet and sorghum. Further north, precipita-
tion diminishes steadily as one travels from east to west. The Indian Ocean coast
receives some 80 cm of rain a year; to the west lie the arid Kalahari and Karoo,
and the Namib desert. Cultivation is possible only where the rainfall is at least 38
cm a year, and over 90 per cent of the population of southern Africa lives in its
eastern half.[3] It is not surprising that until the late eighteenth century territorial
wars seem to have been more common among the Tswana than in more favoured
regions further east, clearly reflecting an intensified competition for scarce
resources.[4] The Tswana greeted each other with the word 'Pula', may it rain.

A coastal strip, the home of the 'Nguni', lies between the Drakensberg
mountains and the Indian Ocean. Some believe it was once covered in forest and
has become grassland as a result of centuries of cultivation and pastoralism.[5]
Much of the rest of southern Africa is over 3,000 feet high. West of the
Drakensbergs, the land slopes away gradually, and the Orange river and its
tributaries flow westward to the sea. In the interior there are vast upland plains –
plattelands – interspersed by high mountains. Further north, the Limpopo flows
into the Indian Ocean.

The Khoisan

Khoisan is an artificial composite term, best used to refer to one of Africa's four
great language families. The peoples whom Europeans once called Bushmen are
now generally referred to as the San, though since it is a derogatory term

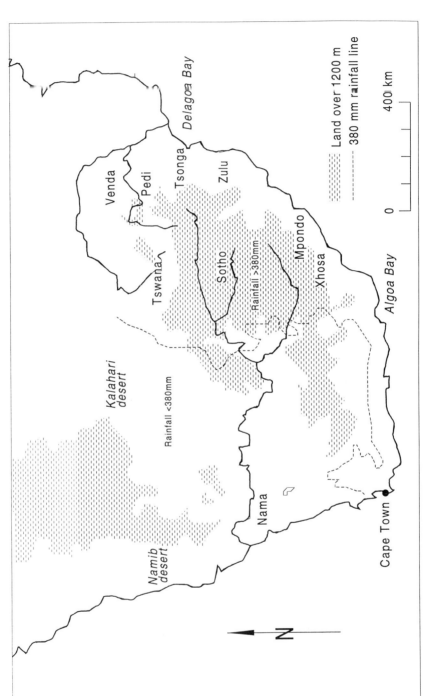

Venda

Pedi

Tsonga

Delagoa Bay

Zulu

Tswana

Sotho

Rainfall >380mm

Mpondo

Xhosa

Algoa Bay

Land over 1200 m

380 mm rainfall line

0   400 km

Kalahari
desert

Rainfall <380mm

Nama

Namib
desert

Cape Town

N

Map 7   South Africa

invented by the Khoikhoi, it is almost as unsatisfactory, and some advocate '[its] consignment ... to the ashcan of history'.[6] Bantu speakers called them Twa. Twa or Cwa is a very widespread term for small-statured hunter-gatherers: it is found, for instance, in Rwanda.

Khoikhoi means 'men of men',[7] and ethonyms such as Korana are related to it. Europeans called the Khoikhoi Hottentots, a derogatory reference to the distinctive implosive consonants ('clicks') in their speech. They spoke dialects of a single language, unlike the San, whose languages were deeply differentiated, and had a sense of common identity. They adopted pastoralism near the beginning of the Common Era, and their first nucleus of settlement was in northern Botswana.[8] By the seventeenth century there were two main branches – the Nama of Namibia and the Khoikhoi of the Cape. They did not smelt iron, and perhaps for environmental reasons cultivated no crop but the narcotic, *dagga*. They rode on oxen and built beehive-shaped homes which were easily transported. Many of their genes are preserved in the modern 'Cape Coloured' population, but not their language or culture. In the seventeenth century, the Nama were moving north through the grasslands of central Namibia, between the coastal desert and the Kalahari. Here they met the Herero, Bantu-speaking pastoralists, moving south. As so often, lack of water and the competition for scarce resources was to precipitate conflict, which dominated their nineteenth-century history.

The Khoikhoi and the San were the only indigenous inhabitants of the Cape, west of Algoa Bay. Like the Aborigines of Tasmania, and the Native Americans of New England, the Cape Khoikhoi and southern San no longer exist as separate peoples; the San are now confined to a few relict bands in the deserts of Botswana and Namibia.

The boundaries between these communities were fluid, and their lifestyles had much in common. In general, the San were hunter-gatherers, but some San kept livestock, and Khoi pastoralists who lost their cattle adopted the hunting lifestyle of the San; if they regained them, perhaps through banditry, they reverted to pastoralism. Ethnic labels, here as so often, misrepresent a fluid and constantly changing reality.[9] The San of the (nineteenth-century) Kalahari have been described in these terms:

It is essential to note the diversity and heterogeneity of the San. They spoke a variety of San (and Khoi) languages, exhibited a variety of physical types, and most important, they lived in a variety of socioeconomic circumstances. While all relied to an extent on hunting and gathering, some lived interspersed with, and worked for, Herero, Ovambo, and Tswana herders. Others kept herds of their own and paid tribute to various overlords. Still others ... lived as relatively independent hunter-gatherers.[10]

In 1850, an observer described San in northern Namibia 'who contrary to most other members of this race, are settled and possess large copper mines and have copper in abundance'.[11]

The Bergdama of Namibia were hunter-gatherers who owned no cattle and spoke Nama. But they had the appearance of black Africans and worked in copper and iron.[12] They cut across conventional categories and remind us of their inadequacy.

Like the peoples of the ancient Sahara, the San created a precious heritage of rock art. In attempting to discover lost cognitive maps we are bound to look for meanings in these paintings, but their interpretation is controversial. Some of them seem to reflect the healing trance dances which were central to San cultures, though there are problems in extrapolating modern ethnographic data back to paintings which may, in some cases, be as much as 26,000 years old.[13] In some areas, the eland is a core symbol and in others the gemsbok. It is a good example of the insight which Leach expressed with reference to totemism – 'good to think with' rather than 'goods to eat'. The eland is especially cherished by God: '/Kaggen does not love us if we kill an eland', and myth relates how, after a ritual was performed, 'all the elands that had died became alive again'.[14] Some paintings depict encounters with African pastoralists and with the *trekboers*. The last San artist died in the nineteenth century.

Much of the San past lies beyond recovery but, paradoxically, one of the most vigorously pursued historical controversies in recent years focusses on this area. In an earlier chapter we noted the work of Lee and his collaborators on the contemporary !Kung San of Namibia and Botswana (p. 67 above). In this view, their hunter-gatherer lifestyle is both ancient and efficient, producing a healthy diet and ample leisure, and marked by its egalitarianism. In Wilmsen's political economy of the Kalahari, their lifestyle is the end product of a long history of domination, their egalitarianism reflects a shared poverty, their isolation lies in the eye of the observer. Once more, a vision of Merrie Africa recedes, and the San are seen as the victims not only of white settlers but of their African neighbours.[15]

'Nguni', Sotho, Tswana

South of the Limpopo, black Africans – all of whom speak Bantu languages – are conventionally grouped into two main categories: the Sotho-Tswana of the high veld, and the 'Nguni', who live in the narrow coastal plain between the Drakensberg mountains and the sea, though the validity of this distinction, which is largely rooted in language, has been questioned.[16] The earliest recorded instance of 'Nguni', in 1589, refers to what later became northern Zululand. In the nineteenth century, it was a synonym for Xhosa. It now refers to the African peoples who live east of the Drakensbergs and south of the Tsonga of Mozambique, but this is a recent 'invention',[17] and no ethnic group considers itself 'Nguni'. Today there are two major 'Nguni' languages which are mutually intelligible: Zulu in the north and Xhosa in the south. The languages of the high veld, Sotho, Tswana and Pedi, are much more deeply differentiated than the Nguni languages. The cultures of the Lobedu and Venda of the northern Transvaal, conventionally regarded as part of the Sotho-Tswana cluster, are closely related to that of the Shona of Zimbabwe. The Venda live in and around the Soutpansberg mountains, and their traditions tell of rulers who came from north of the Limpopo. By the late eighteenth century, the Xhosa had reached the Zuurfeld, between the Bushmans and Fish rivers, and had thus penetrated much further south than the Sotho-Tswana, who still lived to the north of the Orange river. Well before the tumultuous events of the Mfecane, some Nguni migrated to the high veld; in the seventeenth century, a Zizi group from the Tugela valley settled among the Sotho adopting a Sotho totem, Phuthi (duiker), which became their name. They migrated gradually towards the south, and adopted many Sotho words.

Earlier in this study, we noted the many complexities which surround the interpretation of the spread of Bantu speech, agriculture and pyrotechnology in the Early Iron Age. This is all beyond the reach of oral history:[18] 'The Basuto say they come from a place named Ntsuanatsatsu, a kind of big hole with a rock overhanging it, full of reeds, where voices from under the ground may be heard.'[19] Archaeological research has shown that iron-using agriculturalists crossed the Limpopo early in the Christian era. Older ideas of a purposeful Bantu migration to the south have been replaced by a more nuanced concept of ebb and flow. Early Iron Age farmers filled ecological niches underused by hunter-gatherers, but they were also attracted by other kinds of resources, especially the shellfish of the coast. Their advance was halted by increasing aridity or by tsetse fly.

Seven hollow terracotta heads were found at Lydenburg in the eastern Transvaal. They date from *c.* 500 CE, and were found in association with iron and copper beads.[20] The comparison with the distinctive hollow terracotta heads associated with iron-using peoples at Nok in central Nigeria at much the same time is irresistible, but their styles are quite different, vast distances separate them, and there is clearly no connection. The farmers did not create rock paintings. They were more burdened than the San with possessions, which impose, as we all know from experience, the need to acquire more. They were preoccupied with the care of their cattle, the upkeep of their homes, the storage of their grain. They had little time or inclination for art on the rocks.[21]

The Sotho-Tswana have a strong preference for marriage with close relatives, especially cousins, while the 'Nguni' rigidly prohibit sexual relations between kin.[22] The 'Nguni' built beehive-shaped houses of woven branches, plastered with clay, and thatched; the Sotho-Tswana lived in larger and more substantial structures with clay walls and thatched roofs, and, in many cases, stone reinforcement. The popularity of stone on the high veld may reflect the need to conserve wood. The remains of stone foundations and drystone walls of round-houses and cattle kraals on the highveld go back, in some cases, to the fourteenth century, and exemplify the symbolic 'Bantu Cattle Pattern' discussed in an earlier chapter (pp. 99 and 115 above). They have been studied through aerial photography; three different settlement patterns were found, the oldest of which has been attributed to the forebears of the Kwena and Kgata. The Taung have been linked to another of these patterns, and the most common of them, found only in north-west Orange Free State, with the Rolong.[23]

Both Khoikhoi and Xhosa were pastoralists, and some Khoi 'became Xhosa', a process reflected in the fact that a sixth of the words in the Xhosa language contain clicks. Sotho rulers, including Moshoeshoe, made a practice of marrying a San as a junior wife. Ethnic labels are an unsatisfactory shorthand for a reality which was fluid, nuanced and constantly changing. MacKenzie wrote of the word 'Bechuana' (baTswana): 'These people do not use this word of themselves, or of one another; nevertheless they accept it as the white man's name for them, and now begin to use it of themselves.'[24] 'Zulu' has had quite different meanings in the eighteenth century, the nineteenth, and the twentieth. It even had different meanings at the same time. In the 1880s Cetshwayo was asked what he knew of the diamond fields. He said that 'the Zulu people never went to the Diamond Fields; the Natal Zulus did'.[25]

Production

A dominant motif in Southern Bantu societies is their passion for cattle, reflected in a very rich pastoral vocabulary. Their cows are individually named, and songs are composed in honour of favourites. Alberti, who visited the Xhosa in 1803, described the complex patterns into which cattle horns were trained and how the cattle obeyed their owner's whistle, like a well-trained dog. 'The Kaffir's cattle is the foremost and practically the only subject of his care and occupation, in the possession of which he finds complete happiness.'[26]

Wealth could be stored in the form of herds, which offered a certain measure of protection against famine. But above all, cattle were valued as a medium of exchange, needed to obtain wives and, through them, children: 'Cattle beget children.'[27] The ownership of cattle led to an increasing difference between rich and poor, and may also have contributed to an increasing polarisation of gender roles which some find reflected in the ruins of fifteenth-century Zimbabwe.

It is a paradox that although bridewealth payments, *lobola*, could only be made in cattle, Southern Bantu women were rigidly excluded from pastoral tasks. Among the Xhosa, they could not milk or even wash milk pails or walk through the herds.[28] Among the Khoi, on the other hand, women did the milking.

A fish taboo is a culture trait common to the 'Nguni', the Venda, the Shona and many Sotho.

> I do not eat fish
> A fish is a snake
> A water snake
> It makes me ill.[29]

When a southern Tswana people began to eat fish in a time of famine they were called Thlaping, Fish People.

As elsewhere in Africa, work was organised on bases of status, age and gender, and white observers often described the lot of women as oppressive and heavily burdened. A Portuguese shipwrecked on the Transkei coast in 1635, said of the proto-Xhosa: 'The women do all the work, planting and tilling the earth with sticks to prepare it for their grain, which is millet ... They have maize also, and plant large melons which are very good.'[30]

Among the southern Tswana in the first part of the nineteenth century, 'While going to war, hunting, watching the cattle, milking the cows, and preparing their furs and skins for mantles was the work of the men, the women had by far the heavier task of agriculture, building the houses, fencing, bringing firewood.'[31]

Among the Zulu,

The men function as the artisans and pastoralists; the women as the housekeepers and agriculturalists ... To the Zulu man it falls to build the huts and keep them in repair; to erect and renew the various fences ... to hew down the bush ... from such spots as the females are to cultivate; to milk the cows and generally tend all stock ... Many of the elder men are constantly engaged with special offices ... doctoring, divining, metal-working, wood-carving, basket making [etc.].[32]

It is sometimes suggested that European accounts were affected by western preconceptions about gender and manual work, and it is true that women's work was made more attractive by companionship and the sharing of tasks. But there is evidence that some at least resented the multiple duties of their burdened lives; there are many accounts of 'wives in flight from husbands, husbands enforcing their demands, bands of sons in pursuit of their mothers and sisters, and daughters escaping from unwanted, and often much older husbands'.[33] Some women fled from nineteenth-century Zululand to Natal with partners of their own choice.[34]

It has been suggested that the most meaningful category of socio-economic differentiation in pre-industrial southern Africa was not between rulers and commoners, or between cattle owners and clients, but between married men on the one hand and women and single men on the other.[35] Elders wielded power over younger men by their control of bridewealth, and of initiation ceremonies.

Observers commented on the varied and ample diet of the 'Nguni'. Maize was introduced in the eighteenth century and had become a staple by the nineteenth. The Zulu had over forty alternative dishes, including 'boiled maize-grains, toasted maize-cobs, sour clotted milk, boiled sweet potatoes, a mash of pumpkins, [and] fermented sorghum porridge'.[36]

'In the Zulu system', wrote Bryant, 'every kraal is self-contained and self-supporting.'[37] No hamlet was entirely self-sufficient; it needed products from local craft specialists, especially iron workers. Copper was greatly valued, though used entirely for personal adornment or as currency. Many areas lacked copper and iron ores and imported these metals from centres such as Phalaborwa in the eastern Transvaal, where copper was mined for a thousand years. At one iron-smelting site in the vicinity, it is estimated that 48 tons of iron were produced, at the cost (in charcoal) of 7,000 trees.[38] A Zulu story tells how the secrets of metal working were discovered; after a time the people were afflicted by an epidemic which diviners blamed on metal working. As a result, all metal objects were buried, and smiths gave up their trade.[39] (Does this embody an intimation of the hidden costs of metallurgy?) Salt was often scarce, and had to be obtained from areas blessed with brine springs. Salt cakes were manufactured on a tributary of the Oliphant river.[40]

Political organisation

The San, like all hunter-gatherers, lived in small bands with perhaps twenty members. The Khoikhoi lived in larger communities, and the Southern Bantu in units that were larger still, a difference in size rather than kind. 'There were various nations who were distinct in their greatness and their kingship.'[41]

They are often called chieftaincies, though the present writer prefers 'principalities', to distinguish them from kingdoms. This term has the merit of bringing out the similarities between Khoi and other African polities; it mirrors their fluidity. It has been suggested that kingdoms differ from chieftaincies in geographic extent, the centralisation of authority and the existence of hierarchical structures with delegated powers,[42] but in southern Africa the term is used for polities which Africanists elsewhere would not hesitate to call kingdoms.[43]

Communities were sometimes named after a putative royal ancestor ('Xhosa',[44] 'Ngwane') or, among the Tswana, after the totemic animal of the ruling clan (Taung, 'lion', Kwena, 'crocodile').

In general, the 'Nguni' tend to live in dispersed hamlets, the Sotho-Tswana in larger nucleated towns. (The latter phenomenon is often seen as a response to scarcity of water, which created a need to cluster round what rivers there were. An alternative view considers it a response to the tumultuous events of the nineteenth century.)[45] In 1801, it was said that the chief settlement of the Thlaping (southern Tswana) was as large in circumference as Cape Town.[46] Rain-making was the fundamental duty of a king, and in the nineteenth century it became the criterion by which missionaries were judged.[47] 'Nguni' principalities were smaller, apparently because water was more abundant and the complementary pasture types called sweet and sour veld found closer to each other. The states of the southern Sotho were also smaller and tended to cluster in fertile river valleys such as the Caledon.

Polities tended to go through successive phases of fusion into larger units, and of fission. Sotho-Tswana traditions describe the spread of two chiefly lineages from perhaps 1500,[48] the Kwena and Kgatla (a species of monkey). A brother or son of a chief would leave his father's homestead and found a new settlement of his own (a process which was mandatory for the sons of Xhosa chiefs). The original homeland of the Kwena and Kgatla was between the Vaal and the Limpopo, where the stone remains of their villages can still be seen. They spread to the south, intermarrying with the Fokeng, another ancient lineage. It has been suggested that it was their resources in cattle which enabled them to develop new chieftaincies. But it is suggestive that Rolong totems include the kudu (*tholo*, the source of the ethonym), iron and the hammer.[49] Sometimes one has hints of a wider forest of symbols: crocodiles are schematically represented in the ruins of Great Zimbabwe, and an alternative name for the Kgatla was People of the Fire Flames (see p. 113 above).

These totemic 'clans' were not monolithic entities. Many, like the Rolong, had different totems, and the totems are those of the rulers, not the more numerous commoners. Each chieftaincy tended to attract many groups of adherents, each with its own distinctive history.[50] The chain of oral testimony was interrupted by the traumatic events of the nineteenth century, so that it is not easy to discern the lineaments of the remote past. In some cases, the position of earlier 'lords of the land' is fossilised in ritual: in the Pedi state they were given a token tribute of thatch and building poles.[51]

The Ngwaketsi and Ngwato were eighteenth-century Kgatla offshoots; the Ngwato later produced another branch, the Tawana. The Kgalagadi are

Tswana who live on the edge of the Kalahari; in an adverse environment they became fragmented and acknowledged allegiance to more prosperous chieftaincies.

Oral tradition explains fusion and fission in individual terms, the conquests of a hero, the ambitions of rival princely brothers, but it is likely that the underlying causes were often ecological, the pressure of a growing population and expanding herds on resources. Because the ruler was a rainmaker, drought was sufficient reason to challenge his authority.

Both fusion and fission took place in the late eighteenth century and the readiness with which these states split into their component sections suggests that they are best called confederacies. The southern Xhosa split into three sections, and encroaching *trekboers* profited by their divisions. Among the southern Tswana, Tau, a warrior who was killed fighting the Korana in 1760, founded a large but short-lived Rolong state. After his death, several sections, including the Thlaping, broke away.

The Thlaping combined Khoi and Tswana elements, and in the early nineteenth century their ruler was the son of a Kora mother and married to a Kora wife.[52] The Swazi are conventionally called 'Nguni', but their speech and culture have many Sotho elements. The name of the Xhosa principality, Gqunukwebe, reflects its many Khoi members: 'Near [the Xhosa] and with them mix the Gonaqua Hotentots. These the Caffers use as servants and in war time, they also serve them as soldiers; their clothes and lifestyle are precisely alike and they intermarry without differentiation.'[53]

Communities were linked by clientage, trade and intermarriage. Xhosa kings usually obtained their Great Wife and Right Hand Wife from the Thembu and Mpondo. The San traded with Khoi and Xhosa, exchanging ivory for cattle and *dagga*. We should not idealise inter-group relations in the African past. Many wars were fought, and sometimes the San were treated by their African neighbours with brutality and disdain.[54]

Aristocrats had a better diet than commoners; in particular, they were able to eat meat regularly. They wore rare furs and abundant jewellery in copper and other materials. Rulers had much larger homes and their cattle were more beautiful and numerous. Because they had more cattle, they had more wives and more children. John Dunn, a Scot who settled in Zululand in the time of Cetshwayo, had 48 wives and over 100 children.[55] Control of people and cattle bolstered the power of kings, and the power of kings enabled them to obtain more people and cattle. Raiding was only one of the methods they employed: a Swazi king paid no bridewealth for his many wives, but for Swazi royal women (and even royal captives) inflated bridewealth was demanded.[56]

It has been suggested that there was much greater social differentiation among the northern than the southern 'Nguni'.[57] Bryant, having listed the many tasks of Zulu daily life, observes, however: 'In these duties it is important to note that all take part, from the kraal-head, even the chief himself.'[58]

The powers of kings were limited by the geographic mobility of their subjects. Families could and did move away if they disliked an arbitrary ruler. 'Some kraals break up and march towards the borders of the country and there they stay, keeping themselves ready to emigrate to another country.'[59] Tswana kings decided important issues in consultations with an assembly of adult men, *kgotla*. (The Sotho equivalent is *pitso*.)

Drought and other misfortunes were often explained in supernatural terms, as the anger of ancestors, the malice of witches. The Xhosa Gcaleka (d. 1778), who founded the lineage which bears his name, was a sickly man who killed many supposed witches in his pursuit of health. His health did not improve. But in an earlier period, a Xhosa councillor charged with witch execution hid prospective victims in a forest, where they married Khoi.[60]

We have noted the copper mines of ancient Phalaborwa. Eleventh-century and modern pottery from the area are almost identical; this is particularly interesting as the pottery is unique, with no obvious ancestors or relatives elsewhere in Africa. The Phalaborwa, the Lobedu and the Birwa are all Sotho of the north-east Transvaal. They live 400 kilometres east of the centre of Sotho dispersal and are not linked to major Sotho lineages.[61]

Until the late eighteenth century, the political units in Africa south of the Limpopo were relatively small. In the nineteenth, the great upheaval of peoples known as the Mfecane was to change the face of southern Africa for ever.

10

Northern Africa to the seventh century CE

The *Romans* ... carefull Relaters of their great victories, doe speake
little of the interior parts of *Affrica*.

R. Jobson, *The Golden Trade*[1]

PART ONE: TO THE INCEPTION OF ROMAN RULE

The western world has tended to approach the African continent with a
particular set of prejudices – dazzled by the achievements of ancient Egypt,
largely ignorant of those of black Africa. To some extent this is due to historical
circumstances: Napoleon's invasion of Egypt created the science of Egyptology
in its wake and achievements such as a long tradition of literacy or monumental
construction in stone are more readily appreciated by westerners than, for
instance, architecture which exploits the sculptural potential of mud. The
pyramids endure; sculpture in wood in a tropical environment usually does not.
But the culture and language of ancient Egypt are long since dead. The
languages, religions and cultures of black Africa are with us still.

It is extraordinarily difficult to incorporate the history of northern Africa into
that of the rest of the continent. Part of the difficulty is that we know so much
more about it; massive documentation survives from the Egypt of the Pharaohs
and whole books have been written about single reigns. We know the Egyptian
past between, say, 3000 BCE and 1000 CE with a detail and precision which will
never be possible for sub-Saharan Africa, where we glimpse the remote past
darkly, through the windows of language change, archaeology and oral tradition.
Ancient Egypt had a great influence on Nubia, which was, in many ways,
reciprocal. As far as we know, it had no influence at all on the rest of Africa. But
after the Arab conquest of the seventh century, Islamic influences, transmitted
through North Africa and across the Sahara, were to be of incalculable
importance. The history of the Western Sudan, in particular, although the
remote frontier of the Islamic world, was in many ways transformed by its
impact. But that is to anticipate.

Ancient Egypt

A central theme of this book is the interaction between African societies and their
environment. Egypt has been called the gift of the Nile and of the fellahin. In
modern times, it is virtually rainless, depending entirely on the annual flooding
of the Nile. The great river rises ultimately in Lake Victoria Nyanza; it floods

when its tributaries, the Blue Nile and the Atbara, bring a torrent of water and fertile topsoil from the Ethiopian plateau. The Crusaders conceived but never executed a plan to divert them and render the Nile valley uninhabitable. The Palermo Stone lists not only early Pharaohs, but flood levels in their reigns.[2]

Ancient Egypt, the Two Lands, was a narrow habitable strip between the uninhabitable Eastern and Western Deserts (only in the Red Sea hills, the home of the Beja, was settlement possible). Lower Egypt was the Nile Delta, and Upper Egypt the Nile flood-plain, from the Delta to Aswan, a distance of 700 kilometres. Its width varies from 10 to 20 kilometres, and its black alluvial soil contrasts sharply with the red soil of the desert. There was another fertile area in the Fayum, a depression surrounded by desert, to the west of the Nile, which was first exploited under the Ptolemies. It was on the desert edge that grain was stored and the dead buried, leaving the precious alluvial soil free for cultivation.

We have stressed the limited impact of African states on distant provinces. No Egyptian village was far from the Nile, so the central government was able to exercise a much more detailed control. The Eastern and Western Deserts effectively prevented population dispersal and drift, and fostered a sense of insularity and self-sufficiency, while limiting Egypt's impact on other cultures. It was long believed that the Nile valley was too swampy for settlement until about 5000 BCE, the date of the earliest known agricultural settlements, and that people lived on its edges until the process of desertification began. It is now thought that they lived in the Nile valley much earlier, and that it offered ideal conditions for hunter-gatherers.[3] Agriculture was practised in the Fertile Crescent from the tenth millennium BCE on. If Egypt really first adopted agriculture in *c.* 5000 BCE, it is puzzlingly late – later than the Sahara. This may well have been because the natural resources of the Nile valley were so abundant that the hunter-gatherer lifestyle continued to be eminently satisfactory. Alternatively – and this is more likely – earlier agricultural settlements lie buried under Nile silt or under the river itself, which nows lie 3 kilometres east of its course 2,000 years ago.[4] In so-called Predynastic Egypt (the expression reflects the traditional concentration on Pharaonic Egypt), we can discern the origins of the fine craftsmanship for which Egypt became internationally famous – decorated pottery, copper (first annealed and later smelted) and carving in a variety of materials including flint and ivory. Dwellings, then as later, were made of sun-dried brick, and the dead were buried with grave goods. In general lifestyle and socio-political organisation, Predynastic Egypt was comparable with contemporary cultures in Nubia and the Sahara.[5]

In about 3100 BCE there was an extraordinarily rapid and dramatic change: the unification of Egypt into a single state under a king, and the establishment of what, as far as we know, were Africa's first cities. Ancient sources, including Herodotus,[6] attribute these events to a king of Upper Egypt called Menes, who conquered the Nile Delta and built a capital, White-Walled Memphis, on land won from the Nile. (The god of Memphis was Ptah, who caused the earth to emerge from the primeval waters.) It is possible that Menes was not a historical individual but a personification of an era of change – *mn* means to endure.[7] But there is also a contemporary record in bas-reliefs on votive palettes (which evolved from the cosmetic palette, where green malachite was ground for eye shadow), a mace head and a knife handle. A recurrent image is that of violent conquest: A famous palette dating from about 3100 BCE shows a king called Narmer (a form of Menes?) about to club a kneeling captive: the execution of enemies is a recurrent motif in Egyptian art. On one side Narmer wears the White Crown of Upper Egypt; on the reverse the Red Crown of Lower Egypt. He gazes on rows of corpses and, in the form of a bull, breaks down a fortified town and tramples on yet another foe. Another palette shows the king as a lion, savaging the corpses of the slain. A mace-head from much the same time shows a ruler wearing the White Crown and breaching a dyke; he is known only as the Scorpion King. Egyptians were still enacting the ceremony of Opening the Dykes in the eighteenth century CE.[8] This mace shows dead birds hanging from standards. In later years, these birds, *rekhyt*, symbolised the Egyptian people.[9] The image of the monarch as a dangerous predator, lion or crocodile, has many parallels in sub-Saharan Africa. But the archaeological record does not reflect great upheavals, and it is believed that Egypt was unified, not by conquest, but by a long process of 'percolation' from Upper Egypt.[10] The image of the slaughter of enemies belongs to the rhetoric of power.

The association of early state formation and urbanisation with irrigation agriculture has parallels in both the Fertile Crescent and the Indus valley. The growth of the Pharaonic state is usually explained in ecological terms. The annual flooding of the Nile, and the intensive agriculture it made possible, produced the surplus which built the pyramids. But basin irrigation required central organisation to maintain channels, repair walls and so on. The cultivation of irrigated soil was at the heart of the Egyptian state, but paradoxically, early Pharaohs wore pastoral symbols: an animal tail, an artificial beard, a shepherd's apron, crook and flail (for collecting gum).[11]

There are hieroglyphs on the Narmer palette and still earlier examples are known.[12] It is generally believed that the *idea* of literacy came from Mesopotamia; its Egyptian *form* was new.[13] Hieroglyphs were used for inscriptions, and a cursive hand, hieratic, for the transactions of daily life.

It has been suggested that Predynastic Egypt had a population of 100,000–200,0000 and Early Dynastic Egypt one of 2 million.[14] If this is true, it represented a remarkable demographic leap. The population of Egypt may well have been equal to that of the rest of the African continent at this time.[15] The great strengths of ancient Egypt were the fertility of its well-watered soil, at least in the years when the Nile rose as expected, the efficiency of its food production and the technical excellence of its craftsmen. The staples were wheat and barley, made into bread and beer, but an abundance of other crops was grown. Hunting was both a cherished sport and a valuable resource; the Egyptians hunted the migratory birds which visited the Nile in vast flocks, and kept both geese and ducks.[16] A fourth-century CE source stated that hippos were once abundant in the Delta, 'but now they are nowhere to be found, since, as the inhabitants of those regions conjecture, they became tired of the multitude that hunted them and were forced to take refuge in the land of the Blemmyes'.[17]

Egyptian stone workers were famous for their expertise, not only in sculpture, engraving and bas-reliefs, but also in the making of superbly crafted vessels of semi-precious stone such as alabaster. (This skill declined after the introduction of the potter's wheel, early in the Old Kingdom.) The Egyptians invented faience, a brilliantly glazed 'pottery' made of crushed quartz; they both invented and exported papyrus, an immense improvement on Mesopotamia's tablets of clay. It survived for millennia in the dry air of the Nile valley, but not in the Nile Delta. The production of glazes for faience developed into glass working and the Egyptians also made fine linen, which grave robbers sought as avidly as other treasures. Standing at the meeting place of three continents, Egypt was well situated both to profit by trade and to absorb new concepts: the practice, or at least the idea, of agriculture, the idea of literacy but not the form it took, and construction in sun-dried brick. Apart from its perpetually replenished soil, inhabited Egypt was lacking in resources, especially timber, which was purchased from Byblos ('the cedars of Lebanon').

The Egyptians thoroughly exploited the resources of the deserts which surrounded them, including gemstones and precious metals, and mined the turquoise and copper of Sinai. They re-exported minerals and tropical products from Nubia and the Land of Punt, which was probably on the Red Sea coast of Somalia. Engravings of a trading journey there in the reign of Queen Hatshepsut give us a precious glimpse of an otherwise little-known part of Africa through Egyptian eyes – including its people, some black and some caucasoid, and its roundhouses, on a river bank – a uniquely early glimpse of African domestic architecture.[18] Until the later Middle Kingdom, when the more durable alloy, bronze, was introduced, Egypt remained in the Copper Age; the great stone blocks of the pyramids were cut with copper saws and sand. Copper did not replace stone tools, which reached a peak of perfection in ripple-surfaced flint knives. Iron smelting began late by Mediterranean standards, in the sixth century BCE. Herodotus gives us an interesting vignette of Egyptian economic life which sheds light on conventional Greek views of gender roles: 'The Egyptians ... in their manners and customs seem to have reversed the ordinary practices of mankind. For instance, women attend market and are employed in trade, while men stay at home and do the weaving.'[19]

Despite the calm assurance and serenity of their statuary, the ancient Egyptians had their characteristic ailments, including rheumatism and water-borne diseases such as schistosomiasis. Rich and poor suffered severe dental attrition as the result of residual quartz dust in bread, from the grinding process. (The New Zealand Maori had the same problem from sand in shellfish.) The average life expectancy of the upper classes in Greek times was about 36,[20] rather higher than that in Imperial Rome.[21] There are exceptions to every generalisation, however, and Phiops II reigned for ninety-four years.

Egyptian history was to remain full of paradoxes – conservative in some respects and innovative in others. The basic outlines of Egyptian civilisation were achieved very early and its innate conservatism is reflected in the conventions of its art – the frontal eye and body, the head in profile. Ancient Egypt produced a considerable body of literature, which includes the inscriptions on royal tombs known as the Pyramid Texts, works of political and moral advice, and novels such as *The Story of Sinuhe*. The Egyptians were accomplished mathematicians and astronomers, dating their 365-day calendar from the heliacal rising of Sirius.[22]

The Step Pyramid – the world's first great building of cut stone – was designed by the vizier Imhotep (fl. 2680 BCE), a man of great gifts, who was later deified. The largest pyramid was built for Kheops, in *c.* 2590 BCE and is still the world's most extensive stone structure after Cologne cathedral. The Great Sphinx, whose head is that of Khephren, was built to guard the city of the dead which grew up around these pyramids, which were themselves only one element in a larger complex including the great mastabas (rectangular tombs) of queen mothers and consorts. The living, including the Pharaohs, inhabited structures of sun-dried brick. Stone monuments were for the dead.

The construction of giant pyramids did not continue for long and this may reflect a decline in the power of the Pharaohs, or in general prosperity. Historians differ in their attitude to them. Some regard their building as a form of wasteful conspicuous consumption. Others point out that the work was carried out in the agricultural off-season, and that payments to workers, generated from taxation, had the effect of redistributing income over the whole year. But perhaps no society has devoted so much of its resources to the welfare – in this case, the supposed eternal welfare – of single individuals as did Egypt in the age of the pyramids. Nubia's historian writes: 'Impoverishment under the Egyptian Old Kingdom was not confined to Nubia. The peasantry of the northern country suffered almost equal deprivation, if grave goods are any measure . . . The reason in both cases appears to have been the same: the concentration of wealth and commerce in the hands of the pharaoh.'[23]

A twentieth-century Egyptian author said of Upper Egypt: 'I noted that often peasant women, as soon as they had been married and had given birth once or twice, could hardly be distinguished from their mothers. They bore . . . the stamp of their continuous, monotonous, and exhausting work.'[24]

After the Archaic period (the first two dynasties), Egyptian history is conventionally divided into the Old, Middle and New Kingdoms and the Late Period. The Old Kingdom lasted for 500 years, and then collapsed in *c.* 2200 BCE, a crisis caused primarily by a fall in the level of the Nile floods. A bas-relief shows the huddled, emaciated victims of famine;[25] this seems to have been part of a much more extensive drought, which may also have caused the fall of the Akkadian empire and be linked with the conflagrations which engulfed Troy II and Byblos.[26] Ankhtifi, an aristocrat who lies buried a little south of Luxor, boasted, with justifiable complacency: 'All of Upper Egypt was dying of hunger, to such an extent that everyone had come to eating his children, but I managed that no one died of hunger in this nome.'[27]

Egypt was reunited by a prince of Thebes (modern Luxor), inaugurating the Middle Kingdom, which lasted 400 years and was destroyed by invaders, the 'Hyksos', who probably came from Palestine. In 1570 BCE they were expelled by another Theban prince, the architect of the New Kingdom, which lasted slightly less than 500 years. Bell suggests that the fall of the New Kingdom, which was approximately contemporary with the fall of the Hittite empire and of the Mycenaean civilisation in Greece, was also caused by drought and its sinister companion, famine.

The Pharaohs of the New Kingdom built an empire in Nubia and western Asia and carved their great sepulchres out of the Theban cliffs. We have seen how historians of Africa have come to question a historiography which focusses on Great States. Egyptologists have tended to glorify the periods of strength and unity, and regard the Late Period, from 1072 BCE, as one of decline, when Upper and Lower Egypt drifted apart, and the Nile valley was repeatedly conquered by foreign powers. O'Connor suggests a valuable corrective, seeing this period as 'representing complex and subtle responses by a flexible political and ideological system to greatly changed circumstances, but not a fundamental reordering or internal disintegration. Egypt did not need to, and apparently did not, perceive itself as in decline; despite periods of foreign occupation, it remained relatively prosperous.'[28] For a time Egypt was ruled by Nubians and later by the Assyrians, who used iron weapons at a time when the Egyptians were still in the Bronze Age.

There was a brief return to indigenous rule under a Delta dynasty, the Saites, one of whom, Necho (610–595 BCE), cut a canal from the Red Sea to the Nile and is alleged to have sponsored the first circumnavigation of Africa. Political fragmentation did not preclude artistic vitality and cultural innovation. A new cursive script, demotic, was introduced, and Egypt entered the Iron Age.

In 525 BCE, Egypt became a province of the Persian empire. Apart from a period of sixty years, Persian rule lasted until 332 BCE, when Egypt was conquered by Alexander the Great. It was to be ruled continuously by foreigners until modern times.

Religious change

Studies of religions other than Christianity or Islam have often assumed that they were static in an African context. It is recognised in theory that religion was as subject to change as other areas of life, but in practice such developments are not easy to trace. Ancient Egypt is unique in Africa in that its records document religious change over three millennia.

Its cults were always immensely varied and complex, but some generalisations can be made. Egyptian religion had a strong ecological dimension. The concept of Ptah creating the world from watery chaos was linked to the emergence of the earth after the Nile floods. The Pyramid Texts reflect the concept of the Pharaoh as the divine son of the sun, bursting into the heavens after his death. The priests of the sun cult included the foremost intellectuals of their time, including Imhotep. Herodotus noted that 'It is at Heliopolis that the most learned of the Egyptian antiquaries are to be found'.[29] A New Kingdom Pharaoh, Akhenaten, made a remarkable attempt to introduce monotheism, the cult of the Aten, the sun's visible disc, but this religious revolution did not survive his death. Much of what he created was destroyed but his Hymn to the Sun survives as a classic of religious poetry.

The building of pyramids in the Old Kingdom reflected a concentration on the Pharaoh's eternal welfare. After the collapse of the Old Kingdom, private individuals made provision for their own souls, furnishing their tombs with servant statues, Coffin Texts which copied the Pyramid Texts, and so on, in a process which could be called the democratisation of eternity.

Horus, symbolised by a falcon, was identified with Upper Egypt, the storm god, Seth with Lower Egypt. Sometimes Horus is depicted as slaying Seth in the form of a hippopotamus or crocodile, which *may* be iconographically related to St George and the Dragon, and the many African myths which describe a hero who slays a water monster.[30] Amun, the god of Thebes, rose to prominence in the Middle Kingdom and his cult was lavishly promoted by the Theban founders of the New Kingdom. Osiris, corn god, Lord of the Underworld, and slain, dismembered and resurrected king, with his shrine at Abydos, became ever more important as time went on. He offered his devotees personal immortality, as did the other mystery religions of the ancient world. His cult, and that of his consort Isis, were international. Egypt was part of a Mediterranean world. The most detailed visual representation of the Nile in antiquity – the Palestrina mosaic – is found in a town in Italy.

'No woman holds priestly office,' noted Herodotus, 'either in the service of goddess or god.'[31]

Nubia[32]

Nubia has been called a country 200 miles long and five yards wide. The Nile has carved its way deeply into the relatively soft sandstone, so that the flood-plain is narrow and sometimes non-existent, and a series of five cataracts makes river transport difficult. So narrow is the riverain plain that settlement takes the form of strip villages, where, as was said in 1700 CE, 'one house stands directly next to the other, surrounded by the most beautiful [date] palm groves'.[33]

Lower Nubia is now covered by the lake created by the Aswan dam. Because of its aridity it has always had a sparse population and at some periods in ancient history it appears to have been virtually depopulated. Upper Nubia began at the Second Cataract. To the south the rainfall increases, and the kingdom of Meroe developed in savanna grasslands. Like the Egyptians, the Nubians suffered from water-borne diseases – schistosomiasis and river blindness – as well as malaria, tuberculosis and trachoma.

The general pattern of Nubian history – the shift of the centre of political gravity ever further to the south – was undoubtedly shaped by ecology. 'What is now the Nubian desert was, some three thousand years ago, more like the grasslands of the central Sudan today ... Rainfall and vegetation zones have shifted steadily southwards since then.'[34]

In modern times, occasional rains have begun at the Nile bend; it was noted in 1699 that here 'one begins to see trees and dry grass, the rains extending to this region, whereas everything up to this point was watered only by the overflow of the Nile or by machine'.[35] South of this point the date palm disappears and there is enough vegetation to support camel nomads. Further south still, in the latitude of Sennar, there is enough rain to support cattle nomads and cultivation which depended not on irrigation but on rain.

In the early part of the third millennium BCE a people known to us as the A group lived in Lower Nubia. They cultivated cereals, made fine black and red pottery, jewellery and copper tools, and buried their dead with grave goods, which were often imported. They endured raids which were magnified in

Egyptian official panegyric: one Pharaoh is alleged to have taken 7,000 captives and 200,000 livestock. But they seem to have traded on equal terms with their northern neighbour. An Egyptian text describes the export of ointment, honey, clothing and oil to Nubia, and archaeologists have unearthed Egyptian pottery and other artefacts there.[36] In return, Nubia supplied ivory, gold, slaves and a variety of tropical products obtained from further afield.

In about 2000 BCE a new culture emerged called the C group. (One may well ask why there is no B group. The answer is that there was once a B group, which later researchers decided was not a real cultural entity!) The A and C groups are separated by an obscure period of poverty and declining population caused by a fall in the levels of the Nile, perhaps exacerbated by Egyptian raids. Pastoralism was at the heart of their economy and cultural values.

The era of trade gave way to one of military aggression. During the Middle Kingdom, Egypt dominated and exploited Lower Nubia, building gigantic forts near the Second Cataract, but did not rule it. When the Middle Kingdom collapsed, the first major Nubian state developed in Upper Nubia, at Kerma, but the warlike Pharaohs of the New Kingdom turned Nubia into an Egyptian colony, under a governor with the title of 'King's Son of Kush'. Egyptian rule lasted from 1500 to 1000 BCE, by which time Egypt was struggling with invaders for its own survival. Soon, an independent state developed in Nubia. Its first capital was probably at Napata[37] near the Fourth Cataract. Later, it shifted to Meroe on the other side of the great Nile bend, south of the junction with the Atbara.

The tide, in time, turned to such an extent that in 751 BCE the Nubian king, Piankhy, became the ruler of Egypt. His inscriptions cast him in a pleasant light: he spared his conquered enemies while avoiding contact with unclean fish eaters, and grieved for the sufferings of the horses in a besieged Egyptian city, establishing a cemetery for them among the royal tombs at Napata.

In a sense his very invasion of Egypt shows how deeply his people had absorbed its cultural values, because his aim was to protect the sacred city of Thebes and its cult of Amun from the attacks of a Delta prince. Nubian kings ruled Egypt until 664 BCE, when an Assyrian invasion drove them back to their homeland. Even then they saw themselves as a kind of Egyptian government in exile, and used Pharaonic titles such as 'Beloved of Amun' or 'Lord of the Two Lands', the two lands being, not Nubia and Egypt, but Upper and Lower Egypt. The chief state god was Amun of Thebes, and Nubian kings were buried in pyramids, albeit of a different design. For centuries, Nubians went on pilgrimage to the shrine of Isis at Philae. Despite all this, a strong indigenous cultural element survived. Apedemek, the many-armed lion god, has no Egyptian equivalent, but the Nubian experience is an arresting early example of the way in which the colonised absorb cultural values from the coloniser.

There is a fascinating enigma in Nubian history: Ancient Meroitic is not apparently closely related to any other living or dead languages, or to the language which succeeded it. The history of Nubian literacy is a good example of creative adaptation to external stimuli. The Nubians began to write in hieroglyphs and hieratic during the New Kingdom. By the second century BCE, a new alphabet of twenty-three characters, with the world's first written punctuation marks, was being used to write down an indigenous language.

Both language and script are known as Meroitic. The script disappeared suddenly in the fourth century CE and when writing reappeared in the form of Old Nubian, written in a modified Greek script from 795 on, the language bore no apparent relation to Meroitic. We know the phonetic values of Meroitic but not its meaning. It is one of a considerable body of as yet undeciphered ancient languages, which includes Etruscan.[38] Old Nubian is recognisably related to modern Nubian languages; the change is best explained by the depopulation of Lower Nubia during a period of desiccation and its reoccupation by immigrants from the Kordofan area, when the adoption of the water wheel made settlement possible again.[39]

In one of the most famous interviews of the ancient world, reported in the Acts of the Apostles, Philip met a dignitary from Meroe 'who was an important official in charge of the treasury of the Queen of Ethiopia'. There is no doubt that women played a major part in the government of Meroe, and we know the names of no less than five regnant queens.[40] Candace was the title of the Queen Mother but she clearly shared the government with her son. In 28 BCE, when the Romans invaded Meroe, the Candace (probably Amanirenas) was 'a masculine sort of woman and blind in one eye'.[41] It was her generals who fought the Romans and her ambassadors who later negotiated for peace.

The city of Meroe covered almost a square mile and was surrounded by great iron slag heaps which date from early in the Common Era. Treasures from far afield have been excavated there, reflecting the vitality of its trade. It was well known to various writers of antiquity, including Herodotus. Meroe's distinctive art gives us precious glimpses of Meroitic life and its superb decorated pottery, often bearing motifs from the natural world, is among its finest achievements. In the first three centuries CE Meroe declined, until in the fourth century both the monarchy and Meroitic script disappeared. In about 350 CE, Meroe was invaded by the king of Aksum, Ezana, who left a great monument in three languages describing his exploits.

Several factors caused the decline of Meroe, including the loss of eastern trade routes to Aksum and, especially, increasing desertification, which, like the adoption of the camel, increased the power of surrounding nomads.

The Libyans

Human settlement in North Africa forms a series of islands between the desert and the Mediterranean. In Cyrenaica, which the Arabs called the Green Mountain, the altitude attracts sufficient rainfall for pastoralism and mixed farming. Further west, in the Gulf of Syrtis (Sidra), the sea reaches desert latitudes, with a narrow inhabitable coastal strip in Tripolitania. Still further west is the Maghrib, which simply means 'the west' in Arabic – the fertile plains of Tunisia, and beyond them the great Aures and Atlas ranges with their high plateaux and the relatively well-watered coastal Atlantic plains. The vegetation is Mediterranean and crops such as vines, olives and wheat grow well here. The Greeks called the light-complexioned peoples of North Africa 'Libyans' (Libu was a state to the west of Egypt). The Romans called them 'Berbers' (*barbari*, meaning people who do not speak Latin). It has been suggested that when the horse was introduced from Asia, Libyan chieftains used it to establish their ascendancy in the western Sahara. We have a hint of this in Herodotus when he describes the Garamantes of the Fezzan, a powerful people practising oasis agriculture, using chariots to pursue the fleet-footed cave-dwelling 'Ethiopians'.[42] Later on the introduction of the camel greatly increased their mobility and economic strength.

The Libyans worked first copper and later bronze, part of a wider Saharan complex (pp. 69–70 above). It is likely that they later absorbed iron-working skills from the Carthaginians, and that pyrotechnology reached West Africa through Libyan intermediaries.

The Libyans of Libu and Mashwash attempted to settle in the western Nile Delta in about 1200 BCE. Egyptian references to their towns and the valuable booty captured from them, including gold and silver, bronze swords and chariots, suggest a considerable level of prosperity. We can only guess at the reasons for the attempted migration – perhaps demographic or environmental pressure – and at the circumstances (probably trade) which forged their alliance with the 'Foreign Peoples of the Sea' from the Aegean and Asia Minor. Later, Libyan dynasts ruled in the Delta for a time.

Herodotus visited Egypt in the 440s. His account of the Libyans[43] is based on hearsay, a fascinating mixture of fact and mythical stereotypes – 'dog-headed men, headless men with eyes in their breasts (I don't vouch for this, but merely repeat what the Libyans say)'. He describes transhumant Nasamonians who every summer left their homes on the coast to harvest dates at the oasis of Augila, and pays tribute to the piety of the women of Cyrene, who honoured Isis and kept Egyptian food taboos.

Phoenicians, Greeks and Romans

After *c.* 813 BCE, the putative date for the foundation of Carthage, successive arrivals from other Mediterranean countries, Phoenicians, Greeks and Romans, made the Maghrib and Egypt a hothouse of cultural interaction. It is tempting to see, in the history of these years, certain anticipations of later experience. There was a fierce revolt of rural poor and slaves against Carthage after the Second Punic War, and the Libyan kingdoms under their scholar rulers are a classic case of selective modernisation.

Ironically, we know far more about the newcomers than we do about the indigenous Libyans. Carthage (Kart Hadasht, New City) was the most important of a number of Phoenician settlements in the Maghrib. Located near modern Tunis, it evolved as a stopping place on the journey between the Phoenician trading cities of Tyre and Sidon and the kingdom of Tartessos in southern Spain, a source of silver and (re-exported) tin. Ancient Greek sources state that the city was founded by a tragic and possibly historic queen. Virgil's account of Dido's love affair with Aeneas is a work of the imagination but there may have been a real historical figure, the great-niece of the Old Testament Jezebel. Carthaginian history is full of interest – the epic struggles for control of the Mediterranean, first with the Greeks and later with the Romans, the extraordinary journeys of exploration (Hanno may well have reached Mount Cameroon). The Carthaginians grew olives on the fertile Tunisian plains; the only Carthaginian book which is known to have been translated into Latin is a now lost treatise on agriculture by Mago. They collected *Murex* shells, used to produce the purple of kings, on the Atlantic coast of Africa, and traded with African peoples for gold and carbuncles. The latter is a gemstone which has never been identified – yet another mystery of the African past.

But the Carthaginians were harsh and exploitative towards their Libyan neighbours, and their religious practices were notorious in the ancient world for their cruelty. They sacrificed their own first-born children to their implacable gods; modern excavations have uncovered the tiny skeletons.[44]

In 146 BCE the Romans razed Carthage to the ground, giving the manuscripts they found to a Libyan state. As Punic gave way to Latin, these priceless records were lost, and we know its history exclusively from the writings of its enemies.

The Greeks, like the Phoenicians, were driven to trade, exploration and colonisation by the barren nature of their homeland. From *c.* 639 BCE, they settled in Cyrenaica, where their kings were called, alternately, Battos and Arkesilaus, which is almost as confusing as Egypt's long succession of Ptolemies.

Cyrenaica exported silphion, a plant greatly valued for culinary and medicinal purposes. It became extinct in Roman times, either through over-exploitation or as a form of passive resistance. The extinction of any plant or animal species is a disaster – doubly so when, like silphion, its value is proven.

The Greek presence in Egypt was to be of much greater historical importance. Greeks first settled in Egypt as merchants, craftsmen or mercenaries under the Saite kings. They became more important in the 300 years during which Egypt was ruled by a Hellenistic dynasty. As we have seen, Egypt was conquered by Alexander the Great, who founded the city which still bears his name, Alexandria. After his premature death in 323 BCE, his empire was divided among his three generals. Egypt, the richest and politically most important of his conquests, fell to Ptolemy and his successors. There were to be fourteen Ptolemies, the last three of whom were Cleopatra's brothers and her son by Julius Caesar. Cleopatra committed suicide in 30 BCE after defeat at the hands of Octavian (the future Emperor Augustus). She was the only member of this Greek dynasty to speak Egyptian, and killed herself by embracing the cobra, whose image formed part of the Pharaoh's headdress.

In some ways Egypt prospered under the Ptolemies, partly because of the use of mechanical devices to expand the area under irrigation, the ox-drawn water-wheel and the Archimedean screw. The marshes of the Fayum were drained, providing a major addition to Egypt's precious cultivable land, and the introduction of the camel from Arabia facilitated long-distance trade. There was another demographic explosion, from an estimated 3 million in the late Pharaonic period to perhaps as much as 7.5 million.[45] The Ptolemies ruled an empire embracing Cyprus, Cyrenaica and, for a time, areas of Asia Minor.[46] Under the second Ptolemy, the canal between the Nile and the Gulf of Suez was reopened. Merchant fleets explored the Red Sea and later the coast of East Africa, establishing regular trade with India after Hippalos discovered the monsoon winds which bore his name in about 120 BCE. Aksum, with its port at Adulis, was involved in international trade and affected by Hellenistic culture. Despite its greater distance from the sea, this was also true of Meroe, where Greek pottery has been found. Zoscales, king of Aksum, was literate in Greek, like Ergamenes of Meroe.[47] The mummy portraits of the Fayum date from Ptolemaic times and later. Painted in encaustic (hot wax) on wood, they are the liveliest and most realistic portraits from the ancient world.

Thereafter, there were two Egypts – the cosmopolitan Greek-speaking world of the court and of government and of Alexandria, and the world of the peasant. This division was to be writ large on Egyptian Christianity. The scholars of Alexandria were part of an international world of learning. They included Euclid and the Jews who translated the Old Testament into Greek, the Septuagint. Eratosthenes, born in Cyrene in *c.* 285 BCE, made a reasonably accurate estimate of the circumference of the world.[48]

But in the later years of the Ptolemaic dynasty, civil wars and oppressive taxation led to repeated revolts. An apocalyptic text called the *Oracle of the Potter* proclaimed: 'That will be the end of our evils when Egypt shall see the foreigners fall like leaves from the branch. The city by the sea [Alexandria] will be a drying place for the fisherman's catch.'[49]

The Libyan kingdoms

The bases of Libyan civilisation existed long before these events: pastoralism, grain cultivation, bronze technology and international trade. The Libyans responded to new stimuli in creative ways but the tide of cultural influence ran in two directions. The Libyan shrine to Amun at the oasis of Siwa drew many Greek pilgrims, including Alexander himself, and Pindar wrote an ode in honour of a Cyrenian Greek who won a Libyan bride in an athletic contest. Herodotus described statues of Athene in Libyan dress. The Phoenician Baal was equated with Amun (Hammon) and the Libyan goddess Tanit was one of Carthage's main divinities.

The first Libyan kingdoms developed in ancient Mauretania[50] in the fifth century BCE and the last ruler of that nation fell victim to Caligula in 40 CE. We know little about the Numidian kingdoms until the third century BCE. The history of these kings is a tragic one – their drive to autonomy and innovation was frustrated by the rising tide of Roman imperialism and by their ill-fated involvement in Rome's internal power struggles. Syphax, the most powerful Numidian ruler of his day, became a Roman captive at the end of the Second Punic War in 202, having backed the losing side, apparently swayed by his noble Carthaginian bride Sophonisba. When Syphax was imprisoned she offered her hand to Masinissa, another Numidian prince, but he supported Rome, and Sophonisba committed suicide rather than fall into Roman hands. Masinissa was to live happily, if not ever after, at least to the age of ninety, the most powerful and most successful of all the Libyan kings.

He did everything in his power to increase the agricultural productivity of Numidia. It became a corn-exporting centre, and arboriculture was highly developed. He built a palace at his capital of Cirta and issued his own silver coinage inscribed in Punic. His land holdings were so enormous that he left each of his 44 sons an estate of 2,000 acres. It was his persistent invasion of Carthaginian territory which led directly to the Third Punic War and the sack of Carthage.

Masinissa was succeeded by his son, Micipsa, a patron of Greek learning. It was in his reign that the Libyans developed their own script, which was alphabetic with twenty-three characters. His grandson, Jugurtha, fought a long war with Rome which ended with his betrayal and death in a Roman prison. A later Numidian king, Hiempsal (d. 60 BCE), wrote a history of Africa in Punic. His successor backed the losing side in Caesar's struggle with Pompey, committing suicide when Caesar was victorious. Numidia then became a Roman province.

In 33 BCE, the king of Mauretania died without heirs. His kingdom fell to Rome, which in 25 BCE established a client kingdom there under a Numidian prince Juba, who had been educated in Rome. He married the daughter of Mark Antony and Cleopatra. He was a great patron of the arts and learning and wrote a lost work in Greek on the geography of Africa and Asia. To obtain information, he sent out expeditions which went far down his kingdom's Atlantic coast and explored the Canaries. Juba was succeeded in 24 CE by his son Ptolemy, named after his illustrious ancestors. In 40 CE, Ptolemy fell foul of his second cousin Caligula and was put to death, not for rebellion but for his sumptuous dress. Mauretania was annexed by Rome, thus completing a process of Roman colonisation whch had begun with the sack of Carthage. Rome never succeeded in conquering Meroe – the two powers signed a treaty in 21 BCE and Meroe remained independent.

Requiem for Medusa

One of the most haunting images in the mythology of the ancient world is that of Medusa, the female monster who turns men to stone and who is slain in the end by her own mirror image. Medusa is simply the feminine present participle of a Greek word meaning 'to rule over'. The traditional history of Carthage begins with a queen, and Pharaonic Egypt ends with one. Such women were exceptional. The Greek historian Diodorus Siculus, who began his work in about 59 BCE, tells of a nation in western Libya which was ruled by women.[51] A few have taken this as evidence of a forgotten matriarchy but it is nothing of the kind. It belongs to a whole world of mirror images which people invent to define or justify the status quo. (Thus, the witch prefers the night and walks on her hands, because it is 'normal' to prefer daylight and walk in the usual way.) Sophonisba, whose intense patriotism was characteristic of her people, could intervene in politics only through flirtation and death. Pheritima, widow and mother of Cyrene kings, sought reinforcements in Cyprus when her son was overthrown. Its ruler gave her a golden distaff and spindle, 'which, unlike an army, he thought suitable for her sex'.[52]

The contribution of women to society lay primarily, not in government, but in production and trade. But although these societies were, in the main, ruled by men, their religious life was often dominated by goddesses, a common paradox in the ancient world, and, indeed, elsewhere.

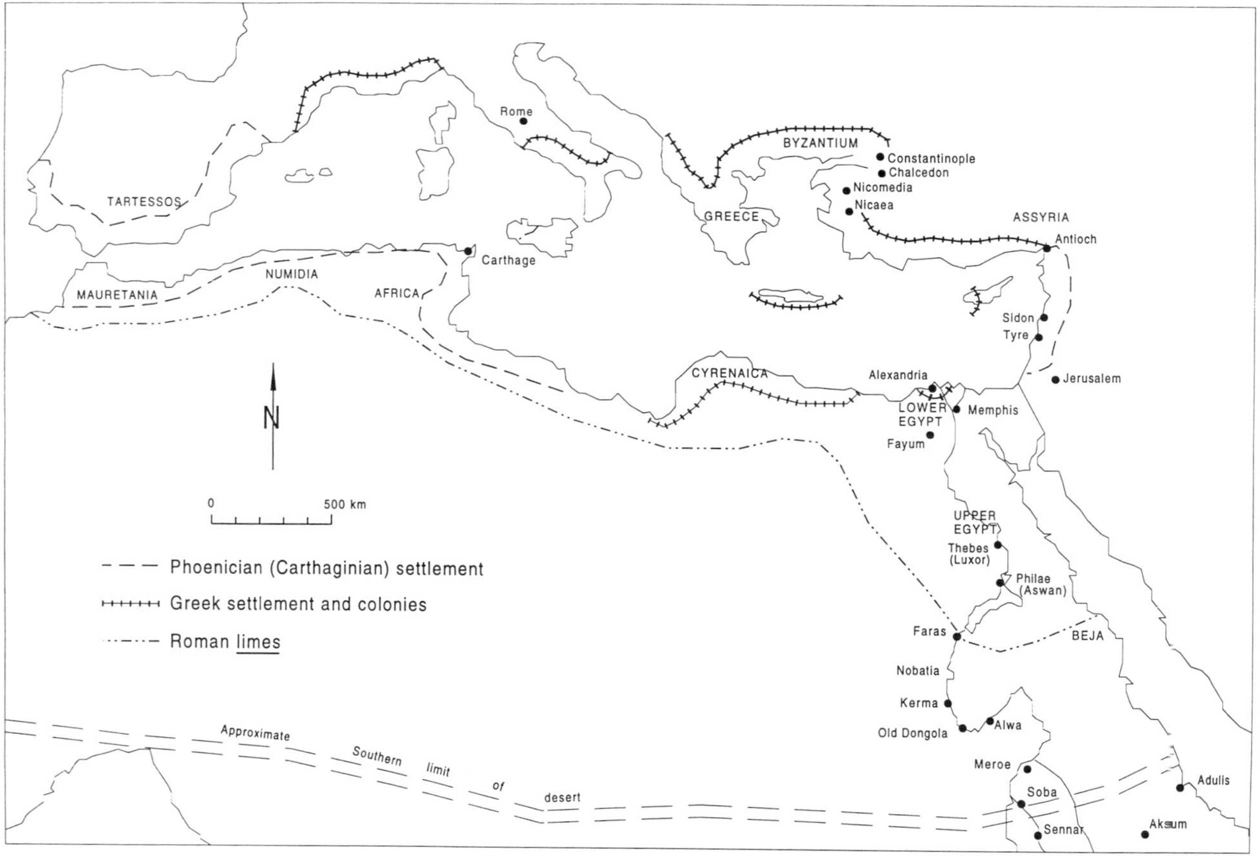

Map 8   Northern Africa in antiquity

Key (legend):

- - - Phoenician (Carthaginian) settlement
++++ Greek settlement and colonies
-··-·· Roman limes

Scale: 0 ____ 500 km

N

Labels on map:

TARTESSOS
MAURETANIA
NUMIDIA
AFRICA
Rome
Carthage
GREECE
BYZANTIUM
Constantinople
Chalcedon
Nicomedia
Nicaea
ASSYRIA
Antioch
Sidon
Tyre
Jerusalem
Memphis
Alexandria
LOWER EGYPT
Fayum
CYRENAICA
UPPER EGYPT
Thebes (Luxor)
Philae (Aswan)
Faras
Nobatia
Kerma
Old Dongola
Meroe
Alwa
BEJA
Soba
Sennar
Adulis
Aksum

Approximate   Southern   limit   of   desert

PART TWO: A ROMAN/BYZANTINE INTERLUDE

Roman Egypt

The history of North Africa and Egypt in late antiquity falls into two sharply contrasted phases: the first is Roman/Byzantine and, in some areas for some of the time, Christian; the second begins with the Arab conquest of Egypt in 639. We should not exaggerate the contrast – Coptic Christianity survived, though as a minority faith; the spread of Arabic was far from uniform, and areas of Berber speech have survived into modern times. And, as many commentators have pointed out, Christian Donatists and Muslim Kharijites had much in common, as did the Christian 'Desert Fathers' and Egypt's Sufis.

It is possible to exaggerate the religious dimension of northern Africa's history.[53] By taking 'Christian' and 'Muslim' as central variables, we run the risk of paying too little attention to other dimensions of the past. The impact of Rome (and later of Byzantium) and of Christianity was markedly different in Egypt and in the Maghrib.[54] The form of government was different: Egypt was directly under the emperor, under a prefect, while the rulers of Africa and Cyrenaica answered to the Senate. It was a distinction which would have meant little to most of their subjects. The most fundamental difference was that Egypt remained part of the Greek-speaking world, whereas in the Maghrib – or at least that portion of it which lay within Rome's fortifications, the *limes* – the urbanised and educated, at least, spoke Latin. The line of demarcation between Greek and Latin speakers was to have profound consequences for the history of Christendom.

But there were also similarities; both Egypt and the Maghrib were important sources of food for the metropolis – first Rome and later, in the case of Egypt, Constantinople. Josephus, writing in *c.* 75 CE, claimed that Egypt provided a third of the corn consumed by the Roman populace, the Maghrib two-thirds;[55] Tacitus pointed out the vulnerability of regimes which rely on imported food, 'For Egypt holds the key, as it were, both of sea and land; and [Augustus] was afraid that anyone occupying that country ... might threaten Italy with starvation'.[56] The history of both Egypt and the Maghrib in Roman and Byzantine times is a palimpsest of the development and exploitation so typical of later colonial governments.

In many ways Roman Egypt was a continuation of the regime which preceded it. The administration of Egypt remained in the hands of Greeks and Hellenised Egyptians, Greek remained the language of administration, and Alexandria a great centre of learning. Egypt was still divided between the Hellenised population of the cities and the native Egyptian countryside. Indian Ocean trade expanded and further improvements were made to the irrigation system. In both Egypt and the Maghrib, there seems to have been a phase of prosperity followed by increasing rural impoverishment of the countryside. Taxation was heavier under Rome than under the Ptolemies, and it became an intolerable burden when the Nile floods failed. Changes introduced by the emperor Septimius Severus in 191–201 CE established a senate in each district or nome. It was collectively responsible for making up any shortfall in taxation, effectively ruining the more prosperous citizens as well as the peasantry. In the late third century, petitioners asked the oracles, 'Am I to become a beggar?', 'Shall I take to flight?', 'Is my flight to end?'[57] It is disquieting to note a suggestion that Egypt was more prosperous under Greek/Roman/Byzantine rule than it was to be again until the nineteenth century.[58]

There were major risings in 152–4 and 172; the latter was the Revolt of the Herdsmen, in the Delta. There were also sinister explosions of ethnic violence in Alexandria, where the Jewish community was repeatedly attacked in the first century CE. In 115 there was a great Jewish revolt against Roman rule which began in Cyrenaica and spread to Egypt, Cyprus and Mesopotamia. The reprisals decimated Alexandria's Jews.

We have seen how the earlier forms of literacy – the hieroglyphs, used on inscriptions, and hieratic, used on official documents – were supplemented by a popular cursive script, demotic. Demotic began to decline in the second century and disappeared in about 450. The latest known hieroglyphs date from 394.[59]

Coptic is demotic Egyptian in Greek characters with extra letters added. The word comes from the Greek word for Egypt, Aigyptos, which in its turn comes from an ancient name for Memphis, the house of Ptah. The script came into widespread use from the late third century on, when the Christian church used it to reach out to the wider population. It symbolised and reinforced the gap between native Egyptian and Hellene which was typical both of the church and of the wider society. But the fact that it was necessary to write in Greek characters rather than demotic shows how pervasive the Hellenistic influence had become.

Thanks to the wealth of surviving documents and inscriptions, the Egyptian common people speak for themselves in a way which is rare elsewhere on the African continent:

This is the grave of Arsinoe, wayfarer. Stand by and weep for her, unfortunate in all things, whose lot was hard and terrible. For I was bereaved of my mother when I was a little girl, and when the favour of my youth made me ready for a bridegroom my father married me to Phabeis and fate brought me to the end of my life in bearing my firstborn child.[60]

The changing fortunes of Rome

It is impossible to understand the changing fortunes of Rome in Africa without some knowledge of the history of the empire generally. Octavian became the first Roman emperor, with the title Augustus. By the time he died, in 14 CE, the empire had reached its greatest extent, except for Roman Britain, which was conquered later. In the centuries which followed, the empire would be increasingly under pressure from populous Germanic peoples from the north. They were all, from the Roman standpoint, *barbari*. Some served as allies of Rome; others were its enemies.

The third century was a time of crisis for the Roman empire, when its very survival was endangered by external threats and rival armies placed ephemeral emperors in power – over twenty of them in less than fifty years. Diocletian (284–305) restored strong government and built a new capital at Nicomedia in modern Turkey, a precedent followed by Constantine, who built the capital bearing his name on the Bosphorus. It was completed in 330, the dividing line between Roman and Byzantine history.[61]

For a time there was an eastern and a western empire. In 410, Alaric's Visigoths conquered Rome itself. The portent shook the Roman world and led Augustine to write his famous *City of God*. Soon after this, the Visigoths and their allies invaded Spain and France. One of these peoples, the Vandals, burst into African history when, between 429 and 573, they established a short-lived kingdom in Tunisia. Until 480, there were shadowy emperors of the west, based first in Ravenna and later in Dalmatia. After that the heir to the traditions of Rome was Byzantium, with its capital at Constantinople.

Justinian (*c.* 527–65) was the most outstanding of the emperors of late antiquity. His great ambition was to reconquer Rome, and the Western empire. In 533 his forces succeeded in driving out the Vandals, who were swallowed up by the surrounding population as if they had never been, leaving not a single word in Berber speech. The Byzantines, unable to conquer Italy, were equally unable to maintain effective rule in North Africa, and when the Arabs invaded the Maghrib the opposition they met was not from Byzantines but from the local Berbers. The spread of Islam would gradually strip Constantinople of its provinces, but the city was not conquered by Muslim forces until 1453. Arabic speakers called it Rum (Rome) and when Turks established a state in Anatolia they called it the sultanate of Rum (see Map 10).

Christianity[62]

The Maghrib and Cyrenaica have long been Muslim, and Christianity in Egypt survives only as the faith of a small (and Arabic-speaking) minority. But in the first five centuries of the Common Era, northern Africans were at the heart of Christendom's great debates. Some of Christianity's most influential and brilliant intellects came from Egypt or North Africa: Origen, Tertullian, Cyprian, Augustine. Alexandria was one of the three great sees of early Christianity together with Rome and Antioch.[63] In the third century, the eastern Maghrib was one of three regions in the world where Christians were in a majority (the others were Armenia and modern Turkey). The mass adoption of Christianity in both Egypt and the Maghrib began in the middle of the third century and was virtually complete by 400. There were many other faiths in northern Africa, including Manichaeanism – a dualist faith from Persia, which for a time won over Augustine. The third-century Neoplatonist philosopher Plotinus was the guiding light of the learned pagans of late antiquity. He came from Upper Egypt and studied first in Alexandria and then in Antioch and Rome, where 'he would never talk about his race, or his parents, or his native place'.[64]

Until the reign of Constantine, who prudently postponed baptism until his death bed, there were periodic persecutions of Christians, though for long periods they were left undisturbed. They were often blamed for disasters: Tertullian complained that if the Tiber flooded or the Nile failed to flood, there was a cry of 'Christian to the lion'.[65]

Coptic spirituality was forged in the sufferings of the martyrs. The Coptic year dates from the accession of Diocletian in 284, because it was late in his reign that the last and most dreadful persecution took place. There were more ways than one of suffering for one's religion. Many Egyptians went into the desert, where they practised a ferocious asceticism, first as hermits and later in religious communities. Scholars speak of the Desert Fathers, but many of the solitaries were women. The pioneer hermit was St Anthony, who underwent a radical conversion at the age of twenty, in 270. Pakhom (d. 346) was a soldier who became a Christian and founded a complex of monasteries for men and for women in the Thebaid.

In the fourth and fifth centuries, the Eastern churches were convulsed by theological controversies on the nature of Christ and on the Trinity. The leading protagonists in the first phase of Christological controversy, Arius (d. 336) and Athanasius (d. 373), both came from Egypt.

Constantine deplored these divisions, seeing a united Christianity as a concomitant of a united empire. In 324, he summoned the Council of Nicaea, which condemned Arius. By the end of the century, Arianism was in decline, except among the Goths, who had been converted by an Arian. (The Vandals were Arians, which greatly embittered the relations with their fellow Christians in Tunisia.) But it was not the end of Christological controversy. A new debate, with momentous consequences for the unity of Christendom, focussed on the relationship between the divine and human natures of Christ.

The Council of Chalcedon, held in 451, was also summoned by imperial authority. It decreed, enigmatically enough, that Christ has two Natures, distinct and indivisible. This was profoundly unacceptable to many Eastern Christians, the Copts among them, who felt that this was to divide Christ and undermine His divinity. After a considerable lapse of time, five Monophysite churches were founded, three of them in Africa – the Coptic, Ethiopian and Nubian churches.[66] Their members have always called themselves Orthodox, never 'Monophysite'. The Copts were passionately opposed to Chalcedonians and called their Byzantine representatives Melkites, king's men. A Chalcedonian patriarch was lynched six years after the council. There was undoubtedly an element of national patriotism in all this, which also took other forms, such as the claim that Jesus was born in the Egyptian city of Herakleopolis.[67] A tenth-century Coptic bishop wrote of this period: 'He forced them to accept the faith of Chalcedon except this monastery alone; for the inmates of it were extremely powerful, being Egyptian by race and all of them natives, without a stranger among them.'[68] When the Arabs invaded Egypt, their task was made easier by the divisions of Egyptian Christians.

The Maghrib

Rome's territories in the Maghrib consisted of the coastal plain, bounded by the fortifications called the *limes*, but excluding the southern steppes and the mountain ranges. The province of Africa, in modern Tunisia, derived its name from the local Libyans, Afri. It became the name of the continent.

Roman Africa produced oil and grain on land which is now almost desert.

'Here lies Dion, a pious man' reads a Numidian epitaph. 'He lived 80 years and planted 4000 trees.'[69] It is an enviable memorial. It is possible that there were long-term climate changes and that the rainfall gradually declined (there is considerable evidence of this on the southern edge of the Sahara). But much of the productivity of Roman agriculture was due to their efficiency in storing and transporting water.[70] Here, as elsewhere in what was once the Roman world, the remains of great aqueducts can still be seen. This, combined with the choice of crops adapted to dry conditions, is at least part of the story. But when the reservoirs and aqueduct systems crumbled into decay, the deforestation which the extension of cultivation had involved was to lead to disastrous erosion, and the continued cultivation of wheat may sometimes have led to the progressive degeneration of the soil. But one should not exaggerate these contrasts; the Aghlabids built aqueducts to carry water to Mahdiyya in the ninth century; the great productivity of the Tunisian plain in the sixteenth was due largely to irrigation; the Moroccan sugar refineries at this time depended on a network of eleven canals and the regency of Algiers, from the sixteenth century, had a water supply drawn from cisterns and aqueducts which many European cities of the day might well have envied.

Resistance to Roman rule sometimes took cultural forms which may have included the conscious adoption of the Punic language after Rome's sack of Carthage. Military resistance often grew out of ecological factors, the response of pastoralists to the steady encroachment of cultivation.

When the Romans built a military road across the route taken by the transhumant Musulami it triggered off a revolt, led by Tacfarinas,[71] who had gained military experience as a Roman auxiliary. He waged guerrilla warfare from 17 to 24 CE, gaining support from both Numidia and Mauretania, until he was finally defeated in a surprise dawn attack. There was another broadly based revolt much later, in 253-62, by a coalition of peoples who called themselves Quinquegentiani, the Five Peoples. Several Roman expeditions struck deep into the desert, and Julius Maternus reached a land of rhinoceroses, which may have been Lake Chad.

In the towns and cities, Latin became the language in daily use. Augustine grew up two hundred miles from the sea but spoke no language but Latin. He tried unsuccessfully to learn Greek. North Africa produced many distinguished lawyers and men of letters, among them the playwright Terence, who, in the second century BCE, came to Rome as a Berber slave and wrote words much loved by historians of cultures other than their own, 'I am a human being, and nothing human is alien to me.'

Many North Africans rose to positions of authority in Rome's service. Septimius Severus, who became emperor of Rome in 193, was a North African of Phoenician ancestry, who spoke Latin with an accent. He married a Syrian princess whose family were royal priests of Baal, and died on campaign in York in 211. Few Romans, if any, made their permanent home in Egypt, but there were many Roman colonists in the Maghrib, some of them demobilised soldiers. New and old cities were built in the Roman style with baths, an amphitheatre, a forum, a gymnasium and so on. Individuals and whole townships were accorded

Roman citizenship; an edict of 212 extended it to the inhabitants of the empire in general. Intellectuals and wealthy land owners thrived in Roman Africa. Its prosperity rested entirely on the labours of the rural poor, some of them peasants with a right to use but not own land, some of them landless labourers, and some of them slaves. They were to find a voice in the Donatist movement.

The growth of Christianity

The first known incident in the history of Christianity in the Maghrib was the martyrdom of five women and seven men from Scilli, in 180. Victor (189–199), the first pope to speak Latin, was a North African, and Perpetua, martyred at Carthage in 202, is one of the four women writers in the first five centuries of the Christian church whose work survives.

The church in the Maghrib cared little for the Christological disputes over which Eastern Christians agonised. They were, indeed, so staunchly Chalcedonian that the Council of Carthage in 550 denounced the pope as a heretic for seeking a *rapprochement* with the Monophysites. But the church in the Maghrib did not escape division. It was torn apart, not by theology but by the experience of persecution itself.

The Donatist church developed out of issues which became acute during Diocletian's persecution, when Christians were asked to hand over their Bibles for destruction. The Donatists, who took their name from their charismatic leader, claimed that those who had given way during persecution should be permanently excluded from the church. The orthodox view was that they should be admitted after repentance. The Donatists formed a strongly based North African church with their own bishops and even, for a time, a pope in Rome. They claimed to be the true vine, pruned of rotting branches, and saw the church as an elect community of true believers. To Augustine, it was bizarre to suggest that God's church was primarily located in Numidia and he compared the Donatists with frogs in a pond who thought they were the universal church. Despite official persecution, the Donatists survived for centuries, and there was a revival in the late sixth century.

The church historian Frend interpreted Donatism as a vehicle for Berber patriotism and a response to socio-economic distress, the protest of urban and rural poor alike against a church increasingly identified with the landowning classes and imperial authority.[72] The Donatists claimed Simon of Cyrene as an Afer like themselves. The Circumcellions, an extremist wing, seem to have first appeared in about 340. It was clearly a peasants' revolt, and they lived in communities near the tombs of rural martyrs, attacking their propertied opponents with the war cry, *Deo laudes*.

... no man could rest secure in his possessions ... At that time no creditor was free to press his claim, and all were terrified by the letters of these fellows who boasted that they were 'Captains of the Saints' ... Even journeys could not be made with perfect safety, for masters were often thrown out of their chariots and forced to run, in servile fashion, in front of their own slaves.[73]

They aided 'any debtor whatever that sought their assistance or protection'[74] and some committed suicide, in pursuit of a kind of martyrdom.

Frend's critics have pointed out that Augustine differed little from the Donatist bishops in his education and economic circumstances, that Donatist apologists apparently wrote only in Latin, and that Donatism was as much an urban as a rural phenomenon. But if one were to write the history of peasant revolts in Africa, one would linger on the experience of the Donatists.

It is one of the mysteries of church history that at some times and places, but not at others, Christians have felt a strong call to convert others. The churches of Egypt and the Maghrib, for all their brilliance and fervour, did not embark on missions to their African neighbours, and the Aksumites were converted by Syrians. In the fifth century, the Roman provinces in the Maghrib were invaded not only by the Vandals but also by worshippers of Baal and Tanit from the desert edge, the Lawata, 'ignorant of the Christian god'. In the Islamic era, the desert was to become a powerhouse of saints and scholars.

Christianity in Nubia[75]

Christianity came late to Nubia, in 543, introduced not, as we would expect, by the Christians of Egypt but by Monophysite missionaries from Byzantium, sent by Theodora, Justinian's redoubtable wife. It was the beginning of over six hundred years of a brilliant Christian civilisation.

The rapid and thorough conversion of the Nubians is reflected in their cemeteries, where the practice of burying the dead with grave goods died out at once. Every pre-Christian Nubian king is known by his grave, but not a single Christian one. The Nubians built splendid churches and basilicas; their fine murals show dark-skinned Nubian royalty and bishops, together with biblical figures and saints. From the eighth century on, manuscripts in Old Nubian were written in Greek script. Pre-Christian religious buildings were often situated far from centres of population, but in the Christian era there were up to six churches in each village. Written records from Christian Nubia include inscriptions and fragments of religious texts, usually Gospels, lives of the saints or liturgical documents. Ibn Selim, an Egyptian visitor to Nubia in about 970, described 'Lovely islands and at a distance of less than two days' journey about thirty villages with beautiful buildings, churches, monasteries and many palm trees, vines, gardens, fields and large pastures'.[76]

There were three kingdoms in Christian Nubia. The northernmost was Nobatia with its capital at Faras. Makuria lay further south, in the great loop of the Nile, between the Third and Fourth Cataracts; its capital was at Old Dongola and in time it absorbed Nobatia. Alodia, or Alwa, with its capital at Soba, was near modern Khartoum. A long-continued process of Arab immigration, analysed in a later chapter, was ultimately to submerge the Christian kingdoms, replacing them with a civilisation which was Muslim and predominantly, though not exclusively, Arabic speaking.

II

Northern Africa from the seventh century CE

> ... the number of its pulpits was the flower of the land ... their
> lightest thoughts weigh as mountains, and their excellence, like the
> sun, is not hidden anywhere.
> The eleventh-century poet, ibn Rashiq, on the *ulama* of Kairouan[1]

Muhammad never visited Africa, but his followers were destined to have an immense impact on the history, not only of northern Africa, but of the Western Sudan and the Swahili coast. Arabic gradually became universal in Egypt and dominant in the Maghrib, where today Berber is spoken by only 1 per cent of the population, mainly in the mountains and on the desert edge. Morocco became a land of saints – 'the earth of Morocco let saints grow as grass'[2] – and was also famed for its magicians.[3] An eleventh-century history of Tahert cited Hadith that the Berbers had played a special role in the defence of Islam, though others were less than complimentary.[4]

Many Berber clans came to claim an ancestor from the holy land of Arabia. It was often suggested that they were the descendants of Jalut (Goliath), in one of the many attempts to synchronise the cognitive maps of the Islamic world with the human geography of Africa.[5] The Sanhaja claimed descent from the pre-Muslim kings of Himyar in the Yemen, and so did the Mais of Kanem, far to the south.[6]

The Islamic era dates from 622 when the Prophet fled to Medina from a Mecca which refused to accept his message. By the time he died ten years later, he was both the temporal and spiritual head of a large Arabian state. He was succeeded by four caliphs, remembered collectively by Sunni Muslims as Rightly Guided, each of whom had been closely associated with him during his lifetime; the fourth, his cousin Ali, who married his daughter Fatima, was assassinated in 661. It was in the reign of Umar (*c.* 634–44) that Arab Muslim armies began to create an empire. They were not, at this time, called Muslims – they called themselves Believers, Mu'min, or Emigrants, Muhajirun. The Believers took Syria from the Byzantines and overthrew the Persian empire. Between 639 and 642 they conquered Egypt. It is a reminder of the homogeneity of the Near Eastern world (easily forgotten in the context of African history) that when the forces of 'Amr ibn al-As first reached Egypt, they were unsure whether they were still in Syria.[7] The Arabs conquered Egypt with the help of Coptic allies, one of whom, the Duke Sanutius, handed over the Egyptian fleet to 'Amr, in return for the recognition of the Coptic church. A garrison city was built at Fustat; it was later to be renamed Cairo, the Victorious. It was not immediately clear that Islam was a new faith community, and the Ishmaelites, as they were called, seemed much like a reforming Christian sect. The Byzantines left Egypt for ever, and the Copts were rid of the hated Melkites. Coptic Christians (until the nineteenth century the only Egyptian Christians) were *dhimmi*, protected, but their men had to pay poll tax, in addition to the dues they paid in common with the rest of the population. Tax collection and irrigation were entrusted to Coptic officials. The Arabs did not seek the conversion of the Copts – for a time indeed, it was prohibited, perhaps because of the fiscal importance of the taxes they paid.

At first, all Muslims were Arabs. Those who joined the community of faith did so by becoming clients of an Arab patron, thus making their *islam*, submission. The word 'Muslim' at first referred to non-Arab believers; by the middle of the ninth century it was used in its modern sense. The manpower for the invasion of the Maghrib and Spain came from Berber clients, *mawali* (sing. *mawla*), a system which lasted until the late eighth century.

Why did Christianity survive in Egypt and die out in the Maghrib? Much has been written on this subject, but in the absence of contemporary evidence – the first Muslim historian of northern Africa wrote in the ninth century[8] – much is speculation. It has been suggested that the Coptic church survived as an expression of national patriotism, though this has been questioned.[9] The church's survival has been explained by economic factors: its rich endowments, the privileged role of Copts in the civil service. Its decline has also been explained by economic factors: conversion to escape poll tax, though this was only one of several fiscal exactions. Some scholars emphasise marriages between Arabs and Coptic women, whose children became Muslims, but the influence of Christian wives is one of the standard explanations for the spread of Christianity in the first place.

'Copt', which originally meant Egyptian, now meant Christian. Christians formed a majority in Egypt until the tenth century; they became a minority, partly as a result of the demographic impact of further Arab immigration, and partly as a result of periodic persecutions. Religious adherence and language were distinct; by the end of the tenth century, most Egyptian Christians still spoke Coptic; by the end of the twelfth, most spoke Arabic. Coptic survived for liturgical purposes, like Latin in the west. Today there are some 4 million Copts in a population of 48 million.

The Maghrib

The Libyans of ancient history become the Berbers of more recent times. It is assumed that the modern Berber languages are the lineal descendants of ancient Libyan; it is not known, however, whether Libyan, like modern Berber, was divided into deeply differentiated branches.[10] Conventional history, in part reflecting the emphases of the Arabic sources, focusses on 'states'. It is important to realise that these tended to be urban islands in a vast rural sea, a fact which historical maps often fail to reflect.[11] A state such as Tahert consisted essentially of a single city, with a certain degree of dominance over the peoples surrounding it. In vast areas, especially in the mountains, there was no city state at all.

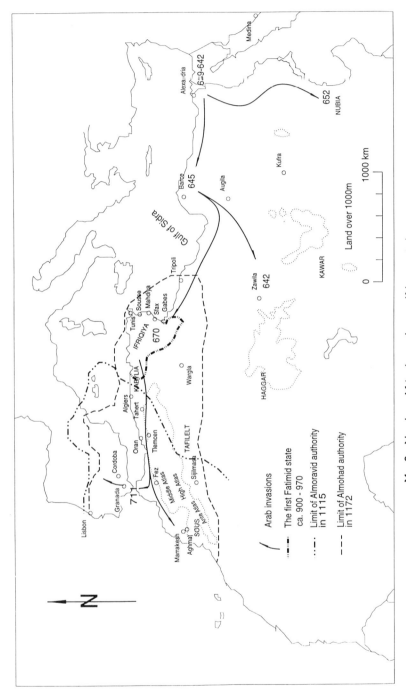

Map 9   Northern Africa (seventh to twelfth centuries)

Medina

Alexa-dria
6=9-642

652
NUBIA

Kufra

Barce
645

Augjia

Gulf of Sidra

Tripoli

KAWAR

Zawila
642

Land over 1000m

HAGGAR

0   1000 km

Soussé
Tunis   Mahdīya
IFRĪQIYA   Sfax
670   Gabes
Wargla

KALBIA

Algiers
Tahert
Oran
Temcen
TAFILELT

Fez
Middle Atlas
High Atlas
Sijilmasa

Cordoba

Granada
Lisbon
711

Marrakesh
Aghmat
SOUS   Anti Atlas

— ·· — Arab invasions

— ·— · The first Fatimid state
            ca. 900 - 970

— ·· —· Limit of Almoravid authority
             in 1115

— — — Limit of Almohad authority
            in 1172

N

Much analysis has contrasted the 'stateless' Berbers with the growth of centralised states. The Berbers and their Arabised descendants were organised into large bodies, united by the fiction of descent from a common ancestor (as were many peoples in sub-Saharan Africa). They called themselves 'Children of': Ait in Berber, Awlad or Banu in Arabic. The great fourteenth-century Maghribi historian, ibn Khaldoun, listed three Berber peoples, the Zanata, Sanhaja and Masmuda, but each of them consisted of many smaller autonomous 'tribes' or clans. Modern historians tend to use these categories, but they have no meaning to present-day Berbers.[12] The Zirids who ruled Ifriqiya for a time were Sanhaja, and so were the Lamtuna of the western Sahara who founded the Almoravid empire. Supposedly 'stateless' Berber clans had a sense of common identity and of territoriality, and a capacity for common action, especially in time of war. As elsewhere in Africa, concepts of ethnicity were partly determined by ecological factors. The Masmuda were agriculturalists of the High Atlas; the Massufa were camel-owning desert nomads. Here, as elsewhere, the line of demarcation between state and stateless is increasingly questioned.

By 645, Arab Muslim forces had conquered Cyrenaica and built a new inland capital at Barce (Map 9). They signed a pact, *baqt*, with Christian Nubia – deterred from wars of conquest both by the fabled skill of its archers and its aridity. For centuries, Nubia was to send 400 slaves a year to Egypt in return for wine, pottery and luxury goods. The *baqt* protected the civilisation of the Christian kingdoms of Nubia but at a price: they were compelled to raid for slaves.[13]

The Maghrib was very different, and the Arabs called it al-Khadra, the Verdant; it was also a valuable source of slaves and *mawali*. When the Arabs asked local people the source of their wealth they were shown an olive pit.[14] The cost of the great mosque at New Fez, in the late thirteenth century, was defrayed from the revenue of the olive oil press at Meknes.[15]

In 670, a garrison was founded at Kairouan, south of Carthage. The name, cognate with 'caravan', means resting place. It was destined to become an important centre of Islamic learning, and a later traveller who asked what its people were discussing was told, 'the names and attributes of God'. Its great mosque, constructed with columns from Roman and Byzantine buildings, was a symbol of the continuities in the Maghribi past.

The Arabs met with fierce opposition, less from Byzantines than from Berbers. A ruler called Kusila defeated and killed the great Arab general Uqba n. Nafi in 683 and seized Kairouan, but met his own death three years later. Ten years later a Berber queen called Kahina, 'the Prophetess', is said to have continued the tradition of resistance, but encouraged her sons to become Muslims. She may have been Jewish or Christian. But the sources date from much later and Kahina may be a misrepresentation of the male name Kahya.[16] If this is the case, the warrior queen never existed, though the story sheds considerable light on these early encounters.

By 705, what are now the plains of Tunisia had become the province of Ifriqiya, and Carthage had risen again, as Tunis. A Berber *mawla*, Tariq b. Ziyad, overthrew the Christian Visigothic kingdom in Spain, creating the province of Andalus. His name is immortalised in Gibraltar, the Rock of Tariq. Kairouan became the centre of a vast province, embracing the eastern Maghrib and Andalus.

The Atlas mountains, rising to a height of 12,000 feet, lay beyond the effective control of any state. They provided summer grazing for desert nomads; agricultural communities lived in the valleys. Penetration from a wider world began in the ninth century, as merchants from Fez explored the route to the copper and silver resources of the Dra river valley and the irrigable land of the Sous. The Islamic frontier extended here informally, as gradually a variety of holy men settled in the mountains, exercising a great influence on the peoples around them.[17]

Shiites and Kharijites

The early Islamic world formed a single caliphate (the word 'caliph' means Deputy, that is, of the Prophet). The fourth caliph, Muhammad's son-in-law, Ali, was overthrown by the first ruler of the Umayyad dynasty, descended from one of the leading families of pre-Islamic Mecca. This family ruled for a hundred years from a capital that was not in Arabia but at Damascus, in Syria. But they did not go unchallenged, particularly by Shiites and Kharijites.

Many believed that the Caliphate belonged rightfully to the descendants of Muhammad, through his daughter Fatima, the wife of Ali, and his grandsons, Hasan and Huseyn. They were called the Shia, the Party (of Ali).[18] The Kharijites were originally followers of Ali who turned away from him when he agreed to submit his claims to arbitration. They believed that sinners should be excluded from the community of the faithful and that the caliph should be elected, and all devout believers eligible. Like many fervently democratic movements, they divided into a number of separate bodies including the Sufrites and the Ibadites. In 739–40, a Berber called Maysara launched a Kharijite revolt which began in Tangiers and spread to Tunisia, but was crushed after a long and bitter struggle.

But it was Shiites, not Kharijites, who overthrew the Umayyads in 850. The new dynasty, the Abbasids, came from Central Asia; they claimed descent from the Prophet's uncle, Abbas, and not from the Prophet himself (hence they did not command the allegiance of Shiites in general). They founded the magnificent palace city of Baghdad (Harun al-Rashid, of the *One Thousand and One Nights*, was an Abbasid).

A fleeing Umayyad prince, after an extraordinary journey, reached Spain in 755 and founded an independent state there which later became the caliphate of Cordoba. Another refugee from the Abbasids, a Sharif,[19] founded the city state of Fez, relying on the support of local Berbers, the Awriba. He died soon afterwards, in 795, but Fez and the Idrisid dynasty survived, and a tradition of Sharifian political authority was created which was to be of great importance later. Seldom can refugees have had so great a historical impact. There were a number of small Kharijite states in the Maghrib; the most famous was the Ibadite Imamate of Tahert, founded in 763 and conquered by the Fatimids in 909. Its dynasts, the Rustamids, were proud of their Persian ancestry – a reminder that

Persian as well as Arabic became an important vehicle for Islamic literature. From the eleventh century on, many Kharijite communities would become Sunni; after the sack of Tahert, its people moved, first to Wargla and then to the Mzab in the Algerian desert, where their faith flourishes still; they speak Berber, 'a small Berber island in a vast Arab sea'.[20]

The Kharijite movement, like Donatism, has been seen as the vehicle of Berber patriotism, its egalitarianism a reaction to the ascendancy of the Arab aristocracy. But this view has been questioned.

Ifriqiya was conquered in the name of the Abbasids, but its governor, Ibrahim al-Aghlab (d. 812), was virtually independent, creating a sultanate modelled on that of his former overlords, with the help of a slave army; he built a palace city, called the Abbasid. In 827, the Aghlabids began the conquest of Sicily (a process which was to take decades) with the aid of volunteers from many lands, including al-Andalus. It was the first new Islamic community established in a non-Muslim country for a hundred years.[21] Egypt also became independent under short-lived Turkish dynasties, the Tulunids (868–905) and the Ikhshidids (943–69). The unity of the Islamic world was lost and would never be recovered.

Social and economic change

As Brett points out, the political fragmentation of the Maghrib went hand in hand with economic unification.[22] The rise and fall of states is only one dimension of the history of these years. Ibadite merchants controlled the emerging trans-Saharan slave trade – an ironic contrast with the belief in democracy within the Muslim community. Then and later, there was no rigid separation between the religious and economic role. One of the sayings attributed to Muhammad was 'Poverty is almost like apostasy', and missionary and merchant were often one. The Umayyad caliph Umar II (d. 717) sent ten religious teachers to the Maghrib, one of whom was called God's merchant.[23] Trade routes ran from north to south and from east to west, through Kairouan to Egypt and beyond to Asia, source of silk and spices.

In antiquity, Egypt and the Maghrib exported agricultural products – wine, oil and corn – to Rome.[24] In the medieval period, both Egypt and the Maghrib excelled in manufacturing, especially textiles, which were produced in a large number of different centres. It was said that Sfax made better cloth than Alexandria. Kairouan manufactured copper artefacts, Tunis ceramics, and Bougie glass. Large quantities of the felt cap westerners called a fez were made in Ifriqiya: at one stage, 2 million were produced a year, in a cottage industry employing 1,500 people.[25] The potters of Jerba exported their wares not only to other parts of Ifriqiya but also to Algeria and the Levant.[26] Ifriqiya produced huge quantities of wheat, olive oil and dates, oranges, bananas and figs.[27] Coastal Morocco exported vast quantities of wheat to the Iberian peninsula from the tenth century on.

In part because of its small population, the history of the Sahara tends to be subordinated to that of the Sudan and Maghrib, except in specialist monographs. Until the late sixteenth century, gold, which was high in value in proportion to its weight, and slaves, which were self-transporting, were the main imports to northern Africa from the south. Gold from the Western Sudan was imported from the third century CE.[28] It made a crucial contribution to the economic and diplomatic importance of the states of the Maghrib, since there was a chronic shortage of bullion in the Mediterranean world and western Europe until New World silver became available. There was also an imbalance of trade between Asia and Europe, to the former's advantage, which meant a steady transfer of African gold, via Egypt, to the East.

Many of the slaves were absorbed into northern Africa; they played an important role in agriculture, especially on the desert edge, and in some periods there was an extensive use of black slave soldiers. Some Moroccan sultans were of part black descent, because of the popularity of concubines from sub-Saharan Africa.

Desert trade provided the livelihood of the northern desert termini such as Sijilmasa, Tuwat, Wargla and Ghadames, and contributed to the prosperity of the coastal cities such as Tripoli. According to one estimate, a ton of gold was carried over the desert routes every year, when the medieval trade was at its zenith, and 6 million slaves were exported across the Sahara between 650 and 1600.[29]

The people of the desert controlled the trans-Saharan caravans. They had a monopoly, both because of their special expertise and because camels could not be bred successfully far from the desert. In the eleventh century, a people from the western Sahara were to create a vast if short-lived empire, stretching from the Western Sudan to Spain.

Pilgrimage became a central institution for Muslims, as it was for their Christian contemporaries. The scholar population of Kairouan was swelled by pilgrims who tarried for a time or permanently. The route from west to east, which carried both trade and tribute, greatly facilitated the Hajj. Some pilgrims from Morocco travelled by sea, while others went overland, and an official pilgrimage caravan left Fez each year.[30] The Hajj linked North African – and later West African – Muslims with the rest of the Islamic world. The Almoravid and Almohad movements began with a returning pilgrim; one of the great state founders of nineteenth-century West Africa was al-Hajj Umar.

New cities

The growth of new cities is an important part of the region's history. We have seen how Tunis arose near the site of ancient Carthage and how Kairouan began as a garrison city and became a centre of learning. Cities founded for religious, political or military reasons often developed a flourishing economic life and attracted migrants from great distances. Fez was situated on a river; the naming of its two banks, Andalus and Kairouan, reflected the origins of the refugees who settled there in the early ninth century.[31] Sousse began as a *ribat* and became a major port. Rabat, the modern capital of Morocco, was built by the first Almohad caliph, who called it Ribat al-Fath, the Ribat of Victory. Not all the new cities survived; al-Mansura was built by a Marinid during the siege of Tlemcen and abandoned almost at once when he was murdered.

The construction of mosques and palaces and city walls absorbed substantial resources. They were a visible reflection of spiritual and temporal hierarchies, the supremacy of Islam and the majesty of rulers. Islam brought new styles of architecture and a tradition of literacy in Arabic first to the Maghrib and later to the Western Sudan. North African crafts included fine filigree work in plaster, which adorned mosques and palaces, and splendid calligraphy in a distinctive script. It is one of the many paradoxes of Maghribi history that both small states and great empires were founded with the indispensable co-operation of 'stateless' Berbers. The Idrisids relied on the Awriba, and the Fatimids on the Kutama. But the Almoravid and Almohad states were founded and ruled by Berbers themselves, who found an inspiration and an ideology in Islam.

Shiites and Kharijites loom large in the dynastic history of the Maghrib, but the vast majority of African Muslims have always been Sunni. The word comes from Sunna, Customs (of the Prophet) embodied in the Qur'an and in the Sayings (Hadith) attributed to him. A large body of legal interpretation grew up around these sources. Four legal schools were founded in the eighth and ninth centuries. The Malikite has always been dominant in North and West Africa, but the differences between the schools are minor.

The Abbasids claimed that they were restoring the golden age of the Rightly Guided Caliphs. The caliph – or Commander of the Faithful – was both a spiritual and temporal ruler. But the disintegration of the empire had important implications – it was no longer coterminous with Islam. In the course of the ninth century, the ruler came to be thought of as a sultan (the word was originally an Arabic abstract noun meaning power) and the interpretation of religion was left to scholars, *ulama*. In the course of African history, they were destined to be sometimes the advisers of rulers and sometimes their critics and opponents. On a number of occasions the *ulama* were to found new states, taking over the function of the ruler.

Maghribi Christianity had died out by the twelfth century after a long period of decline. Various reasons have been suggested for its disappearance – the divisions between Catholics and Donatists, the economic and other rewards of service in Muslim armies. But Maghribi Christianity survived long after the extinction of Donatism and may have died out because it lacked the monastic tradition, which was a powerful agent in preserving the traditions of the Coptic church. Learned Muslims were well aware of the People of the Book who preceded them, and searched in the ruins of Roman Hippo for the cathedral of 'Augodjin, a great doctor of the Christian religion'.[32] The Jewish communities of the Maghrib survived; they were to be reinforced when their co-religionists were expelled by the Spain of the Reconquista. Rabbis in Algiers guided the Jews of Tuat on issues such as how to keep the Sabbath while crossing the Sahara.[33]

The Sufis were mystics – the name comes from their garment of coarse wool. Originally, they were spiritual athletes who devoted their lives to the arduous pursuit of God through asceticism and prayer. The Sufi way was handed down from master to disciple and by the nineteenth century the Sufi orders had many thousands of adherents, only a few of whom were practising mystics. It is a classic instance of the routinisation of charisma.

Dhu'l Nun al Misri ('the Egyptian'), a saint of Nubian parentage who died in 860, was one of the founders of the Sufi way.

The Maghrib has always had a tradition of holy teachers; their tombs became places of pilgrimage, like those of the Catholic and Donatist saints who went before them, and the stories of their lives acquired a rich patina of the miraculous. They founded dynasties of saints, each generation providing one or more heirs to the charisma of its holy predecessors. They were called *murabitun* – men of the *ribat* or fort. The reference was originally to devotees who kept watch in coastal *ribats* and devoted themselves to prayer. In the form 'marabout', it is the generic term for an Islamic teacher or Sufi in Francophone Africa.

Gender

Much has been written on the way in which Islam has affected the position of women:

One group denies that Muslim women ... are any more oppressed than non-Muslim women or argues that in key respects they have been less oppressed. A second [says that] the Quran ... intended gender equality, but this was undermined by Arabian patriarchy and foreign importations. An opposing group blames Islam for being irrevocably gender inegalitarian.[34]

All this has exact parallels in the history of Christianity. The Fatimid sultan al-Hakim not only ordered women to stay at home but forbade shoemakers to make shoes for them. 'One day the inhabitants of Cairo came across an effigy made in the image of a veiled woman holding a piece of paper insulting and cursing al-Hakim because he forbade women from walking in the streets.'[35] Ibn al-Hajj, a cleric who was born in Fez and died in Cairo in 1336/7, was one of many who denounced women in religion's name, quoting the Hadith: 'You are lacking in mind and religion.' When Cairo was afflicted with plague and famine, the Mamluk sultan Barsbay was advised by the learned that they were caused by the failure of women to remain in seclusion.[36]

But women created spaces for choices in their own lives: in fourteenth-century Cairo, they counted Saturday and Sunday as days of rest as well as Friday! They visited the baths and the tombs of saints, met for picnics by the river, and went boating and swimming.[37] We know of all this only because of the writings of the male moralists who denounced them.

Women Sufis and scholars tend to enter the historical record only as the prelude to an account of a distinguished son. A fifteenth-century Moroccan woman was called 'the ninth copy' of the Qur'an in her household, since her knowledge of it was so precise.[38]

Production was gender-specific, though much of the evidence comes from a later date. In the Maghrib men were responsible for cultivation, while women ground the grain and cooked, and collected water and firewood. An eighteenth-century observer described how, 'they strap their nursing babies to their back and walk two or three miles from home in search of water'.[39] In the coastal towns, women spun and men wove, but in the countryside women did the spinning, weaving and dyeing, making not only cloth but also tents and carpets.[40] The pastoralist's tent (which women erected) was divided by a curtain into male space, devoted to hospitality, and women's space, for cooking and weaving.

In general, men dominated the public arena, and women's role was thought to lie in the domestic and private sphere, but a few aristocratic women played an important role in national affairs. Zainab, widow of the Mamluk sultan Inal, died in 1479, at the age of eighty. A chronicler paid tribute to her: 'She enjoyed such prestige during the reign of her husband that she administered state affairs, influencing both appointments and dismissals.'[41]

A contemporary of Zainab's, Fatima, daughter of Sultan Tatar, chose a very different path. She refused the marriage arranged for her, squandered a fortune on dissipation, and died deeply in debt; her life was untypical but determined by her own choices.[42]

The poor

The sources tend to focus on religion, warfare, and the rise and fall of kings. The poor had other preoccupations. There is some evidence that the prosperity of Egypt declined under Arab rule. In 891, al-Ya'qubi claimed that its revenue had fallen from 14 million dinars at the time of Amr ibn al-As to 3 million; al-Maqrizi, an Egyptian historian who died in 1442, made similar claims.[43]

Egypt's tradition of rural discontent – noted in Roman times – continued. There were a number of revolts in the Delta between 725 and 832 and many peasants avoided taxation by leaving the land, as their forebears had done under the Romans, a trend the authorities tried to suppress by requiring passports. There was a Berber revolt in the Maghrib in *c.* 734, a protest against tribute in slaves and lamb skins. In 826, black slaves in the Djerid revolted, armed with axes and spades.[44] Tens of thousands of black slaves, the Zanj, worked in grim conditions draining the swamps of southern Iraq. There were slave risings there in the 750s and 770s, precursors to the famous revolt of the Zanj in 869.[45]

As time went on, many émigré Arabs also came to experience a sense of relative or absolute deprivation. In the early days of Islam, the Believers were virtually identical with a victorious army. By 642 there may have been 20,000 Arabs in Egypt, and each new governor came with an entourage of thousands, many of whom settled in Egypt permanently.[46]

But when the age of expansion ended, the payment of the army became a problem and it was necessary to limit its numbers. Unpaid soldiers in Egypt rebelled on a number of occasions. From the late seventh century, those entitled to serve in the army were listed in registers and received a salary, and those excluded felt themselves deprived. In 834, a caliph began his reign by ordering the governor of Egypt to end the whole system of registers. The Abbasids relied less on Arab volunteers than on Turks, one of whom, in 868, became the independent ruler of Egypt. 'The bedouins found themselves back where they had begun: as an external proletariat.'[47] The results were momentous, for many Arabs chose to migrate into the Maghrib and into what is now the northern Republic of Sudan, where Arabic gradually became the majority language. Others were absorbed into the peasant population of the Nile valley, their presence contributing to the gradual adoption of Arabic speech.[48]

The Abbasids held power for a little less than a hundred years. Baghdad was called the City of Peace, but the period was troubled by civil wars and regional breakaways. We have noted the virtual independence of Egypt and the Maghrib. Finally, in 945, the Buwayhids, a dynasty from near the Caspian Sea, seized Baghdad, retaining the Abbasids as figureheads. The collapse of the caliphate augmented the importance of Egypt as a centre of Islam and of Arabic civilisation.[49]

The Ismailis

The next attempt to found a universal caliphate began in the Maghrib. As we have seen, the Shiites believed that the headship of the Islamic community was the rightful prerogative of the descendants of the Prophet. They rejected all the Rightly Guided Caliphs but Ali, and also the Umayyads and Abbasids. Ali loomed large in their spirituality, as did his son, Huseyn, who died fighting overwhelming odds. They believed that this spiritual headship was handed from father to son. There are many who claim descent from the Prophet, and the Shiites have always been divided among supporters of different claimants. Two groups, the Ismailis and the much larger Twelvers, agree on a line of six Imams, or spiritual heads, ending with Ja'far al-Sadiq (the Authentic), who died in 765. The Twelvers traced the line through Ja'far's son Abdullah to the eleventh Imam, who died as a child in 874; they believe that the twelfth Imam is in hiding, until he returns as the Mahdi, the Rightly Guided One, at the end of time. Twelver Shia became the official religion of Persia in the sixteenth and seventeenth centuries. The Ismailis consider a different son of Ja'far, Ismail, to be the seventh and last Imam.

The Ismailis believed that the End was imminent; theirs was a revolutionary creed, often disseminated in secret. They appealed to the poor, to whom they promised the overthrow of those in high places. One group of Ismailis, the Carmathians, founded a state in Arabia. Their most spectacular success, however, was first in Ifriqiya and later in Egypt. The Abbasids first rose to power in Khurasan, on the eastern frontier of the Islamic world, while the Fatimid caliphate was founded in the Maghrib, the distant west.

Three empires in the Maghrib: (I) the Fatimids (Maps 9 and I0)

Three successive empires were founded in the Maghrib between the tenth and the thirteenth centuries, ruled respectively by the Fatimids, the Almoravids and the Almohads. Each was inspired by an ideology rooted in Islam. It has been said that they began as sects and ended as empires.[50] Each, at its greatest extent, stretched far beyond the Maghrib and each began on the desert edge or in the mountains. In the words of Geertz: 'The formative period both of Morocco as a nation and of Islam as its creed ... consisted of the peculiar process of tribal edges falling in upon an agricultural center and civilising it. It was the periphery of the country, the harsh and sterile frontiers, that nourished and in fact created the advanced society which developed at its heart.'[51]

The Fatimid state was founded by Ismailis (the name reflects the fact that the dynasty claimed descent from Fatima). It is one of the paradoxes of North

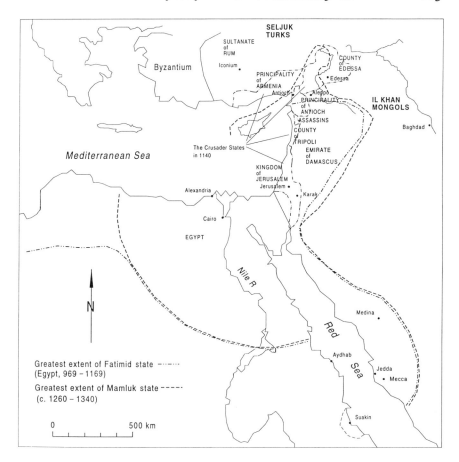

Map 10   Egypt and the Near East: Fatimids and Mamluks

African history that they succeeded in founding an empire among overwhelmingly Sunni populations.

A Syrian Ismaili missionary (*da'i*, caller), Abu Abd Allah, went to Ifriqiya, with momentous consequences, in 893. He built up a following among the Kutama, a branch of the Sanhaja, who lived in the mountains on the western borders of the Aghlabid state. They probably saw him simply as a holy preacher, without realising the distinctiveness of Ismaili belief. Such was his success that the man who claimed to be the Mahdi, Sa'id b. Husayn, left Syria and joined him. The Aghlabid state was overthrown, a task made easier by the shortcomings of its later members – the last Aghlabid sultan came to the throne through parricide. Said became the first Fatimid ruler, adopting the name Ubayd Allah, and building a new capital, al-Mahdiya, on the coast,[52] a step which contributed to the decline of Kairouan. In 911 he had Abu Abd Allah put to death, presumably afraid of too powerful a subject.

To the Fatimids, the conquest of Ifriqiya was only the first step in establishing a universal caliphate. They made several unsuccessful attempts to invade Egypt; at first they had more success in conquering the city states of Sijilmasa, Tahert and Fez. The ruler of Andalus reacted to the Fatimid regime in the name of Sunni orthodoxy, by taking the title of Caliph, unifying Muslim Spain and invading Morocco. But the most dangerous challenge to the Fatimids' regime in the Maghrib came neither from Cordoba nor from Baghdad, but from a great revolt in 943–7, led by a Kharijite holy man called Abu Yazid, the Man on a Donkey. His forces took Kairouan but were ultimately defeated. There was, of course, a tension between the exalted role expected of the Mahdi and the actual position of the ruler of an earthly state. Ubayd Allah claimed that he was merely the precursor of his son, who was the hidden Imam, and who succeeded to the throne in 934, with the exalted title of al-Qa'im, Bringer of the Resurrection, and ruled until his death in 946. The writings of a noted theologian, al-Qadi'l Nu'man, did much to establish the respectability of the regime in Sunni eyes but the Ismaili faith did not take root in either the Maghrib or Egypt. It remained the preserve of the ruling dynasty and its close associates. On the whole, despite differences in their theology, the Fatimids remained on amicable terms with their subjects.

In 969 the Fatimids realised their dream of conquering Egypt, leaving a Berber deputy in the Maghrib. In time, his family, the Zirids, became independent, reinforcing their legitimacy by claiming descent from ancient rulers in the Yemen. A related family, the Hammadids, founded a separate kingdom further west, later establishing a new capital at Bougie. But these were relatively small states and Morocco lay far beyond their boundaries. In 1057 the Zirid sultan left Kairouan, and the city declined thereafter. The encomium quoted at the beginning of this chapter was written in nostalgia for a vanished age of greatness.

On the Atlantic coast, a prophet called Yunus founded a state among the Barghawata, claiming that his grandfather, Salih, had come with a Berber Qur'an and would return as the Mahdi. Their faith, though deeply indigenised, was heterodox, and this probably limited their appeal. It was the orthodox Almoravids who would found an empire. Another prophet, called Hamim, preached a Berberised form of Islam south of Tetuan.[53] Probably as a result of Shiite influences, there was a great proliferation of such figures in the Maghrib, but they lie beyond the scope of a general history.

The Banu Hilal

As Arab migration into the Nile valley continued, many bedouin migrated to the west. The people of rural Cyrenaica think of themselves as either Mrabitin – descended from the original inhabitants – or Sa'di, descended from nine conquering Arab clans.[54] Bedouin who acquired a collective identity as the Banu Hilal and Banu Sulaym settled in the western oases, later migrating, first to Ifriqiya and then to the Atlantic plains of Morocco and to Shinquit (modern Mauritania). According to ibn Khaldun it was the Fatimid caliph who sent them to Ifriqiya, when the Zirids began to assert their independence. The story has often been repeated, but it appears that the migration began much earlier, and lasted for centuries.[55] Slowly, Arabic supplanted Berber in much of the Maghrib, and Arabs and Arabised Berbers became indistinguishable. A legend-encrusted account of the adventures of the Banu Hilal forms the theme of an oral epic which is still sung in the Maghrib.

The Banu Hilal, like the Vandals, have had a bad reputation. Ibn Khaldun compared them with a great swarm of locusts laying waste the land, and his words have often been echoed by modern scholars. 'It was an evil day for North Africa when, in the eleventh century, the Banu Hilal poured out of Egypt westward along the coast ... The Banu Hilal systematically pillaged every town and destroyed every solid building they encountered ... Land dependent on irrigation went out of cultivation and reverted to desert.'[56]

The evidence, however, has been subjected to new interpretations.[57] Ibn Khaldun died in 1406; he was as distant from these events as we are from the English Civil War. The Banu Hilal undoubtedly contributed to the political fragmentation of the Maghrib, though this was not necessarily an evil, and it is inconsistent to applaud the Arabs as bearers of civilisation in some contexts and as agents of catastrophe in others. In many – though not all – cases, pastoralists and farmers lived in symbiosis. In Tunisia, nomadic pastoralists left their food supplies in the care of settled villagers.[58]

The Banu Hilal played a military role in the lands of the West, providing cavalry for its rulers, 'while their leaders became princes, generals and barons in their own little fortresses. This character their descendants retained down to the fifteenth century.'[59]

The Fatimids in Egypt

It was the Fatimids who built Cairo, the Victorious, near the garrison city of Fustat. They saw the conquest of Egypt as a step in the establishment of a universal caliphate. It was a goal they never attained but their domains reached well beyond Egypt; for the first time since the Ptolemies, Egypt ruled an empire in Asia Minor. The Fatimids ruled Damascus from 978 to 1076, and Syria was divided into Fatimid and Byzantine spheres. They gained prestige from the fact that, with Carmathian support, they became the guardians of the holy places, Mecca and Medina.

The Fatimids added more strands to the complex web of Shia sectarianism. The caliph al-Hakim, eccentric, if not mad, was a persecutor of Jews and Christians; he died mysteriously in 1021. He claimed to be divine, and the Druze in the Lebanon and southern Syria accept this.

When the caliph al-Mustansir died in 1094, a child, al-Mustali, was proclaimed his heir. He is the progenitor of another line of hidden imams, the Tayibi. The Ismailis of Syria and Persia rejected al-Mustali in favour of his adult brother al-Nizar. The Nizari, based in Persia and Syria, continued the original revolutionary goals of the Ismailis; they were called the Assassins. Until 1256, there was a Nizari state in Alamut; after this the Nizaris moved away from revolutionary activity and became a quietist and mystical movement. In 1845, a Nizari imam who was the first Aga Khan transferred the headquarters of the movement to India. Many of the Indians who settled in colonial East Africa were Twelvers or (Nizari) Ismailis or Bohra – yet another Ismaili group which dates from the Nizar–al-Mustali schism. They became prosperous merchants, a world away from the fiery zealots of Alamut.

The Fatimids were patrons of the arts, seeking to equal the splendours of the Abbasid court. They built the great mosques of al-Hakim and al-Azhar ('the fair', one of the praise names of Fatima), and lived in legendary splendour. But like the Abbasids, their power declined. For a time the process was arrested by effective viziers. But their ultimate collapse was caused, not by their individual inadequacies, but by a dramatic change in the balance of power in the Near East, a theme to which we return later in this chapter.

Three empires in the Maghrib: (2) the Almoravids

The Idrisids and Fatimids came from the east and founded states in the Maghrib with the support of Berber peoples. The Almoravid empire was created and ruled by the Lamtuna section of the Sanhaja, Berbers of the Western Desert. The earliest account of them was written in the late ninth century.

He who travels from Sijilmasa to the south, making for the land of the Sudan . . . will be met in the desert by a people called Anbiya, of the Sanhaja, who have no permanent dwellings. It is their custom to veil their faces with their turbans . . . They subsist on camels, for they have no crops . . . Then the traveller will reach a town called Ghust [Awdaghust] . . . It is the residence of their king, who has no religion or law.[60]

The *litham*, a black veil covering the faces of Sanhaja men below the eyes, has survived into modern times. It was to become the distinguishing badge of a ruling caste, and Muslims from other cultures were often perturbed by the fact that men wore veils, but women did not, and by the latter's freedom.

The author of the passage cited above came no closer to the Sahara than Egypt. Ibn Hawqal, who visited Sijilmasa in 951–2, described the great volume of Saharan trade and the power of the Sanhaja and Massufa, who levied tribute from caravans, acted as guides and exported salt to the Bilad al-Sudan.[61]

It is not easy to chart the gradual progress of Islam in the Sahara and the Western Sudan. It was introduced by clerics and merchants (scholars disagree as to the relative importance of their respective roles[62] and indeed they were often the same person). The jurists of Kairouan issued rulings on various aspects of desert trade just as the rabbis of Algiers did, albeit with different variables in mind.[63] It seems likely that Islam spread among the people of the Western Desert in the early tenth century. Al-Muhallabi, writing in 985, said that the people of Awdaghust were Muslims.[64] In the first half of the eleventh century, a Sanhaja nobleman called Tarashna went on pilgrimage to Mecca and died fighting a holy war in the Bilad al-Sudan.[65]

Another Sanhaja aristocrat, the Juddala Yahya ibn Ibrahim, went on pilgrimage in 1035/6, and discovered in the course of it the inadequacies of his people's knowledge of Islam. The pilgrimage has often been a prelude to a life of social and political activity; the traveller gains a wider perspective which enables him to see the weaknesses of his own society more clearly.[66]

Yahya ibn Ibrahim sought unsuccessfully for a teacher willing to live in the desert among the scholars of Kairouan. He found one in the southern Atlas mountains, the fiery ascetic Abd Allah ibn Yasin. Ibn Yasin practised a harshness which far exceeded the dictates of orthodoxy[67] and became so unpopular among the Juddala that he was forced to leave for a time[68] but later he attracted a solid nucleus of fervent followers who called themselves al-Murabitin, people of the *ribat*. A *ribat* is a fortified settlement (in this case probably a spiritual rather than a physical edifice, a community of the like-minded)[69] and Almoravid is the Spanish form of this name. According to a contemporary source, the Almoravids fought with the support of black Muslims from Takrur against the Juddala.[70] Yahya b. Umar, another Sanhaja nobleman, came to lead the movement and his people, the Lamtuna, to form the core of its support. There were, of course, other variables besides the purely religious, not least the desire for ethnic and economic dominance. They were to forbid other peoples to wear the *litham*, and began by conquering the crucial commercial centres on the margins of the Sahara. In about 1055 they conquered the northern and southern termini of the desert route from Ghana to Morocco, first wresting Sijilmasa from Zanata control and then taking Awdaghust from Ghana. They also captured a town much further east, Tadmekka, the desert port of Gao.[71]

One source suggests that this was yet another instance of expansion driven by hunger. 'In the year 1058/9 their country suffered a famine so ibn Yasin ordered the weaker ones to go out to the Sus ... They gathered for themselves something of value and returned. Then they found the desert restricting.'[72]

There was an intrinsic austerity in the desert way of life, and puritanism came naturally to desert dwellers. At Sijilmasa, ibn Yasin 'chopped up the instruments of music and burned down the shops where wine was sold. He abolished non-Koranic levies and taxes ... he placed a governor from Lamtuna in charge and retired to the desert.'[73]

In a famous passage ibn Khaldun suggested that the Almoravids conquered Ghana itself, though this has been questioned.[74] There is some evidence to suggest that the Almoravids of the south may well have founded a state which is not mentioned by the Arab geographers, incorporating ancient Ghana. This would explain their notably abundant supply of gold.[75] Abu Bakr's son Ibrahim is described as black, and a twelfth-century source states that 'the amir of Ghana is related to [the Barbara] and used to be one of them'.[76] A mysterious passage tells of the visit of a black king from the desert edge state of Zafun to the Almoravid capital of Marrakesh. He rode his horse into the palace. 'The Commander of the Muslims met him on foot, whereas the [king of] Zafun did not dismount for him ... he was tall, of deep black complexion and veiled.'[77]

Ibn Yasin died fighting the Barghawata in 1059, and Yahya b. Umar was killed in a desert battle with dissident Juddala in 1066. His brother, Abu Bakr, led the Almoravids to a successful conquest of Morocco, perhaps at the request of its clerics,[78] but relinquished its rule to his cousin ibn Tashfin and returned to the desert, where he died in 1087. Morocco, which had been, for the most part, beyond the effective frontiers of Roman, Byzantine and Arab Africa, became a unified state for the first time. The Almoravids made no attempt to invade

Ifriqiya, perhaps because its rulers were Sanhaja; their advance to the east stopped at Tlemcen.

Ibn Tashfin was the real architect of the Almoravid empire. He founded a new capital at Marrakesh in 1070, conquered Fez in 1075, Ceuta in 1083, and invaded Andalusia in 1085. The Umayyad caliphs of Cordoba had been the defenders of Sunni orthodoxy, but by 1031 their state had disintegrated into fifteen small polities ruled by Berbers, 'Slavs' (Europeans) or Arabs. The Reconquista – the reconquest of Spain by its Christian kingdoms – had begun; they seized Toledo in 1085; in this situation of crisis, the leadership of the Almoravids was acceptable. (The Spanish folk hero known as the Cid died fighting them.) But there were many tensions between the reformers from the desert and the urban sophisticates of Andalus.

Ibn Tashfin did not take the title Caliph, in deference to the claims of the distant puppet Abbasids. The Almoravids were Sunni, adherents of the Malikite school of law,[79] and laid great emphasis on its strict application. Probably relatively few Sanhaja actually emigrated from the desert to Andalusia or the Maghrib. The culture of the latter was more profoundly affected by the westward thrust of the Banu Hilal. But the effects of the movement were far-reaching. Orthodox Sunni Islam replaced the rich variety of Maghribi belief which had preceded it – Idrisid and Ismaili Shi'ites, the Barghawata, the different Kharijite bodies – though there are still Ibadite communities in the Mzab. Cultural and other linkages between the Western Sudan, the Sahara, the Maghrib and Andalusia were strengthened. As so often, the vanquished took the victor captive and Andalusian architects built mosques and palaces in the Maghrib. On the Niger bend, the marble tombs of early eleventh-century Gao royals, which were carved in southern Spain, have been found.[80]

The Almoravids struck large quantities of fine dinars, often in Spain, in the most extensive minting of gold in western Europe since the Romans.[81] They were copied by Alfonso of Toledo, whose dinars were known as *le morabeti alfonsi*.[82] At a later period, the Muslim world would adopt the Maria Theresa *thaler*, the symbol and reflection of profound transformations.

Trans-Saharan trade flourished: 'The people of the city of Aghmat [near Marrakesh] are opulent wealthy merchants who go into the Sudan with numbers of camels . . . During the dynasty of the Mulaththamun [Veiled Ones] there were none richer or in easier circumstances than they.'[83]

Despite its vast extent the Almoravid state was short-lived – it was challenged by the Almohads in the Maghrib during the long reign of ibn Tashfin's son Ali (1106–43). It was during his reign, too, that Seville and Cordoba fell to the Reconquista.

A number of reasons have been adduced for the rapid decline of the Almoravid empire: the exclusiveness of its Sanhaja rulers, the unacceptability of their puritanism, the vigour of the Reconquista. The sheer size of the empire militated against its survival – no state has ever succeeded in maintaining control of areas both north and south of the Sahara. The Almohads who supplanted the People of the Ribat followed a teacher who critiqued their legalism, emphasising the devotional and mystical elements in Islam.

Three empires in the Maghrib: (3) the Almohads

'Almohad' is a Spanish form of an Arabic word, *al-muwahhidun*, which means Proclaimers of the Unity of God. All Muslims are unitarians: the name reflects the theology of the movement's founder, Muhammad ibn Tumart (*c.* 1080–1130).[84] Ibn Tumart was a man of the Masmuda, agriculturalists of the Ante-Atlas, who have retained Berber speech into modern times. He went on pilgrimage, studied in Baghdad and Damascus, and was influenced by both the mystical writings of al-Ghazzali and the theology of al-Ashari, who rejected anthropomorphic readings of the Qur'an, interpreting it allegorically. In the early days of Sufism, the excesses of the more extreme of its practitioners tended to alienate the orthodox; the Persian mystic, al-Hallaj, was executed for blasphemy in Baghdad in 922. Al-Ghazzali, a Baghdad scholar who became a wandering sufi, contributed to the reconciliation of the legal and mystical traditions, though there was always a tension between the two. His books were burnt by the Almoravid ruler Ali. Abd al-Qadir al-Jilani (d. 1166) was another scholar of Baghdad who is revered as the founder of the oldest Sufi order.[85]

In 1121 ibn Tumart returned to the Maghrib, beginning his public career by denouncing the lifestyle of the people of Bougie. Later, he engaged in public debate with the Almoravid theologians of Marrakesh. He settled in the Ante-Atlas, where he built up a large following and, in time, claimed to be an infallible Mahdi.[86] Shortly before his death, in 1130, he came into conflict with the Almoravids, making an unsuccessful attempt to capture Marrakesh. He died the head of a small and obscure community in the mountains, but his disciple, Abd al-Mumin (d. 1163), a Zanata Berber from west of Oran, converted when ibn Tumart visited Bougie, took over the leadership, gradually building up a large independent state in the High Atlas. The succession of a Masmuda by a Zanata was a notable triumph of ideals over ethnic allegiance, though the tensions between the Mahdi's clan and the claims of the ruling family were not settled until shortly before Abd al-Mumin's death.[87] In the 1140s he began to challenge the Almoravids, and in 1147 he captured Marrakesh, which became his capital. He invaded Ifriqiya in 1152/3 and 1159/60, recapturing Mahdiya from the Normans, who had seized it some years before, and his son carried the jihad successfully into Muslim Spain. Unlike the Almoravids, he adopted the title of Caliph, the Deputy of the Mahdi, ibn Tumart.

Like the Almoravids, the Almohads came to absorb much of the culture of Andalus, and their far-flung state led to the strengthening of economic and cultural exchanges. Like their predecessors, they minted fine dinars with the gold of the Bilad al-Sudan. The Almohad caliph Abu Yaqub was the patron of the Andalusian philosophers ibn Tufayl and ibn Rushid ('Averroes'), and encouraged the latter to write his commentary on Aristotle. His son, Abu Yusuf, banished Averroes to a village.[88] A black poet from Kanem, Abu Ishaq Ibrahim, lived at Marrakesh at this time.[89]

Soon, the Almohad empire fell apart, weakened by succession disputes and revolts. The Almohads lost both territory and prestige in Spain; the caliph Abu Ya'qub died fighting the Christians in Spain in 1184, and in 1212 the Almohads experienced a crushing defeat at the battle of Las Navas de Tolosa. By 1276, Christians had regained the whole of Spain except Granada, which fell in 1492, that extraordinary year which also saw the expulsion of the Jews and Columbus' 'discovery' of America. A branch of the Almoravids settled in the Balearics, whence they launched an ultimately unsuccessful invasion of Ifriqiya.

Abd al-Mumin encouraged the settlement of Arab nomads from Ifriqiya, the Banu Maqil, in coastal Morocco, an area largely depopulated by the conquest of the Barghawata. This migration led to the further extension of Arabic; as in Ifriqiya, the presence of Arab nomads added an important element to the local power equation, symbolised by the fact that when one of the Marinid sultans (the successors of the Almohads) went in public procession, he was escorted by a Zanata Berber on one side and an Arab on the other. Later, the Banu Maqil migrated into Shinquit.

Like its predecessor, the Almohad state collapsed in part because of its sheer size. To Sunni Muslims the Almohads were heretics, not because of their stress on the spiritual nature of God, but because of the claims made for ibn Tumart, as the infallible Mahdi. Caliph Abu Yusuf seems to have doubted this, and a later caliph, the great-grandson and namesake of the first al-Ma'mun, repudiated it energetically.[90] But in doing so he struck at the basis of his own authority.

In 1236/7, Ifriqiya became an independent state under the Hafsids, who were originally Almohad governors. Whereas the Arabs ruled from Kairouan and the Fatimids and Zirids from Mahdiya, they adopted Tunis as their capital. Although Hafsid Tunisia went through periods of weakness and disunity, it survived until 1574. There was also a smaller independent state at Tlemcen, and in Morocco a Zanata dynasty, the Marinids, overthrew the last Almohad caliph in 1269, establishing an independent state with its capital at Fez, where they built a new palace quarter. The resultant double city, with its separate administrative and commercial capitals, was reminiscent of its counterparts in the Western Sudan. The Marinids, like the Almohads before them, were divided, and lost prestige by their inability to stem Portuguese aggression on Moroccan soil. After a period of expansion, the kingdom shrank to an enclave round Fez. The last Marinid ruler was overthrown by a revolt of local Sharifs and killed in 1465, but six years later the Sharifs were overthrown by the Wattasids, kin of the Marinids and their former viziers. Like their predecessors, they ruled a small enclave at Fez but were unable to expel the Portuguese from their outposts on the Atlantic coast. The last Wattasid sultan was put to death in 1554.

The Sufi tradition became firmly entrenched in the Maghrib in the time of the Almohads, though scholars disagree as to whether this was a reaction against their puritanism or a response to their encouragement of the mystical way.[91] Dynasties of holy men played a leading role in the life of the local community, 'saints of the Atlas'.[92] The charisma of the original saint was inherited by some of his – often very numerous – descendants. Sidi Abu Madyan ('Boumédienne'), originally from Andalus, was one of the key figures in the history of Maghribi Sufism. Al-Shadili ('Chedli'),[93] originally from Ceuta, was his disciple at one remove, who taught in Egypt and died on pilgrimage.

Although the Sharifian revolt in fifteenth-century Fez failed, the real dynamic of Moroccan history was to lie not with successive sultans, but with a rising tide of popular support for Sufi saints and for the Sharifs who claimed descent from the Prophet, usually through Idris, the founder of Fez.

Egypt: on Turks and Crusaders

At some periods, events in Asia Minor have been of crucial significance in Egyptian history. From the eleventh century on, it became entwined with that of the Seljuk and Ottoman Turks, the Mongols and the Crusaders.

From time to time, the nomadic peoples of the steppes of Central Asia have exploded out of their homeland; the underlying causes, economic or demographic, are debated. Braudel compared the movement of the Arabs out of the hot deserts of Arabia in the seventh century with that of the Turks from the cold deserts of southern Russia in the tenth, the first movement associated with the camel, the second with the horse.[94] There is a Turkish proverb that a nomad does not need to go anywhere, but needs to be on the move.[95] Again and again, 'barbarians' from the east have invaded Asia Minor and eastern Europe; the Romans called them, collectively, Scythians. These migrations were never reversed, as the rivers which feed into the Caspian provide better pasture than the arid steppes of the invaders' homeland.[96]

The Turks, one of the peoples migrating west from a homeland in Central Asia, have impinged on the history of Egypt and the Maghrib in many ways. They were divided into many independent clans which were identified by the name of a real or putative ancestor. The Ghuzz Turks included the Seljuks and Ottomans. The former, zealous converts to Sunni Islam, invaded the Near East in the eleventh century; they conquered Iraq and Iran, sweeping away the Buwhayids, and invaded Syria, driving a wedge between the Fatimids and Byzantines, and setting up a number of small principalities.

The First Crusade (1099–1109) was to a large extent a response to the Seljuk advance. Medieval Christians, like their Muslim contemporaries, had a tradition of pilgrimage and of reverence for holy places. Jerusalem was sacred to both Muslims and Christians; the Umayyads had built a mosque there as a symbolic appropriation of their Jewish and Christian past, and Muslims came to see Jerusalem as the point of contact between earth and heaven. The Crusaders, whom Muslims called Franks, sought salvation, adventure and principalities, not necessarily in that order. In the First Crusade, they established a chain of small states headed by the kingdom of Jerusalem, but inland from the coast the Turkish principalities ruled. The brooding desert fortress of Karak, the fortifications of Acre, preserve a memory in stone of the Frankish moment in the long history of the Holy Land. Inevitably, Christian–Muslim relations became polarised and embittered.

Saladin and the Ayyubids

The Ayyubids ruled Egypt for eighty years, between the periods of Fatimid and Mamluk rule. Salah al-Din, whom the Crusaders knew as Saladin, was a Kurd in the service of the Turkish ruler of Damascus. Fatimid Egypt was in deep decline, and both Franks and Turks aspired to control its resources. In 1169 Saladin and his uncle overthrew the last of the Fatimids, restoring Egypt to Sunni rule. From his Egyptian base, Saladin carved out an empire in Syria and fought the Crusaders; he captured Jerusalem in 1187 and came close to expelling them from Palestine, but did not in the end succeed. To his contemporaries, both Muslims and Crusaders, Saladin was the epitome of chivalry, magnanimous in victory, so generous that he died with his treasury almost empty.[97] Saladin died in 1193; his heirs, the Ayyubids, ruled Egypt and Syria as a conglomerate of principalities until 1250. The Crusaders retained their attenuated states largely because of their internal divisions.

Perhaps the most enduring consequence of the Ayyubid interlude was the strengthening of the Sunni element in the world of Middle Eastern Islam. Egypt went through something of a cultural renaissance, manifested, among other ways, in an efflorescence of Arabic mystical poetry, closely associated with the Sufi way. Ibn al-Farid (1181–1235), one of the greatest of the mystic poets, was born and died in Cairo. But the Ayyubids ruled Egypt for less than a century; they were overthrown, not by Franks or by other external enemies, but by their own Mamluks.

The Mamluks

The rulers of successive empires in Egypt and the Maghrib relied on armies of differing ethnic composition. The Maghrib and Andalus were initially conquered by Arabs and Berber *mawali*. The Tulunids and Fatimids relied heavily on sometimes turbulent black slave soldiers; they revolted in Cairo, in the reign of the last Fatimid caliph.[98] The Almoravids excluded their non-Sanhaja subjects from the army, and made greater use of Christian mercenaries – there was a church in Marrakesh.[99] The Almohads and Marinids did the same, as did the rulers of Tlemcen.[100] The Ayyubids relied on Mamluks, who later supplanted them.[101]

The word *mamluk* is based on a root which means 'owned' and is often translated 'slave soldier', but although Mamluks were indeed purchased as children, they spent their lives as free, powerful and privileged men. They were trained as horse archers, a highly skilled avocation requiring many years of training; during this time they became Muslims and were freed at the age of eighteen. The elite among them were the royal Mamluks, who numbered about ten thousand. At the time of the fall of the Ayubbids, most of Egypt's Mamluks were Kipchak Turks, a people scattered by the Mongols. The great Mamluk sultan, Baybars, was a Kipchak. A ninth-century Arab writer stated that the Turks 'have become in warfare what the Greeks are in philosophy'. Some were Kurds or Slavs;[102] a majority in the later Mamluk period in Egypt came from the Caucasus; they were never Arabs, for Muslims could not be enslaved. Their children could not be Mamluks, though they were privileged townsmen.

The Mamluks were a distinctive institution, virtually peculiar to the Muslim world (Christian Georgia also employed slave soldiers of Turkish origin). They were first employed on a large scale by the Abbasids in the ninth century. We have noted the career of ibn Tulun, the Turk who founded a short-lived dynasty in Egypt; his father had been sent as a slave to Damascus. The Fatimids made some use of Mamluks, but it was under the Ayyubids that they became of dominant importance, financed by Egyptian agriculture. The Mamluks collected the revenues from large fiefs, work carried out previously by tax collectors.

In 1249, Crusaders, led by Saint Louis of France, occupied Damietta in the Nile Delta and seemed on the brink of conquering Egypt. At this juncture the sultan, al-Salih Ayyub, died. The crown prince succeeded him briefly but was unpopular and power was soon seized by the Mamluks, who had won the battle of al-Farikskur, when Louis and his nobles were captured and thousands of their followers killed. (Louis was ransomed; he died in 1270, besieging Tunis, pursuing the same impossible dream.)

Ayyub's concubine, Shajar al-Durr, was proclaimed sultana, and married to the first Mamluk sultan. She had him killed out of jealousy and was put to death herself, having first, legend claims, destroyed her jewels so that no other woman might wear them.

The Mamluks were to rule Egypt until 1517 – one episode in the millennia of foreign rule in its long history.

The Mongols

The Mongols, like the Turks, were horse archers from Central Asia, but comprised a distinct ethno-linguistic group. A leader of genius who took the title Genghiz Khan, Lord of the World, created an empire which stretched from Persia to Korea. The Mongol conquest of Persia and Iraq augmented the importance of Egypt as a leading Muslim nation. After Genghiz' death in 1227, his empire was divided into independent khanates, but the Mongol advance to the west continued. In 1250 Baghdad was taken, and the puppet Abbasid caliph put to death. The Mongols invaded Syria, but their seemingly inexorable advance was permanently halted by the Mamluks in 1260, at the battle of Goliath's Spring, often regarded as a crucial turning point in world history. Like all generalisations, this has been qualified: the Mongols were destined to return several times to Syria, and in any case, their long-term impact in the countries they did invade was limited. They became Muslims, and were much influenced by the cultures they ruled – another instance of the conquered taking the victor captive.

The Mamluks ruled Syria and Palestine from Egypt, finally expelling the Crusaders, a process completed, with terrible bloodshed, at the fall of Acre in 1291. Their victories over Crusaders and Mongols gave them a certain legitimacy, which they enhanced by preserving a line of puppet – and probably spurious – Abbasids in Cairo. The high cost of purchasing and training prospective Mamluks was sustained by the agricultural sector, and by a strategic location in international trade. Egypt re-exported the spices of Asia and sent textiles and ceramics to Russia in return for wood, furs and slaves. It was, of course, an exchange of manufactured goods for raw materials and human labour, the reverse of the situation which was to pertain in the external trade of sub-Saharan Africa.

The economic decline of Egypt began with the Black Death in the mid-fourteenth century. This was not the first time when plague had been recorded in the eastern Mediterranean: there was an outbreak in the sixth century in the reign of Justinian.[103] The impact of the Black Death has been much debated, and it has been pointed out that the standard of living of the individuals who survived may well have risen. But from the point of view of the Egyptian state, the loss of over a million people was a catastrophe without parallel. Bubonic plague became endemic and led to famine, since there were too few labourers to till the soil. It also affected the whole Mamluk system, since children became more difficult to obtain in the depopulated recruitment areas.

As the supply in the southern Russian steppes dried up, Circassians began to be recruited; in 1382, the Bahri (Kipchak) sultans were succeeded by the Circassian Burji Mamluks.[104]

From about 1400 Egypt was plunged in an ever-deepening financial crisis; it was intensified rather than ameliorated by the measures taken to combat it, such as drastic devaluation and the establishment of state monopolies, which drove many merchants into exile in India. The high price demanded by the Egyptian state for spices gave an extra impetus to the quest for an alternative route to India, to break its middleman role.

Meanwhile, other powers arose in the east. Another great conqueror from the steppes of Central Asia, Timur or 'Tamberlaine', embarked on wars of expansion which ravaged prosperous Syria. But it was the rise of the Ottoman Turks which was to have a direct effect on the history both of Egypt and of the Maghrib.

The Ottomans – the people of Othman – expanded first in the Balkans and then in Anatolia. They were defeated by Tamberlaine but this proved to be only a temporary setback. In 1453 they captured Constantinople, and with it the unchallenged leadership of the Muslim world. In 1498 Vasco da Gama reached India, and the Portuguese began to challenge Muslim control of Indian Ocean trade. The Mamluks made determined efforts to expel them, but were unsuccessful – not surprisingly, as their training and skills were in land-based warfare. The Portuguese, moreover, had firearms, which the Mamluks made little use of, wedded to a dream of chivalry which was already archaic, the horseman armed with nothing but his sword, bow and personal courage.

Many of the generalisations once made about this period have been eroded by modern scholarship. Egypt was not ruined as a result of the sea route to India – its economic decline had begun long before.

The Mamluks fell in the end to firearms, but not to the Portuguese: the Ottomans defeated them in Syria in 1516 and in Egypt the following year, largely by their effective use of powder weapons.

Nubia

By the end of the fifteenth century, Christianity in Nubia was virtually extinct, due not to foreign conquest but to the same process of bedouin immigration which led to the Arabisation of the Maghrib and Shinquit. The sheer impact of their numbers overwhelmed the Christian kingdoms, so that both the Islamic faith and Arabic speech became the norm. Ibn Khaldun wrote a moving requiem for Christian Nubia: 'Their kingdom was torn in pieces and the Juheina Arabs took possession of their country ... Not a trace of kingly authority remained in the country, and the people are now become bedouins, following the rains about as they do in Arabia.'[105]

At this time, the tradition of making fine pottery on the wheel had been lost and henceforth it was hand-made by women. Imported goods disappeared in the archaeological record; apparently both manufacturing and trade were affected by the disturbances of the times.[106] In 1315 the government of Egypt imposed a Nubian Muslim as the king of Makouria and in 1317 Dongala cathedral officially became a mosque. The tiny Christian splinter kingdom of Dotawo lasted until the late fifteenth century. Further south, the Christian kingdom of Alwa (Alodia) seems to have survived to about 1500. In 1523 a traveller visited its capital, Soba, and found it in ruins. Four hundred years later, local Arabs still swore an oath in the name of 'Soba the home of my grandfathers and grandmothers, which can make the stone float and the cotton boll sink'.[107]

Famine and disease

Famine and pestilence, dread Horsemen of the Apocalypse, are seldom absent for long in northern African history. We have mentioned the impact of the Black Death in Egypt; its 'terrible ravages'[108] were equally evident in the Maghrib in the late fourteenth century, and there were further outbreaks in the fifteenth, one of which is said to have killed 400,000 in the towns (where cramped living conditions always encouraged its spread) and 100,000 in the country.[109] Epidemics wrought their havoc on populations ravaged by hunger, and killed or weakened the workers needed to plant and reap a harvest. Hunger and disease were to be persistent motifs in northern African history in the centuries to come.[110]

12

The North-East

The original of the Abyssins, like that of all other nations, is obscure, and uncertain.

Jeronimo Lobo, in the early seventeenth century[1]

Somalia, Ethiopia and the southern Republic of Sudan do not constitute a usual unit of academic analysis (Map 11). Ethiopian history, like that of Egypt, has traditionally been a separate discipline, focussing on Aksum and the Solomonic monarchy. The fall of Haile Selassie in 1974 led to historical studies with different emphases, a good example of the way in which the study of the past is shaped by the realities of the present.[2] The name 'Abyssinia' is an unacceptable alternative to 'Ethiopia', because it refers only to the speakers of Ethiosemitic languages. Some scholars, however, make a conscious choice of 'Abyssinia' to refer to the past, a kind of shorthand for Amhara dominance, and boundaries more circumscribed than those of the modern nation.[3]

In north-east Africa, religion has long been a catalyst of identity. A distinctive form of Christianity defined the cultural perimeters of the Solomonic monarchy. Virtually all Somali have long been Muslims; most trace their ancestry to a putative Arab ancestor some twenty or twenty-five generations ago. Like comparable traditions elsewhere, this tells us less about physical descent than of a desire for personal identification with the homeland of Islam. Yet it is in a sense paradoxical that the inner core of national identity was symbolised by foreign descent; similarly, for much of Ethiopia's history, its kings have claimed descent from a putative son of Solomon and the queen of Sheba.

Somalia has few written records of great antiquity, apart from visitors' accounts of the coast; before the nineteenth century the Nuer and their neighbours have none at all. Aksumite inscriptions and Ge'ez manuscripts illuminate the Ethiopian past, as do sources in Arabic. Scholars, as so often, have tended to focus on literate societies to the neglect of others. There are three chapters on Aksum in the relevant volume of the UNESCO History of Africa, and a fourth on its South Arabian antecedents.

Here, as elsewhere, the pattern of life has been largely determined by the environment. The Beja are desert nomads who live near the Red Sea. This ethonym is an Arabic word, cognate with bedouin. The Somali live in a predominantly desert environment, and much of their history can be best understood in terms of competition for scarce pasturage and wells. Highland Ethiopia is saved by its altitude from aridity; its long conflicts with adjacent

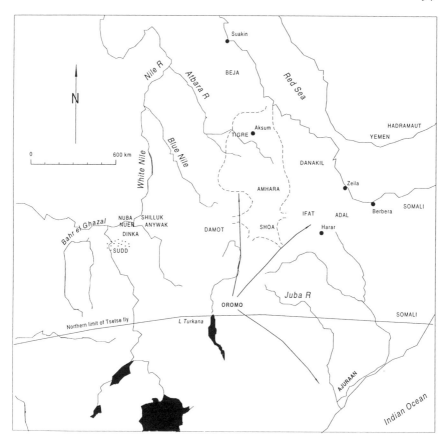

Map 11   The North-East

Muslim sultanates had an ecological dimension, as those living in the desiccated lowlands attempted to settle on the more fertile plateau.

Many large rivers have their origins in the Ethiopian highlands, carving deep canyons which impede communications and foster separate regional identities. Two-thirds of the Nile's waters originate here, mainly via the White Nile (Bahr el Jebel) and the Sobat. South of Lake No, the Bahr el Jebel flows into the Sudd. The word means barrier in Arabic; it is a tangle of watery vegetation, described almost two thousand years ago by two centurions Nero sent to discover the source of the Nile: 'we came to immense marshes the outcome of which neither the inhabitants knew, nor can anyone hope to know, in such a way are the plants entangled with the waters'.[4] The basin of the Bahr el Jebel and the Bahr el Ghazal, the home of the Nuer and their neighbours, is a zone of ecological extremes, with yearly phases of flooding and aridity, the context of their transhumant pastoralism. Further north lie the Nuba mountains, the home of many small and fragmented peoples.

In all these dramatically different environments, the local inhabitants developed an appropriate way of life and technology and an intimate knowledge of available resources, investing a familiar landscape with religious and symbolic meanings. The Konso live in stony hills in the far south of Ethiopia, and construct stone walls, terraces and pillars: 'Stone is as much a part of Konso life as soil. Their use of stone ... conveys a sense of harmony, order, and industry, and is in these respects a true expression of their values.'[5]

In north-eastern Africa, as elsewhere, ethonyms are often unsatisfactory, suggesting compartmentalised identities which are far removed from the ebb and flow of actual group interactions. 'Galla' was used until relatively recently for the people who call themselves Oromo. It is an Amharic word, with pejorative overtones. 'Sidama' is an Oromo word meaning non-Oromo.[6] 'Shankilla' is another pejorative ethonym used by Amharic speakers to refer to the lowlanders of the south and west. Yet one of these peoples, the Gumuz, has adopted it.[7]

Much of the African past must be seen through the eyes of racist and uncomprehending Europeans. But there was also racial prejudice in inter-group relations within Africa. The Amhara despised both Oromo and Shankilla, and their disdain is fossilised in proverbs ('Even if you wash them, stomach lining and a Galla never will come clean') and in the niceties of language which distinguish part-Shankilla descent to the seventh generation.[8]

The Somali peninsula

The word 'Somali' first appears in a Ge'ez hymn of the early fifteenth century.[9] Today, some 3 million Somali live in the Somali Democratic Republic, often called Somalia. Many modern African states struggle with the problem of the conflicting demands of multifarious ethno-linguistic groups, but all Somali have a sense of ethnic identity rooted in language, religion and the structure of their macroclans – though this has not precluded internal conflict in the past or present. A key goal of Somali nationalism has been to reunite Somalis divided by colonial boundaries:[10] a million Somali live in Ethiopia in the Ogaden, a quarter of a million in Kenya, and 100,000 in Djibouti.

Their early history must be gleaned from archaeological and linguistic evidence, supplemented by the accounts of travellers to the coast. Cosmas Indicopleustes was a sixth-century Alexandrian merchant turned monk, who wrote a book called *The Christian Topography*, with the intention of proving that the world is flat. On other issues, he was more reliable. 'The region which produces frankincense is situated at the projecting parts of Ethiopia ... The inhabitants of Barbaria, being near at hand, go up into the interior and engaging in traffic with the natives, bring back with them any kinds of spices, frankincense' and other items which they exported to the Yemen, India, Persia and Adulis, the port of Aksum.[11] Somalia, like Arabia, was valued as a source of myrrh and frankincense. These exports are depicted in Egyptian engravings of trading journeys to Punt and their importance is mirrored in the language of antiquity – 'Arabia *felix*'.

Most travellers' accounts concentrated on the coastal enclaves; a vignette from a ninth-century scholar in China sheds light on the pastoralists who in the twentieth century have formed 65 per cent of the population. 'The land of Po-pa-li [Barbaria, that is, the Somali peninsula] is in the south-western Ocean. The people do not eat any cereals but they eat meat: more frequently even they prick a vein of one of their oxen, mix the blood with milk and eat it raw.'[12]

The consumption of blood is a widespread pastoral trait in north-east Africa,[13] and it would be an anachronism to attempt to link this reference with any modern ethnic group. It sheds light on the antiquity of blood consumption, and reminds us of the paramount and enduring importance of pastoralism in the Horn of Africa.

The evidence of language makes it virtually certain that the original home of Eastern Cushitic speakers, such as the Somali and Oromo, was in southern Ethiopia, north of Lake Turkana. Eastern Cushitic languages began to diverge in the second millennium BCE, and nineteen out of a total of twenty-four are still spoken there. Somali is so closely related to Rendille, spoken by camel nomads in north Kenya, that the two are grouped as Somaloid.[14]

The Somali seem to have lived in the Horn of Africa for some two thousand years. Why they left a relatively well-watered zone where mixed farming is possible to live in virtual desert is totally obscure. Although most Somali are pastoralists, there are farming communities in the south, in the valleys of the Juba and Shabeelle rivers. Some at least are probably of Bantu descent. They were despised by the pastoralists, as the Maasai despised their farmer neighbours. Significantly Somali divides into two major dialects, one of which is spoken in this southern area.

The tsetse belt begins at 4 degrees north of the Equator. Camels were domesticated in South Arabia, in the Hadhramaut – not as pack or riding animals, but for their milk, and as a form of accumulation. They were probably first used as pack animals in the incense trade, between south and north Arabia. The Somali and their neighbours do not ride camels and make relatively little use of them as pack animals; they rely heavily on their milk and value them as a way of accumulating wealth. They were brought to the Horn of Africa from South Arabia in the early period of domestication and reflect its distinctive characteristics.[15]

Camels, used in the drier north, and cattle, more common in the south, have specific respective advantages and disadvantages. Camels are hardier and can travel further in search of forage, but cattle multiply more rapidly. These basic facts have many implications for pastoralist lifestyles and social organisation. Like the pastoral Fulbe in West Africa, the Somali practised transhumance, moving to lush wet-season pastures in the rains and clustering round inherited wells in the dry season. A typical social unit had two or more herders and about a hundred stock. To deal with the ecological crises common in a barren land, the Somali developed various strategies which may be compared with those documented elsewhere in Africa. They relied above all on their detailed knowledge of the environment and the physical mobility which enabled them to take advantage of its varied resources. Just as destitute Maasai took refuge with farming or hunter-gatherer communities, drought-stricken Somali left their women, children and elderly members with relatives in coastal towns to lessen the demands on their herds. They kept a large number of stock, so that they could sell or slaughter the surplus in times of drought. Different clans formed alliances and offered each other access to wells and pastures when disaster threatened, for the impact of drought was often local. They could also turn to other occupations, such as collecting gum and incense for sale on the coast. If all else failed, a clan would enter into clientage with another, in order to use its wells and pastures. Pastoralists followed conscious policies of conservation, refraining from the use of dry-season pasture during the rains.

On the northern and southern peripheries of Somalia, cosmopolitan ports developed, with a partially Arab culture: at Zeila (Seylac) on the Gulf of Aden, and Mogadishu on the Benaadir coast. Interestingly, this Arab element was not in evidence in the many smaller coastal towns in between. Each clan was linked with a specific town, and some coastal communities underwent a process of 'bedouinisation' due to nomad immigration. This is documented in Mogadishu from the sixteenth century on.

The physical mobility of the pastoralist, the fluidity of power structures, and the absence of fixed boundaries are all, perhaps, different faces of the same social reality: 'the precise location of a pastoral group in space ... is an ambiguous enterprise ... the ... end of each tribal territory is devoid of boundary'.[16] All modern Somali belong to one of six macro-clans, only one of which is confined to a particular region. Each claims a common ancestor twenty or twenty-five generations removed. Al-Idrisi, an Arab geographer at the Sicilian court, mentioned one of them, the Hawiyya, in the early twelfth century. Macro-clans were essentially a social device, facilitating the sharing of regional resources by diverse herding groups. There were also some fifty exogamous clans, which were, of course, much smaller than the macro-clans. The lowest unit of common action comprised those who agreed to pay blood wealth for each other, that for murder, for instance, being the alternative to reprisal killings and lasting feuds.

Nomads acquire few possessions and build few structures which endure. There is therefore an especial interest in burial sites excavated west of Lake Turkana, which seem to have been the work of Eastern Cushites in *c.* 300 BCE.[17] Most of those buried there were adult males, and the rocks were decorated with engravings of cattle brands.

The Lake Turkana tombs were made of great stone slabs, some of which weighed as much as 10.5 tons. It is tempting to link them with the modern Konso, the only Eastern Cushites who bury their dead in cemeteries. The prediction of weather changes was crucial in this region; weather experts were highly esteemed, and part of their craft was a knowledge of astronomy and astrology. Modern Eastern Cushites have a sophisticated 12-month 354-day calendar based on the risings of seven stars. One of these megalithic burial sites has a series of basalt pillars aligned to the rising of all seven.

Clans rarely acted as decision-taking units, and when they did, policy was determined at an assembly of adult males. But despite this, and despite the physical mobility of herding groups, a number of states did develop, when a group rose to dominance, perhaps through control of scarce resources, especially wells. The Ajuraan established a state in southern Somalia, between the Juba and Shabeele rivers, sixteen to twenty generations ago. Tradition stresses the orthodoxy of their beliefs and the harshness of their rule; they are associated with stone wells and other structures which still exist. These oral traditions are replete with familiar stereotypes. The line began with an Arab progenitor first encountered in a tree; the Ajuraan were allied with a legendary race of giants, the counterparts of the small-statured autochthenes we have noted elsewhere. But at the heart of the myth there is a kernel of historical truth. In the early seventeenth century, the Ajuraan were overthrown in a popular rising, yet another instance of the nemesis which befell tyrannical kings.

The northern Muslim principalities

We know more about the sultanates which grew up to the east of the Ethiopian plateau, sustained in large part by their control of the trade routes from Zeila to the interior. They seem to have been dominated by Ethiosemitic, rather than Eastern Cushitic speakers. The first Muslims in the area were merchants, who maintained peaceful relations with Christian Ethiopia for centuries. Christian–Muslim conflict began in the twelfth century, the time when the earliest known sultanate was created in the region – Shoa, situated east of the plateau of that name. Ifat was a powerful successor state in the same region, which flourished for a hundred years until defeated by Ethiopia in 1332. Adal, on the Harar plateau, was founded in *c.* 1520 and was actively supported by the distant polity of Mogadishu.[18] The Imam Ahmad, who almost destroyed the Christian kingdom in the sixteenth century, waged his campaigns with the aid of Somali troops, and these holy wars also attracted many Arab immigrants. There were many other smaller and sometimes transient principalities: one Arabic source mentions the 'seven Muslim states of Ethiopia'.[19]

North–south migration

Although the Somali originally migrated from south to north, during the last millennium there has been considerable reverse migration. In a sense, since it is a move from an arid zone to a more favoured one, it requires little explanation though, as Cassanelli points out, where survival depends on knowledge of the environment, movement to an unfamiliar one is not undertaken lightly. Periods of drought may have contributed to the expansion of camel-owning groups; camels could survive in areas where cattle could not, but their close cropping of available fodder caused the environment to deteriorate to a point where the latter could no longer survive. Pressure from Arab immigrants may also have had the effect of displacing Somali pastoralists further south.

Somali women

Where Somali poetry speaks with passion and desire, it expresses a thirst for God rather than human love. The world we have described up to this point is a male one. Somali women endure the hardships and deprivations of the nomadic life and also an additional insecurity, since they are readily divorced. They are excluded from public worship in the mosque and are subjected to the most extreme form of genital mutilation – not only clitoridectomy, but also infibulation.[20] According to Ioan Lewis, 'Somali women have a strong and explicit sense of sexual solidarity and feelings of grievance and antagonism towards men', and often find solace in the *zar* spirit possession cult,[21] which is also popular among women in Cairo and Ethiopia. Here, as elsewhere, spirit possession cults have a special appeal to women, and to poor and marginalised men. There are currently over a hundred *zar* spirits, whose roles women enact in a parody and critique of the society in which they find themselves.[22]

Ethiopia

Conventional histories of Ethiopia fall into two main phases, the first dealing with Aksum, the second with the Solomonic monarchy. Between them, from 1050 to 1170, was the brilliant if short-lived era of the Zagwe (that is, Agaw) kings. Historians have tended to focus on the Amharic monarchy to the exclusion of other Ethiopian peoples but more recent work provides a salutary corrective to this tendency.[23]

The evidence of language

Aksum was founded by Semitic-speaking immigrants from south-east Arabia (the modern Yemen) who settled in northern Ethiopia, among an Agaw (Central Cushitic) population. The conventional date, based on archaeology, is *c.* 600 BCE, but linguistic evidence suggests that Ethiosemitic diverged from South Arabian before 2000 BCE.[24] If, as seems likely, the Afroasiatic phyllum first evolved on the African side of the Red Sea, this was in fact a reverse migration.

Aksum's composite culture was symbolised in the folk etymology which interprets 'Aksum' as an Agaw word for water coupled with a Semitic word for ruler.[25] The language of Aksum developed into Ge'ez, which incorporates both Cushitic and Greek elements. Spoken from *c.* 400 to *c.* 900 CE, it then became the classical written medium of Ethiopian literature and liturgy, playing a role similar to that of Latin in medieval Europe. The script evolved from the consonantal writing of South Arabia and Aksum, with vowels added; it is thought to have influenced the alphabet of Armenia.[26]

There are some seventy distinct languages in Ethiopia, most of them Afroasiatic.[27] It is difficult to ascertain the relationship between the Ethiosemitic languages because of the high incidence of mutual borrowing. They are variously divided into two or three branches which separated in the first millennium BCE. North Ethiosemitic – Tigre and Tigrinya – is spoken on the northern edge of the Ethiopian plateau, and in Eritrea. They are 'the most archaic living Ethiosemitic languages'.[28] There are 3.5 million Tigrinya speakers. Tigre, not to be confused with Tigrinya-speaking Tigre province, has 120,000 speakers, desert nomads on the shores of the Red Sea, closely linked with the Beja, some of whom speak Tigre as a second language.

There are fifteen Southern Ethiosemitic languages and dialects, including the Gurage cluster, which were not, in the past, written down. Spoken by some 500,000 people, they lack the Greek and Cushitic elements of the northern branch.[29] It seems likely that they are not descended from Ge'ez, but represent separate South Arabian contacts, probably an immense number of trade or other encounters over centuries. Central Ethiosemitic (Amharic and related dialects, with 7,800,000 speakers) is intermediate between North and South Ethiosemitic and has interacted closely with both. It has been much influenced by the liturgical language, Ge'ez, and independently incorporates much Cushitic vocabulary and syntax.[30] Amharic speakers have also absorbed a number of Cushitic culture traits such as the fish taboo. It is likely that Amharic is the end product of 'a process of pidginization and creolization'.[31]

The original Amhara heartland was in Wello, east of the Blue Nile and its tributaries, the Bashilo and Wanchet, and west of the escarpment which overlooks the Danakil plains, but Amharic is now the first language of many, such as the Falasha, who were originally Agaw speakers.

Ethiosemitic speakers were not contiguous with the Ethiopian Christian monarchy. We have noted their dominance in the northern sultanates, and most Gurage have practised traditional religion into modern times.[32] Modern Muslim Ethiosemitic speakers are called Jabarti. There are four branches of Cushitic (five, before Omotic was recognised as a separate entity). There is only one North Cushitic language, Beja, spoken by Red Sea desert nomads – the Blemmyes of antiquity. Central Cushitic comprises Agaw and related languages, Eastern Cushitic includes Somali and Oromo and Southern Cushitic survives only in tiny enclaves far to the south. Beja in the extreme north and Iraqw in the extreme south preserve the most archaic features (the conservatism of the periphery is quite common in language history and is paralleled, among Romance languages, by archaic survivals in Sardinian). Agaw was once the language of much of the Ethiopian highlands; today it survives only in scattered enclaves. Omotic languages are spoken only in south-west Ethiopia by fifty small, distinct ethno-linguistic groups.[33]

Ancient Aksum

For many centuries both Ethiopians and South Arabians have crossed the narrow straits which separate them. An Aksumite king invaded the Yemen in the sixth century CE, and Muslim Habasha (Ethiopian) slaves established an emirate there in the eleventh and early twelfth centuries. As we shall see, both Habasha and Himyar became important metaphors in the historical and social discourse of the Western Sudan. At some historical periods, the Red Sea has been a flourishing commercial waterway; at others a backwater, when trade was attracted to the Persian Gulf instead. The Ptolemies developed Red Sea trade, as did the Roman and Byzantine rulers of Egypt after them, and Aksum, with its Red Sea port, Adulis, prospered accordingly. It seems to have taken over much of the commercial role of Meroe, an entrepot where African products were exported in return for a wide range of international merchandise. Aksum was a cosmopolitan enclave on the edge of the Hellenistic world. We have mentioned the first-century king Zoscales, who was literate in Greek, as doubtless were many of his subjects. Buddhists, Jews and Egyptians practised their respective religions in Adulis, and by 400 CE there were Aksumite traders in India and Ceylon. Unlike Meroe, Aksum minted its own currency; its splendid stelae, towers of solid masonry, with non-functional doors and windows, were an early manifestation of a major indigenous tradition of monumental architecture in stone, which later found expression in the rock-hewn churches of the Zagwe kings.

In Egypt and the Maghrib, the first Christian converts were humble people, often women. In Aksum, the first recorded Christians were at the king's court. Ezana, a contemporary of the first Christian Roman emperor, Constantine, was converted to Christianity by Graeco-Phoenician brothers from Tyre. One of them, Frumentius, became the first bishop of Aksum. Ezana's earlier inscriptions honour the Aksumite gods Mahrem, Baher, Meder, and the South Arabian Astarte, goddess of the evening star.[34] His later ones reflect first a generalised monotheism and then a definite adherence to Christianity. It is likely that there were Christians in the trading community who had already disseminated their faith, as so many Muslim merchants in Africa were to do later. It is possible, too, that he was influenced by the illustrious example of Constantine. Kaplan has interpreted his conversion in terms of Horton's famous thesis, that as a community establishes linkages with a wider world, its local divinities become less appropriate to its needs.[35]

The Ethiopian church became part of the Monophysite movement; this allegiance was strengthened by the work of Syrian missionaries, remembered as the Nine Saints. Christianity was to be fundamental to national identity both in Aksum and in its successor states. Until the advent of Islam, Aksum was part of a great continuum of Christian nations in Egypt, Nubia, Syria and Arabia. Afterwards, it became increasingly isolated, and trade was deflected away from the Red Sea by the attractive power of the new Abbasid capital, Baghdad. The Ethiopian church continued to obtain its head, the *abuna*, from the Coptic church in Egypt, a complicated process when this became a minority body under Muslim rule.

We know relatively little about Ethiopian history beween *c.* 500 CE and the accession of the Zagwe kings in 1050. No internal records survive, and we rely on glimpses in Arabic sources and the records of the Patriarchate of Alexandria. Perhaps because of pressure from the Red Sea nomads, the capital shifted south to Kubar, apparently in the Lake Hayq area, an interesting parallel to the general shift southward in Nubia, noted elsewhere in this book.

The gradual colonisation of areas further south, their incorporation, where possible, into the Christian-Ethiosemitic plough agriculture culture sphere, is the central theme of Ethiopian history for over a thousand years. The view from within, the writings of Ethiopian chroniclers, focusses on the Christianising impact of monks and monastic schools, and the conquests of kings. Modern scholarship has laid increasing emphasis on ecology and political economy.

The kingdom and the periphery

One of the few Africanists with a global perspective, the anthropologist Jack Goody, has explored the social implications of varying economic systems in a series of immensely influential books which have a direct bearing on our understanding of Ethiopia.[36] He argues that in feudal Europe technological improvements, especially the plough, made land a scarce resource and enabled individuals to create a surplus, which in turn supported an elite class. Women's inheritance rights, especially the dowry, led to arranged marriages within social classes. In most of Africa, the limitations of hoe agriculture prevented the accumulation of this kind of surplus. Land was relatively abundant. Ruling elites relied, not on land rights but on tribute and imposts on trade, and there were few barriers to marriage between social classes. Ethiopia, he believed, was an exception, its plough economy mirrored in greater social stratification.

Ethiopian specialists, however, seem agreed that its nobility controlled tribute rather than land. Even the former was precarious, since the king could revoke the right to levy it at any time. The peasants were divided between tenants and landholders; the word for the former was cognate with 'smoke', mirroring their precarious tenure. The artisan castes, as we noted in another context, could not own land at all (pp. 95–6 above), and the Amharic word for lord means to vanquish or expropriate. Donham makes suggestive comparisons between the authority of the church, the relationship of lord and peasant, and male control of the household. The lord's field worked by peasant labour was *hudad*, which also means Lenten fast.

An Amharic proverb states, 'A woman and a donkey can't be kept straight without the stick,'[37] but the marginalisation of women was not peculiar to Amhara. A book written in Harar stated that all knowledge can be reduced to 4,000 precepts, which in their turn are reducible to four. The first is, do not trust women.[38]

Ethiopian society could be defined as rapacity tempered by potential mobility; since descent was reckoned in both male and female lines, most peasants had some noble forebears, and could hope to enrich themselves in war.

Since the nobility did not control production, they had little interest in innovation. An Armenian built a windmill for a sixteenth-century Ethiopian king, which the latter dismantled, since he could not transport it on his journeys round his kingdom, 'as if', noted an observer, 'the device could serve only where he himself happened to be and not the people of his entire kingdom'.[39]

Various factors made it necessary to keep extending the tribute-paying area, among them the increasing independence of provincial elites, who tended to retain the surplus extracted; environmental degradation as the result of intensive farming; and 'the growing adeptness of peasant resistance'.[40] All Ethiopia's successive capitals have been placed on high ground overlooking both tribute-paying countryside and trade routes. Ethnic divisions as perceived by Ethiopians – Amhara, Oromo, Shankilla – reflect at least in part the degree of economic assimilation to highland society. 'The "Shankilla" of the lowlands were in effect unassimilable as much for ecological as for ethnic reasons; their lands could not be turned over to the plough.'[41]

Whatever the shortcomings of Amharic society, the ideology of the Christian monarchy rose above ethnic consciousness. It created a national identity, to which non-Ethiosemitic speakers could subscribe, albeit often at the cost of their own language and culture. Beyond its boundaries, the Omotic polities adopted Amharic political vocabulary and symbolism.

Studies of Ethiopian history in the nineteenth and twentieth centuries often focus on peasant resistance.[42] The records of a thousand years earlier stress the resistance of rulers. In the mid-tenth century, a queen who 'ruled with complete independence in her own country' (probably Damot) waged a long and successful struggle against the Aksumite monarchy. The struggle had an ideological dimension: she was hostile to Christianity, and her forces sacked churches and killed a Christian king.[43] The traditional chronicle of Shoa begins with a queen, 'Badit, daughter of Maya'. We know her name but nothing of her life. In the case of the queen of Damot, we know a little of her life but not her name.

Between a militant Islamic world to the north and hostile traditionalists to the south, Abyssinians felt increasingly isolated and beleaguered. There was an increasing sense of identity with ancient Israel,[44] and Ethiopia became Siyon, her people identified with the Twelve Tribes of Israel.

Lalibela, the greatest of the Zagwe kings, rebuilt Jerusalem on Ethiopian soil, complete with the Mount of Olives and Calvary. A strong sense of identification with the Old Testament, a religious sensibility attuned to the sacred places, threads its way through the African independent churches in the twentieth century. It is no coincidence that they are called Ethiopian.

Ethiopians kept the Sabbath holy as well as Sunday and observed Jewish dietary taboos. Old Testament precedents confirmed their devout kings in polygamy: they had four principal queens. Ethiopians fasted with a severity unparalleled in Christendom. In the nineteenth century, they exported coffee but were forbidden to drink it. Their church is unique in that it springs direct from its Hebraic roots, uninfluenced by Greek philosophy.

Gebre Christos, patron saint of lepers, was a king's son who renounced his wealth and prayed for leprosy in order to share the sufferings of Christ. His prayer was answered.[45]

There is no more potent myth in African history than the legend which traces the 'Solomonic monarchy' to the son of a union between Solomon and the Queen of Sheba, who is thought to have brought the original Ark of the Covenant to Ethiopia. The first reference to the legend is in the tenth century; it was gradually elaborated until it reached its final form in the *Kebra Nagast*, Book of Kings, first written in Arabic in the early fourteenth century. A composite work, distilled originally from oral tradition, it was recorded by Tigrinya scribes from Aksum but became the founding charter of an Amharic monarchy, a monarchy which always recognised the spiritual primacy of Aksum.

The Zagwe kings reigned only from 1150 to 1270. Their capital, Adefa, was 350 kilometres south of Aksum, and Lalibela's rock-hewn churches are their enduring memorial. It seems that the Solomonic legend was elaborated in their time as an ideology of opposition. The new dynasty was founded by a nobleman from Amhara. That it has been generally described as 'Solomonic' and seen as a restoration, that in modern times Haile Selasse claimed the title of Lion of Judah, shows the myth's extraordinary tenacity and persuasiveness. After the Zagwe fell, Ethiopian kings ceased to build in stone. The dynasty which replaced them was peripatetic, moving from one region to the next, and exacting tribute until the local capacity to support the court was exhausted. It tackled the problem of political disunity in draconian fashion, imprisoning all princes but the children of the reigning king in a mountain-top fastness at Gishen.

The new kingdom was only one of many independent states. The foundations of its expansion were laid in the reign of Amda Siyon (1314–44), whose conquests were so great that he was called, with pardonable exaggeration, a ruler over ninety-nine kings. Zara Ya'qob (1434–68) extended its boundaries still further. It was not only political authority which expanded, but also the Amharic language and culture sphere and the Christian religion. Zara Ya'qob insisted that his new subjects be tattooed with an acknowledgement of the Trinity. Even in its heyday, the medieval monarchy was far smaller than the modern state of Ethiopia, which owes its boundaries to the expansion of nineteenth-century rulers.

It inherited endemic conflict with the Muslim sultanates. The greatest of the Muslim generals was the imam Ahmad, whom Ethiopians remember as el Gragn, the Lefthanded. He won an epic victory over the Christian kingdom in 1529 which almost, but not quite, destroyed it, creating an alliance which included Somali clans and Abyssinia's long-standing foes in Shoa and elsewhere. But Ahmad was defeated and killed in 1543, in one of the decisive battles of African history, and the alliance, already under strain, died with him.

In all these wars it was the peasants who suffered most. It was said in the seventeenth century, 'The Poverty of the Souldiers impoverishes the Countries through which they march.'[46] A nineteenth-century emperor put it more succinctly: 'Soldiers eat; peasants provide.'[47] Some peasant risings are on record; one in the late seventeenth century was led by Isaac the Inciter, a member of one of the marginalised metal-working castes. 'After him went all the foolish and wicked who were escaping from poverty.'[48]

The Falasha

Falasha is a pejorative but familiar name for the people who call themselves Beta Israel, the Ethiopian Jews whose conversion probably dates back to Judaic influences from South Arabia. Originally Agaw speakers, the language survives only in their liturgy, and they now speak Amharic. They had no knowledge of Hebrew or the Talmud. By the early fifteenth century they had been defeated by the Amharic monarchy and allowed to keep their land only if they became Christians. They were forced either to withdraw to economically marginal areas or to turn to crafts. They preserved their literature and culture in part by adopting monasticism. In the seventeenth and early eighteenth centuries, they became partially assimilated in Amharic society, acquiring land and titles. But in the Age of the Princes (1755–1855) they became increasingly marginalised, associated with the evil eye, and ever more rigidly identified with blacksmithing and pottery making.[49] This well-documented example sheds light on patterns of caste formation elsewhere.

Marginalised occupational castes – smiths and tanners, and sometimes potters and hunters – are widespread in Ethiopia. Often, they play important religious and magical roles. It has been suggested that they reinforce the self-image of the dominant society by embodying the Other. Because they are on the edges of society, they can more readily mediate with the spirit world.[50] There are striking similarities with caste in the Western Sudan. But in the latter case, we have accounts from within,[51] which show that their members perceive their own role, not as marginalised, but as one of supernatural power – in the words of an important book on the subject, a realm of knowledge, power and art.

The Nuer and their neighbours

The basin of the Upper Nile, dissected by its tributaries the White Nile and the Bahr al-Ghazal, is one of the most extreme habitats in the world. In the rainy season it is covered with floodwaters, and settlements cluster precariously on mounds crowded with herders and cattle. If grazing is inadequate, stock must be taken on perilous journeys through crocodile-infested waters. Here, as elsewhere, river crossing is a seminal metaphor in oral tradition. In the dry season, the plains are arid and sun-parched, life is sustainable only near river banks, and stinging flies torment people and cattle alike. In recent times, the Dinka and their neighbours have been decimated by famine and war, but the shadow of death has never been far from their arid homeland.

> My grandmother, my grandmother, Aluel,...
> She came with a glory which God denied:
> A great lady who bore multitudes of children,
> But consumed her hoes digging their graves.[52]

The largest ethnic group, the Dinka, numbered just over a million according to the 1955–6 census, the Nuer just under half a million – though estimates vary considerably[53] – the Atuot[54] 50,000, the Luo of the Bahr-al-Ghazal 16,000. These ethnonyms are highly artificial. 'Dinka' is a British adaptation of an Arabic form of Jaang, a pejorative name applied by the Nuer to defeated neighbours. But, more profoundly, we must ask in what sense were 'Dinka' and 'Nuer' (or 'Jieng' and 'Naath') meaningful categories in pre-colonial times? It seems clear that in the past the most significant social unit was not 'Jieng' but sections such as Rek or Bor, many of which were widely dispersed, like the Somali macro-clans. The Nuer and the Dinka speak different Western Nilotic languages, which are more closely related to each other than to any others.

The Nuer are almost entirely surrounded by Dinka and, at least since the nineteenth century, have been expanding at the latter's expense. Evans-Pritchard, in a passage which is an interesting example of an anthropologist's unconscious identification with the values of the people studied, writes: 'Nuer have a proper [*sic*] contempt for Dinka and are derisive of their fighting qualities ... These boasts are justified both in the unflinching bravery of the Nuer and by their military success.'[55] To ask when the 'Nuer' separated from the 'Dinka' is, of course, to revert to the oversimplifications we have just critiqued. A number of attempts have been made to answer this and allied questions on the basis of linguistic evidence, despite the problems created by diversity of dialects and mutual borrowing. Ehret suggests that proto-Western Nilotic was spoken before 2000 BCE and that proto-Nuer/Dinka and proto-Luo developed about 3,000 years ago.[56]

The peoples of the upper Nile basin have few possessions but their cattle. Nineteenth-century western observers, confusing material simplicity with intellectual and cultural poverty, despised them. In 1866 Samuel Baker called the

White Nile 'a place where man is represented by so abject and low a type that the mind repels the idea that he is of our Adamic race ... The mind is as stagnant as the morass which forms its puny world.'[57]

Thanks to the justly celebrated anthropological studies by Evans-Pritchard and Lienhardt, the closely related religions of the Nuer and Dinka are now perhaps more widely appreciated than those of any other African people. In their analysis, the life of the Western Nilotes is permeated by a consuming passion for cattle. Their languages are rich in cattle terminology: there are several hundred terms for cattle colour configurations; both men and women take cattle names, and songs in praise of a cherished ox are a major form of oral literature. The very ethonym Atuot comes from *tuot*, bull.

More recent studies have pointed to certain imbalances in these classic works, including their agnosticism about many aspects of historical process. Evans-Pritchard believed that 'even a tentative reconstruction of their historical relations with each other which led to the formation of two distinct cultures is out of the question'.[58] The romantic identification with male pastoral values led to the relative, but not absolute, neglect of fishing and cultivation.[59] Of central importance in the diet, both are mainly the sphere of women, who also milk the cows. In a sense, male pastoral values are a form of false consciousness, bearing little relation to the real facts of production, which are, indeed, mirrored in myth and ritual. The sacred leader of a Dinka community is the Master of the *Fishing* Spear. Dinka myth tells of a time when people could subsist on a single grain of millet, and that the earth and sky separated when a woman struck the heavens while pounding grain. Kir, the culture hero who led the easternmost Nuer, the eastern Jikany, to their present home, was born in a pumpkin. These persistent agricultural and piscatorial metaphors are closer to the realities of subsistence than the romantic values of pastoralism. The separation of Nuer and Atuot is attributed to a dispute over inherited cattle. The Atuot ancestor obtains the valuable calf and the brothers separate for ever. The Nuer tell much the same story, of how a Dinka obtained a cow by deceit and thereafter the Nuer legitimately regained cattle by force of arms. Another Nuer myth, cited earlier in this book, tells how the primordial cow sought revenge for her mother's death by causing disputes among people about debts and bridewealth. The proto-Dinka, it seems, divided into different ethnic groups when they acquired cattle and, with them, the need for control of pasture and water.[60]

Recent excavations of mounds at Dhang Rial, in an area now inhabited by Dinka, showed that between the eighth and the thirteenth centuries CE, they were inhabited by people who kept cattle, hunted and fished. They wore jewellery made from iron and mollusc shells, their pottery was decorated with twisted cord roulettes and they made clay images of humpless cattle. There were traces of permanent habitation.[61] It is noteworthy that the skeletons found here and elsewhere lacked the dental evulsion which is an important parameter of identity for modern Western Nilotes. Later the clay images were of humped cattle and the permanent dwellings disappeared. Did the local people adopt the hardier zebu cattle, and with them a transhumant lifestyle? Did consequent territorial expansion, in search of water and pasture, set off a chain reaction which led to

the migration of Luo speakers far to the south, which is dimly imaged in myths
about conflict over the inheritance of cattle?

The expansion of the Nuer at the expense of the Dinka is well attested in the
nineteenth century and seems to be a much older phenomenon. It has been
interpreted in ecological terms (the relative lack of high ground for wet-season
settlement in the Nuer heartland), in demographic terms (the increasing pressure
of people and herds on resources) and in cultural terms (the need to raid for
stock for bridewealth).[62] These explanations are not mutually exclusive; rather,
they present different aspects of the same phenomenon. The Nuer, it seems
universally agreed, grew out of a 'proto-Dinka' culture base. One of the basic
dimensions of their sense of identity was their predatory relationship with the
regularly raided Dinka. Although more numerous, the Dinka seem to have
offered little resistance. The Nuers' success has been attributed to their greater
capacity for co-ordinated action, the segmentary agnatic lineage a 'predatory
mutation' for this purpose.[63] In this sytem – also found among the Berbers and
among many far from predatory agricultural communities – the entire society is
conceptualised as the descendants of a single ancestor. The members of a
component lineage – the descendants, for instance, of a putative grandson of the
founder – can act together when their common interests are at stake but do not
do so otherwise.[64] Johnson has questioned many of these theories: 'the theory of
segmentary opposition works better in principle than in practice. We find Nuer
siding with Anuak against Nuer . . . It is an exaggeration to describe the Nuer as
acephalous . . . By the 1930s Nuer society was not so much acephalous as
decapitated.'[65] Having conquered the Dinka, the Nuer proceeded to incorporate
at least some of them into their own society. Among the Lou, as many as 75 per
cent were of Dinka descent: 'The peculiarity is that, having emerged, the Naath
proceeded to incorporate Jieng to such an extent that they became again, in a
secondary sense, more than half Jieng themselves.'[66]

The Spear and the Bead

There are few episodes in the history of ideas in Africa which are more
fascinating than the permutations of the myth of the Spear and the Bead, found
not only among the Nuer, Dinka and Shilluk, but also, far to the south, among
the Luo-speaking Alur and Acholi.

The Shilluk (or Collo) are the most northerly of the Luo-speaking people, and
their riverain kingdom is perhaps Africa's most famous instance of sacred (or
'divine') kingship, expressed in terms of the culture hero, Nyikang, first Shilluk
and first king. A story which is in essence the same is told both by the Shilluk and
the Luo of the Bahr-al-Ghazal to explain their parting.[67]

Nyikang threw a spear belonging to his brother Dimo at an elephant, and the
wounded beast carried it away. Dimo refused to accept a substitute spear and
Nyikang was forced to embark on a long, dangerous journey to recover the one
that was lost. He reached the land of elephants, who proved to have both a
forgiving nature and a penchant for metamorphosis. An old woman, variously
called the Mother or Queen of the Elephants, gave him the spear and he returned
home. But the journey had a dreadful sequel. Dimo's child swallowed a bead

belonging to Nyikang; substitutes were refused, and the child was cut open to recover it. The brothers then parted for ever.

A virtually identical story is told by the Acholi and Alur of Uganda and Zaire, far to the south. In this southern version, the brothers (with different names) parted at a still identifiable point on the White Nile called Pubungu. They drove an axe into the river bed as a symbol of separation. The dry river bed has sometimes been taken as a reference to drought; the Pubungu diaspora, widely accepted as historical, is conventionally dated to the fifteenth century (see p. 138).

Among the Nuer and Dinka, the Spear and Bead stories are told independently. In one version, it is a cow which is sacrificed and becomes a clan totem, and in another, it is a cobra which is speared, and snakes which in due course not only return the spear but provide a bride.

Modern Nuer and Dinka, other than the western-educated, have no contact with or knowledge of their southern cousins such as the Alur. These stories belong to an ancient substratum of West Nilotic culture. That they have been preserved so tenaciously shows their profound significance to those who preserve them.

Like all myths, these stories have many dimensions of meaning. As in *The Merchant of Venice*, they emphasise the folly of insisting on one's pound of flesh.[68] The magnanimity of 'dangerous' wild animals or snakes – the elephants and cobras – contrasts with the cruelty of humanity. The Nuer or Dinka paid bloodwealth in cattle for loss of life; the only alternatives were a perpetual feud or physical separation.

The Dinka and Nuer have no kings, and beads and spears (other than the ritual spear of the Dinka Spearmaster) are of little importance to them. Among the Alur and Shilluk, they are emblems of royalty, and the myths at one level describe a struggle for political power. The Shilluk call their royal beads, collectively, Nyikang, and an Alur king at his accession put a bead in the mouth of his dead predecessor in 'a symbolic re-enactment of the myth in which Nyabongo's son swallowed the bead of Thiful'.[69] The dead child stands for all the human sacrifices which have enhanced the sacred character of African rulers. In a text collected among the Luo of the Bahr-al-Ghazal, the 'feelings of sorrow and revenge' it produced are explicit, as is the sense that life is infinitely more precious than property: 'Now that my daughter has died because of your daughter's cowrie we shall separate, it is not possible to live together any more, we shall never meet again on this earth.'[70] A figure previous analysis has overlooked is the 'old woman', who is variously depicted as the queen or mother (the two are, in this context, synonyms) of the elephants. The old woman is a recurrent figure in African myth. She plays a central role in the traditions of origin of the Turkana of northern Kenya and the Kaguru of central Tanzania.[71] Among the latter, the old woman and the fire she lights have been interpreted as a metaphor for the creation of society. Her significance in the land of the elephants remains obscure. Perhaps it is an instance of mythical inversion: in the real world, brothers struggle for power; in the mythical land of anthropomorphic elephants, an old woman is dominant.

Insofar as the story of the spear and the bead is part of a far-flung network of

Nilotic culture, the mytheme may be seen as part of an ancient shared heritage. But at Cabinda, far away, in the Kongo culture zone, a virtually identical story is told – the spear carried away in an elephant's side, the search, the return with magical gifts – and the insistence on the recovery, not of a swallowed bead, but of a banana eaten by a child. In this case, it is the second brother, not the child who is the victim, and he becomes a slave.[72]

13

The Western Sudan

There were Mallams and holy men in the country in such numbers that God alone could count them. But their history is not known because no one has written books about their country.

Muhammad Bello on Ahir, in c. 1812[1]

Environments

The Sahara has often been compared with a sea; its southern edge is the sahel, a word Arabic in origin which means shore; – 'Swahili' is another form of it. But it is much more varied than any ocean, broken by rocky massifs such as the Haggar, and dissected by the beds of rivers long since dry. The great northward sweep of the Niger bend carves its way deep into the desert, making irrigation possible along its banks. Latitude and rainfall go together with almost mathematical precision. The desert has less than 200 mm of rain a year; rainfall increases by 200 mm with every degree south.[2]

Desert and sahel merge imperceptibly into each other; further south, the sahel, equally gradually, becomes savanna – a park-like landscape dotted with the legend-encrusted baobab and the shea butter tree. It was said of Sundiata (see p. 225 below) that his southward conquests ended where the shea butter tree ceased to grow. The savanna is the home *par excellence* of grain cultivation, especially of millet and sorghum. Gradually, as one moves south, the vegetation becomes more abundant and the staples change, until the landscape is crowded with fruit trees, yam, maize and cassava plots, and oil palms.

Continuing climate change probably provided the context for much savanna and sahel history. Rainfall began to increase from the beginning of the Christian era, and 700–1100 CE was a relatively wet period, followed by a dry phase from 1100 to 1500.[3] The desert-edge state of Ghana flourished in the wet phase and declined in the dry phase – the time of Mali's greatness (Map 12). It was during the dry phase that the government of Kanem moved south to Borno. Trans-Saharan trade routes expanded in the wet phase, when conditions were less adverse than they later became. Not all scholars agree that the decline of Ghana or the shift to Borno were caused by long-term climatic change. Another view is that the fall of these oasis states, which grew up on the desert edge and were sustained predominantly by trade, was a reflection of their inherent fragility,[4] and that the profits of long-distance trade were no substitute for a regular agricultural surplus.

The history of the Western Sudan can be interpreted in ecological terms as the

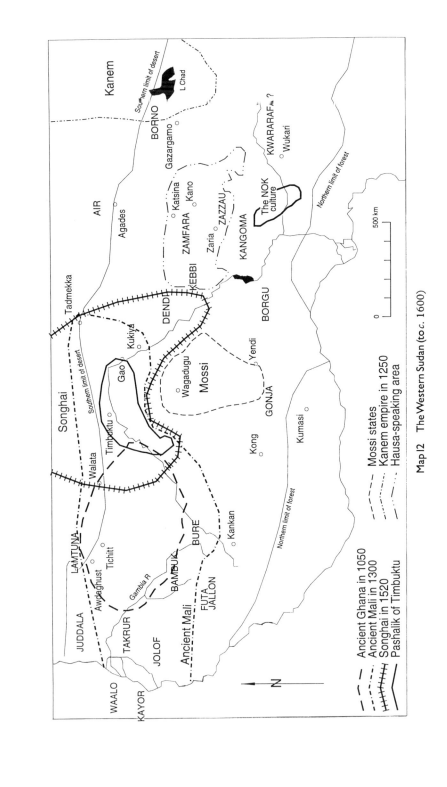

Map12 The Western Sudan (to c. 1600)

Kanem

Southern limit of desert

L. Chad

BORNO

Gazargamo

AIR

Agades

Katsina

ZAMFARA

Kano

Zaria

ZAZZAU

KWARARAF ?

Wukari

KANGOMA

The NOK culture

Northern limit of forest

Tadmekka

KEBBI

DENDI

BORGU

Songhai

Southern limit of desert

Gao

Kukiya

Wagadugu

Mossi

Yendi

GONJA

500 km

0

Walata

Timbuktu

Kong

Kumasi

Northern limit of forest

LAMTUNA

Tichitt

JUDDALA

Awdaghust

Gambia R

BAMBUK

BURE

Kankan

TAKRUR

JOLOF

Ancient Mali

FUTA JALLON

WAALO

KAYOR

N

Ancient Ghana in 1050

Ancient Mali in 1300

Songhai in 1520

Pashalik of Timbuktu

Mossi states

Kanem empire in 1250

Hausa-speaking area

ebb and flow of a power balance between the peoples of different ecological zones. The ascendancy of the Soninke was followed by that of the desert Almoravids; the rise of the savanna empire of Mali followed, and when it declined, the desert Tuareg controlled Timbuktu. Imperial Songhai's hegemony reached far into desert latitudes, until it was conquered by an army from Morocco in 1591. In the eighteenth century the Tuareg invaded the Niger valley.[5]

The lower the rainfall, the greater the risk of famine. In savanna and sahel, hunger was commonplace, at the end of the dry season and the beginning of the rains. An eleventh-century king of Malal became a Muslim when a cleric prayed successfully for rain, and fourteenth-century Kanem was called a land of famine. Descriptions of more recent famines shed some light on its ravages in the past. In Borno in the 1830s, 'They starved for four years. Not a drop of rain fell from the skies. They were forced to eat carrion and the leaves of trees, donkeys, horses, and even resorted to cannibalism. Then they repented – and the rains came.'[6]

The desert and the camel

In the often echoed image of the Qur'an, the camel was the ship of the desert. There were indigenous camels in the Sahara in prehistoric times but they died out, and the camel which transformed the life of its people was originally domesticated in South Arabia. In the Sahara, unlike South Arabia and Somalia, it was valued above all as a pack and riding animal. Its ability to survive for long periods without water and to carry heavy loads made it possible to continue trade between the Western Sudan and the Maghrib after the desertification of the Sahara. It was so efficient as a pack animal that the use of wheeled vehicles died out in vast areas: there was 'a dearth of vehicular traffic from Morocco to Afghanistan',[7] and goods exported from Kano to Timbuktu were sent through the desert rather than through the savanna. As this example indicates, camel routes went from east to west as well as from north to south.

The first written mention of the camel in North Africa dates from 46 BCE; it had become commonplace by the third and fourth centuries CE. Camels were bred in the desert by the Tuareg and could flourish nowhere else. They could not live further south than the northern limit of cereal agriculture – an imaginary line from the mouth of the Senegal to the confluence of the Blue and White Nile, south of which donkeys and water transport were all-important. But donkeys, like horses and most cattle, could only live in the savannas, north of the tsetse belt. The great states of the Western Sudan rose and fell within these perimeters.

Before ancient Ghana

The Arabic sources, and modern books based on them directly or at one or more removes, stress the contribution of trans-Saharan trade to the empires of the Western Sudan. In the late eighth century, a scholar at the court of the Abbasid caliph in Baghdad referred to 'Ghana the land of gold'.[8] While acknowledging that Ghana clearly began earlier than this, older histories of the Western Sudan tended to take it as their starting point. A Catalan map of 1375 shows a veiled merchant on a camel approaching the dark king of Mali, who holds a gold nugget in his hand. The frequency with which it is reproduced in modern books reflects a historiography focussed on Great States and long-distance trade.

In recent years, archaeological excavations have shed ever more light on settlements more ancient than the first mention of Ghana. It is now widely recognised that the growth of states, long-distance trade and social differentiation began much earlier, probably in association with a late, rapid and diversified adoption of agriculture,[9] and in at least some cases, the spread of iron working.

Dhar Tichitt in southern Mauretania is now virtually desert but the striking stone remains of villages can still be seen there. In about 2000 BCE its people were hunters and gatherers who lived on the edges of freshwater lakes, made pottery and ground-stone axes, and painted wild fauna on canvasses of rock. In a period of aridity, the area was abandoned for a time. By 800 BCE, villages had been built on the escarpment with defensive walls, over half the grain imprints were of domesticates, and pastoralism was important. After 300 BCE, there are no more villages. Instead, there are paintings of mounted warriors and inscriptions in *tifanagh*, the script of the Tuareg.[10]

The walls enclosed considerable areas and imply a population much greater than the area could sustain in modern times. It is difficult to explain this – or the extensive cereal cultivation – unless the rainfall was higher than it is now. On architectural and other grounds, the inhabitants of Tichitt are thought to be ancestral to the Soninke, the people of ancient Ghana.

Towns grew up on the middle Niger from the middle of the first millennium BCE; they were conglomerates of many smaller centres, which may well have been the homes of different occupational groups.[11] They clearly antedated the advent of pyrotechnology. The first evidence of iron was dated to *c.* 200 CE and the first copper to *c.* 400 CE; they reflect trade rather than production, since the ore of neither is found locally. Old Jenne was occupied from *c.* 250 BCE until it was abandoned, at some time before the early fifteenth century. It is likely that Old Jenne was originally involved in east–west rather than trans-Saharan trade, exporting food by river to desert-edge Timbuktu. Between 700 and 1100, settlement in the area was ten times as dense as it is today, and there were forty towns and villages within a radius of 25 kilometres. The commercial city of Jenne is first mentioned in written sources in the late fifteenth century and its growth was linked with the adoption of Islam. The first Muslim king asked the *ulama* to pray for the growth of trade.[12] It became a great commercial centre, trading in foodstuffs as well as gold and kola from the Akan area, and salt from the Sahara. 'Jenne is one of the greatest Muslim markets, where traders carrying salt from the mines of Taghaza meet traders with the gold of Bitu ... It is because of this blessed town [Jenne] that caravans come to Timbuktu from all points of the horizon.'[13]

Megaliths and tumuli

Megaliths and tumuli are found throughout the world: the fascination of Stonehenge, for example, is perennial. Complexes of megalithic monuments and tumuli dating from late in the first millennium CE are found in the Senegambia and in the Inland Niger Delta. Over 16,000 such sites are known. In the Inland Delta they are associated with iron and copper jewellery and multiple interments, which are probably evidence of human sacrifice. Dressed stone pillars on the middle Gambia date from *c.* 600–800 CE. In Senegal, over 6,800 megaliths and tumuli are known, and excavations have revealed grave goods of copper, brass and gold, dated to the eighth to twelfth centuries. One had a large collective burial, again evidence of those sacrificed with a great lord.[14] In 1068 al-Bakri described the burial of a king of Ghana in a wooden chamber in a great mound, with his servants and treasure. This is clearly part of the same cultural complex.[15] Megaliths and burial mounds are found elsewhere in Africa.[16] They reflect a huge expenditure in energy and resources and hence a society which produces the surplus that makes it possible. Insofar as they are funeral complexes, they are legacies of kings, imposing on an otherwise forgetful landscape the memory of their existence.

Nok and Kangoma

Some of the most remarkable memorials of the distant past are to be found in an area which in recent times has been one of small-scale polities and sparse population. The Nok culture area in central Nigeria is remarkable for the development of an early and sophisticated iron technology (from the sixth century BCE) and for powerful and distinctive terracotta sculpture. The modern inhabitants of the area were, until recently, accomplished metalworkers who made elaborate pots and, in some cases, terracotta finials. The Anaguta made ornate mortuary pots; these pots are totally unknown to the world of scholarship, and only to be found, very properly, on old Anaguta graves. African village life often manifested an arresting degree of continuity, which contrasts with the fragility and ephemeral nature of so many empires, whether African or ruled from Europe. The Nok culture did not 'decline'; particular phases of its peoples' complex and varied life appear in the archaeological record, discovered by accident, in the course of open-cast mining.

Last has written a fascinating reconstruction of an obscure state called Kangoma, which flourished in the western part of the Nok culture area. He believes that it was the precursor of the much more famous Hausa kingdom of Zazzau, with its capital at Zaria,[17] founded by Gunguma. There is still a town called Kwangoma and an ethnic group called Kagoma which represent the north-eastern and south-western ends of ancient Kangoma, separated by the incursion of the Gbagyi ('Gwari'). When the gold of the Kaduna valley was discovered, there was an influx of Wangarawa merchants and new towns sprang up, first at Turunku, long since abandoned, and later at Zaria, whose walls include the ancient ritual centre of Kufena. Other central Nigerian kingdoms are mentioned in Arabic sources, but for the most part they are so vaguely described that identification is impossible.[18]

The area is full of the relics of ancient settlements which are little known or studied. At the end of the nineteenth century, one of them was described near the Niger–Benue Confluence.

There were three huge walls built of rock and stone, built across the entire breadth of the mountain ... Behind the second and third walls were deep ditches. The walls were about 12 feet broad, and about 10 feet high. The old chief told me that there are many traditions about these walls ... he said that the walls were about 1000 years old.[19]

Desert trade

Saharan trade was the vehicle for the transmission of ideas, but it was, of course, the prospect of profit which encouraged merchants to make the dangerous desert crossing. 'The richest gold mine on earth is that of Ghana ... Deserts and fear of the Sudan bar the way to it.'[20] The gold exported from Ghana came from Bambuk, south of the upper Senegal. The gold fields of Bure, which were eight times as productive, were further east, at the headwaters of the Niger, and seem to have come into production later, in the thirteenth century.

The gold of the Akan forests was mined from the early fifteenth century,[21] if not earlier, and taken to Jenne along a Dyula trade route, through the market town of Bitu (Beghu), to be exchanged for Saharan salt. Such was its economic importance that its existence was known to foreigners far away. At the beginning of the sixteenth century, a Portuguese visitor to the coast observed: '200 leagues from this kingdom of Mandingua is a region where there is abundance of gold; it is called Toom [the Akan are called To in Malinke] ... the inhabitants of the town called Beetuu ... go to this country of Toom to obtain gold in exchange for merchandise and slaves which they take thither.'[22] Later in the century, a physician at the Moroccan court wrote of kola coming from 'a place called Bitu where there are mines of gold and gold dust'.[23] After the inception of Atlantic trade, much of the gold was deflected to Europeans on the coast, and the trade in slaves became relatively more important, as did a wide range of other exports, including worked leather and ostrich feathers.

Gold was of great importance in the political economy of the Maghrib, but in the Western Sudan it was probably less significant than the capture of slaves for export and for local deployment. A son of one of the Askiyas boasted that a prince could capture as many as a thousand slaves in a day. Meillassoux ascribed the rise and fall of the states of the Western Sudan to the practice of slave raiding: on the one hand, the sale or deployment of slaves generated revenue but on the other hand the wars which obtained them spread the boundary of empire ever further, so that potential sources of slaves were ever more distant from the metropolis.[24] He contrasted the survival of merchant cities such as Kong, with 'the glory and the ruin of the Sudanese "empires" '.

Slaves were exported north across the Sahara, in numbers which may not have fallen far short of those which crossed the Atlantic.[25] Far fewer reached their final destinations than were enslaved; both those who survived the desert journey and those who did not endured horrific sufferings. More women crossed the desert as slaves than men: ibn Battuta travelled with a caravan of 600 slave girls.[26] The high price of eunuchs reflected the fact that although many boys were subjected to the ordeal of castration, only one in ten survived. Religion justified the Muslim slave trade: 'the reason for slavery is non-belief' said a famous scholar of sixteenth-century Timbuktu. It was forbidden to enslave free Muslims (though this not infrequently happened) and enslavement was seen as a kind of apprenticeship in faith. The relative ease with which those enslaved in Muslim countries gained their freedom meant that there was a constant demand for fresh slaves.

As in the Atlantic slave trade, the large-scale export of slaves tended to lead to their increased role in domestic production. Another consequence of domestic slavery was a redistribution of population from small-scale societies to the vicinity of major cities. At various points in this study we have noted mysterious densities of population, much greater than those of the present day. Some can be attributed to climate change; some may reflect the involuntary migration of the enslaved.

Trade between different ecological zones tended to be the preserve of merchants of specific ethnic origins: Sahara trade was dominated by North Africans and the Moors and Tuareg of the desert; the routes between Jenne and the gold fields were controlled by Mande traders, the Dyula or Wangara. Originally, they operated within the Mande heartland but by the sixteenth century they had reached the sea. The relative importance of the southern termini of the desert trade routes changed as time went on, the general pattern being a move from west to east. At the beginning of the thirteenth century, trade shifted from Awdaghust to Walata, further east, which in its turn was displaced by the river port of Timbuktu, originally a Tuareg settlement, a century later. 'The market had previously been at Biru [Walata]. Caravans used to come there from all points of the horizon. The pick of scholars, pious and rich men from every tribe and country lived there ... Then all these gradually moved to Timbuktu ... The building of Timbuktu was the ruin of Biru.'[27] Some trade routes led to the Nile valley through the central Sahara, from Mali and from Kanem, but because of their dangers, the sultan of Egypt prohibited their use for a time, and the oases were abandoned.

Regional trade

Trade between the adjacent zones of sahel and savanna, with their contrasting and complementary resources, was far more important than the camel routes across the desert – certainly in bulk, probably in value, and undoubtedly in the role it played in the daily life of the peoples concerned. It figures much less prominently in Arabic sources, which were based on information from those involved in trans-Saharan commerce.

Timbuktu was a major grain market, and Jenne was an entrepot both for textiles and for a wide range of foodstuffs including rice, millet and fish. It was able to withstand a siege by Sunni Ali, which lasted for (a symbolic) seven years, seven months and seven days.[28]

The most important import to the Western Sudan was salt from a chain of mines worked by slaves, which stretched across the Sahara – Awlil, in Mauretania, Taghaza, Taodeni and Bilma, north of Kanem. The location of the first of these is unknown, and since the word means a 'depression' it may be a generic term rather than a specific site.[29] The people who lived at the mouth of the

Senegal, in the area which was to become the Wolof state of Waalo, exchanged grain for pastoral products with the desert nomads to their north, and sent fish and salt eastward by river, in return for millet.[30] In the late nineteenth century, the Tuareg of Ahir were importing 7,500 tons of millet from the savanna each year as well as their clothing requirements, in return for salt and natron from Bilma, and dates and livestock.[31]

A wide range of goods was imported across the Sahara; many items obtained in this way were also produced locally – cloth, jewellery, swords and other metal artefacts. Horses were imported, both from the Maghrib and from the sahel; the difficulty of the journey is reflected in the fact that in Borno, in the 1520s, fifteen or twenty slaves were exchanged for one horse.[32] The result of these imports has been called a cavalry revolution, a theme to which we return later in this chapter.

The coming of Islam

By the late fifteenth century, all the known rulers of major states in the Western Sudan were Muslims. The Western Sudan was the furthest frontier of the Islamic world, and local Muslims were well aware of this. Muhammad Bello wrote in c. 1812: 'I am living on the fringe of the Soudan – the Soudan where paganism and dark ignorance prevail.'[33] The coming of Islam was of enormous significance to the peoples of both the Sahara and the Sudan. Islamic education led to literacy in Arabic and made its more advanced students part of an international world of learning. At lower levels, literacy tended to be limited and specialised and Arabic was used for a restricted range of subjects but not for daily discourse. At the desert town of Walata, in its heyday, there lived scholars and merchants from 'Egypt, Awjila, Fezzan, Ghadames, Tuat, Dara'a, Tafilelt, Fes, Sus, Bitu, and other places',[34] and the Persian poet Di'bil lies buried in Zawila in the Fezzan. Scholars migrated in both directions: Abu Ishaq was a black poet and scholar from Kanem, who lived for a time at Marrakesh and died in Spain in 1212.[35] Four hundred years earlier, an Ibadite governor in North Africa spoke the language of Kanem; we do not know whether he was a much-travelled merchant or of Kanem origins.[36]

Al-Maghali (d. 1504) was a scholar from Tlemcen who visited Katsina, Kano and Gao. Various pieces he wrote for the benefit of local rulers explored 'the obligations of princes' and the relationship between Islamic ideals and the realities of politics, and were to be of seminal importance to the jihadists of a later day, but his memory is tarnished by the role he played in the massacre of the Jews of Tuwat.[37] Many conversions can be explained in terms of the prestige which accrued to the learned and prosperous merchant community. The conversion of kings was a two-edged sword, because their authority was intimately connected with traditional religion. Elements of syncretism are explained in these terms as a partial accommodation to the status quo. But Islam, as an international faith, was particularly appropriate for the successive empires which developed in the sahel and savanna; traditional religion was ethnic, hence divisive. The period of transition was often mirrored in urban geography, in the twin cities found in Ghana and Gao, or in the multiple centres of political authority which characterised early Kanem. Islam was more firmly rooted in courts, urban life and merchant communities than in the countryside. In Egypt and the Maghrib, Islam was introduced from above, and spread through conquest. In the Western Sudan it was introduced not by kings but by merchants and clerics, who were excluded from political power. In some areas, at least, the jihads were to reverse all this, and place power in the hands of clerics, though not of merchants.[38] The conversion of rulers was sometimes a response to an ecological crisis. In eleventh-century 'Malal' (?Mali) there was a long drought, which traditional rituals could not alleviate. The prayers of a Muslim visitor brought rain: 'So the king ordered the idols to be broken and expelled the sorcerers from his country. He and his descendants after him as well as his nobles were sincerely attached to Islam, while the common people of his kingdom remained polytheists.'[39] This episode, reminiscent of the contest between Elijah and the priests of Baal, may well be a symbolic statement of the total power of God, rather than a historic incident; it is paralleled in later Ibadite writings.[40]

There is a sense in which religious encounters are the most visible aspect of a multitude of social, economic and political relationships.[41] 'The frontier ... was ... an area where ethnic and societal transformation took place.'[42] What is preserved of these encounters, whether glimpsed from distant Baghdad, or encoded in oral tradition, is their most spectacular manifestations: wars, and the conversion of kings. 'The Zumum came out to meet him, naked and with iron spears in their hands. Their king was riding on a horned beast of enormous size ... he proceeded to fight very bravely, but then al-Rayan defeated him. They retreated into marshes, jungles, caves and rugged mountains, where al-Rayan could not follow them.'[43]

The incident is mythical, but non-Muslim peoples on the edge of empires were often displaced to marginal environments. And there were other forms of resistance, as a fourteenth-century source makes clear:

They bring gold dust to [the ruler of Mali] each year. They are uncouth infidels. If the sultan wished he could extend his authority over them but the kings of this kingdom have learnt by experience that as soon as one of them conquers one of the gold towns and Islam spreads and the muezzin calls to prayer then the gold begins to decrease and then disappear ... When they had learnt the truth of this by experience they left the gold countries under the control of the heathen people and were content with their vassalage and the tribute imposed on them.[44]

Traditional religion often continued to flourish, despite proximity to Islam, and important monographs describe it this century among the Bambara and the Hausa.[45] It has been said that the most important dialogue between Christianity and traditional religion in Africa takes place in the hearts of individual Christians. The same is true of Islam.

Genealogy as metaphor

Muslim scholars attempted to locate the historical experience of the Western Sudan on familiar cognitive maps, hence the proliferation of legends which state that the founder of the Hausa states came from Baghdad, or that the ancestor of the Mali royal clan was Bilal, the black companion of the Prophet.[46] A myth of Himyarite (that is, pre-Islamic Yemeni) descent was recorded of the Seyfawa dynasty of Kanem in the thirteenth century[47] and was a core statement of identity among the Sanhaja of the western Sahara.[48] The Yemen, in Arabic thought, is often 'the South'. Himyarite descent provides ancient and noble – albeit non-Islamic – forebears.

The Muslims of the Western Sudan, feeling themselves to be on the periphery of the Islamic world, welcomed this kind of identification, and contributed to it. Muhammad Bello, whose *Infaq al-Maysur* is a fascinating piece of intellectual history, summarised various current theories about the origins of the Tuareg of Ahir.

It is said that these Tuareg are the remnant of the Beriberi who scattered at the time when Afrikiya was conquered by the Muslims. And the Berbers are of the children of Abraham. Others say they are descended from the Yajuju and Majuju [Gog and Magog] whom Dthukarmene imprisoned. A certain band got out and did much harm. They married Turks and Tartars. Others again say they are descended from Jinns.[49]

The history of non-Muslims living adjacent to Muslim areas was interpreted in the same way. Muhammad Bello stated that the Yoruba were descended 'from the kindred of Nimrud'.[50] In the late nineteenth century, Borgu, in north-western Nigeria, was divided into five kingdoms, whose people spoke one of two unrelated languages. Their sense of unity was rooted largely in the myth of descent from an immigrant king, Kisra, who lived in Mecca but was not a Muslim, and finally died in Bussa. Kisra is the Arabic form of Khosrau, the name of the Sassanid Persian kings, none of whom, clearly, came anywhere near Nigeria. Muslim scholars, perhaps encountering traditions of another 'Kisra', made the identification; the people of Borgu accepted it[51] somewhat in the spirit of Yoruba of a past generation who welcomed the idea that their ancestors came from Egypt.

The cavalry revolution

It has been aptly said that events are shaped by the means of destruction as well as by the means of production. It was in the fourteenth century that the savanna states embarked on a series of innovations which amounted to a revolution in the technology of warfare, including the importation of large horses from the Maghrib. Horses had reached West Africa much earlier, but their size gradually declined to that of ponies. There is a sculpture of a horse and rider among the Igbo-Ukwu bronzes, and there are references to horses in the Western Sudan in ninth- and tenth-century Arabic sources.[52] It was possible to breed large horses in the Western Sudan but they were still scarce and expensive. The introduction of saddle, stirrups and bit made the cavalry charge and combat at close quarters possible. Helmets, chain mail, and quilted protection for horses were introduced in Kano in the reign of Kanajeji (1390–1410).[53] Significantly, he is also remembered as a successful slaver. Cavalry was not always invincible – at the outbreak of the Sokoto jihad, Fulbe archers, lacking horses and armour and using light bows with a range of thirty paces, were able to defeat the heavy cavalry of Gobir:

Yunfa fled from bare-legged herdsmen
Who had neither mail nor horsemen.

It has been argued, both in the context of European and of African history, that the cost of acquiring and sustaining horses placed considerable power in the hands of the aristocracy. In West Africa, it has been argued that the converse is true, and that only the king had the wealth to acquire and especially maintain horses, a labour-intensive business since they were stall-fed. Largely because of trypanosomiasis, horses could not survive for long south of the Western Sudan. Bas-reliefs show the oba of Benin on horseback, supported by two attendants. The northern Igbo bought horses but did not ride them; they were sacrificed at the funerals of Big Men or by those aspiring to the prestigious title of Horse Killer.

The Mande connection

Much of the history of this period is intelligible only in the context of the many ramifications of the Mande language family, a subject greatly complicated by the proliferation of alternative ethonyms, Bamana/Bambara, Mande/Manding, Dyula/Wangara, and so on. Ancient Ghana was dominated by the Soninke, whose language is one of four in the Northern Mande subgroup, the others being Susu/Jalonke, now spoken far to the south in Sierra Leone and Guinea, Vai, spoken in Liberia, and Mandekan. Mandekan is a generic name for a family of languages which includes Dyula, Malinke and Bambara; it is a grammatically simpler form which may have evolved as a trade lingua franca.

South East Mande includes Bussa, on the north-western Nigerian border, and Dan and Gio, spoken in Ivory Coast. South West Mande includes the Sierra Leone languages Mende and Loko. Some of these categories may be modified by further research, but it is noteworthy that the east–west bifurcation of language is paralleled in masking cults – Simo among the Susu and Jalonke, Poro among the Vai/Komo.[54]

'Ethnic' identities were determined by occupation and religion as well as by language. The Dyula were a long-distance merchants, called Marka on the Niger bend; the Fulbe, ideally, pastoralists, the Bozo and Somono fishermen. The Dyula were Muslim, and the Bambara 'pagans'. The social reality was fluid and changing, there was a Muslim presence in the Bambara states, and some Dyula were not Muslims. 'It was not uncommon for FulBe to become Bozo, Bozo to become Somono, and ... animist farmers to become Maraka Muslim tradition-alists.'[55] Most Marka identified themselves as 'white' (the black were the recently converted).

Ghana: a state of the desert edge

Conventional histories of the Western Sudan are dominated by great empires – Ghana, Mali, Songhai, Kanem-Borno – but each was an agglomeration of polities, and each was surrounded by independent states. We know a good deal about some of them, such as Mali, and a little about others, such as Takrur. In some instances, we know only their name and inevitably some have slipped through the net of history altogether. As Muhammad Bello said of Ahir, in the words which form the epigraph of this chapter, 'their history is not known because no one has written books about their country'. [56]

Ghana was a state of the Soninke. They are now widely dispersed, and have, in some cases, long since lost their Soninke speech, but they still preserve the memory of an ancient kingdom called Wagadu. Its people worshipped a sacred snake, who was honoured with an annual human sacrifice, and who replenished both rain and gold. But the snake was killed, the gold disappeared, and the land became desert. It is an extraordinarily vivid symbolic representation of the decline of a kingdom, the advent of Islam, and the degeneration of the environment. Al-Bakri, writing in 1068, describes snake worship but ascribes it to the Zafun, who were probably Soninke too. [57] Living in Cordoba, he obtained details about Ghana from travellers, which included the magnificence of its king: 'This Tunka Menin is powerful, rules an enormous kingdom, and possesses great authority.' [58]

He described a capital in transition between traditional religion and Islam. The Muslim town had twelve mosques surrounded by 'wells of sweet water' and vegetable gardens. The royal capital, six miles away, had its own mosque, but was also a stronghold of traditional religion. 'Around the king's town are domed buildings and groves and thickets where the sorcerers of these people live.' Long-distance trade sustained the court: imposts on the import and re-export of salt, copper and other merchandise, which were exchanged for gold from Bambuk, the Ghana king retaining all nuggets found.

The great fourteenth-century historian, Tunis-born ibn Khaldun, summarised two hundred years of Western Sudan history in brief compass.

Later the authority of the people of Ghana waned and their prestige declined as that of the veiled people, their neighbours on the north ... grew ... These extended their domination over the Sudan, and pillaged, imposed tribute and poll-tax and converted many of them to Islam ... the rulers of Ghana ... were overcome by the Susu ... Later the people of Mali ... vanquished the Susu and acquired all their possessions. [59]

Whether in fact Ghana was overthrown by the Almoravids has been questioned, [60] and in any case, both its decline and the adoption of Islam were probably gradual processes.

Today the site of the capital of ancient Ghana is on the desert edge. Was there a process of increasing desertification, due either to drought or to human agency – overgrazing or neglect of the wells? Al-Idrisi wrote eloquently of a deserted oasis on the route to Egypt, in words which shed light on the decline of other desert towns.

... a ruined town called Nabranta. In the past it was one of the famous cities, but according to what is related, sand overwhelmed its dwellings until these fell into ruins, and covered its waters until these dried up. Its population diminished and at the present time only their remnants live there, clinging to the remaining ruined homes out of affection for their native place. [61]

A state of the savanna: Mali

Mali was a state of the savanna, its people the Malinke or southern Mande.[62] Western histories, like this one, explain the rise and fall of states in socio-economic, political or ecological terms. This is not the perspective from which the Mande view their own past, as reflected in their epic poetry. The Mande epic poem is an extraordinary literary creation,[63] and this is acknowledged in an episode where heroes struggle, not for an empire, but for a song.[64]

The epic of Sundiata tells of a historic hero who probably lived in the early thirteenth century and led his people to freedom from a Susu overlord.[65] Its explanation of events is supernatural, and the conflict between Sundiata and the Susu king, Sumanguru, is one between magicians. Tradition is explicit that Sundiata's predecessors were Muslims – perhaps because this was a necessary implication if the dynasty was founded by Bilal – but Sundiata's powers are rooted in traditional religion. Sundiata was a cripple in his childhood, his mother was a hunchback, his great general, Fakuru, a dwarf with an abnormally large head. Perhaps heroes are physically disabled to show the overriding importance of the spirit. Both Sumanguru and Fakuru were blacksmiths.

The fluctuations of Mali's fortunes are associated largely with the strengths and weaknesses of its kings. Perhaps Mali never developed an infrastructure sufficiently strong to outweigh personality. Ibn Battuta, who visited the Western Sudan, paid tribute to the power of royal women, and described an attempted coup by the king's chief wife. 'She was his partner in rule according to the custom of the Sudan, and her name was mentioned with his from the pulpit.'[66] Mansa Musa (1312–37) was Mali's most famous king. His munificence in Egypt when he was on pilgrimage devalued gold there, and 'Rex Melly' and 'Mussa Melly' appear on contemporary European maps. He brought back with him an Andalusian poet and architect, whose remains rest in Timbuktu. Modern historians – even, ironically, those most critical of conspicuous consumption in the contemporary Third World – have tended to praise the splendours of these kingdoms. The price was paid by the gold miners. In the vivid language of hyperbole, an early Portuguese source describes the gulf between the one who mines gold and the king who profits by it: 'The gold mines are seven in number. They are shared by seven kings ... The mines are extremely deep down in the earth. The kings have slaves they place in the mines ... Children are born and raised in these mines.'[67]

Gold was not always mined by slaves, though it would be surprising, in slave-owning societies, if they were not sometimes deployed to do work which was both laborious and dangerous. In Bambuk, gold was mined by family groups, to augment their income in the dry season, working shafts up to 20 metres deep, which sometimes collapsed. Gold mining was organised on gender lines: men dug out the ore, while women extracted the gold, and the two groups divided the gold equally. The gold fields were not particularly rich, as the poverty of modern Mali indicates. But at a time of year when farming was impossible, any supplementation of the family income was welcome.[68]

Saharan salt was mined by slaves; ibn Battuta gave a vivid description of their environment:

Taghaza is a village with nothing good about it ... its houses and mosque are of rock salt ... It has no trees but is nothing but sand with a salt mine ... Nobody lives there except the slaves of the Massufa who dig for the salt ... the water there is brackish. It is the most fly-ridden of places.[69]

Mali survived, though in a shrunken and weakened state, throughout the period of the rise and fall of imperial Songhai. Its king attacked Jenne unsuccessfully in 1599, but his forces were defeated by the *arma*. This is the last mention of Mali in Arabic sources. Tradition states that the Bambara and Fulbe sacked Niani, its capital, early in the seventeenth century.[70]

Songhai

Ghana and Mali were Mande states but Songhai is the westernmost branch of the Nilo-Saharan language family. Its people were riverfarers, and when Sonni Ali planned to conquer the desert town of Walata, he began to construct a canal. Songhai is sometimes described as the third of the great empires of the Western Sudan, but its origins were as ancient as those of Ghana.

Its first capital was at Kukiya, the centre of a state founded by fishermen from Dendi, on the modern Nigerian frontier. They encountered farmers, 'owners of the land', in the classic meeting of stranger and settler which is at the heart of so many West African political charters. The founder of its first dynasty secured his position by slaying a fish dragon, just as Bayajida, the Hausa culture hero, slays a magical snake in a well.

Gao was a later capital; it lies in desert latitudes, but irrigation and river transport are made possible by the enormous northern sweep of the Niger, and rice was cultivated in slave plantations along the river banks, which were perhaps more productive then than they have ever been since.[71] Its location gave it a strategic role in trans-Saharan and riverain trade.

'Kawkaw' is mentioned in the oldest extant Arabic account of West Africa, in the first half of the ninth century.[72] A little later it was called 'the most important and powerful' state in the Western Sudan, acknowledged as overlord by vassal states whose rulers are 'kings in their own lands'.[73] There were twin towns, as in Ghana, 'one being the residence of the king and the other inhabited by the Muslims ... Their king is a Muslim.'[74] For a time Songhai was part of the Mali empire, regaining its independence when the latter declined.

Sonni Ali (1462–92) was the second founder of Songhai, a figure similar to Sundiata, rooted in traditional religion despite his Muslim forebears.[75] He conquered Timbuktu and Jenne, and expansion continued under his successors, as Mali contracted to the Malinke heartland, south of the Niger Inland Delta. His successor, Askia Muhammad, was a committed Muslim who went on pilgrimage only three years after his seizure of the throne, spending a fortune in gold like Mansa Musa before him.

It is a mistake to see the conversion of princes solely in terms of *realpolitik*, but the empire's western expansion meant that it embraced many non-Songhai peoples, for whom Islam was a more appropriate ideology than the ethnic shrines where Sonni Ali worshipped. At its greatest extent, the Songhai empire was the largest state ever created by West Africans; its influence extended from the Senegal to the western marches of Hausaland; Kebbi, in north-western Nigeria, was founded by a Songhai general.

For a hundred years, the politics and trade of the Western Sudan were dominated by two giants: Songhai and Borno. In 1591, the Songhai empire, weakened by epidemic disease and the internecine struggles of its royal family, was shattered by an invading Moroccan army. It was largely a victory of firearms and a mercenary professional force over traditional weaponry. (Further east, sixteenth-century Borno imported both firearms and mercenaries.)

The links with Morocco did not last (p. 270 below). The invaders and their descendants founded a small state, the Pashalik of Timbuktu, which gradually became independent. They married Songhai women, and in time became one with the conquered. 'Today the descendants of these Andalusians and Moroccans are no more than a high-status caste of cobblers in Timbuktu, their only link with their military past being their right to carry a sword.'[76] The heirs of the Askias retreated to Dendi, the original Songhai homeland.

In the eyes of a Timbuktu historian, influenced by the fact that many local scholars had been killed or exiled by Moroccan forces, the sequel was catastrophic. 'Security gave way to fear, prosperity to misery and unhappiness, and well-being to calamity and distress.'[77] This was an exaggeration; trade and scholarship continued to flourish, and the frontier of Islam to advance.[78] Clearly, much of life went on unaffected by the changing shape of the political superstructuture.

The Senegambia

Futa Toro – ancient Takrur – was a long narrow state along the Senegal river. It was some 400 kilometres long and 16 to 24 kilometres wide, with barren steppe to the north and south.[79] 'Futa is a double barrelled gun,' say its people, referring to the combination of flood-plain and upland cultivation.[80] Away from the river, wells were dug which were as much as 30 metres deep.[81]

Takrur may well have been the state which produced the megaliths and tumuli of the Senegal valley. War-Djabi, who died in 1040/1, was its first Muslim king. A thirteenth-century Arabic account describes 'a section who have become sedentary and live in towns and a section who are nomads in the open country',[82] that is, the Tukukor and the Fulbe who, despite the latter's migrations, speak the same language, which is related to Wolof. A European map of 1339 locates 'Felle' and 'Tochoror' near the Senegal.[83]

Further south, on the Gambia, there are many Mandingo communities, who trace their origin to the westward thrust of Mali in the time of Sundiata. Early European visitors were told of a distant overlord: 'The Mandinga kingdom begins in the Gambia river ... the king of Mandinga is called Mandimansa.'[84] But Mali declined, and its tributary provinces became independent.

When the Portuguese reached the Senegambia in the fifteenth century, they found a chain of Wolof- or Serer-speaking coastal kingdoms, Waalo, Kayor, Baol, Sine and Salum, which were tributary to an inland sovereign, the Burba Jolof. Tradition claims that the Jolof empire was founded by Njajan Njai, who came from Futa Toro, emerging from the river with a Qur'an in his hand, and that the first Jolof kings had to recite the entire Qur'an before they could be enthroned.[85] Jolof imported horses from North Africa and the desert edge on such a large scale that one scholar writes of a 'cavalry revolution'.[86]

In the first half of the sixteenth century the coastal provinces broke away, beginning with Kayor, a change usually assumed to reflect resources acquired from Atlantic trade, as the Portuguese brought horses there by sea from the Maghrib. Kayor and the Serer state of Salum became the most powerful of the coastal kingdoms.[87] An alternative theory suggests that Jolof declined because a new dynasty, the Denianke, founded by Koli Tenguella in Futa Toro, cut off its access to Saharan trade and horses.

Dyula and Jakhanke

Dyula was a generic name for Mande-speaking Muslim merchants who travelled great distances, often founding settlements far from their original homes. They were an enduring commercial and cultural presence in Hausaland, and one of their number may well have founded a new dynasty in Katsina. As ibn al-Mukhtar explained in the seventeenth century, this 'ethnic' label was largely an occupational one: 'the Wangara and the Malinke are of the same origin, but whereas the Malinke are the warriors, the Wangara are those traders who travel from one end of the world to another'.[88] The English merchant, Richard Jobson, was called a Dyula.[89] Those who settled among the Bambara became the Marka, and those who settled among the Mossi became the Yarse, in each case adopting the language of their hosts.

Jobson, who visited the Gambia in 1620–2, found the Dyula learned and hospitable,

... going in whole families together, and carrying along their bookes and manu-scripts, and their boyes or younger race with them, whom they teach or instruct in any place they rest with them ... howsoever the Kings and Countries are at warres, and up in armes ... yet still the Mary-bucke [marabout] is a priviledged person and many follow his trade, or course of travelling, without any let or interruption of either side. Notwithstanding there is none of these Mary-buckes but goe armed.[90]

The influence of these Muslim traders in spreading Islam and developing long-distance trade was incalculable. It was said of those who carried salt to the gold fields, 'They trust each other without receipts, written agreements, or witnesses.'[91] They tended to live in existing states rather than found new ones, but at a later date Kankan (in modern Guinea) and Kong (in northern Ivory Coast) were exceptions. The Jakhanke were Soninke-speaking clerics with a strong commitment to peace. Their name came from the town of Diakha in Massina, founded in the twelfth century. In 1500 they established a new Diakha far to the west, on the Bafing near Bambuk, led by a culture hero al-Hajj Salim, who is said to have gone seven times on pilgrimage. Diakha was a sanctuary: 'they gave it the epithet, city of God'.[92]

There is a tendency to identify Muslim clerics with Muslim traders, but the equation is not always acccurate. The Jakhanke owned slaves, whom they employed in agriculture, in order to free their own energies and time for study. The Wangarawa who settled in fifteenth-century Kano, were not merchants but Jakhanke on pilgrimage.[93]

Beyond the Bilad al-Islam

Sources in Arabic shed more light on Muslim states than on their 'pagan' neighbours. The tenth-century author ibn Hawqal, in words somewhat reminiscent of Trevor-Roper in the twentieth, explained:

We have not mentioned the land of the Sudan in the west, nor the Buja nor the Zanj, nor other people with the same characteristics, because the orderly government of kingdoms is based upon religious beliefs, good manners, law and order, and the organisation of settled life directed by sound policy. These people lack all these qualities ... Their kingdoms, therefore, do not deserve to be dealt with separately.[94]

It is likely that some of the stereotypes found in the Arabic sources (such as cannibalism, and perhaps silent trade by barter)[95] were deliberately created by Sudanese merchants, to discourage their Maghribi or Saharan trading partners from going directly to the source of gold. The Bambara and Mossi kingdoms and Gonja were, in the eyes of Muslim chroniclers, 'pagan' states. There was, in fact, a considerable Muslim presence in both, but it was not the official state ideology. Their rulers stood somewhere between traditional religion and Islam, absorbing elements from both traditions,[96] and Muslim merchants and clerics settled freely within their boundaries. There was an official in Dagomba called Chief of the Muslims. The Bambara kingdoms of Segu and Kaarta were founded in the eighteenth century and thus lie beyond the time span of this chapter.

The Mossi kingdoms[97]

In the savanna north of the Akan forest, a complex of related kingdoms was established; it is Wagadugu which is properly called Mossi, but the name is more loosely used for the whole complex as well. The title of the king of Wagadugu, Mogho Naba, means Lord of the World. The relationship between the kingdoms is conceptualised in terms of descent from a single ancestor, Na Gbewa, who founded a state in the north-east of modern Ghana in the early fifteenth century. *Nakomse*, 'possessors of power' whose success was based on their cavalry, conquered the indigenous peoples and exacted tribute from them. Some local peoples fled, but most became commoner classes in the new state. The languages of the indigenes belonged to the Voltaic or Gur family, and in time the invaders became Gur-speaking.

The earlier form of organisation was small scale, centred round a land priest and earth shrines. Some peoples in this area still live in small territorial units under the ritual leadership of a Priest of the Land, the custodian of an Earth shrine, which is thought to be, significantly, fatal to horses.[98] It seems probable that these narratives are less a relation of historic events than a concentrated metaphor of socio-political relations.

The Mossi kingdoms were located between two economic zones, and well situated to profit by trade between them in gold and kola nuts from the south, salt and livestock from the north. Arabic sources record a number of attempts to invade the territory of their northern Muslim neighbours, in accounts which have much the same ideological overtones as 'Kwararafa's' wars with Hausaland and Borno. It has been surmised that the Mossi sought access to the rich middle Niger region and the southern termini of desert trade, and on one occasion their campaigns reached as far as Walata, on the desert edge.

The capture of slaves – used within the kingdoms rather than exported beyond them – was of major importance to these states, and their cavalry preyed on peoples in small-scale polities such as the Dogon and the Tallensi. It was not until the nineteenth century that the Mossi supplied captives to the Atlantic slave trade. It is said that it was the twenty-seventh Naba, who reigned from 1855 to 1894, who had 'the idea of selling captives taken in war'.[99]

Gonja

In the mid-sixteenth century, Mande horsemen founded the kingdom of Gonja between the Black and the White Volta and ultimately displaced the Mossi kingdom of Dagomba eastward, to modern Yendi. According to an eighteenth-century Arab chronicle, the ruler of Mali had dispatched an expedition to Bighu, to complain that tribute in gold was not reaching him; instead of returning, his soldiers founded a new state, and adopted the language of the local people, Guan, while remaining a ruling caste, the Ngbanya.[100] The pattern is obviously similar to that of the Mossi traditions, and here, too, a memory of the past is preserved in the ritual opposition of Earth shrines and horses.[101] The Gonja state attained its greatest extent in the long reign of Jakpa Lanta (1622–66) but in the mid-eighteenth century it became a tributary of Asante. Gonja seems to have relied on raiding for slaves, who were then exchanged for gold. This was perhaps the only way to sustain a powerful state in an arid region. '... on the northern edge of the forest of Ghana, there flourished in central Gonja, probably in the fifteenth to seventeenth centuries an interesting culture, especially between the Black and White Volta. This land, now a poverty-stricken wilderness, waterless for half the year and suffering from soil erosion, was thickly populated.'[102] As so often in African history, scarcity underlay the predations of a warrior state. The political economy of Muslim states which relied on slave raiding had much in common with it.

Kanem-Borno

Kanem was a state to the north-east of Lake Chad whose ruling dynasty, the Seyfawa, abandoned their homeland for 'Kaga', the clay plains of Borno,[103] in the fourteenth century. Ancient Ghana, Mali and Songhai have long since disappeared, but Kanem's successor state, Borno, survived until the beginning of colonial rule. The Seyfawa ruled until the early nineteenth century, one of the longest surviving dynasties in world history.

The earliest references are to the Zaghawa, possibly a form of Zanj. Today, the

Zaghawa are a pastoral people far to the east, on the borders of Chad and the Republic of Sudan. In the past, it was clearly a generic name for the black nomadic peoples of the Central Sudan, speakers of Nilo-Saharan languages such as Teda, Daza and Tubu, a language family to which modern Kanuri belongs. Kanem means 'south' in Tubu. A legend first recorded in the twelfth century ascribes the state's foundation to a hero from the Yemen called Sayf ibn Dhi Yazan.

It is possible that the concentration of political power was associated with iron working, since there are many blacksmith kings in the Chad basin. Centralised institutions and a sacred monarchy grew up among a nomadic people on the desert edge. According to a late ninth-century source, 'the Zaghawa ... live in the place called Kanim. Their dwellings are huts made of reeds and they have no towns.'[104] This early account describes not one but five states in the area; one has a Zaghawa king, one is hostile to Kanem (but has a king whose title seems to be a form of 'mai'), and a third is in a tributary relationship to 'the king of ThBYR'.[105] A tenth-century account contrasts the poverty of their material culture with the elaborate ideology of sacred kingship. 'Their houses are all reed huts as is also the palace of their king, whom they exalt and worship instead of Allah.'[106] Some of the sources hint that the environment was too barren to sustain the burden of king and court. 'Their king, despite the feebleness of his authority and the poverty of his soil, shows an inconceivable arrogance. It is a land of famine and austerity.'[107]

Lacking the gold which sustained courts further west, Kanem exported slaves to the Fezzan and profited by its control of the salt and natron of the Kawar oases.

Umme Jilme, in the late eleventh century, was the first Muslim Mai – and possibly the founder of the Seyfawa dynasty – but there had clearly been an Islamic presence in the kingdom long before. He died on pilgrimage, one of a long succession of kings from the Western Sudan who endangered both their thrones and their lives in that most perilous of journeys. The next mai but one drowned in the Red Sea on his third pilgrimage.

There was an undoubted tension between the appeal of Islam and the religious sanctions of sacred kingship. A mysterious story tells how Mai Dunama Dibbalemi (1210–48) opened a sacred object, the *mune*, and a time of troubles followed. Does this symbolise an onslaught on traditional religion? Since the *mune* was a heavily wrapped Qur'an, was it Muslims who objected? It is significant that an identical story is told of the last Hausa king of Kano.[108]

Dunama is said to have extended his empire's frontiers to the Fezzan, to have built a hostel in Cairo for his compatriots and to have begun the process of resettlement in Borno, which was completed in the reign of Umar ibn Idris (1382–7), who 'took out his armies and all his possessions and his people into Kaga: and down to this day none of our rulers have ever returned to Kanem to re-establish their residence there'.[109]

The most obvious reason for leaving Kanem was the fact that the flood-plains of Borno were far more favourable for agriculture than Kanem was, but there were other factors: a mai complained of the depredations of Arab immigrants from the east, the forebears of the Shuwa.[110] Ironically, in the light of the kingdom's long involvement in the slave trade, he lamented his subjects' enslavement. Borno sources emphasise the role played by the closely related Bulala, who founded an independent state at Lake Fitri, and expelled the Seyfewa in concert with Kanem's local inhabitants – a fascinating case study of the evolution of ethnic identity, and of conflict at least partly rooted in 'corruption, oppression and injustice'.[111]

Royal women played a major role in both Kanem and Borno. It is claimed that an eleventh-century mai was imprisoned for a year by the queen mother, the magira, and during the minority of Mai Idris Aloma, in the sixteenth century, Borno was ruled by his sister, A'isha.

Wandala and the Sao

Borno was not uninhabited when the Seyfawa arrived. The indigenous people, called the Sao in traditional sources, are popularly thought to have been giants because of the huge mortuary pots they left behind. The word may mean 'city', and they have left many traces of their settlements to the south of Lake Chad, on mounds arising from the flood-plains of its great tributaries, the Chari and Logone, where terracotta sculptures and ornaments of bronze have been found. The conflict between the immigrant Kanuri and the Sao lasted from the thirteenth to the seventeenth centuries. The Just-So Sao, as one account calls them, were Chadic speakers, and some are referred to by recognisable ethonyms, such as Kotoko.[112] Two hundred years after the Seyfawa left Kanem, the royal chronicler, ibn Fartuwa, depicted their plight with unconscious pathos.

It [Mai Idris Aloma's campaign] largely consisted in building camps near the pagans, and settling Muslims in their vicinity, so as to allow them little empty country. Secondly, constant attacks on their territory in the hot season and winter so that they got no rest. Thirdly, cutting down their crops in the wet season ... Thus matters went on till the pagans became very weak. Before the age of our Sultan, they used to wander about in the land of Bornu ... Idris stopped all this.[113]

Some submitted and gradually became part of the Kanuri people, while others moved away, often forming smaller centralised polities on Borno's periphery. Oral tradition remembers this defensive adaptation as state formation by Kanuri immigrants.[114] The most powerful and best known of these was Mandara, or more correctly, Wandala. In 1459, the Italian Fra Mauro drew a map of the world which included Mandara (the Kanuri form of Wandala) and Marghi.[115] In 1573, another Italian, Anania, published a universal history, which mentioned, in addition to the Sauo, who gave their name to a huge navigable lake full of fish, Marghi, and 'Mandra', with its capital at 'Craua' (Keroua, the first Wandala capital).[116]In the eighteenth century, the Marghi still lived in small-scale polities, practising traditional religion, while Wandala, in the plains, had become a unified Muslim state. In the sixteenth century Wandala exported iron, and by the eighteenth, it also exported slaves.

Other ethnic groups took refuge in the mountains, where they suffered from increased overcrowding and periodic famine, but continued to sell smelted iron to Wandala. The profound paradox is encapsulated in a modern statement: 'The

Wandala are clever. They bought our iron, then used it to make the shackles that they held us with.' The sale of slaves enabled Wandala to buy horses, the basis of military power. Influenced by Borno, its ruling class became Muslims – a source of cultural dominance over the *kirdi* of the mountains. In the nineteenth century, when Borno's power increased, the Wandala shifted their capital and stored food in the mountains. It would have been easy for the *kirdi* to remove it, but they did not do so. They continued to trade with Wandala, purchasing much-needed salt and dried fish in return for iron and for slaves, whom they obtained by preying on each other.[117]

The Hausa kingdoms

In the sixteenth century, when Songhai and Borno dominated the Western Sudan, the Hausa kingdoms were a buffer zone between them. Ethiopia was called 'Habasha' ('Abyssinia') in Arabic, and the word was often used as a metaphor for the Hausa (baHabshe is 'Hausa' (singular) in Katinsa dialect, and 'Bagauda', the name of the legendary Kano state founder, means 'the Copt').[118] The modern name of the Maguzawa – rural non-Muslim Hausa – comes from *magus*. Hausaland has been well served by its historians. A number of brilliant reconstructions, which are in many ways complementary, have shed much light on the many ancient settlements which antedated the formation of the historic kingdoms of Kano, Zazzau and so on. They included Dalla Hill, at Kano, and Santolo, 18 miles to the south-east, where there was another hilltop shrine. Pauwa and Samri were ancient settlements in Katsina. The capitals of the various kingdoms were often on their northern edge; the older cult centres to the south were foci of potential opposition: 'terms for "south" became a recurrent feature of Hausa political geography'.[119]

Hausa is a Chadic language; since all other Chadic speakers are to the south or east, it is overwhelmingly probable that Hausa settlement spread from east to west;[120] many Chadic speakers have undoubtedly been absorbed by the Kanuri. The Chadic-speaking Ngas and Mwahavul live on the Jos plateau; they are radically different from the modern Hausa, in dress and lifestyle, and represent an ancient thrust to the south, as do the Goemai in the Benue valley. The Gwandara are another central Nigerian people, who claim that their ancestors left Kano rather than become Muslims; their speech is still recognisably Hausa, but without Arabic loan-words.

We see the early history of Hausaland through a glass darkly, glimpsing it through various traditional histories. One of the best known myths tells of a prince of Baghdad called Bayajida or Abuyazid. He travelled to Hausaland after a sojourn in Borno (an early nineteenth-century version calls him a slave of the mai),[121] perhaps a folk memory of origins on the Borno borderland, or a reflection of Borno political and cultural dominance.

At Daura, he killed a snake which lived in a well, and married the state's regnant queen (there is a similar tradition of marriage with a regnant queen in Wandala). The myth is explicit that state formation preceded the hero's arrival; a local author anticipated modern scholarship in 1824 when he pointed out that there were 'kings in these countries before the sons of Bawo'.[122]

According to a Daura version, Bayajida had six sons by three wives: Gazaura and Bagauda, who founded Daura and Kano; Gunguma and Duma (Zazzau and Gobir); Kumayau and Zamna Kogi (Katsina and Rano). The inclusion of small and insignificant Rano and the exclusion of indubitably Hausa Zamfara have been adduced as further proof of eastern origins. In the years when the Hamitic hypothesis flourished, this story was seen as a creative invasion by charismatic Berbers, a theory which has long been discredited.[123]

According to the 'Kano Chronicle', the city's first settler was Barbushe, 'a black man of great stature and might, a hunter, who slew elephants with his stick and carried them on his head about nine miles', a figure very like the traditional image of the Sao.[124] 'Then came Bagoda with his host and was the first Sarki of this land.'[125] 'The Song of Bagauda' ascribes the growth of the state to the creation of a surplus in agriculture, which drew immigrants in a time of famine, an enlargement of scale with political consequences: 'There was no chief, no protecting wall ... The elders said: let a chieftaincy be established. They appointed Bagauda, the protector.'[126]

Barbushe 'was skilled in the various pagan rites'. The central theme of the first section of the 'Kano Chronicle' is conflict between successive kings and the custodians of these ancient mysteries which centred on a sacred hill, Dala, and a magical grove.

The late fifteenth century was a watershed in Hausa history, marked by the growth of centralised political authority, the building of city walls, the cavalry revolution, and a more widespread acceptance, at least in urban circles, of Islam. 'In Yakubu's time (c. 1452–63) the Fulani came to Hausaland from Mali, bringing with them books on Divinity and Etymology.'[127] New dynasts came to power – in Katsina, Korau, who owed allegiance to both Islam and the Earth cult, and whose name lives on in the emir's palace, which is called *gidan Korau*, Korau's house. It is possible that he was one of the Wangarawa.

The name of the kingdom of Zazzau, or Zegzeg, may well be based on Zanj. The 'Kano Chronicle' tells of the conquests of a fifteenth-century semi-legendary Sarauniya (king's daughter) of Zazzau called Amina. At the beginning of the nineteenth century, her exploits in central Nigeria were regarded as historical.[128] Was she a historical figure? There were many titled, fief-holding women in the Hausa kingdoms – eight such ancient titles were known in Daura alone[129] – but it seems unlikely that any of them were permitted to embark on a career of military conquest. How do we explain the persistence of 'queens' in tradition, their absence in more recent centuries? The simplest explanatory theory is symbolic inversion: the location in the remote past or in distant lands of the opposite of the familiar.[130]

Colonialism shaped perceptions of Nigeria, which later politics perpetuated, distinguishing between 'the North' on one hand and 'the Middle Belt' on the other. Historically, they are inextricably connected, and many migrants from Hausaland settled in the south, drawn by its resources of iron, salt and tin, part of a wider Hausa diaspora which was to reach as far as Asante. The great mask complex, Magiro, was found both in Katsina and among peoples far to the south.

Kwararafa

The mysterious state of Kwararafa threads its way through Hausa and Borno history; it is a 'pagan' state of the south, full of symbolic significance in Hausa perceptions of their own past. Korau and Amina, among others, are said to have waged war against Kwararafa, which, in its turn, in the sixteenth and seventeenth centuries repeatedly invaded the Hausa kingdoms but, oddly, without any lasting political or cultural result. The mais of Borno fought similar wars with the 'Kwana'. These traditions are generally associated with the Benue valley people known in written sources as Jukun (a Hausa ethonym), who call themselves Wapan and who are widely known as Apa. The Aku of the Jukun settlement at Wukari is one of Africa's best known instances of sacred kingship.

Colonial ethnographers saw the Jukun as the collective *éminence grise* of central Nigerian history, playing a role similar to that of (mythical) Hamites further north. Undeterred by the fact that the Jukun speak a Benue-Congo language, with its linguistic relatives in central Nigeria and the Cross River area, colonial ethnographers made them 'a Hamitic or half-Hamite ruling caste'.[131] Nor is this the only difficulty. The identification of Jukun, Apa, Kwana and Kwararafa goes back to at least the mid-nineteenth century, but modern Jukun have no memory of Kwararafa or a supposedly martial past, and Kwararafa invasions ended mysteriously in the seventeenth century. In the nineteenth, the Jukun lived, not in a unified kingdom, but in a number of small communities in the Benue valley. It is possible that Kwararafa was a generic name for non-Muslim peoples from Dar al-Harb, the Land of Unbelief. It may well have been a multi-ethnic federation, which acted together for specific purposes and then disbanded. History is about change, and it is not impossible that the Jukun embarked on military expansion in the seventeenth century and were preoccupied with ritual in the nineteenth. A similar transition is well documented in early seventeenth-century Benin.

Many central Nigerian peoples have a tradition of an ancient migration 'from Apa', but in some of these cases, linguistic evidence makes a historic relationship very unlikely. The Idoma speak a Kwa language, related to Igala and Igbo, whereas Jukun is a Benue-Congo language. But Idoma ancestral chants sing of an ancestral home in Apa, in the Benue valley.[132]

Masking cults

We began this study by pointing out the difficulty of doing justice simultaneously to structure and process. Any organisation of a historical narrative involves reductionism, a concentration on a small number of themes and areas from many possible variables. Inevitably, in a western academic study, the categories are drawn from western thought: government, religion, production, trade, and leave out much of a densely textured and complex reality. A good example of this is the masking cult, which has hitherto been mainly studied by art historians and anthropologists. Masking cults are readily borrowed; communities are attracted by their spectacular appearance, and their supernatural power fascinates while it terrifies. They form large cultural complexes, common to numerous ethnic groups. The centre of the Magiro cult, which the Hausa call Kakan Tsafi, the Grandfather of the Sacred, was at Kwaterkashi, an area of granite outcrops near modern Gusau. It was important in the Hausa kingdom of Katsina, and was found among the Gbagyi and many other peoples of west-central Nigeria,[133] cutting across the artificial modern distinction between 'North' and 'Middle Belt'.

Abvwoi and *ku* form a similar complex in the region Nigerians call 'Southern Zaria'.

> O how is ku?
> O ku the wasp
> O the red ku
> O the white ku
> O the yellow ku

The colours reflect its supernatural character, the wasp its danger. Like many such cults, it appeared in public in the form of a masked dancer or of mysterious voices, 'audible ghosts'.[134]

Jankai, Red Head, Hausa in name and dress, with a distinctive headpiece of red seeds, is a much-feared mask found among many ethnic groups in central Nigeria, which seems to reflect a perception of Hausa culture and political power. Its antiquity and provenance are unknown.[135]

In Nigeria, these cults are the exclusive preserve of male initiates, though some acknowledge a 'mother', who is always an older woman; one of their most important functions is to maintain control over women, the uninitiated young, strangers and slaves. Material collected early this century in southern Zaria states: 'The idea of forming a "Dodo" [mask] society originally started in the village of Agabi a number of years ago. Two men were bewailing the fact that their wives were constantly running away from them and that their children were getting out of hand. They put their heads together to seek a remedy.'[136]

The relationship between gender, power and secret cults is explicit in the myths which describe the genesis of a Nupe witch eradication cult. In one version, a king's government was paralysed by his mother's interference, until a diviner invented a mask which swallowed her up. An alternative version states that the mask was created in a time of disorder: 'The older women, especially, caused much trouble.' Only one person resisted – an older woman, who was put to death by the older men.[137] This explicit polarity between the male masking cult and the woman witch is not peculiar to Nupe. 'God made things double,' say the Ebirra, 'masquerading for men and witchcraft for women.'[138]

Caste: blacksmiths and griots

In an earlier chapter,[139] we drew attention to one of the great mysteries of the African past, the existence of very similar occupational castes in Ethiopia and the Western Sudan. There is also an independent and somewhat different area of occupational castes on the Nigeria–Cameroon border.[140] There is a vast and ultimately connected complex of castes among Mande speakers and their neighbours, such as the Wolof, Tukulor, Songhai and Tuareg, some fifteen ethnic groups in fourteen modern nations.[141]

Both occupational castes and masking cults were, in a sense, an embodiment of supernatural presences. Men and women were born into a caste and inherited particular magical powers and capacities. In the masking cult, the supernatural presence was the masked figure or the unseen voice. Often, caste and mask were explicitly linked: Mande smiths 'own' the terrifying Komo initiation cults, and among the Gurage of Ethiopia they play the leading role in a women's secret cult.[142] Mande society was divided into the free, the casted and slaves: the free were either peasants or aristocrats; the casted, who could be neither enslaved nor killed in war, formed small minorities – some 5 per cent of the Soninke and Bambara population – and unlike many of their Ethiopian counterparts, they could own land. In pre-colonial times they often did not need to farm, and prospered by plying their trades. Casted and free did not intermarry. The structure of castes varied in different ethnic groups; they included metal workers, leather workers and bards, griots. Their wives were often potters, and male and female caste members were, respectively, responsible for circumcision and clitoridectomy, thus forging adult social identity. Casted men produced a great corpus of sculpture, including masks. The free were excluded from these avocations.

The position of the casted was profoundly paradoxical. They could not be kings, but were often royal advisers and messengers. In 1352–3, ibn Battuta described the power and splendour of Dugha, the Mali king's griot and spokesman. It is significant that he saw bards in masking costume: 'the poets are called *jula* [modern Mande *dyeli*, bard] ... Each of them has enclosed himself within an effigy made of feathers, resembling a [bird called] *shaqshaq*, on which is fixed a head made of wood with a red beak. They stand in front of the sultan and recite their poems.'[143]

This is the earliest account of caste, but the institution is clearly much older. The griot was the custodian of Mande oral literature, and, to a large extent, of the community's knowledge of its own past and sense of identity. The blacksmith was of crucial economic importance. By entrusting circumcision and clitoridectomy to the casted, the Mande placed their children's lives in their hands. Why were they marginalised?

Caste structures prevented those in a position of potential power from actualising it – the casted smith, rather than the Blacksmith King. The linking of craft skills with group endogamy meant both that children were trained in crafts from an early age and that society was not flooded with an unviably large number of, for instance, leather workers. But the essential reason is that these amazing transformations require magical powers, which are dangerous to those who approach too closely. 'A blacksmith is born into a caste which enables him ... to transform the shapes of iron, earth and wood, and to survive the forces unleashed by his transformations.'[144] They may well have found a special meaning in the City of Brass of Arabic folklore.

Smithing, like circumcision, is dangerous to the practitioner, protected only by inherited and acquired magical powers. But there is a sad symbolism in the fact that early European visitors referred to the casted as Jews (the marginalised of early modern Europe), and the usage still survives in Portuguese Creole.

Although the casted were excluded from both kingship and warfare, in Mande epics, sung by casted griots, Sumanguru is a Blacksmith King and Fakuru a blacksmith general,[145] In the world of oral literature, they reclaimed spheres from which Mande society excluded them.

14

West Africa: from the savanna to the sea

A gha se Edo, Edo rre.
The closer one gets to Benin, the farther away it is.
An Edo proverb[1]

Environment

There is no satisfactory name for that vast expanse of West Africa which lies between the savanna and the sea (Map 13). Historians sometimes write of Upper and Lower Guinea, but this is the language of the seventeenth and eighteenth centuries, meaningless to modern West Africans. Its history is shaped both by outward circumstances and by a hidden dynamic of cognitive change, which can only be recaptured through the surviving art of the distant past, and through present-day myth and ritual.[2] These are ambiguous voices – but there are sometimes no other voices to be heard.

There is no clear line of demarcation between the savanna and Guinea, or between their histories.[3] The vegetation changes imperceptibly as one goes south; little of the original ground cover survives in huge areas of what conventional maps still show as the forest zone, but which is now covered with cultivated plots, interspersed with secondary bush, and economic trees, especially the oil palm. In 1894, it was observed: 'As far as I could see, it had been entirely cleared of the original forest, only a few of the larger trees being left here and the area round the villages or in plantations. The fields seemed to be almost entirely devoted to yam cultivation.'[4]

Between the Cameroun mountains and the Bandama river in Ivory Coast, yam is the traditional staple, now often supplanted by the less nutritious cassava or by crops for export, such as cocoa; further west, the staple is rice. The cultivation of land covered by rainforest involved herculean efforts: it has been estimated that to clear one acre of virgin rainforest required the removal of between 300 and 700 tons of vegetation.[5] The words used of Asante in a book published in 1929, are much more widely applicable.

Ashanti is a country covered for the most part by dense primordial forest. To win a plot of land from these sombre unlit depths ... to reach its rich virgin soil beneath the tangle of lianas and living, or dead and decomposing, vegetation that covers the land, was a task that ... might have seemed almost impossible for individual effort. Gigantic trees had to be removed, huge fallen trees which a man could hardly climb.[6]

According to a widely cited model, the Akan first cleared the forest with the aid

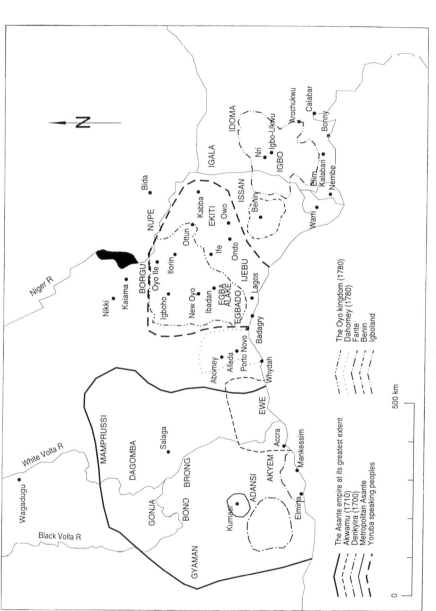

Map 13 Lower Guinea

of slave labour, in the fifteenth and sixteenth centuries,[7] thus laying the foundation for the creation, first of principalities, later of states. If this is true, it suggests a difficulty: why were the Akan forests cleared so much later than those of, for instance, southern Nigeria? West of Lagos, for reasons which are not fully understood, the savanna meets the sea, a fact which goes far to explain why the cavalry kingdom of Oyo expanded in this direction. But great states could and did develop in the forest zone and one of the major remaining areas of rainforest is near the city of Benin.

The Atlantic coast is sometimes a zone of pounding surf beaches and some-times of intricate waterways and swamps – the latter form most of the coastline of Nigeria. Specialist communities of fishermen and salt makers have lived here since time immemorial, exporting dried fish and salt far into the interior. The name of the coastal town of Jakin, in the Republic of Benin, means 'supplier of salt'.[8] In Elmina, fishing fleets of seven or eight hundred canoes would set out together.[9] Canoemen often travelled long distances through the coastal water-ways – from the Gold Coast to Angola, if we can believe a seventeenth-century visitor.[10] The coast was a frontier, the outer edge of civilised space, until the arrival of European merchants transformed its economic and cultural life. It was often ecological factors which shaped a sense of ethnic identity; Oyo was a cavalry state, but 'the Owa [of Ilesha] has everything but a horse's stable', and a minor ruler on the borders of Oyo and Ilesa thatched half his roof with bere grass, and half with forest leaves![11] A savanna god forbids his devotees to drink palm wine and a forest god prohibits guinea corn beer.[12] The names of Igbo groups often refer to the environment they lived in – Agbaja and Enugu, uplands, Anaocha, barren ('white') land.

Famine and disease

Because rainfall was higher, killing famines were probably less common in Guinea than in the savanna. But food shortages recurred every year before the harvest; it was forbidden to eat the new season's yams before the New Yam festival, to prevent hungry people from eating immature tubers (and dying of famine later). On the lower Niger, nineteenth-century missionaries watched with consternation as families sold one of their number to buy food for the rest.[13]

Drought was not the only cause of famine; it was sometimes due to 'the dreadful swarms of grasshoppers or locusts, which ... spread all over the country in such prodigious multitudes, that they darken the very air ... At other times ... immense swarms of small birds, and of ants and pismires, will do such mischief to their fields, that no less a dearth must ensue.'[14]

The Nok terracottas sometimes show pathological conditions, and certain Ife sculptures depict elephantiasis, rickets and anacephaly. The Yoruba god of herbalism, Osanyin, has one arm, one leg and a damaged voice.[15] In the twentieth century, some West African nationalists suggested placing the mos-quito on their national flags. It was not entirely in jest. West African diseases had a devastating impact on European visitors with no inherited immunity and proved to be one of the most powerful forces preventing white settlement. West Africans suffered particularly from helminthic and insect-borne diseases. Malaria was not peculiar to Africa but it was present in West Africa in a particularly deadly form, falciparum.

Sickle-cell anaemia is a genetic disease found among black Africans which causes episodes of agonising pain and kills its victims in childhood or young adulthood. Those who carry the gene, but do not suffer from the disease, have some immunity against malaria; this is also conferred by other abnormal blood haemoglobins found in West Africa. Sickle-cell anaemia probably underlies the concept of the Returner – *abiku* in Yoruba, *ogbanje* in Igbo, the child who repeatedly dies and returns, tormenting the unfortunate parents.

Guinea worms, like jiggers, were crippling, though they could be removed by a skilled practitioner. Smallpox was endemic, its spread limited by local forms of inoculation.[16] Bosman said of the Gold Coast in 1700: 'The National Diseases here are the *Smallpox* and [Guinea] *Worms*; by the former of which in these thirteen or fourteen Years time thousands of Men have been swept away ... This *Worm-Disease* is frequent all the coast over.'[17]

He also described a different affliction, manifested by a ravenous appetite, which may be linked with the mysterious and much-debated dirt eating which was common in slaves on American plantations, and often proved mortal.[18]

Smallpox epidemics led to witchcraft accusations, which sometimes caused as many deaths in poison ordeals as the disease did.[19] The Yoruba so dreaded it that they addressed its god, Sopona, by euphemisms, as the Greeks called the Furies the Kindly Ones. Dahomey kings introduced this cult, but two of them died of smallpox. River blindness (onchocerciasis) is caused by a filarial worm, transmitted by a fly, appropriately named *Similium damnosum*, which also causes a skin itch so intense that some victims have committed suicide. It has blinded thousands in the Volta river basin and has led whole communities to abandon the well-watered river valleys; generations later, when the disaster has been forgotten, people return and the whole cycle begins again. As late as the 1930s, the cause was not understood; doctors blamed it on vitamin deficiencies and urged people to eat spinach![20] Sleeping sickness, caused by tsetse fly, was another scourge which forced people to leave fertile lands and much-loved homes.

Small-scale states

West Africa has a much greater population than the rest of black Africa, and in some regions, such as southern Nigeria, it reached rural densities comparable with the Nile valley. In large areas, such as the great quadrant east of the Niger and south of the Benue, people lived in small-scale village democracies. Some have postulated a link between small-scale states and population densities – the result of centuries of perhaps unconscious preference, a predilection for the relative freedom of village life, rather than the exactions of kings and the rapacity of urban merchants. 'An option for the peasant oppressed by debt is to flee to such a society. "Deep rural" societies would tend, therefore, to gain population (and a reputation for harbouring drop-outs, runaways and criminals).'[21] There is little hard evidence that this actually happened, but villagers cherished their freedoms, circumscribed though they were. *Igbo enwero eze* (the Igbo have no kings) is a core statement of Igbo identity, and one of the best studies of the Igbo ever written is called *The King in Every Man*. It well reflects the complexity of our subject that it is written about a (small) kingdom.

Before the early nineteenth century, the Egba section of the Yoruba lived in 153 separate polities; here too it was proverbial that 'Egbas have no king, they are all of them like masters'.[22] Oral traditions which may well reflect later perceptions rather than actual events sometimes bear witness to a reaction against kingship at the heart of kingdoms. Egharevba records a (probably mythical) phase of what he calls republican government in pre-dynastic Benin.[23]

Many small states had sacred kings. The Berom of the Jos plateau numbered 119,000, according to the 1963 census, and lived in eighty separate polities, each with a sacred *gwom*.

It seems clear that many larger states – Igala, Benin and the Yoruba kingdoms among them – grew out of the fusion of small polities into a larger conglomerate, a transition which may well have occurred, in at least some cases, in the fifteenth century. The north-east Yoruba retain the small-scale structures which probably characterised the Yoruba kingdoms initially.[24] A memory of this time is preserved in myth and ritual and in extant political structures; sometimes it is fossilised in town design, the Benin city walls do not form concentric rings, like those of Ife, but mirror the fusing together of small independent polities.

The distinction between towns and villages located in Great States and those outside them is more apparent than real. In a very real sense, the power of the court did not extend far beyond the capital and historical maps – including those in this book – which suggest blocks of territory like modern nations, where the impact of government is equally felt everywhere, are misleading. Distant towns sent tribute, which was sometimes essentially symbolic and a description of the Lunda empire in Central Africa is much more widely applicable: 'a chain of political islands in a sea of woodlands occupied mostly by dispersed villagers recognising no overlord at all'.[25]

To flourish, a state required three things: trade, population, and enough military power to dominate its neighbours, or at least to hold its own.[26] These variables were interwoven, and the desire for an increased population was as true of small villages as it was of kingdoms. The incorporation of captives was one response to this need and, in general, communities welcomed immigrants. According to one legend, an early owa of Ilesha complained that he had too few subjects, and more were created for him out of sticks![27]

Villages, like kingdoms, were involved in trade, which often sprang naturally out of the needs and products of different ecological zones – salt from the Benue brine springs was exchanged for hoes and spears from the Jos plateau, in each case passing through many hands. Sometimes villages in much the same kind of environment traded with each other for reasons which were not primarily economic. They imported ritual objects, or purchased items which they produced equally well themselves, in order to foster closer links with their neighbours. On the Jos plateau, the Rukuba acquired tobacco, tomatoes and cord from the Irigwe in exchange for grain.[28]

If the need for people, and involvement in trade were universal, the military pursuit of dominance was not. On the Jos plateau, war between villages was governed by strict conventions; the attackers gave advance warning, and warfare stopped after the first casualty. These conventions were sustained when they fought the British, at enormous cost. 'They never made a sneaky attach [*sic*] such as creeping through the grass in the night ... their battles were arranged by due notice and a definite date and time fixed, like a football match.'[29]

Urban life

Life in an urban environment, even when people were engaged in agriculture, represents another distinct cultural choice which is particularly characteristic of the Yoruba. (Scholars disagree about the extent to which the Yoruba option for urban life was a response to the dangers of the nineteenth century, or whether it was an earlier phenomenon.) The Ijesa kingdom has 134 towns and villages, and 70 quarters in the capital, Ilesa.[30]

We have seen how, in the Jenne area in the first millennium CE, there were dense urban networks and a population much greater than that found in modern times.[31] The same is true of the Benin kingdom. The walls of the Edo and Issa region have been called 'the world's largest ancient monument' and are several times as long as the Great Wall of China. Their average height is 4 metres, and although most seem to date from the fifteenth and sixteenth centuries, the time of Benin's greatness, Benin is not at the centre but at the periphery. These ruins imply that the rural population in the area was ten times what it is today.[32] At the beginning of this century, missionaries came upon the walls and associated moats: 'Tradition says they are the work of a giant, son of one of the kings of Benin, who lived generations ago ... the names of the towns are forgotten, and the ruins are covered by thick bush.'[33]

Language, identity and history

Many of the peoples of Guinea speak Kwa or Benue-Congo languages (and it is noteworthy that some scholars have questioned the dividing line between them). The Kwa-speaking region is broadly identical with the yam belt. It includes Igbo, Igala, Idoma, Ijo, Yoruba, the Aja languages (Ewe, Fon and Gun) and the Akan languages. Deeply differentiated, they clearly reflect millennia of historical continuity. 'Rough basic vocabulary counts suggest that Yoruba, Edo and Ibo may have started to diverge not much less than 4,000 years ago ... There is no reason to suppose that the divergence of these languages from a parent stock has not taken place side by side more or less *in situ*.'[34] Linguistic intrusions, and especially areas of Mande speech such as Susu or Vai, are clearly related to specific historical migrations.

Early European records reflect continuity in ethonyms and toponyms which is perhaps surprising. In the mid-fifteenth century, early European visitors to Senegal encountered Geloga/Geloffa/Gyloffa/Jalofo in much the present home of the Wolof, who were often referred to by the name of the Jolof kingdom.[35] An account of what is now southern Nigeria, written at the beginning of the sixteenth century, mentions Geebuu (Ijebu-Ode), Beny (Benin), Opuu (Igbo), Jos (Ijo) and Subou (Sobo/Urhobo).[36]

Oral traditions for this early period tend to focus on dynastic origins. It is often far from clear whether they reflect real historical individuals or are personifications of phases of historical experience. There is a tendency for modern scholars to understand oral traditions in symbolic and mythical terms, which may lead us, on occasion, to overlook a deposit of historical fact. After the fall of Accra in 1677, its royal family founded a new state at Little Popo. If this had not been documented in contemporary sources, historians would solemnly debate whether the Little Popo tradition of founders 'from Accra' was a mythical construct! Oral traditions, here as elsewhere, often take the stereotypic form of the cliché – the immigrant hunter who founds a kingdom, or the animal(s) who rescue a people, either by providing a bridge across water or by covering their footsteps during their flight. A common mytheme tells of a person – sometimes a ruler – who sacrifices her child or her own life to save a kingdom. Moremi does this in Ife legend, and in Igala tradition the Attah's daughter voluntarily offers herself up when her father is reluctant to do so. The Baoulé of Ivory Coast tell of a fugitive queen who threw her son into a river, whereupon a ford appeared. This particular example emanates from folk etymology (*ba-ule*, 'they threw').[37]

Many oral traditions, especially those preserved in the framework of a dynastic kingdom, are, in a sense, elitist in their preoccupation with kings and wars. They sometimes shed light, almost incidentally, on an economic base which is vividly depicted in eye-witness accounts from a later date. An account of the Gold Coast, written in the mid-sixteenth century, described local craftsmanship: 'All their cloth, cordes, girdles, fishing lines, and all such things, which they have, they make of the bark of certaine trees, and thereof they can worke things very prettily, and iron worke they can make very fine, and all such things as they doe occupy, as darts, fishhookes, hooking yrons, yron heads and great daggers . . .'[38]

In the late seventeenth century, Barbot described Efutu (a Guang-speaking polity with its main port at Cape Coast): 'It has many well built towns, full of inhabitants . . . The blacks of this kingdom apply themselves, some to tillage, others to fishing, or boiling of salt; others to press oil and draw wine from the palm-trees; and others to trade, either on their own account or as brokers for the inland blacks.'[39]

The Igbo culture sphere

It is impossible to write African history without the familiar shorthand of 'Yoruba' or 'Igbo', but there was no sense of pan-Yoruba or pan-Igbo consciousness, except among the victims of the transatlantic slave trade.

'Igbo' may have originally meant 'community', and is still widely used in this sense. Niger Igbo called themselves 'Olu' and thought of 'Igbo' as the people of the interior, to whom they felt themselves superior, partly because of their broker role in trade. To the Igbo of the interior, the Olu, with their traditions of migration from elsewhere and their little kingdoms, were not really 'Igbo' at all.[40] Ethnic labels, in the nineteenth century and earlier, often meant little more than 'us' and 'them'.

Language and the findings of archaeology suggest that 'the Igbo' have lived in much their present homes from the dawn of human history. 'We did not come from anywhere and anyone who tells you we came from anywhere is a liar. Write it down,' said an elder of Mbaise in 1972.[41] Most scholars regard the Owerri, Okigwe, Orlu and Awka areas as an Igbo heartland. The peoples of this area have no tradition of migration from elsewhere and modern demographic maps reflect its extraordinarily high population density. Why did people concentrate on sandy uplands of limited fertility, with frequent water shortages, rather than the river valleys with their alluvial soils? Several answers have been suggested, none wholly convincing: the original vegetation was more easily cleared, riverain sites were subject to periodic flooding, at risk from marauders in canoes, and, as early missionaries discovered to their cost, infested with mosquitoes.

Nri and Igbo-Ukwu

It is in this heartland that the holy centre of Nri grew up, and the ancient treasures of Igbo-Ukwu were discovered. At its greatest extent the Nri sphere of influence covered perhaps half of Igboland; nevertheless, it constituted its ritual heart, like Ife, among the Yoruba. Both are encrusted with legend, and in both, ancient sculptures and other treasures have been found. 'The street of the Nri family is the street of the gods, through which all who die in other parts of Iboland pass to the land of Spirits.'[42]

The Eze Nri is a ritual figure rather than a king. Chosen, after an interregnum, through manifestations of supernatural powers, he is installed after a symbolic journey to Aguleri, on the Anambra river. Here, by magical means, he collects stones from under the water, undergoes a symbolic burial and exhumation, and is anointed with white clay, symbol of purity. When he dies he is buried seated in a wood-lined chamber.[43] The Igbo myth of the creation of the world is located, not at Nri, but at Aguleri: 'All the first things happened at Aguleri. There the land was made dry and food given to the world.'[44]

Nri and Aguleri are part of the Umueri clan, a cluster of Igbo village groups which traces its origins to a sky being called Eri, and, significantly, includes (from the viewpoint of its Igbo members) the neighbour kingdom of Igala. The land, originally a quagmire, was dried by the bellows of an Awka smith; the chameleon, a magical being, walks with great care because it was created in the world's morning.[45] Nri tradition provides a mythical charter for the foundations of Igbo life: yam and cocoyam were obtained at the cost of the death of Nri's son and daughter, an oil palm and a breadfruit tree by the sacrifice of slaves.

Although bloodshed is inherent in this historical charter, for many centuries the people of Nri have had a strong commitment to peace, rooted in the belief that it is an abomination to pollute the sacred Earth. 'The white men that came started by killing those who did not agree with their rules. We Nri never did so.'[46]

The Nri sphere of ritual influence was probably at its greatest between 1100 and 1400.[47] Nri ritual specialists, distinguished by their facial scars (which are shown in several Igbo-Ukwu sculptures) and by their ritual staffs of peace, travelled far afield, purifying the earth from human crimes and introducing a variety of ritual practices, including the *ozo* title system, and *ikenga*, the cult of the right hand, 'with which a person works out a successful living in this difficult world'.[48] This ritual pre-eminence is the reward for Nri's original distribution of the food he had acquired at such great cost.[49] The four-day week and its associated markets were brought by strangers bearing baskets of fish[50] – a condensed symbolic statement of the beginnings of trade between the landlocked Igbo and Niger Delta fishermen (and salt processors).[51] In 1911, the names of nineteen Nri were recorded. The list is not easy to translate into chronological terms, partly because of the long interregna.[52]

In Africa, as elsewhere, many of the most important archaeological discoveries have been made by accident. In 1938, a farmer was digging a cistern in his compound at Igbo-Ukwu, nine miles from Nri, when he stumbled upon remarkable bronze sculptures. More than twenty years elapsed before the area was professionally excavated, and much longer before the excavations were published. When they were, they revealed the existence of a hitherto unsuspected Igbo Bronze Age in the ninth century CE. The dating did not go unchallenged, but it has never been disproved.[53] Many of the finds – which included a treasure hoard and a dignitary buried in a sitting position in a wood-lined chamber, with slaves and valuables – were immediately explicable in terms of later Nri culture. A bronze depicts a woman with *ichi* facial scars; only one woman had these scars – the eldest daughter of the Eze Nri. The incised designs on the pottery were very similar to modern woodcarving patterns. One motif of surface decoration was a snake with an egg in its mouth, a praise name for the Onitsha king. The finds also included several fine specimens of textiles.

The implications of the excavations were far-reaching. They showed the antiquity of Igbo textile and metal-working skills, which are well attested in the nineteenth and twentieth centuries. (And yet in 1922, a colonial official had written, 'The local Ibo is virtually ignorant of the art of working metals and is hopelessly backward in arts and crafts ... Indigenous trades, such as that of weaver, the brass-worker, or tanner, are unknown.')[54]

The Igbo-Ukwu excavations suggested that the institution of sacred kingship, which still flourishes at Nri and among the riverain and western Igbo, was much older than could have been deduced from oral tradition alone. The finds yielded evidence of a hitherto unsuspected involvement in international trade, hundreds of miles from the southern termini of the Saharan routes: there was a great treasury of beads, some of glass and some of carnelian, many of which seem to have originated in Venice and India. Much research has been devoted to the raw materials used in the sculptures: tin bronze and leaded tin bronze, which may have been obtained in ancient mines in Abakaliki in eastern Igboland.[55] They depicted, among other things, a horse and a seashell. Nri is far from the sea, and because of tsetse fly, horses cannot survive there.[56] The dignitary was buried with slaves and ivory; the economic importance of both is mirrored in oral tradition, and Ogbuenyi, Elephant Slayer, is a widespread personal title.

The artistic idiom of Igbo-Ukwu is unique. The bronzes, cast by the lost-wax method, often replicate forms from the natural world, such as a shell or a calabash, but are covered with intricate decoration, sometimes featuring insects. They are a triumph of the metal caster's art. There is a sense in which they exist in puzzling isolation, though at nearby Ezira bronzes were also found covered with elaborate lace-like decoration, and there are seventeenth-century drawings of finely worked swords, attributed to the Igbo.[57]

Bronze is only one of many sculptural media; it has attracted perhaps disproportionate scholarly attention because of its durability and its value in western eyes. Much sculpture, among the Igbo as among other West Africans, was in wood or terracotta. Sculpture in unbaked clay is intrinsically ephemeral, but this medium was often chosen to honour Ala, the sacred Earth. The *mbari* houses of the Owerri Igbo are not dwellings but collections of clay sculpture, part of the Earth cult; once completed, they were allowed to crumble away.[58]

Social idioms

In modern times – and undoubtedly much earlier – the eastern Igbo lived in village groups; although the area is now one of the most densely populated rural areas in Africa, this is not apparent, and scattered homes are surrounded by the ubiquitous oil palm and other indigenous and introduced trees that have economic value. They derived their common identity from maps in the mind, which traced their origin to a putative ancestor. The western Igbo, who also traced their descent to an apical ancestor, lived in nucleated settlements. The genealogical calculus was mirrored in the organisation of space, each quarter tracing its origin to a son or grandson of the founder.

The idiom of genealogy was an extremely precise guide to relationships at all levels – within the village, and between the independent communities which comprised the village group and the wider 'clan', and an inherent flexibility made it possible to incorporate strangers. There was an evident need to find a beginning in an otherwise endless chain of father–son successions, and this is found in the myth of the stranger from elsewhere – the earth or the sky, or a hunter from far away.

The details of Igbo village democracy varied. We have glimpses in nineteenth-century descriptions, but the first systematic analysis dates from this century. Much can, however, be extrapolated back to a much earlier period. It was said in the 1920s that Igbo communities were ruled by ancestors and divinities. They were dominated by the male elders – in many communities, titled elders – who were closest to the world of the ancestors; the structures of local government included a hierarchy of personal achieved male titles, age grades, and one or more secret societies.

In Asaba,[59] the age grade of men aged from 58 to 68 formed the town's governing body, but only those who held personal titles had an effective say; these were not inherited but achieved, in a process which required both lavish expenditure and a state of ritual purity. Younger male age grades had specific duties appropriate for their age. There was also a secret society, dominated by younger men. By the late nineteenth century, there were 500 holders of the highest title, *eze* (king). Tradition claims that there was originally only one king, and the title was multiplied as a defence against a 'grasping and avaricious' ruler.[60] Several individual titles were borrowed from Benin, and there was a single titled woman, the *omu*, Market Queen.

The details of local government varied in different areas. In Awka, enriched by its blacksmiths and other itinerant specialists, there was a structure of nine titles; in the 1970s, twenty-six men held the highest title, *ozo*, and it was thought the number had been lower in the past.[61]

Water spirits

The names of places and of divinities shed considerable light on the past, often reflecting submerged cultural complexes, in a past so remote that it is difficult to glimpse, let alone understand. Alaenyi means 'land of elephants' – in an area where elephants are no longer found. The town of Asaba was originally called Ahaba or Araba. Its tutelary divinity is a river goddess dressed in white, called Onishe. Mbiri is a different western Igbo community; its tutelary goddess also lives in water and wears white; she is called Araba.[62]

East of the Niger, in the Okigwe area, the goddesses Ihuku, Lolo and Imo live in the streams which bear their names; in the past, cult slaves, *osu*, were dedicated to them, and human beings sacrificed; their fish are sacred and may not be eaten, and before a disaster, Lolo's crocodile would cry out for four days in warning.[63]

The Igbo's southern neighbours, the Kalabari of the Niger Delta, have filled its waterways with a myriad of brilliant presences, the water people, richly dressed and living in splendid towns under the sea. Each village celebrates them, together with the heroes and the ancestors, in an annual cycle of thirty to fifty masked plays.[64] The Kalabari see them as a rich source of cultural innovations; it is a form of false consciousness, for the Kalabari invented the new dance or play themselves. Further east, on the rain-drenched forested slopes of Mount Cameroun, Bakweri women practise a spirit possession cult of *liengu* sea spirits, miles from the sea and in a forest environment.[65]

The Yoruba culture sphere

The word 'Yoruba' originally referred to Oyo, and was first used in its modern sense by a missionary in 1832. It reflects a common language, but one with marked dialectal differences, a body of shared religious concepts and socio-cultural patterns, none of which are common to all Yoruba. Not all the Yoruba kingdoms shared the tradition of a founder prince from Ife – but Benin did.

'Yoruba' Oyo looked on 'Yoruba' Ilesha or Ijebu as alien. The Ijebu 'were, before the [British] conquest the most exclusive and inhospitable of tribes'.[66] Foreigners absorbed and reflected these stereotypes. 'I was now among a strange people, [the Ijesha] of bad repute among the [Oyo] Yoruba, with a language somewhat difficult and liable to suspicion.'[67] The primary unit of identification, here as elsewhere, was the kingdom – *ilu* in Yoruba, *oman* in Twi. These varied greatly in size, from the vast Oyo empire of the late eighteenth century to small principalities such as the Sixteen Kingdoms of Ekiti.

Ife, like Nri, is famous both for its ritual pre-eminence and for its ancient sculpture. Here, tradition claims, the world was created, by separating the water from the dry land: 'from thence the sun and the moon rise, where they are buried in the ground, and all the people of this country, and even white men, have come from that town.'[68]

The enormously rich world of Yoruba myth and ritual has fascinated many scholars; few peoples in black Africa have been so intensively studied. Not surprisingly, their legends do not fit together to make a tidy whole, and historians differ radically in the way they interpret them. The gods of Yorubaland are sometimes understood as kings who were divinised in cults after their death, sometimes as divinities who have in tradition been given an unhistorical human face. Sango is alternatively the god of lightning or an early Alafin of Oyo who entered the pantheon after his death. Obatala is the creator god or an early ruler of Ife. Oduduwa is a different creator god or an immigrant to Ife who overthrew Obatala and created his own kingdom. In a further variant, Oduduwa is Obatala's wife! The cult of Obatala is of great importance in Ife religion, as is the royal cult of Sango in Oyo. The worship of Ogun, god of iron, is centred at Ire in Ekiti.

Ife tradition tells of early settlers called Igbo (the word has a different tonal structure from the name of the ethnic group, to which it is totally unrelated). Some scholars regard this as a historical indigenous population, but Igbo means 'bush', and the legend may describe the conquest of nature by human culture. A heroic woman, Moremi, is said to have destroyed the Igbo by discovering the secret of their raffia masking costumes. This is one of a number of African legends which praise a woman who betrays her husband in the interests of her kin.

The Yoruba kings, who claim the jealously guarded right to wear a beaded crown, all claim an ancestor from Ife, 'the sons of Oduduwa'. In some versions, these number sixteen. This is a symbolic number: Ife is the centre of Ifa divination, obtained by casting sixteen palm nuts, and based on a corpus of sacred literature in sixteen sections.[69] Regional variants in myth are often politically determined: Oyo tradition states that the first Ooni (king) of Ife was a slave, and it seems likely that traditions of an Ife supremacy were elaborated as an ideology subversive of Oyo hegemony.[70] An Ijebu man said in 1901, 'I deny that Oyo is the capital city of Yoruba land. Ife, the cradle home of the whole Yorubas and the land of the deified Oduduwa, has been recognised by every interior tribe (including Benin and Ketu) for all intents and purposes as the capital city.'[71] The Oduduwa traditions can also be interpreted as a narrative of local chieftains and guild heads in the Ife area. (Ogun the blacksmith, Osanyin the physician.)

Some have suggested that Ogboni, the secret male cult of the sacred Earth, is an institutional relic of an ancient past; two of its officials have the names of pre-Oduduwa kings, and its songs stress 'the rights of certain ancient local lineages *vis-à-vis* all "Interlopers" '.[72] Ogboni was found in Oyo, Abeokuta and elsewhere – but not in Ilesha. In Ilesha, there are three ancient chieftaincy titles called *ogboni*, which are linked with the Benin forest, and are the headships of local towns;[73] like the Igala Mela in Igala, or the Uzama in Benin, they are an institutional fossil from a time before the dynastic kingdom. They have the same associations as the secret cult: elders, metal and the earth. Do they share common historical roots, which evolved into different forms but retained the same name? There are some 'kings' at Ife who own beaded crowns they may not wear – a relic of otherwise vanished and forgotten polities.[74]

Ife was a substantial town between the ninth and the twelfth centuries, with a splendid court, magnificent sculpture in terracotta and bronze, and elaborate potsherd pavements (these are also found, presumably independently, in Borno). Tradition associates the Ife pavements with a tyrannical woman ruler,[75] one of many apparently mythical woman royals who thread their way mysteriously through early West African history. The court may well have been sustained by the profits of Ife's glass industry; it died out before the nineteenth century, when glass was mined as if it were a mineral resource. Its origins in human technology forgotten, it was thought to be a gift from the gods. Yoruba royals wore abundant jewellery, and crowns were embroidered with beads in a symbolically significant pattern. They also symbolised the wounded herbalist god Osanyin: 'There was once born an amazing child. He came into this world with shining beads in many colours gleaming about his body.'[76]

Ife is internationally famous for its terracotta and bronze sculptures. The latter are quite different in metal content from their counterparts in Benin and Igbo-Ukwu: some are leaded brass, and some of almost pure copper. Willett has calculated that the whole of the copper and copper alloy work from Ibo-Ukwu weighs 70 kg, and that from Ife 170 kg. A single caravan across the Sahara carried four times as much.[77] They are cast, like the Igbo-Ukwu sculptures, by the lost-wax technique; the metal is very thin, reflecting both its scarcity and the artist's superb virtuosity. But in style and subject matter, they are entirely different from the sculpture of Igbo-Ukwu. Most of the Ife bronzes are busts, idealised portraits, and one is a mask in the same style. They are thought to date from *c.* 1100 to *c.* 1400. Only thirty Ife bronzes are known to exist, and it is possible that they came from a single hand. There is a much larger corpus of terracotta sculpture, some, but not all, in the same style. Several bronzes depict a victim awaiting sacrifice, gagged so that he cannot curse his executioner. Like the multiple interment at Igbo-Ukwu, they are a mute reminder of the underside of African history.

One of the mysteries of the Yoruba past is the contrast between Ife's importance in myth and the wealth reflected in its sculpture on the one hand, and its lack of political power in recent centuries on the other. Was an era of political strength succeeded by one of political decline, when ritual became all-important? Ilesha, only twenty miles away, was probably founded in the early sixteenth century, and it may have taken over much of Ife's political role.[78] A legend states that the ancestor of its first king, Obokun, was Oduduwa's youngest son, and that it was he who performed his father's burial rites, leaving behind a mere custodian at Ife.

Oyo, destined to be the largest of the Yoruba kingdoms, grew up on the northern edge of Yorubaland, hundreds of miles to the north of modern Oyo, which is a nineteenth-century foundation.[79] The lightning god, Sango, is said to have been an early Alafin, an overambitious magician who brought disaster on his court, was abandoned by his people, and committed suicide. In some versions he enters the ground by passing an iron chain into the earth; the same story is told of the Nupe culture hero, Tsoede. The Yoruba say of Sango, *Oba koso* (the king does not die). But *koso* is not a Yoruba word[80] and Oyo history is interwoven with that of its neighbours, Nupe and Borgu.

The original Oyo capital was founded in the eleventh century; it became a larger city in the fourteenth.[81] Tradition suggests that it began as a small state – its putative founder, the Ife prince Oranmiyan (who is also the 'founder' of Benin), lacked a beaded crown and seized one from a neighbouring king. Significantly, he is remembered as a youngest son. Nupe forces drove the Alafin and his court into exile for about a hundred years, from the early sixteenth century to the early seventeenth. Nupe successes may well have been due to their cavalry.[82]

Tradition claims that Oyo was ruled by a woman, Iyayun, during a long regency in the late fifteenth century. 'She wore the crown, and put on the royal robes ... and ruled the kingdom as a man.'[83] It is a sad irony that later the Alafin could not have a living mother. The Ondo state looks back to a mythical woman founder, sometimes described as the exiled mother of twins. Ilesa has traditions of no less than six early women Owa (rulers). Peel suggests that they were men, described as women to exclude their heirs from the succession,[84] but it is likely that these and similar stories are really examples of a pattern we have noted previously – the use of inversion, to define and affirm the status quo.

Benin

When the first European visitors arrived in the late fifteenth century, Benin was already a substantial kingdom. Tradition tells of thirty-one *ogiso* whose rule preceded the dynastic kingdom – the number is symbolic, intended to mirror the king list. In the annual *iron* festival, the transition is re-enacted: the Uzama, chiefs of ancient title, challenge the Oba and are defeated, holding out their archaic crowns. The *ogiso* are thought to have lived on the eastern side of Benin, and it is here, near Agbor, that Benin tradition locates the beginning of the world – a primal morass, the delicately stepping chameleon.

Present-day tradition describes a dynastic founder from Ife, the much-travelled Oranmiyan, and Ife is also seen as the source of bronze-casting skills. Early European sources describe Benin's links with a great sacred king, possibly the Ooni of Ife or the Attah of Igala. Thornton has made the arresting suggestion that the Oranmiyan tradition developed later, as a result of the well-attested presence of Yoruba functionaries at the Benin court, an employment of free foreigners comparable with the role of slave courtiers and generals elsewhere.[85]

Early Benin was a small state among others; it fought bitter wars against Udo, some twenty miles away. The name of the now extremely obscure town of Urhonigbe means 'ten gates', a gibe at Benin, which had nine. Ewuare, who ruled in the fifteenth century, was a warrior and magician who vastly expanded the kingdom, and destroyed its capital, building a new city from its ashes. He created the basic structure of Edo government by founding an order of Town Chiefs. He was the architect of much royal ritual and is said to have obtained royal beads from the sea divinity Olokun. His daughter was later offered the throne, but was prevented from reigning by mortal illness (a tradition comparable with that of Ife's tyrant queen – the impaired woman born to rule).

It has been claimed that people fled from centralised states to the freedom of village democracies,[86] but great states were more often the subject of admiration and emulation. Many western Igbo towns have Bini titles and the Bini ceremonial sword, *ada*, and some claim a founder from Benin, as did the ruling families of two small coastal kingdoms, Warri and Lagos.

Igala, Nupe and the forest of symbols

The southern Igala share a border with the northern Igbo and a certain sense of ultimate identity is mirrored in the mythical charter of the Umueri clan, but the Igala language is much more closely related to Yoruba. The Igala have four distinct traditions of dynastic origin; clearly, they cannot all be taken literally, especially since a leopard is one of the putative founders! Traditions collected in the nineteenth century refer to a dynast from Yorubaland who supplants an indigenous 'Okpoto' king. Traditions collected in the 1960s describe, with much circumstantial detail, a dynastic founder from Benin. A third version ascribes the origins of the dynasty to the Jukun of Wukari. All versions of Igala tradition agree that the apical ancestor of the royal clan is Ayagba om (son of) Idoko, preceded by four shadowy figures, Abutu Eje (leopard), Agenapoje, Ebelejonu and Idoko. Ebelejonu was a woman ruler who married a captive Igbo hunter, who became the first Ashadu. All versions agree that Ayagba led a great war of liberation against the Jukun, achieving victory by ritual means when his daughter, Enekpe, offered herself as a living sacrifice, the remedy suggested by a Nupe diviner.

The kingship rotates between four branches of the royal clan, and when an Attah dies, his subclan members resign their offices. Nine high officials, the Igala Mela, reflect an earlier period of small-scale government, and are the custodians of the sacred Earth shrine. To the anthropologist Boston, these traditions have no historical content: they are a mythical charter for the checks and balances of later Igala politics.[87] The Ashadu is an important official, but the myth makes him the descendant of a slave. The Attah's eminence is balanced by the indignities endured by the Attah elect, who is regarded, like Ebelejonu, as the Ashadu's wife.

There were ten Attahs between 1834 and 1956, with an average regnal length of twelve years. Applied to the full current king list, this yields a mid-seventeenth-century date for Ayagba – assuming his historicity. Benin invaded the Igala kingdom at the beginning of the sixteenth century, and there are probable references to it in early European sources. Sargent, a member of the Dalhousie school, has worked out a dynastic chronology which begins in *c.* 1477,[88] but despite his many 'tie-ins', few scholars, perhaps, feel confident about its reliability. Igala tradition refers to a Nupe diviner; Nupe tradition describes a dynastic founder called Tsoede, who was the son of an Attah of Igala. Tradition emphasises his vast cavalry. Is he a historical figure[89] who can be dated to the early fifteenth century[90] or a personification of a period of historical experience?[91] A political entity called Nupe threads its way through the early history of Oyo, Zazzau and Katsina. Ibn Battuta, who visited the Western Sudan in 1352–3, referred to a powerful state on the Niger called Yufi; this is generally taken to be a reference to Nupe (Nufi).

Numerous traditions connect Oyo, Nupe, Benin and Igala, and complex linkages are also found in their art. The kings of Igala and Benin have identical masks, the former in bronze and the latter in ivory. The face painted in beads on the crown of a Yoruba Oba has an obvious similarity with the masks worn by members of secret male cults. The birds which surmount it recall the cluster of iron birds at the apex of a Bini or Yoruba herbalist's staff. Bird clusters are also found in Ogboni sacred sculpture, which is made of bronze, a symbol of immortality.

Until recently, there was a mysterious group of bronze sculptures in Nupe, in villages near the Niger. One, a seated figure, is so clearly in the Ife style that it is sometimes called the finest work in the Ife corpus. Two of the statues are known as the Gara image and the Jebba bowman. On the tunic of the former and the forehead medallion of the latter is a distinctive figure which art historians sometimes call the snake-wing bird.[92] It has a triangular head and long wings like snakes, which are sometimes grasped by feet which are like hands. This is a familiar motif in Yoruba and Benin art; in the latter corpus, it is sometimes found together with a figure with a human head and torso, and curved legs in the form of fish or snakes, which has been linked both to Olokun symbolism, and to an early paraplegic oba. On the forehead medallion of the Gara image is a face with snakes protruding from its nostrils, and with horns and a projecting tongue. In Benin art, this represents the sacred aspect of kingship, the magician who is able to breathe forth snakes. The wide currency of these images is in part explicable through trade, war booty and the diplomatic exchange of gifts. But they reflect a world of symbolic meanings which transcended ethnic boundaries,[93] and whose centrality is quite explicit: 'the priest of Agemo at Imosan ... when shown a drawing of a crown with veil, birds, and frontal faces, immediately exclaimed: "The very history of the Yoruba"'.[94]

Masks, kings and gender

The legend of Moremi reflects the antiquity of mask societies. In Nigeria, they are always a male preserve, though some have a post-menopausal 'mother'. Some must be joined by all freeborn adult males, and adolescent initiation becomes the rite of passage to adult life. Others, such as the Yoruba Ogboni, are the preserve of a few. Some, such as Ekpe in Calabar, consist of a number of levels; an initiate aspires to reach ever higher levels and discover the cult's innermost secrets. The lower levels of Ekpe were open to slaves, but in general – and Ekpe itself is no exception – masking cults acted, as we saw in the last chapter, as an agency of social control over women, children, slaves and foreigners, and there is often a sense of the polarity of male masking cults and witches, perceived as women, often with specific reference to their role in economic life.[95] The riverain Igbo believe that witches gather in the market place by night, in the guise of astral birds, and in Nupe, the leader of the guild of women traders is also thought to head a coven.

Egungun is a masking cult, widespread but not universal in Yorubaland, which represents the male dead in their collective aspect. Its head was a member of the Oyo Mesi, a royal council of seven great officials. The Ifa divination corpus includes an account of how the witch would kill children, until

> The Human Being went back to his Ifa priest
> And performed the sacrifice which he previously neglected . . .
> He put on the robes of his Egungun.[96]

'The original three cloths of Egungun were of the colour red. They terrorised the witches.' [97]

The Aja-speaking peoples

The Ewe of Ghana and Togo, the Fon or Aja of ancient Dahomey and the Gun of Porto Novo (both in the modern Republic of Benin) all speak much the same language. Barbot referred to 'the *Fidafians* [of Whydah] using the same language as those of *Ardra*' and to 'their uniformity of manners and practices'.[98] The Ewe/Aja/Gun are now divided by the boundaries of no less than four modern nations, two of which are anglophone and two francophone. This, and the diversity of their ethnyms, means that their essential unity is often not realised, even by other West Africans. The Ewe call the Gun and Fon – but not themselves – Aja, and western Yoruba, such as the people of Ketu, do likewise. Because of this a new name, Gbe, has been suggested for their common language[99] but it has not yet won general acceptance. Aja-speaking communities trace their origins to the inland town of Tado, which has much the same ritual supremacy as Ife among the Yoruba. Some traditions say that Tado was founded by a migrant from Yorubaland, either from Ketu or from Oyo. From Tado, tradition claims, one section moved west to Nuatje, also in Togo, the centre from which the Ewe trace their origin. Both Tado and Nuatje have substantial earthworks.

It seems likely that the Tado tradition does not reflect real historical movements but is essentially a charter of social relations. Some traditions speak of a leopard ancestor and others of an escape from royal tyranny, in myths which are strikingly similar to others told in far distant parts of Africa (the king who placed thorns in the mud to be trodden for a building).[100] But in the last three hundred years or so, there have been well-attested cases of the formation of states after a migration, usually of a small body of royals and their entourage rather than whole populations. Refugee royals from Accra founded Little Popo in the late seventeenth century, and dynasts from Allada did the same at Porto Novo in the early eighteenth. If these movements were not fully documented, we might well believe traditions about them to be charters of social relations.

Different Aja-speaking groups made different political choices: the Ewe remained in the decentralised villages which probably originally characterised all Aja speakers. There are hints that kingship sometimes evolved out of clan headship – the Aja word for 'king' was *Ahosu*, which originally meant 'clan head'.[101]

The hundred Anlo villages were on the coast in a zone of lagoons, sandbanks and barren clay soils, where cultivable terrain was very limited. All Anlo are members of one of fifteen clans, obeying the same ritual prohibitions, respecting the same totem, and tracing descent from a common ancestor. As with the Asante, or the Igala - but unlike the Igbo – clan members do not live in a single area but are scattered through many different settlements.

The conventional view is that clans are very ancient (a founder whose descendants are ever more numerous). But in the case of the Anlo, it has been suggested that the clans were developed in the late seventeenth or early eighteenth centuries to protect their limited areas of agricultural land, when refugees reached the area from the west.[102]

The Akan

The study of language relationships sheds a great deal of light on the history of the Akan-speaking peoples and their neighbours.[103] Volta Comoe languages fall into three main branches – western, central and Guang. The western branch consists of two languages spoken by small ethnic groups in Ivory Coast. The central branch has two sections, Bia and Akan. Bia includes Agni and Baoulé, also spoken in Ivory Coast, and Aowin and Sefwi, found in western Ghana. Akan divides into three dialect clusters: the northern dialect of Brong, and Asante and Fante. The last two languages are known as Twi. Linguistic evidence suggests that the original home of Volta-Comoe was western Brong-Ahafo, near the present Ghana–Ivory Coast frontier, and that western Brong was the original point of dispersal for Akan. It is noteworthy that the type site for the Late Stone Age Kintampo culture is in this area.

The Fante lived on or near the coast; further east, Ga and Dangme were spoken, and there were some Guan-speaking enclaves. The relationship between language and population is complex; a lineage in Accra speaks Ga and regards itself as Ga, but its ancient heritage of oral literature is in Akan.[104] Some Akwapim towns, such as Mamfe, changed from Guang to Akan, and Kpone changed from Dangme to Ga.[105]

The use of the word Akan has changed over time, and is chronically ambiguous.[106] Its most appropriate modern use is linguistic, referring to speakers of Akan languages. In Twi, the prestigious term *akan-fo* meant 'us', 'the true people', as opposed to *apoto-fo*, 'them', 'foreigners'. In modern academic discourse 'Akan' is 'inclusive and fixed rather than exclusive and situational', a usage apparently derived from nineteenth-century Basle missionaries.[107]

Early European visitors wrote of 'Heccanys', 'Hacanys' and 'Quiforo' (Twifo, the Twi people). Forms of 'Akan' thread their way through sixteenth- and seventeenth-century records, and disappear in the eighteenth century. It is likely that the earlier references are to specific states, and though there is no general agreement on the identification[108] Akani (and Adansi) were clearly located in the Pra-Ofin basin. Guang is now spoken by scattered communities along the Black Volta and Volta, as well as near the coast in south-eastern Ghana. The linguistic evidence suggests a move from north to south. It is likely that Guang was once much more widely spoken, and that in some areas it has been supplanted by Akan.

The earliest Akan states developed north of the forest, in Bono and Bighu (Bitu), a commercial centre on the Dyula trade route to Jenne.[109] The area has yielded iron-working dates from the second century CE,[110] though settlement would have begun long before involvement in far-flung trade routes. There were Brong and Dyula quarters in Bighu; the former claim that they originally came from a hole in the ground; this hole was an ancient water cistern, surrounded by grinding hollows and traces of the Kintampo culture.

In 1895, the Gold Coast historian Reindorf wrote: 'Adanse [the Pra–Ofin basin] was the first seat of the Akan nation, as they say by tradition: there God first commenced with the creation of the World.'[111] Neolithic tools have been found near Kumasi, and the area was sparsely settled and cultivated from that time. In the fifteenth and sixteenth centuries, there was a major transformation; the forest was more densely settled, and there was extensive clearance.[112] Oral tradition remembers this in terms of woman 'ancestors', descending from heaven or emerging from the ground. They were not properly ancestors at all – they imposed a social order on existing populations. The Brong do not have the great totemic matriclans of the forest Akan. What these myths describe is the growth of a new socio-economic order.

The capital of the Asante kingdom, founded in the late seventeenth century, was at Kumasi, about fifty miles within the rainforest zone.[113] There was an earlier settlement twenty miles further south which the Asante regarded as a sacred shrine: 'The *Asante Hene* ... sent a yearly offering to "Santemanso", whence he came.'[114]

In the sixteenth and early seventeenth centuries, the forest Akan exported gold and imported labour; they purchased slaves from both the Dyula to the north (these apparently came from the small-scale societies of the Volta basin) and the Europeans in the south; these captives were rapidly absorbed in Akan society. Small states were founded by entrepreneurs, Big Men, who used slave labour to mine gold and clear the forest.

Gold was extracted, sometimes by slaves, and sometimes by family units; as in Bambuk, men hacked out the ore from shafts which were sometimes as much as 30 metres deep. Women extracted the gold from the ore and also panned for alluvial gold on river banks. The labour involved was enormous – the maximum amount which a woman could wash in a day was 50 pounds of soil; in the 1880s, this earned a profit of between 2s 6d and 10 shillings.[115]

The number of the matriclans has changed over time; Bowditch referred to twelve in 1819; eight were listed by the Asantehene in 1907. They have almost ceased to exist. 'For a quite surprising number of Asantes today, clan affiliation is a matter no longer within, or but vaguely within, the level of consciousness.'[116] Wilks suggests that the matriclans evolved as a way of organising labour in the era of forest clearance; when this had been done, they declined, and the size of the unit of production shrank to the lineage. The Anlo developed clans as a way of protecting access to land and the Asante as a way of controlling labour.

Mane and Sape

Stone sculpture is relatively rare in West Africa, but in some areas there are great numbers of stone statues, the provenance and date of which remain obscure. Many of the 295 monoliths which survive on the upper Cross River, in eastern

Nigeria, are of markedly phallic shape,[117] and there are hundreds of stone carvings at Esie, on the northern edge of Yorubaland.[118]

The most studied, and in some ways the most interesting, stone sculptures have been found in inland Guinea, Sierra Leone and Liberia. Carved out of soft soapstone, they are called *nomoli*, and are sometimes dug up by farmers and used in religious rituals.[119] Well over a thousand examples are known.[120] They were often found together with brass rings, and seem to have been made before 1500. The modern inhabitants of the area where they are found are the Kissi and Bullom, who are now separated from each other by the Mande-speaking Kono and Mende.

The presence of these and other Mande speakers in the coastal area reflects a number of separate incursions, one of which was the well-documented invasion of the 'Mane' in the mid-sixteenth century: 'The old Sapes say that these nations come every hundred years to make war in this country.'[121] 'Sape' was a generic term for the earlier inhabitants of the area, and it should be noted it included, as well as the proto-Kissi and proto-Bullom, other peoples who live outside the area where stone sculptures have been found, such as the Temne and Limba. A Portuguese visitor said in 1625, 'all these nations are called in general "Sapes", in the same way that in Spain several nations are called "Spaniards" '.[122]

The Mane profited by the disunion of the Sape to conquer their towns one by one. They recruited new troops from recently conquered peoples, the 'Sumba'. It was so much like the Jaga in Central Africa that many contemporaries – and even a modern historian – identified the two, despite the vast distance between them. It is now generally accepted that the Mane were proto-Vai;[123] the proto-Mende and proto-Kono were earlier immigrants. The Mane were not always victorious – they were defeated by another Mande-speaking people, the Susu. European slavers, as so often, made a profit from war: 'Our ships . . . behaved like birds of prey, when they saw the woods burning as they went along, they hoped it would be to their advantage.'[124] It has often been assumed that the Mane invasion ended the sculpting of nomoli, but this artistic tradition apparently ended earlier. Early foreign observers were unanimous in their praise of local craftsmen. 'In this land they make ivory necklaces more delicately carved than in any other country, also very fine and beautiful mats of palm-leaf.'[125] As in Benin, contact with European traders was a source of stimulus to an already thriving artistic tradition; one manifestation of this can be found in the so-called Afro-Portuguese ivories, made by African artists for European patrons: 'In Serra Lyoa the men are very clever and inventive, and make really marvellous objects out of ivory of anything you ask them to.'[126] But there is evidence that this tradition was disrupted. 'It is the fault of these foreign kings [the Mane] that the country is so poor, because they have captured so many master craftsmen, and . . . have committed so many vexations on the indigenous people that these latter have become less and less concerned and have given up the exercise of their arts.'[127]

The cultural patriotism characteristic of Mande peoples is reflected in the uniformity of the Manding dialects over vast geographic areas, a uniformity which was strengthened by the performances of itinerant bards, and by the practice of sending youths back to the Mande heartland to acquire an education and a bride.[128]

Poro and Sande

The spread of male and female masking cults such as Poro and Sande has been interpreted as part of an ancient cultural heritage of West Atlantic speakers. Alternatively, it has been attributed to Mande immigrants, who founded lodges to facilitate their economic activities and as agencies of Mande acculturation.[129] They were willingly joined by local people, probably because of the prestige of Mande smiths and long-distance traders – the Mane, like the Susu, are described in early sources as expert iron workers. What is distinctive about the masking cults of Sierra Leone and Liberia is the existence of a parallel association for women.

Modern myths collected among the Gola give a mystic primacy to women: 'In the beginning ... there was Sande. Women were the custodians of all ritual.'[130] The men's cult, Poro, was created when war threatened the 'ancient days of peace and perfect order'. They found a forest monster which they subdued and which became the Poro spirit. The association between masks and real or imaginary forest animals is a common one – an astral leopard is central to Ekpe (p. 356 below). This became an agency of male control, but Sande and Poro still 'rule the country' for alternating periods.

Fernandes wrote of men's and women's cult lodges, at the beginning of the sixteenth century. Alvares de Almada described an audible incarnation of a spirit which speaks through a voice disguiser, at which time non-initiates must stay indoors.[131] The fullest account comes from Dapper, a Dutchman writing in the mid-seventeenth century. Like Fernandes, he was a compiler, and never visited West Africa.

They have another custom which they call Belli-Paaro. They say that it is a death, a resurrection, and incorporation in the assembly of spirits or souls, with whom the members appear in the bush ... But this is kept secret from the women and from unknown men, for they pretend that the spirits eat this food ... They receive the Belli-Paaro mark very seldom, that is, only once every 20 or 25 years. And they tell amazing things about it. Namely that they are killed, cooked and completely transformed ... Just as the men have the Belli mark, so the women have the mark of their society.[132]

A hereditary woman official played a major role in Poro ceremonies. Much has been written on these cults in modern times.[133] It is not always understood that they are an authentic manifestation of the mystic's way – the initiate is reborn with a new identity. They functioned as agencies of socialisation and social control, and were an important element in government.

Despite the importance of women's cults, a valuable study of the modern Kono of Sierra Leone reflects the same gender hostility as that which emerges so clearly from Nigerian male masking cults.[134] Women were seen as dangerous, and as especially destructive witches – a hostility due to their divided allegiance, between the village into which they were born and the village they joined by marriage. The worst possible crime a witch could commit was to penetrate the Poro grove in the guise of a man.

Conclusion

Much of this chapter is based on the eyewitness accounts of early European visitors. Through this glass we perceive, if somewhat darkly, a world which their presence had scarcely modified. In West Africa there were two moving international frontiers – the Islamic/trans-Saharan and the Atlantic. Sometimes the two met – notably in the Senegambia. Some whole regions were totally unaffected by either until the twentieth century. But for many areas of Africa, external factors were of ever-growing importance from the seventeenth century on. They are writ large on the third section of this book.

Part III

Regional histories to *c.* 1870

15

Northern Africa

Three things elude confidence; the sea, time, the prince.
Sidi Lahcen Lyussi of Morocco (d.1691)[1]

I have nothing to learn from Machiavelli ... You need not translate any more of him.
Muhammad Ali (d.1848) to a translator[2]

PART ONE: TO 1800

Introduction

We saw in an earlier chapter how the Arab invasion led to the spread both of Arabic and of Islam. In a sense, the sixteenth century marked the beginning of a period of 'Turkish' dominance, in Egypt and the eastern Maghrib – 'Turks' being a blanket expression which embraced not only Ottomans but also Kurds, Muslim Greeks and Albanians. They constituted ruling enclaves in Egypt, Tunis, Algiers and Tripoli (though not in Morocco) and, at a later date (1820–80), in the Sudan. But, unlike Arabic, the Turkish language and culture did not take root, and ultimately disappeared. The links with the Ottoman empire, though not entirely meaningless, were increasingly restricted – to military support in time of crisis, and to the periodic recruitment of janissaries from Anatolia or Istanbul.[3]

Whether in 'Ottoman' Algiers or Sharifian Morocco, the peoples of the countryside chose different ways of interacting with the central government. Gellner, writing of Morocco, makes a distinction which also applies to the rest of the Maghrib, between the government allies who collected taxes, the subjects who paid taxes, and those who paid none.[4] Governments sent periodic tax-collecting expeditions into the countryside, but some clans allied with the central authority, in return for exemption from taxes and for local autonomy. Fiscal exactions were at the heart of perceptions of authority – *makhzen*, the word for government, means treasury, and taxes were called *al-naiba*, the affliction.[5] There was a persistent tradition of rural revolt and of banditry.

Famine and disease

Famines and epidemics are a recurrent motif in the history both of the Maghrib and of Egypt in this period. Some of the epidemics seem to have been typhus, and many were of 'plague' – this is sometimes clearly bubonic plague, but was also used to refer to deadly epidemic diseases in general. Famine and disease are also, of course, writ large in sub-Saharan Africa, but the greater amplitude of written source material north of the Sahara means that they are more fully documented there, and it is not easy to tell whether they were more prevalent. The Moroccan famine of 1776–82 drove some to cannibalism.[6] 'You see very few old men in Morocco.'[7]

The trade and other linkages of the Mediterranean world exposed its populations to new diseases, and plague was sometimes carried by returning pilgrims to Maghribi populations made vulnerable by their poverty. There was a particularly tragic case in 1492, when Jews expelled from Granada after the Reconquista brought an epidemic (probably typhus) to Fez, and 20,000 died. It had originally been brought by French troops from Cyprus. This may have been the origin of an epidemic which struck both Tunisia and the oasis of Tuwat in 1494.[8] In the 1520s, Leo Africanus suggested that there were plague epidemics of the Maghrib every ten, fifteen or twenty-five years – always with great mortality.[9] In 1520, there was a famine in Morocco so terrible that for a long time other events were dated by it.[10] It has been suggested that the population of Morocco fell from 5 to under 3 million between the early sixteenth and nineteenth centuries.[11] The people of the desert edge and, to a lesser extent, of the mountains were safe from bubonic plague because its vector, the flea, could not survive there.[12]

The view from the Bilad al-Siba

A distinction has always been made, in Moroccan thought, between the *bilad al-makhzen*, the realm of government, and the *bilad al-siba*, the realm of dissidence, which lay beyond it, and which varied in extent at different times, but comprised about half the country.[13] The French distinguished *le Maroc inutile* – the steppes which merge into desert, the great mountains – from *le Maroc utile* – the fertile Atlantic plains.[14] The question of *makhzen* and *siba* has been much debated,[15] but it is certain that much of the dynamic of Maghrib history lies outside the narrow sphere of the former. The limited scope of the *makhzen* was to make modernising initiatives difficult in the nineteenth century. Much of Morocco lay beyond the sultan's writ; the Berbers of the High Atlas and the desert edge had basically the same kind of organisation as the Igbo or the Nuer, which anthropologists call segmentary. The appropriateness of the segmentary model has been much debated,[16] and the details of Berber 'traditional' organisation varied. Some analyses make the leff, or inter-clan[17] alliance of central importance, but a Berber politician told an enquirer he had never heard of it until it was explained to him by a French official![18]

Most studies of the Berbers are anthropological, not historical, and often located in a timeless ethnographic present.[19] Nevertheless, much is undoubtedly applicable to a more remote past. Not all the features mentioned here were universal, and different scholars emphasise different elements.

Clans, large or small, were united by their descent, at least in theory, from a common ancestor, who was usually, but not always, male – a famous family of sharifs in northern Morocco takes its name from a noblewoman, Raysun.[20]

The genealogical model, here as elsewhere, was flexible enough to accommodate newcomers – 'only 49 per cent of Central Rifian lineages are homegrown'.[21] Sometimes, the symbolic, rather than historic, reality is evident – the Banu Yazid are not descended from an ancestor named Yazid but were originally called Ziyada, Increase.[22] The Berber word *Ait* means 'people of', which could refer to location rather than descent; it came to have the latter meaning, influenced by the Arabic word *Banu*.[23]

As in segmentary societies elsewhere, the myth or reality of common descent underlay units at different levels – the family, the lineage, the village, the clan. As the unit became larger, the genealogical depth became greater. Sometimes common action at one level was appropriate, and sometimes at another. In the often-quoted words of an Arab proverb, 'I against my brother; I and my brother against my cousin; I and my brother and my cousin against the world.'[24]

Oases, which depended on the equitable sharing of irrigation water, were particularly striking examples of elaborate social organisation without the coercion of central government – it has been said that groundwater in the Sahara is a social rather than a natural factor. 'These "hydraulic" societies functioned without the state.'[25]

The role of the arbiter was much older than Islam – it was inherited by lineages of 'saints', whose many social functions included that of adjudicating in conflicts – such as those which arose when transhumant pastoralists competed with mountain farmers for land and water. Several villages constituted a Fifth, and several (not necessarily five) Fifths made up a clan. At each of these levels, there was a popular assembly of males of arms-bearing age. We have noted the leff, or alliance. The Fifths would elect a clan leader, who held office for a year only;[26] the lineages of saints provided continuity. The blood feud was a core institution, and so was the procedure whereby the kinsmen of an accused man swore a corporate oath on his innocence. The marabout shed no blood and swore no oaths.[27]

The practice was perhaps less democratic than the theory – 'the majority are "more equal" than the minority, who ... have never participated in this system.'[28] In times of crisis, provincial warlords tended to seize power – a process well documented in the nineteenth century.

A changing Mediterranean world

Histories of the Maghrib tend to devote too much attention to external relations on the one hand, and to the rise and fall of dynasties on the other. It is, however, impossible to understand the history of northern Africa without paying at least some attention to events which lay outside it. In Morocco, the sultanate shrank to an enclave round Fez, and the last Wattasid ruler died in 1554. A Spain united in 1469 by the marriage of Ferdinand and Isabella conquered the last Muslim state in al-Andalus in 1492. Ten years later, Spanish Muslims were forced to choose between baptism and exile; in 1609 the New Christians were expelled as well. The exiles went to North Africa, taking with them, inevitably, a bitter sense of injustice. They settled in the towns, adding another strand to the complexities of Maghribi culture; they had little in common with the people of the countryside.[29] Jewish refugees from Spain also went to the Maghrib, where an ancient and prosperous community of their co-religionists already existed, only to find that a sense of encirclement encouraged the persecution of vulnerable minorities. The Jews of Tuwat were massacred, the survivors seeking safety in conversion or flight. Some fled to the Mzab, where they prayed each year at the Passover, 'Next year at Tamantit.'[30]

Portugal, where the Reconquista was completed much earlier than in Spain, obtained its first foothold in North Africa with the capture of Ceuta in 1415. By 1501 Portugal controlled all the Moroccan towns on the Atlantic coast but one, while Spain seized a number of strategic points on the Mediterranean, between Oran and Tripoli. They were motivated by economic and strategic factors, and by fears of reprisals from those whom they had expelled. Neither had the resources to offer a serious challenge to North African governments, but they profited from their fragmentation and by a weakness which intensified with Spain's and Portugal's successes. It was firearms, including artillery, which gave the Iberians a decisive advantage over the light Maghribi cavalry.

To the seventeenth-century mystic, Lyussi, the divisions of Morocco were a symbol of his own heart.

> My heart is scattered through my country.
> One part is in Marakech, in doubt.
> ... another in Meknes with my books
> ... another in Mulwiya [in the Middle Atlas] among my tribesmen.
> O God, reunite them. No one can do it but you.[31]

Both Spain and Portugal were soon to concentrate on empires further afield. Just as power relations were transformed by artillery and hand-held firearms, the global distribution of resources was transformed in the early fifteenth century by new maritime technology, particularly by the caravel, with its superior manoeuvrability and carrying capacity.[32] Their outposts on the Atlantic coast of Morocco led the Portuguese to a progressive exploration of the African coastline – each year they ventured a little further, until in 1498 Vasco da Gama sailed around the Cape of Good Hope to Calicut. In 1492, Columbus reached the New World in the service of Spain, and in 1519–22, Magellan circumnavigated the globe. Suddenly, the known world became enormously larger. Until the end of the fifteenth century, Muslim shipping had dominated the Indian Ocean. In the centuries that followed, the maritime technology of western Europe gave it a dominant position in global commerce – the era of merchant capitalism. What was the effect on trans-Saharan trade, and the economy of the Maghrib, when Europeans began to trade directly with West Africa? The main commodities carried north across the desert in medieval times were gold and slaves; now most of the gold was deflected to European merchants on the coast, and the imports of silver from the New World made it less vital to Europe's economic life in any case. The slave trade continued; the trade routes of the western Sahara declined, while those further east, that is, those linking Borno and Hausaland with the Fezzan and Tuwat, became more important. The commodities of Saharan trade diversified, and items such as gum arabic, ivory, wax, leather and ostrich feathers became more important. After 1600, the large resident communities of European merchants at ports such as Tunis and Algiers gave an extra stimulus to desert trade.[33]

The loss of a broker role in both the Guinea gold trade and the Asian spice trade undoubtedly lessened the income both of Maghribi governments and of their merchant communities, and reduced the diplomatic importance of Morocco, in particular. The Berbers of the High Atlas or Kabylia were not affected.

Most of the European enclaves in North Africa proved ephemeral, though Spain still rules Ceuta and Mellila.[34] And though Christians and Muslims were often at war, and relations between them were further exacerbated by corsairing, they were also linked by trade, and merchants from many European nations lived and prospered in Tunis, Algiers or Tripoli. There they bought and sold a complex mix of raw materials and manufactures, which it is interesting to compare with Roman times, when northern Africa exported grain, wine and olive oil.

It seems likely that northern Africa had a positive balance of trade with western Europe – a situation which changed in the nineteenth century – and a negative balance with India, which was adjusted with gold.[35] The ports of the Maghrib both imported and exported cloth, dyes and copper; grain was exported, but also purchased when the crops failed.[36] Although North African cloth production was highly developed, luxury fabrics for the elite were also imported (a comparable situation existed in sub-Saharan Africa). 'Moroccan leather' was famous, some of it re-exported from the Western Sudan. Most slaves were absorbed in the Maghrib, but some were exported to Europe, especially after the Black Death. Until the Portuguese developed a sea route to India, the re-export of spices from Asia, via Egypt, was of great economic importance.[37] European merchants also willingly bought goods seized from their compatriots by corsairs.

From the mid-fifteenth century, the Portuguese acted as maritime carriers in African trade. They bought copper and woollen cloth on the Moroccan coast for resale in West Africa, as well as Barbary horses, both for export to the Senegambia and for their home market. They even transported copper ore from the Sus, where it was mined, to the point on the Moroccan coast where it was smelted. Moroccan raw sugar was exported from the eleventh century on, and from the early sixteenth century it was processed locally in large state-owned refineries.[38] After 1541, saltpetre, used in the manufacture of gunpowder, was exported to England. But soon, Moroccan sugar was eclipsed by that of Brazil and the western world found other sources of gunpowder.[39]

This kind of international commerce was irrelevant to the majority of Egyptians or Maghribi. Trade was indeed important to them, but it was trade of a different kind. In the central High Atlas, pastoral clans exchanged wool for grain, dates and salt. 'The Abdi, very short of cereals but famed for their wool, must export or die.'[40] On the limitations of history from without, the words of Laroui are salutary: 'They put too much stress on piracy ... on commerce (which was marginal), on diplomacy ... and on local chiefs (petty condottieri) ... Many present-day Maghribi historians allow themselves to be dazzled by these false riches and judge the greatness of a king by the number of ambassadors he sent to the court of England or Spain.'[41]

Westerners called the Maghrib Barbary – like Berber, the word comes from the Roman word, *barbari*. The Muslims of the Maghrib and al-Andalus were called Moors (a word which has the same ultimate root as the name of the Roman province of Mauritania). Some Europeans distinguished between black and 'tawny' Moors,[42] but the word often acquired a sense of 'black' – as in *Othello*. This reflects the demographic impact of centuries of importing slaves and concubines from the Bilad al-Sudan. The Marinid sultan Abu l'Hasan was called the Black, in the mid-fourteenth century, and Mulay Ismael, in the seventeenth, was the son of a black mother. But there was also a pejorative element – the Moor became the Other, black in 'identification . . . with the black fiend'.[43]

Morocco

Geertz has written of the simultaneous existence in Morocco of three great cultural complexes – *siyyid*, *zawiya* and *makhzen* (government). The *siyyid* complex was the – characteristically rural – cult of dead saints and their tombs, the continuing spiritual authority of their descendants. There was a natural tendency for holy men to claim descent from the Prophet – the Sharif, with his distinctive green turban. Ever since a refugee Sharif founded Fez, Morocco had had a special link with this tradition, and many of its people claim sharifian descent.[44] Morocco was to be reunited by two successive dynasties of Sharifs from the south. The second great complex was that of the Sufi orders, the *turuq*, and their lodges, *zawiya* – the word means corner, or nook, a refuge from the dangers of the age. By the 1930s, a fifth of Moroccan men belonged to one of them,[45] and they were also of great importance in western Algeria and, as we shall see, in the Western Sudan. It has been suggested that inland towns such as Fez, Tlemcen or Kairouan, which could not participate in the burgeoning commercial life of the coast, sought an alternative role in supporting the sufi orders.[46] *Turuq* is often translated 'brotherhoods', but there is evidence of women's participation in the nineteenth century, and in Egypt at an earlier date. When the sphere of the *makhzen* shrank, the vacuum was filled by a phase of historical experience which historians often call the maraboutic crisis. There was a certain symbolism in the deaths, in 1465, of the last Marinid sultan of Fez, and the founder of the Jazuliyya, a powerful Sufi brotherhood, based in southern Morocco. Al-Jazuli made his base at Afughal, in the Sus, and had 12,000 followers at the time of his death.[47] One of his disciples then made war on the sultans of Fez, carrying the corpse of his master with him until his own death in 1485. He claimed to be guided by the spirit of al-Khadir – a powerful figure in the spirituality of the Maghrib and the western Sahara.

A family of Sharifs from the Dra valley, whom history knows as the Sa'adians, rose to prominence in the early sixteenth century. It is usually claimed that the name was given them by their successors, in the seventeenth century, to discredit their claim to Sharifian ancestry, implying that they were descended from the Prophet's foster mother, Halima al-Sadiyya. It may be a corrupted form of 'those who are happy' – an expression used for Sufis – and have been adopted by the Sa'adians themselves to stress their Sufi linkages.[48] But its significance may be wider – the people of Cyrenaica distinguish between the Sa'adi and the Marabtin. The former, named after a woman of the Banu Sulaym called Sa'ada, are the nine clans who rule by right of conquest; the Marabtin are in a client relationship to them.[49]

Muhammad al-Sadi, who died in 1517, took a leading role in opposition to the Portuguese. He made his headquarters at Afughal, and took the name al-Quaim, once held by a Fatimid caliph.[50] He was originally a minor cleric[51] who founded a dynasty, winning support for his visionary claims, less for himself than for his two sons. Each of them ruled a kingdom in southern Morocco, until in 1540, the younger, Muhammad al-Mahdi, deposed his brother and reigned alone, taking the title of caliph. The Sa'adians had captured Marrakesh in 1524. Muhammad al-Mahdi took Fez from the last Wattasid sultan thirty years later, but like the Almoravids and Almohads before him, preferred the southern city as his capital. Sa'adian hegemony extended as far south as the oasis of Tuwat.

From the 1530s on, the Sa'adians acquired firearms, and in 1541 Muhammad gained much prestige by capturing the Portuguese fort at Agadir, breaching the walls with cannon. He formed close commercial and other links with the British, who had a common interest in opposing the Iberian kingdoms. By 1550, the Portuguese retained only three of their coastal garrisons – Ceuta and Tangiers, in the Straits of Gibraltar, and Magazan, on the Atlantic coast. All this has often been interpreted as proto-nationalism, but eschatology was probably more important.[52] There was a tradition that the Mahdi would come from the Sus, a claim made for al-Jazuli.

The purchase of firearms and the expense of foreign mercenaries led inevitably to heavy fiscal demands and Muhammad became estranged from the marabouts, the dynasty's original supporters – in 1547, he massacred the heads of the Sufi orders at Fez.[53] He was assassinated by one of his own Turkish mercenaries ten years later. One of Africa's early modernisers, he concentrated, perforce, on firearms and the exports needed to obtain them.[54] The modernisers of the nineteenth century were to do much the same.

Having fought their way to power, the Sa'adians came close to losing it by their internal power struggles. In 1578, the rash young king of Portugal invaded Morocco in support of a deposed king, whose successful rival was a Turkish-speaking Ottoman protégé. All three died in a single day at the battle of Alcasar, which Europeans called the Battle of the Three Kings. Morocco's victory contrasts with the defeat suffered by the Ottomans at Lepanto, a few years earlier. The younger brother of the dead sultan, Ahmad, the posthumous son of Muhammad al-Mahdi, emerged as a strong and unchallenged ruler. He ruled Morocco till his death in 1603, taking the honorific, al-Mansur, the Victorious. He built up a large mercenary army, trained in firearms – as much to win his independence from the marabouts as to guard against external threats. Despite the export of sugar and saltpetre, this military machine made great financial demands. It was natural for a Sa'adian, whose family came from the desert edge, to look towards the south for resources.

Like his father and uncle before him, al-Mansur contested control of the Sahara salt mines of Taghaza with Songhai, but by then they were nearing the end of their productivity. His famous conquest of Songhai[55] was undertaken despite the opposition of the *ulama*, who were against such a perilous expedition against a Muslim ruler. He was motivated partly by the desire for direct access to the gold of the Western Sudan, but he seems also to have dreamed of a great international caliphate, and the presence of the Ottoman Regencies made it impossible to expand further to the east.

The Moroccan forces which invaded Songhai numbered four thousand, and were mainly converts to Islam[56] – their common language and that of their leader, Judar Pasha, was Spanish. They crossed the Sahara and defeated a much larger Songhai army at the battle of Tondibi in 1591, a success due to their professional discipline and their firearms. The conquest brought little permanent benefit to Morocco, and the flood of gold which ensued proved ephemeral.

When al-Mansur died in 1603, the struggles of his sons destroyed their inheritance. Significantly, they turned to Spain and the Ottomans, respectively, for support[57] (it was almost a re-enactment of the alignments of Alcasar). For a time, Morocco disintegrated into a number of small states, some, such as Dila, based on a *zawiya*, and others, such as Marrakesh, ruled by a local chieftain. Then another Sharifian family from the northern Sahara succeeded in establishing its supremacy – the Alawites, kin to the Sa'adians, who came from Sijilmasa, in the oases of Tafilalt.

Mawlay Rashid, who came to power in the 1660s was the effective architect of their fortunes. (A Sharif is addressed as 'Mawlay, my lord' – it was the customary title of the Alawites.) He was succeeded by his half-brother, Ismail (1672–1727), the son of a black mother, who founded a new fortress city at Meknes. He established his hegemony over shaykhs and marabouts by establishing an army which included not only Arab (Banu Maqil) and European mercenaries but also 30,000 or more black slaves, most of whom had previously been employed in agriculture. To support the army, he exacted heavy taxation. It is ironical that Sharifs originally rose to power with the support of the Sufi brotherhoods, and that first the Sa'adian, Muhammad al Mahdi, and then the Alawite, Ismail, found themselves in conflict with them. A legend tells how Lyussi reproached Mulay Ismael for his harshness to the labourers who built the walls of Meknes.[58] The famous Sufi centre at Dila was founded in the mid-sixteenth century. Its members attempted to establish an independent state and for a time captured Fez, but Ismail suppressed the rising with such severity that Dila's very location is debated. There was another expedition to the south, and, from this time on, Moroccan troops, called Orman, played a considerable role in the internal politics of Senegal.[59] After Ismail's death, another period of political fragmentation followed, and although the dynasty still survives, his successor was deposed five times.

Partly because of the gold of the Western Sudan, the Moroccan sultan had a prominence in international affairs in the sixteenth and seventeenth centuries which would soon disappear. Radical scholars point out, correctly, that it did little good to the majority of Moroccans, and that it was precarious because it rested on wealth produced outside Moroccan boundaries.

The Regencies

In Morocco, the Sa'adians and Alawites began their journey to power in the rural south, and went on to conquer the cities. The Maghribi states which Europeans called the Barbary Regencies and the Turks the Western Provinces began with the conquest of Mediterranean ports, and remained essentially urban in character. It is a paradox that the genesis of modern Maghribi nations, other than Morocco, lay in the activities of adventurers from the eastern Mediterranean. It is a further paradox that historians tend to describe these states as 'Ottoman' and to stress corsairing, but in many ways the Ottoman links were tenuous, and corsairing was of marginal economic importance to society as a whole – though not to the ruling group.

Corsairing, was 'official' piracy, in the employ of a government, or at least obedient to its policies, directed to political and religious ends. As the case of Drake reminds us, it was not peculiar to Muslims. It flourished in impoverished areas of maritime southern Europe, and most corsairing captains were originally Christians from Corsica, Sicily or Sardinia, or other Mediterranean lands – though Reis Hammada, who led the Algiers fleet during the Napoleonic wars, was a Berber from Kabylia.[60] Corsairing sprang as much from poverty as from religion, but for some – such as the expelled Muslims of al-Andalus – it acquired the dimensions of a crusade. The wrongs of the Spanish Muslims were an important motive for Barbarossa, as his autobiography reveals.[61]

Muslim corsairing began long before the Regencies were founded – in the thirteenth century, Mahdiya had a fleet 'to wage pirate warfare against the Christian countries',[62] but as western shipping became dominant in the Mediterranean, the corsairs had an additional incentive.

A history of Spain is subtitled 'From frontier to empire'.[63] The history of any of the Barbary Regencies could be subtitled 'From frontier to nation'. The first state founded by corsairs was Algiers, a coastal town which was, at the time, of little political importance. The leading role was played by Muslim Greeks from the island of Lesbos who, like the people of al-Andalus, had little reason to love westerners. Aruj and his three brothers took to corsairing when young; he was captured in a battle in which one of his brothers was killed, and spent several years toiling in the galleys of the Knights of St John of Malta – foreign military rulers, like the Mamluks – before he was ransomed. He then founded a corsairing centre on the island of Djerba, off the coast of Tunis, attracting many followers, who venerated him as Baba (father) Aruj. He became ruler of Algiers, on the boundary between the spheres of influence of Tlemcen and Tunis – and as such posed a threat both to the Spanish coastal enclaves and to local Muslim rulers. He and a third brother lost their lives in 1518, during an attempt to capture Tlemcen, leaving the youngest, Hayreddin (Khayr al-Din, Gift of God), in command. He is best known in western history as Barbarossa, Red Beard. He was forced to leave Algiers for a time, but recaptured it in 1525, creating a good harbour by constructing a long breakwater.

In 1518, Spain sent a great Armada to take Algiers, but it was scattered by a storm. The same thing happened in 1541 – God blew and they were scattered – and Algiers came to seem invincible, 'the Whip of the Christian World, the Terror of Europe, Bridle of Italy and Spain, Scourge of the Islands'.[64] By the late sixteenth century, Algiers had an estimated population of 61,000 and was called the richest city in the Maghrib,[65] and seven countries paid it tribute to ensure the safety of their shipping.[66]

The Barbarossa brothers realised that they needed access to greater resources, which they obtained from the Ottoman sultan, who sent a contingent of infantry in return for their allegiance. These janissaries were obtained as children as tribute from Christian communities, and brought up as Muslims – much like the Mamluks.

The aptitudes and training of the Ottomans were in land-based war. They used the skills of the corsairs to challenge Spanish control of the Mediterranean, part of a wider conflict which ended with a truce in 1581. With the exception of a single expedition from the Red Sea to India in 1538, Turkish naval activity was confined to the Mediterranean, where galleys were used.

Hayreddin was appointed admiral of the Ottoman fleet and in 1534 left Algiers for ever; he had laid the foundations of a modern nation, in a career entirely devoted to other goals. Gradually his successors expelled the Spaniards from their outposts in the Maghrib, until they were left with only Oran, which Spain retained until 1791.[67] In 1574, forces from Algiers captured Tunis, where for forty years the Hafsids had survived as Spanish puppets.

Tripoli was invaded by Spain in 1510, and handed over to the Knights of Malta. It was recaptured by a corsair called Darghut ('Dragut') in 1551. Like the Algiers corsairs, he accepted Ottoman sovereignty, and, like Hayreddin and his immediate successors, held the military title Beylerbey, Commander of Commanders. The oasis area of the Fezzan to the south remained independent under its own sultan but paid tribute and Cyrenaica, too, was gradually incorporated, so that the Regency of Tripoli was the precursor of the modern state of Libya.

The title of Beylerbey was soon given up, and the three Regencies became Ottoman provinces, each under a pasha sent from Istanbul for a three-year term. In time, the links with Istanbul weakened – a reflection of the decline of the Ottoman empire,[68] a complex phenomenon which lies beyond the scope of this study. The respect for Turkish institutions and culture remained and the janissaries still wore Turkish dress. Algiers was the Regency where Turkish links were most evident; the indigenous element was strongest in Tunisia, where Arabic became the official language, and the bey had to have Turkish documents translated into 'pidgin Moorish', a trade lingua franca.[69] Unlike Arabic, Turkish had no more lasting an impact than the language of the Vandals.

The Regencies: changing government

The distinctive premise of government in the Regencies – as in Egypt under the Mamluks – was that political power was the preserve of those born abroad – 'Turks by birth and Turks by profession'[70] – corsairs and janissaries, represented by a council of captains called the Taifa, and one of officers called the Diwan, respectively. Since the corsairs were often at sea, government was controlled by the janissaries. At first they were sent from Istanbul; later, they were recruited directly, often from Anatolia. They were organised and paid in a highly democratic fashion, and promoted by seniority – the highest position, that of general (*agha*) was held for two months, an egalitarianism which contrasted oddly with their monopoly of power *vis-à-vis* the local population. The *kulughlis*, offspring of a Turkish father and a local mother, were another distinct group; except in Tripoli, they were kept in a subordinate position.

Historians have tended to criticise the government of the Regencies as alien and predatory. Whether they were more rapacious than other governments of the time is not easy to tell, though periodic revolts clearly reflected some dissatisfaction. In 1588, for instance, a Mahdi arose east of Tripoli who was not defeated until 1592, and then only with the aid of outside reinforcements, and in 1603–8, the Berber ruler of Kuko fought a war against Algiers.

Soon, the paths of the Regencies diverged. Algiers was a military oligarchy, headed for a time by the *agha* and later by another military figure, the dey, chosen by the council of janissary officers, the Diwan. There were twenty-eight deys between 1671 and 1830, of whom fourteen died through assassination.[71] Muhammad ibn Uthman, dey from 1766 to 1799, tried unsuccessfully to found a royal dynasty.

In both Tunis and Tripoli, hereditary monarchies emerged in the seventeenth century. Murad Bey (1612–31) seized power in Tunisia, with the title of Dey, and in due course his position was recognised by Istanbul; in the late seventeenth century the dynasty he had founded destroyed itself by civil war. In 1705, Husayn bin Ali, the son of a Cretan father and a local mother, reluctantly took on a leadership role in the face of a threat from Algiers. He was not a janissary, but a member of the cavalry, *spahi*; the dynasty – which held the title, not of dey but of bey – survived until Tunisia became a republic in 1957. In Tripoli, a member of the *kulughli* class, Ahmad Qaramanli, came to power in 1711; his descendants retained power until 1835, when the Ottomans took advantage of their divisions to reassert their authority, with the compliance of the western powers.

Egypt was ruled by a foreign military class from the thirteenth to the nineteenth century (indeed, since Muhammad Ali came to Egypt as a Macedonian officer in an Albanian regiment, the tradition did not end with his regime). The Regencies were ruled by a foreign military class from the sixteenth century until the imposition of colonial rule.[72] A French visitor to Egypt in 1778 said: 'I could not help being surprised at seeing so numerous a body of men voluntarily submitting themselves to seven or eight thousand foreigners, who have no other employment than their destruction.'[73] He explained this apparent paradox in terms of national character – until the end of the colonial era and beyond it, outsiders were to distinguish between Africa's martial and supposedly non-martial peoples.[74] In 1808, the population of the Algiers Regency was estimated at 3 million, the number of 'Turks' at 10,000, and of kulughlis at 5,000.[75] Despite their internal divisions, these minorities retained their power by military training and firearms, and through the fragmented nature of any opposition. Men's social identity was reflected in their dress – diwan members wore gold lace on their turbans, janissaries wore Turkish uniforms, complete with pistols and scimitar. Women's all-concealing clothing hid their individual identity. They were secluded, but not powerless; 'the women of Algiers maintained their position in urban life through their control of food, honor, sex, sons, inheritance, and the supernatural ... Excluded from the religious and intellectual life of male society, females of all elements of society visited women who were reputed to have control over the spirits.'[76]

There was, as we have seen, considerable opposition in the first phase of Ottoman rule, but this was often deflected by the perception that the Regencies represented Islam *vis-à-vis* European encroachment. By the eighteenth century, the Regency governments were increasingly oppressive, as they attempted to compensate for the revenue lost by the decline in corsairing[77] by heavier taxation. Partly because of financial constraints, they recruited fewer janissaries. To excessive taxation were added the afflictions of famine and plague. In the late eighteenth and early nineteenth centuries, there were a number of risings against Algiers. Several were linked with the Darqawa, a Sufi brotherhood founded in the eighteenth century, whose members adopted the life of the wandering dervish, dressed in rags.[78] Algeria's divisions were to facilitate the French conquest, from 1830 on.

Egypt

From 1517 on, Egypt was a province of the Ottoman empire, subject to a pasha, who was sent from Istanbul, together with janissaries. Later, these were recruited locally.[79] But there was another element in the power equation, which distinguished it from the Regencies – the Mamluks survived and continued to recruit as before. In time, a new ruling class developed, army officers, called beys, who were usually of Mamluk origin. From the 1630s, they were the effective rulers of Egypt, so that the distinction between Mamluk and Ottoman Egypt is more apparent than real. As in the Maghrib, a local, if not indigenous, military elite had succeeded in gaining virtual independence from the Ottoman empire. They continued to send tribute to Istanbul, which was, it has been estimated, much the same as that remitted to Rome under Augustus![80] They extracted taxes so heavy that there were periodic revolts; a vicious circle resulted, of larger mercenary armies and escalating military expenditure. On a number of occasions Islamic scholars led these revolts – their failure, and that of the clerics of Dila in Morocco, contrasts with the great states founded by clerics in the Western Sudan, at this time and later.

Egypt had lost its middleman position in the spice trade, but until the early eighteenth century, its merchants made great profits from handling coffee.[81] As this trade declined – partly because of coffee production in the Antilles – and as Egypt's cloth exports also slumped, there was an increasingly unfavourable balance of trade.

Ali Bey, whose career in some ways anticipates that of Muhammad Ali, created an international army of mercenaries, with firearms and artillery. He is usually called the Great, and aspired to be a king. Contemporaries called him the Cloud-Catcher, because of his vaulting ambition, but he died in 1773, at the hands of one of his own henchmen.

Changing international relations

The rise and fall of different individuals or families within the framework of a military class is only the superficial face of northern African history. The seventeenth century was the golden age of corsairing, and of the Regencies. In the eighteenth, and still more in the nineteenth, there was an ever-increasing gap between the Muslim world and the economic and political power of the West, which was both symbolised and reflected in the widespread use of the Maria Theresa thaler in the Muslim world. Dated to 1780, it was produced in Trieste; it was so popular in northern Nigeria, in the nineteenth century, that it was counterfeited in Kano.[82]

In the eighteenth century, corsairing survived by preying on the weak, attacking small coastal vessels, and the western powers used it for their own ends. An English politician said in 1783: 'the great nations should suffer the Barbary pirates as a check on the activities of the smaller Italian states and America'.[83]

Histories of Egypt stress the instability and rapacity of late eighteenth-century government. The nineteenth-century Egyptian historian al-Jabarti wrote of the early 1780s: 'This year passed like the previous one, with hardship, dearth, a poor Nile and continued disturbances. Expropriations and oppressions by the grandees went on and on ... the country was ruined, the roads became the prey of highwaymen.'[84]

When Ibrahim Bey asked the clerics for prayers, one of them replied, 'How do you expect God to receive our supplications and prayers when the mamluks and soldiers day and night pillage, ravage, hit, kill, without fearing chief or notable?'[85]

Valensi emphasises the prosperity of the first two-thirds of the eighteenth century in Tunisia, which was described in 1770 as 'a vast storehouse of all kinds of grain'.[86] She contrasts this with a period between 1770 and 1830, when natural afflictions – drought, famine, cholera and plague – ravaged Tunisia, which began to import grain rather than exporting it, relying on exports of olive oil instead.[87] Most studies take 'decline' or 'stagnation' for granted, whether in the Maghrib, Egypt, or the Ottoman empire. This has been questioned by Roger Owen in a vigorous and stimulating rethinking of the issues involved. He points out, for instance, that a diminution of the powers of central government *vis-à-vis* the provinces is not necessarily undesirable.[88]

In the nineteenth century, northern Africa would be caught in a downward spiral of underdevelopment and the process of colonial conquest would begin – themes to which we return in a later section of this chapter.

Ethiopia: Oromo expansion

The expansion and socio-political transformation of the Oromo (formerly called Galla) is the dominant theme of Ethiopian history in the late sixteenth and seventeenth centuries. Until then, they lived in a small area in the extreme south of Ethiopia, not far from the modern frontier with Kenya.[89] In the first half of the sixteenth century, they exploded out of this homeland, invading the Ethiopian and Harar plateaux to the north, filling a vacuum created by the Christian–Muslim wars. Abyssinian expansion was deflected to the north-west – at the expense of the Beta Israel. Some Oromo migrated south and east, reaching Malindi, and displacing Bantu coastal peoples further south. In the nineteenth century, the tide was to turn, and Somali and Maasai pressure led them to retreat north of the Tana river. Today, there are two Oromo groups in northern Kenya – the Boran, and the much smaller Orma, whose Maa-speaking neighbours, the Samburu, regard them as a source of ritual knowledge.[90]

The advance of the Oromo was, in a sense, a process of what has been called 'reCushiticisation'. Their relatively recent and rapid spread is mirrored in the fact that, although Oromo speakers are now found over a vast area, they all speak dialects of a single language. Its closest relative is Konso, spoken in southern Ethiopia.[91]

The reasons for this kind of migration, and the factors which made it possible, remain obscure. It is possible that it was caused by population pressure, and it was clearly facilitated by the *gada* system.[92]

Gada was a system of eleven named generational – not age – grades, following a forty-year cycle. A man could not father a son until he reached the fortieth year of the cycle (daughters came later!) and all a man's sons, of whatever age, joined the system five grades behind him. The fifth grade was obliged to take lives in war; it was ritually connected with a grade of the same name 280 years earlier, and bound to repeat its achievements or atone for its failures.[93] They often fought other Oromo, and their warlike spirit sprang largely from competition for scarce resources.

The danger the Oromo posed to the Ethiopian state was not immediately apparent. Traditionalist in religion, they offered less of an ideological challenge than the Muslim sultanates, and as pastoralists they moved into underexploited ecological niches.

An Oromo section was divided into two exogamous moieties, each with a sacred leader and medium called the Kallu. Among the Kenya Boran they are descended from a mysterious figure who appeared long ago, discovered by a member of a marginalised caste of hunters and smiths. He told the Boran, 'God bore me. Only along the road of prayer have I come: I have nothing else. I have men's blessings.'

The Oromo did not form a unified state, nor did they have a sense of common identity. Some were assimilated by their neighbours. They played a dominant role at the Ethiopian court when the capital was at Gondar, in the eighteenth century.

In many ways, *gada* was dysfunctional; it required the deaths of infants born before the appropriate time, and because it was based on generation, rather than age, it was possible for the warrior grade to be full of children, or the old. But it was central to Oromo identity. 'When the gada customs were destroyed, everything else was also destroyed. When gada no longer existed, there was no justice ... And the oxen refused to fatten.'[94]

Ethiopia: the Agaw

We have seen how Aksum was a composite of Semitic and Agaw elements, and how Ethiopia was, for a time, ruled by Agaw kings. The extension of the Ethiopian state, and its cultural and often linguistic absorption of Agaw communities, continued, and is better documented for more recent centuries. Some pockets of Agaw speech survive as 'isolated – even if dwindling – islands' from Eritrea to Gojjam.[95] After the Ethiopian state centre shifted to Gondar, at the end of the sixteenth century, intensive attempts were made to control the Agaw living south of Lake Tana. They came to identify profoundly with the Amharic culture of the court – to the point of incorporating their own past into the Solomonic myth, claiming that their ancestor, Adil, was a cousin of the first Menelik and came with him from Jerusalem. In the sixteenth century, they were predominantly traditionalists, and allied with Ahmad against the Ethiopian state. They were conquered in a series of campaigns from the late sixteenth century, and this province became 'a veritable bread-basket for the royal court at Gondar'.[96] The conquest was completed by the Ethiopian king Yohannes, in a series of campaigns in the late seventeenth century. 'Then every Agaw who lives in the middle of Sikut ... was terrified, took refuge at a church ... and said ... "I shall become Christian and submit to the king and pay tribute and I shall do whatever the king orders me to do." '[97] But Yohannes ('the Saint') is highly thought of in modern Agaw tradition, and his invasion blamed on the machinations of local enemies – a remarkable example of the phenomenon so well described by Frantz Fanon, where the conquered internalise the values of the conqueror.

PART TWO: THE NINETEENTH CENTURY

In many ways, the experience of northern Africa before 1870 anticipates that of sub-Saharan Africa at a later date. The characteristic dynamic of ongoing underdevelopment is evident – the ruinous mushrooming of foreign debt, the formation of privileged foreign enclaves, the usurpation by external forces of economic and other controls in nominally independent states – palaeo-colonialism rather than neo-colonialism.

The European nations sought their own ends in the name, not of their own enrichment and aggrandisement, but of ideals – in the nineteenth century, free trade and the abolition of slavery and corsairing figured prominently among them. In the medieval period, Egypt and the Maghrib exported manufactures such as fine textiles; in the nineteenth century, they came to rely ever more on the export of a small number of primary products – cotton in Egypt, olive oil in Tunisia. (It should be noted, however, that the manufacture of the fez in Tunisia continued until 1881.)[98] Partly because of the land and labour that crops such as cotton demanded, and partly because of an exploding population, they became ever more dependent on food from abroad. They imported, in addition, an ever-increasing volume of foreign manufactures, creating an unfavourable balance of trade. As in western Europe, many traditional occupations became obsolete; the import of factory-made cloth threatened the spinner and handloom weaver, and railway construction took away work from camel and donkey drivers. Sugar, coffee and, later, tea, began as the luxuries of kings and ended up as the necessities of the common man and woman. None of the three has any food value; a Maghribi poet sang, with more insight than he knew

> As for tea, you see,
> The Christian, who knows full well you are his enemy,
> Catches you with his cannon balls and his bales of tea ...
> The enemy catches you in the belly ... He brings sugar loaves.[99]

The crisis was as much spiritual as political. Muslims agonised over the strength and aggressive dynamism of Europe, so clearly exemplified in Napoleon's invasion of Egypt in 1798, and over the decline of the Ottoman empire, the world's greatest Muslim state. They responded to the situation in a number of different ways. The Wahhabi of Arabia were fundamentalists, urging a return to the Qur'an, highly critical of the Sufi orders – views, on the whole, welcomed by Moroccan sultans. The Wahhabi attack bred a reaction among the *turuq*, which expanded greatly in the nineteenth century. Some major new Sufi orders were founded, among them the Sanusiyya and the Tijaniyya, and both old and new orders played a major role in the events of the time. A considerable number of women joined the Tijaniyya and Rahmaniyya, and on several occasions women headed *zawiya* of the latter movement.[100]

It is noteworthy that some of the most successful attempts to resist foreign encroachment were traditional and Muslim in inspiration – a rising against the French, led by a Qadiriyya shaykh in west Algeria, the Mahdist state in the Sudan, from 1881 to 1899. This was also true in the early years of this century – the twenty-year struggle in Somalia led by the patriot and poet Sayyid Muhammad Abdallah Hassan, until his death in 1920, or the state founded in the Rif in northern Morocco, from 1920 to 1926, by Abdul Krim the Learned.

Resistance was only one possible response to the economic and military dominance of the western world. An important body of nineteenth-century Muslim thinkers advocated the mastery of western knowledge, especially in the sphere of technology. The original Ottoman conquest of Egypt, in the early sixteenth century, was made possible by their use of firearms; as time went on the technology, including the military technology, of western Europe came to outstrip both the Ottomans and the powers of northern Africa. Rifa'a al-Tahtawi, an Egyptian cleric who lived in Paris from 1826 to 1831, was an early exponent of this view. Although his original education was in Arabic, he mastered French, his voracious reading embraced Racine, Rousseau, Voltaire and Montesquieu and he worked for many years as a translator.[101] Men of this kind tended to be advocates of parliamentary democracy – a recent growth in the West at that time. Paradoxically, it was just as a body of western educated supporters of democracy developed that the spread of colonialism robbed them of a say in the affairs of their own countries. Tahtawi wrote, 'There is a moral obligation on those who share the same *watan* [country], to work together to improve it and perfect its organisation in all that concerns its honour and greatness and wealth.'[102]

French control of Egypt lasted for only three years, from 1798 to 1801, and the colonial era in northern Africa began with the French conquest of Algiers, in 1830. It was untypical of its time and most colonial jurisdictions were established later. The Ottomans reasserted their authority in Tripoli, with western compliance, in 1835; it was invaded by Italy in 1911. Tunisia fell to France in 1881, and the conquest of Morocco began in 1907. Nineteenth-century Egypt acquired, for a time, its own imperial domain, ruling the Sudan from 1820 to 1881, when its hegemony there was ended by the creation of the Mahdist state. This lasted until 1898, when it fell, in effect, to the British. The conquest of Algeria began in 1830, and took decades, and this was equally true, at a later date, of Morocco. Many wars were fought against colonial jurisdictions, several of which led to the creation of what were, in effect, short-lived independent states.

As in sub-Saharan Africa, foreign invasion was greatly facilitated by local divisions; to take one example among many, the French invasion of Algiers was aided by Tunisia. Sometimes there is something of the pan-Islamic consciousness colonial authorities always dreaded. Napoleon turned back from the siege of Acre in Palestine because of the valour of its defenders – who included a contingent led by a Moroccan.[103]

Egypt under Muhammad Ali is one of Africa's most famous cases of an attempt – albeit one which was in many ways unsuccessful – to modernise and westernise. In the past, historians tended to assume that industrialisation, western education, and parliamentary democracy were in themselves a Good Thing, and interpreted the nineteenth-century experience of northern Africa in terms of success or failure in attaining this goal. It is now realised that phenomena such as year-round cultivation or industrialisation exacted a great human cost, and that the changes of the nineteenth century led to a growing gap between rich and poor.

In a model which fits Egypt and Tunisia better than the rest of the Maghrib, Brett has divided the nineteenth-century history of northern Africa into the Age of Muhammad Ali, the Age of Ismail, and the Age of Cromer.[104] The first was characterised by modernising initiatives, under an absolute ruler; the second saw several short-lived experiments in constitutional government. The third, which lies beyond the time span of this volume, is the period of the Scramble for Africa and the formation of colonial governments.

Egypt under Muhammad Ali

The French left Egypt in 1801, and the daughter of the Shaykh al-Bakri, who had mixed with the French and worn European dress, was executed,[105] an obscure episode amid more momentous events.

In the years which followed, there was a power struggle among Mamluk and Ottoman factions, in the course of which Muhammad Ali, who had recently come to Egypt as an officer in an Albanian regiment in Ottoman service, made himself supreme. He did so with the support of the Cairo clerics and populace, who may well have regretted it later. They were reacting against the chronic conflict and rapacity of the former governing class, and some of the poor sold their clothes to buy weapons. It was a rare moment in Egyptian history, almost suggestive of the French Revolution, when the poor acted with decisive effect – one of the urban leaders was a greengrocer.

Muhammad Ali soon made himself independent of his local supporters, and in 1811, he massacred a group of beys,[106] ending over five hundred years of Mamluk dominance. The survivors fled to Nubia. It is a paradox that Muhammed Ali, who had so much in common with his Mamluk predecessors, is remembered as a moderniser. It is said that he modelled himself on the great Mamluk sultan, Baybars, and he officered his new army with his own Mamluks.[107]

The linguistic situation reflected the intrinsic complexity of society. All Egyptians spoke Arabic, but Muhammad Ali and his entourage spoke Turkish – he reproached one of his sons for preferring Arabic. When he founded a translation bureau to make western scientific and technical texts available, it worked in both Arabic and Turkish, though the latter gradually died out after 1845. The language of the court was French, and remained so, even after Arabic became official in 1870. In Tunisia, Hamuda Bey (1782–1814) seems to have been the last of his line to speak Turkish; Ahmad Bey wrote to Istanbul in Arabic, as he did not wish to sign a document he could not read.[108]

Muhammad Ali's aim was that of the Cloud-Catcher – to found a strong dynasty, ruling over an independent and powerful Egypt. This meant building up a modern army and civil service, expensive undertakings which he sought to finance primarily through cotton exports. Ironically, one of his regime's main achievements, the expansion of cotton production, was to turn Egypt into a dependent monoculture. Egypt had grown short-staple cotton for many centuries. From 1818 on, it was replaced by a superior long-staple; soon, it had become Egypt's leading export, and by the 1880s, it comprised 80 per cent of all exports.[109] Production was expanded by extending the irrigation system and introducing year-round cultivation. Cotton had, we are told, a great advantage from the viewpoint of the ruling class – 'the fact that it could not be eaten by the peasants'![110] The expansion of production to feed French or English cotton mills was a classic case of growth without development. It was growth, moreover, which exacted a great human cost; the work it required, knee deep in water, now lasted all year, and there was a great increase in waterborne and other diseases. In the 1920s, an Egyptian described, in Upper Egypt, 'the victims of bilharziasis and malaria – all those young men [*sic*] in full manhood whose faces disease had rendered deathly pale. Hypertrophy of the spleen had swollen their stomachs. They had become monsters of whom it was impossible to say whether they were youths or old men.'[111] Thousands died of hunger and exhaustion in the course of forced labour on the canals. A system of state monopolies meant that the government purchased all produce, reselling it to both Egyptian consumers and foreign merchants at a profit.

A number of factories were established, beginning with the munitions factories and shipyards which reflected Muhammad Ali's primarily military aims, and came to include textile mills, sugar refineries, and tanneries. At first they relied, not only on foreign technical experts, but even on foreign workers. The obstacles were enormous, as Egypt lacked both iron and coal – the energy problem was not to be solved until the mid-twentieth century, with the construction of the Aswan dam. In 1841, the western powers forced Egypt to accept free trade, and without protective tariffs Egyptian industries could not survive. This abortive attempt at industrialisation had the unintended consequence of undermining Egypt's traditional handcraft industries; this in its turn was one of a number of factors contributing to a deterioration in the position of peasant women.[112]

Rather than incorporating new elements in the curricula of traditional Islamic schools, Muhammad Ali created a parallel system of secular education. Twentieth-century colonial governments were to do the same thing in Muslim areas such as northern Nigeria, and the long-term consequences were momentous. The ancient mosque-university of al-Azhar continued to produce graduates, but their employment prospects declined, just as they opened up for the western-educated.[113] Western education was largely geared to military aims – the medical school was originally intended to train army doctors. Initially, expatriate teachers were used and then Egyptians trained in Europe, until sufficient locally trained personnel were available. Muhammad Ali learned to read himself, at the age of forty-seven, and sternly regulated the studies of his sons.[114]

He and his successors made extensive use of foreign experts, among them French military men, unemployed after the Napoleonic wars. His first campaigns were waged in the name of the Ottomans – first, with success, against the Wahhabi rising in Arabia, in 1811–19, and then, in 1824, against the Greek nationalists, but here his victories were cancelled out by the intervention of the western powers. In the 1830s, his forces invaded and conquered Syria. The West preferred an enfeebled Porte to a dynamic and aggressive Egypt, and he was forced to withdraw from both Arabia and the Levant. He did, however, succeed in gaining Ottoman recognition of the hereditary right of his family to be viceroys in Egypt.

Egypt's conquest of the Sudan had longer lasting effects. In 1821, separate Egyptian armies conquered the Funj sultanate and Kordofan – but not Darfur. The new rulers of the Sudan, locally known as the Turkiyya, included Ottomans, Albanians, Greeks and Kurds. The invasion of the Sudan was inspired by the desire to eliminate the Mamluks who had settled in Dongola, and to create a black slave army, but a high mortality rate among Sudanese soldiers soon led Muhammad Ali to rely on the conscription of the fellahin. He had also hoped to obtain gold, but little was in fact forthcoming – though he went to the Ethiopian borderland, at the age of seventy, to inspect the situation! In the Sudan, he could seek military glories without provoking the intervention of the western world. There was a rising in 1822–3, which failed, and was followed by extensive emigration from the regions ruled by the Turkiyya. Their administrative capital, Khartoum, then a minor town, developed into a centre of great commercial importance.

The invasion of the Sudan led to the exploration of regions further south. The Turkish sailor Salim Qabudan – the unfamiliarity of whose name contrasts with the celebrity of a Livingstone – went up the White Nile twice between 1839 and 1841, finding his way through the tangled vegetation of the Sudd, and reaching modern Juba.[115] (Livingstone began his travels in 1841, and the European exploration of the Great Lakes area came considerably later.) At the time, it seemed a unique gateway of opportunity to the African interior, and especially an opportunity to purchase ivory.

At the end of his life Muhammad Ali was forced by the western powers to open the trade of the Southern Sudan to their nationals. From the 1850s on, the merchants of many nations penetrated the Bahr al-Ghazal and beyond, in search of ivory; their armed retainers often seized slaves or cattle. The European presence was short-lived, and soon the area was dominated by Egyptian or Sudanese warlords, who are generally referred to as the Khartoumers. Initial contacts had been peaceful; the escalating violence which afflicted the area was due less to slave trading, which Gray calls 'minor and secondary', than to cultural differences and problems of communication.[116]

The army was divided between a Turco-Circassian officer class and Egyptian conscripts. In time, Egyptians joined the officer class but still felt themselves marginalised. The first Egyptian nationalist movement, in the 1880s, was to spring from their sense of grievance.

It was the peasantry which paid the price for Muhammad Ali's policies. Women in full Muslim dress sweltered in the new factories, and fellahin mutilated themselves or fled to the hills, the cities, or even the Levant to avoid conscription. Factory workers were paid little, and charged for defective work or machinery repair. It is not surprising that the factories were repeatedly attacked by arsonists,[117] and that there were several rural revolts – one of them dominated by handloom weavers.[118]

There were famines, due to fluctuations in the levels of the Nile, and epidemics of plague and cholera; in one of these alone, half a million people perished. But despite this, the population increased – another paradox of under-development.[119]

The Suez Canal and the Khedive Ismail

On his deathbed, the old pasha said ambiguously that his children would reap what he had sown. It was his youngest son, Said, whose regime lasted from 1854 to 1863, who signed the Suez Canal agreement, a step which Muhammad Ali had always refused to take, recognising that it would erode Egyptian sovereignty. The terms were disastrously unfavourable – Egypt provided 45 per cent of the capital, unpaid corvée labour, and large tracts of land.

In the early nineteenth century, western powers had seen northern Africa as a source of raw materials such as cotton and wool. With the development of the steamship, and the opening up of the resources of Australia and the Americas, the emphasis shifted to the search for markets and a field for investment.[120] To Britain, in particular, with an empire in India, the area was of key strategic importance, and in the 1850s a railway was built from Alexandria to Suez, providing an overland route from the Mediterranean. After the opening of the Suez Canal in 1869, the route it provided to India became a key element in British policy. In one interpretation, it set off the chain of events which led to the Scramble for Africa.

In many ways, Muhammad Ali's grandson, Ismail (1863–79), continued his policies. He had the same admiration for the western world, the same enthusiasm for education and development, the same desire to create an African empire. Western education, neglected by his two predecessors, became a priority once more, and his third wife, Jashem Afet Hanum, opened the first school for Egyptian girls in 1873. At great expense, he obtained firmans from the Ottoman sultan, which gave him the quasi-royal title of Khedive and allowed the succession to follow the laws of primogeniture. But Ismail plunged ever more deeply into debt, borrowing from European bankers on unfavourable terms. Much was deducted in fees and commissions and of £68 million borrowed, only £49 million actually reached Egypt. The same thing happened in Liberia, on a much smaller scale, at the same time. Some of this borrowed capital went on modernisation – street lights, or the improvement of Alexandria harbour – the cost of which was greatly increased by European rapacity. Some was squandered on various forms of conspicuous consumption. Ismail attempted to take back

Said's more disastrous concessions – the supply of labour for canal construction, labour which was needed in agriculture, and the provision of land for a fresh-water canal and agriculture between Suez and the Nile, and was forced to pay an indemnity of £3 million. In contrast with his grandfather's absolutism, he introduced a representative assembly – indeed, at one time he hoped to be Prime Minister.[121] But his ever-increasing indebtedness destroyed his political inde-pendence and forced Ismail to sell his Suez Canal shares to Britain in 1875. Until 1956, it was to be a foreign-controlled enclave on Egyptian soil, generating profits which Egyptians did not share. Large numbers of Europeans settled in Egypt, their numbers rising to 50,000; since they were exempt from Egyptian law and taxation, by the system of Capitulations, they constituted, in a very real sense, an *imperium in imperio*.[122] In Ismail's time, the system was amended – so that one common court for foreigners replaced seventeen different ones. But the system itself lasted until 1937.

Although a law of 1871 recognised peasants' ownership of their land, flight from the land continued, in response to heavy taxation, forced labour and conscription. The viceregal family and their entourage accumulated great estates.

Ismail shared his grandfather's dream of an African empire, though nothing permanent was achieved and it proved yet another drain on his financial resources. In 1863, Speke and Grant descended the Nile from Lake Victoria Nyanza to Cairo; it was now hoped that the Nile would prove a highway to the great kingdoms of the south, but this was not to be. Said had attempted unsuccessfully to establish a government outpost on the Sobat confluence. Ismail created a province of Equatoria (now northern Uganda, and the adjoining area of the Republic of Sudan) partly in response to western anti-slavery sentiment, but little was achieved. In the Bahr al-Ghazal, a powerful local warlord, Zubayr, was appointed an Egyptian governor. He conquered Dar Fur, and for a moment created one of nineteenth-century Africa's new empires; he made the mistake of returning to Cairo, where he was immediately imprisoned, and his son was unable to defend his father's conquests. Some of Zubayr's supporters joined the forces of the Mahdi; others followed one of his lieutenants, Rabih, who established a military state in the Bahr al-Ghazal. Realising that it was impossible to stem the rising tide of Egyptian and British imperialism, he led his forces in an epic migration to the west. He invaded Borno in 1893, and was killed fighting the French in 1900. Samori made the same discovery – it was not possible to escape colonialism by migration in the Africa of 1900.

Ismail made several unsuccessful attacks on Ethiopia; Egypt's holdings in the Sudan expanded into a vast but short-lived tropical empire which included Dar Fur and Equatoria and the southern shore of the Red Sea. Like his grandfather, he tended to rely on foreigners, among them Charles Gordon, who served as the Governor-General first of Equatoria and later of the Sudan. He was to die at Khartoum, in Egyptian employ. The long-term consequence of Egyptian im-perialism was that the peoples of the south, such as the Dinka, were to form a single nation with the Arabised north, which despised them. For much of the time since independence, they have been at war.

By 1876, Egypt was on the brink of bankruptcy, and Ismail owed nearly £100 million.[123] The major European powers moved in to protect their shareholders' interests – and in 1879 he was deposed. His son succeeded him, transparently a figurehead.

The army was a focus of embryonic Egyptian nationalist consciousness, critical of the Turco-Circassian court, of the continuing link with Turkey, and of political mismanagement generally. In 1882, under the leadership of Urabi Pasha the Egyptian (the name is significant), it briefly dominated the political scene – only to be conquered by an invading British army. Urabi Pasha went into exile – but the ideals he advocated – democratic government by Egyptians – were never wholly forgotten. At the very time a substantial class of western-educated Egyptians had developed, Egypt became a virtual colony.

The Mahdist state in the Sudan[124]

The ineffectiveness of the educated advocates of democracy in Egypt provides a striking contrast with the success of the Mahdi in the Sudan. Muhammad Ahmad, a shaykh from a Sharifian family, created a great theocratic state in an area of political and ethnic fragmentation. In 1880–1 he had visions which led him to believe himself the Mahdi, the Rightly Guided One who would restore the world to justice in the last days. Mahdism is a belief with a special appeal to the poor and marginalised, and in the Sudan it proved a revolutionary ideology, canalising hatred of corrupt and oppressive Egyptian rule. In 1885, his forces captured Khartoum. General Gordon's death in the doomed city reverberated around the English-speaking world – the Mahdi had tried to spare his life and had urged him to convert to Islam. Soon afterwards, he himself died in an epidemic. But the movement survived, led by a Deputy, Khalifa, until 1898, when Kitchener's guns mowed down the flower of its army at Omdurman. In a sense, it was the last of the Islamic states of the Sudan, discussed in the chapter which follows. It is dealt with briefly here because it lies outside the time frame of this volume.

Tunisia

In many ways Tunisia's experience parallels that of Egypt. Ahmad Bey (1837–55) was another enthusiast for modernity; he founded a conscript army, with western-style uniforms and drill, and established short-lived factories, largely to supply its needs. Like so many Maghribi rulers before him, he built a palace city – but his was decorated with paintings of Napoleon's victories. In 1846, Tunisia led the Islamic world in abolishing slavery – it was an institution of marginal importance to its economy, but it ended the importation of Mamluks. Shortly before his death, he sent a contingent to support the Turks in the Crimean war, financing the venture with loans and the sale of family jewels. From 1861 to 1864 there was a short-lived experiment with parliamentary institutions.

Tunisia had the same weaknesses as Egypt – heavy taxation, increasing foreign indebtedness, the existence of a large and privileged European enclave. A man's conscription in the army was mourned more intensely than his death. In 1864 the burden of excessive taxation led to a great revolt, in which landowners and clerics took part, as well as the peasantry. It was a revolt which failed, leaving the peasants poorer than before, subjected to punitive fines, which drove them to the money-lenders. It ended the brief phase of constitutional government.[125] As so often, social and political disasters were followed by drought and by epidemics of cholera in 1865 and typhus in 1867.

As in Egypt, it was the growing burden of foreign debt which undermined the independence of the state, and in 1869 an international commission was set up which controlled expenditure. In this unpropitious situation, Tunisia embarked on an experiment with constitutionalism and reform which was of great symbolic importance to later nationalists.

Khayr al-Din (1810–89)[126] reached Tunis as a Mamluk; he was the last and arguably the greatest of Africa's Mamluk rulers. In 1873, after a distinguished public career, he was appointed Prime Minister, and, unlike his venal predecessors, proved to be both efficient and honest. His attack on corruption struck a chord, and civil servants willingly accepted a salary cut. But like many of Africa's modern military rulers, he saw reform as 'efficiency' rather than radical economic restructuring, and inherited a situation where much national income went on debt servicing. In 1877, alienated both from the foreign powers and the bey, he was dismissed, and left Tunis for ever. In 1881 Tunisia became a French protectorate.

Algeria

E. J. Hobsbawm once wrote that 'colonialism makes its victims its defenders'. It is a theme which is writ large on African history. Algiers, like the other Regencies, sent supplies to Napoleon's army in Egypt, and gave the French an interest-free loan as well. In 1830, the French conquered Algiers (not Algeria), almost by accident. They took this step because of domestic political considerations, as Charles X made an (unsuccessful) attempt to bolster up his failing government. The minister of war had written in 1827 that 'it would be a useful distraction from political trouble at home'.[127] The next regime – the July monarchy – considered various options, including withdrawal, but in the end, they stayed. It has always been difficult for metropolitan governments to give up overseas territories without losing face, and it was doubly so for the French in the days when the British ruled India. The original intention was to limit their control to coastal cities such as Algiers, Oran and Bougie, but colonial boundaries had an inveterate tendency to advance until they met another colonial jurisdiction.

Algerian responses to the French presence anticipated, in many ways, the situation elsewhere in Africa after the Scramble. There was no united or universal resistance, and the process of invasion, as so often, was facilitated by the divisions of local people. These, of course, reflected the complexities of power relations before the fall of Algiers. Initially, the French presence seemed a new element which conflicting factions could use to advantage. In many cases, it was only after the elapse of time that the true implications became gradually evident. As a French commission in 1833 admitted, the military regime committed many atrocities, including the virtual extirpation of the Ufiyya – a contemporary account describes how their bracelets were sold in the markets of

Algiers, with severed wrists still attached. A mosque was turned into a Catholic church, although the French had promised to respect Islam; the bones from a cemetery were left scattered after road construction; bizarre as it seems, there is evidence that they were sold to sugar refineries in Marseilles.[128]

Hajj Ahmad, the Regency bey of Constantine, led a war against the French in eastern Algeria in the name of the Ottomans, until his defeat in 1837. It was followed by a major war in the west led by Abd al-Qadir, a shaykh of the Qadiriyya – it was an area with strong links with Morocco, and a long history of resistance to the Regency government. He began by signing a pact of coexistence with the French, which Hajj Ahmad condemned as a betrayal. He gradually created what was, in effect, a new theocratic state, in what was once the independent state of Tlemcen – building granary fortresses, acquiring firearms, and minting his own coinage. But he could not match the resources of the French, and by 1843 he was a fugitive, though other leaders rose, who continued the struggle. He surrendered in 1847, and became a political exile, first in France and later in Damascus. There were to be many political exiles in early colonial Africa. Kabylia was not conquered until the 1850s.

The French had won Algeria, but at a price, and in the late 1840s, it was absorbing a third of its armed forces.[129] It was the progressive alienation of land, and an ever-rising tide of European settlement, which influenced Algerian lives most profoundly. By 1846, there were 110,000 European settlers (almost the same number as the army). By 1870, their numbers had risen to a quarter of a million, and the economy and infrastructure were geared to their needs. By 1870, 674,340 hectares of farmland and 160,000 hectares of forest had been alienated. In 1867, the falling price of grain, the reduction in arable land, and crop failures led to famine, in which 300,000 or more Algerians died.[130]

The great rebellion of 1871 began with the refusal of Algerian troops to take part in the Franco-Prussian war, but spread far more widely – a fire which fed on the suffering of a plundered and dispossessed people. It did not form a single co-ordinated movement, a fact which – as so often in African colonial history – greatly facilitated its suppression, as did the shortage of arms. Two-thirds of the indigenous population took no part.[131] It was savagely punished with land seizures and fines – the latter were increased by interest, and not paid off until 1890. In 1954, Algerians were to take up armed revolt once more, this time with success.

It had been hoped that Algeria would be a source of the tropical products once supplied by Haiti, such as sugar and coffee. But it proved unsuitable, and came to duplicate the products of France itself – wheat and wine.[132]

Morocco

The completion of the Suez Canal made Morocco, as well as the Red Sea, of greater strategic significance to the western world, for the new waterway was useless unless shipping could reach it freely. The fact that colonial rule was not imposed in Morocco until 1911 was due to the divisions of potential colonisers. Sultan Mawlay Abd al-Rahman said in 1871, 'Morocco is like a threadbare garment, if the slightest force is used it will be rent and go to pieces.'[133]

In the late sixteenth century, Morocco was a major international power; by the nineteenth it was, to European observers, the 'sick man of the west'.[134] The power of the Moroccan sultan to effect change or resist external aggression was limited by the geographically restricted impact of central government. In 1844, when the British Consul complained of pirates, he was told: 'these lawless men must most often be seen not so much as common subjects, but as savage bandits, who are outside the domain of the law and are not at present subject to its authority.'[135] Some observers realised that what some called anarchy others called freedom and Moroccans themselves retained a striking confidence in the value of their own culture. 'All men are equal except those who inherit sanctity. Every Moor considers himself to be as good as another Moor, and far superior to any European.'[136]

Like their counterparts elsewhere in northern Africa, the rulers of nineteenth-century Morocco were confronted with major policy decisions – should they attempt to modernise, on the lines of the western world, should they seek closer links with the western world, and expand trade links, or should they follow a policy of isolation? They were well aware of foreign precedents. In the 1820s, Maghribi merchants warned statesmen in northern Nigeria about the British. ' "By God" said the Marroquin, "they eat the whole country – they are no friends: these are the words of truth." '[137] In the 1890s, Mawlay Hassan observed that 'The Sultan of Turkey had ruined his Empire by cultivating relations with foreign powers'.[138]

Under Mawlay Sulayman (1792–1822) it was illegal to export goods to Europe (but not to import them) until the ban was lifted in 1817. This has been interpreted in religious terms, but in the contemporary Ottoman empire, it was a basic economic policy – 'Turkey seized upon the fanciful idea of becoming rich, prosperous and mighty, by letting nothing go out of, and to let everything come freely into, her dominions.'[139] The fundamental dilemma was the source of revenue – whether this should be derived from customs, or by taxing the countryside; the latter choice led to rural unrest and to a return to export trade, including the export of grain.[140] 'It is instructive to compare this situation with that of Tunisia, where the accent was emphatically upon the taxation of the countryside instead of the towns ... Whereas in Tunisia the centralisation of government went together with foreign trade, in Morocco the two impulses appeared as alternatives.'[141]

The reliance on foreign trade – which was continued by Sulayman's successors – had the great disadvantage that it placed Morocco at the mercy of western powers; as in Egypt, Britain was able to enforce free trade. In 1860 the Spanish invaded Tetuan, demanding a heavy indemnity as the price for withdrawal, which swallowed up three-quarters of customs' revenue. Mawlay Hassan (1873–94) adopted, in response to this, a 'recourse to the interior,'[142] travelling constantly round his dominions in an attempt to assert his authority. (There was nothing particularly novel about this – it was standard practice in feudal Europe, in Ethiopia, and in many states of sub-Saharan Africa.) Like Ahmad Bey in Tunisia, he attempted to build up a modern army, but was frustrated, partly by financial constraints and partly by the western profiteers who sold him firearms 'of every type except those in use in the most modern armies'.[143] He bought a cruiser but was unable to man it and it was sold to Colombia.[144] And as the peoples of the Bilad al-Siba acquired firearms as well, the net effect was essentially centrifugal.

From the 1850s onward an increasingly unfavourable balance of trade plunged Morocco into the fatal pattern of external indebtedness which ruined both Egypt and the other Maghrib governments. There is the same pattern – inflation, the export of raw materials, the increased dependence on imports, a privileged European enclave, and a much larger number of Moroccan 'protégés' in European employ, who were exempt from Moroccan law and taxes and enriched themselves accordingly – 'the *Hydra, Protection* which is depriving this Government of its lawful taxes and of all jurisdiction over Moors'.[145] A declining income from taxes led to heavier taxes in the countryside; as in Egypt, a few became very rich, while the peasants found themselves in a prison of increasing misery. In 1867, the Dukkala were paying a tax on livestock thirty times that prescribed in Islamic law.[146] There was a great expansion in banditry; this, together with famines and epidemics, weakened the state still further.[147]

European victories undermined the prestige of the sovereign. The French defeated a Moroccan army in 1844 in a clash which sprang from the campaigns of Abd al-Qadir, and we have noted the later conflict with Spain. Colonial conquest was forestalled largely by the rival ambitions of those European powers involved in Moroccan affairs who were (understandably) blamed for all the country's varied economic ills. In 1908 Sultan Abd al-Aziz was replaced by his brother, Abd al-Hafiz, but a dynastic reshuffle could not halt the pattern of events – a task which was probably no longer possible. In 1912, Abd al-Hafiz signed a treaty which made Morocco a French protectorate, and was deposed soon afterwards. He joined a Sufi order, and wrote poetry in honour of the mystical way.

The Sanusiyya[148]

Al-Sanusi (1787–1857) was an Algerian scholar-saint from Oran who influenced the history of Cyrenaica and the Sahara profoundly. Like al-Hajj Umar, he went on pilgrimage and remained in the East to study; he was deeply influenced by the kind of spirituality which had inspired the Wahhabi in Arabia. He returned to North Africa, setting up lodges of a new brotherhood in Cyrenaica where his teachings were eagerly welcomed – westerners called him the Grand Sanusi. He returned to Mecca for some years, but finally died in Africa, and his work was ably continued by his sons. The centre of the movement was at first on the coast of Cyrenaica, then further inland, and finally in the heart of the Sahara, moving ever further from the tide of European influence. In Libya, the Sanusi lodges gradually built up political and economic power. But the special mission of the Sanusiyya was to the nomads of the desert and Sanusi holy men resolved their disputes and encouraged trade. They rejected the Mahdi as an imposter. It is ironical that an order so hostile to European influence worked within the context of Saharan trade, which ultimately supplied the markets of Europe. The Grand Sanusi's grandson was to become head of the order in 1916, and later, king of Libya.

Ethiopia

Ethiopians remember the late eighteenth and early nineteenth centuries as the Era of Princes, a time of incessant conflict between rival warlords when the authority of the king, with his capital at Gondar, existed in name only. Ethiopia was also divided by the religious tension between Muslims and Christians, and the Ethiopian church itself was torn by obscure doctrinal controversies. It is a strange irony that this divided state preserved its autonomy into the modern world, whereas great African states elsewhere were swept away by colonialism.

The Dajazmach Kasa (1818–68) seized supreme power in 1855, taking the throne name Tewodros (Theodore): many expectations clustered around it, for it was believed that a king of this name would restore peace and prosperity after a time of war and famine. Such expectations naturally flourished among a peasantry plundered in successive wars, and there are some similarities with the rise of Mahdism in the Sudan. The evils from which he was to liberate Ethiopia included the rule of women!

Tewodros was deeply religious, and often called himself the slave of Christ.

He is persuaded that he is destined to restore the glories of Ethiopian Empire, and to achieve great conquests ... his faith is signal: without Christ, he says, I am nothing; if he has destined me to purify and reform this distracted kingdom, with His aid who shall stay me: nay, sometimes he is on the point of not caring for human assistance at all, and this is one reason why he will not seek with much avidity for assistance from or alliance with Europe.[149]

His great goal was to restore the strength and unity of the Ethiopian state. He was extremely anxious for access to western technology, and especially western arms. Tewodros came to the throne as a reformer but he spent his reign fighting an unending series of rebellions. The area under his control shrank steadily, and reverses – which included the death of his beloved wife – so distorted his character that he became increasingly violent and prone to alcoholism, and some have considered him insane. He forfeited the support of the church in 1860, when he attempted to reduce the number of clergy and to give the surplus land to tax-paying peasants.[150]

He had hoped to negotiate with the western powers as an equal. When a letter to Queen Victoria, seeking technical aid, went unanswered, he took several missionaries hostage. The British government sent an expedition under Napier, at great expense, to rescue them (it would have cost much less to respond to Tewodros' initial request). On Good Friday, 1868, his army was decimated by British forces. Tewodros sent his hostages away in safety and, then, on Easter Monday, died by his own hand. It is a bitter irony that the pistol was a gift from Queen Victoria. He had dreamed of uniting Ethiopia and conquering Jerusalem and, indeed, the world.

The British expedition was not intended to create a colony and soon withdrew. But Ethiopia was subject to external pressure from both Egypt and the Mahdist state. The completion of the Suez Canal augmented the strategic importance of the Red Sea – it led to the British capture of Aden and to what became French and British Somaliland. Italy began the conquest of Eritrea in 1883 and aspired to invade Ethiopia, but was overwhelmingly defeated at the battle of Adowa in 1896.

Yohannes (1871–89), like Tewodros before him, had his power base in northern Ethiopia – where the closely related Semitic languages, Amharic and Tigre, were spoken, and Monophysite Christianity prevailed. The south was dominated by Menelik, the prince of Shoa, who according to a prior agreement succeeded him when he was killed fighting the Mahdists and reigned from 1889 to 1913.

More than any other single individual, Menelik was the architect of modern Ethiopia. His conquests to the south dramatically expanded the frontiers of the state, and he founded a new capital, Addis Ababa. Menelik's 'internal colonialism', like that of Egypt in the Sudan and Equatoria, has been much criticised; the unity of the new Ethiopia was fragile, and after the overthrow of the Solomonic monarchy, in 1974, it began to break apart.

Conclusion

What are we to make of the unsuccessful attempts to modernise, the growing tide of colonialism? To contemporary western observers, it reflected political incapacity, the dead weight of a bankrupt political tradition. But it is clear that although the problems of, for instance, Egypt's viceroys were intensified by errors of political judgement, at the heart of their dilemma was the great imbalance between the economic and military resources of Europe and the Muslim world, which was in its turn largely the product of the Industrial Revolution. They acted within the limited range of possibilities the European powers allowed them; Muhammad Ali's attempt to industrialise failed because western pressures forced him to abandon tariff barriers. Much of the experience of these years – the increasing burden of external debt, the power of foreign enclaves, the growing poverty of the rural sector, the unsuccessful experiments with industrialisation, the famine and disease against which human initiatives seemed powerless – anticipates, with tragic exactitude, the experience of the twentieth century. This is not the whole story, and in the nineteenth, as in the twentieth, century, there were grounds for optimism as well as despair.

16

The Western Sudan in a time of jihad

The people were not created for the benefit of kings, but rather kings for the benefit of the people.

Nasir al-Din (d. 1674)[1]

The cleric gives birth to the chief, and the chief to the pagan.

Fulbe proverb[2]

The background

Between the late seventeenth and the late nineteenth centuries, a number of attempts were made to found new theocratic states in the Sudan. Not all succeeded, but those which did rewrote the political geography of the Western Sudan (Map 14).

The process began in the far west, in Mauretania, with an ultimately unsuccessful rising led by Nasir al-Din (d. 1674), and ended far to the east, with the Mahdist state (1881 to 1898). The development of these states was cut short by conquest – sometimes by another African state, as when the Umarian state defeated the caliphate of Hamdallahi, but more often by the imposition of colonial rule. In some cases, the very process of state formation was affected by conflict with colonial or quasi-colonial powers.

There had been comparable movements in the Sudan earlier – Takrur, the Almoravid empire, Wadai. Familiarity tends to dull our awareness of what an astonishing achievement the nineteenth-century jihads were. The scholars of Dila in Morocco, and Kairouan in Tunisia, tried to do the same, but were unsuccessful. Futa Toro was located in ancient Takrur, but most of the jihadist states were new political entities. The Sokoto caliphate was one of them, and its component emirates included ancient states such as Kano, and new ones such as Bauchi and Fombina. The jihads were particularly attractive to the Africanist scholars of the 1970s, including the present writer,[3] because they seem to offer a precedent of reforming leadership and successful state formation. Here as elsewhere, the tide has turned. Historians now lay greater emphasis on the human cost of the jihads, the sufferings of the enslaved and raided. Rulers such as al-Hajj Umar or Samori were once hailed as pioneers of modernity, but the main form it took was the adoption of western firearms.

The states founded by jihad had their contemporary critics, as well,[4] but no human society has ever succeeded in ridding itself of oppression and injustice, and sometimes it has been the states that began with the highest ideals which

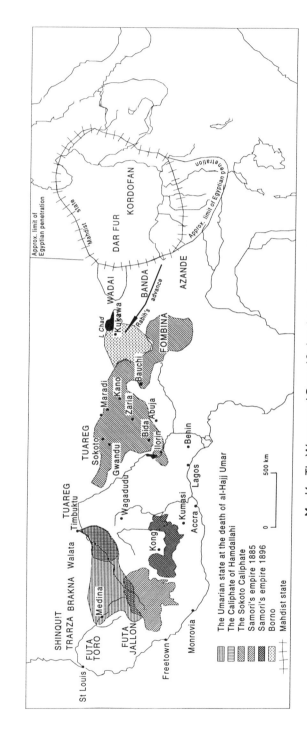

Map 14   The Western and Central Sudan: the nineteenth century

have in the end inflicted the greatest suffering. In non-Islamic African cultures, the dominant language of political discourse was that of kinship; it characterised both the relations of kings and subjects and of slave and free, and in itself did much to ameliorate them. The founders of the new states always recognised their obligation to obey Islamic social ideals, whatever the shortcomings of their practice, and Uthman dan Fodio's precepts, if followed, would solve many of the problems of contemporary Africa.

One of the swiftest ways of destroying a kingdom is to give preference to one particular tribe over another ... Every governor of a province should ... combat every cause of corruption which occurs in his country and forbid every disapproved thing ... and he should strive to reform the markets and set right the affairs of the poor and needy.[5]

The West African jihads have often been seen as among a number of responses to a situation of international crisis in the Islamic world, but its manifestations, though not unknown there, were far from being central preoccupations in the Western Sudan. What their leaders were concerned with, above all, was the local situation – manifestations of unbelief or oppression. They judged their world in terms of the guidelines of scholars of the past, especially the fourteenth-century jurist al-Maghili,[6] and found it wanting.

Some have suggested that a crisis at the heart of the Islamic world was counterbalanced by its vitality on the periphery. Perhaps the appearance of decline and crisis is itself an illusion, created by focussing on the fate of empires, to the neglect of other manifestations of religious life.

It was widely believed that the thirteenth Islamic century (1785–1882) would see the end of the world. Uthman dan Fodio believed that the end was near; he denied that he was the Mahdi, but in every century there is a Renewer, a Mujaddin, who precedes him. Like al-Maghili before him and Amadu Lobbo and al-Hajj Umar after him, Uthman believed that he was such a one. He thought, indeed, that he was the last Renewer before the Endtime.

Few West African religious leaders went on pilgrimage. Al-Hajj Umar owed much of his reputation to his standing as a pilgrim. Uthman dan Fodio never did this, though both his teacher, the Tuareg Jibrin ibn Umar, and his uncle were pilgrims. Some West Africans went on pilgrimage and never returned. Salih al-Fullani (1752–1803) was a scholar from Futa Jallon who remained at Mecca and was acclaimed as one of the two Mujaddids of his time.[7]

Most of the leaders studied in this chapter were members of Sufi brotherhoods. Their history is a striking instance of what has been called 'the routinisation of charisma'. Trimingham distinguishes three phases – the 'golden age' of mysticism, succeeded by the stage of the *tariqa* (Way, plural *turuq*) and then by that of *ta'ifa* (Organisation).[8] In the eighteenth and nineteenth centuries, many new *turuq* were founded; they were so different from their predecessors that some write of 'neo-Sufism'. The Sufi orders became mass movements, emphasising obedience to a shaykh who could trace his line of authority to the movement's founder. Their founders typically justified their actions in terms of visionary experience, and claimed the authority of the Prophet himself.[9] In a mass movement, not all were practising mystics. The *turuq* filled a need for religious community, and provided for the needy and poor among their members. In modern Hausaland, the popular definition of Sufism is 'being good'.[10] The earlier *turuq* were not exclusive and Uthman dan Fodio joined three. He was a member of the Qadiriyya, and had a great personal devotion to its founder, but it contributed little to the mobilisation of support for his jihad, whereas in the case of al-Hajj Umar, his office as a khalifa in the Tijaniyya was crucial.

This *tariqa* was founded by a Sufi from southern Algeria, Ahmed al-Tijani, who died in Fez in 1815. He forbade its members to join any other brotherhood and made exalted claims which members of other *turuq* resented – it was the last of the *turuq*, superseding all others and the Mahdi would be a Tijani.[11]

The combination of the roles of Sufi and scholar – an expertise in both *tasawwuf* (mysticism) and *fiqh* (jurisprudence) – was a distinctive hallmark of West African Islam, as was, very often, its rural rather than urban setting.[12] Uthman was a scholar as well as a Sufi, as were many women and men of his family, and al-Hajj Umar is said to have vanquished the scholars of Cairo in debate. Not all the jihad leaders were learned. Ahmadu, the founder of Hamdallahi, was far from erudite, and it may have been this, as much as his puritanism, which estranged him from the learned of Timbuktu. Some clerics[13] in Futa Toro had difficulty in corresponding in Arabic.[14]

Those who fought in the jihads included devout scholars who embraced the struggle in the hope of paradise, and those who hoped to grow rich from plunder and the capture of slaves. (These are points on a continuum, and not necessarily mutually exclusive.) The first emir of Kano had so little property that he lacked the sacrificial ram needed for a festival. Yakubu, first emir of Bauchi, dug his own grave; it was said of him:

> You flow like a river until you have become a river
> Among the people, until there is no one thirsty on earth.[15]

There was a chronic tension between the statesman and the saint. It is said that Umar wept after his first victories, but in his last years he was sometimes guilty of great cruelty.[16]

Social and economic factors

The history of the Western Sudan from the late eighteenth century on has usually been written as if it falls naturally into three phases – the states which existed before the jihads, the jihadist states, and colonial jurisdictions. All this begs many questions – the kingdoms which the jihadist leaders denounced for their unbelief were, to varying extents, identified with Islam, and the jihadist states did not always put their ideals into consistent practice. There is a tendency for narratives to revolve round a romantic concentration on statesmen and saints – another version of the Great Men theory of history. Studies which focus on the changing relations of production bring out significant continuities. From this perspective, the differences between 'pagan' Segu and al-Hajj Umar's empire are more apparent than real; each was a warrior state, and in each, slave labour was crucial.[17]

Were the societies in which jihad was preached gripped by a real crisis –

reflected less in 'unbelief' than in oppressive government, or did the jihadists condemn them unfairly, from the viewpoint of an intolerant puritanism? If there was a real social crisis, should it be linked with the Saharan and/or Atlantic slave trades? The evidence is complex and contradictory. The jihads began in the Senegambia and Futa Jallon, where society was militarised and polarised by Atlantic trade.[18] The growth of Atlantic trade enriched Muslim merchants and may well have made them dissatisfied with their subordinate political status. But the jihadist leaders were not merchants.

A recent study claims that the Atlantic slave trade had a significant impact on Hausaland from the 1780s on, and that dan Fodio should be seen as 'a Muslim William Wilberforce'[19] opposing, not slavery in general, but the enslavement of free Muslims. On the other hand, it has been suggested that one of the advantages in defining a Muslim in narrow terms was that it increased the numbers of those who could be legally enslaved![20]

Slave labour was of such great importance in these new states that some have written of a slave mode of production. Ahmadu of Hamdallahi, for all his idealism, refused to abolish servile and casted status.

There seems to have been a long period of diminished rainfall in the late seventeenth and early eighteenth centuries. During the Senegambia famine of 1681, 'many sold themselves for slaves, only to get a sustenance'.[21] The mid-eighteenth century saw an ecological crisis in a Western Sudan afflicted by drought, locusts, famine and epidemics.[22] In 1757, the French commander of St Louis released 500 slaves he could not feed.[23] Its exact impact on political and religious history has yet to be fully explored. The famine of the mid-eighteenth century may have destroyed the first Segu state and the rise of the Sokoto caliphate has been linked with the recovery which followed; all this is partly speculation. Ecological crises may well have intensified attachment to religion, and made believers readier to embark on hijra.[24]

The Fulbe dimension

There is a recurrent pattern in African history, where a Muslim leader creates a new political unity among pastoralists living in scattered clans, and infuses them with a new militancy and religious and political consciousness. The Almoravids and Almohads were a case in point, and so, in the nineteenth century, were the Sanusiyya of Libya.

The jihads in Futa Toro, Futa Jallon, Sokoto and Hamdallahi were led by Fulbe, and the Umarian state was founded by Tukulor, who are sedentary Fulbe. All but one of the flag bearers who carried the jihad in Gobir further afield were Fulbe, though there were many Tuareg and Hausa among dan Fodio's supporters. Previously, with one exception, Fulbe had not ruled over unified states,[25] but had lived for the most part in transhumant clans.

One of the most remarkable aspects of West African history is the tremendous eastward expansion of the Fulbe, from a home on the middle Senegal. By the 1950s, it was estimated that of some 6 million Fulbe, only 3 per cent were in their original homeland.

By the nineteenth century, they had reached modern Chad and Cameroon, and had overlapped with another body of migrant pastoralists, the Shuwa Arabs, who had travelled across the central Sudan from the Red Sea.

An understanding of the Fulbe is particularly bedevilled by the diversity and inaccuracy of ethnyms. The Fulbe are called Peul in French, Fula in Sierra Leone, and Fulani in Nigeria. Their language is called Pulaar on the Senegal, and elsewhere Fulfulde. On the Senegal, they call themselves Halpulaar, but elsewhere Fulbe. The Woodabe are 'red' Fulani – referring to their typical – but not invariable – olive complexion and aquiline features.

The Tukulor of Futa Toro are sedentary, rather than nomadic Fulbe; the Torodbe ('those who beg for alms') – Toronkawa in Hausa – were clerical Tukulor. The word originally meant simply Muslims with some knowledge of their faith. After the jihads, the Torodbe became a hereditary caste; figures which may be too high suggest that the Tukulor comprise 55 per cent of the modern inhabitants of Futa Toro, and Torodbe 45 per cent of Tukulor.[26] Throughout the Senegambia, clerics tended to be Torodbe. They 'believe themselves to be ... the first people in the world, the chosen children of God, for they alone, among the Muslim peoples, they say, properly observe the law of Muhammad'.[27]

It is possible that the Fulbe diaspora was a response to alternating phases of plenty and scarcity; in periods of good rainfall, human and livestock populations built up to a level which the environment could not sustain when conditions were less favourable – hence the recurrent need to migrate. The basic mobility of transhumant pastoralists made it easier for them to embark on longer migrations.

The needs and lifestyles of farmers and pastoralists were often complementary; and the movement of pastoralists was facilitated by the fact that they filled an underused ecological niche. Cattle could be pastured on land which had too little water or nutrients for successful farming; Fulbe cattle manured the fields and pastoralists exchanged milk for grain. But sometimes stock trampled the crops, farmers rustled Fulbe cattle, or both groups competed for scarce water.

Fulbe pastoralists resented the cattle tax, *jangali*, imposed by the rulers of the Hausa kingdoms; those living in the small Mandingo kingdoms south of the Gambia had similar complaints, and tradition remembers the occasion of the jihad of 1867 as the seizure of a Fulbe sheep.[28] On the Gambia in the early seventeenth century, it was observed: 'In some places they have settled Townes, but for the most part they are still wandering ... These people live in great subjection to the *Mandingo,* under which they seene to groane, for he cannot at any time kill a beefe but if they know it, the black-men will have the greatest share.'[29]

Only a small minority of Fulbe were clerics, and many were not Muslim at all. The seventeenth-century Timbuktu chronicles, the *Tarikh al-Sudan* and the *Tarikh al-Fettash*, describe the pastoral Fulbe of Massina as pagan.[30] In Fombina, the South Land, fasting was seen as a distraction from the care of the herds, so thirty men fasted for one day each, on behalf of the community.[31] But Adama, who led the jihad there, was a scholar-saint; when his soldiers plundered newly defeated Wandala, he prayed (successfully) that they would be repulsed. In the jihadist states, the Fulbe were not only a ruling elite but developed a sense of being a chosen people, Fulfulde a sacred language second only to Arabic, in which scholars wrote didactic poetry.[32]

> I will cite the classical sources in Fulfulde
> to aid you in understanding. As you hear them, accept them.
> To each in effect only his own language
> allows him to grasp what the classics have to say . . .
> To remain in incertitude about the great obligations
> is not sufficient for speaking, nor indeed, for acting.[33]

We have seen how the ropes of fictitious genealogies bound the Muslims of the African periphery to the heartland of Islam. The Fulbe reinforced their role as a chosen people by claiming descent from the Arab conqueror, Uqba.[34]

Clerics and warriors

The history of the Senegambia has often been interpreted in terms of conflict between Muslim merchants and clerics on one hand and syncretist or 'pagan' kings and warriors on the other. The reality was more nuanced and complex. Many clerics were not merchants, and the jihads were waged against rulers who considered themselves Muslims. They were accused of unbelief, for jihad could only be waged against unbelievers. We know them only from the writings of those who overthrew them and should not exaggerate either their oppressiveness or their syncretism. The learned and devout Ahmad Baba of Timbuktu (1556–1627), who was exiled to Marrakesh in 1592, listed the countries he believed to be Muslim: 'Bornu, Kano, Songhai, Katsina, Gobir, Mali and some of Zakzak . . . Also the majority of the Fulani, except a group beyond Gao, as we have been informed, who are said to be *kaffir*.'[35] When the deposed king of Gobir, Yunfa, was fleeing for his life from the jihadist forces he said the obligatory prayers, albeit at the wrong time.[36]

The identification of the Wolof kings with Islam has often been masked by their predilection for alcohol. In 1848, when Christian missionaries wished to work in Kajoor, the king said that they would be welcome as merchants, provided they brought liquor, but not as religious teachers: 'far from receiving the law of God from others, it is we who teach it to the world. Kajoor is completely converted and needs no one to teach it.'[37]

Al-Kanemi, who was to stem the tide of jihad in Borno, pointed out that much of what was condemned was sin rather than unbelief. 'No age and no country is free from its share of heresy and sin.'[38] Uthman dan Fodio himself wrote a number of essays condemning 'a group of *talaba* [students] who accuse the ordinary Muslims of unbelief'.[39] The Hausa or Senegambian kingdoms were 'Muslim' in the same way that medieval Europe was 'Christian'; there were differences in degree of commitment and understanding. Becoming a cleric was not becoming a Muslim; it resembled initiation into a particular community; slaves, the casted and royals seldom became clerics.[40]

Clerics – like Fulbe pastoralists and Dyula merchants – were traditionally excluded from political power. When they suddenly laid claim to it, the

exisiting elite found the transformation of accustomed roles profoundly dis-
concerting.

Rural protest

West African Islam has often been understood as an urban phenomenon, and
cleric and merchant have sometimes been regarded as synonymous. In fact,
many clerics shunned trade, though it was commerce which gave cities such as
Timbuktu and Jenne the resources to sustain a community of scholars. After the
collapse of the great empires, Islam moved into the countryside.[41] None of the
jihadist leaders came from towns, or were associated with the court, and none
were merchants.

A challenge to the status quo did not come from its beneficiaries. Dan Fodio
denounced the court mallams, and Ahmad Lobbo was at loggerheads with the
clerics of Jenne and Timbuktu.[42] But after the jihads, the Hamdallahi government encouraged Fulbe pastoralists to settle in towns.[43]

Paths of peace

Not all clerics accepted the necessity of the jihad of the sword. Many disavowed
the Sword of Truth, and believed that jihad should be waged only in the heart –
the Jakhanke, as noted earlier in this study, have always been linked with
pacificism. 'The King has asked and given us a choice about taking up arms and
joining battle and on the other hand about building a fortress. We have said, if
we are asked to build a fortress we shall build it, and if we are asked to take up
arms and join battle, we shall build a fortress'.[44]

The first jihad was led by a cleric from Shinquit; he broke away from the
traditional distinction between clerical and warrior callings, though his eventual
failure reinforced it. The Sahara produced many scholars and saints – the
austerity intrinsic to life in the desert probably fostered a tendency to focus on
the eternal and the Muslims of the desert have always had a great impact on the
people of the Bilad al-Sudan.[45]

One of the most celebrated desert saints was a shaykh of the Qadiriyya, Sidi al-
Mukhtar (1729–1811). He was a member of the clerical clan, the Kunta, and
believed that he was the Renewer of his time. He opposed the jihad of the sword,
and believed Muslims should work by attraction, and especially by drawing
recruits into the turuq. A later Kunta cleric warned al-Hajj Umar: '*Jihad* leads to
kingship and kingship to oppression; Our present situation is … safe from the
error to which *jihad* leads.'[46]

Al-Mukhtar advocated the acquisition of wealth – in the case of the Kunta, the
link between cleric and merchant is evident. In the words of his son, 'After
acquiring a substantial grounding in the religious and mystical sciences [the
Kunta] would concentrate on accumulating wealth.'[47]

The justification of the jihad of the sword was by no means self-evident. It is
noteworthy that dan Fodio, al-Hajj Umar and others only embarked on it after
they had been commanded to do so in a vision. They needed this kind of direct

divine authority before they could embark on something so hazardous and so momentous.

The Senegambia

More than any other part of Africa, the Senegambia was simultaneously involved in Atlantic and trans-Saharan trade. The Sahara is more densely populated in the west, because the ocean moderates its climate. Its impact on the Bilad al-Sudan was correspondingly intense. The Senegambia extends between two shores – the ocean and the sahel. In the economic sphere, the Atlantic zone proved dominant; in the world of the spirit, trans-Saharan influences were stronger, and most Senegalese are now Muslims.

The proportion of the community who were slaves increased in the era of Atlantic trade; as elsewhere, there was a great difference between those obtained as captives and those born into a society. Most of the enslaved were engaged in manual work, but there was also a class of rich and powerful military slaves, *tyeddo*, the exact counterparts of Egypt's Mamluks. Muslim reformers often denounced their rapacity and violence; the *tyeddo* drank heavily, and demarcated their corporate identity in ways not dissimilar from the *rugaruga* of nineteenth-century East Africa – bright clothes, jewellery and long hair. In modern Wolof, the word means pagan. 'They were brave without compare,' wrote a Frenchman in 1876. 'Without any exaggeration they may be likened to our brave medieval knights.'[48] There were also the hereditary casted occupations such as blacksmiths and minstrels (griots), who were often more prosperous than the free peasantry; their numbers were relatively low. The griot had immense influence; he carried the king's standard into battle and, like the *tyeddo*, was identified with traditional religion.

The Atlantic slave trade led to an expansion of domestic slavery – Park, travelling in the Niger bend area at the end of the eighteenth century, thought that slaves outnumbered the free by three to one.[49] In 1904, it was estimated that two-thirds of the people of Bundu were slaves, and a modern study of the Tukulor suggested that 20 per cent were of slave descent and 6 per cent were casted.[50]

Atlantic trade increased the resources available to kings, and the tyeddo often plundered the peasantry; there are many parallels elsewhere in Africa to this growth of warlordism. Senegambia was 'marked by the most terrible violence, and most of the time, free men were taken, were rendered captive without reason and sold . . . so that they could buy for themselves horses, silver, guinea cloth and trade liquor'.[51]

Waalo, near St Louis, was enriched by customs duties, and the support of foreign merchants sometimes saved a ruler's throne. But the growth of the groundnut trade, from the 1830s on, strengthened the economic role of the peasant cultivator.

Colvin sees the Senegambian jihads as attempts by a clerical group not unlike a caste to obtain political power from which it was excluded. Barry interprets Nasir al-Din's jihad as 'a grass-roots vehicle of revolt and resistance'.[52] A casted jeweller, Diile, led an ultimately unsuccessful revolt in Kajoor in 1827–30.[53]

Mauretania and Shurr Bubba

The early jihads developed, not in the Islamic heartland of Jenne and Timbuktu, but on its western periphery, where they spread across two ecological zones. The first, which was ultimately unsuccessful, was led by a cleric from the deserts of southern Mauretania, Nasir al-Din (d. 1674), and is remembered as Shurr Bubba.

In modern Mauretania, traditions of Shurr Bubba are a foundation myth for contemporary perceptions of social structure. These structures are in fact more ancient; reality, as one might expect, is more nuanced and contradictory than the model.[54] The language of the overwhelming majority is Hassaniya, a dialect of Arabic, and Znaga Berber survives in small pockets. The 'Moors' are descendants of Arabised Berbers and Berberised Arabs. In contemporary perceptions, Mauritania is dominated by two noble castes – the warrior Hassani, who trace their descent to Hassan of the Banu Ma'qil, and the clerical Zawaya. One should not exaggerate their differences – both were nomadic pastoralists, and in Shurr Bubba, the Zawaya took to arms. There were other, subordinate castes – the _zenagha_ (herders, cultivators and warriors) and the black _harratin_, of freed slave descent, and casted smiths and griots.[55]

Shurr Bubba was undoubtedly a response to a situation of political and ecological crisis – it was a time of drought, and Moroccan forces, in alliance with the Hassani, were raiding for slaves who were intended for the Moroccan army.

Initially, the jihadists were dramatically successful, overthrowing the rulers of Futa Toro, Jolof, Kajoor and Waalo, and replacing them with 'masters of prayer'. The Tukulor were divided – some, led by the Torodbe, supported Nasir al-Din, others, including the royal family, the Hassani. Nasir al-Din opposed the export of slaves and appealed to popular hostility to the traditional rulers – 'God will never permit the kings to pillage, slaughter and enslave their subjects.' But he died in battle, and traditional rulers re-established their authority, with the help of firearms bought from the French on the coast.

Nasir al-Din's vision was a purely supernatural one – reflected in the usage which called his followers the _tubenan_, the penitents.[56] According to Barbot, the people of Kajoor believed that his teaching would lead to miraculous harvests; they did not plant, and a famine followed.[57] After the movement failed, the Hassani established two emirates north of the Senegal river – Trarza and Brakna – where the Zawaya were in a tributary relation.

Shurr Bubba came to underpin the distinction between warrior and clerical clans – the former living primarily by raiding and the protection of caravans, the latter by commerce. Like 'Dyula', these were occupational rather than ethno-linguistic categories – some members of warrior clans became clerics, and some clerical clans raided with enthusiasm.[58]

Bundu

The jihad led by Malik Sy in Bundu (d. 1700) was in a sparsely peopled area with a number of different ethno-linguistic groups; it created a new polity which endured until it was dissolved by the French in 1905. He and his followers came from Futa Toro. His jihad created a Fulbe Muslim elite who prospered by trade and the control of slaves, like their counterparts in the Futas. A recent study focusses on pragmatism as its defining characteristic.[59]

Futa Jallon

The jihad in Futa Jallon, like that in Bundu, created a unified state where none had existed previously. For generations, pastoral Fulbe had migrated into Futa Jallon, an inland massif in modern Guinea, where the Gambia, Senegal and Niger rivers rise. Here, they formed symbiotic relationships with local agricultural peoples – Susu and Mandinka-speaking Jalonke. After the defeat of Nasir al-Din, some Torodbe joined them. The Fulbe became increasingly wealthy in cattle and slaves, and sought commensurate political power; they formulated this goal in Islamic terms.

The jihad in Futa Jallon began with a meeting of nine clerics, in 1726; they elected Karamoko Alfa as their leader, chosen for his piety and learning (both names mean Teacher, in Mandinka and Fulfulde respectively). When he died in 1751, he was replaced by his cousin, Ibrahim Sori, an outstanding military leader. He adopted the title almami, like Nasir al-Din and Malik Sy before him. In future, the descendants of Alfa and Sori would compete for the office. The new Fulbe ruling class prospered by selling provisions and slaves to European merchants on the coast. They established slave villages, whose inhabitants grew food both for their overlords and for sale.[60] Over half the population was of servile status. It is a particularly clearly documented case of the social polarisation which so often accompanied Atlantic trade. But Futa Jallon also became a famous centre of Islamic learning, and among those who came to study there was al-Hajj Umar.

In 1845, a cleric called Alfa Mamadu led a revolt of the Hubbu (from *hubb*, Arabic for love); he died in 1854, but the movement survived until wiped out by Samori in 1884. But the Hubbu, too, lost their initial idealism, and became a community of brigands; they did not abolish slavery.[61]

In the mid-nineteenth century, another local Muslim lamented: 'Honesty has disappeared, government and religion have become corrupt ... Each one is occupied with looking after himself.'[62]

Futa Toro

The jihad in Futa Toro took place in an established state, ruled by the Denianke. They were closely identified with Islam;[63] the *satigi* (king) who died in 1702 spent his days in Qur'anic study. In a familiar quest for illustrious ancestors they claimed that their dynastic founder, Koli Tenguella, was a son of the great Sundiata.[64]

For much of the eighteenth century Futa Toro was in turmoil. Its rich agricultural resources and extended frontiers made it both attractive to aggressors and difficult to defend and it lacked the canoe fleet of imperial Songhay. Moors and Moroccan 'Orman' invaded it repeatedly and French trade on the Senegal also had a divisive impact. The jihad grew out of this situation, and the ecological crisis to which we have already referred. It was a movement of the Torodbe, and its first leader was Sulayman Bal; after his death, in the 1770s, Abdul Kader Kan became the first Almami. He had once studied under a Mauretanian woman shaykh, Khadija.[65] He was overthrown and killed in 1806 – a fate he had prayed for, fearing his position of power would jeopardise his own salvation.[66]

The Torodbe became a propertied oligarchy, and the original religious impetus was soon lost. The Almamis were weak, holding power, on average, for a year each, as did the French Governors of St Louis, in the first half of the nineteenth century!

Uthman dan Fodio and the foundation of the Sokoto caliphate

The states in the Futas and Bundu were small and divided, and drifted far from their initial ideals. The jihad which led to the creation of the Sokoto caliphate had much more far-reaching consequences. It created a vast conglomerate of states extending some 1,400 kilometres from east to west and 700 kilometres from north to south. It was justified by a large corpus of theoretical writings, in part occasioned by a dispute with al-Kanemi of Borno. Uthman dan Fodio (1754–1817) was its undisputed authority figure, but the task of practical leadership was shared by others – notably his brother, Abdullahi, his second son, Muhammad Bello, and his son-in-law, the vizier Gidado. Abdullahi and Muhammad Bello led the wars in Gobir and shared the administration of the caliphate. Muhammad Bello succeeded his father as caliph of Sokoto, while Abdullahi ruled the western section, Gwandu. Bello died in 1837, and Gidado in 1842. The Sokoto leadership had a continuity which was to be signally lacking in, for instance, the Umarian state.

The jihad broke out in the Hausa kingdom of Gobir. Far from being in decline, Gobir was at the height of its military strength and territorial expansion. It was the pastoral Fulbe who seem to have been undergoing a crisis – some had returned to Hausaland, from a Borno afflicted by a series of ecological disasters. Like their kinsmen elsewhere in West Africa, they resented demands for taxes and were subject to the risk of enslavement – 'the political and social "space" for Fulbe was being closed down'.[67]

Uthman dan Fodio lived on the borders of Gobir, at Degel, a rural Torodbe settlement. The jihad was to overthrow the Habe rulers not only of Gobir but of the ancient states of the Hausa heartland – Kano, Katsina, Zazzau, Daura. The jihadists failed to conquer Borno, but the kingdom was shorn of its eastern provinces, and the descendants of al-Kanemi replaced the Seyfawa. The jihad spread far beyond Hausaland; the descendants of a Fulbe mallam became rulers of Nupe, and a Muslim rising in northern Yorubaland led to the creation of the emirate of Ilorin. In some cases, new states were created in areas of political fragmentation – Bauchi is an instance, and so is Fombina, often called Adamawa after its founder.

The Hausa kingdoms and Borno had been Muslim for centuries. It was a critic who said of nineteenth-century Borno, 'Indeed there are not to be found in these countries ordinary people more scrupulous than they in reciting the Qur'an and reading it and memorising it and writing it out. And the ordinary people did not cease to be thus down to the beginning of this jihad.'[68]

The Shehu – as dan Fodio is always called in Hausaland[69] – denounced the Hausa kings for syncretism and various forms of oppression, the taking of bribes, and illegal taxation. Jihad was, he said, obligatory against a king 'who mingles the observances of Islam with the observances of heathendom, like the kings of Hausaland for the most part'.[70] The debate was a fundamental one. How oppressive were the Hausa kings? To what extent was the religious practice of the courts tinged with syncretism? What was the religious condition of the country-side, or of the towns? There is no one answer, and inevitably, the Hausa kings are judged by the writings of their enemies.

Later, al-Hajj Umar was to elaborate a distinction which was often made between the jihad of the heart, the jihad of the word, and the jihad of the sword. All three are well exemplified in the life of the Shehu. He began his career as a teacher at the age of twenty, preaching in Hausa, and writing learned works in Arabic and didactic verse in Fulfulde. From 1789 on, he experienced a series of visions, in one of which the founder of the Qadiriyya gave him 'the Sword of Truth, to unsheath it against the enemies of God'.[71]

His relationship with successive sultans of Gobir was fraught with tension; finally, a clash led the Shehu to embark on hijra to its boundary. His small band of followers defeated the forces sent in pursuit. In the words of one of the defeated Hausa kings, the jihad was like a spark which turns into an uncontrollable blaze.

The early jihadists fought fearlessly, in the certain expectation of paradise, using the Fulbe bow against the armoured cavalry of Gobir in battles which many of them did not survive. The Hausa kings fought for their inheritance with courage and tenacity, and a small band of scholars, however devoted, could not have overthrown them. The jihad succeeded because it won much wider support. The Shehu's supporters, as we have seen, included Hausa and Tuareg as well as Fulbe. Fulbe pastoral clans – each under its leader, the *ardo* – responded, motivated largely, it seems, by grievances such as cattle tax and problems with local farmers. The Hausa kings were given an opportunity to accept the jihad. Only one – the devout Jattau of Zazzau – did so, and he died a little later. Five successive kings of Katsina died fighting the jihadists; the last of them threw himself into a well in his despair.[72]

By 1810, the jihad had succeeded in the old Hausa kingdoms – Gobir, Katsina, Daura, Kano and Zaria. It had narrowly failed in Borno, though three emirates were carved from its western provinces, and it set a chain of events in train which replaced a thousand-year-old dynasty, the Seyfawa, with the descendants of a Kanembu mallam whom history knows as al-Kanemi. In Bauchi and Adamawa, long years of struggle with local communities had begun. The Ilorin and Nupe emirates were founded in the 1820s, Kontagora in 1859.

The emirates had a high degree of autonomy and several of the Hausa kingdoms survived in an attenuated form – the court of Zazzau moved south to Abuja, and there were other displaced Hausa kingdoms on the desert edge, among them Maradi.

The initial impulse was never wholly lost. But inevitably, success and the passage of time adulterated the first idealism, and Hausa poets came to castigate the shortcomings of the Fulbe rulers in much the same way as that in which Uthman denounced the Hausa kings. A mid-nineteenth-century poet from Kontagora urged the Fulbe

> Do not act proudly because of this world,
> Do not strive for wealth ...
> Do not despise the people of this world,
> People of the bush and of the scattered villages.[73]

The impact of the Sokoto jihad went far beyond changes of government. Islam became more widely and deeply rooted, though elements of traditional religion survived, especially in the countryside. In time, Hausa took the place of Fulfulde as the vehicle of didactic literature, recited and written in *ajami* (modified Arabic script).[74] To an ever greater extent, Islam became part of the unquestioned fabric of daily life.

The Shehu was a strong advocate of the education of women, and condemned scholars who 'leave their wives, their daughters, and their captives morally abandoned ... without teaching them what God prescribes should be taught them'.[75] His wives, Hauwa and Aisha, were noted Sufis. His daughters – Hadiza, Fatima, Hafsatu, Safiya, Mariam and Asma'u – wrote poetry and prose in Fulfulde and Hausa. Asma'u, the best known, is the author of fifty-two extant works; she devoted herself to education, and founded a women's religious movement which still survives.[76] But the practice of keeping women veiled and in seclusion expanded under the new regime, and was facilitated by the enslavement of large numbers of captives, whose labours both made it possible for women to live in seclusion and freed the energies of scholars for literary pursuits and a life of prayer.

The caliphate of Hamdallahi

The caliphate of Hamdallahi maintained an independent existence only from 1818 to 1862 and was much smaller than the Sokoto caliphate, or the successor state of al-Hajj Umar. It was probably the most purely theocratic of the jihadist states, and the one which departed least from its original ideals. It was founded in the Inland Delta of the Niger, and included the ancient commercial and religious centres of Jenne and Timbuktu. It is possible that state formation in the area had been impeded by the fact that it lay within the boundaries of successive empires – Ghana, Mali and Songhai.[77] But the region produced the surplus to sustain the apparatus of government, thanks to a strategic location on long-distance trade routes, river transport, and fertile agricultural land.

The Bambara kingdom of Segu was the dominant power in the region when the jihad broke out. (The people generally known as Bambara called themselves Banmana and spoke a dialect of Malinke.) The Segu state had been founded relatively recently, by Biton or Mamary [Muhammad] Kulibali (d. 1755). Tradition claims that he was a hunter and stranger, who became the head of the young men's age grade (*ton*) with the help of water spirits. He attracted slaves and debtors to its ranks, and became a king – a notable instance of the transformation of traditional institutions. He did not, however, succeed in founding a long-lived dynasty, perhaps because of the catastrophic drought and famine of the mid-eighteenth century. In 1765, N'gola Diara, a first-generation captive, succeeded in seizing power, and his heirs ruled Segu until it was conquered by al-Hajj Umar in 1861. It reached its greatest extent in the reign of his son, Mansong.

To Muslim chroniclers, Bambara was synonymous with 'pagan', but there was a considerable Muslim presence in Segu. When Mungo Park visited it in 1796, he observed that 'Moorish mosques are found in every quarter' and called the city – whose population he estimated at 30,000 – 'a prospect of civilisation and magnificence which I little expected to find in the bosom of Africa'.[78] Kaarta was a smaller state, founded in the sahel among Fulbe and Soninke by the unsuccessful opponents of Biton Kulibali.[79] Bambara slave warriors despised farming, and practised a conspicuous consumption reminiscent of the *tyeddo* of Senegal.

The Niger bend was an area of considerable ethnic diversity – its peoples included Dyula (called Marka locally) and Bozo, who fished the waters of the Niger and its tributaries. Timbuktu and its environs were dominated by Tuareg. Massina, well watered and fertile, was particularly attractive to Fulbe pastoralists, who had been settled there since the early fifteenth century.

The founder of the Caliphate of Hamdallahi, Ahmadu Lobbo of the Bari clan, was a Fulbe of Massina, who spent his youth in study and in cattle herding. Like Uthman dan Fodio, he was a member of the Qadiriyya, which he joined in Jenne; he sought dan Fodio's blessing on his own movement, though the Kunta shaykhs of the desert influenced him as well.[80]

Ahmadu began his jihad against the Fulbe *ardoen* of Massina in 1818,[81] a rising of Fulbe pastoralists against Fulbe pastoralists.[82] The ardoen were not pagan – they had Muslim names[83] – but they were in a tributary relationship to Segu, which the Fulbe experienced as oppressive, because of its seizure of people and cattle.[84] Ahmadu was initially supported by the Sokoto and Timbuktu religious leadership; they were later alienated when he ceased to pay deference to their teachings, and claimed the title Commander of the Faithful. Although slaves flocked to his banner, Ahmadu did not abolish casted and servile status. Nor did he conquer Segu – the two states co-existed in embattled hostility until the arrival of an external enemy, al-Hajj Umar, drove them to a brief and uneasy alliance. Like other jihadist states, Hamdallahi gained much of its revenue from war.

Dan Fodio lived in retirement, entrusting government to others. Ahmadu kept it in his own hands, but went to great lengths to ensure that it kept to his theocratic ideals. He is said to have invited a hundred scholars to write an essay on Islamic government, selecting forty of them to serve on his Council.

He built a new capital at Hamdallahi ('Praise God'), where he made provision for the poor and for pilgrims, and prohibited not only alcohol but also tobacco, and dyed cloth. He insisted on the seclusion of women in walled compounds, and appointed an overseer of the market to avoid fraud. He came into increasing conflict with Jenne and Timbuktu – his new city threatened the former's economic role, and he destroyed its mosque, on the grounds that it was too ornate. The Kunta, for all their attachment to the Qadiriyya, led a number of risings against him in Timbuktu – the element of urban–rural conflict which is evident in other jihads. The Fulbe clerics of Hamdallahi seem to have been positively hostile to commerce.[85]

Ahmadu died in 1845 and was succeeded first by his son, then by his grandson – both were his namesakes. In the latter's reign, Hamdallahi was overthrown by the forces of al-Hajj Umar, and the holy city of Hamdallahi did not long survive this defeat.

Al-Hajj Umar (c. 1794–1864)[86]

Al-Hajj Umar Tal was born in humble circumstances in a Futa Toro he left permanently, apart from brief visits, in 1820: 'He was permanently marked by his perceptions of a failed revolution, discriminatory regime, and vulnerable society.'[87] It was not until 1852 that he was commanded in a vision to embark on the jihad of the sword; he created an empire in the last twelve years of his life.

Other jihad leaders established new governments in the societies where they lived. Umar founded a short-lived empire, not in Futa Toro, where he was born, nor in Futa Jallon, where he settled for a time, but on the Niger bend; he did so with the support of *émigré* Fulbe/Tukulor from his homeland – one of the major migrations of recent West African history. He could not lead a jihad in Futa Toro because it was a Muslim state. Moreover, French encroachment on the Senegal undermined the region's stability and autonomy.

An imperial structure was imposed by a Senegambian and Guinean 'west' upon a Malian 'east'. When this structure tried to encompass the Masina Fulbe as well, it broke at the seams and the ephemeral empire shrank back to a series of garrison islands in a generally hostile sea. The imperial *jihad* and its successor states stressed Fulbe colonisation and privilege, not the creation of the institutions of islamization ... This structure was highly successful for conquest. It was decidedly less so for administration and the spread of Islam.[88]

Umar joined the Tijiniyya before he began his pilgrimage in 1825. In Mecca and Medina, he attached himself to the Tijani khalifa for the Hijaz, and became a khalifa, winning respect for his sanctity and learning. He left Arabia in 1831 – his return journey took nine years, six of which were spent at Sokoto. He also visited Massina, gaining a quite exceptional first-hand knowledge of West Africa's jihadist states.[89] In 1840 he founded a community of scholars, not in Futa Toro but on the eastern borders of Futa Jallon, at Jegunko; he attracted large numbers of followers and built up large reserves of firearms. Most of his followers were Fulbe and Tukulor, recruited in Futa Toro. In 1849 the community moved east to Dinguiray.

In 1852, when he was fifty-eight, a heavenly voice urged him to embark on a jihad. His writings reflect his inner struggles – he was glad of the hostility of the Almami of Futa Toro, for he might otherwise have been tempted to become 'one of the venal scholars who ... mixed with the *sultans*'.[90]

Dinguiray was situated in the small animist Mandinka state of Tamba, where the initial victory of Umar's forces attracted many new recruits; this enabled him to wage war on the Bambara kingdoms, beginning with Kaarta, which fell after a long struggle in 1856. Expansion to the north-west brought him into conflict with the French, who were moving inland from their older settlements on the coast. Modern oral traditions remember the history of the period as a clash between two great protagonists – the French governor Faidherbe[91] and al-Hajj Umar. In 1857 his forces laid siege to the French fort at Medina, which was under the command of a Eur-African, Paul Holle. He placed on the gate a sign which read, 'Long live Jesus!!! Long live the Emperor [Napoleon III]!'[92] The symbolism of the conflict echoes down the years.

After this, Umar and the French reached an informal *modus vivendi*. Umar, his forces decimated, decided to concentrate on war in the east, against the 'pagan' Bambara. Thousands followed him from Futa Toro, sometimes as a result of coercion. Faidherbe wrote to its rulers in 1860, 'your country is depopulated and ruined. It's no longer a country but a desert.'[93] In practice, though not in theory, the jihad acquired strong ethnic overtones – Fulbe/Tukulor versus Mande speakers.[94] The main interest of the French was in the peanut-producing area of the Senegambia, which they continued to control. Many Senegambian Muslims chose to co-operate with the French, rather than resist or emigrate.[95]

Ahmadu III of Hamdallahi joined forces with Segu, his erstwhile enemy, to resist the invader. The conflict between two Muslim Fulbe states was a tragedy – Umar felt it necessary to write a lengthy theoretic defence of his actions, in which he accused Ahmadu of apostasy – collaborating with 'pagan' forces against Muslims – in a debate reminiscent of that between al-Kanemi and Muhammad Bello. In 1861, Umar's forces conquered Segu, the next year, Hamdallahi. Soon afterwards, the Massina Fulbe revolted and besieged Hamdallahi in 1864. Umar, who was there, managed to escape, but was killed in the caves of the Dogon cliffs.

After Umar's death, his sons contested the succession, and his empire broke apart.[96] No one had the stature and charisma to take his place. His chosen heir, Amadu Seku, controlled the area around Segu, while his nephew, Tijani, suppressed the rising in Massina and established his own authority there. Aguibou, destined to become the collaborator of the French, ruled Dinguiray.

Because of its multi-ethnic character and its use of firearms, the Umarian state was once seen as a prototype of the modern nation,[97]but a recent study describes it as a state sustained by war and the capture of slaves, much like Segu. In 1894, over half the population of Segu were thought to be slaves.[98]

The immigrants from Futa Toro became a new aristocracy, and this intensified a Bambara sense of animist identity, which survived until the fall of the Umarian state.[99] Sinsani ('Sansanding') lies across the Niger from Segu. In 1890, its ruler wrote, 'Most of the population has left ... [We have nothing] but weariness and poverty ... we have nothing in our hands but hunger.'[100]

For decades, Amadu tried, like his father, to avoid war with the French by diplomacy. His father succeeded by expanding eastward, but in the years which followed his death, French pressure intensified. In 1881, the construction of a railway to the interior started, dividing the empire in two. Samori Touré suggested the two Islamic powers make common cause, but in vain. In 1890, the French conquered Segu, placing a Bambara on the throne. Ahmadu fled to

Massina, and tried, too late, to ally with Samori and the ruler of Sikasso. He embarked on hijra to the east, and died three years later, before reaching Sokoto. His cousin and faithful companion, Muhammad Tal, said, 'the respect that was due to him continued to be showed to him by all the princes and chiefs among whom he sojourned'.[101]

Maba (d. 1867) [102]

The Gambia was another area of great ethnic diversity, where Wolof and Fulbe lived side by side with Mande-speaking Mandingo and Soninke (Sarakollé). They were divided between animists or lax Muslims called, somewhat misleadingly, Soninke[103] and Marabouts – the consumption of alcohol was a line of demarcation between them and the former, including the local kings. The expansion in peanut exports attracted many migrant workers – often devout Muslims – to the Gambia. This influx affected Soninke–Marabout relationships, and Muslims felt that they were oppressed by 'pagan' kings who imposed heavy taxes and restricted access to land. The old order was in crisis, and traditional cults were in decline.

In 1861, Maba Diakhou Ba, the son of a Torodbe father and a Wolof mother, preached a jihad in Baddibu, one of fourteen small Mandingo states on the Gambia. The jihad soon spread to Salum. He had devoted himself for years to the jihads of the heart and word, and took up arms[104] in a reluctant response to oppression. He had met al-Hajj Umar – tradition says they prayed together three nights and three days – and called his capital Nioro, after the capital of Kaarta. The state he founded was quite small, and retained its independence for only six years. Maba was killed in battle in 1867; in the years that followed, the Gambia was ravaged by war, in which marabouts, for whom war had become a way of life, struggled for power.[105] But he left as his legacy a great extension of Islam in the Gambia – over 80 per cent of the people of the former Mandingo kingdoms were Muslim by the middle of the twentieth century.[106]

Maba converted Lat-Dior, the Damel of Kajoor, and the Damel's nephew, Alboury N'Diaye, who became Burba Jolof in 1875. Lat-Dior was for a long time the prototype of the modernising ruler, exporting vast quantities of groundnuts. When the French began to build a railway through Kajoor, it led inevitably to conflict, and Lat-Dior was deposed and replaced by a French nominee, but he continued to struggle against the French until his death in 1886. On that day, he foretold that he would say his evening prayers with Maba, who had died twenty years before.

Samori Touré c. 1830–1900[107]

Samori Touré founded an empire in the Western Sudan, but it was not a jihadist state – he began his career as an illiterate soldier of fortune, with a very limited knowledge of Islam. His attachment to Islam intensified after he founded an empire, which was destroyed almost as soon as it was created by French colonial encroachment. He first came into contact with the French in 1881 and was finally arrested by them in 1898: 'no other confrontation between colonised and coloniser had ever lasted so long without the former surrendering his liberty'.[108]

The Dyula are usually regarded as Mande-speaking Muslim merchants, but Samori's father was a Dyula who neither traded nor practised Islam – a good example of the fluidity of quasi-ethnic categories. Yves Person subtitled his definitive life of Samori, 'a Dyula revolution', but this did not begin with Samori. In the early eighteenth century, Seku Wattara led a rising against the Senufo and created the first independent Dyula state, Kong, in modern Ivory Coast.[109] He called himself, not Almami, but Fama, a traditional Malinke title. Kankan, another Dyula city state, also became independent in the late eighteenth century.

Samori rose to power in the highlands of eastern Guinea, at a time when they were torn apart by the ambitions of rival Dyula clans and traditional Malinke principalities. These groups, of course, spoke the same language and had much in common, and the tolerant relations between Dyula Muslims and Malinke animists are reflected in the former's belief that all just men, including animists, would be saved.[110] The Dyula revolution was linked with Atlantic trade and with the increased volume of foreign trade which followed the foundation of Futa Jallon. This made the Dyula richer; they traded, among other things, in firearms, and their lack of political power was perceived as a contradiction, which they were now able to remedy. They were undoubtedly also encouraged by the many examples of successful state formation which surrounded them.[111]

In 1835, a Dyula cleric from Kankan called Mori-Ulé Sisé founded a new state called Medina. A complex set of conflicts followed, in which both Dyula clans and Malinke ruling families were involved, and some Dyula fought on the latter's side. Mori-Ulé was killed in 1845.

After a period as a trader, Samori fought on the side of the Sisé clan – tradition claims that they had captured his mother and that he took this step with the hope of securing her release. He himself was a member of the Turé clan; the first head of independent Guinea, Sekou Touré, was his descendant. Later, he built up his own army. Through his brilliant gifts as military strategist, and his ability to exploit the divisions of Dyula and Malinke clans and to win the devotion of his soldiers, he founded, first a small state in his native Konyan, and then an empire, with its capital at Bissandugu. In 1867 he took the title of Fama. He won the support of the Dyula by keeping their trade routes open and opposing the exactions of local chiefs. As his state expanded, he identified increasingly with Islam – some believe that he was politically motivated, and sought a unifying ideology for his new empire. But his policy of Islamicisation was to spark off a major revolt. In middle age, he devoted himself to Qur'anic study; and in 1884 he renounced the title Fama for that of Almami.

Had he lived in an earlier age, he would have been remembered as the founder of one of West Africa's great empires, the Sundiata of his time. But like al-Hajj Umar before him, he came into conflict with French imperialism. After a period of conflict, he signed a treaty with France in 1886; with a later amendment, this gave the French a protectorate over his empire. A series of reverses followed and Samori's attempt to conquer Sikasso ended in disaster. This was followed by a great rebellion against him; opposition to his regime was fomented by the French, and exacerbated by his policy of Islamicisation, but it was due, above all, to the suffering caused by his wars. Samori suppressed the rising, but experience had taught him that he could not defeat the French. In 1891 they captured Bissandugu and, like Umar before him, Samori determined to create a new empire further east.

In his retreat, he followed a burnt earth policy which left devastation behind him. He created a new empire in northern Ivory Coast and Burkina Faso, transferring the apparatus of the state hundreds of miles to the east. His last years were a struggle for survival – it was no longer possible to emphasise Islam or education. Umar, in the 1850s, was able to retreat to areas beyond the reach of colonialism. By the 1890s, no such area existed. Samori was captured in 1898, in the Liberian interior, and died in exile two years later.

Samori, like Umar, has been described as a modernising ruler. He realised that the success of the French was due to their modern weaponry; in the 1890s, he obtained many modern guns, which were repaired by Malinke blacksmiths. He copied the resources of the invader to a remarkable extent – even to uniforms and bugle calls. But he did not have the resources to defeat an international empire. Assessments of Samori differ. Africanist scholarship has stressed his military genius, the rapid modernisation of his army, the boundless courage and loyalty of his forces, his enthusiasm for education, the tremendous feat of logistics and organisation involved in relocating an empire. But the human cost was enormous – many were killed or enslaved, or died in the famines which his burnt earth policies caused; he destroyed the prosperous Dyula city of Kong. He originally generated revenue in a variety of ways, including a public field in each village, and the Buré gold fields were at first within his frontiers but lost when he moved to the east.[112] In his desperate last years, he came to rely increasingly on the sale of captives. When Sekou Touré sought political support in the 1950s, he was asked, 'You will not sell us into slavery?'[113]

Changes: the sacred landscape and the written word

The rise and fall of states is only one dimension of the Islamic history of the Western Sudan in this period. Islam became more widely and deeply rooted, a change reflected in place-names and other features of the landscape.

Reverence for sacred landscapes threads its way through 'traditional' religions – in Morocco popular Muslim piety appropriated this insight, and the Atlantic became a saint, or the abode of saints. In Sokoto and Gwandu in the early 1880s 'not only in the busy towns, but in the fields and by the dusty pathway, the observant traveller will see here and there places marked off by stones, with orthodox mihrab or niche, indicating the Kihlal or Point of Adoration'.[114]

Mecca and Medina became increasingly common toponyms, and Tamba, the first of al-Hajj Umar's conquests, was renamed Dabatu, the Excellent, a synonym for Medina. There was an increasing amount of pilgrimage to the tombs of local saints, including that of Uthman dan Fodio.[115] Education and literacy, including literacy in vernacular languages, first Fulfulde, and later Hausa, expanded,[116] and the number of children attending Qur'anic schools increased – a development facilitated by the extensive employment of servile labour.

Some clerics went on to specialised studies in fields such as grammar, law and theology.

A different Western Sudan: the view from the periphery

Up to this point we have analysed the view from the centre, and concentrated on the clerics who founded new states or instituted new governments in old ones. The boundaries between Sokoto and Hamdallahi were agreed on, as if the entire Western Sudan was under the jurisdiction of Muslim states. But there was a different world in the Western Sudan – the world of those who resisted the jihadist states or whose lives were little affected by them. In many cases, those who resisted most effectively lived in the hills – the *montagnards* of Wandala, the Jos plateau or Ningi.

Old, established states were destroyed by the jihads, and 'the people of the bush and of the scattered villages' suffered greatly from slave raids and the exaction of tribute. 'All the earnings of the [Oworro] people seem to go towards the support and maintenance of the Nupes.'[117]

Umar Nagwamatse was a grandson of Uthman dan Fodio who carved out a state for himself from 1857 onwards, which became the emirate of Kontagora. He was known as the Destroyer, and said that he would die with a slave in his mouth. His exactions contrasted starkly with the moderate tribute previously collected by Hausa Zazzau.

The southern emirate of Nassarawa (Victorious) was founded in 1835. Its forces destroyed the ancient Ebirra polity of Panda in 1854. Soon afterwards, Panda's refugee king spoke to a visitor.

Ama Dogo, the Filani war chief, offered the condition of paying one hundred slaves as an annual tribute; and the king said he feigned compliance with these terms, till he had recovered as many of his people as they were able to ransom; and that he would never go to Panda again ... he said, if they complied and paid one hundred slaves one year, in the next they would require two hundred, and where were they to get them? and that they detested war, trade being their chief employment.[118]

Similar experiences are still vivid in contemporary oral traditions: 'The Mada people suffered incessant raids from the Hausa of Keffi ... The Mada pushed into the thick forests around or climbed the surrounding hills, because the horses could neither climb high land nor enter forests ... Once a whole village was routed and the citizens carried away.'[119] Keffi means stockade, and sometimes the name became synonymous with a slave settlement.[120]

In 1846, sixteen Hausa mallams, led by Hamza, left Kano emirate as a protest against taxation, and settled in the Ningi hills.[121] They succeeded in forming an alliance with the local people (who lived in small-scale polities) in part through Hamza's prowess as a magician. Hamza was killed in battle in 1849, but Ningi survived – its ruler entitled simply Mallam. Hamza was a mystic, with a concern for social justice not unlike that of dan Fodio himself – but directed, not against Hausa kings, but Fulbe emirs. 'I will deliver you from ... the Fulani who are unjust ... who impose upon you things which you cannot pay.' Ningi was recognised by the caliphate in the 1870s but, like the emirates themselves, relied on the revenue derived from slave raiding and all but one of its rulers died a violent death. But in the late nineteenth century, those who escaped from slavery often found refuge in the Ningi hills: '[Haruna] had gathered some heathen tribes and escaped slaves under his flag ... His robberies spread fear and horror among the farmers and traders ... Fugitive criminals, escaped slaves were accepted by him.'[122]

Ningi defined its corporate identity largely in relation to the caliphate. But it is a distortion of highlander history to see their lives primarily in terms of their relationship with their powerful Muslim neighbours. The Anaguta are a tiny people, numbering perhaps 5,000, who lived on ridge settlements near the modern city of Jos. Their name means People of the Bow; the bow, and their hilltop homes, were core symbols of identity, as distinct from the Berom, horsemen of the plateau.

Anaguta traditions vividly reflect the horror felt in the local community when its members were enslaved. It is said that the Anaguta originally sent human tribute but desisted when they learned that those sent were coated with clay and turned into statues (a powerful statement of the dehumanising effects of enslavement). In 1873, the Anaguta and their allies defeated an invading Bauchi contingent led by the Chiroma. This episode, confirmed by Bauchi sources, was ritually re-enacted each year into modern times.[123] Modern Anaguta have adopted Hausa speech and dress, but have become Christians, not Muslims.

Bauchi impinged much less on Anaguta lives than their immediate neighbours. To some of these they were bound by the closest ties of friendship, by shared festivals and shrines and communal hunts – by intermarriage or, alternatively, by a joking relationship. Only the Rukuba – whom they perceived as ferocious and numerous – were their enemies. There are probably some 5,000 Anaguta and 12,000 Rukuba. One of the most powerful spiritual presences in the ritual life of the Anaguta – and of many other central Nigerian peoples – is the dangerous masked spirit, Jankai, who has a Hausa name and wears Hausa dress. It is a powerful symbolic expression of the power, danger and attraction of Hausa culture, as seen from the periphery.

If one moves inside a nineteenth-century Anaguta world – which is not easy to do, as they believe that safety lies in secrecy – one discovers a world which is invisible in general histories. The Anaguta prided themselves on their well-stocked granaries; they lamented their small numbers, and longed for abundant children. Sometimes they acquired more people from their neighbours, in exchange for grain. They were not slaves, but cherished wives or adopted sons.[124] This was also true of the Berom – 'A slave was expected to behave as a perfect son.'[125] The history of the Anaguta is lost in a general survey, or in an account which focusses on the jihadist states. They are included here because the present writer researched their history and culture. Historians criticise histories which focus on Great Men and Great States, but the history of tiny ethnic groups tends to elude us.

17

The Eastern and Central Sudan

For ... the countries of Bagirmi, Waday ... and Dar-Fur ... besides the information to be gathered from the natives, only a few detached and obscure statements have been handed down to us.

Heinrich Barth, in 1852[1]

The Central Sudan tends to become invisible in general histories of Africa, or more precisely, balkanised, subsumed in narratives centred on 'West Africa' or 'the [Eastern] Sudan'.[2] It has been much less thoroughly studied, partly because of the scarcity of written source material from before the nineteenth century.

Historians tend to concentrate on centralised kingdoms, and the Central Sudan is no exception – there are fine studies of Borno, Dar Fur, and the Funj kingdom of Sennar. But the population of much of North Central Africa is sparse and scattered, and many of its peoples, such as the Gbaya and the Banda, living in small decentralised hamlets, have been studied by anthropologists rather than historians. Their small settlements formed wider linkages in various ways – the marriage alliances made necessary by exogamy, blood brotherhood, and shared cults.[3]

It is a zone where three of Africa's great language families meet: Chadic, as we have seen, is a branch of Afroasiatic, and Adamawa-Eastern, sometimes called Adamawa-Ubangian, is a subdivision of Niger-Congo, while Central Sudanic languages belong to the Chari-Nile branch of Nilo-Saharan.[4] Ehret located their speakers' homeland in the upper Bahr el-Ghazal; David, on the grounds of climate change, to its north.[5] Clearly, they have spread from east to west.

Adamawa-Ubangian, on the other hand, has spread from west to east. It has two branches – one is a 'dense cluster' of Adamawan languages in or near north Cameroon, while the Ubangian languages (Banda and Gbaya among them) are spoken by peoples scattered over a vast expanse of the central African savanna. These language facts seem to imply many centuries *in situ* for the former, a recent diaspora for the latter.[6] The easternmost Ubangian speakers were the Azande,[7] destined to be divided by colonial jurisdictions between the Belgian Congo (now Zaire), the Sudan, and the French colony of Oubangi-Chari (now Central African Republic).

The original inhabitants of Borno, before the Kanuri incursion, almost certainly spoke Chadic languages, related to Hausa. The Kotoko and Musgu, people of the flood-plains of the Logone and Shari rivers, south-east of Lake Chad, are on the eastern boundary of the Chadic language family.

In the Central Sudan, even more, perhaps, than in the other geographic regions studied in this book, there are no obvious boundaries. Borno looks both eastward and westward. Its ruler, at the time of colonial conquest, began his career in the Eastern Sudan, and its history is closely entwined with that of neighbours to the east and south-east, Wadai and Baghirmi. Its nineteenth century is also inextricably interwoven with that of the jihads in Hausaland, but perhaps the main reason why we tend to include it in the Western Sudan is the fact that it now forms part of Nigeria!

The Eastern Sudan: Arab immigrants

In an earlier chapter, we noted the process of Arab immigration – most of it via Egypt – into the Maghrib, Shinquit and the Republic of Sudan. In earlier Nubian civilisations, the riverain cultivators had been dominant; in a radical transition, the balance of power was now transferred to the nomads of the steppe and desert.[8] Nubian Christianity died out and Islam spread, in part through the demographic dominance of the Arabs, in part through the dedication of missionaries such as Ghulamallah, in the early fifteenth century. The son of a Yemeni, he 'went out with his sons to the land of Dongola, because it was in extreme perplexity and error for lack of scholars'.[9] Wherever Arabs settled, Islam took root; as in the Maghrib, Arabic was widely adopted, but in some areas, the older languages survive. Along the Nile, from Aswan to near Dongola, the Nubians, long since Muslims, retain their language and a cultivator's lifestyle, but define themselves as of Arab ancestry. 'According to their own traditions the present [1813] Nubians derive their origin from the Arabian bedouins.'[10] From Dongola to Khartoum, the banks of the Nile are occupied by Arabised Nubians, the Ja'aliyin, who are also predominantly cultivators. Away from the river live the Juhayna, camel nomads who are closest, in language and culture, to the original Arab immigrants. Further to the west, in Dar Fur and Kordofan, are the Baqqara, cattle-owning pastoralists, who speak Arabic and also claim Juhayna ancestry. Some pastoralists migrated still further to the west – the Arabic-speaking Shuwa, who reached the Lake Chad area, where they overlapped with the Fulbe, migrating from the west.

The Ja'aliyin and Juhayna are overwhelmingly dominant in the Arabised Sudan, so much so that these ethnyms have become synonymous with farmer and pastoralist.[11] Each of these cultures, in its modern form, is the result of centuries of cultural exchange and environmental adaptation. Like the peoples of Somalia, the Maghrib and the Western Sudan, they laid great stress on genealogies which claimed Arab ancestry; a sixteenth-century scholar is said to have produced an Abbasid ancestry for the Ja'aliyan and a Sharifian one for the Funj. As in the Maghrib, a cult of saints and of their tombs was of great importance; their domed shrines are scattered all over the northern Sudan, a physical reflection of the *baraka* of the holy.[12] The peoples of the Sudd, such as the Nuer and Dinka, discussed in an earlier chapter, remained outside this Islamic and Arabic-speaking world, and in modern times those who have left their traditional religion have become Christians. The gulf in religion, language and culture has contributed to the civil war which has bedevilled the Republic of Sudan for much of the time since Independence.

The peoples of the Eastern Sudan used a distinctive form of ethnic labelling, based on colour coding. The Funj were the Blues, the Abdullab the Greens, the Ja'aliyan 'Mixed', the Arabs Yellows, while the Reds were peoples high on the Blue Nile who wore red ochre. *Abid* were slaves, imported from the south and west.[13]

A number of Juhayna groups were brought together by a leader called Abdallah Jamma, the Gatherer, who seems to have been linked with the prosperous Red Sea port of Sawakin.[14] They overthrew the kingdom of Alwa, and acquired a collective identity as the Abdullab, with a capital near the confluence of the Blue and White Niles, not far from Soba. They were conquered by the Funj, in 1504, and from then on paid them tribute. The Abdullab used their strategic location to exact payments from transhumant pastoralists – 'to catch all the Arabs that had flocks, who . . . were every year . . . obliged by the [tsetse] fly to pass . . . to take up their abode in the sandy desert without the tropical rains'.[15]

The Funj kingdom of Sennar

In 1772, the explorer James Bruce recorded traditions about the foundation of the Funj kingdom, at the beginning of the sixteenth century: 'In the year 1504, a black nation hitherto unknown, inhabiting the western banks of the [White Nile] . . . made a descent, in a multitude of canoes . . . upon the Arab provinces.'[16]

It is generally accepted that they were driven north by the Shilluk, but their immediate victory over the Abdullab seems unlikely for a conquered and refugee force. Like the Dinka after them, they are likely to have been attracted by a much more propitious physical environment. Their kings were called the black sultans, and the first of them, Amara Dunqas (1503–33), was a well-documented historical figure. Tradition claims that the Funj conquered the Christian kingdom of Alwa; it is thought more likely that this was done by the Abdullab, who were in their turn defeated by the Funj, and became a tributary state on the kingdom's northern boundaries. Later, they revolted and became virtually independent. The Funj capital was at Sennar on the Blue Nile. It was well to the south of the capital of Alwa – an example of the way in which the centre of political gravity moved ever further south. The heart of their kingdom was the 'island' between the Blue and White Niles, but the Funj raided for slaves far to the west, in the plains of Kordofan. The first sultan may have been a Christian, but his successors became Muslims almost at once, and the veiled king, with his slave courtiers, kept many of the customs of the pre-Islamic era. Princesses were married to vassal kings, and their sons brought up as hostages at the royal court. Like their counterparts in the Western Sudan, the Funj heavy cavalry wore chain armour and helmets, and carried swords which were blessed by holy men and handed down as heirlooms in noble families. Arabic became a lingua franca, but Funj survived as a court language, dying out in the eighteenth century.[17] The Funj drove back an Egyptian invasion in 1589, and the boundary between the two states was established near the Third Cataract. In 1618–19, Ethiopia invaded Sennar, but retreated almost at once. From 1630 on, the 'Dinka', despite their small-scale political organisation, expanded into Funj territory, and the latter allied with the Shilluk against them.[18]

Sennar was a wealthy cosmopolitan centre, like ancient Meroe, enriched by gold and slaves. Egyptians, Ethiopians, Jews, Portuguese, Greeks and Armenians were among its resident merchants. In 1700, a visitor said 'that in all Africa . . . Sinnar is near to being the most distinguished trading city. Caravans are arriving continually from Cairo, Dongola, Nubia, from over the Red Sea, from India, Ethiopia, [Dar] Fur, Bornu, Fezzan and other kingdoms.'[19]

But the state declined in the eighteenth century, and fell victim to Muhammad Ali's Egypt in 1821.

States of the Central Sudan

Two hundred megaliths in what is now the west of Central African Republic reveal the existence of an otherwise unknown centralised state there two thousand years ago. We know nothing of the people who erected them. Leo Africanus, writing in the 1520s, described a kingdom between Borno and Nubia called Gaoga, founded by a black slave who seized his master's property, bought horses with the proceeds, and raided for slaves. His grandson was ruling at the time of Leo's visit.

This *Homara* hath greatly enlarged his dominions, and hath entred league with the Soldan of Cairo … diuers merchants of Egypt, and diuers inhabitants of Cairo present most pretious and rare things unto him, and highly commend his surpassing liberalitie. This prince greatly honoureth all learned men, and especially such as are of the linage of Mahumet.[20]

Unlike the other states he mentions, which are readily identified, Gaoga remains mysterious; Barth identified it with the Bulala state at Lake Fitri[21] and one interpretation locates it in Dar Fur, but there are other possibilities, and the verdict must remain 'Not Proven'.[22]

The historical kingdoms of the Central Sudan – Dar Fur, Wadai, Baghirmi – date from the seventeenth century or later, the time when Islam first became firmly established there. This is, of course, much later than the foundation of the early states of the Western Sudan, and the advent of Islam there, and this undoubtedly reflects the fact that the desert routes which linked the Central Sudan to the east and north were much more difficult and dangerous, and hence less travelled.

These kingdoms raided for slaves, some of which were exported across the desert routes, as was ivory and other relatively minor commodities such as ostrich feathers. Wadai had no direct desert route to the Maghrib until the early nineteenth century. The literature on the kingdoms of the Central Sudan emphasises slave raiding, that on the jihadist states of the Western Sudan lays much more emphasis on religious ideals. But the latter, as we have seen, also raided for slaves, and it may well be that the difference is more apparent than real, and reflects the lack of early eyewitness accounts of the geographic heart of Africa. The earliest firsthand account of Dar Fur (if we exclude Leo's Gaoga) was published in 1799, and based on a visit from 1793–6.

Dar Fur

The powerful Keira sultanate of Dar Fur[23] dates from the seventeenth century. Dar Fur is in much the same sahelian latitudes as Kanem, but its altitude attracted rain, and it lay between a desert zone, sparsely peopled by camel nomads, and a savanna zone, where cattle nomads, the Baqqara, pastured their herds. It was an area of linguistic diversity and Fur, the language of its dominant group, seems to lack close local relatives.

Fur traditions recorded in the nineteenth century told of three successive dynasties founded by Wise Men from the East – the core cliché of Sudanese history. Each dynasty belonged to a different ethnic group – the Daju, the Tunjur and the Fur. Both the Daju and Tunjur are identifiable peoples, found over a large area of the Sudan. Tradition claims that the last Daju sultan was a tyrant, and that his people persuaded him to mount an antelope, which carried him off to Chad! The third dynasty, the Keira, was overthrown by a warlord from Khartoum in 1874.[24]

A dangerous trade route, the Forty Days' Road, linked Dar Fur to the Nile. In 1663, a visitor to Egypt wrote: 'To the west of Cairo lies the land of Fur, to which caravans repair frequently in order to purchase slaves. From that country [the caravan] brings as goods, ostrich feathers, tamarind, elephant tusks, pitch-black male and female slaves, and even little children.'[25]

A connecting route went to the Western Sudan, and Hausa and other pilgrims travelled through Dar Fur to Mecca; sometimes, rather than continue their journey, they chose to remain in the Central Sudan.

The Fur obtained slaves by raiding their southern neighbours, whom they viewed collectively as Fartit. In a sense they despised their culture as 'pagan', and justified enslavement because through it captives were incorporated in the Islamic world. A Fur song brings out these stereotypes clearly – Hausa and Kanuri lords regarded the mountain people of the south in much the same way.

> The people who live in Fartit are slaves and (yet) go free.
> They know nothing at all, neither good nor evil.
> These heathens who eat men, are barbarians and go around naked . . .
> We Fur go and bring them among us and teach them our Islam;
> And they live happily among us.[26]

But they also have traditions which claim that Fur and Fartit are brothers. Many of the slaves were retained in Dar; some served in regiments, others worked in agriculture, and a few rose to become powerful officials.[27]

Wadai

Wadai was situated between Dar Fur and Kanem, in another area of linguistic diversity – nineteenth-century informants listed forty languages (or dialects). It was subject to Dar Fur in the period of Tunjur rule, until a cleric called Abd al-Karim founded an independent sultanate there in the early seventeenth century.[28] Different traditions state that he came from the Hejaz, and that he had studied in Baghirmi, or Borno. Some of the Tunjur had Muslim names, and they clearly identified, to some extent, with Islam, but nineteenth-century traditions interpreted Abd al-Kerim's war as a jihad – 'the idea of overthrowing the pagan dominion of the Tynjur, and of founding in its stead a new kingdom based on Islamism'.[29]

We see these events through a glass, darkly. One source – which has parallels elsewhere – suggests the way in which an honoured guest could become the master.

Then the Sultan of the Tunjur gave him his daughter to wed, and said, 'pray God for me'.
But he prayed on his own behalf and so the Sultan died, but the 'Sherifs' rule Wadai till now.[30]

Wadai seems to have gone through the same kind of transition Kanem underwent centuries earlier. There are hints linking Abd al-Karim to pastoralism – the site of his capital was found during a search for lost calves, and he came to power with the assistance of camelry. But his heir built a capital at Wara, with a mosque and palace in brick. It was not until the early nineteenth century that a direct route to North Africa from Wadai was discovered. But it was far from isolated: there was only one person from Wadai in nineteenth-century Freetown. He had studied in Dar Fur and Kordofan, and at Zeila in the Fezzan.[31]

Baghirmi

Baghirmi grew up further south, still further from the desert trade routes, east of the Shari river and south-east of Lake Chad. It was on the eastern edge of the Fulbe diaspora. Traditions recorded by Barth state that Abd al-Karim of Wadai studied in Baghirmi, at 'one of the the places in that region where ... Fulbe had settled from early times, and among them a family which, by means of undisputed sanctity and learning had begun to exercise a considerable influence in the introduction of Islamism'.[32]

The region had been raided by Kanuri slavers for centuries – Mai Idris Aloma was mortally wounded when on campaign there and died by Lake Alo – hence, 'Aloma'.[33] Despite this, an independent kingdom grew up which raided for slaves and mirrored the culture of the Kanuri state in a way strikingly like that of Wandala. The first Muslim ruler was a contemporary of Abd al-Karim. A late eighteenth-century sultan went on pilgrimage, and is credited with a wider dissemination of Islam.[34] Baghirmi paid tribute to Wadai, and both waged war with Borno. Baghirmi was far from the desert trade routes and obtained imported goods via Wadai or Borno.[35] But the people of Wadai are said to have coveted the fine indigo cloth of Baghirmi, because they lacked the art of dyeing.[36] When the Wadai sultan Sabun conquered Baghirmi in the early nineteenth century, he seized fine cloth and silver which had been acquired in raids in Borno or on its caravan route to the north.[37] Barth, in the mid-nineteenth century, assessed the Baghirmi cavalry at 3,000, those of Wadai and Dar Fur at 5–6,000 and 10,000 respectively.[38]

Borno in the nineteenth century[39]

Al-Hajj Muhammad al-Amin al-Kanemi was born in the Fezzan, the son of a Kanembu cleric and an Arab mother. When the Sokoto jihad began, he was living south of Lake Chad in a rural community of scholars, much like dan Fodio. Like him, he acquired great influence through his personality, piety and learning, to which was added the prestige of one who had completed the pilgrimage.

Local Fulbe invaded Borno's eastern provinces, taking the capital, Gazargamu, in 1808. They did so initially without the knowledge of the Sokoto leadership – Muhammad Bello wrote to the Mai, 'As for your country we do not know how warfare broke out there [except for what he was told by his emissary] ... As for your country we have no knowledge of the state of its faith or its sultans.[40] Nothing is more attractive in these Muslim leaders than their belief that political issues could and should be solved by debate, their ongoing concern for right conduct. The tide turned against the Fulbe, and al-Kanemi was given the credit, though it seems his role was confined to prayer and the provision of amulets. He was given a province of his own, and attracted followers drawn largely from 'the discontented of other countries', especially the desert.[41] Like dan Fodio, he was called Shehu – it became the official title of the dynasty he founded – and he built his own capital at Kukawa.

From 1809 to 1813, the mai, Dunama, blamed for his nation's reverses, was deposed and replaced by his uncle. In 1813, al-Kanemi restored him to power, and gradually Dunama realised that the kingmaker had become a king. In 1820, he conspired to have him killed; the plan misfired, Dunama died in battle, and al-Kanemi struck his own seal, symbol of sovereignty. He had had greatness thrust upon him, and, like dan Fodio and al-Hajj Umar, remained chronically ambivalent about his own success.[42] When he died, in 1837/8, his sons succeeded him; the mais survived as puppet kings until 1846.

The political convulsions in Borno may well be linked with famine and pestilence recorded in the late eighteenth century.[43] Informed Borno opinion attributed the kingdom's weakness to a catastrophic defeat at the hands of Wandala.[44] Barth, our source for this, also described 'the whole eastern part of these northern provinces ... laid waste and depopulated' by the Tuareg.[45] To the east were the hostile sultanates of Wadai and Baghirmi. The problems caused by war and ecological crises and the incursions of hostile neighbours were compounded by the mais' indifference to their people's plight. In famine time, the Seyfawa 'indulged in luxury and ostentation, while the kingdom was falling to pieces'.[46] In the early sixteenth century, it was said of the mai, 'He is at perpetual enmitie with a certain people inhabiting beyond the desert of Seu ... the King seemeth to be marveilous rich; for his spurres, his bridles ... yea and the chaines of his dogs ... are of golde ... He had much rather pay his debts in slaves than in golde.'[47] The export of slaves across the Sahara remained the most important source of government revenue in the Borno of the Shehus. As it usually did, the slave trade enriched the elite: 'The chief motive [of a slaving expedition] consisted in the circumstance of the coffers and slave-rooms of the great men being empty.'[48] A Kanuri nobleman's song runs:

The peasant is grass, fodder for the horses.
To your hoeing, peasant, so that we can eat.[49]

Gradually, the North African slave market declined; for a time, ivory and ostrich feathers were important, but demand for these fell during the European depression of the 1880s. In 1883, the then Shehu, Bukar, attempted 'splitting the calabash', taking half or even more of the peasant's property.[50] Into this weakened and polarised society was to sweep, in 1893, a general from the east – Rabih, a lieutenant of the Mahdi.

The central savanna in the nineteenth century

Several themes emerge clearly in this period – the enlargement of scale, reflected in the foundation of new if short-lived states, among them the Mangbetu kingdom and the Azande principalities, and later, in the 1890s, the sultanate of Kuti. Trans-Saharan trade went through a phase not only of strength but of expansion. To the slave raiding of local kingdoms were added the depredations of warlords from the east, the Khartoumers. Two of them were particularly successful – al-Zubayr, who conquered an empire which then evaded his grasp, and Rabih, who ended his life as lord of Borno.

Mangbetu and Azande

The Mangbetu of north-eastern Zaire are Central Sudanic speakers, noted for their artistic creativity. A lord called Nabiembali founded a kingdom there – but in the 1850s his sons and grandsons fought for his inheritance, founding new states in the process. In 1872, the ruler of the central kingdom was killed by traders from the Nile, who dominated the area until the rise of the Mahdi in the 1880s.[51]

Some fifty other ethno-linguistic groups, some of which were, like the Azande, Ubangian speakers, were totally or partially absorbed in the latter's cultural and political complex.[52] Azande tradition told of a homeland in the west, near the Mbomu and Shinko rivers, and 'true Azande' were called Mbomu. They did not form a single united state – princes of the royal clan, the Avongara, endeavoured to establish their own kingdoms, which numbered about fifteen by the 1880s. They lived on the margins of the savanna and the forest, and kept no cattle because of trypanosomiasis. In the colonial period, they were to be compulsorily resettled away from the riverain locations they preferred, in an attempt to eradicate sleeping sickness.[53]

Although they absorbed other ethno-linguistic groups, 'Azande' culture was a composite, with many borrowings. Even *benge*, the key ingredient for their main system of divination, was obtained in forests to the south, the probable source of the practice itself. It was so central to Azande culture that their internal wars have been called conflicts between two oracles.

Traders and warlords

The trade routes through the central Sahara continued to carry a considerable volume of traffic until the early twentieth century.[54] A new route[55] was discovered by chance and enthusiastically developed by Sabun, sultan of Wadai (d. 1813); it linked his kingdom with Benghazi – slaves and ivory were exported, and after 1870 changes in ladies' fashions in Europe created a demand for ostrich feathers. In Chapter 15, we noted the growth of the Sanusiyya in the central Sahara; its lodges both assisted the development of this trade route and were sustained by it.

The *jallaba* were itinerant traders from the Khartoum area who carried goods on donkeys or bullocks to Kordofan, Dar Fur and Wadai, purchasing small quantities of slaves and ivory. This very extensive informal network, which offered no threat to existing political structures, grew much larger in the nineteenth century, though it began much earlier – one of Abd al-Karim's companions was called the Jallaba. Some *jallaba* traded among non-Muslim peoples further south, such as the Azande. While they travelled great distances from the east, another trade diaspora spread in the west, as Hausa and Kanuri merchants moved through Adamawa and beyond.

When Muhammad Ali became *de facto* ruler of Egypt, he endeavoured to carve out an empire in the Sudan; in 1821 his forces seized Kordofan, formerly tributary to Dar Fur. (see p. 317 above). From the 1840s on, the vast area west of the Nile was invaded by armed merchants, who are conventionally and conveniently called the Khartoumers. They were very different from the *jallaba* – they had large bodies of followers armed with firearms and they established fortified settlements called *zeriba*, from which they raided for slaves and ivory. As elsewhere in Africa, the ivory frontier receded; when the elephants of the Bahr al-Ghazal neared extinction, the Khartoumers and their followers moved west into Dar Fur, which their most powerful member, al-Zubayr, defeated in 1874, only to spend the rest of his days imprisoned in Cairo.[56] Egypt's control of the Sudan was abruptly ended by the Mahdist rising.

Some of al-Zubayr's followers joined the Mahdi, others followed one of his lieutenants, al-Rabih, who expanded his army with captives, and in 1893 and 1894 conquered Baghirmi and Borno respectively.

Social change

The violence of the mid and late nineteenth century in the northern savannas had many socio-economic consequences; for defence purposes, people tended to collect in larger settlements, which were often stockaded. Domestic slavery expanded and social polarisation increased. Some took refuge on hilltop settlements; raiding, flight and resettlement led to smallpox epidemics, and in many areas, cassava supplanted the traditional grains, because it was less susceptible to marauders. Some regions suffered absolute depopulation.[57] All this has many parellels elsewhere – the Tonga who lived near Lake Malawi also planted cassava because it was less likely to be taken by Ngoni marauders. In the Central Sudan, as elsewhere, famine and disease were the invisible background to the rise and fall of states, and to colonial conquest. Ali Eisami was born in Borno, in about 1786, and enslaved in 1812. Many years later, he remembered the Borno of his youth. 'About two o'clock in the afternoon, we looked to the west, the Kaman-locusts were coming from the west . . . When the time of the locusts was past, the famine Ngeseneski took place ... After it, the pestilence came, and made much havoc in Borno, completely destroying all the elderly. Next, the wars of the Fulbe came up.'[58]

In the late seventeenth century, there were seven years of drought and famine in Wadai; seed-corn was exhausted, and was, tradition claims, miraculously replenished by an ant. In the 1840s, a claimant to the throne succeeded, with Dar Fur help, in defeating a Wadai weakened by 'severe famine'.[59] *Plus ça change* ...

18

The Atlantic slave trade

The name of the world is not world; its name is load.

A Kuranko proverb[1]

In the modern world, a situation where the forces of western capitalism erode the autonomy of nominally independent states and distort their economies tends to be called neo-colonialism. One is tempted to call the era of the Atlantic slave trade palaeo-colonialism.[2]

The historian must avoid both of two extremes – exaggerating the impact of external trade (for whole areas remained unaffected) and failing to recognise how far into the African continent the forces of merchant capitalism were to penetrate. Enslaved Bambara from the Niger bend walked some 500 kilometres to the sea, and slave coffles often travelled comparable distances in West Central Africa. The capital of the Oyo empire was much the same distance from the sea, as the crow flies, but its history, as we shall see, was profoundly modified by Atlantic trade. Some states, such as the Kazembe's kingdom in northern Zambia, were part of trade networks which extended to both the Atlantic and the Indian Ocean.

The frontiers of the Atlantic factor were not identical with the geography of enslavement. Imported goods passed from hand to hand, sometimes taking years on their journey, finally reaching those to whom both the ocean and Europeans were merely a myth. Slaves and ivory from the Zaire river, above Malebo Pool, reached the coast, and European goods travelled in the opposite direction, together with stories of the white men, the returning dead from the depths of the sea.[3]

Within the Atlantic zone, not all states were equally affected. Some restricted the impact of the slave trade by deliberate policy – Benin is a notable example – or were protected by geography (like some of the peoples of the Jos plateau). Even in the areas most radically affected by Atlantic trade, history was, of course, shaped by many other factors as well. Even in states such as Dahomey, where there is abundant primary documentation and a wealth of academic studies, scholars disagree profoundly about its impact.

It is, in a sense, artificial to separate the Atlantic slave trade from the enslavement of those destined for domestic servitude or for export across the desert, and at some places and times captives were divided among these three destinations. The Senegambia was located between the zones of Atlantic and Saharan trade, and was deeply involved in both.

Understandings: from within

Throughout this study, we have tried to recreate histories of ideas, the way in which Africans themselves constantly reinterpreted their changing world. Often, they critiqued the era of international trade by contrasting it with an (? imagined) Golden Age in the past: 'the discerning Natives account it their greatest Unhappiness, that they were ever visited by the *Europeans*. They say that we Christians introduc'd the Traffick of Slaves, and that before our Coming they liv'd in Peace.'[4] A Yao traditional historian in East Africa saw the past in much the same way,[5] and so did Ga notables who lived on the Accra plain in the 1740s.[6]

In an earlier chapter, we discussed the basic contradiction between wealth and people as loci of value. The slave trade sacrificed the latter to the former, as traditions found over vast areas make explicit. 'The cowries we were told, were obtained in the ocean. These cowries were obtained by throwing human beings into the ocean ... These corpses were then dragged out of the ocean and the cowries plucked off ... I do not know where this ocean was.'[7]

The terror which slaves experienced was intensified by the common belief that Europeans intended to eat them.[8] Mungo Park spoke with slaves travelling from Segu to the Gambia: 'A deeply rooted idea that the whites purchase negroes for the purpose of devouring them ... naturally makes the slaves contemplate a journey towards the coast with great terror.'[9] Cannibalism is part of the image of the horrific Other; it was often attributed (in many cases falsely) by Europeans to African societies.

In West Central Africa, traditional images of witchcraft contributed to the concept of the enslaved soul; it is recorded in the seventeenth century, and was to have a long life.[10] When Baptist missionaries reached the lower Congo in the late nineteenth century, they found that 'It was thought that the dead were bought by white men, and that their spirits worked for them under the sea'.[11] A document written as recently as 1969 explains, 'The Catholics have a kingdom of the blacks, under the earth, the grave. When a black man dies, the whites keep him chained under the earth.'[12]

A story is told at Cabinda of a beautiful woman who offered a villager wealth beyond imagining. 'Then she sang another song and steamers appeared on the water in great hosts.' But there was a price to pay – he must never again see his father, and the price, in the end, proved one he was unable to pay. 'And with such sadness, Mavungu changed back to what he had formerly been, and in sorrow he died.'[13]

Each of these powerful, indeed unforgettable, stories – the slave who becomes a living bait for cowries, the villager who rejects a wealth attained by the sacrifice of family life – condemns the slave trade, the inhumanity with which individuals and families were sacrificed to the divinities of power and profit.

In Africa, both slave owners and slaves tended to blur the realities of the situation by euphemisms and the language of kinship – the master was called 'father', and the vast number of 'wives' in royal households reflects the fact that many were slaves, employed in manual work. The actual transaction was often concealed from those most directly affected, who often did not realise, for a time, that they had been sold.[14]

Understandings: from without

The historiography of the Atlantic slave trade is particularly rich and complex. One of the earliest debates concerned the reasons for its abolition, once regarded as one of the 'few totally unselfish international operations'.[15] A pioneering work by the West Indian historian Eric Williams, which appeared in 1944, suggested that the slave trade helped generate the capital for England's industrial revolution, and was abandoned both as a result of the declining profitability of the West Indian plantations, and in response to the evolving needs of industrial capitalism, in particular for the markets provided by a free labour force.[16] Much subsequent research has been inspired by his seminal study, generating debates which have much in common with controversies over the profitability or otherwise of colonialism, and many of his conclusions cannot be sustained.[17] In any case, the motives of European abolitionists and the relationship of the slave trade to economic growth in England or the Americas are marginal to a history of Africa, and we do better to focus on the ongoing debates on the demographic and social impact of Atlantic trade on African societies.

Slave trade studies must be understood in the context of a much wider debate. In the first chapter of this study, we introduced dependency theory, the view associated in African studies especially with Immanuel Wallerstein, Samir Amin and Walter Rodney. In essence, this presents a global view of history, and depicts the successive eras of merchant and industrial capitalism as a process which enriched the western world, and underdeveloped the periphery.[18] The ramifications of this model are enormously far-reaching, and it underlies a controversy about the San of the Kalahari. It has been challenged because it does not acknowledge the autonomy of the local region's history, which becomes a reflection of change in western Europe. It has also, significantly, been challenged by European specialists[19] in debates which would lead us too far beyond the perimeters of this book.

Studies of the slave trade written in the 1960s and early 1970s tended to go to one of two extremes. Left-wing historians such as Basil Davidson or Walter Rodney (or, indeed, the present writer) tended to depict the Atlantic slave trade as totally destructive,[20] the ruin of Merrie Africa. Rodney believed that domestic slavery did not exist in Upper Guinea previously, and Davidson – and the present writer – suggested that the slave trade not only turned Benin from the gracious city depicted in early descriptions to a City of Blood but also led to a decline in its art![21] But there was another, Africanist school which described the slave trade in terms which seemed to minimise the harm and pain it caused. Fage wrote of the 'close correlation, between economic development (and political development because indigenous commercial activity was largely king or state-directed) and the growth of the institution of slavery'.[22] To radicals, this approach seemed to whitewash Europe's crimes in the past – and perhaps, by extension, in the present. It was in fact more generously intentioned; it was rooted in a historiography which stressed African rationality and enterprise. The only alternative seemed to be a scenario where Africans were either victims or compradors.

My own work on the Igbo was in the radical tradition.[23] Fage's high and well-merited standing in West African studies meant that studies of the same area in the Africanist tradition – notably Northrup's *Trade without Rulers*[24] – were more generally accepted and are still more widely cited. And yet the finest modern scholarship on the impact of the Atlantic slave trade on West and West Central Africa stands in the radical tradition,[25] and substantiates many of its claims – that the slave trade engendered violence and warlordism, increased social polarisation and led in at least some areas to an absolute decline in population.

Much research has been done since the radical/Africanist debates of the early 1970s, and some elements in the original radical analysis have been discarded. There is, for instance, abundant evidence that domestic slavery was well established in many areas before the onset of Atlantic trade, and the idea that Benin art declined is based on a now discarded chronology, as well as invalid suppositions about what constitutes great art. Scholars are now more ready than I once was to see merit in the various commodities African societies imported in return for slaves. But the debate continues. Eltis has claimed, in a widely cited study, that both the Atlantic slave trade and its suppression had little effect on Africa, and that the export of slaves comprised an insignificant proportion of Africa's total economic activity. He suggests that even when the West African slave trade was at its peak, in the 1780s, Atlantic imports probably represented well below 5 per cent of African incomes,[26] that 'significant depopulation was unlikely', and that a much smaller proportion of West Africa's population 'emigrated' between 1781 and 1867 than left the British Isles, Portugal or Italy (over a different time period).[27]

Manning, who based his demographic projections on innovative, if controversial, computer simulation studies, believes the population of West and West Central Africa declined between 1730 and 1850,[28] and that total slave exports (including those in the Indian Ocean zone and those exported to or through northern Africa) meant that the population of sub-Saharan Africa in the latter year was 50 million, rather than 100 million.[29] He and others argue for social transformations so far-reaching that they amount to a change in the mode of production.[30]

The proliferation of slave trade studies, often conducted with great methodological sophistication, has led to an ever more detailed and nuanced understanding of the subject, with considerable areas of general agreement.

The statistics of the slave trade

An estimate of the numbers involved is the indispensable prerequisite to understanding the impact of the external slave trade on African societies. Until 1969, a figure of 15 million landed in the Americas was commonly cited. In that year, Curtin published a seminal study based on an exhaustive study of published sources.[31] He concluded that 9,566,000 slaves *were landed*, mainly in the Americas. Radicals initially greeted his projections with suspicion, viewing it as another variant of the ameliorationist hypothesis (fewer slaves so less harmful). Historians of all ideological persuasions now pay tribute to the extraordinary extent to which his figures have been confirmed by later archival research, which was, of course, inspired by his study. A total of 11,863,000 *exported from* Africa has been suggested – which is much closer to Curtin's order of magnitude than the guesstimates which preceded his work on the subject.[32]

It is important to realise that a census of slaves documented in written records will always be lower than the actual number exported. Not all records survive, and aspects of the trade – such as the activities of smugglers, interlopers and slaving captains who packed more slaves on board than the law allowed[33] – meant that many participants had a positive interest in concealment. It has been suggested that these areas of uncertainty invalidate all statistics,[34] or mean that they are far too low.[35] Both statements may well be true, but the general scholarly consensus is that the figures are remarkably accurate.

It is clear that the total demographic impact of the slave trade was much greater than the number of slaves exported. Many lost their lives in wars or raids partly or wholly motivated by the hope of gaining slaves. Many more died *en route* to the coast, while awaiting purchase in slave barracoons, or during the Middle Passage. Estimates of all this vary. Lovejoy suggests that these losses amounted to '6–10 per cent at the port of departure and 10–14 per cent or more *en route* to the coast' when the slave trade was at its height.[36] This may well be conservative; an eighteenth-century Loanda merchant claimed that slavers lost 40 per cent of their captives between the original point of purchase and embarkment.[37]

Enslavement and gender relations

The demographic impact of the slave trade, of course, depended on the age and gender of the enslaved.[38] Perhaps two-thirds of those exported were males; plantation owners in the New World preferred youths and young men – 'none to exceed the years of 25 or under 10 if possible, among which so many men, and stout boys as can be had seeing such are most Valuable at the Plantations'.[39] This, combined with African captors' tendency to retain enslaved women, led to gender imbalance both in the societies where the enslaved originated and in those in which they were incorporated as domestic slaves. An excess of women over men is documented in a census taken in Portuguese Angola in 1777–8.[40] Sometimes male slaves in Africa were left without wives or children.[41] The contradictions in Barth's account mirror the contradictions inherent in domestic slavery: 'The quiet course of domestic slavery has very little to offend the mind of the traveller: the slave is generally well treated ... I have come to the conclusion that marriage among domestic slaves is very little encouraged by the natives; indeed I think myself justified in supposing that a slave is very rarely allowed to marry.'[42]

The export of young males had serious social consequences. Since the young and strong were exported abroad, the proportion of economically productive members declined, and the burden on them became greater. The export of males meant that a heavier workload fell on women. It was said of Whydah in the early eighteenth century, 'it is normally the women who support the men either by their work or their trade'.[43] An increasing male involvement in war – including slave raiding or defence against raids – had the same effect. Since hunting and pastoralism and (sometimes) fishing were male pursuits, the protein in the diet may well have declined.[44]

Polygyny is undoubtedly much older than Atlantic trade; the new imbalance between women and men seems to have led to its expansion and, in matrilineal societies, to a growth in female pawnship (which meant that a man's children belonged to his own lineage). A Portuguese visitor to the Bissagos Islands in 1669 observed, 'there are blacks there who have twenty or thirty wives, and no one has only one'.[45]

Royals and aristocrats were often keen to marry slave wives, apparently because they lacked a supporting network of kin. A Jesuit noted in the Bissau area in 1616, 'If a noble takes his own slave for a wife, and she gives him some displeasure, he will sell her along with her child.'[46] This was undoubtedly exceptional, and many West African kings were the sons of slave mothers. One of the most clearly documented results of the slave trade was an increasing gulf between rich and poor. This was reflected in conjugal arrangements. According to Bosman, an important man in Whydah had forty to fifty wives, the king from four to five thousand (many of whom were in fact domestic slaves). This meant, as was noted later, leaving 'the lower class unprovided with female companies', and prostitution was prevalent.[47]

In the eighteenth century, 25 per cent of the slaves exported were children; the percentage had risen to 40 per cent in the nineteenth century.[48] In south-east Africa it rose as high as 61 per cent.[49]

Manning has suggested that the process which led to some 9 million slaves being landed in the New World between 1700 and 1850 entailed the capture of 21 million, of whom 7 million became domestic slaves and an additional 5 million died within a year.[50] Such figures are necessarily speculative, but the order of magnitude they suggest is significant. Enormous though they are, their demographic impact was probably less than that of child mortality, famine and disease.[51] In time of famine, the sale of a family member for food may have reduced mortality rates in two ways – there were fewer mouths to feed, and with the payment obtained those remaining could buy provisions and seed.

The slave experience

What statistics do not reflect, of course, is the immense pain suffered not only by each individual enslaved but by their families. Miller's superb study describes, in harrowing detail, the sufferings of captives on their journey in shackles to the coast, in the barracoons, and in the *tombeiros* (floating tombs) which carried them to the New World.[52] In the barracoons, slaves slept in their own excrement, and corpses were often left unburied to save the cost of interment,[53] although African cultures lay a very great emphasis on mortuary rituals. Slaves were branded not only with ownership marks but, in Angola, with a cross as proof of baptism. There is no greater irony than the fact that, in

Portuguese settlements, slaves had to be baptised Christians when sold, and could be sold only to Christians.

Scurvy was so common that it was called *mal de Loanda*, the Luanda sickness. Dysentery was epidemic, causing appalling suffering for the slaves who lay shackled below decks.

Occasionally, despite all the odds against them, the slaves revolted successfully and ran the ship ashore (where, far from their homes, they were usually enslaved once more). On one occasion they put the crew in longboats, thus giving them a chance of survival.[54] Some committed suicide and many more attempted it.

To the sufferings of the enslaved must be added those of their families – parents deprived of their children, and children of their parents, husbands deprived of their wives, and wives of their husbands. Oga was an Iyala from what is now central Nigeria. Eleven of his thirteen children died,

and the eldest of the two remaining was about twenty years of age when a friend sent him to buy a slave, returning with whom they were attacked by a wild cow which killed the slave. The friend then wanted to sell the messenger as a restitution for the loss of his slave: but Oga, rather than have his son lose his liberty, offered himself as a slave and was accordingly sold.[55]

On the 'Slave Coast' (between the Volta and Lagos) cowries were the most important import. The growth of a commercial economy, and the inequalities it engendered, encouraged the spread both of gambling and of indebtedness. Gambling, as Law points out perceptively, parodied the vagaries of the market. A king of Whydah tried unsuccessfully to ban the practice.[56] Bosman said of its people, in the 1690s: 'They are very great Gamesters, and willingly stake all they are masters of in the World at play; and when Money and Goods are wanting . . . they stake first Wife and Children, and then Land and Body.'[57]

The readiness to gamble even the freedom of one's relatives may well reflect the way in which Atlantic trade subordinated life and freedom to the cash nexus. The enslavement and sale abroad of defaulting debtors – or even of members of the debtor's village – was a different manifestation of the same phenomenon.

The changing pattern of the slave trade

One of Curtin's most valuable contributions was his analysis of the way in which the impact of the Atlantic slave trade varied with time and place. Later studies have modified details of his conclusions, but the general pattern he established has stood the test of time amazingly well. In a book published in 1983, Lovejoy suggested the following totals for slave *exports* from Africa during the Atlantic trade.

Period	Volume
1450–1600	367,000
1601–1700	1,868,000
1701–1800	6,133,000
1801–1900	3,330,000
Total	11,698,000[58]

The export of slaves began on a very small scale indeed, and at first trade in other commodities was more important. Some black slaves were taken to Portugal, and others to various Atlantic islands, including the Cape Verdes and São Tomé, where sugar plantations were established, anticipating those established later, on much the same lines, in the New World. It was in 1532 that the first slaves were sent directly to the New World from West Africa, rather than re-exported from Portugal. At first they worked as miners; sugar planting developed in Brazil from the 1540s on.

It was not until the 1630s that the Atlantic slave trade developed on a large scale. Two factors caused this change – one was the entry of other European nations, among them the Dutch, English and French, into African and Atlantic trade, ending the virtual monopoly hitherto enjoyed by the Portuguese. The other was the vast expansion in New World slave plantations, from the 1640s, beginning with sugar production in the British and French West Indies. By the eighteenth century, there were also tobacco plantations in Virginia, and cotton became the most commercial important crop in the *ante bellum* South. But there was always a strong linkage between sugar and slavery. Why was an African enslaved labour force employed in the New World? As Curtin pointed out long ago, much of the answer lies in epidemiology,[59] since New World populations were decimated by Old World diseases, especially smallpox. According to some estimates, there were 100 million inhabitants in the New World in 1492, and 5 million by the early seventeenth century.[60] An Indian from Yucatan described it all, in words which are strikingly similar to the way East Africans spoke of the arrival of jiggers and cholera. 'There was then no sickness; they had no aching bones ... they had then no smallpox ... At that time the course of humanity was orderly. The foreigners made it otherwise when they arrived here.'[61]

Africans had a high level of disease resistance. There is, moreover, a general consensus that prices paid for slaves in Africa were low, so that, despite the costs of transport and losses through mortality, European merchants made a profit. Assessing the prices paid by Atlantic merchants for slaves is a matter of great complexity – currencies varied, over time, as did the purchase price of the goods offered, and the goods themselves. In 1682, it was said of trade at St Louis, 'The negroes are bought for ten francs each and resold for more than 100 crowns ... it costs less to buy a slave than it does to ship him across the Atlantic.'[62]

At the same port, in the 1750s, a slave cost between £10 and £12, at a time when a year's supply of millet for one person cost £2.75.[63] Slaves were cheap because, to the initial captor, they were a 'free good' – Thomas and Bean elaborate an extended comparison with ocean fisheries.[64] As Law points out, with characteristic insight, the price of slaves is only indirectly relevant to African history, because the value Africans placed on imports bore no necessary relationship to their original cost to European slavers.[65]

We have seen how a central imperative of African governments was the need for people, and how many regions were underpopulated. Why then were people sold abroad? The problem is a complex one, to which we shall return.

Changing regional distribution

One of the most striking facts to have emerged from the various statistical studies of the slave trade is the dominance of West Central Africa. It exported more slaves than any other region; while other areas, such as the Slave Coast or the Niger Delta, peaked at particular periods, it was of importance throughout the whole period of the slave trade. Possibly 40 per cent of all slaves exported in the Atlantic trade came from Angola or the Congo river basin.[66] The ethnic identity of slaves changed as time went on, and there was a tendency for the slaving frontier to move ever further inland, until it reached the Lunda heartland and the Kazembe kingdom in Zambia.

The Slave Coast was an important source in the eighteenth century and the first four decades of the nineteenth. The large numbers of Yoruba enslaved at the very end of the slave trade had a great impact on Afro-American cultures in Brazil, Cuba, and elsewhere.

The Niger Delta produced relatively small numbers of slaves from the late fifteenth century on, as did Upper Guinea and the Senegambia, which was more prominent in the first phase of the Atlantic slave trade than it was ever to be again – 20 per cent of all slaves exported to the New World in the 1520s may have been Wolof, 8 per cent Serer and 8 per cent Malinke.[67] By the eighteenth century, the Senegambia was a minor supplier, and most of those sold there were Bambara from far inland.[68]

The export of predominantly Igbo slaves from the Niger Delta expanded vastly from the late seventeenth century on, and still more during the eighteenth. John Barbot was a French slaver who visited the area twice between 1678 and 1682. He wrote of 'a vast number of slaves of all sexes and ages' sold there.[69] Slave exports from the Niger Delta and the Cross River peaked in the late eighteenth century – Lovejoy suggests an average of 17,000 a year in the 1790s.[70] An English slaver who made ten voyages to Africa between 1786 and 1800 stated that 20,000 slaves were sold annually at Bonny alone, and 50,000 over a twenty-year period at Calabar.[71]

Alternative exports

Even when the export of slaves was at its height, Atlantic trade had other dimensions. The relative importance of other forms of commerce was particularly great in the sixteenth century. Initially, the Portuguese had difficulty in providing goods which Africans wished to buy, and often generated the funds to pay for their own purchases by acting as carriers in internal African trade. They brought African textile workers to the Cape Verde Islands and sold the cloth they made on the mainland in return for gold, slaves, pepper and other commodities.[72] They bought raffia cloth, camwood and elephants' tails (a treasured symbol of authority) in Loango, and sold them in Luanda.[73] They exchanged slaves, cloth and akori from the Niger Delta for gold on the Gold Coast[74] (which was thus at first an importer rather than exporter of slaves). Akori was a gemstone which has been the subject of several studies but has never been identified with certainty. The Portuguese also purchased local pepper, but it could not compete on the European market with the Asian variety. Thomas Windham bought gold, ivory and slaves in Benin; a later English visitor, in 1588, wrote, 'The commodities that we brought home were pepper and Elephants teeth, oyle of palme, cloth made of cotton wool very curiously woven, and cloth made of the bark of palm trees.'[75] In 1620–1, Richard Jobson was offered slaves in the Senegambia. 'I made answer, We were a people, who did not deale in any such commodities, neither did we buy or sell one another, or any that had our own shapes.'[76] By the late eighteenth century, Britain bought more slaves than any other European nation. Throughout the seventeenth century Whydah exported cloth and akori. In 1705 it was said, 'apart from slaves, nothing else can be bought here'.[77] Ivory and copper were originally the most important exports from Loango. After 1630, slaves became ever more important.[78] Despite this, trade in multiple commodities continued during the era of the Atlantic slave trade. As in East Africa, the need to provision slave ships often proved a stimulus to agriculture – there were thriving farms for this purpose near Whydah and in parts of Fante. The people of Tori, inland from Whydah, profited in two ways from foreign trade – the export of food, and banditry.[79]

Slaving captains sometimes bought ivory as well, as an insurance policy, 'seeing in that Commodity there's no Mortality to be feared'.[80] The Senegambia, although continuing to supply some slaves, also exported a variety of different products, including gum arabic, gathered on the desert edge and used in the textile industry. 'The principal goods the French have in return for these commodities from the Moors and Blacks, are slaves, gold-dust, elephants teeth, bees-wax, dry and green hides, gum-arabick, ostrich feathers, and several other odd things . . . [and] provisions.'[81] It would be a mistake to think that the impact of 'legitimate' trade was always beneficial: gum arabic was collected on the desert edge by slaves; much of the gold was alluvial, but some was mined in deep and dangerous shafts.

Gold was the most valuable export, apart from slaves, though its production was highly localised. In a widely cited article, Bean suggested that the value of West African gold exports exceeded that of slave exports until 1650. A recent study suggests that, between 1623 and 1632, slaves comprised 36 per cent of the exports of western Africa *by value*, gold 27 per cent, and ivory 3 per cent, followed by hides and malaguetta pepper.[82] Nearly all the gold came from the Akan area.

A major though unintended consequence of both the slave and ivory trades was that commerce in other commodities expanded, as long-distance traders seized the opportunity of dealing in other items as well. The Bobangi, carrying slaves or ivory on the upper Zaire, filled any surplus space in their canoes with local products.[83] In the second half of the seventeenth century, Gold Coast canoemen copied European merchants involved in coastal trade and began to carry goods between the Gold and the Slave Coasts.[84] This had both positive and negative consequences – it benefited the consumer, but, like foreign imports, sometimes undermined local craft industries. It generated real economic growth, in that it more fully utilised potential productive capacities.[85]

The mode of enslavement

The social and demographic impact of enslavement depended largely on how slaves were obtained – were they criminals, who would otherwise have been put to death, or the innocent victims of kidnapping and war? Alvares de Almada said of the Senegambia in 1594, in words which have innumerable later parallels, 'The slaves which they own and sell they enslave by war or by judicial decisions, or are kidnapped.'[86] Barbot visited the same area just under a hundred years later and reported:

Those sold by the *Blacks* are for the most part prisoners of war ... others stolen away by their own countrymen; and some there are who will sell their own children, kindred or neighbours ... The kings are so absolute, that upon any slight pretence of offences committed by their subjects, they order them to be sold for slaves ... Abundance of little *Blacks* of both sexes are also stolen away by their neighbours, when found abroad on the roads or in the woods ... In times of dearth and famine, abundance of these people will sell themselves to prevent starving.[87]

In 1850–2, the distinguished missionary linguist, Koelle, collected data from 210 language informants in Sierra Leone, 179 of whom were ex-slaves. Of those who gave details about the mode of their enslavement, 34 per cent had been taken in war, 30 per cent kidnapped, sometimes by fellow townsmen, 7 per cent had been sold by their rulers or relatives, 7 per cent sold in settlement of a debt, and 11 per cent enslaved as a judicial penalty.[88] (These categories were not mutually exclusive – it is likely that those sold by relatives were either redeeming a debt, or expiating a crime.)

The dominant mode of procuring slaves varied with the region – in the Bight of Biafra it was kidnapping, in the Bight of Benin, war. Bosman said of Whydah, 'most of the Slaves that are offered to us are Prisoners of War'.[89] Sometimes the wars would have been fought anyway. In the often quoted words of Kpengla, who ruled Dahomey from 1774 to 1789, 'In the name of my ancestors and myself I aver, that no Dahoman man ever embarked in war merely for the sake of procuring wherewithal to purchase your commodities ... Did Weebaigah [Wegbaja] sell slaves? No; his prisoners were all killed to a man.'[90] But it is clear that the prospect of making a profit from selling captives encouraged a general militarisation of life, and that the distinction between legitimate war and banditry depended very much on one's point of view.

In south-eastern Nigeria, kidnapping was the dominant mode of enslavement. 'The great Bulk of them [slaves] were such as had been taken in piratical Excursions, or by Treachery and Surprise.'[91] Olaudah Equiano (c. 1745–89), an Igbo who fell victim to the slave trade as a child, described a society where kidnapping was an offence punishable by enslavement, but was so common that when children played together, it was necessary to keep watch. Despite this, when he and his sister were at home alone, they were kidnapped by two men and a woman.[92] Those who sought the judgement of the oracle at Arochukwu were enslaved when found guilty, but by its nature, this process is unlikely to have provided large numbers of slaves.

There is much evidence that the slave trade led to a distortion of legal processes and an increase in witchcraft accusations. 'Many slaves are made in the Sherbro from the bare terrors of Red Water.'[93] 'Mr Baggs was almost universally informed by the black brokers that crimes constituted one of the ways by which they were doomed to servitude: that the revenue of the kings of the country depended on the sale of slaves, and that they therefore strained every nerve to accuse and condemn.'[94]

Much the same point was made in the 1730s, in the Senegambia: 'Since this Slave Trade has been us'd, all Punishments are changed into Slavery; there being an advantage on such condemnations, they strain for Crimes very hard, in order to get the benefit of selling the Criminal.'[95] On the other hand, some of those exported as slaves would have been executed otherwise.[96]

Ecological pressures – which at their most disastrous led to famine – are a recurrent theme in this study. They interact with the slave trade in many different ways. It was common for individuals to be enslaved as a direct or indirect result of hunger – either from a general famine or a family crisis. One of the texts of terror in the substantial corpus of slave recollections is the story of Swema, a Yao born in 1855, who was sold as a child to pay for two sacks of grain, buried alive when apparently dead, and miraculously rescued from the grave.[97]

To condemn the African merchants and kings who sold slaves to foreigners as villains or fools is almost as unsatisfactory as to praise them as creative statesmen. If people were the central value of African political cultures, why were they sold abroad rather than incorporated into the captor society? Sometimes captives *were* incorporated, and the growth of domestic slavery is a very clearly documented and widespread concomitant of the Atlantic slave trade.

In some cases, rulers did attempt to limit the export of slaves. At first it was copper, rather than slaves, which the Kongo kingdom exported. Later, when enslavement became a danger even to the ruling class, its king tried unsuccessfully to restrict it: 'our country is being completely depopulated, and Your Highness [of Portugal] should not agree with this nor accept it as in your service'.[98] But the slave trade continued, and by the mid-seventeenth century, the Kongo state was in ruins. Benin was more successful in limiting human exports.

It was more common for statesmen to enforce a prohibition against the export of slaves from within their own boundaries. Futa Toro, Futa Jallon and Bundu prohibited the export of their own nationals as slaves, though their people were sometimes slave traders, and they profited from the passage of slave convoys through their territories.[99] Osei Kwame (1777–98) introduced a similar law in Asante.[100] These regulations show, clearly enough, that rulers recognised the contradiction between the export of people and a culture which stressed the importance of adherents. Miller suggests that rulers may first have become involved in Atlantic trade in the quest for goods with which to reward and attract adherents. Goods were used to create obligations among their recipients, to retain their allegiance and provide a form of insurance against scarcity – in time of dearth, the obligations were called in.[101]

But if kings and Big Men initially welcomed foreign merchants in search of rare goods to reward supporters and enhance their political influence, the results were often quite different. The slave trade sometimes weakened central governments by enabling local lords to fight their way to power and wealth. It was said of Ibadan in the 1850s, in an era when domestic slaves supplied the demands of 'legitimate' trade – 'Slave-raiding now became a trade to many who would get rich speedily.'[102] A career as a warlord sometimes laid the basis for enduring political power – the rise of the kingdom of Dahomey may be a case in point.[103]

Slavery and social polarisation

Domestic slavery did not begin with Atlantic trade, but it expanded as a consequence.[104] After the export of slaves ended, in the nineteenth century, domestic slavery expanded. It was often geared to the production of commodities for the export market (clove plantations in Zanzibar) or to their bulking and transport (palm oil, in southern Nigeria). Manning estimates that the number of slaves in Africa and in the New World were much the same from the seventeenth to the early nineteenth centuries, and that after 1850, there were more slaves in Africa.[105]

Some enslaved children were bought and cherished by the childless. David Pepple was sold to a childless woman who 'treated me exactly as a son'; but after a year she was forced to sell him to satisfy a creditor.[106] These were societies where parents were sometimes forced to part with their own children when disaster threatened. But there was a special vulnerability in the enslaved child.

Some slaves were exported whose lives would otherwise have been lost in religious sacrifices – Dahomey, which practised human sacrifice on a large scale, is a good example. But there is considerable evidence that unsaleable and surplus slaves often ended up as sacrifices and that, as a consequence, human sacrifice increased.[107] De Marees' account of the Gold Coast, published in 1602, spoke of rulers finding employment for the crippled and blind.[108] At the end of the century, it was said that 'several poor wretched Men, who through Age or Inability are become incapable of Labour, are sold on purpose to be made Victims in these accursed Offerings'.[109] In 1718, the kings of Whydah and Allada forced foreign traders to buy old, diseased and disabled slaves – 'blind, cross-eyed, lame, limp or mutilated'.[110] After the second Dahomey invasion of Whydah, in 1728, 'all the old and young they catched that was not vendable they kild and butchered after a very barbarous manner'.[111] In Igboland, unhealthy slaves were taken to Uburu to be sold for sacrifice to the spirit of the brine springs.

Imports

What did African communities import in return? The answer varies at different times and in different places. In the first phase of Atlantic trade, southern Nigerian communities imported brass and copper bracelets used for personal decoration and currency; beads and cloth were other early imports. Ryder comments, 'strictly utilitarian articles were conspicuously absent ... None of these things was vital to the strength or survival of Benin.'[112]

Textiles came to be by far the most important import, in West and West

Central Africa as a whole – they comprised half the goods sent to Angola,[113] and a slave was often called a 'piece', that is, of cloth. At first, imported textiles came from India; later they were manufactured in Europe, following Indian patterns. In a sense this is surprising, because many African communities made textiles of the highest quality. In the Kongo kingdom, European observers compared the various weaves of raffia cloth with damask, tatteta and brocade.[114] In Nigeria, the Ijebu sold blue and striped cloth to European merchants at Lagos and Allada; they then took it to the Gold Coast, Gabon, Angola and Brazil. In the seventeenth century, the people of Benin exported some 32,000 cloths in a two-year period.[115]

Did foreign imports destroy local textile industries? In the long run, this was to be the case, but until the late nineteenth century it seems clear that imports supplemented local production rather than undermining it. Miller suggests local industries were not weakened before 1830; in Nigeria, local cloth production still flourished in the late nineteenth century. Imported cloth increased the variety available; in Africa, as elsewhere in the world, dress reflected social standing, and an increased supply of cloth made clothing more accessible to the poor.[116] Sometimes imported cloth was unravelled and the thread woven locally. Not all cloth was put to a productive use – it was often buried with the dead (as is still, in many areas, the case today). A late nineteenth-century missionary, working in the old Kongo kingdom, described 'the scrupulous care with which they use up, in funeral wrappings and expenses, all the cloth that a dead man leaves, breaking even the crockery that was his'.[117]

The next most important imports in West Central Africa were spirits, such as Brazilian sugar brandy, and tobacco. Alcohol was the second most important import by value at Luanda in the late eighteenth and early nineteenth centuries.[118] Spirits were adulterated with water, and pepper was then added to disguise the deficiency. In the 1890s, it was estimated that a case of spirits for the African trade cost 1s 9½d including bottles, case and contents![119] Indigenous drinks – millet beer, palm wine or mead – were far more nutritious, and the westerners who sold trade spirits often mocked their purchasers for drunkenness. Some African rulers were teetotallers and others restricted the consumption of alcohol – including locally made beverages. This is true of Ghezo of Dahomey and his heir, Glele, of Kazembe III Lukwesa in Zambia (d. 1805) and of the Tswana king, Kgama (d. 1923).

Currency, in the form of cowries, was the most important import on the Slave Coast followed by metals and textiles. Iron, used for agricultural tools, dominated until the 1690s, and copper (used for currency and personal adornment) afterwards. Brazilian tobacco was in great demand from the eighteenth century on.[120]

The patterns of imports reflected the priorities of African consumers. Atkins, who visited West Africa in 1721, said: 'the Windward and Leeward Parts of the Coast are as opposite in their Demands, as in their distance. Iron Bars, which are not asked for to Leeward, are a substantial Part of Windward Cargoes ... Cowreys ... at Whydah. Copper and Iron Bars at Callabar.'[121]

Adams advised a prospective merchant planning to take £1,000 worth of cargo to Bonny to include £630 worth of guns and gunpowder.[122] Guns and firearms were the third most important import, by value, in West Central Africa. The evidence is paradoxical. Guns and ammunition were essential for the African trade; in Portuguese settlements, where arms imports were prohibited, they were smuggled in. But guns for the African market were so inferior that they often did not work, and were frequently more of a danger to their owner than to anyone else – all that prevented them from exploding was the inferior quality of the gunpowder. In the mid-nineteenth century, it was calculated that a safe musket cost over 16s to make, while guns for Africa, from 'Sham Damn Iron', cost 5s 3½d.[123] But in the late eighteenth century, West Africa imported between 283 and 394 thousand guns per annum, and the Congo-Loango area, some 50 thousand.[124] This is incomprehensible if the arms were both useless and dangerous.

A paper written in 1971, in the heyday of Africanist scholarship, suggested the guns were used for ivory hunting and protecting the crops. (Its author was undeterred by the fact that there is no evidence of the latter phenomenon!) Inikori, reverting to an older model, suggests they were used to collect slaves. Miller agrees that they were used in war and contributed to the growth of a warlord class, but claims that their efficacy was mainly symbolic – though none the less real for that. 'In a direct sense, the gun interposed European technology between rulers and their subjects ... Guns made ... new men into a distinct genre of warlords ... [But] European weapons ... need not have been fired with accuracy to achieve effects comparable to the legendary knives and spears wielded by the African kings of old.'[125]

Iron bars were an import like textiles – they supplemented a local product where the supply, at least in some areas, was clearly less than the demand. In the Niger Delta, they became a unit of account, in terms of which other imports were valued. In the twentieth century, indigenous smelting died out; in earlier periods, imported iron supplemented rather than destroying it, and a more abundant supply of iron led to more knives, cutlasses, hoes and so on. This in its turn made a major contribution to agriculture.

In the short run, currencies – such as cowries or copper manillas – facilitated economic transactions; in the long run, cowries in particular were so devalued by uncontrolled imports from East Africa that they became useless for all but the smallest purchases.[126] In the end, the cowries for which such a price was paid became valueless and their owners abandoned their treasure: 'the bitter decision to abandon them as junk. Stocks of ... cowries hoarded by being buried in the ground, a testimony to centuries of accumulation, have since been abandoned in their permanent graves'.[127]

The general trend in slave trade studies, even among radicals, is to emphasise the value of the imports. But often the profits were either hoarded or squandered. Duke Ephraim of Calabar imported a prefabricated house which he did not live in but filled with assorted objects from Europe, which were soon in a state of confusion and decay.[128] The Africanist defence is that it proved his creditworthiness! The Asantehene, Osei Tutu, built a stone house, full of a mixture of treasures and junk, which Africanists tend to call a museum, but which McCaskie has interpreted in symbolic terms. 'The Asante were and are acutely aware that their culture, in the most literal sense, was hacked out of nature. And this understanding ... engendered the abiding fear that ... the fragile defensible space called culture would simply be overwhelmed by an irruptive and anarchic nature.' European imports of all kinds were hoarded, to strengthen the realm of culture against the realm of nature.[129]

The imports: interpretations

Scholars disagree about the value of the goods imported in the slave trade era – what is at issue is not the facts, but the way in which they are interpreted. In 1973, I wrote of 'the extraordinary inequality of the exchange', pointing out that some imports duplicated Africa's own products – iron, copper, textiles, salt – and that others were positively harmful – trade spirits, inferior muskets.[130] Others put forward a very different picture – it was suggested that cloth, iron and salt became more abundant, which benefited the poorer consumer. Later studies suggested that iron imports reduced the wood used in furnaces, and hence meant fewer trees were felled.[131] A recent book by Thornton points out that before 1650 Africa imported nothing which was not also locally produced. He stresses the quality and quantity of African production of metals, cloth and so on, so that the Atlantic trade provided a wider range of consumer choices.[132] He explicitly critiques the 'radical' historiography of Rodney and others, but is essentially advancing one of its central tenets, that the imports were superfluous. Regional variations show, in one sense, the power of choice of the African merchant. But although they could enforce a preference for guns or cowries, they could not break free from a dynamic which in the long run underdeveloped Africa and helped build the 'developed' western world. Even if some of the imports brought positive benefits, these were clearly outweighed by the sufferings of the enslaved, the wars and kidnapping, the distortion of judicial processes and the loss of life. Africa exported Africans, as well as gold, ivory and other items of relatively local significance. In return it obtained consumer goods, and some items which by any reckoning were positively harmful – inferior guns, trade spirits, tobacco. When the slave trade came to an end, Africans themselves pointed out that centuries of European contact had not led to development. In Zambia, in 1886, the Lozi king Lewanika expressed concern about the economic future of his country when the elephants had gone and ivory exports had ended. Coillard reassured him: 'I pointed out to him the fertility of his country, and that if the chiefs would give themselves up to the cultivation of cotton, tobacco, coffee, sugar-cane, etc, they would soon find that it would be an inexhaustible source of riches for them.'[133]

In the twentieth century, Bulozi exported people as labour migrants.

Alien corn: new crops, and the Atlantic factor

A Kuba king who lived at the beginning of the seventeenth century is said to have lost weight through lack of appetite. His wife – honoured for her action by a title which still survives – obtained chili pepper from the Lele, which remedied the situation.[134] This particular anecdote may be symbolic, though it is told of a historical king. But it reminds us that one of the most important consequences of the Atlantic factor was the introduction of new foods, which, in their turn, affected demography, work patterns and gender roles. In late nineteenth-century Shaba, there was a song which ran, 'Lombe, you remember, introduced potatoes, and what was reckoned poison is now staple diet.'[135]

Two of the most important introductions were of maize and cassava. Cassava has less nutritional value than indigenous grains, but it thrives on poor soil and survives in the ground indefinitely. Moreover, it is the inedible stem and not an edible tuber or grain which is planted, a not inconsiderable matter for those living on the edge of hunger. Since it requires laborious processing to remove toxicity, it added to women's workload. Often, it was the food of the poor, or slaves, the prosperous opting for the traditional carbohydrate staple – 'The banana is the bread of the wealthy, as cassava is that of the poor.'[136] Maize withstood disease, humidity and birds better than indigenous cereals, and made a double or even triple annual harvest possible. It was the rural staple in mid-seventeenth-century Kongo, but the nobility ate millet.[137]

Cassava is first mentioned on the Loango coast in 1612[138] and had reached the Lunda heartland by 1650. In the late seventeenth century it was adopted in the kingdom of Mutombo Mukulu, whose inhabitants called themselves the Cassava People.[139] Still further east, in the Upemba depression, the praise song for a title at the Kinkonja court ran:

> Lord of the little cassava root
> Its leaves are eaten and its root is crushed.[140]

American crops are first documented in inland Senegambia in the 1720s, but were clearly present earlier.[141]

The demographic impact of these changes is uncertain. Cassava often spread along slave trading routes. Its calorific contribution, and role in protection against famine, may have been offset by its lack of nutrients, and it has been suggested that women's additional workload contributed to miscarriages, and perhaps abortions.[142] Whatever the benefits of these new crops, the price the Atlantic factor exacted, in suffering and social dislocation, was clearly exorbitant. It has often reminded me of Keats' image of Ruth.

> She stood in tears amid the alien corn.

Diseases: old and introduced

We saw in an earlier chapter how a considerable number of deadly diseases were endemic in Africa. Some of them were carried to the New World as an unintended consequence of Atlantic trade – yellow fever (which seldom affects Africans), hookworm, river blindness, and virulent falciparum malaria.[143] Malaria seems to have been the most important cause of death in the *ante-bellum* South. Yellow fever ravaged the Caribbean, especially Trinidad. Because of their inherited immunities, those of African descent were less affected – this, in its turn, reinforced racist stereotypes, because it seemed to reflect 'racial' differences.[144] River blindness was carried to Guatemala, Mexico and Venezuela.[145]

A number of afflictions were brought to Africa from the New World. Jiggers (sand fleas) disabled countless thousands of Central and East Africans in the late nineteenth century.[146] Syphilis was brought back from the New World by the first European visitors.[147] It is closely related to yaws, a non-venereal disease indigenous to Africa which is also caused by the spirochete *Treponema* – they cannot be differentiated under a microscope. It spread in central Africa from the late nineteenth century on, and has greatly affected population growth in some areas. Because of the similarity to yaws, it is not easy to identify in travellers' accounts; it may be among the various afflictions Barbot described among the peoples of modern Liberia, in the late seventeenth century.

The *Meazles* kill abundance, and formerly in the land of *Hondo* swept away the best part of the people. They think this distemper was brought in by some *Europeans* at the beginning of this century . . . The *Small-Pox* also ravages this country very much, and kills very many of the natives. The *Head-ach* is very violent . . . The *Bloody-flux* is also common, and sweeps away multitudes of the *Blacks*. The *Quojas* [Kono] *Negroes* affirm, they never knew of the bloody-flux till it was brought from *Sierra Leona* in the year 1626, eight months after the *Dutch admiral* Laun had left that place. They are also much aflicted with *Cankers* [?syphilis] . . . which perhaps may be occasioned by their extraordinary luxuriousness with women.[148]

The ravages of smallpox, which this account mentions, suggests that new and virulent strains may have been introduced from Europe, as were possibly, but not certainly, tuberculosis and bacillary pneumonia.

Conclusion

Many of the details of the original radical model are now generally rejected, and Eltis' estimate, that the sale of slaves seldom exceeded 10 per cent of the total domestic product of African societies, is widely accepted.[149] The profits made by slavers were less than was once thought, and the wealth of West Indian plantation owners was more likely to be channelled into conspicuous consumption or political ambitions in England than into industrial growth.

But the underlying model, of a trade which underdeveloped Africa and developed the western world, is still valid, and even when the slave trade was abolished, Europeans continued to buy commodities such as cloves or palm oil which depended in some way on slave labour. When nineteenth-century explorers such as Livingstone described the sufferings of slave coffles, it became part of an image used to justify the missionary onslaught on African religions, the colonial usurpation of African political autonomy. The Atlantic slave trade conflated all black Africans into a common identity, which was then identified with slavery. It was forgotten that many other peoples had also been enslaved,[150] and racism flourished in a world the enslaved had helped to build.

19

West Africa to 1800

The trade of slaves is in a more peculiar manner the business of kings, rich men, and prime merchants, exclusive of the inferior sort of *Blacks*.

Barbot, in the late seventeenth century[1]

A foreign presence on the coast

In the era of Atlantic trade, European merchants distinguished the various parts of the West African coast with the names of the commodities they came to seek – the Grain Coast (the reference is not to cereals but to malaguetta pepper), Ivory Coast, still the name of a modern nation, the Gold Coast, which became the name of a British colony, and the Slave Coast, which, like 'Gold Coast', is still often used as a unit of academic analysis. The names symbolise an ever-increasing involvement in Atlantic trade, which was to institute social changes so far-reaching that they have been called a change in the relations of production. It is not easy to evaluate the relative importance of external trade and the continuing internal dynamics of each culture and its interaction with its environment – 'a people in a landscape'. There are infinite permutations – and we see each region through the eyes of different scholars, who bring to their research different understandings of historical process and method.

The involvement of West and West Central Africa in international sea-borne trade began in the late fifteenth century. West Africa had long been linked with a wider world, across the trans-Saharan trade routes, and goods obtained in this way had penetrated deep into Guinea. The volume of trade was limited by the exigencies of desert travel; the export of slaves imposed immense sufferings on individuals, but this was in a sense counterbalanced by real benefits, such as access to literacy in Arabic, and to an international world of Islamic learning. But the victims and the beneficiaries were not, of course, the same. In some areas, the agents of Saharan and Atlantic trade were in direct competition. The Portuguese founded a trade post at Arguin in Mauretania, with the express intention of deflecting goods from the desert trade routes. On the Gold Coast, they may have purchased 500 kg of gold a year in the late sixteenth century, and 700 kg in the early sixteenth – perhaps half the gold formerly exported along a Dyula trade route to the north.[2]

The Portuguese reached the estuary of the Senegal in 1446, Sierra Leone in 1460, the Zaire river in 1484. In many ways, their initial impact was quite minor, though it led to significant changes at the Kongo court. But in the long run, it was one of the great watersheds in the history of sub-Saharan Africa, a transition from an age where local production, local initiatives and local ideas were all-important to one where, in at least parts of Africa, social and political institutions were distorted by the successive demands of merchant and industrial capitalism.

The nature of the European presence changed as time went on. Until the end of the sixteenth century the sea-borne trade of western Africa was dominated by Portugal, though even then it was unable to exclude other nationals, Spaniards and Englishmen among them. Portuguese exploration and overseas commerce was a state enterprise; for a time, the crown exchanged commercial rights in West Africa for the exploration of a certain amount of coastline each year.

It proved impossible to exclude 'interlopers', and in the seventeenth century an ever-increasing number of European nations became involved in the trade of western Africa, and acquired forts on the Gold Coast. The French, English and Dutch (who captured São Jorge da Mina in 1637) were dominant, but other European nations had a foothold there for a time, including Denmark and Brandenberg. The seventeenth century was the heyday of Chartered Companies such as the Royal African Company, which undertook military and administrative duties in return for a commercial monopoly. They failed for much the same reasons as the Portuguese had failed – the impossibility of excluding commercial rivals, or of competing with them when carrying military and administrative costs. There would be a new era of Chartered Companies in Africa in the late nineteenth century. By the eighteenth century, attempts to sustain a commercial monopoly in different parts of Africa had ended. Some forts and factories were still maintained by government agencies; by 1800, Portugal, England, Holland, Denmark and France still had land establishments in West Africa.

New states

One of the most striking aspects of the history of this period is the rise and fall of Denkyira and Akwamu, and the growth of Dahomey, Asante and Oyo, from small principalities to large and powerful states. The expansion of Oyo dates from the early seventeenth century, the rise of Dahomey and Asante from the early eighteenth. Oyo relied on cavalry, imported from the savanna at great expense in return for European imports (which were obtained on the coast in return for slaves). Asante and Dahomey made extensive use of firearms, paid for largely by slaves. A recurrent motif, even in kingdoms thought of as 'absolute', was the changing balance of power between the king and his officials. There was conflict between the king of Dahomey and his officials in the 1730s. Near the end of his reign, in 1748, the Asantehene Opuku Ware introduced administrative changes which he had to abandon because his chiefs rebelled.[3] This kind of cleavage was much more protracted and dramatic in Oyo, where the Alafin was peculiarly vulnerable, because his great officials could require his suicide.

In recent years, much attention has been paid to the revenues of African kingdoms; they included some or all of the following: provincial tribute, a share of booty taken in war, imposts on trade (and sometimes the direct involvement in trade of a sovereign's representatives), the agricultural production of royal slaves, and death duties, levied on the estates of the wealthy – the source of the Asantehene's praise name, Ogyefo, the Taking One. Tribute had a symbolic dimension, and was sometimes nominal – bere grass to thatch the alafin's roof, water carried from the Niger to the Oba of Benin.[4] The extent of central government's fiscal demands varied considerably. Dahomey, in its tributary years, paid Oyo 40 men, 40 women, 40 muskets, coral and 400 bags of cowries annually, while the town of Saki paid two rams and ten bags of cowries.[5] These payments were an inconvenience rather than an unbearable burden. But in Kea's analysis, the financial exactions of the Akan political class in the seventeenth century were severe enough to drive peasants off the land.[6] Rulers, oppressive or otherwise, needed to reward supporters and distribute largesse, and a reputation for meanness could lead to their overthrow. Village democracies paid no taxes, though boys and men contributed labour to public works instead. Among the southern Igbo, the Okonko society maintained footpaths and was repaid by levying tolls; its brightly coloured toll booths, which have long since vanished, made an impression on early European visitors.[7]

Sierra Leone

The study of language families is the key to much Sierra Leone history. For many centuries, a dominant theme was the Mande factor, mirrored in the name of the country's largest ethnic group, the Mende. There were a number of different Mande migrations into the area,[8] and many of the modern nation's people speak Mande languages such as Kuranko and Susu, which are inter-intelligible, as, to a lesser extent, is Yalunka.[9] The Temne, the second largest people of modern Sierra Leone, speak a West Atlantic language, most closely related to Baga and Landuma, more distantly to Bullom, Sherbro, Krim and Limba – the ancestral forms of these languages were clearly spoken by the region's inhabitants before the Mande incursions. Their culture, however, was influenced in many ways by those of Mande speakers.

The Temne lived in states headed by sacred kings, and share a tradition, probably not to be taken literally, of migration from Futa Jallon.[10] When a king died, he was thought to return there, to be restored to health and return as his successor. Temne speakers did not form a monolithic or uniform bloc; one scholar spoke of their 'extraordinary degree of heterogeneity', and an older study observed, in words applicable to many other ethnic groups as well, 'Strata upon strata seem to have been laid down, in the course of ages, folk upon folk, flowing in from the north, the northwest, and the northeast ... Through wars and marriages [they] have been absorbed the one into the other, so that the mass is now completely, or nearly completely metamorphosed into new groups or crossings.'[11]

West Atlantic speakers were much influenced, not only by Mande immigrants, but also by Dyula traders. They adopted the Mande system of large eponymous clans, the origins of which are reflected in their Mande names, and which created horizontal links between a vast number of independent communities.[12]

Sierra Leone was of relatively minor importance in the total pattern of Atlantic trade; ivory, camwood and slaves were exported, and the Royal African Company had two factories located on Bunce and York Islands. Certain English slavers founded families which gradually became African, such as the Caulkers and the Clevelands, with their power base on the Banana and Plantain Islands. Some coastal peoples opposed the slave trade. Tomba – who in 1721 fell victim to enslavement himself – 'was a Leader of some Country Villages that opposed them [slave traders] and their trade at the River Nunes.'[13]

In the late eighteenth century, it was said of the Baga, 'they will not allow Europeans to settle among them, and the reason assigned for their conduct is that they dislike the slave trade'.[14] The Kru took a great pride in the tradition that they had never been enslaved.

The Gold Coast

In 1698, Denkyira conquered Assin, one of a number of flourishing commercial polities in 'Akani' or Adansi, in the Pra–Ofin basin, later to be the heartland of the Asante kingdom. In the sixteenth and seventeenth centuries, there was a flourishing commercial system, dominated by gold merchants from Adansi.[15] Large caravans travelled between the inland states and the coast; near the European forts, broker corporations developed which Kea, following his sources, calls captaincies, but which have much in common with the Canoe House system of the Niger Delta. Rich merchants were called *abirempon*, Big Men; books in the Trade and Politics tradition called them merchant princes, an expression first used in a Gold Coast context in 1903.[16] They tended to invest their profits in the acquisition of office, which then generated more wealth. In the 1640s, when a wood carrier earned about 144 dambas of gold per year, this cost nearly 39,000 dambas.[17] Cultivators paid tribute in gold, in kind and in labour. 'The farm is my domain, the land is the chief's domain.' Kea suggests that between a quarter and a half of a peasant family's production was creamed off by taxation.[18]

Some moved to the towns, and endeavoured to improve their situation by trade. With some exaggeration, a Portuguese factor described the dynamics of social change in 1618, in words which are not irrelevant to other places and times: 'Because of the many commodities the Dutch have brought and are still bringing, all have abandoned farming and have become and are still becoming merchants.'[19]

Those who did not prosper sometimes became brigands and preyed, above all, on merchants. Seventeenth-century experience anticipated a phenomenon which has become sadly familiar in modern Africa – the association of poverty with violent crime.[20] It was evident at Keta, in the lagoons east of the Volta: 'there are few wealthy men among the *Cotos*, and the generality being very poor, many of them turn strolling robbers about the country, and do much mischief'.[21]

The dominance of the *obirempon* declined in the late seventeenth and early eighteenth centuries. The new elite were the *awurafram*, masters of firepower, leading regiments of musketeers, who grew rich by seizing and selling captives – a process little different from panyarring and banditry. In the eighteenth century, armies and states grew larger; in some areas there was an absolute decline in population, and a movement away from urban life and the commerce of Adansi declined, though gold mining continued.[22]

Two *oman* – Denkyira in the west and Akwamu in the east – rose to dominance some distance from the coast, in the seventeenth century. Denkyira was in the heart of the gold-bearing area – 'The inhabitants of *Dinkira* are vastly rich in gold,' noted Barbot,[23] some twenty years before it was overthrown by Asante in 1701.

Akwamu was founded in about 1600, when members of the Abrade matriclan migrated to the hinterland of Accra, which was conquered in 1677. Its capital was Nyanaoase – 'the Frenchmen whom I sent there assured me that they had never seen a place of greater beauty'.[24] Akwamu was located to the east of the gold-bearing area; despite this, 'the King and his Nobles, or rather, Favourites, are so very rich in Gold and Slaves, that I am of Opinion this Country singly possesses greater Treasures than all those we have hitherto described taken together'.[25] They excluded potential commercial rivals, such as the Akyem, from the sea, both by force of arms and by the common stratagem of creating adverse stereotypes. 'They painted us Europeans as horrid; that we were sea monsters.'[26]

Akwamu was the first Akan polity to make extensive use of firearms, and in the eighteenth century the archer was replaced by the musketeer.[27] It seems to have preyed on its own citizens – a body of young men known as *sika den*, black gold, devoted themselves to panyarring in its service.[28] Akwamu's dominance bred a reaction, and its capital was sacked by a coalition of Akan states led by Akyem, in 1730. The whole area was dramatically depopulated by flight, violent death and enslavement.[29] The Gold Coast became a net exporter rather than a net importer of slaves, and in 1725 Dutch merchants complained that it would be more appropriately named the Slave Coast, since gold was scarce and slaves abundant.[30]

The refugee Akwamu court, like that of Accra fifty years earlier, founded a new polity east of the Volta; the presence of these émigré states added to the militarisation of life on the Slave Coast.

Asante

No African state has been more fully studied than Asante. Africanist historians, among whom Wilks was pre-eminent, analysed its past in a way which emphasised the similarities between Asante and European history: 'the institutional structure of the state, in respect of "army, bureacracy, taxation, trade, diplomacy" ... came to resemble in many respects that of the absolutisms of post-Renaissance Europe'.[31] This was, essentially, a salutary reaction against the racism of many of the sources from which any history must be reconstructed, which tended to depict Asante and other African kingdoms as bloodthirsty tyrannies. It was 'an Asante history resonant with the needs and hopes of the early days of an independent Ghana'.[32] My own early work was in this tradition,[33] but there were large areas of documented historical experience which this model excluded, such as the persecution of witches and the prevalence of human sacrifice.[34] It left out much of what Africans themselves considered important, especially, perhaps, in the sphere of 'traditional' religion. The exercise was, in the last analysis, condescending; African cultures were cast in a mould comparable with, and similar to, their western counterparts, as if this was the only way they could be validated in western eyes.[35]

There are similar debates about Dahomey. A paper published in 1974 called 'Fly and elephant parties: political polarisation in Dahomey' discussed Dahomey's Annual Customs in quasi-parliamentary terms. The Annual Customs, thought to have been introduced by Agaja in the 1730s, were large-scale human sacrifices in honour of royal ancestors.[36]

The Asante state began, not with conquest, but with an alliance between a number of small principalities, which acknowledged the ruler of Kumasi as their head, the Asantehene. The first holder of this office was Osei Tutu, who reigned from *c.* 1695 to *c.* 1717. The new kingdom was modelled, to a large extent, on Akwamu, the source of many of its institutions. A sense of national identity was forged in resentment at Denkyira hegemony and in its successful overthrow. This identity focussed on political symbols, the introduction of which was associated with the priest Komfo Anokye – the Golden Stool, where the *sunsum* (soul) of the Asante people resides and the Seventy-Seven Laws which bear his name.

The new kingdom expanded with extraordinary rapidity; by the death of Osei Tutu's heir, Opuku Ware, in 1750,[37] it covered much of modern Ghana and parts of modern Ivory Coast and Togo. Northern expansion ended in the savannas, with the conquest of Gonja, Mamprussi and Dagomba. When he died, a Gonja chronicler wrote, 'Peoples of all the horizons feared him very much.'[38] In the reign of Opuku Ware, four Dutchmen set up a distillery in Kumasi, and thread was used from unravelled imported cloth as an input in the weaving industry,[39] an interesting example of selective modernisation.

Much of the dynamic of Asante expansion came from the sale of gold and slaves in return for firearms. The state was at once an importer of slaves from the north and an exporter of war captives to the European slavers on the coast. In the decades of military expansion, war itself generated much revenue, in the form of plunder, tribute and captives. By the end of the eighteenth century, expansion had reached its limits. The decline of the slave trade in the early nineteenth century led to an increasing reliance on revenue from commercial transactions, as bulk imports from the coast were broken down into smaller units in return for gold dust.[40]

Despite its warlike image, the accumulation of wealth, and especially gold, remained a core Asante value, and *obirempon* was a rare prestigious title. The insignia of its holder included an elephant's tail. The core symbols of royalty included not only the famous Golden Stool but also a Golden Elephant's Tail, emblem of wealth. It is noteworthy that the latter – but not the former – symbol fell into abeyance in the late nineteenth century.[41] When an office holder died, his possessions reverted to the Asantehene, who returned at least some of his wealth to his heirs.

The war between Nature and Culture remained a perennial motif in Asante thought.[42] Large trees were planted at new settlements, and when they fell, their fall was thought to presage the dissolution of society.[43] When an Asantehene died, it was said, 'A great tree has fallen.' Umbrellas – an important political symbol – had a similar meaning.

At the annual festival called *odwira*, which celebrated the harvest and honoured the dead royal ancestors, the king addressed the Golden Stool, in words which provide an apt summary of his culture's values:

> Golden Stool who first came into existence on a Friday . . .
> We beseech you for life and prosperity of life . . .
> May the nation grow in prosperity.
> Grant that fertile women bring forth children,
> Grant that our farms yield abundantly.
> Grant that the hunters kill meat.
> Let those who dig for gold find much
> So that I can get some to uphold my Kingship.[44]

The Fante

Kingship and matrilineal inheritance are at the core of perceived Akan identity, but both the Fante and Baoulé lived in small-scale states, and their cultures embodied both patrilineal and matrilineal elements. The Fante and the Asante speak the same language, Twi, and the dialectical differences which exist are due to changes in Fante since they were first recorded.[45] The Fante had the same matriclans as the Asante, and their members often offered each other hospitality. The sacred grove of Mankessim, 10 kilometres from the coast, was for the Fante a ritual centre comparable to Santemanso among the Asante, and an oracle of considerable importance.[46] The Braffo was a military leader and judge acknowledged by all Fante, but each of the nineteen[47] Fante polities was independent. In the words of Bosman, at the beginning of the eighteenth century:

If the *Fantyneans* were not in perpetual Civil Divisions, the circumjacent Countries would soon find their Power by the Irruptions into their Territories . . . Here is no King, the Government being in the Hands of a Chief Commander whom they call their *Braffo* . . . he is . . . somewhat closely restrained by the old Men, who are a sort of National Councellors . . . besides these every part of *Fantyn* hath also its particular Chief.[48]

In 1707 they formed a confederation, headed by Abora, largely in response to the danger presented by the growing power of Asante, but this kind of alliance for military aims was fragile – they were 'divided into so many petty Republicks, and always at war among themselves'.[49]

The political fragmentation of the Fante and the other peoples of coastal Ghana has been attributed to the disruptive effects of the European presence. (But the rise of Kajoor and other coastal states in the Senegambia has been attributed to their access to foreign trade.) By the mid-eighteenth century, there were thirty forts along 500 kilometres of coast, and although each of them paid rent to a local ruler, African autonomy was inevitably undermined. But these small-scale states may also reflect cultural choices at a deeper level.

The Baoulé

The Baoulé of Ivory Coast are the westernmost Akan, and the relative neglect of their history[50] contrasts with the great output of research on Asante. Their traditions claim that they fled from the Asante heartland after the death of Osei Tutu, in *c.* 1717, but Baoulé and Twi are deeply differentiated, which suggests that they separated much earlier. Linguistic evidence suggests that Twi speakers moved east and Baoulé speakers west, from a home in western Brong.[51]

Among other Akan, important areas of life were shaped by matrilineal inheritance – matrilineages collectively owned land, and matrilineal descent determined inheritance and succession to office. Among the Baoulé, the core institution was the homestead, which could expand rapidly through the acquisition of extra wives and through the incorporation of captives as 'fictive kin'. One could join such a homestead by right of either matrilineal or patrilineal descent. Among the Asante, cross-cousin marriages were preferred, but the Baoulé had strict rules of exogamy.

The kola trade

Kola nuts were one of the major exports of the Akan forests. They were a stimulant acceptable in the Islamic world, and their high caffeine content enabled porters, farmers and others to sustain intense exertion despite hunger and fatigue. They were highly perishable, so their transport over vast distances required specialised skills.

An important caravan route ran from Asante to Hausaland, through Gonja and Borgu. Hausa or Hausanised groups bought kola in Asante, in return for natron from the desert and slaves, as well as textiles and other Hausa manufactures. Clapperton met a caravan of a thousand men and women and a thousand pack animals in Borgu in 1826, and saw more foreign imports there than he did in Yorubaland.[52] In colonial times, Borgu became an impoverished backwater. Kola was among the many commodities traded between Hausaland and what is now central Nigeria; a river between Katinsa and Nupe was called the River of Washing away Poverty.

'The Slave Coast'

The area Europeans came to call the Slave Coast – a name first used in the 1690s – extends from the Volta to the Lagos Channel, and is predominantly, though not exclusively, populated by Aja (Ewe, Fon, Aja, Gun) speakers.

By the early seventeenth century, Allada was the leading Aja polity. It first appeared on a map of the 1480s but was clearly more ancient.[53] In the mid-seventeenth century, the coastal polity of Whydah, previously subject to Allada, gained its independence and from 1671 on, it dominated the external trade of the coast. The total demographic impact of the Atlantic slave trade is a complex and much disputed question,[54] but there can be little doubt that it caused regional depopulation in some areas. Seventeenth-century observers stressed the density of the population round Whydah, whereas in the nineteenth century they were struck by its absence, and elephants – once extinct in the area – had returned. Swift, with more insight than he knew, wrote of geographers who

> o'er inhabitable Downs
> Place Elephants for want of Towns.[55]

It would be simplistic to attribute this demographic decline simply to the export of captives; depopulation was caused as much as anything by wars – the Atlantic slave trade clearly contributed to these wars, since they were, at least in this region, the main source of slaves.

Dahomey

The kingdom of Dahomey, or Fon, was founded in the second quarter of the seventeenth century. A great deal of scholarly attention has been devoted to its history, and in particular to the impact of the slave trade. Dahomey was founded by a prince who ruled from *c.* 1625 to *c.* 1650; eighteenth-century sources describe him variously as a bandit and as the leader of mercenary soldiers (the two are not, of course, mutually exclusive).[56] Originally tributary to Allada, it expanded dramatically under Wegbaja (*c.* 1680–1716), whom tradition remembers as the first king, and still more so under his successor Agaja (*c.* 1716–40), who conquered Allada and Whydah, in 1724 and 1727 respectively. The refugee royals of Allada founded a small state further east, at Porto Novo. Tradition that Dahomey's rulers were descended from an Allada prince, and ultimately came from Tado, may well have been late eighteenth-century inventions, intended to give greater antiquity and legitimacy to a new kingdom and dynasty.[57]

But while Dahomey fought its way to the sea, it was itself repeatedly attacked by the cavalry of a distant inland kingdom, Oyo. Although the invaders could not spend long periods of time so far from their home base, in the end Dahomey agreed to pay tribute, a situation which lasted until 1823. There was a civil war when Agaja died, and there was, at times, serious conflict between the king and his officials. In the face of all this, Dahomey not only survived but acquired a degree of military strength which was to enable it, in the nineteenth century, to launch repeated invasions of Yorubaland.

In a classic example of 'Africanist' interpretation, Akinjogbin suggested that Agaja initially intended to suppress the slave trade, but that this proved impracticable; it is now generally agreed that he hoped to profit more from Atlantic trade by cutting out the coastal middlemen.[58] Dahomey was a state geared to war where the king wielded authoritarian power over his subjects, who were sometimes described as his slaves.[59] Akinjogbin believed that Dahomey represented a new political ideology, quite distinct from the older idiom of kinship.[60] But there were many continuities between Dahomey and the states which preceded it and, as Akinjogbin himself pointed out, the king of Dahomey was sometimes called Dada, Father.[61] The rhetoric of kinship blurred the hard lines of owner–slave and ruler–subject relations; the reality was much the same.

Much of Dahomey's success was due to its early and rapid adoption of firearms. Agaja said in 1726, 'Boath I and my predecessors were, and are, gret admirers of fire armes, and have allmost intirely left of the use of bows and arrows.'[62] War captives belonged to the king, who paid soldiers a pound each for the living, and considerably less for the heads of the dead. At the time, slaves were sold to Europeans for fifteen pounds each, so this generated considerable revenue, much of which was redistributed as largesse.

In time, Dahomey developed a middleman role, and other nations exported slaves through its ports, but in the late eighteenth century Oyo began to make increasing use of alternative trade routes further east. There was a strong emphasis on law and order, and it was said in 1728 that since Agaja 'cuts off the head of whoever steals only a cowry, one travels in his country with more security than in Europe'.[63]

The Dahomey court relied heavily on the energies and abilities of women. The food for the court was grown on plantations by slaves, among whom women predominated.[64] Each major official had a counterpart at court called his 'mother'; through these women, the king was able to keep a check on their activities. The aspect which struck outsiders most forcibly was the role of women in the army. In the eighteenth century, some of the king's wives formed the royal bodyguard. Under Ghezo, in the early nineteenth century, they became a major fighting force, whom Europeans tended to call Amazons.

The Yoruba culture sphere

Historical writing on the Yoruba for this period is dominated by the rise and fall of the Oyo empire. Even at its greatest extent, it was never identical with the Yoruba-speaking area; Dahomey paid it tribute for a considerable time, and large areas of Yorubaland, including Ijebu, Ijesa and Ekiti, lay outside it.

In the early seventeenth century Abipa reoccupied Old Oyo, after perhaps a century of a court in exile, for much of which time the Alafins ruled from Ighboho. Johnson claimed that Ifa divination and the Egungun mask cult were introduced during the period of exile, the latter, it is said, from Nupe.[65]

It seems likely that Nupe's original success in driving the Alafin from his capital was due to its cavalry, and that Oyo began to expand when it began to import horses from the north, an expensive undertaking financed by obtaining European goods from the coast in return for slaves, and re-exporting them in return for horses and captives with the skills of grooms and cavalrymen.[66]

Abipa's successor was Obalokun, whose name means King at the Sea; tradition attributes the inception of Atlantic trade to his reign. He made a disastrous attempt to invade Ilesa, which lies south-east, in the forest zone, where horses were of little use.[67] He was succeeded by Ajagbo, remembered for his long reign and his military successes. He created the office of Are-One-Kakamfo – a war leader, based outside the capital, who was usually the ruler of a provincial town. A later Kakamfo was destined to play a decisive role in the empire's fortunes.

The eighteenth century was a period of expansion, and Oyo reached its greatest extent under Abiodun (d. 1789). But Johnson heads the relevant chapter, 'a succession of despotic and short-lived kings'; every Alafin between Ajagbo and Abiodun died a violent death, which may well reflect an unresolved tension in their relationship with their cabinet of great officials – the Oyo Mesi, headed by the Basorun. It has been suggested that the Alafins strengthened their own position by employing slave officials, the *ilari* in the palace, and the *ajele*, who collected tribute in the provinces and thus disrupted the balance of power. But the Alafins were chronically vulnerable, both because the Oyo Mesi could order their suicide and because the Basorun was also the head of the army. In a justly celebrated essay, Goody suggested that the use of firearms encouraged autocracy and the employment of slave soldiers, while the cost of acquiring and maintaining horses strengthened the aristocracy because, at least in West Africa, it required resources greater than those of even a great king.[68] The theory, though not universally accepted or applicable, may well shed light on the political fortunes of Oyo.

For twenty years the Basorun Gaha usurped effective power – he was overthrown by the Alafin Abiodun, with the help of provincial rulers, in 1774. In Johnson's traditional history, written in the late nineteenth century, Gaha is remembered as a were-elephant, who was defeated when old age weakened him and his magic failed.[69]

Under Abiodun, the Oyo state reached its greatest extent, and established control over a route to the sea, east of Dahomey's sphere of influence. Such was its importance that the Alafin's sons ruled the small towns on the way.[70]

Tradition remembers Abiodun's reign as an Indian summer of prosperity; before the deluge. 'In Abiodun's time we weighed our money in calabashes. In Awole's time we packed up to flee.'[71] But the process of decline was already evident – Oyo was defeated by the Borgu kingdom of Kaiama in 1783 and by Nupe in 1790.

The fall of Oyo

Few themes in West African history have been as extensively debated as the reasons for the fall of the Oyo empire. Traditional history ascribes it to the weakness of Awole and the effects of his dying curse. Modern historians vary in the relative emphasis they place on two sets of circumstances – the conflict between the Alafin and his high officials, and the breaking away of tributary states.

Abiodun overthrew Gaha with the help of provincial rulers. Awole was overthrown in 1796 in a revolt led by a provincial ruler, Afonja, the Kakamfo and governor of Ilorin. He had hoped for the throne; disappointed, he turned Ilorin into an independent principality. Oyo went through a period of near collapse – at one stage there were three Basoruns, and for a time the throne was vacant.[72]

In the late eighteenth century, the Egba revolted under the leadership of Lisabi the Liberator, killing the Ajele sent to collect tribute. Lisabi himself died in battle soon afterwards; he is remembered as a statesman and patriot, who fostered the export of kola nuts to the north and said that he fought so that the Egba could wear the finest cloth. Dahomey made an unsuccessful attempt to break away from Oyo in the reign of Agonglo (1789–97) and finally succeeded under Gezo, in 1823. Oddly enough, Oyo sovereignty survived longest in its remotest province – the Egbado corridor to the sea.

Afonja had revolted in alliance with Oyo Muslims, inviting a Fulbe cleric,

Salih ('Alimi'), to assist him. He may well have been influenced by the role of Mallam Dendo in Nupe; like the kings of Nupe and Borno, he had taken a step which would lead to his own destruction. In 1817, Alimi proclaimed a jihad, in which he was supported both by local Muslims and by the many northern Muslims who had become Oyo slaves. An enslaved Kanuri remembered: 'After I had been there four years, a war arose: now, all the slaves who went to the war became free, so when the slaves heard these good news, they all ran there.'[73] They protected kind masters, took revenge on harsh ones, and called themselves *jamaa*, like the first jihadists in Gobir. Afonja, who was not a Muslim, could not control the forces he had aroused, and he was killed in 1823/4. Alimi died at much the same time and his son, Abdulsalami, obtained a jihad flag from Sokoto and became the first emir of Ilorin.

Benin

Benin is a notable example of a kingdom which limited the export of slaves and encouraged alternative forms of commerce by deliberate state policy; the sale of male slaves – much more popular than women with European slavers[74] – was prohibited from the early sixteenth century to the end of the seventeenth. The Edo preserved the multiple character of trade by deliberate policy, going to the extent of forcing their customers to buy camwood they no longer needed.[75]

At first, copper, beads and textiles were imported in return for pepper and ivory, and for cloth and slaves, which were re-exported to the Gold Coast. African pepper was soon supplanted in European markets by Asian varieties. Foreign trade was marginal in the total life of the kingdom, but it reinforced the wealth and prestige of the court and reinforced – or created – the image of the great Olokun, god of the sea, source of beauty, wealth and creativity (notable in a landlocked kingdom). The Yoruba goddess of the sea, also Olokun, is similarly linked with wealth and creativity, as are the water spirits of the Niger Delta. Atlantic trade gave the Bini access to abundant copper, and led to a renaissance of Edo sculpture. There are over 900 copper plaques, which may well have been influenced by European book illustrations. The stylistic variety of Benin art reflects the abundance of imported copper. Why did the same thing not happen at Ife? Probably the tradition of bronze casting had died out before the advent of Atlantic trade.

Benin had whole quarters of craftsmen, ivory carvers, brass smiths, woodcarvers, leather fan makers and other specialists, such as astrologers and drummers. The prosperity of the craftsmen was proverbial. 'Smiths and woodworkers will never suffer from poverty.'[76]

In the sixteenth century, there was a series of warrior obas, one of whom successfully invaded Igala. The last of them, Ehengbuda, died in the creeks of Lagos at the beginning of the seventeenth century. Perhaps as a result of this disaster, the kings who followed were *rois fainéants*, living secluded in their palaces while their great officials ruled. At the end of the seventeenth century there was a civil war, and another powerful king, Akenzua, emerged triumphant. He reintroduced the export of male slaves, probably in order to rid himself of his enemies.

The history of Great States inevitably focusses on their rise and decline, and the fortunes of dynasties. But in any meaningful index of well-being, Benin was no less prosperous in the days when external expansion ended, and the obas lived in seclusion.

Small-scale polities: the Igbo

The Akan and Igbo social ideals of the Big Man – the Akan *obirempon* or Igbo *ogaranya* – were virtually identical, but in the centuries which saw the rise of Denkyira, Akwamu and Asante the Igbo continued to live in small-scale polities. This probably reflects cultural choices at the deepest level, choices no less real for being in large part unconscious. A geographer counted 2,240 separate village groups east of the Niger, to which we must add the western Igbo.

If taken literally, Igbo genealogies would suggest not only a considerable movement of peoples in the sixteenth and seventeenth centuries but a general pattern of migration in an anti-clockwise direction![77] This time depth, although considerable, does not reflect the great antiquity of settlement which population densities, dialectical differences and archaeology suggest. This is, in a sense, inevitable – genealogies are bound to undergo attenuation, especially since they are preserved in families, not by dynastic bards. But many of these traditions are mutually reinforcing, and if we reject them as memories of real events, we are left with a different problem – that of myriads of mutually corroborative genealogies, and other traditions.

There is some evidence that Igbo communities were moving towards larger groupings in the quest for security, and that these alliances were then described in a genealogical idiom – it is difficult to explain in any other way the cluster of towns which call themselves the Children of King Chima. An expanded volume of commerce, both between the small-scale states of Igboland and with their Cross River or Ibibio neighbours, seems to have encouraged the building of ritual linkages between them. The best known is undoubtedly that associated with Arochukwu.

The Arochukwu connection

Arochukwu is located on the Igbo–Ibibio borderland. By the time the earliest first-hand accounts were written, it consisted of nineteen villages, some of which claimed an Igbo, others an Ibibio and still others an 'Akpa' origin. The details of traditions of origin vary (in some, Igbo slaves rise against Ibibio overlords) but in general they tell of a war between Igbo and Ibibio villages, in which 'Akpa' armed with firearms played a decisive role. Genealogies suggest that these events occurred in the early seventeenth century; the mention of firearms may be an anachronism – like the tradition that a primal morass was dried by the bellows of an Awka smith! The Akpa may be a Cross River people; it is more likely that they came from southern Igbo market towns.[78] Some scholars take the dates these genealogies suggest fairly literally; others believe that these traditions have no historical foundation and are the mythical charters for the trade routes controlled by the different Aro villages.[79]

Oral traditions suggest that the Akpa had traded with the Delta before the advent of Atlantic trade, exchanging smoked meat, plantains and camwood for salt, fish and shrimps. The expansion of a small local shrine (according to some versions, an Ibibio shrine) into a great regional oracle is thought to have occurred soon after Arochukwu's foundation. In a sense it was exploitative – its fees, like those of other oracles, were high, and those it found guilty seem to have been sold abroad as slaves. It provided an impartial arbiter for local conflicts, and may well have prevented much bloodshed, but 800 western Ijo went to consult it in the 1890s, of whom only 136 returned.[80]

The Aro founded many settlements – an Aro local historian suggests 98 – the largest and best known of which were founded by trusted slaves. They were full-time merchants, trading in slaves and imported goods, and were probably the only Igbo group who did not farm, relying on food purchased from their neighbours. They formed a symbiotic relationship with martial Cross River Igbo who fought only for glory, and made use of their services when force was required. Their goods were carried, not by slaves, but by specialist contract porters. Both Aro at home (Aro *ulo*) and Aro abroad (Aro *uzo*) had a sense of common identity and pride which has never left them.

The Niger connection

On the lower Niger, linkages of a different kind flourished. Oral tradition suggests that a number of immigrants, some of Igbo origin and some from Igala, joined small existing riverain communities in the sixteenth and seventeenth centuries. In the nineteenth century, this kind of settlement was still going on, usually by Igala riverfarers who were thoroughly at home on the water, as were the people of the Igbo kingdom of Aboh, strategically located at the apex of the Niger Delta. Some riverain peoples were landlubbers, who took no part in canoe traffic and preferred to catch their fish in ponds – which is compatible with an original inland home. Tradition seems to suggest immigrant entrepreneurs, who responded to the opportunities of Atlantic trade, albeit at several removes from the frontier of direct contact. Nnebisi, the putative founder of Asaba, grew rich by ivory hunting, and used his wealth to acquire slaves.

The first European visitors to the lower Niger from 1830 on described an elaborate structure of interlocking markets, fed by canoe traffic governed by well-understood conventions. Traders from Nembe, Aboh and Igala brought trade goods in large canoes and exchanged them at a sandbank market near Asaba. There was another sandbank market north of Idah, which attracted trade canoes from Nupe and other regions further north. The Nupe travelled in big house-boats, where they lit fires, cooked and slept, and which could make 20–25 kilometres upstream a day, against a strong current.[81]

Although it doubtless expanded in the years of Atlantic trade, canoe commerce on the lower Niger is clearly much older.[82] There is a reference to trade in beads at Aboh ('Gaboe') in a seventeenth-century compilation,[83] and Opuu, the name Pereira used for the Igbo in the early sixteenth century, was, at least in the nineteenth century, a northern (Igala and Nupe) name for them, and may reflect north–south trade links.[84]

Awka[85]

In an earlier chapter, we noted the ritual pre-eminence of Nri over much of Igboland, and the ancient bronzes of Igbo-Ukwu. Awka is close to both, and in the nineteenth century (and undoubtedly much earlier) it was famous for its itinerant blacksmiths. Smithing was a jealously guarded craft, the preserve of certain villages, each of which had its own journey route to avoid competition. The smiths took it in turns to travel abroad, and it was compulsory to return home for the Otite festival, to ensure that all were safe. There were other famous communities of specialist iron workers – such as those of Abiriba. Like the travelling merchants of Arochukwu, the Awka smiths escorted clients to an oracle, in this instance dedicated to Agbala, the Earth. There were other oracles – one of the best known was called, significantly, Igwe-ka-Ala, Sky is greater than Earth.

Broker states of the south-east

A considerable number of small trading states grew up along the coast between the western Niger Delta and Cameroon. The many similarities between them are often masked by the fact that they spoke different languages – Itsekiri and Urhobo in the western Delta, Ijo in the central and eastern Delta, Efik in Calabar, and Duala in the Cameroon estuary. In modern times they are also divided by an international boundary. The Delta states which became famous in the centuries of Atlantic trade, such as Nembe (Brass), Bonny and Elim Kalabari, had been founded long before, perhaps by 1200. The Duala settlements date probably from the late sixteenth century, Calabar from the early seventeenth. There were and are many other Ijo villages in the Niger Delta, but only a small minority ever became involved in Atlantic trade. The Delta was a maze of waterways and mangrove swamps, and farming was out of the question. Its villages originally relied on exporting salt and dried fish, in large trade canoes, to the interior, in return for yams, livestock and other foods.[86] It was perhaps the villages already most involved in long-distance trade which exploited the new frontier of opportunity and developed a broker role.[87] Many of them even had to import the canoes on which all transport depended.

> Big as the mangrove grows
> It makes no canoes.
> The Nembe make no canoes.[88]

Atlantic trade modified local institutions in many ways. The building block of the social order was originally the lineage; the *amanyanabo* was the head of the village assembly. His powers increased in the era of Atlantic trade, as foreigner merchants paid *comey* (customs), and through his role as community spokesman, until he was described as a king. The lineage gave way to the Canoe House, a trading corporation which one could join, not only by being born into it, but by choice or by enslavement. It maintained the language and ideology of the family – the master was 'father'. The lowest level was that of the recently acquired slave, but through commercial acumen and ability it was possible to rise to House headship. The Canoe Houses went through a continuous process of fusion and fission, as weaker ones were absorbed by the more successful, and stronger ones produced new satellite Houses. Rival clusters of Canoe Houses contended for economic and political dominance.

The influx of Igbo slaves sometimes threatened to submerge Ijo language and culture – it was possible, in the early twentieth century, to write of 'the members of the Ibo tribe, who form the chief inhabitants of the Niger delta'.[89] The Kalabari developed social mechanisms to protect the hegemony of their own language and culture and in particular the Ekine cult acted as an agent of acculturation.[90] The Bonny people did not, and by the 1970s, were struggling to revive Ibani, which was near extinction.

There was an increasing gap between rich and poor – 'The fisherman who went where he wished in his fishing canoe became the "pullaboy" in a large trade canoe.'[91] Wealthy merchants accumulated valuables for which they often had little practical use and which were sometimes lost in the fires which periodically ravaged the Delta towns. King Perekule of Bonny 'accumulated and buried enormous manillas, silver and brass wares, demijohns of rum, arms and ammunition, copper rods for war canoes and numerous coral and glass beads'.[92] It is a classic instance of growth without development.

Calabar

The Efik of Calabar have a sense of distinct identity from the Ibibio hinterland, although they speak the same language. It is a good example of the uneven spread of historical research, that two substantial books have been written on Calabar,[93] while the history of the far more numerous Ibibio remains almost unknown.[94] The original home of the Efik was in Ibibioland, on the Enyong creek, near Arochukwu. They left it in *c.* 1550, sojourned for a time at Uruan and settled in Calabar in the early seventeenth century. Calabar was a conglomerate of settlements, best known to historians by their European names. The earliest was at Creek Town, followed by Old Town and Duke Town. Each was nearer the sea than its predecessor, which tradition ascribes to a desire to have better access to European shipping, and it would also seem inherently likely that the initial migration was also due to the attraction of Atlantic trade. The difficulty is that the first recorded vessel there was in 1668.[95] The growth of Arochukwu itself may well have been due to Atlantic trade – perhaps to a desire to play a broker role between the early port of Rio del Rey (east of Calabar) and the smiths of Abiriba. It is possible that the rise of Arochukwu and the foundation of Calabar were connected.[96]

The Ekpe relationship[97]

Ekpe or Ngbe was a secret mask cult which flourished in the Cross River area, in western Nigeria and eastern Cameroon. Both words mean leopard, and each Ekpe lodge had a stone which housed a leopard in astral form. A new lodge would buy Ekpe secrets from an existing one; each had a number of grades – there were nine in Calabar – which the initiate endeavoured to ascend, penetrating ever further into its secret/sacred lore. Ekpe transcended ethnic boundaries – it began among a small Cross River people, the Ekoi, and was adopted by some eastern Igbo clans, by the eastern Ibibio, and by the Efik. There is an excellent modern ethnography of Ekpe among the Banyang of Mamfe, in Cameroon.[98]

Like many other male cults, it was an important agency of social control, and through it initiates maintained their control over women and slaves. It was said of mid-nineteenth-century Calabar, 'The sound of "Egbo Bells" and the name of "Egbo Day" are enough to terrify all the slave population of Duketown.'[99] It was such an effective debt-collecting agency that some Europeans joined it. A government official, the ethnographer Amaury Talbot, who worked among the Ibibio and Ekoi from 1907 on, said of Ekpe, 'Before the coming of the white man this institution ruled the land, and even now it has more influence in many ways than government itself.'[100] Like the Arochukwu oracle, or the Lemba cult on the Zaire river, it provided a bridge between small ethnic groups and thus facilitated trade relationships. It may also have protected the successful against witchcraft accusations. Ekpe was much more than a form of government or a device for maintaining control over subordinate groups. Talbot wrote that 'a considerable amount of hypnotism, clairvoyance and spiritualism is taught ... some of the powers of Nature are known and utilised by initiates, in a way forgotten or unknown to their white rulers'.[101] The dimension of perceived mystical experience is easily overlooked in histories traditionally geared to Trade and Politics.

Nsibidi

A number of scripts were invented in West Africa in the nineteenth and twentieth centuries – the best known being those of the Vai of Liberia and the Bamum of Cameroon. These were alphabetic, and clearly a response to the stimulus of western forms of literacy. Nsibidi was a script found among a number of Cross River peoples which owed nothing to foreign exemplars – each symbol is an ideograph, as in Chinese. Because each symbol represented a concept, it could be used between peoples speaking different languages; over 500 signs are recorded, and there is reason to believe that they were only a small part of the whole. There are suggestions that it was used by the Ekpe society, but there is a record of a school where children were taught the signs. A curious aspect of Nsibidi, as recorded by three separate observers in the early twentieth century, was that many of the signs dealt with love affairs! It seems likely the ideographs dealing with religion and war were kept secret – and that the choice of signs to explain to European officials was an elaborate joke,[102] as well as a way of protecting the realm of the secret/sacred from outsiders.

The Duala

The Duala, like the Efik, were a small ethno-linguistic group, and have never numbered more than 20,000.[103] They developed a broker role in ivory, and there was a brief upsurge of the slave trade in the late eighteenth and early nineteenth centuries. The socio-political organisation was similar to that of the Niger Delta, dominated by Big Men or Merchant Princes, who headed Canoe Houses which acted as trading corporations, staffed with kin, slaves and voluntary recruits, and which contended for dominance. Slaves collected palm oil and kernels from the hinterland and often rose to positions of power and affluence, but when a man of slave descent founded a new 'town' he was put to death – though the town survived. Europeans called the major 'town' heads King Bell and King Akwa. There was a network of masking cults, common to the Duala and inland peoples; like Ekpe, they enforced debt repayment, filled a judicial role, and cemented links between those involved in trade relations. But whereas the Efik Big Men used Ekpe as an agent of social control, the slaves of Douala sometimes used mask societies to strengthen their position *vis-à-vis* the free and the Bell and Akwa segments tended to support rival masks. The dominant one, Jengu, was found among a number of peoples, including the 'Pygmy' Baka.[104]

A composite coastal culture

One result of the European presence on the coast was the growth of new and distinctive cultural forms. Some have described this complex as a trade culture, but its ramifications were much more far-reaching. Commercial conventions were, indeed, part of it; trade was regulated by commonly agreed conventions, which, especially in the nineteenth century included very extensive 'trust' or credit. Since European and African merchants did not share a common currency, they made extensive use of abstract units of account, to set a value on a wide range of different commodities, the ounce and accy of gold on the Gold Coast, and the iron bar in the Niger Delta.

As Austen points out in his valuable study of the Duala, inequality was built into many aspects of the relationship. White traders took African wives, and broker communities such as the Duala took wives from hinterland peoples, but not vice versa. Pidgins – English, French or Portuguese – flourished in the trade culture, and the languages of the coastal brokers often became a lingua franca further inland – Duala is an example. Europeans invented new names for their African trading partners, who, of course, had names already – it was a symbol and a reflection of inequality. Sometimes these new names indicated respect, or were neutral – Captain Hart, Duke Ephraim – but often they marginalised or ridiculed the recipient – Jumbo Manilla, Long John.

Some Efik learned to write, and perpetuated the knowledge in their own schools; the diary of an eighteenth-century Efik trader, written in pidgin, reflects this tradition.[105] On the Gold Coast, a few youths were taken to Europe by traders or missionaries, and some attained a high level of education, but none exercised much influence on his return. One of them wrote a treatise in Latin defending the slave trade; their profound cultural alienation was reflected in the fact that some forgot their mother tongue.[106]

Those of mixed African and European descent were often prominent in the trade culture; like the *prazeiros* in Zambezia, their descendants were soon almost indistinguishable from other Africans, except for their names and western dress. They tended to cling to Christianity to define their distinct identity, but were often marginalised by Europeans – 'profligate villains, a bastard race'.[107] In

Sierra Leone, they sometimes chose to reside on islands – another symbolic assertion of a distinct identity.

The coast culture manifested itself in many ways – we have noted the Afro-Portuguese ivories. In the tiny state of Warri, in the western Niger Delta, Catholicism was the religion of the court from the 1570s to the 1730s; unvisited by missionaries for long periods, its faith was sustained by the devotion of successive rulers. A king who came to power in 1733 turned against it, apparently because of drought. At the end of the eighteenth century, an English sailor described, in the palace, the relics of an age which was past: 'we were much surprised to see, placed on a rude kind of tablet, several emblems of the Catholic religion, consisting of crucifixes, mutilated saints, and other trumpery ... A large wooden cross, which had withstood the tooth of time, was remaining in a very perfect state, in one of the angles formed by two roads intersecting each other.'[108]

20

West Africa 1800 to 1870

> I ... do not see what concerns you in the affairs of Djoloff, Cayor, Baol, Sine and the rest of Saloum.
>
> Ma Ba to Faidherbe, in 1864[1]
>
> Trade is our sole object in West Africa.
>
> A British Foreign Office official, in 1898[2]

Europe and Africa, 1800–1870: a conspectus

The relations between Europe and tropical Africa were gradually transformed in the course of the nineteenth century. The transatlantic slave trade slowly drew to a close, a process which in West Africa was not completed until the 1860s. Various forms of 'legitimate trade' developed, but insofar as commodities were produced, gathered or transported by slave labour, the change was often more apparent than real. As late as 1906, Adansi chiefs pointed out their reliance on domestic slaves – if they were freed, 'then no more towns in Ashanti ... all our drums, blowing horns, swords, elephant tail basket carrying and farming works are done by these'.[3]

In many cases, the decline of the slave trade began before its abolition, and the growth of legitimate trade occurred independently and began in the slave trade era. An emphasis on European 'abolition' is now seen as just one more variant of a Eurocentric history.

Paradoxically, the anti-slavery movement reinforced white racism, a sense of moral superiority which conveniently overlooked the fact that it was European slavers who created the Atlantic slave trade in the first place. 'When I told one, this morning, that the slave trade was a bad thing, and that White people worked to put an end to it altogether, he gave me an excellent answer. "Well, if White people give up buying, Black people will give up selling slaves."'[4]

The foreign presence looms large in historical studies of the nineteenth century, mainly because they tend to be based on source material written by imperial proconsuls, foreign traders and missionaries. The result is both misleading and Eurocentric, a narrative dominated by the decline of the Atlantic slave trade, the growth of 'legitimate' trade, and colonial or quasi-colonial encroachment. It is easy to forget that the lives of many African communities were little affected by these changes.[5] Even on the Gold Coast, where European forts and trading posts had existed for centuries, local trade was more important, and the Fante sometimes stopped foreign trade for years at a time: 'The wants of the natives [the Fante] are few and those easily satisfied.'[6] The emir of Kontagora once said that Europeans were fish, who would die if they left the Niger.[7] By 1870, colonial or quasi-colonial jurisdictions were still confined, in the main, to small coastal enclaves. Even in Senegal, the French sphere was effectively confined to the coastal commercial centres and a few forts and trading posts on the Senegal river.

The impact of industrial capitalism

In Europe, the eighteenth century was a time of transition between merchant and industrial capitalism.[8] It was once claimed that it was the profits of centuries of international trade – or more specifically, of slave plantations and the slave trade – which made the Industrial Revolution possible; but as we saw in an earlier chapter, the links are by no means self-evident, and the whole question is, like the factors underlying the Scramble for Africa in the 1880s, much debated by scholars working in this field.

Industrial capitalism required both imported raw materials and external markets; cotton manufacturing, which was central to its development in Britain, was totally dependent on both. When Britain enjoyed an unchallenged industrial dominance, it did not need tropical colonies with their associated human and financial costs, to sustain its economic interests. Much of the Scramble was to be motivated by a fear that other nations would establish colonies and surround them with tariff walls: 'the scheme ... for keeping the French away from the Niger & Oil Rivers'.[9] But Free Trade was more than a stratagem which suited the most advantaged competitor. To many, it embodied a compelling dream of international co-operation and harmony, almost part and parcel of Christianity itself.

Not all authorities agree that 'the' Industrial Revolution occurred at all (some emphasise a long sequence of innovations rather than a sudden change) but it is clear that, from about 1750 onwards, revolutionary developments took place in the technology of production, with the first advances being in the British textile industry. In 1760, the machines used in British cotton textile manufacture were 'nearly as simple as those of India'[10] – or Africa. A familiar succession of inventions, among them Hargreaves' spinning jenny (1770) and Crompton's 'mule' (1779), meant that by 1825 it took 135 hours of human effort to spin 100 pounds of cotton, a task which would require 50,000 hours of manual spinning.[11] The power loom had a similar effect on weaving. In the eighteenth century, the new technology was powered by the traditional means of wind and water; in the nineteenth, the invention of the steam engine revolutionised not only factory production but also both land and ocean transport.

It has often been pointed out that Africa played a comparatively minor role in the global picture of European commerce – 'at no time did West Africa account for as much as one per cent of total British trade'.[12] French trade with black Africa comprised 'a derisory 0.65 per cent of total French commerce'.[13] Even Egyptian cotton was subsidiary to the main source – the southern United States, – though one that became crucially important during the American civil war.

Foreign encroachment, however, was motivated as much by the possibility of future profits as by present realities ... 'The mills of Manchester ... will yet shout for joy through the cotton wealth of the Niger districts'.[14] The Niger districts, in fact, despite growing cotton for local looms, continued to export palm oil. Asaba people, when urged by the Royal Niger Company to plant cotton, thwarted the project by first boiling the seeds!

Commerce and Christianity[15]

There was a great expansion of Christian missionary involvement in Africa in the nineteenth century. It was rooted, often unconsciously, in the same profound sense of moral and cultural superiority, and the belief that technological advance and other forms of progress went hand in hand; sometimes Christianity and technological development seemed to be inseparable. In June 1840, there was a great meeting at Exeter Hall, to discuss the proposed Niger expedition. One of the speakers said: 'there was no worldly policy so sure as that which was based on Christianity ... He anticipated the day when they might obtain wool and indigo in great quantities from Africa ... Africa was populous and the population was unsophisticated; might not artificial wants be created for them?'[16]

Queen Victoria advised Sagbua, and other Abeokuta rulers, in 1848: 'commerce alone will not make a nation great and happy, like England. England has become great and happy by the knowledge of the true God and Jesus Christ.'[17]

When Livingstone prepared to return to the Zambezi, he said – the unconscious ordering of his words is significant – 'I go back to Africa to make an open path for commerce and Christianity.' 'The Book says you are to grow cotton, and the English are to come and buy it,' explained his interpreter.[18]

Much has been written on nineteenth-century missionaries, but outside Freetown they had, for the most part, little impact, their teachings appealing in the main to the disinherited of traditional society, the witches and the slaves. When the CMS founded a mission in Bonny in 1864, it was slaves who initially welcomed its teachings; they built little chapels in the inland markets, where they repeated, word for word, the sermon they had heard in the mission church. Their masters were not pleased – 'they never sent their boys to be "Bishops" in Ibo, but to "Trade"'.[19]

In 1897, after decades of missionary endeavour on the lower Niger, a CMS worker there wrote, 'In a small district we perhaps touch one percent of the people ...'[20]

The decline of the Atlantic slave trade

In 1807, the British Parliament passed legislation prohibiting its own nationals from taking part in the slave trade; it was not the first nation to do so – the Danes passed such a law in 1792, which came into effect ten years later – but it was a significant step, since in the eighteenth century two-thirds of all slaves exported to the New World were carried in British ships. Other nations followed suit, often as a result of diplomatic pressure, and a British naval squadron off the West African coast enforced the ban; nine-tenths of slaving vessels eluded it, but it was an undoubted deterrent. (There were also French and American squadrons, liberating captives at Libreville and Monrovia, respectively, but the small numbers landed reflected the limited nature of their operations.)

There is no more telling commentary on the inadequacies of 'abolition' and anti-slavery squadrons than the fact that between 1800 and 1870 an estimated 552,500 slaves were exported from the Bight of Benin, 407,500, from the Bight of Bonny (Biafra) and 326,000 from the vast extent of coastline from Senegal to the Gold Coast.[21] These figures may be compared with the 160,000 released by the naval squadron.

The export of slaves ended at different times in different places – it was already in decline by 1807 on the Gold Coast, and ended there in the 1820s,[22] a process reflected in the Asantehene's decision, in 1822, not to accept slaves as tribute any longer.[23] Most Niger Delta ports stopped exporting slaves in the 1830s; the trade lasted longest in Nembe, which was relatively inaccessible – an 1857 visitor recorded that the last slaver had called three years earlier, and that the barracoons had fallen into disrepair.[24] The involvement of Lagos in Atlantic trade began in the 1760s, with the export of slaves and Ijebu cloth.[25] The former ended when a British consul was stationed there in 1851, beginning the erosion of the small principality's sovereignty. It became a British colony ten years later. In the Windward Coast (modern Liberia and Ivory Coast) the slave trade declined from the 1820s on and disappeared in about 1840.[26] It lingered until 1864 in the region between Sierra Leone and Guinea, which the British called the Northern Rivers and the French the Rivières du Sud.

'Legitimate trade' and domestic slavery

As the Atlantic slave trade gradually declined, it was replaced by what is often called legitimate trade – the export of primary products. The volume of this trade, and of the goods imported (which vastly exceeded the imports of earlier centuries) was remarkable. Exports included palm oil, peanuts, ivory, gum and hardwoods; at a period later than that covered by this book, palm kernels, wild rubber and cocoa were added to the list. In 1879, Tetteh Quarsheh brought cocoa seedlings from Fernando Po to Akwapim. It is seen in modern Ghana as a symbolic turning point, but in fact the Basle mission had introduced cocoa in the 1860s, and it had been taken up enthusiastically, often by pioneer Christians such as David Asante.[27] It spread to western Nigeria in the 1880s. Liberia exported the world's finest coffee, until, in 1876, specimens were sent to a Trade Fair in America; Brazil acquired these varieties, and Liberian coffee exports declined.

With the exception of coffee, cocoa and peanuts, these products were hunted or collected in a wild state, rather than emanating from the core of African productive activity – farming, pastoralism or craftsmanship.[28] Although 'legitimate' in comparison with the slave trade, they often depleted an irreplaceable natural resource, such as the forests of Sierra Leone. This was not peculiar to Africa. In Canada, the beaver frontier receded before the Iroquois, and on its Pacific coast the sea otter became a rarity.

In Europe, palm oil was used in the manufacture of soap, of candles and, before the discovery of mineral oil in California in 1850, as a lubricant. It was also used as a coating in the process of tin plate manufacture.[29] Palm oil production was a traditional but extremely labour-intensive activity, usually organised on gender lines. Men (often, slaves) cut down the clusters of nuts – a task which sometimes led to injury or death – and women extracted the oil, which was originally used in traditional cuisine. Its export had begun during the slave trade era – palm oil and pepper flavoured the carbohydrate staple given to the slaves during the Middle Passage, and Calabar was an important exporter of palm oil from the eighteenth century on.[30]

In the first half of the nineteenth century, the palm oil and slave trades co-existed. In a map published in 1823 the eastern Niger Delta and Calabar are called the Palm Oil Coast;[31] by the 1850s, it was exporting 16,000 tons of palm oil annually,[32] as against 4,000 to 5,000 tons from Lagos, and 7,000 tons from Whydah and Porto Novo.[33]

Because it was bulky and difficult to transport, palm oil could only be exported where navigable rivers flowed. At first the palm kernels were discarded; later they too became an important element in export trade, a development pioneered by the Sierra Leone Eur-African, Charles Heddle. Four hundred nuts had to be cracked to produce a pound of kernels. They were to be used in the manufacture of margarine (invented in 1869) and for cattle food.

There was less demand for palm oil in France, because of consumer resistance to yellow soap! Peanut oil, however, could be used to make soap of the desired hue (blue). Peanuts are indigenous to Latin America, and were introduced to West Africa in the sixteenth century. Their commercial production began on the Gambia in the early 1830s, and in Senegal in the early 1840s,[34] and by the 1880s the region was exporting some 29,000 tonnes of unshelled peanuts a year.

The growth of peanut exports brought with it a demographic and socio-economic revolution. Free migrant workers came from great distances in the interior to grow peanuts commercially. By 1848, 'The Sera-Wollies [Sarakollé] and Telli-Bunkas ["people of the east", i.e. Mandinka/Bambara] ... frequently [came] from distances of not less than 500 or 600 miles in the interior'.[35] These migrants were to play a leading role in the Soninke wars on the Gambia. Whereas the slave trade strengthened 'kings and rich men', the peanut trade strengthened the peasantry,[36] who supported a succession of marabouts against both rulers and the powerful slave soldiers, *tyeddo*. In time, the *tyeddo* died out as a separate class and became one with the peasantry. Many became Mourides, joining a new brotherhood founded by Ahmadu Bamba (1850–1927). They devoted themselves to agriculture, and found in this new *tariqa* a measure of social and economic security in a rapidly changing world. The new export commodities were not, of course, evenly distributed – the Niger Delta and Calabar exported palm oil, Sierra Leone hardwoods, the Senegambia peanuts, Mauretania gum. Gum, collected on the desert edge, was an input in European textile manufacture – by 1800, its exports were equal in value to those of slaves on the Senegambia. They boomed between the 1830s and 1850s, and ultimately declined because of the increasing use of artificial substitutes.[37] Camwood, a dye wood exported from Sierra Leone for centuries, was similarly supplanted by chemical dyes.

By the nineteenth century, the elephant populations near the coast were almost extinguished; ivory never had a dominance in West African export trade comparable with its role in East and Central Africa, though small quantities were exported at a number of different ports. In Asante, royal elephant hunters were among the select few who enjoyed royal protection on the Great Roads, but ivory was so scarce that much had to be imported from Kong, and the transition from tribute paid in slaves to tribute paid in gold and ivory created problems. It was said in 1820 that 'the difficulty of paying the annual Tribute in Gold or Ivory is so much greater than when it was paid in Slaves that almost every district is in a state of insurrection'.[38]

A number of independent studies have shown how trans-Saharan trade, far from being eclipsed by the sea-borne traffic of the nineteenth century, actually expanded. In the early nineteenth century, the ivory from Adamawa and northern Cameroon sold to Europeans on the coast was estimated at 60 tons.[39] By the 1850s, much of it was being deflected, by the enterprise of Hausa traders, to trans-Saharan routes, with the result that 50 tons were exported across the desert annually, and only 6 to 10 from the Cameroon coast. From the 1860s, much of it was acquired by European merchants on the Niger and Benue. Sixty tons of ivory represented the slaughter of 2,000 elephants; it was used for knife handles, piano keys, combs and billiard balls. So much for 'legitimate trade'.

We have seen how less than 1 per cent of Europe's trade was with Africa; African producers of vegetable oils competed with other sources of oil – tallow from Australia and elsewhere, cottonseed oil from the United States and sesame oil from Egypt – and with other sources of the same commodities, such as peanuts from India (especially after the opening of the Suez Canal). They had little control over prices, which were affected by worldwide changes. A Gold Coast palm oil trader 'rapidly glanced over his dispatches and suddenly shouted – "Hurrah for my oil! There's a murrain among the cattle in Russia; my oil must go up." And so it did.'[40]

Where Europeans attempted to establish farms or plantations on African soil, they invariably failed. In the 1820s, the French attempted to cultivate cotton and indigo on the Senegal. It was a failure, as was the model farm set up at Lokoja during the 1841 Niger expedition and immortalised by Dickens as Mrs Jellaby's Borioboola-Gha.[41] Many expatriates came to realise that they had less expertise in tropical agriculture than the African farmer. An agriculturist from Toronto who came to Nigeria at the beginning of the twentieth century 'with the aim of teaching the natives improved methods of cultivation' discovered that 'he had nothing to teach them'.[42]

Domestic slavery

Where export commodities were produced or transported by slave labour, the transition was essentially one from the export of slaves to the expansion of domestic slavery in Africa. Much the same price was obtained for a slave and for a ton of palm oil, which took 250 days to process.[43]

There is some evidence that human sacrifice expanded in the nineteenth century – when the external demand for slaves disappeared, prices fell, and it became correspondingly less expensive.[44] Human sacrifice seems to have expanded in Benin from the 1830s on, perhaps because the king responded to a sense of encirclement and threat by recourse to ritual.[45] Human sacrifice definitely increased in the Niger Igbo town of Asaba, in the late nineteenth century.[46] But it was said of Aboh (where forty slaves, purchased for the purpose, were sacrificed at the funeral of Obi Ossai in 1845), 'this practice is gradually dying out at Abó, if it is not altogether extinct'.[47] There seem to have been two contradictory impulses at work – towards an expansion of human sacrifice, as slaves became cheaper, and a tendency to reject it, sometimes in response to western influences. In the Efik state of Calabar, 300 slaves were killed at Duke Ephraim's death in 1834,[48] but in 1850–1, the slaves banded together as the 'Blood Men' and obtained the abolition of the practice.[49]

Slave revolt and flight seem to have become more common in the nineteenth century – or perhaps they are more fully documented. We saw in an earlier chapter how slaves fled to Ningi; they took control of Warri, in a time of crisis, and intervened in Calabar life, as we have seen, by immensely effective joint action. The slaves of Ondo played a decisive role in a civil war in the 1850s; they did not seek a social revolution – as in Warri, those involved were palace slaves, loyal to a particular prince.[50]

Flight was more common than revolt. When the Landers visited the Egbado town of Ijanna, they observed: 'Perhaps the extraordinary decrease in the population of Jenna has arisen from the desertion of slaves, who embrace the opportunity, whilst their masters are from home ... of running away.'[51] It became much more common when colonial jurisdictions were imposed; the numbers resident in the palace in the Yoruba kingdom of Owo fell from 3,000 to 100, as both wives and slaves ran away.[52]

A challenge to governments

It has been suggested that the end of the slave trade caused a 'crisis of the aristocracy'.[53] The argument is that the slave trade generated wealth for an elite, while the export of palm oil or peanuts put profits in the hands of the peasant producer. The total quantity of imports increased and prices fell, suggesting that goods from abroad became more generally available.[54] The experience of the Senegambia supports a model of traditional rulers and their traditional entourage in crisis, and an empowered peasantry, but one should not exaggerate the democratisation of external trade. 'None but kings and great men trade here, the same as myself.'[55]

The Asantehene, Osei Bonsu, also pointed out the dangers of accumulating captives – who, at the time, numbered 20,000. 'Unless I kill or sell them, they will grow strong and kill my people.'[56] Glele of Dahomey told a visitor in 1863, 'the customs of his country compelled him to make war, and that unless he sold he must slay his captives.'[57]

The slave revolt the Asantehene feared sometimes eventuated. 'In 1756 the slaves of Foutah Jallon revolted, and declaring themselves free, left the country in great force, and proceeding towards Foutah Boundou, built and established themselves in a strong town ... which was repeatedly attacked by the Soolimas and Foulahs without success.'[58]

Rulers often responded to the decline of the slave trade by appealing for what would now be called development aid. In 1842, an Efik ruler wrote from Calabar:

We can't sell slaves again, we must have too many men for country, and want something for make work and trade. And if we have some seed for cotton and coffee we could make trade, plenty sugar cane live here; and if some man would come teach way for do it, we get plenty sugar too; and then come man must come teach book proper.[59]

It has been said of modern Calabar that its main form of production is independent churches!

In 1848, the chiefs of Abeokuta wrote to Queen Victoria: 'We want ... those who will teach our children mechanical arts, agriculture, and how things are prepared, as tobacco, rum and sugar.'[60]

Ghezo ruled Dahomey from 1818 to 1858. In 1848, he explained his predicament, as he perceived it:

The state which he maintained was great, his army was expensive ... [The palm oil trade] was a slow method of making money, and brought only a very small amount of duties into his coffers. The planting of coffee and cotton had been suggested to him; but this was slower still. He held his power by an observance of the time-honoured customs of his forefathers; and he would forfeit it, and entail upon himself a life full of shame, and a death of misery, if he neglected them.[61]

In 1841, the British signed a treaty with Ossai, the ruler of Aboh, in which they promised regular commercial visits if he stopped trading in slaves; the next steamer arrived in 1851. By then, Ossai was dead. The nineteenth century provides many interesting examples of selective modernisation. Jaja did not see Christianity as part of modernity, and remained attached to traditional religion throughout his life; he founded a secular school with an expatriate teacher and attempted to break the stranglehold of expatriate firms over the export trade. In Dahomey, Ghezo limited human sacrifice, restricted the death penalty and campaigned against alcoholism[62] and reflected on what should be changed and what retained.

As many of the old absurd customs, which still existed, were of a comparatively harmless nature, he had hitherto permitted them to remain, as he considered it dangerous amongst a people so long accustomed to these usages to revolutionise the whole at once; but he approved of commencing with the most unreasonable and injurious, and gradually progressing, as in fact he had done.[63]

Open and closed societies

The dialectic between African societies and colonial jurisdictions and other manifestations of a foreign presence has resonances which go far beyond 'resistance', or 'new elites', or 'mission'. The challenge to traditional rulers lay as much in the mind as in the changing structure of export trade. It was, in a sense, a transition from a closed society to an open one, though probably its earlier state was more 'open' than this formulation would allow. African states were both challenged and undermined by the presence of alternatives. In 1859, the

Balogun of Ibadan supported the right of the crown prince Adelu to succeed his father as Alafin of Oyo, rather than die with him, pointing out that 'as many of the Yoruba laws were broken through the late wars, and we had come to a new time, he did not see why the law concerning the successor should not be broken too'.[64]

Adelu was able to challenge the conventions of Oyo society; the vast majority were powerless to effect change in this way, but often registered their dissatisfaction with the status quo by moving. Many emigrated from Asante to the coast in search of greater economic opportunities, and it is no coincidence that many of the early converts to Christianity were drawn from the enslaved, lepers, mothers of twins, old women thought to be witches. The black Settlers and Recaptives of Sierra Leone and Liberia had moved still further from traditional worlds. With profound irony, when they attempted to create a new society, it was built in the image of the oppressor, complete, in the case of the latter, with Capitol and Senate.

The overthrow of Agonglo, king of Dahomey, in 1797, may have been due to his apparent readiness to become a Catholic.[65] Osei Kwame, Asantehene from 1777 to 1801, lost his throne because of his sympathy for Islam. 'These and other innovations were of a tendency to alarm the great captains; they feared, it is said, that the Moslem religion, which they well know levels all ranks and orders of men, and places them at the arbitrary discretion of the sovereign, might be introduced.'[66] At Bonny, where a mission was introduced in 1864, it was said, 'the fear of some of the Chiefs is that, should Christianity progress more than it is now ... civilised ideas naturally will follow & a revolution may take place'.[67]

Asante and Fante

Asante's period of imperial greatness lasted little more than a hundred years. The first Asantehene died in 1717 (or perhaps 1712) and the kingdom reached the zenith of its power in the reign of Osei Bonsu (1801–24). As in Oyo, this occurred immediately before a decline.

The nineteenth-century histories of Asante and of the small Fante states on the coast are inextricably interwoven. It is paradoxical that Asante conquered powerful northern kingdoms such as Gonja but never succeeded in establishing lasting control over the much smaller polities on the coast, despite repeated invasions in the eighteenth century. Various explanations have been put forward for this, among them the fact that the Fante had direct access to the sellers of firearms – but the Asante (who did their best to prevent their northern neighbours from acquiring them)[68] imported firearms in large quantities – a report of 1742 refers to an Asante regiment of 5,000 musketeers.[69] The Fante states succeeded in acting together in times of crisis. It is possible that Asante rulers hesitated to come into too close a proximity to the European settlements on the coast, with the implicit challenge they presented to Asante values.

There is more evidence about the motives for such an invasion – not least, resentment at the exactions of coastal middlemen, and their not infrequent disruptions of trade. 'Ashantees take good gold to Cape Coast, but the Fantees mix it ... ten handkerchiefs are cut to eight, water is put to rum.'[70] The invasion of the coast in 1807, however, was occasioned not by economic considerations, but by the fact that the Fante sheltered two chiefs who were refugees from the Asantehene's wrath. The Asante were initially successful, and the king took the name Bonsu, Whale. But the Fante never accepted Asante suzerainty, and a succession of wars followed; the coastal region bore the brunt of it all, and Dupuis, perhaps with some exaggeration, wrote that in much of Fante and Assin 'the population [is] extinct, the plantations more or less destroyed, and the forest relapsing to its original growth'.[71] Some towns were abandoned, among them Abora. It reminds us that war and depopulation were not always caused by the slave trade.

The British tended to ally with the Fante, the Dutch with Asante. An eighteenth-century governor analysed the underlying considerations. 'The Dutch ... urge the insolence of the Fantees ... Whereas, say they, if the whole Gold Coast was under one powerful prince, there would be only him to satisfy ... but ought they not to consider that we derive the supremest Advantage from the mixt government of the Fantees?'[72]

It has been said that in 1823–4, the fourth Fante–Asante war became the first Anglo-Asante war,[73] but it was not British intervention but Fante patriotism which prevented Asante from conquering to the sea. Two years later, the Asante suffered a crushing defeat at the battle of Katamanso. The forces which defeated them – largely by means of new technology, the Congreve Rockets – comprised sixty Europeans and some 12,000 Africans.[74]

His chosen name symbolised the importance of the southern factor, but Osei Bonsu felt a profound sympathy for northerners and Muslims; some of his correspondence was conducted in Arabic, using Muslim scribes, and there was a Muslim school in Kumasi.[75] But he also employed a Dutchman as a secretary, and the Kumasi elite stood between two world religions and two forms of literacy. An Asante prince, John Owusu Ansa (1822–84), was educated abroad in the 1830s, and later worked devotedly in Asante service; he and his sons were to be leading advocates of westernisation.

The ending of the Atlantic slave trade was an inconvenience rather than a catastrophe. Palm oil exports began on the Gold Coast in the 1840s, but were always insignificant in comparison with those of the Niger Delta – 1,870 tons a year in the 1850s.[76] It was impracticable for the Asante to take part in this; they exported some ivory to the coast, and gold both to the north and to the south, but with reluctance, both because supplies were limited and because they preferred to retain the latter, the core symbol of their culture. They obtained luxury cloth in the north in return for salt, kola and small amounts of European goods.[77]

The trade route which ran from the Akan area through Gonja to Hausaland was much older than these events. According to the 'Kano Chronicle', it was in the reign of Yakubu, in the mid-fifteenth century, that 'merchants from Gwanja began coming to Katsina'. The trade expanded greatly in the late eighteenth and nineteenth centuries, and many Hausa merchants settled permanently along the route. A new market town grew up at Salaga, which was, claimed Dupuis, twice the size of Kumasi.[78] The kola trade generated income which was used to purchase firearms, ammunition and imported iron at the coast. It was not until cocoa production developed, from the 1880s on, that a major export crop, in

demand in European markets, was available. It is important to remember that
here, as elsewhere, local production and markets were far more important than
export trade and agriculture and cloth manufacture flourished, as did the
goldsmiths' art.

Years of decline

The years after the death of Osei Bonsu are usually depicted as, in the words of
an eminent Ghanaian historian, a period of 'decline, disintegration and
defeat'.[79] This is, of course, to equate 'rise' and 'decline' with empire; the sphere
of Asante hegemony shrank to north of the Pra, and the central government was
weakened by a civil war in 1831.

There was an enduring division of opinion among the Kumasi elite about the
desirability of war, especially in the south, which was often mirrored in the
sensibility of individuals. Osei Bonsu himself, veteran campaigner that he was,
claimed, with some justice, 'that it was a maxim associated with the *religion he
professed* never to appeal to the sword while a path lay open for negotiation'.[80]
Kwaka Dua reigned from 1834 to 1867; for most of this time, he supported the
peace party. Late in his reign, he yielded to pressure and embarked on a number
of campaigns, including one to the south.

McCaskie writes perceptively of the transitions of the mid-nineteenth century:

> It was in this period that Asante became massively exposed to novel options, to
> different (and even contradictory) ways of looking at the world ... This period
> represented a watershed in the understanding of values and beliefs ... The 'genera-
> tion' of 1880 was further removed from that of 1830 than that 'generation' had been
> from any of its predecessors throughout Asante history.[81]

He stresses the rapacity of Kwaka Dua, the frequency of executions, the many
Asante who sought security and new frontiers of opportunity in the south.[82]
Significantly, his invasion of the south was occasioned by the harbouring of a
fugitive who contravened an Asante law against keeping gold nuggets. He was
the last Asantehene to create a Golden Tail.

The next Asantehene, Kofi Karikari (1867–74), swore at his coronation that
his 'business should be war'. There was a further invasion of the south, which led
to a 'British' invasion of Kumasi, which succeeded largely because its troops
were equipped with up-to-date weaponry, including Enfield rifles. Like other
colonial wars, it was fought largely by black troops. Kumasi was sacked and a
huge indemnity in gold exacted; the king was deposed on charges of plundering
the treasures from the royal graves, charges which, of course, reflected his
impoverishment.

The Gold Coast

The numbers of the western-educated expanded greatly in the mid-nineteenth
century, largely as a result of the growth of mission schools. By the mid-
nineteenth century, nearly a thousand children were being educated by the
Wesleyan Methodists' schools, and it was said of them that they would 'bear a

comparison of their proficiency with English children of the same standing'. Many chiefs had a secretary – often a son – and humbler individuals made use of the western-educated as scribes, producing a large volume of written communication.[83] Princes were often among the first Christians – in a matrilineal system, they had no claim to the throne.

Many observers commented on the Fante passion for trade. In the words of a book published in 1853, 'There was not a nook or corner of the land to which the enterprize of some sanguine trader had not led him', including Kumasi.[84] Fante traders carried Christianity far into the interior; a Methodist mission was established in Kumasi in 1843, but languished, 'the people being afraid to expose themselves to the ire of the king, whose frown is indeed death for people becoming Christians'.[85]

In about 1850, the iron steamer replaced the wooden sailing ship as the standard form of ocean-going transport.[86] Trading operations and ownership of shipping – which went together in the slave trade era – were separated, and it became possible for African merchants to become importers and exporters on their own account. Some attained considerable wealth – 'There were merchant princes in those days'[87] – which was often invested in the education of their children.

In the mid-nineteenth century, a number of Africans held high positions in Gold Coast local government. James Bannerman, a Eur-African and prosperous merchant, served as Lieutenant-Governor in 1850, and came close to being appointed Governor. James Africanus Horton and W. B. Davies, British-trained doctors from Sierra Leone, served on the Gold Coast; the writings of the former were to make a remarkable contribution to local political developments.

The pattern of socio-political change was profoundly paradoxical – at the very time a western-educated elite developed, with a commitment to constitutional self-government, the autonomy of African polities was steadily eroded.

At the beginning of the eighteenth century, Bosman stated that the English and the Dutch had the same power in 'Fantyn', 'that is, none at all'.[88] At the beginning of the nineteenth the British, Danes and Dutch all held forts on the Gold Coast. Their relationship to local states was that of tenant and landlord; the 'Notes' which recorded this, and the payments made accordingly, loomed large in African conflicts.

The British forts belonged to the Company of Merchants; founded in the slave trade era, the company did not prosper, and in 1821 the forts were placed under the Governor of Sierra Leone. It was, it was said, like trying to govern Barbados from Cork.[89] In 1824, the Governor of Sierra Leone, Sir Charles MacCarthy, died fighting the Asante. In the wake of this disaster, it was decided to give up the forts on the Gold Coast, but when protests were made, it was decided to hand them over to a Council of Merchants. Its President was George Maclean, who reached the Gold Coast in 1830, and remained there until he died in 1847. The history of those years was later summarised by the elected king of Cape Coast. 'In the days of Governor MacLean, the Governor in a very peculiar, imperceptible and unheard of manner wrested from the hands of our Kings, Chiefs, and head men their power to govern their own subjects.'[90]

In 1843 the Crown took over the forts again; in 1844, a series of treaties, known collectively as the Bond, formalised the legal powers which Maclean had acquired informally. In 1850 the Gold Coast became a colony separate from Sierra Leone, and the British purchased the Danish forts. Two separate enclaves remained in Dutch hands, which made it impossible to generate revenue from customs. An attempt was made to introduce direct taxation – a poll tax – which generated so much hostility that it was abandoned. It was opposed because most of the proceeds went on the costs of collection, and only 8 per cent on roads and schools.[91]

In 1865, a Select Committee of the House of Commons looked into the whole question of British possessions in West Africa. It resolved that new acquisitions of territory would be 'inexpedient', 'and that the object of our policy should be to encourage in the natives the exercise of those qualities which may render it possible for us more and more to transfer to them the administration of all the Governments, with a view to our ultimate withdrawal from all, except, probably, Sierra Leone'.[92] Its contents were soon known to the Gold Coast elite, who naturally believed that their aspirations were compatible with British policy. It was one of the factors which led to the creation of the Fante Confederation, West Africa's first experiment in western-style democracy.

The Fante Confederation

Africanus Horton's book, *West African Countries and Peoples*, included a political blueprint for a Kingdom of Fante and a Republic of Accra.[93] The Fante Confederation was a deliberate attempt to put his ideas into practice. It drew on the tradition of popular agitation which had opposed the poll tax, and anxiety both at the Asante invasion of 1863, and at a proposal, never implemented, to exchange forts with the Dutch – since local people were not consulted, they felt themselves to be, in the words of the *African Times*, bartered like bullocks.

Three successive constitutions were drawn up, at meetings where Methodists played a dominant role. The second, adopted in 1871, owed much to the writings of Africanus Horton. It made provision for a king/president and national and representative assemblies. A seal was struck and a supreme court created. But the movement soon collapsed, partly because of internal rivalries, partly because Britain acquired the forts of the Dutch, Asante's traditional allies, so that the peril which had driven the Fante together seemed to recede. Begun in the confidence of British support, the movement could not withstand British hostility, especially since its leaders were educated men who looked largely to the colonial government for employment.

In 1865, Joseph Aggrey was elected king of Cape Coast. A tireless critic of British encroachment,[94] he was deported to Sierra Leone for his temerity, and died soon after his return.

The cultural encounters of the coast took many forms. The *asafo* of the Fante[95] were first described in the mid-nineteenth century, but are clearly older. Originally regiments, they are now ceremonial bands; some have women's sections. Members wore elaborate uniforms and carried flags. One Cape Coast company had a Union Jack and a side drum among its emblems, another a bugle, a telescope and a clock.[96] This kind of parody of the paraphernalia of power was very common, and the Asante contructed imitation telegraph poles after the invasion of Kumasi.

Dahomey

Both Asante and Dahomey were states with a strong ideological commitment to war and a history of eighteenth-century expansion. Dahomey, unlike Asante, had succeeded in conquering to the sea, but whereas Asante ruled a vast northern empire, Dahomey paid tribute to the northern kingdom of Oyo. In the Gold Coast, the European presence developed gradually into a colonial state. In southern Dahomey, until the late nineteenth century, foreigners had no independent power, and the Brazilian slaver Francesco Felix da Souza (d. 1849) was in royal employ, as Chacha of Whydah. As in the past, the Dahomey state relied heavily on women officials and soldiers. 'The palace was the nerve centre of the kingdom ... Several thousand people inhabited the palace – all women, apart from a few eunuchs.'[97] The so-called Amazons played a major role in Dahomey's foreign wars, and were destroyed as a fighting force during the French conquest.

In 1818, Gezo seized the throne from his brother, with the help of Brazilian slavers. He was to reign until his death in 1858; his son and heir, Glele, reigned until his death in 1889, a dynastic history strikingly more stable than that of many European states at the time, including France.

Gezo ended the annual tribute to Oyo. Dahomey became the aggressor, launching successive invasions of western Yorubaland, partly in search of slaves and glory, partly in the desire to control or dislocate a rival trade route to the sea. A woman soldier said in 1850, 'War is our great friend; without it there is no cloth, no armlets; let us to war, and conquer or die.'[98] The new city of Abeokuta bore the main brunt of defence; Dahomey was unable to conquer it, and experienced several major reverses. 'People have no time for peaceful pursuits: war, war, war is alone thought of, and the King gives them no rest. Many of these Chiefs complain of this, and seem heartily tired of it.'[99]

The foreign forts at Whydah were abandoned, and reoccupied when palm oil exports began, at first on a small scale, in the 1840s. In 1850, 'the exports from Whydah [were] slaves and palm-oil'.[100] In 1852, it was discovered how to remove palm oil's distinctive orange coloration, and thus make it acceptable to the French soap market. The slave trade declined steadily, and da Souza ended his days in poverty. Two events in 1851 – the abolition of the Brazilian slave trade and the posting of a British consul in Lagos – heralded the end. A few slaves were exported in the 1850s, and the last slaver left in 1865.[101] Much palm oil was produced by individual villagers; some Big Men, including the king, responded to the decline of the slave trade by establishing oil palm plantations. One of them owned a thousand slaves.[102] Palm oil was transported by canoe on the river Ouémé and on the coastal lagoons. In the early twentieth century, and perhaps earlier, it was also rolled in barrels to the sea.

When the French invaded Dahomey in 1890, the slaves, who were largely Yoruba, seized the opportunity to return home. 'The Fon later claimed, during their passage through the country, [they] did more damage than did the invading French army'.[103]

The Yoruba culture sphere: the struggle for supremacy

In an earlier chapter we saw how the Oyo empire collapsed, soon after attaining its greatest extent, and how the rebellion of a disappointed aristocrat led to his own death and to the formation of the new Emirate of Ilorin. Yoruba history in the nineteenth century is one of tumultuous change; it is possible to see it as a time of warlordism and great human suffering, or as one of creative innovation – in a sense, both are true. Relatively few Yoruba had been enslaved in previous centuries; as a result of nineteenth-century wars, Yoruba culture has left an enduring imprint on black civilisations in Cuba and Brazil; nowhere is this more evident than in the religion called Santeria, which combines Catholic elements with Yoruba divinities such as Ogun, god of iron, or the river goddess Oshun.[104]

The Landers visited Old Oyo shortly before its final defeat, and commented on a prevailing fatalism. 'The walls of the town have been suffered to fall into decay; and are now no better than a heap of dust and ruins ... unconcern and apathy pervade the minds of the monarch and his ministry'.[105]

By 1833, the capital had fallen to Ilorin, and so had many of its tributary towns. Atiba was a son of Abiodun, who had established an independent polity at Ago Oja, far to the south. In 1836, he was offered and accepted the Oyo throne, but instead of fighting to regain the ancient capital, he transformed Ago Oja into a New Oyo.

Many Oyo Yoruba fled to the south, and not only the capital, but other important towns such as Igboho were abandoned; there was a major shift of the population, and a diffusion of Oyo culture traits, such as the cult of Sango, and the narrow loom operated by men.[106]

In the south, new states grew up. Kurunmi led a group which settled in a deserted Egba town called Ijaye. Another group of Oyo refugees, led by Oluyole (like Afonja, an Oyo royal in the female line), founded the new city of Ibadan. Atiba granted them the Oyo titles of Kakamfo and Basorun, respectively; he had the prestige of an ancient name, but was a minor player in the conflicts and power struggles of the time, and for all its illustrious precedents, New Oyo remained a lesser power. The new order was dominated by Ibadan, Ijaye and Abeokuta; each lacked a traditional oba with a beaded crown. The divorce between the realities of power and a tradition of reverence for kings may well have had a destabilising effect,[107] as did their close proximity to each other. It had been the declared objective of Ilorin to dip the Qur'an in the sea.[108] In 1838, its southward advance was halted by Ibadan at the battle of Oshogbo, one of the decisive conflicts of Nigerian history.

The war in the south

While Oyo fought Ilorin in the north, its vassal state, Owu, was engaged in a completely different conflict in the south, first with Ife and then with Ijebu, which ended in its destruction in 1817, largely because the Ijebu had firearms.

The war grew out of kidnapping at Apomu market, intended to procure slaves for sale at Lagos.[109]

An account written thirty years later described how the conflict engulfed the small independent polities of the Egba. 'From this time, town after town was destroyed, many of the young and vigorous that escaped banded together and became the scourge of other towns, until every town was destroyed in the country and Abeokuta became a stronghold to which all that escaped the wars ultimately fled for refuge.'[110]

Abeokuta ('under the rock') was founded in *c.* 1835; here the original Egba settlements preserved the memory of their past and the individual titles of their former princes.

Ibadan was a military republic dominated by warlords and their retainers, Ijaye a dictatorship ruled by Kurunmi. In the 1860s, they fought for supremacy, in a war which ended in the latter's destruction. Ijayi was remembered as one of the most beautiful of Yoruba cities, a model of town planning.[111]

Ibadan carved out an empire in the east, among the small states of Ekiti and in Ilesa. They did not acquiesce in defeat, but formed an alliance, the Ekitiparapo, and fought the invader. The Egba and Ijebu were also involved in what proved to be the last of the Yoruba wars, from 1877 to 1886. Horses were now of marginal importance, except in Ilorin, and firearms became all-important – hence, access to the sea was essential for survival.

Africanus Horton had dreamed, not only of a 'Kingdom of Fantee' and a 'Republic of Accra', but of an 'Empire of the Eboes' and a 'Kingdom of the Akus', with its capital at Abeokuta.[112] Neither eventuated, but Abeokuta did embark on an experiment in modern government, with the creation of the Egba United Board of Management in 1865.[113] The Basorun became the President General and the Seriki the High Sheriff. The leading light behind it was G. W. Johnson, a Sierra Leonian tailor of limited education. They set up a postal service and a court, but Johnson's influence declined as time went on, although he renounced his British citizenship and adopted an Egba name.

Social change

These wars were fought with a ferocity which was probably untypical of earlier conflicts. People starved in the besieged cities – in Ijayi, children sold their freedom for a plate of beans. The people of the Ekiti town of Ikoro were besieged by Ibadan for a year, and reduced to eating banana stems and roots. When it fell, rather than lose their liberty, the men killed their own wives and children, burnt their homes, and immolated themselves in the flames.[114]

When the export of slaves ended, captives were increasingly employed on plantations. When Ibadan was asked to renounce its eastern empire, its representative explained, 'the Ekiti were their wives, their slaves, their yams, their palm oil etc.'.[115] Johnson, a Yoruba historian of the late nineteenth century, observed, 'Slave-raiding now became a trade to many who would get rich speedily.'[116]

Urbanisation was a striking characteristic of Yoruba history in this period, and the tendency to live in cities or towns, even for people engaged in agriculture, has remained a characteristic of Yoruba life. Scholars disagree as to whether it was an older phenomenon or a response to the wars of the nineteenth century.

It would be a mistake to interpret the history of these years in terms of enslavement and war alone. It was said of Atiba's successor that 'he loved his people and would never allow any of the princes to distress the poor with impunity'. When food was scarce he would flood the market with crops from the royal farms – 'my children must not starve'.[117]

Ketu was a western Yoruba kingdom, vanquished by Dahomey late in the nineteenth century. In 1853, when Adebia had been king for twenty years, Samuel Crowther paid him this tribute:

He does not buy slaves to keep, but only has such as are given him for presents, who live in the palace and are considered free ... Adebia ... may be classed among those who study to keep their people in peace and safety. He sends his people to no war ... he tries to make them happy, and encourage them to industry ... The Egunguns of Yoruba, and the Oro and Ogboni of the Egbas, are not allowed in the town of Ketu: they are looked upon as inventions which spoil the country; so women may walk as freely at night in the town of Ketu as in the streets of Sierra Leone.[118]

The Niger Delta

In much of West Africa, external trade was marginal to the daily life of ordinary people. Many of the items sold in the markets were locally made; it was largely rulers and great officials who were affected by the fluctuations of Atlantic trade, because they needed firearms, and items such as spirits, tobacco and luxury cloth to reward their supporters and to demarcate their own elite status. The broker states of the Niger Delta, such as Bonny, Elim Kalabari and Nembe (Brass), were situated on pockets of dry land in a wilderness of mangrove swamp. They could not farm, and had long since abandoned the salt processing and fishing on which they had once relied. In the late nineteenth century, they underwent a crisis, caused, not by the transition from the slave trade to the palm oil trade, but by developments which threatened their broker monopoly.

In nineteenth-century Bonny, the monarchy declined; in a trading community, its indebtedness undermined its prestige. Political life was dominated by the struggle between two rival Canoe Houses, Anna and Manilla Pepples, dominated by merchant princes who had once been slaves. The most famous of them, Ja Ja, was brought to Bonny as a slave when he was a boy; for a time he was a pullaboy on the great trade canoes. He struggled up from these humble beginnings to become first a respected trader and then head of the Anna Pepple House. In 1869, in a move of great boldness, he led his supporters to a new island home at the mouth of the Imo river, which he called Opobo, cutting Bonny off from its oil markets, and leaving it 'a ruined and impoverished Country'.[119] He ruled his island kingdom for eighteen years, and then fell victim to British encroachment, carried into an exile from which he did not return alive. Elim Kalabari had a not dissimilar history – a long struggle between rival Canoe Houses, and an exodus to a new inland site, led in this case by Will Braid in 1879. In the end, not one but four new settlements were founded on the northern edge of the Delta, and Elim Kalabari was deserted.

The Warri capital was located on the Forcados river. Its economic life was destroyed, not by the foundation of new settlements further inland, but by the shift of trade to an anchorage preferred by European captains on the Benin river, 80 kilometres away. This left the king without revenues or subjects. King Akengbuwa died in 1848 and, not surprisingly, he is remembered for his severity. Two sons, who succeeded him in turn, died soon afterwards, and for a time, affairs were controlled by royal slaves.[120] The interregnum which followed lasted until 1936. A visitor noted in 1884, 'The town of Warri is a mere shadow of its former greatness, the broad streets being overrun with lime trees and bush.'[121]

The Governor of the River had previously been a royal official. Now he became a substantive ruler in his own right. The last and most famous holder of the position, Nana, came to power in 1883; eleven years later, his apparently impregnable fort was taken by the British.

Individual slaves enjoyed considerable social mobility, but there was a great social gap between the merchant elite and the paddlers on the trade canoes, or, in the case of Calabar, the workers on plantations. In 1904, a missionary wrote of the latter: 'I have visited a number of farms or "Pindis". They are full of Ibos. These poor Ibos, so numerous, have furnished all the slaves of Calabar, Bonny, Brass etc ... And so all the chiefs have one, two or three storeyed houses, furnished like chateaux in Europe.'[122]

The commercial roles of Warri, Elim Kalabari and Bonny were destroyed when breakaway groups created new settlements at strategic locations, and one set of African brokers was supplanted by another. A more profound change occurred when the whole middleman economy was first challenged, then destroyed, as foreign traders gained direct access to the interior. The coastal brokers were always aware of the danger, and did what they could to prevent it. The most obvious path to the interior was the Niger.

The lower Niger

An older historiography made much of Africa's European 'explorers'; Africanist scholarship reacted against it, pointing out that their 'discoveries' were already well known to innumerable Africans. 'Exploration' paved the way to direct commercial contacts with a wider world, and ultimately to colonial conquest. Partly, but not entirely, because of the importance of water transport, nine-teenth-century 'explorers' tended to be obsessed with rivers and their sources – Livingstone died looking for the source of the Nile. In West Africa, there was a particular fascination with the course of the Niger, and with the fabled city of Timbuktu, which Caillié succeeded in visiting in 1828. In 1795, Mungo Park travelled inland from the Gambia and reached the Niger at Segu. In 1805 he returned, with a large expedition, none of whose members would survive, intending to follow the river to its outlet. After a journey of 1,500 kilometres, he drowned in the rapids at Bussa in north-western Nigeria.

Europeans had traded on the coast for centuries, but knew little of the interior. One writer claimed that the ivory sold on the Cameroon coast came from elephants who had died of thirst in the desert or had sunk in an adjoining (and mythical) morass![123] Despite centuries of trading in the Bight of Bonny, Europeans first learnt that the 'Oil Rivers' were the Delta of the Niger when the Lander brothers followed the great river to the sea in 1830. In 1841, the British government sponsored an ambitious expedition to the Niger in response to the urgings of anti-slavery interests, but a third of the Europeans involved died, and little was achieved. In 1854, a further expedition, led by a Scottish doctor, William Balfour Baikie, survived the disease environment of the lower Niger, thanks to the regular use of quinine. In the years that followed, a number of commercial firms established trade posts on the Niger, employing Sierra Leonian staff. The Church Missionary Society founded a new mission on the Niger, headed by Samuel Ajayi Crowther, who first rose to prominence as a member of the 1841 and 1854 expeditions and became an Anglican bishop in 1864. Its members, too, were all Africans from Sierra Leone.

Previously, the commerce of the lower Niger had been dominated by riverfarers from Nembe, Aboh and Igala. Now, their role was undermined. 'A long time ago the Abohs were regarded as the most powerful amongst their neighbours, both for riches and strength, and as such were feared by all . . . they could not describe their feelings to me whenever they saw ships laden with merchandise passing away from them to villages further up.'[124]

The 1860s and 1870s were an Indian summer for educated West Africans. Henry Venn, for many years the Secretary of the Church Missionary Society, was an advocate of the 'euthanasia' of foreign missions, in favour of independent local churches. Idealism and pragmatism went hand in hand. African agents, whether in mission service or the commercial world, were paid far less than Europeans, and were more resistant to tropical diseases.

The year 1879 was a turning point for the Sierra Leonians on the lower Niger. In that year, a European was given charge of the Niger Mission's finances; by 1883, most of its members had gone 'by disconnection, dismissal and resignation'.[125] When the aged bishop died in 1891, he was replaced by a European. In 1879, too, the man history knows as Sir George Goldie amalgamated the competing firms on the Niger as the United African Company. In 1884, it obtained a charter to govern, as the Royal Niger Company, which it used to exclude its rivals, the Sierra Leonians and the Nembe traders.

The Igbo interior

Igbo enwero eze, the Igbo have no kings. Though a few Igbo polities did in fact have kings, it is a core statement of Igbo identity. But one of the themes which emerges most clearly from the detailed histories of these numerous tiny states is the growth of a wealthy class of robber barons on the one hand and an expansion of domestic slavery on the other.

Oral tradition describes the prevalence of kidnapping and the insecurity it engendered, giving a picture which published slave narratives from the late nineteenth century confirm. 'One day 4 of us went to cut wood in the farm, 2 men met us in the bush and said that "me papa" owed him and caught me, the rest of the girls ran away.' The girl became a domestic slave at Okrika. A boy's father left him with a neighbouring people, where he felt he would be safe from kidnappers. 'But whilst playing about one afternoon, with others of my companions mindful of no danger, 12 of these man-stealers rushed out from the forest nearby and singled me from my mates, and away they go dragging me along with them.'[126]

The social mechanisms introduced to obtain captives endured long after the slave trade ended.

There was a large increase in the number of domestic slaves owned by rich individuals. Oral traditions tell of a man from an Igbo village who blamed his fellow townsmen for their refusal to 'swallow smaller snakes so as to grow richer'. Finally he pronounced a curse of equality on the whole people. 'I tried to grow rich, you refused. I told you to grow rich, you refused. From henceforth, all of you will be equal.' Then he packed his belongings, and went to his mother's kindred at Igbo-Ukwu.[127]

Many of the wars in nineteenth-century Igboland, however, had no apparent links with external factors. The Cross River Igbo, such as the Abam and Edda, had a martial culture, and only a hero – a man who had taken an enemy head in battle – was allowed to have a wife. The Cross River Igbo fought enthusiastically in other people's wars, for glory, not for gain. Sometimes the Aro made use of their services. In the Awka area, a coalition was formed to resist them and defensive towers were built which were still standing in the mid-twentieth century.

In the 1860s, a prophet arose in the Onitsha hinterland, who called himself the Restorer of the Primitive Style. He sent forth delegates, with a message of social criticism and reform, 'to warn the Ibos that they had deviated from the primitive custom – selling things at a higher rate, above the standard for the lower classes to purchase; hence stealing is so painfully practised and the pernicious system of selling children away is very great ... Best of all every man is to lay aside his weapon of war.'[128]

Sierra Leone[129]

From the late eighteenth century on, in Sierra Leone, two themes have been emphasised, often to the neglect of others – the Creole enclave at Freetown and the process of British encroachment. Africanist scholarship – my own included – tended to linger on the achievements of the Creoles, which anticipate the work of African professionals in modern times, and their lives have had a special meaning for historians from Anglophone West Africa. But there were less than 100,000 Creoles, who were vastly outnumbered by the several million people in the hinterland of what later became the modern nation of Sierra Leone. To these, Freetown was little more than a distant name, as it was, indeed, for the Kuranko a hundred years later.

Quite different factors shaped their lives, such as the spread of Islamic influences from the north, especially after the eighteenth-century foundation of Futa Jallon. Susu and Fulbe migrated southward, and one of the latter became king of Yono, on the Mende–Temne borderland, with the title Fula Mansa.[130]

A Foulah Mohomedan from the Futa country journeyed into the Mendi country, and residing there, in time became wealthy and renowned for the efficacy of his charms ... and marrying many wives, he soon became allied to most of the principal Chiefs of the country, and the owner of many slaves. At his death his eldest son ... took to war as his occupation ... and conquered a vast extent of country now known as the Yonnie district.[131]

In the eighteenth century, Susu immigrants gained control of the Temne state of Port Loko, where, following the Futa Jallon model, their leader took the title Almami. In 1816, the Temne overthrew him, led by a chief who took the Muslim title of Alkali, judge. It was now only subchiefs who were called Almami![132]

Temne society was divided into a northern sphere, influenced by Islam, and a southern sphere, where traditional secret societies, especially Poro, retained their ancient supremacy, creating an enduring 'bifurcation of Temne country into "Muslim" and "Society" chiefdoms'.[133] Bilale, was a slave in a Susu state near the Great Scarcies, the son of a Koranko mother and a Susu chief. When the latter died, some of Bilale's relatives were sold to pay his debts. In 1838, he led a band of men, women and children to freedom. Susu who came in pursuit were defeated, and the fugitives took refuge among the Limba, who had their own conflicts with the Susu, establishing a new town, with a name which means Bitter Brook, which they defended successfully for decades. 'Slaves from Layah, Tasaing and other places of the Soosoo country found their way to Billarlie.'[134]

New states were created and some older ones fell apart. In the 1820s, there was a centralised Kuranko kingdom, whose king was 'the most powerful chief between his country and Sierra Leone [sc. the Freetown enclave] ... his authority extends as far as the banks of the Niger'. In the 1880s, the region was invaded by Samori's forces, and when the British came to establish a colonial administration among the Kuranko, they found them divided into twenty-five principalities.[135]

In the course of the nineteenth century, the southern half of Sierra Leone became Mende-speaking. At first, the Mende lived inland, separated from the sea by the Sherbo and the Vai. They expanded towards the west, but their language and culture spread much further, and by 1896, 'the constantly advancing wave of Mende influence has already practically inundated the land of the Sherbros'.[136]

The Creole experience

The Creole enclave at Freetown grew out of the slave trade and the anti-slavery movement. As we have seen, there is an extensive debate about the respective roles of economic self-interest and of idealism in the abolition of the British slave trade, but it is generally agreed that the anti-slavery movement could not have succeeded had not a climate of opinion been created where slavery was unacceptable. Two eighteenth-century West Africans, the Igbo Olaudah Equiano and the Fante Ottobah Cugoano, were among the propagandists who contributed to this change of heart. Both had been enslaved and had won their freedom; both became educated Christians and settled in England; both wrote books.[137] Equiano was a tireless public speaker and one of the architects of Sierra Leone. He was to have been Commissary of the new settlement, but was dismissed before the ship left England.

Freetown was planned as a Province of Freedom, a small independent state of free black settlers, earning their living from agriculture. It was financed by the British government, in part as a way of solving a social problem – the 'black poor' of London. To its supporters, notably the veteran philanthropist Granville Sharp, its importance lay in the fact that it would undermine the slave trade by showing that it was more profitable to trade with free people. In the words of Equiano: 'A System of Commerce once being established in Africa, the Demand for Manufactories will most rapidly augment ... In proportion to the Civilisation, so will be the Consumption of British manufactures ... The Abolition of diabolical Slavery will give a most rapid and permanent Extension to Manufactures.'[138]

In 1787, 341 black men and 70 white women landed in the area where Freetown now stands, on the peninsula which the Portuguese, in the late fifteenth century, had called Lion Mountain. It was not a colony, but an independent polity with its own constitution, drafted by Granville Sharp, who based it, with unconscious ethnocentricity, on his understanding of Anglo-Saxon precedents. Land was purchased from the local Temne king, who affixed his mark to a treaty he did not understand. It was to lead to bitter conflict and marked a radical departure from the older landlord–stranger relationship. It is profoundly ironical that the first permanent alienation of land in West Africa was the result of black settlement.

The settlers landed in the rainy season, and almost starved. In 1789, the settlement was sacked by the local Temne – it was the end of the Province of Freedom. Some settlers were enslaved and others made a living from the slave trade.

The Sierra Leone Company was founded in 1791; it was essentially a philanthropic enterprise and its directors were to suffer great losses. In 1792, over a thousand more black settlers arrived; they had supported England during the American war of independence and been resettled in the bitterly cold environment of Nova Scotia, promised farms which, in many cases, they were not given. They were joined by 550 Maroons, whose forebears had escaped from slavery in Jamaica and set up an independent state there. They were defeated in 1795 – with the help of hunting dogs – and relocated in Nova Scotia.

Like Cugoano and Equiano, the Settlers were committed Christians – usually Dissenters. Their piety amazed observers – 'I never met with, heard of or read of, any set of people observing the same appearance of godliness.'[139]

When Sierra Leone became a colony in 1808, there were fewer than 2,000 Settlers. They were to provide a role model for a great new influx, that of the Recaptives or Liberated Africans. When the British naval squadron intercepted slavers on the high seas, it was impracticable to restore their living cargoes to their widely scattered homes. Instead, they were taken to Freetown, and settled, under missionary tutelage, in villages whose names mirrored a country they had never seen: Leicester, Regent. In time, 74,000 Liberated Africans were resettled in Freetown, transforming the Creole community. They had been violently torn away from their own culture and families and in a sense had no choice but to embark on a new life; they became Christians and learnt to speak English and to read, and chose new names. Syble Boyle adopted the name of the naval vessel which rescued him, HMS *Sybille*.

They found it easier to earn a living from trade, often in goods from confiscated slave ships, than from agriculture. Some, such as the Nupe John Ezzidio, the Hausa Emmanuel Cline, or the Igbo William Henry Pratt, acquired great wealth, and many more attained a solid prosperity, investing their money in housing and their children's education. By 1860, 22 per cent of the colony's population was in school (the figures for England and Prussia at that time were 13 per cent and 16 per cent.)[140] Gradually the line of demarcation between Settler and Recaptive disappeared; a new people came into being, called Creole, or Krio. A few local people were also incorporated in Creole society, often by joining a Creole household as a child. John Macaulay Wilson (d. 1826), who trained as a druggist in England, was a Bullom.

By the middle decades of the nineteenth century, there was a substantial Creole middle class of merchants and professionals. We have already noted the doctor and author Africanus Horton, who spent his working life on the Gold Coast. Another Creole physician, J. F. Easmon, was the first to isolate blackwater fever. Sir Samuel Lewis, a formidable lawyer and Mayor of Freetown, was the first West African knight – though not the first Creole lawyer. Creole society produced its own historian, the schoolmaster A. B. C. Sibthorpe.

In 1827, the Church Missionary Society founded a teachers' training institution, Fourah Bay College. Its first pupil was the future bishop, Samuel Ajayi Crowther, a Yoruba, born in *c.* 1806, and enslaved in the war which destroyed his home town of Osogun. In 1876, Fourah Bay College began to award degrees from the University of Durham. Not all the Creoles became Christians; some 5 per cent were Muslims and kept to their original faith, sometimes sending their children to Futa Jallon for education. Converted Recaptives often preserved elements of their traditional religion and culture. In response to missionary rebukes, one said, 'We were born in another country, this fashion we learned from our fathers. What they did we do too.'[141] The seventeen largest ethnic groups – the Seventeen Nations, of whom the Yoruba, or Aku, were by far the largest – formed committees to resolve inter-ethnic conflicts.

Krio is a pidgin which evolved among the Liberated Africans, incorporating elements of Maroon and South Carolina dialects, which became the language of the Creole community. A Krio letter written in 1860 runs: 'We say na God made we and all thing for true. Then we na fraed again, we say country fashion, him na true God ... O Scroo Masser, we heart good now, we heart sweet now, we heart laugh now.'[142]

As a nineteenth-century Creole writer pointed out, the 'ideas it embodies are not English, but native; it is the collection of means whereby Sierra Leoneans express their thoughts *naturally* and without effort'.[143]

The Creole diaspora

In 1839, three Yoruba bought a ship and carried passengers to Badagry. It was the first step in a massive Creole diaspora; they left Freetown, sometimes in search of their original home, sometimes seeking wider economic opportunities. In the words of Africanus Horton,

... they are to be found in every part of the coast sighing after gold in the capacity of merchants, traders and clerks – in the French colony of Senegal; in the rivers Gambia, Casamanza, Nunez, Pongas, Sherbro and Galinas; in the Liberian Republic; on the Gold Coast; in the Kingdom of Dahomey; in Lagos and Abeokuta; in the Niger; at Bonny, Old and New Calabar, the Cameroons, Fernando Po, the Gaboons and the Islands of St Helena and Ascension.[144]

Where the Saro led, the missionary societies often followed and Wesleyan Methodists and the CMS established missions among the Yoruba, where black and white missionaries worked side by side. Samuel Crowther, ordained an Anglican clergyman in 1843, worked among the Yoruba before he took charge of the Niger Mission.

The Creoles looked outward to other parts of West Africa, and had relatively little to do with the indigenous peoples of Sierra Leone. There were, of course, exceptions, and Peter Hazeley was called the Apostle of the Limba. But in the mid-twentieth century, the Kuranko still spoke of Freetown as if it were another country, Saralon.[145]

The decline of the Creoles

From the 1880s on, the fortunes of the Creole community declined, in a transition similar to events in Liberia and the Gold Coast. As British rule in the area expanded and more white officials arrived, they tended to look on the Creoles as rivals, and increasingly discriminated against them. Economic changes worked against the Creole merchant, as big foreign firms moved into the interior and Syrian pedlars filled the humble economic niche once exploited by Liberated Africans. Some Creole fortunes were destroyed in litigation, or by the multifarious needs of extended families.

Victorian Freetown – or Lagos – was modelled on English exemplars. The Creoles played cricket, enjoyed Gilbert and Sullivan and rejoiced to be called Black Englishmen. Sometimes, they referred to England as home. Because of this, they suffered particularly acutely when they were condemned by white observers. The hostility of colonial Europeans to those whose culture came closest to their own – also evident in India – is a historical oddity. Richard Burton and Winwood Reade were among the visitors to nineteenth century Freetown who described it with an envenomed hostility. Because of their celebrity, their writings influenced public opinion in Britain, and were profoundly distressing to the Creoles themselves. Much later, a Creole writer reflected:

The upset of the Sierra Leonian began with the upset of thought of his white rulers concerning him ... A day came when white thought began to be changed, white feeling began to be altered, and white action began to be fitted to the thought and feeling ... Segregation was the first blast of the trumpet; then other things and other things.[146]

Edward Blyden, who chose to make Liberia his home after bitter experiences of racial injustice, once asked a Creole why no reply had been been made to one of these attacks. He replied, in Krio, 'Who dat go wase powder pon condo?' (Who would waste their powder shooting a red-headed lizard?)[147]

Liberia

The Americo-Liberians[148]

The modern history of Liberia, like that of Sierra Leone, begins with black colonists, in this case from America. The initiative was taken by Paul Cuffee, a Quaker ship's captain of African and Native American parentage, who took a party of black immigrants from America to Freetown in 1816. He died the following year, and the enterprise was taken over by the American Colonisation Society. It was financed largely by white slave owners, who feared that a free black population would undermine the institution of slavery. After a false start in the Sherbro, the first party of settlers landed at Cape Mesurado in 1822; the local ruler, warned by the example of the Temne, ceded them land only at gunpoint. The new settlement was called Monrovia after the American president of the day.

In 1822, there were 1.75 million blacks in America, a seventh of whom were free. Fewer than 12,000 ever chose to emigrate to Liberia, and half of those had been freed on condition that they do so. Most American blacks preferred to remain in America and struggle for a share in an inheritance their labours and sufferings had done so much to create. The Settlers were often fourth- or fifth-generation Americans; they spoke no African language and had lost their immunity to tropical diseases, so that many died soon after arrival. They identified closely with America, and were to reduplicate its institutions – a White House, a Capitol, a Frontier Force. Liberia became independent in 1847. America was one of the last countries to recognise it – in 1862– a bitterly felt slight.

In Freetown, Liberated Africans greatly outnumbered the Settlers. In Monrovia, only 5,700 Liberated Africans were landed; they were called Congoes, reflecting the ethnic composition of the first arrivals. In Freetown, it was the Liberated Africans who created a bridge between Creole and indigenous cultures – albeit, for the most part, cultures far away. In Liberia, the bridge was lacking, and the Americo-Liberians often regarded local peoples with as much fear and hostility as any white settler. Lott Carey, the Baptist pastor from Virginia who played an important role in the first years of the settlement, blew himself up in 1828 while making gunpowder to use against them. Local people were invisible in the country's motto – 'The love of liberty brought us here.' The 1847 Declaration of Independence begins, 'We the people of Liberia were originally the inhabitants of the United States of America.'

Like the Creoles, they found it impossible to earn a living from agriculture, and turned to trade. In time, other small Americo-Liberian settlements were founded along the coast. The largest of them was Maryland – again, its very name mirrors the bitter irony at the heart of the Americo-Liberian experience, the profound identification with the society which had oppressed them or expelled them. From 1836 until his death in 1851, its Governor was John B. Russworm, an early black graduate and co-founder of the first Afro-American newspaper.

A profound hostility between Eur-Africans and blacks divided the Americo-Liberians for many years. Blyden was fanatically opposed to the former, whom he tried to exclude from Liberia. The conflict was rooted in socio-economic distinctions – the Eur-Africans, whose fathers were white slave owners, tended to be propertied and better educated. Joseph Jenkins Roberts, who became the first Governor of part-African descent in 1841, had one African great-grandparent! The Eur-Africans tended to form a wealthy elite, reinforcing their corporate identity through Freemasonry and Episcopalian or Methodist church affiliation. The Republican Party was dominated by Eur-Africans, the True Whigs by blacks. The former, except for the presidency of Edward Roye (1869–71), ruled Liberia from 1847 to 1878, the True Whigs thereafter, until the whole edifice of Americo-Liberian hegemony was shattered in 1980.

Like their counterparts in Sierra Leone, the Liberian business community prospered until about 1870 and some individuals, Roberts and Roye among them, were among West Africa's merchant princes. They exported coffee, sugar, camwood, palm kernels, ivory and raffia fibre, often in locally made schooners, and they imported Brazilian rum and tobacco and European cloth.

Their economic role declined thereafter, partly because of the depression of the 1870s and 1880s, partly because they were unable to compete with the big foreign steamer lines. English shipping stopped calling at Monrovia in 1858, and transatlantic sailings were irregular. Camwood was replaced by artificial dyes, sugar met competition from the growing European beet sugar industry, and Liberia lost its monopoly of fine coffee.

The growth of colonialism affected Liberia adversely in many ways, not least the fact that British and French merchants preferred to trade in their own colonies; the United States, which might have seemed Liberia's obvious trading partner, had a much closer source of tropical products in Latin America.[149] In the mid-nineteenth century, the Liberian elite were typically involved in business; later, they concentrated on politics and law.

As so often in twentieth-century Africa, a lack of resources led to an ever greater poverty and indebtedness. Roye attempted to raise a loan abroad, to finance education and the creation of much-needed infrastructure. But it was raised on disastrously unfavourable terms, and plunged the nation into lasting debt. Roye himself was overthrown in a coup and drowned trying to swim to safety.

Because of its political and economic weakness, Liberia lost territory to British and French colonial neighbours. Losses to Guinea were particularly serious, because the Nimba mountains are among the world's best sources of iron ore.

There was always a paradox in the Liberian thrust to the interior. On the one hand, they laid claim to the coast and its economic hinterland. But the further inland they expanded, the more of a minority the Americo-Liberians became, among peoples who even in modern times have often referred to them as 'white'.

Indigenous peoples

As so often, colonial boundaries cut across cultural and linguistic continuities. There are Vai, Gola and Mende on both sides of the Sierra Leone–Liberia frontier, and the Grebo, Krahn, Gio and Mano live both in Liberia and Ivory Coast.

Liberia is a small country with sixteen ethnic groups, virtually all of whom lived in small-scale polities. The 1962 census put the total population at just over a million, with only two ethnic groups – the Kpelle and the Bassa – over 100,000. Many of its peoples belonged to the great Mande language family, and the Mande invaders of the sixteenth century were probably proto-Vai. All but the Bassa, Kru and Mandingo had Poro and other comparable secret societies.

It is one of the many paradoxes of Liberian history that, although the Settlers fought a number of wars with indigenous peoples and often looked down on them, the latter were among the West African communities who welcomed the modern world most enthusiastically. The Vai coast – Cape Mount and Gallinas – was one of the last centres of the West African slave trade. Islam began to spread there in the eighteenth century, and by 1826 it was said that there was a Muslim teacher in every village. In 1822, the Americo-Liberians settled at Monrovia, not far to the south. In response to these frontiers of literacy, the Vai invented a script of their own in the early 1830s. 'An old man dreamed that he must immediately begin to make characters for his language, that his people might write letters, as they did at Monrovia.' The script was then devised by a committee,[150] and has survived in family use to this day, though for general purposes it has been replaced by written English. Why did they invent their own script in the first place? Perhaps it was a symbolic way of creating a distance from Monrovia.

The Kru and the closely related Grebo lived on Liberia's southern coast; the enthusiasm of foreign visitors for the Kru makes an odd contrast with their hostility to Americo-Liberians and Creoles. The reason, of course, was that the Kru played an indispensable role in their own activities, to which the western-educated posed an actual or potential challenge. West Africa shipping stopped specially in Liberia to pick up Krumen, and they had their own settlement in Freetown. They were brave and skilful seamen and canoeists, whose services were needed, in particular, to transport goods through raging and shark-infested surf. They worked in gangs, each under its own headman, the only one who could flog them, and they prided themselves on the tradition that they had never been enslaved. They invested their earnings in wives, and ultimately retired after two or three decades at sea. They also played a major role in Sierra Leone, as woodcutters: 'they never desert their employers in danger or distress; they are constitutionally brave ... they are the life and soul of the trade on the coast; without them the cargoes could not be stowed, nor could boats be manned.'[151]

The Grebo, Kru and Vai opposed Americo-Liberian hegemony for decades. In 1873, Christian Grebo organised the Grebo Reunited Kingdom, following the Fante example; they won a military victory but did not win their independence.

In 1910, William Wade Harris, the Grebo who was to be the most successful of all Christian evangelists in West Africa, had the vision which changed his life when he was a political prisoner in a Monrovia gaol.

Alien encroachment

West African rulers frequently had a clearer understanding of international events than is often realised. In northern Nigeria, al-Kanemi wrote to Muhammad Bello, pointing out the dangerous precedent of the British conquest of India. No less than five African states sent ambassadors to warn Masaba of Nupe that the British were 'a very dangerous and encroaching nation'. In 1860, the chiefs of Bonny refused to sign a treaty with a British consul. 'One of these expressed to me his dread of our government doing what he said the French had done at Gaboon – namely induce the Chiefs to sign a treaty whose meaning they did not understand, and then seize upon the country.'[152]

In 1849, John Beecroft was appointed consul to the Bights of Benin and Biafra. A clause in his letter of appointment, which was crossed out, perfectly encapsulated British ambiguities – the government had 'no intention to seek to gain Possession, either by purchase or otherwise, of any portion of the African continent in those parts'.[153] In 1879, Salisbury minuted: 'Governor R has had no better occupation for his spare time than to annex some place with an unrememberable name, near Dahomey on the lagoon ... Really, these proconsuls are insupportable ... I have implored the Colonial Office to recall Governor R.'[154]

In 1881, King Bell and King Akwa of Douala invited the British to establish a colonial jurisdiction there. The Colonial Office refused, much in the spirit of the famous 1865 resolutions: 'the climate of all parts of West Africa is very pestilential and prejudicial to the life and health of Europeans. Past experience shows that the extension of British occupation would probably lead to wars with the interior native tribes, and heavy demands upon the British taxpayer.'[155]

When the French established a Protectorate at Porto Novo in 1882, and the Germans obtained treaties in Cameroon a year later, all this was to change.

Understandings

We have seen how the dialectic between wealth and people threads its way through the records of the past and is reflected in witchcraft beliefs and the idea that cowries were obtained with human bait. A famous study of Latin America analyses the way in which the inhumanity of industrial capitalism was interpreted by poor peasants or miners, in terms of a Faustian pact with the Devil.[156] This has many parallels in African thought; an interesting example is a commentary on 'legitimate' trade recorded at Medina, high on the Senegal, at the end of the nineteenth century.

[In the time of Faidherbe], says Silman, we thought that all the remarkable objects the Europeans brought were made by the Devil. Why did Europeans come to look for peanuts? Simply because it is the Devil's favourite food ... They were people who got their merchandise from the Devil and could only live on water. Because of this, we called them toads . . .

The other day, an old Soninke told Silman, 'I used to speak French, but now I don't understand it any more . . . In Faidherbe's time, the Frenchman was a toad, who only went ashore to give us gifts . . . Today the White . . . goes everywhere and treats us like slaves. Today I don't understand French any more!'[157]

21

Central Africa

manama: power stemming from the men one has bought or acquired
lyeme: ordeal to be undergone because one becomes too wealthy
J. Calloc'h, *Vocabulaire Française–Ifumu (Bateke)* (Paris, 1911)[1]

Introduction: the impact of Atlantic trade

The population of West Central Africa has always been low; it is often described as underpopulated, though the frequency with which famines occurred suggests otherwise. When the population of a given area expanded, it often led to a crisis – this happened in the Chokwe heartland in the mid-nineteenth century, as a result of a build up of population by the acquisition of captive women. In good years, people tended to expand into marginal areas, but when the rains failed, they were forced back into the river valleys, often in a servile or client relationship. The coast was barren, and rainfall diminished steadily as one went south – hunger and drought are recurrent themes in the poetry of the Ovambo, people of the northern Kalahari, on the southern margins of Angola.[2]

Perhaps 40 per cent of all the slaves exported in the centuries of the Atlantic slave trade came from West Central Africa.[3] This probably did not lead to absolute depopulation in the region as a whole, because, as we have seen, the great majority of those exported were men, creating a gender imbalance which impacted both on marriage patterns and on the distribution of work.

The introduction of New World crops, especially cassava and maize, helped sustain a denser population, but the dangers of the slave trade era encouraged settlement on mountain tops or in forests, chosen for their safety rather than for their suitability for cultivation. The Chokwe illustrate the paradoxes which resulted; they opted for a forest home and their staple was cassava. Their name means, 'those who fled' (from the wars of the Ovimbundu),[4] but in the late nineteenth century, they conquered much of the Lunda empire.

The history of West Central African societies in this period is shaped by a number of dominant themes – the impact of Atlantic trade, the varying exigencies of specific environments, and the profound cultural preferences which led some to opt for the vertical structures of the kingdom and others to prefer the horizontal linkages of ritual associations.[5] Some states were strengthened, at least in the short run, by external trade, and others were undermined by it.

The commerce between the coast and the interior was dominated by three trade routes. One great complex of trade canoe routes followed the Zaire and its many tributaries, above Lake Malebo. Further south, land routes ran eastward from the ports of Luanda and Benguela, which were long dominated by the inland broker states of Kasanje and Matamba. The peoples of the small kingdoms of the Loango coast came to combine a broker role on the coast with caravan trade to Mpumbu, overlooking Lake Malebo; they developed a new identity as the Vili. The Bobangi, canoetarers on the Zaire above Mpumbu, developed an ethnic identity in the same way. The way in which the Vili, a coastal people, travelled inland was exceptional. It was more common for slaves or commodities to pass from one middleman to the next; since each exacted a profit, prices were inflated in the process. In the region which later became Gabon, goods were exchanged in a potlatch, a sequence of competitive exchanges of gifts.

Atlantic trade affected peoples who had never seen either a European or the sea. For centuries, the strangers were confined to the coast; even in Angola, as we shall see, they did not penetrate far inland. The first European to see the Zaire river above Lake Malebo was Stanley, in 1877. But for centuries, inland peoples had heard rumours of strangers from the spirit world who purchased Africans in order to feed on their life force, who dyed cloth with their blood and processed their bones into gunpowder. Their king was Mwene Puto, Lord of the Dead.[6] The Europeans had their own strange images of the African interior. 'No Christian has ever been there ... The air is so unhealthy, that if a stranger travels by night by the light of the moon, his head will swell up and become as large as two.'[7]

The slaving frontier and associated trade routes moved steadily to the east, until, in the eighteenth century, they reached what is now Zambia. Goods travelled vast distances from hand to hand – in the late nineteenth century it took as long as five years for a barrel of gunpowder from the coast to reach people living on the Zaire above the equator.[8] And yet the lives of these distant villagers were profoundly affected by these changes.

Foreign presences

The first Portuguese vessel anchored in the Zaire estuary in 1483. At first, the main commodity the new arrivals bought was copper from Mindouli, north of the Zaire, supplemented by ivory, raffia cloth, pelts and honey.[9] By the 1520s, they had begun to buy slaves, destined first for the sugar fields of São Thomé, and later for the insatiable markets of the New World; soon, the trade in slaves eclipsed all other exports. The Portuguese began to trade on the Loango coast in the 1570s, and Luanda, the original nucleus of Angola, was originally settled by clandestine traders evading the authority of the crown. In 1615 trade was developed at Benguela, for the same reasons. Angola, founded by a charter of 1571, was Africa's first colony, which African forces confined for decades to the unhealthy coastal lowlands around Luanda.

The Portuguese did not enjoy a monopoly of external trade for long, and before the end of the sixteenth century Dutch, English and French vessels had begun to raid their settlements. The Dutch began to trade in Loango in the late sixteenth century, and it became the centre of their commercial interests in West Central Africa (they briefly seized Angola in the 1640s). They were not, at first, purchasers of slaves, for which they had no use until they obtained their first possessions in South America.

The English and French played a major role in the eighteenth-century slave trade from the area. Like the Dutch, they had a commercial advantage over the Portuguese, both in the better quality and range of their imports and in their readiness to sell firearms and ammunition (prohibited by the Portuguese crown). The British were in a particularly strong position, as the manufacturers both of the most acceptable textiles and of the flintlock, which was a *sine qua non* for African trade.[10]

The large-scale importation of firearms, often via Loango, began in the eighteenth century, and often those with access to guns fought their way to power, then and later – a pattern which, as in West Africa, contrasts oddly with the evidence of their poor quality. In 1759, only 200 of 4,000 trade guns examined were in good order.[11]

West Central Africa was always of minor importance in Portugal's global perspectives, in comparison with Asia and Brazil, or even with the auriferous regions of Africa itself. Even when they enjoyed a virtual monopoly, they did not constitute a single monolithic presence, and the nature of their impact varied with time and place. São Thomé was originally an uninhabited island; the Portuguese began to settle there in the 1490s, founding sugar plantations worked with slave labour – a prototype of those which later developed in the New World. After the Oba of Benin prohibited the export of male slaves in 1516, the planters of São Thomé obtained their slaves in West Central Africa, both for local use and for sale further afield. But the sugar of São Thomé could not compete with that produced in the New World and the viability of its plantations was undermined by recurrent slave revolts, with the result that the settlers came to gain a living from slave trading, and from acting as carriers in coastal trade. Their interests were often at variance with those of the Portuguese crown and its agents. Those who came to West Central Africa were, on the whole, men who were marginal and relatively impoverished in their own society, and this was the cause of much of their rapacity and violence. Those who braved the disease environment of sub-Saharan Africa were lesser nobles, struggling merchants, or younger sons. Their ranks included debtors, criminal *degradados*, Gypsies and Jews, then as later the victims of supposedly Christian Europe. Most died within a few months or years of their arrival. They turned to slave trading, in many cases, because of the failure of other initiatives such as agriculture or the quest for minerals. Like the slaves, but to a much lesser degree, they were the 'casualties of merchant capital'.[12] Those who survived ended up impoverishing and depopulating the regions they had hoped would enrich them.

The immigrants married local women and an Afro-Portuguese community developed; its members retained Portuguese names, European dress, and varying amounts of the Portuguese language, and of degrees of attachment to Christianity. These things were cherished because they helped to define what was, perhaps, an elusive sense of identity. By the eighteenth century, this Creole community was competing for trade with metropolitan Portuguese; these struggles were often the dynamic behind the expansion of the slaving frontier in the interior.

Three kingdoms

By the fourteenth century – and perhaps earlier – a number of small principalities had coalesced into three states near the lower Zaire – the Loango, Kongo and Tio kingdoms. The Kongo state was by far the largest. The Tio state was a confederacy of lords under a sacred king, north of the Zaire near Lake Malebo. Loango was the largest of three small kingdoms on what became known as the Loango coast; its people spoke a dialect of kiKongo.

These states had much in common – matrilineal institutions and much shared political symbolism and vocabulary. There is some evidence that the culture of the Tio area was ancestral to the others: 'All the blacks who live along this [Loango] coast derive their laws and customs from those of Pombo [Mpumbu].'[13] These linkages were expressed in the idiom of kinship, the story of a woman with four sons – muTeke, muKongo, muWoyo and muVili.[14]

The Kongo[15]

Few African states have been as thoroughly studied as the Kongo kingdom. An abundance of missionary visitors, in particular, left very detailed written records, and there is a particular fascination, for western scholars, in the court's early adoption of Christianity and of literacy.

When the first Portuguese visitors reached the coast of West Central Africa, the Kongo kingdom was a substantial state, extending from the Zaire to Luanda Island. Its capital, Mbanza Kongo, later called São Salvador, was 200 kilometres inland. It had a population of perhaps half a million people.

Like so many African states, it was superimposed on many tiny principalities, each with a sacred priest/ruler, who survived as *kitome*, ritual figures with many of the restrictions of a sacred king.

The Mane Kongo was selected from the male members of a group of aristocratic clans, Mwissikongo, and his power rested essentially on his astute manipulation of the products of the ecological zones into which the area naturally divides – *nzimbu* (shell money from Luanda Island), salt from various coastal locations, and palm cloth from the interior. The Mane Kongo welcomed the Portuguese and was baptised as João; white was the colour of the spirit world, and the strangers' supernatural standing was confirmed by their foreign tongue, exotic appearance, and association with the sea.

João soon seems to have regretted his action; when he died, in 1506, there was a civil war, won by the pro-Portuguese and pro-Christian contender, Nzinga Mvemba, whom history knows as Afonso, and who reigned until his death in 1543. The Portuguese assumed he was the heir, as the oldest son of the king's principal wife. Since his mother was not a member of the Mwissikongo, he had, in a matrilineal society, no right to succeed at all. An older historiography saw him as a Christian idealist, struggling unsuccessfully against the slave trade,[16] but he sometimes opposed and sometimes supported it, depending on whether it strengthened or weakened his regime. Like the kings who came before and after him, he cemented political alliances by means of multiple marriages.[17] He may well have seen in Christianity a new ideology appropriate for a non-traditional king. This does not mean that he was insincere, and there was much evidence, in the centuries which followed, of the depth of Kongo attachment to the new religion.[18] Henceforth, the throne was monopolised by his descendants.

In the short run, the Portuguese presence strengthened the Kongo monarchy, and foreign goods augmented the resources available to the Mane Kongo to reward his followers. Successive kings imported firearms and employed Portuguese mercenary musketeers. At first, the Portuguese bought products such as copper and local cloth. Pereira noted at the beginning of the sixteenth century: 'In this land of Maniconguo there is no gold ... but there is much fine copper and many elephants ... we barter the copper and ivory for linen ... In this Kingdom of Kongo they make cloths of palm-leaf as soft as velvet, some of them embroidered with velvet satin, as beautiful as any made in Italy.'[19]

But soon external commerce was overwhelmingly dominated by the sale of slaves, who were at first mostly obtained at markets outside the kingdom, and especially at Mpumbu, the strategic nature of whose site is reflected in the fact that it was roughly the future location of Kinshasa and Brazzaville. It thus became a great entrepot for both local and exotic commodities.

No slaves had been sold there previously; they were called people acquired with *nzimbu* (Kongo shell money).[20] A route from Mpumbu to the sea ran through Mbanza Kongo, and a new class of Afro-Portuguese long-distance traders developed, called *pombeiros*, those who travel to Mpumbu.

In 1568, the Kongo kingdom was almost overthrown by a people called the Jaga, who seized the capital, sacked villages and burnt churches. The king was forced to take refuge on an island in the Zaire river and returned to power only with the help of Portuguese forces from São Thomé. Nearly three hundred years later, a visitor was shown a swamp near the capital, formed by the tears of a local divinity, grieving over this invasion.[21] Much has been written on the identity of the Jaga; they were an inland people – perhaps the forebears of the modern Yaka – and their rising may well have been a response to the pressures of the slave trade.[22] Alternatively (and the two models are not necessarily incompatible), they may have been seeking to make a greater profit from it by cutting out the middlemen. The root of their name, *aka*, means stranger or brigand.[23] Not all the slaves sold by the Kongo elite were acquired outside the kingdom's borders, and rapacious nobles often preyed on the peasantry. As early as the reign of Afonso, there is evidence of kidnapping, and in the seventeenth century fathers branded their sons to protect them from enslavement – the implication being that they were already someone's property.[24]

The profits of enslavement progressively distorted the patterns of social life. If someone broke a borrowed calabash, no repayment was acceptable but a slave, and it was said in the mid-seventeenth century that 'they are more often moved to war to acquire a quantity of slaves ... than for political needs and matters of state'. Alvaro II had a large slave army,[25] and some thought, by then, that slaves outnumbered the free. Male slaves carried out the traditional agricultural tasks of women as well as those of men; their labours, combined with the impact of new crops, sustained an enlarged court. Literacy in Portuguese, perpetuated in local schools, enabled successive kings to keep records, and correspond both with the provinces and with European powers.[26] By the seventeenth century, Kongo subjects paid a poll tax, which was collected in cash, and other dues were payable as well. Thornton suggests that these were not a heavy burden – the poll tax in Soyo was two mabongo; it cost between 80 and 120 mabongo to marry.[27] But villages were built away from the main roads, out of the way of travelling notables and their retinues.

> To collect the tribute they almost always need to use violence, and this requires a lot of time and work . . . The collectors, if they are not well accompanied, risk losing their lives because of the evils they inflict on the . . . country-inhabitants to get them to pay. These, oppressed and vexed, frequently rebel, and if they cannot avenge themselves in any other manner, expel them from the country.[28]

Sometimes peasants restricted production, to reduce the amount which could be appropriated – they 'refuse to sow abundantly and to raise cattle, [because they] would rather suffer penury than to work for someone else'.[29] It was said that when nobles fought nobles or peasants peasants, the casualties were low; there were more deaths when they fought each other.[30]

The king expelled by the Jaga went on to rule for nineteen years; his successor, Alvaro II, also had an exceptionally long reign (1587–1614), clear evidence of the kingdom's recovery. Alvaro II attempted to break free from the control the Portuguese and the merchants of São Thomé exercised over his state's external relations by sending an ambassador to the Pope. He was held in Lisbon for three years – a symbol of Kongo's difficulties in joining the commonwealth of Christian nations on equal terms. Like Afonso I before him, Alvaro asked in vain for technical aid. The foundation of the Portuguese colony of Angola in 1571 did not immediately weaken the Kongo state – the main thrust of Angola's expansion was eastward into Ndongo and, by importing large quantities of Kongo cloth, for sale locally, it may have strengthened its economy. In the course of the seventeenth century, the Kongo state became weaker and more fragmented. Soyo, a Kongo province to the south of the Zaire estuary, successfully asserted its independence from the 1640s on. 'Towards the sea-coast are many lords who, although of inferior rank, usurp the title of king.'[31] In 1665, the king and many of his courtiers were killed by – largely African – Angolan forces at the battle of Mbwila. The kingdom never recovered, and for a long period the capital was deserted.

In this situation of crisis, a woman prophet emerged – Vita Kimpa, baptised as Beatrice, who claimed to be the medium of St Antony. Her teachings were a fusion of traditional religion and Catholicism, and she proclaimed that Jesus and His Mother were black and locally born. Both nobles and poor responded to her teaching, and Mbanza Kongo was reoccupied. She was burnt at the stake for heresy in 1706, her baby son narrowly escaping the same fate.[32]

A little later, Pedro IV (d. 1718), refusing to make war on a rebel, said:

> in no way would he make war, as it was the continual warfare which had already destoyed the kingdom, and also the Faith. Nor did the Congolese want any more troubles. They were already tired of being like beasts in the fields and wastelands:

outraged, murdered, robbed and sold, and their relatives, wives and children killed on all sides.[33]

The unified Kongo kingdom had gone for ever, and the patrimony of its kings shrank to the area round their much diminished capital. Atlantic trade tended to go north to the Loango coast and an independent Soyo, or south to Angola and Benguela. Christianity did not die out, but mutated into profoundly indigenised forms. Literacy survived and the Kongo elite corresponded on banana leaves because of the high cost of paper. The memories of a dramatic and remarkable history survived, and a certain intangible mystique continued to surround the king.

The Loango coast

The three small kingdoms on the Loango coast – Loango, Kakongo and Ngoyo (with its capital at Cabinda) – were first involved in Atlantic trade in the 1570s, the time when the Luanda colony was founded. They had longstanding economic and cultural links with the interior – coastal metal workers would travel every season to the mines, where they would extract, smelt and cast iron and copper and bring it back to the coast. As we have seen, their culture seems to have been influenced by that of the Tio. The institutions of Loango, in their turn, influenced those of their northern neighbours, as far away as the Gabon estuary.[34] Until the 1670s, few slaves were sold and the main export was ivory. The Portuguese also purchased copper, elephants' tails, local cloth and camwood, which they sold in Angola in return for slaves. Some of the cloth was used by the Angolan government to pay its soldiers at inland garrisons.[35] The Dutch settled in Loango from 1593 on, buying ivory and camwood. The ivory frontier moved inland, as elephant populations were exhausted, and by the mid-seventeenth century it had reached Lake Malebo.

In the last third of the seventeenth century, the pattern of Atlantic trade on the Loango coast changed dramatically; almost a million slaves were exported between 1660 and 1793, more than a quarter of a million more by 1835. Here too there is evidence of an increasing degree of social oppression, and people were enslaved for trifling offences.[36]

In the third quarter of the eighteenth century there was a protracted dispute between king and aristocracy, and the sovereign who died in 1787 had no successor for over a century, partly because no one had the wealth needed for the ceremonies, and partly because the ritual prohibitions surrounding the office were incompatible with participation in foreign trade.[37] (In Calabar, the ritual role of the Ndem Efik also declined for this reason.)

Lemba[38]

Between the Zaire and the Kwilu-Niari rivers and the coast and Lake Malebo, a cult called Lemba flourished; it is first documented in the mid-seventeenth century, and died out in the 1930s. It was 'a drum of affliction', a type of cult organisation which is found over vast areas of Central Africa and has been well described in Zambia. In this case, the afflicted were the prosperous – rulers and merchants – who felt their success made them vulnerable to the envy of others and to sorcery. It is ironic that this malaise was experienced by the apparent beneficiaries of Atlantic trade.

Dapper described the shrines of seventeenth-century Loango, such as Kikokoo, a sculpture of a human being, located on the coast near a cemetery. 'It is said that Kikokoo is there to protect the dead, and to prevent sorcerers from making them leave their graves to force them to work and to go fishing with those of the night. This *nkissi* [charm, cult object] also presides over the sea, prevents storms and tempests, and brings ships to safe harbour.'[39]

Another *nkissi*, Boessi-Batta, was carried by African merchants on trading journeys, although it weighed ten or twelve pounds.[40] In Janzen's interpretation, it represented the ambiguity of goods from afar, their danger and attractiveness.[41] The myth of the enslaved soul is clearly rooted in concepts of witchcraft: 'the belief that no one dies except through the malice and enchantment of his enemy, who, by the same spells, revives him, transports him to deserted places, and makes him work there to enrich himself. The murderer feeds him on food without salt, for if the victim tasted salt, he would pursue his killer to the limits.'[42]

The Tio kingdom

The Tio are part of an ethno-linguistic grouping generally known as the Teke (a Kongo ethonym).[43] The Tio plateau is relatively barren and can sustain only a low population – not because of lack of rain, but because the soil (Kalahari sands) cannot retain moisture. An early sixteenth-century account of the area states that 'we do not know of any profit to be had there'.[44] It was proximity to the copper mines of Mindouli and to Lake Malebo which gave it commercial importance. Lions flourished in its savanna environment and were central to its political symbolism – the king used his magical powers to send them forth against his enemies. He was a ritual figure whose sway did not extend beyond his capital, Mbe. He had close symbolic links with iron working – a sacred fire was kept burning throughout his lifetime, and a great official was called Owner of Anvils. The king was the custodian of a powerful spirit, Nkwe Mbali, Court of the Lion, which lived in a cataract; water from it 'cooled' the state when witchcraft, disease or famine threatened to consume it. The king was forbidden to see the Zaire river or Lake Malebo, and real power was in the hands of local lords. They were wealthier than the king, who gave away much of his property in the course of his installation, and each owned a ritual object called *nkobi*, the contents of which came partly from Loango and symbolised 'the ocean, wealth, peaceful relations and power'.[45] Again, we have the symbolic expression of wealth and power from the sea.

The Bobangi

Those involved in commerce inland from the Loango coast acquired a new identity as the Vili, and the same process occurred on the Zaire and its tributaries. The people who became the Bobangi gave their name both to the Ubangi river (which they called Mai ma Bobangi) and to the French colony of Oubangui-Chari.[46] They had so much in common with the Tio of Lake Malebo that early observers thought they were the same people;[47] here as elsewhere, ethnic labels, although useful,

> slip, slide, perish,
> Decay with imprecision, will not stay in place.[48]

They were originally fisherfolk, living on the few scattered mounds which rise above the inundated forest, and exchanging fish for grain and other vegetable foods. Their transformation into a new ethnic group, engaged in long-distance canoe trade, occurred in the late eighteenth and nineteenth centuries. They dealt mainly in slaves and ivory, but they also increased the volume of inter-regional trade, filling otherwise unused canoe space with a variety of goods. Merchants developed links with traders from other communities by intermarriage and blood brotherhood, and Bobangi became a lingua franca, shared with another river-faring people, the Ngala; it developed into liNgala, one of the major languages of modern Zaire. Villages expanded and hived off new settlements, largely by the continual incorporation of captives, in a process which recalls the history of the trading houses of the Niger Delta. The egalitarian world of the fisherman gave way to a much more polarised society, consisting of wealthy trader-chiefs on the one hand and the enslaved on the other. Birth rates were low, and a modern researcher found few Bobangi to study.

The popularity of gambling, which we have noted in the context of the Aja states, and which sometimes ended with the loser's enslavement, reflects the triumph of the cash nexus. There was a belief – which has parallels in distant parts of Africa – that an individual could only gain great wealth by a pact which involved the deaths of one or more family members, and traders relied on magic, sometimes involving a human sacrifice, to pass the river's whirlpools.[49] After the foundation of the misnamed Congo Independent State in 1885, Europeans took over this riverain trade, driving out the Africans who had pioneered it. Exactly the same thing happened to the Brassmen on the lower Niger, in the era of the Royal Niger Company.

Angola

In 1571, the grandson of Bartholemeu Dias was given a charter to found a proprietary colony in Luanda, an area where the Portuguese had traded clandestinely since the beginning of the century. (Virginia is a later example of a proprietary colony.) By the terms of the charter, he was bound to encourage white settlement. The new colony began in the lee of Luanda Island, the source of the Kongo kingdom's shell currency, which soon became inflated and worthless, due both to uncontrolled exploitation and the import of foreign shells.[50] The cowrie currency of West Africa shared the same fate at a later date.

Some hoped to develop a land route across the continent and shorten the journey to India, but above all the Portuguese were attracted by reports of inland silver mines at Cambambe. After thirty years of conflict and much loss of life, they reached the area, only to find that the mines did not exist. There was a real mineral resource 80 kilometres south of Luanda – deposits of high-quality salt, which remained outside Portuguese control. Refugees from slavery in Luanda often came to work there.[51]

The name Angola came from the title of the ruler of the Mbundu state of Ndongo, the Ngola a Kiluanje, Conquering Ngola. The new settlement was a coastal enclave, much smaller than the modern nation, with a single inland settlement. Angola was Africa's first colony. When the mirage of silver disappeared, its economy rested on the export of slaves, and a Portuguese king prohibited further prospecting for minerals, lest it disturb the slave trade![52] In West Africa, slaves were acquired by purchase. The trade was indeed violent, but the violence occurred at the time of the initial capture. In Angola, many slaves were obtained as tribute or as war booty. Sixteenth-century observers commented on the density of the population round Luanda; in the seventeenth century, they described an empty landscape from which the local people had fled. The Pende were among them; they settled far inland on the middle Kasai. 'From that time until our day the Whites brought us nothing but wars and miseries.' 'The white men spat fire and took away the king's salt pans.'[53]

The Ngola's kingdom

The state of the Ngola a Kiluanje, with its capital 160 kilometres from the sea, is often referred to as Ndongo; it was probably quite small when the Portuguese first began to trade in Luanda. The initial result of Atlantic trade was to strengthen and expand it, as it raided for slaves for the planters of São Thomé. In 1579, the Portuguese began to advance inland from Luanda. Successive Ngola succeeded in holding them at bay for forty years, confining them to a coastal enclave and an isolated fort 150 kilometres inland. When they were finally defeated it was largely by African agency – the forces of the Imbangala. The effective conquest of Ndongo began in 1605 and was complete by 1621. A puppet king remained in office; when a later Ngola attempted to reassert his independence in 1671, he was overthrown and his capital became the site of a Portuguese fort. It was exactly a hundred years since the original Angola charter.

The Imbangala

In the late sixteenth and early seventeenth centuries, a ferocious people called the Imbangala played a major role in the affairs of what is now northern Angola, led by a king with the title of Kinguri. They are said to have practised infant sacrifice and cannibalism, and to have forbidden marriage and procreation. In an earlier chapter we described a Lunda tradition on the borders between myth and history – the story of the princess who marries a noble hunter and inherits her father's kingdom, and of her patricidal dispossessed brothers, Kinguri and Kinyama, who leave for distant lands. The former is said to have led his followers to the Atlantic, until they wearied of his cruelty and starved him to death. It was once thought that Kinguri was a historical king who led the Imbangala to the west.[54] In a celebrated monograph, Miller interpreted this and other traditions in terms of a system of perpetual titles, so that it was the lineage attached to the Kinguri title which migrated.[55] He has now reinterpreted the same data[56] and sees the Imbangala as local people who adopted an extreme lifestyle in response to the impact of the Atlantic slave trade and to famine (perhaps reflected in the story that the Kinguri starves to death). They adopted the ideology of a Lunda title – the common phenomenon of ascribing ritual prestige to what is distant. In the 1620s they left the barren coastlands again and settled in the fertile valleys of the Kwango river.

They were, of course, very similar to the Jaga, with whom they have sometimes been identified. Contemporaries drew comparisons with the Mane invasions, documented in West Africa in the early sixteenth century, and the ferocious martial culture of the 'Zimba' in Zambezia. They are comparable, but entirely distinct historical phenomena, all of which are best understood as a response to famine.

The Imbangala were the most successful warriors of their place and time. They allied with the government of Luanda in 1611, and their wars provided slaves for the Atlantic trade. In 1665, Angola defeated the Kongo forces at Mbwila with their help, which was probably decisive.

During the long death agonies of the Ndongo kingdom, two new states were established still further in the interior, in the Kwango valley, Matamba and Kasanje. The Kasanje kingdom was founded by the Imbangala; their king was called the Kinguri, and the Portuguese called him 'Our Jaga', but they soon abandoned the extremes of their former lifestyle, and 'became Mbundu'. They had probably, indeed, always been Mbundu, and Imbangala is a code name for a desperate and anguished phase in a long history. Kasanje prospered from slave raiding and carefully maintained a broker role between the interior and the sea.[57]

Nzinga (*c*. 1580–1663)was the sister of the last effective Ngola a Kiluanje. She seized power with the support of royal slaves and formed an alliance with the Imbangala in 1624, the Portuguese supporting a rival claimant. She left the dissolving state and founded a new kingdom at Matamba, a choice determined at least in part by its tradition of women rulers.[58] In 1656, the old queen allied with the Portuguese and became a Christian.

Nzinga assumed a man's persona; she wore male dress – her husbands dressed as women – and led her armies in person. She was succeeded by her sister, Barbara, and queens ruled for 80 of the 104 years following her death.[59] These rulers still called themselves Ngola a Kiluanje, although they lived some 200 kilometres away from the original kingdom; the state was often called Jinga, or Nzinga.[60]

There were other inland states which also played a broker role; one of them, the Holo kingdom, shared this tradition of woman rulers; they are depicted in statuary as stern figures with a male physique.[61]

Benguela

The export of slaves from Benguela began in 1615, the result of a diaspora of merchants of mixed Portuguese and African descent, fleeing the exactions of the

Portuguese government's representatives at Luanda. Some of them settled inland in places such as Caconda; by the nineteenth century they had acquired an 'ethnic' identity as Ambakistas or as Ovimbali.[62]

The Ovimbundu (who speak uMbundu) live on the Benguela plateau and are the largest ethnic group in modern Angola, a fact which contrasts oddly with their relative neglect in the literature. The ethnym, like that of their northern neighbours (Mbundu who speak kiMbundu), is of Kongo provenance – the names are the same, the prefixes differ. Both Ovimbundu and Mbundu spoke Western Bantu languages[63] and had many culture traits in common. The former were also linked by tradition and cultural ties to peoples of the south and east, and an Ovimbundu state in the south-west belonged to the Southern Bantu Cattle Complex. There were thirteen or fourteen separate kingdoms, with different traditions of origin. Fetu, which tradition suggests was the earliest settlement, was radiocarbon-dated to late in the first millennium CE.[64]

Imbangala warlords established their hegemony among the Ovimbundu. The traditions of Wambu tell of a 'Jaga' conqueror who was killed by his subjects because of his cannibalism[65] – like the story of the Kinguri's death, it may preserve an echo of a time of famine. By the eighteenth century, Ovimbundu rulers were locked in constant wars, which supplied slaves to Benguela in return for firearms. In time the slaving frontier reached the upper Zambezi.[66] The Ovimbundu came to organise huge caravans which carried slaves, ivory and wax from Bihe to Benguela. Diseases travelled along these routes as well – among them smallpox, variously called 'great suffering' or 'great punishment'.[67]

The Lunda empire

The heartland of the Lunda empire was on the Lulua, a tributary of the Kasai, almost equidistant from the Atlantic and Indian Oceans. The origins of the Lunda state are lost in the world where myth and history meet, the world of the hunter-prince Chibinda Ilunga. Its expansion into an empire seems to date from the eighteenth century. Each king built a new capital in the same general area, and visitors commented on their excellent layout and and on their cleanliness[68] – in the early nineteenth century a Lunda ambassador was disappointed by Luanda.[69] Land was abundant and labour scarce; long before they exported slaves to the coast, the Lunda raided for captives, who were settled on plantations near the capital in a familiar pattern of 'internal colonisation'.[70] By the eighteenth century, cassava had become the staple food; the Lunda took it to Zambia when the Kazembe state was founded; perhaps it was this new crop which made their remarkable expansion possible.

Much regional economic exchange took the form of tribute and largesse: slaves, copper, raffia cloth, salt, and foodstuffs such as cassava flour or dried fish, were collected under the supervision of officials called *tukwata*. In return, the king redistributed prestige and luxury items, which were often foreign imports, once the tide of Atlantic trade reached the heartlands.[71]

The export of slaves to the Atlantic seaboard seems to have begun in the eighteenth century; they were obtained partly through raiding and partly through distortions of the judicial system. In 1848 a visitor was told that the end of the slave trade would revive the death penalty.[72] The trade route to the west ran through Kasanje. In 1680, a visitor there described (apparently) Lunda traders who visited it to exchange palm cloth and ivory for salt.[73] Like many broker peoples, the merchants of Kasanje encouraged horrific stereotypes to keep European merchants and inland peoples apart. In 1808, the Lunda king, the Mwant Yaav, overcame these ideological barriers and initiated direct contacts with Luanda.[74]

The Kinguri legend is part of a wider Lunda saga – his brother, Kinyama, is said to have migrated south, founding principalities among the Lwena (Lovale) on the modern Zambia–Zaire frontier. Do these traditions describe real migrant dynasts, or were they invented in response to the prestige of a great empire, which led local leaders to 'become' Lunda (or Luba)? In the case of Kinguri and Kinyama, the latter seems more probable, but sometimes real Luba or Lunda immigrants founded dynasties 'on the edge of empires'. These historical or ideological links found expression in the payment of tribute and in the reciprocal exchange of gifts.

The Ndembu are a small people who live, like the Lwena, on the Zambia–Zaire frontier and were the subject of celebrated anthropological studies by the late Victor Turner. He found that they had little in the way of myths and that their world view was implicit in 'the forest of symbols' in the rich world of their ritual events. Ndembu tradition tells of Lunda immigrants, led by the Kanongesha, who founded a state among the indigenous Mbwela, and this seems to mirror substantial historical truth – albeit expressed in the conventional stereotypes of southern savanna history.[75] The immigrants explicitly acknowledged the ritual rights of the original inhabitants, who, as so often, are still represented by a titled official.

The Kazembe's kingdom, on the Luapula (which divides northern Zambia from Zaire), was founded in the eighteenth century by an official from the Lunda heartland. A visitor in 1799 noted that the dynasty had come from the Lualaba sixty years earlier in an eastward thrust in search of salt and copper, and the aristocracy, while now speaking Bemba, has Lunda praise names.[76] The second Kazembe founded a kingdom on the Luapula in *c.* 1740 but continued to send tribute to the Lunda court.

Migrants – or ideas – travelled westwards as well as eastwards. In the early eighteenth century, Lunda adventurers established principalities on the Kasai, both among the recently arrived Pende and among the Yaka, taking, in the latter instance, the sinister title Mwene Puto.[77] The name (like that of the Alafin of the inland kingdom of Oyo who is remembered as King at the Sea) was a vivid symbol of the importance of the Atlantic factor. Were migrants – insofar as real individuals are involved – refugees moving away from a powerful central government, or were they sent by the Lunda court to exploit new economic opportunities, as seems to have been the case with the Kazembe? The foundation of the Kazembe's kingdom led to the creation of economic links with the Indian Ocean economic zone. In the eighteenth century, it exported ivory to the east through Bisa intermediaries; by the end of the century, the local elephant population was declining, and the Bisa sought ivory in the Luba kingdom on the Lomami.[78]

In 1806 and 1812, two *pombeiros* from Angola, Baptista and Anastacio, crossed the continent to Mozambique, and returned; the journal of their travels has been published,[79] but their relative obscurity makes a striking contrast with the fame and plaudits accorded Livingstone.

The Lozi kingdom[80]

The Lozi state grew up in the Zambezi flood-plain, in what is now western Zambia. The plain is 160 kilometres long and its width varies from 16 to 48 kilometres. Some versions of tradition link its ruling family with the Lunda. What, if any, kernel of historical substance they contain is obscure, but it is not irrelevant that in the nineteenth century the Lozi absorbed Mbunda immigrants from Angola and accepted their leaders as Lozi princes.[81]

The power of royal women threads its way through Lozi history; it is symbolically affirmed in the tradition that the first king, Mboo, who probably lived in the seventeenth century, inherited power from his mother, Mbuyu. She lives on in the Zambezi, in the form of a white cow.[82] There were approximately eleven reigns between Mboo and the Kololo conquest in 1840.[83]

The advantages and disadvantages of life on a flood-plain which was covered with water for part of every year are reflected in symbols which mirror the power of the great river – it was thought to be the home not only of Mbuyu but of a dreadful water snake and of a buck, whose hooves constantly changed its course. The fact that one of eastern Africa's major states grew up here reflects the triumph of human effort over the environment. As the waters rose, the people retreated to artificial mounds. When they rose still further, they migrated to the wooded uplands beyond the plain, led by the king in a royal barge constructed of materials provided by the whole kingdom; it was a symbol of Lozi mastery of the environment.[84] When the waters fell, crops were planted in the fertile silt and the Lozi would say, 'Here hunger is not known.'[85] The exploitation of the flood-plain demanded continuous effort – not only in farming and the creation of mounds but also in the construction of canals and dams and fish weirs. The complementary resources of forest and flood-plain encouraged trade (the people of the plain imported the very wood they needed for their canoes) and much was creamed off in tribute. A description from 1887 undoubtedly rings true of an earlier period. 'Just now, one sees in every direction long strings of people laden with burdens ... it is the king's tribute; honey, pelts, wild fruits, the fishing tackle, mats etc – the produce of the fields, of the chase, and of industry. The queen has her tribute like the king.'[86]

The court kept far more tribute than it redistributed and the surplus sustained it in luxury; the wife of the seventh king would bathe in milk and ask, 'What is it to lack?'[87] Some elements in the Lozi state were similar to those elsewhere, such as the seclusion of the sacred king, but others were distinctive. The Lozi were divided into territorial units and also into non-residential service units (sing. *likolo*, pl. *makolo*). Only the king could create a new one. They are often called regiments, but women and children also belonged to them and their duties included tasks such as salt production. Office-holders were commoners, re-cruited and trained as children. Their most senior members held a double-flanged clapperless iron gong, a symbol of authority through much of Central Africa.[88] There was a subordinate court in the south; its first ruler was a woman, and after 1871 this practice was restored. The custodians of the royal graves enjoyed much authority, as they were the mediums through whom dead kings spoke. There was a council of women at the court, called Mothers of the King, headed by the Queen Mother, but it was not revived after 1864.[89]

In 1840, Bulozi was conquered by the Kololo, Sotho-speaking warriors from the south, who ruled it for twenty-four years and then were overthrown, leaving their language as their most enduring legacy. The Kololo interlude is discussed in the chapter which follows, in the context of the Mfecane.

The Luba Lomami kingdom

The culture hero Chibunda Ilunga is the archetypal Luba royal, a central motif in oral literature and in sculpture.[90] But despite their reverence for princes, the Luba did not form a single unified state; there were several Luba kingdoms, one of which, on the Lomami, expanded greatly in the late eighteenth and early nineteenth centuries. This seems to have been a response to long-distance trade – an attempt to control Bisa caravan routes and later to acquire new sources of ivory and slaves. By the mid-nineteenth century, it extended from the Lubilash to Lake Tanganyika but, like the Lunda empire, it was to fall apart in the late nineteenth century.[91]

A Luba diaspora

Many of the peoples of Shaba and Zambia, the Bisa, Lala and Chewa among them, claim that their ruling family was of Luba origin. Kanyok was a satellite Luba kingdom which finally won its independence. The story of Citend, the Kanyok princess who flees from Luba oppression, is best understood as an ideological charter of this process.[92] The Bemba of Zambia have a myth of political origins which in its richness and complexity recalls the foundation myths of the Luba heartland itself.[93] It tells of a Luba prince who married a woman from the sky, with ears as large as an elephant's, a member of the Crocodile clan. He married her; their offspring built a great tower which collapsed, killing many; the king punished them and tried to kill them with a concealed game pit. The story tells of incest, of a flight by princes with seeds in their hair, a journey across the Luapala and past Lake Bangweulu. The Mushroom clan stayed behind, to become the ruling clan of the Bisa; another migrant became a Lala king. Finally the Bemba kingdom was founded, with its capital named Crocodile. The dangerous predator, which feeds on its own kind, is, here as elsewhere, a symbol for monarchy. There were twenty-five Bemba kings before 1896; the system of succession means that their reigns were fairly short, and a seventeenth-century origin for the kingdom has been suggested. But in this case – as in that of 'the Kinguri' in Angola – it is likely that ideas travelled, rather than individuals.

The nineteenth century: the changing face of external trade

In Central, as in West Africa, the external slave trade took a long time to die, and the mechanisms for procuring slaves endured when the external demand ended, so that it was often followed by an expansion in domestic slavery. In 1847 the Mwant Yaav told a Portuguese visitor, in words which echoed those of his counterparts in West Africa: 'It is customary for us to sell as slaves those who commit murder or robbery, and those who are guilty of adultery, insubordination, and sorcery; and having a great number of slaves, what can I do with them but put them to death if I cannot find purchasers for them?'[94]

In the 1820s, the value of the slaves dispatched from Luanda was still ten times that of its wax exports.[95] The main markets for slaves were in Cuba and Brazil. Brazil became independent of Portugal in 1822 and its legal slave trade ended in 1830, but illegal imports continued until 1850. It was then easy for anti-slavery forces to blockade the island of Cuba. São Thomé had often acted as a clearing-house for slaves, and in the last two decades of the nineteenth century many were imported to work on its cocoa plantations. They were called *serviçaes*, indentured labourers, or 'slaves' writ large. As the slave trade declined, Luanda was impoverished – in 1847 its revenues were less than those estimated for the Lunda state.[96]

The export of slaves came slowly to an end, but the diverse social mechanisms which had been created to supply the demand endured. Sometimes enslavement was a concomitant of famine and when drought afflicted Kisama, in 1857, children were sold by their relatives for three or four bowls of maize flour.[97] The export of slaves was often replaced by the export of products collected, cultivated or processed by slaves – slaves paddled the canoes of the Bobangi and, in many cases, they added to the size of a labour force organised on gender lines. Chokwe women, some of them acquired through purchase, processed wax and later rubber.

It was the plantations and fisheries of southern Angola which came closest to a slave mode of production. On that desolate coast, where even drinking water was at a premium, slaves from inland homes with no knowledge of the sea were forced to go fishing. They were brought by sea from more populous lands further north, and became the Kimbari, a classic example of the evolution of ethnicity. The fish were dried by enslaved women and exported, first to the Zaire basin and later to feed the workers on the cocoa plantations of São Thomé.[98] The representatives of industrial Europe sought markets and raw materials in tropical Africa, but the goods supplied by Central Africa were quite marginal to its needs – ivory for piano keys, wax for candles. The elephant frontier, as we have seen, continually receded, creating a crisis for states which had grown to rely on the income it generated. Orchila, a dye-bearing lichen, was another product collected in the wild, and in 1844 Angola's main exports by value were ivory and orchila,[99] but the demand for the latter disappeared with the invention of chemical dyes.

Plantations were founded on a relatively small scale, sometimes by Portuguese leaving an independent Brazil. A mix of slave and free labour grew cotton, coffee and sugar cane, which was made into brandy for local sale, *aguardente*.[100]

On the Loango coast slaves cultivated oil palms and processed palm oil. Peanuts were grown for export both by slaves and by free peasants. The growing concentration on export crops may have worsened the food shortages to which west central Angola was prone anyway. The Konfo had produced food surpluses to provision slave caravans; by the 1860s, they were growing peanuts and coffee for export, and buying food.[101]

The Portuguese outlawed slavery in 1875; it was the legal form rather than the reality which changed, in part because slave owners were not compensated. Some slaves escaped and others became bandits, as did many free peasants whose land was lost to plantation owners. Here as elsewhere, Atlantic trade led to a greater social polarisation – a class of prosperous merchants on the one hand, an expanded body of slaves on the other. In many instances – Kongo, Loango, the Tio kingdom, Kasanje – it modified the balance of power within states, as merchant princes became more powerful at the expense of the king. The complexity of regional currencies both reflected and symbolised the intricacy of economic life. By the late nineteenth century, the major currencies at Lake Malebo included the brass rod – soon destined to supplant the others – a length of imported cloth, a length of raffia cloth, and shell money. Locally produced lead and copper ingots had been replaced by brass rods. In the Cataracts area, a bead was used as currency. Like many other currencies, the brass rod became smaller as time went on. Ivory and slaves were paid for in a package of cloth, gunpowder and guns.[102] Currencies were not multi-purpose – food was bought with rods or shell money and raffia cloth was used for social prestations such as bridewealth.

The Chokwe

The Chokwe were well situated to profit by the economic changes of the nineteenth century.[103] They lived in forests which were full of bees (valued for honey as well as wax), and were skilled hunters and blacksmiths, able to keep the guns used for elephant hunting in good repair. They desired little in return for their wax and ivory but guns and wives. The acquisition of slaves or pawns as wives was of particular importance in matrilineal societies, because their children belonged to the husband's lineage. Its rate of increase was otherwise limited to the reproductive capacities of its own women. In patrilineal societies, Big Men could expand their lineage rapidly by marrying many wives.

Since their own women were never given to outsiders and they continued to acquire wives by purchase, the Chokwe population expanded. Demographic pressure, combined with the infertile soils of their homeland and the progressive extinction of its elephants, led the Chokwe to embark on a series of migrations into the Lunda heartland in about 1850. At first their interests were complementary; the Chokwe preferred a forest habitat and the Lunda a savanna one, and each people kept one tusk from every elephant killed. The ivory was carried by Ovimbundu caravans to Bihe and Benguela, or through Kasanje to Luanda.

From the 1870s on, the Chokwe themselves turned to the caravan trade. Rubber exports from Benguela began in 1869 and thus lie beyond the time span of this study; like ivory, rubber was a resource soon wiped out by intensive exploitation. As the numbers of immigrant Chokwe grew, they turned from guests in the Lunda heartland to dominant warlords, burdening the caravans of others with arbitrary exactions, profiting by the internal conflicts of Lunda dynasts and capturing the Lunda capital in 1886. In the Lunda heartland, too, ivory supplies dwindled; earlier observers had commented on its prosperity; now they were struck by its poverty. The Chokwe soon lost their recently acquired sphere of influence to the new imperialisms of the time, but their expansion continued, and today they are to be found in eastern Angola, Zaire and Zambia.

While the Lunda empire fell to adventurers from the west, the Luba Lomami state was overrun by warlords from the east, who succeeded largely because of their access to firearms and the rivalries of local princes. Msiri created a short-lived state in Shaba, considered in the last chapter of this study.

Gabon

The coastal peoples of the region which became Gabon – the Mpongwe in the vicinity of modern Libreville, the Orungu further south, on the Ogowé – developed their own broker role and culture. The Ogowé reaches the sea in a maze of waterways, and it was not until the nineteenth century that Europeans realised they were the delta of a single river – the parallel with the Niger is apparent. Gabon has always been sparsely populated; in the nineteenth century, there were about 5,000 Mpongwe and much the same number of Orungu. John Newton visited the area in 1743; many years later he noted that 'the most humane and moral people I ever met with in Africa were on the River Gaboon, and at Cape Lopas; and they were the people who had the least intercourse with Europe at that time'. [104]

The Gabon coast, like that of Cameroon, played a minor role in Atlantic trade compared with the Niger Delta, the Loango coast or Angola. In the seventeenth century, the Dutch dominated its trade – ivory was the major export, and the coastal brokers were purchasers rather than sellers of slaves. In exchange for their ivory, 'they desired no other goods than men and iron'.[105] Here as elsewhere, a composite trade culture developed, and the elite adopted European dress and titles, 'King Jacobus' in the eighteenth century, 'King Denis' in the nineteenth. A visitor to the Mpongwe in 1838 found that some spoke French and that one man had served in the French army.[106] Like other broker peoples, they married women from the interior but did not provide Mpongwe wives in return. The export of slaves first became significant in the last third of the eighteenth century.[107] It lasted until the 1870s, as illicit slavers hid in its myriad waterways and smuggled slaves to São Thomé.

In 1839 and 1842, French representatives signed treaties in the Gabon estuary, as they did in what later became Ivory Coast, in order to check British encroachment in an area where their merchants were dominant. In 1848, Libreville was founded as a settlement for slaves liberated by French naval action, on a site destined to become first a colonial and later a national capital. The numbers of freed slaves settled there were minuscule and, in contrast with the Creoles of Sierra Leone, did not lead to a lasting distinct community. The name Libreville fossilises this episode in the past. At one stage the French considered leaving, but the settlement had momentous consequences for the future; Gabon was to become first a colony then an independent nation conspicuous for its attachment to France. It was the first foothold in what became the vast expanse of French Equatorial Africa – the modern nations of Gabon, Congo-Brazzaville, Central African Republic and Chad.

In the 1860s and 1870s, European merchants developed direct links with the interior, buying rubber as the elephant herds vanished. They eroded the broker role of the Mpongwe, whose numbers declined catastrophically, in part at least because of venereal disease. In 1842, a missionary called King Denis 'one of the most remarkable men I have met in Africa'. Twenty years later, it was said, 'Today he vegetates ill and without strength, his authority gone, his house fallen into ruin, his sons wretched drunkards.'[108]

The Fang are the largest ethnic group in modern Gabon; they appeared on the coast in the mid-nineteenth century, having travelled through the forest from the Sanaga river region in southern Cameroon, in a complex mosaic of migrations which sheds much light on the ancient expansion of the Bantu. Some traditions suggest that they fled from mounted enemies (whom it is tempting to identify with the Fulbe of Adamawa) but the historical reliability of this has been questioned.[109] The Fang, like the Igbo or the Berbers of the High Atlas, lived in small-scale segmentary societies, with genealogy as the guiding principle of group identity. They expanded by a kind of leapfrogging movement similar to the expansion of the Tiv in central Nigeria at much the same time. It is clear that they were drawn to the coast by the prospect of direct trade and, in particular, by the same image of rich spirit beings from the sea which prevailed in the Kongo kingdom in the early sixteenth century.[110] A modern scholar said that they have 'adopted a thousand novelties and search to explore and conquer in all domains'.[111]

Towards colonialism

In the year this book ends, there were four islands of colonialism in Central Africa – the Portuguese enclaves at Luanda, Benguela and (from 1840) at Moçamedes, further south, the French enclave at Libreville. In the years to come, Central Africa would be balkanised into a large number of colonial jurisdictions – the Belgian Congo, the four colonies of French Equatorial Africa, Portuguese Angola; Spain ruled Fernando Po and a small enclave on the mainland. Kamerun was a German colony, divided into French and British Mandates after the First World War.

Colonial conquest was to be facilitated by the fact that African societies were weakened by decades of violence and by widespread epidemics. The trade caravans carried infections as well as commodities; the smallpox epidemic of 1864 killed thousands, as did a later outbreak in 1872–3.[112] There were so many famines in the 1870s that a doctor wrote, 'The majority of inhabitants of this land are mummies rather than human beings.'[113] Jiggers were accidentally introduced by a ship from Brazil in 1872 and spread like wildfire; a well-known affliction in West Africa, where they were efficiently removed, their unfamiliarity wreaked havoc in Central and East Africa, dooming many to gangrene and death.

The first accounts of sleeping sickness date from the 1870s; its ravages caused depopulation in some areas. In some cases, it was caused by an influx of workers into tsetse-infested areas during railway construction. Labour migration also caused many deaths from malaria, as those lacking acquired immunities worked in mosquito-infested regions.[114] Here as elsewhere, depopulation could cause the spread of tsetse, as the balance between cultivated land and the wild was disturbed. A vicious circle was created, as tsetse caused further depopulation.

In Central Africa, as elsewhere, some profited from the changes of the nineteenth century, though many who lived by the sword also perished by it. But if cults of affliction flourished and spread, it was because so many felt themselves to be afflicted.

22

Southern Africa

Peace is like the rain which makes the grass grow, while war is like the wind which dries it up.

Moshoeshoe of Lesotho[1]

The growth of settler society at the Cape

The European presence at the Cape began as a resting place on the long sea journey to India, an opportunity to replenish supplies of water, grain, fruit and vegetables. In 1652, the Dutch East India Company founded a station there – the period of Company rule was to last until the British occupied the Cape in 1795, in the context of a protracted war with France. It was briefly restored to the Dutch in 1803–6, and then reverted to Britain.

In 1658, the first shipload of slaves was landed. Two-thirds of them were to come from Madagascar and many of the rest from Indonesia. White settlers tended to oppose their baptism, in case it led to their emancipation, and many became Muslims, converted by a succession of religious leaders, some of whom were not slaves but Asian political exiles.[2] By 1798, there was a slave population of 25,754, a free one (excluding the Khoikhoi and San) of 21,746.[3]

The first white farmers were the Company's former employees, who were soon joined by immigrants, and although many of the later were Germans or Huguenots, they became absorbed in a dominant Dutch Calvinist culture. The *trekboers* adopted a pastoral lifestyle not unlike that of African pastoralists and, like them, they migrated ever further in search of new pastures. To the north-west, diminishing rainfall limited their possible advance. To the north-east, they were to come into conflict with another body of advancing pastoralists – the Xhosa. In the seventeenth century, perhaps 20,000 San and between 100,000 and 200,000 Khoikhoi lived south of the Orange river. Their relations with the newly arrived Europeans began amiably – they were happy to exchange sheep and cattle for tobacco, copper and iron. But as time went on, the Khoi lost ever more of their land, livestock and political autonomy. They fought several wars against the Company to regain them, but in vain. Many came to work for white farmers, who relied heavily on their pastoral skills. In 1713, laundry brought ashore from a passing fleet introduced smallpox, and the Khoi were decimated. By the end of the eighteenth century, much Cape Khoikhoi culture had been eroded, including the language, which gave way to Dutch. A Nama told Robert Moffat, 'I have been taught from my infancy to look upon Hat men (hat-wearers) as the robbers and murderers of the Namaquas.'[4] By the 1770s, the *trekboers* had

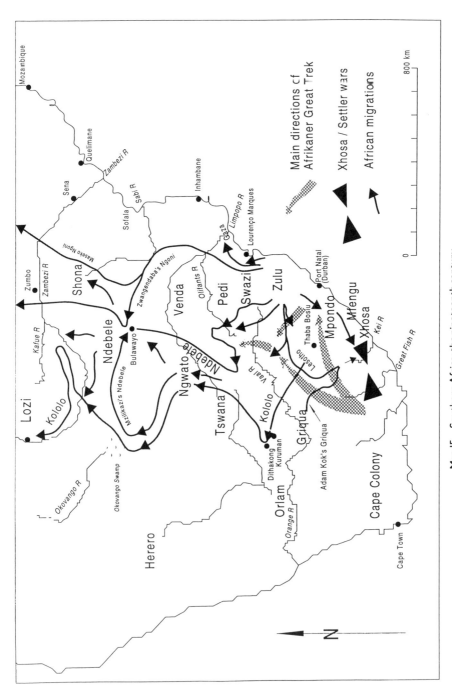

Map 15 Southern Africa: the nineteenth century

reached the Sneeuwberg mountains, peopled by the San. Here, adults were killed on a scale approaching genocide, and children captured for a life of virtual enslavement. 'The Dutch government, from 1774 to 1795,' wrote Philip, 'made a merit of extirpating Bushmen' and went on to describe much the same policy under the British.[5] The great historian E. J. Hobsbawm once wrote, 'Colonialism makes its victims its defenders.' Khoi fought in the Sneeuwberg on the settler side; later they served in the Cape Regiment. The last area of San settlement in Cape Colony was in its most arid part, south of the modern frontier with Namibia – it is still called Bushmanland. In the 1850s, *trekboer* commandos waged wars of extermination there. 'The women threw up their arms crying for mercy but no mercy was shown them.' 'Parties were in the habit of going out to hunt and shoot any Bushmen they might find.'[6]

The Khoi and the slaves were often hostile to each other and Khoi sometimes assisted in the recovery of fugitives. Perhaps they redirected the rage they felt towards the powerful white aggressor but could not safely express, but because there were so few women in the slave community there was increasing inter-marriage between them. The Khoi and the slaves were the progenitors of the modern 'Cape Coloured' – a term first used in the nineteenth century, a category imposed on those it purports to define. They spoke Afrikaans but no African language, and in religion and culture were indistinguishable from the white community. They now choose to be called 'black' or 'Cape Folk'.

In the eighteenth century, there was a considerable amount of cohabitation across 'racial' lines and it has been estimated that 7.2 per cent of the Afrikaner gene pool originated outside Europe.[7] The pastoral *trekboers* adopted many elements of the lifestyle of their African neighbours – they kept Khoi fat-tailed sheep, dried game strips (biltong) in the Khoi style, wore Khoi sandals and sometimes lived in Khoi-style houses. Dutch gave way to Afrikaans, a form of Dutch with a simplified syntax and many African loan-words. But increasingly, social life was rigidly segregated, a development symbolised by the creation of a separate branch of the Dutch Reformed Church for 'Coloured' in 1857.[8]

Many of those who were oppressed, exploited and marginalised by white settler society endured it for lack of an alternative. There were terrible penalties for slaves who escaped, and little prospect of success, though some still made the attempt, and fugitives' camp fires on Table Mountain could be seen from Cape Town. Bartolomeu Dias called the Cape, Cabo Tormentuoso. The name was soon changed but was enduringly true for both slaves and Khoisan under European hegemony.

Some Khoi, former slaves, and people of mixed descent sought freedom beyond the settler frontier. One of their leaders, a Khoi fugitive from a settler farm, called Afrikaner Jager, became a devout Christian before he died, in 1823. But

he became the more bewildered, especially when he thought of the spirit of the Gospel message, 'Good-will to man.' He often wondered whether the book he saw some of the farmers use said any thing on the subject; and then he would conclude, that if they worshipped any such being he must be one of a very different character from that God of love to whom the missionaries directed the attention of the Namaquas.[9]

His son, Jonker, reverted to banditry.

These new frontier societies were originally called Orlam (in Malay) or Bastaards; later, they called themselves Griqua (in Khoikhoi). Like the *trekboers*, they engaged in cattle herding (and raiding), hunting and trade; some turned to agriculture.

The Griqua Republic was situated at the confluence of the Orange and Vaal rivers; in 1813 it acquired a written constitution and later it struck its own coinage. When Andries Waterboer became its elected leader in 1820, he began to study political science – 'Minos, Lycurgus and Solon were names unknown to him ... He felt his deficiencies and thirsted for information.'[10] A number of small independent Griqua settlements were founded, all of which, in time, were swallowed up by the advance of colonialism. We should not, of course, idealise them – they were deeply implicated in both cattle raiding and slave capture – but recent studies have gone to the other extreme; the Griqua, in some accounts, have become the Other, responsible for much of the era of turbulence we call the Mfecane.[11]

Dominance and survival:[12] the Mfecane

The process of fusion and fission which is so evident in earlier history took place on such a dramatic scale in the first half of the nineteenth century that the difference becomes one, not of degree, but of kind. These tumultuous events are, by a convenient if modern convention,[13] called the Mfecane (an apparently 'Nguni'-based word) or Difaqane/Lifaqane in seSotho/seTwana. They have their origins in the late eighteenth century, in conflicts between three northern 'Nguni' communities – the Ndwandwe, Mthethwa and Ngwane (who were the proto-Swazi). The year 1817 is sometimes taken as the beginning of the Mfecane proper[14] – the year in which at least some Ngwane were driven from their homeland by the Ndwandwe, led by the ferocious magician and warlord, Zwide.[15] Sobhuza's Ngwane fled to what later became Swaziland, named after his heir, Mswati, one of two modern independent nations which owe their genesis to these events. Conflict among northern 'Nguni' groups continued and Dingiswayo, leader of the Mthethwa, was killed fighting the Ndwandwe; the vacuum created by the Mthethwa's defeat and disintegration was filled by Shaka, the architect of what soon became Zululand, an enigmatic and controversial figure, to whom we shall return. His forces defeated the Ndwandwe, some of whom fled to Mozambique; others, after a further unsuccessful struggle, became incorporated in the new Zulu state. This was only the beginning of a dramatic chain of events which was to transform ethno-linguistic groupings and political history, not only in Africa south of the Limpopo, but in modern Zambia, Zimbabwe, Malawi and Tanzania.

Partly because the interpretation of these events has real relevance for the contested politics of contemporary South Africa, historians disagree profoundly in their interpretation of them.

It seems clear that the upheaval in northern Nguniland, and the chain of events which followed, was ultimately rooted in ecological factors and in social processes which were caused, or intensified, by the impact of external trade – the export of ivory from Delagoa Bay (now Maputo). The suggestion that the conflicts were caused by the pressure of an expanding population on the limited grazing and arable land between the Drakensbergs and the sea is not a new one.[16] It has been the subject of much controversy, which has produced increasingly nuanced interpretations. Eldridge has pointed out that greater population densities can be achieved by growing crops rather than herding cattle[17] – this runs counter, however, to deeply entrenched Southern Bantu cultural preferences. Guy has suggested that the northern 'Nguni' competed for different *kinds* of grazing, needed at different seasons.[18] Archaeological research shows little evidence of long-term environmental deterioration in the northern 'Nguni' area.[19] There is some evidence that this occurred among the Tswana, where rainfall was lower and their large nucleated settlements may have caused environmental deterioration – trees were felled to make room for houses and cultivated fields, and wood was needed for building, firewood and smelting furnaces. All this meant that different areas were deforested when their locations were periodically shifted.[20] In 1802, it was said that the neighbours of the Thlaping had '22 capital places'.[21]

Studies of tree ring growth, complemented by oral tradition and written evidence, show that among the northern 'Nguni' there was a period of good rainfall in the late eighteenth century; the introduction of maize may also have fostered greater population densities. This was followed by a succession of droughts, producing killing famines – in 1800–3, 1812 and 1816–18 – the very period when militarised kingdoms emerged. Drought was an affliction which extended far beyond Nguniland. Among the Thlaping, in 1820, 'All the elderly people ... asserted that in their young days, the Krooman [Kuruman] was a great river ... No stream now ever flows within its banks.'[22]

The other contributing factor was trade – more specifically, the trade in ivory at Delagoa Bay, from 1750 on.[23] Cobbing suggested that it was a trade in slaves there that initiated the Mfecane, but it is clear that this was insignificant before the mid-1820s, and thus that it was a consequence, rather than a cause, of the Mfecane.[24] A 'decided aversion' to the slave trade was described among the people of Delagoa Bay as late as 1823; northern 'Nguni'-speakers in general refused to sell slaves until the arrival of the displaced Shangaan and Ngoni.[25] We have seen repeatedly in this study how control of external trade contributed to the formation of a ruling class. Ivory, of its nature, is a rapidly diminishing resource, and it seems likely that its depletion exacerbated existing political rivalries. Both Dingiswayo and Shaka showed a positive interest in the trade of Delagoa Bay; the latter tried to develop trade links with the Cape as well. Beads, brass and cloth predominated among the imports, valued, as we have seen, as a resource to win political support, and as famine insurance. Later, guns became of overwhelming importance.

Shaka

It was once believed that Shaka created a kingdom with the help of social and military innovations – the use of the stabbing rather than throwing spear, the 'head and horns' battle formation, and above all the *butho* age-grade regiment, and that it was by their means that displaced Nguni-speakers such as the Khumalo (Ndebele) achieved their successes. It is now generally accepted that these practices developed earlier among other northern 'Nguni' groups – the *butho* date from the mid-eighteenth century[26] and that these fixed battle forma-tions were often disastrous when used against horsemen with firearms.

The Mfecane has traditionally been interpreted in terms of Shaka's wars and the chain reaction they set up. This is mirrored in the title of Omer-Cooper's pioneering study, *The Zulu Aftermath*. It has always been recognised that the Mfecane had its roots in events which predated Shaka – the Ndwandwe, Ngwane, and Mthethwa conflicts, the flight of Sobhuza and his followers. Some recent writers have questioned the importance of the Zulu role and modified it in some details,[27] but it remains generally accepted that the rise of the Zulu state is central to these events.

Historians are now hesitant to endorse historical interpretations which stress the role of Great Men, but there are few more compelling examples of the impact of personality on events than the contrasting careers of Shaka and Moshoeshoe. Here again, the scholars disagree. Omer-Cooper stressed the creative role of Shaka himself and the other leaders of the Mfecane such as Mzilikaze; this was part of an Africanist reaction against racist stereotypes, but it led him to downplay the pathological aspects of Shaka's tragically flawed character.[28] Cobbing suggested that Shaka has been maligned, and that white traders created a daemonic picture of the Other to suit their own purposes – but has not provided an alternative biography.[29] Golan claims that many of the details of Shaka's life story, such as his 'illegitimate birth' and early period of exile are literary clichés.[30]

The accounts from which we know him – like all historical sources – are skewed by the prejudices and interests of their writers. It was a correspondent in a Cape newspaper, *The Colonist*, in 1828, who pointed out that 'The character and objects of Chaka it is not to be expected should be favourably represented by the tribes he had ruined, or threatened to destroy.'[31]

But thousands were killed on Shaka's orders, and the deaths of his mother and grandmother were followed by a holocaust. His panegyric, like so much other African literature in this genre, is explicit in its denunciation.

> King, you are wrong because you do not discriminate,
> Because even those of your maternal uncle's family you kill.[32]

Its imagery has the constant motif of danger – lion, leopard, horned viper – and repeatedly he is hailed as Destroyer, Devourer. (This is not simply literary convention; the praise song of one of his predecessors concentrates on his physical beauty, and of another on his meanness!)[33] Perhaps because of the traumas of his early life, Shaka's mental outlook can best be described as pathological. He and his mother spent a period in exile, as did Dingiswayo. Shaka won renown in the latter's army, and succeeded his father as ruler of the Zulu – then a small group. He did not permit the birth of offspring, reflecting a morbid fear of mortality, which was also evidenced in his pathetic anxiety to purchase hair oil, as a supposed prophylactic against old age. In the words of a Qwabe woman contemporary, 'A man would be killed though he had done nothing, though he had neither practised witchcraft, committed adultery nor stole ... A person like Tshaka is like a wild beast, a creature which does not live with its own young.'[34] His praise name was Dlungwana, the Ferocious One, and in the end he was put to death by a trusted *induna*, and his two half-brothers.

Shaka concentrated power in his own hands, appointing *induna*, officials, who were commoners and answerable to himself alone. Traditional initiation ceremonies were given up; instead, young men spent a period of years in age-grade regiments, devoting themselves not only to war but also to care of the royal herds. The burden of daily work in the homesteads fell heavily on women. The *butho* lived near one of a number of royal households, headed by royal women (not Shaka's wives, for he shunned marriage). An ideology which glorified young male warriors had the effect of marginalising women.[35] Men could not marry till they left the *butho*, and girls often resented their marriage to older men and sometimes eloped.[36]

Movements of peoples

A map of an Mfecane 'octopus' (showing migration patterns) has become unfashionable,[37] but the movements it depicts are historical, and unintelligible unless located in time and space. The warrior bands which left Natal and sought a home elsewhere were quite small – numbered in hundreds – but they absorbed captives on such a scale that they grew into nations. Each movement had a domino effect, as those dispossessed of their land and cattle fell on their neighbours in order to survive. Many of the migrants, including the Ndebele and the Ngoni, were originally northern 'Nguni'; but the Kololo, who conquered the Lozi kingdom, were seSotho-speakers from the highveld. The band who became the Shangaan settled relatively close to their original home, in southern Mozambique. Those who travelled furthest reached Lake Victoria Nyanza.

The ambitions of rival generals, the tendency for the population to build up to a point where the environment could not sustain it and for raiders to run out of communities with cattle or grain to plunder, led to repeated secessions and renewed migrations – the dream which led Zwangendaba to Tanzania was a vision of red cattle. They fought for survival, not only with the local inhabitants at different points on their journey, but often with each other.

The speed and degree of assimilation varied. The 'Nguni' of Gaza maintained a distinct identity; like other invaders, they feared the witchcraft of the defeated, which was believed to have caused the death of Soshangane. Among the Ndebele and Ngoni, the descendants of the original 'Nguni' formed an aristocracy; the most recently acquired captives were the lowest class, occupied in farm work. The Ndebele had a three-tier system in Matabeleland, an 'Nguni' aristocracy, a class comprising those of Sotho/Tswana descent, and the most recently absorbed level, those of Shona descent; intermarriage was rare and discouraged.

But life in these warrior states was a career open to talent, and first-generation captives sometimes attained high command. The incorporation of very different peoples into a single military and pastoral state was, in a sense, a triumph, but the agglomeration of peoples from different ethno-linguistic groups, the minority situation of the aristocracy, and the strain of travel and war created their own stresses. These found a characteristic expression in witchcraft accusations and executions, such as those which darkened Zwangendaba's last years and compli-cated the question of his heir. An important dimension of southern African history in the nineteenth century was enlargement of scale, the foundation of new states of varying size. Some, like the Swazi kingdom, relied heavily on ritual. A notable example of this was the Lobedu state, in the north-eastern Transvaal. In about 1800, its sacred kings were replaced by queens, when Majuji I acceded to the throne after a period of intense conflict between the king and his sons, her brothers. The queens were 'transformers of the clouds', their essential attribute the power to make rain; to the Zulu they were the greatest of all rainmakers. Three successive queens were succeeded by their daughters (the genitor's identity remaining secret). Like other sacred rulers, they were expected to be free from sickness or physical imperfection and to die by ritual suicide. Majuji I ruled until 1850, and her successor, Majuji II, the historical prototype for Rider Haggard's *She-Who-Must-Be-Obeyed*, until her death in 1894, which was followed by drought, locusts, rinderpest and famine.[38] The fourth Majuji died in 1981.[39] Other successful rulers had a much more secular outlook and relied heavily on the acquisition of horses and guns, as Moshoeshoe did. The Ndebele stayed closest to the Zulu prototype, though they modified their military organisation in significant respects, but they too came to recognise that guns were essential for survival.

The defeated

Histories of the Mfecane inevitably concentrate on the victors, but not all the migrants established new kingdoms or found a lasting home. Some names in the history of these years are unfamiliar, because the peoples concerned have ceased to exist as a separate entity.

The Hlubi were neighbours of the Ngwane, who fled inland after a bitter dispute about cattle – the domino effect followed. The Hlubi conquered the Tlokwa, then ruled by a queen, Ma Nthasisi, in the name of her young son Sekonyela. The Tlokwa fled, in their turn, and founded a new kingdom in modern Lesotho, which survived until it was defeated by Moshoeshoe in 1853.

It was soon the turn of a group of Ngwane, under Matiwane, to flee inland after a Zulu attack in 1822. They defeated their old enemies, the Hlubi, absorbing many of them in their own ranks, and attempted to settle in the Caledon valley. Attacked by both the Ndebele and Moshoeshoe's followers, they recrossed the Drakensbergs in the hope of settling in southern Nguniland. This brought them close to Cape Colony, and they were defeated in 1828 by the British, who believed them to be Zulu. Matiwane returned to Zululand, where he was put to death on a flat-topped hill, which has since borne his name.

One of the most famous battles of these years (famous largely because of missionary involvement) was fought between the Thlaping, southern Tswana, with the help of mounted Griqua with guns, and two of the marauding displaced peoples of the Difaqane, the Phuting and the Hlakwana. The former's victory, despite their smaller numbers, was an object lesson in the value of guns and horses which was not lost on African kings. The Hlakwana, killed or absorbed by the victors, vanish from the historical record.

Many defeated and displaced 'Nguni' settled among the Mpondo and Xhosa as clients; they were called Mfengu, beggars, and evolved into a new ethnic group. Not surprisingly, the Mfengu were avid enthusiasts for Christianity, education and modernity in general.

Many fugitives who reached Cape Colony were called, generically, Mantatees. They were once identified with the Tlokwa; it is now recognised that it is a blanket term covering different ethnic groups.

The Pedi kingdom

The Pedi kingdom in the Transvaal expanded rapidly in the late eighteenth century under Thulare (1790–1820). It was conquered in 1826 during the Mfecane – this is usually attributed to the Ndebele, though Delius, the historian of the Pedi, has made a case for Zwide's Ndwandwe. The Pedi state was restored by Sekwati, one of Thulare's younger sons, and despite the dangers posed by both the Zulu kingdom and the voortrekkers, it maintained an independent existence until 1879, when it was conquered by British forces, as was the Zulu kingdom.

It is instructive to compare interpretations of state formation in the Transvaal with debates on the origins of the Mfecane. Much the same theories are put forward. A growth in human and cattle populations in the eighteenth century, aided by the general tendency to higher rainfall, may have led to intensified competition for resources. Alternatively, drought, on record in the time of Thulare's father, may, as so often, have created competition for scarce resources. The growth of the kingdom was aided, not only by international trade through the port at Delagoa Bay, but by the Pedi's broker role in regional trade – which included the products of Phalaborwa metallurgists. In the late eighteenth century, trade at Delagoa Bay declined, when the Portuguese succeeded in excluding other nationals, and Thulare's wars can be seen as part of a contest for a diminished commerce.[40] These explanations, of course, are not mutually exclusive.

Swaziland

We have seen how Sobhuza led a small band of warriors to modern Swaziland, south of the Pedi kingdom. They chose this new home for its agricultural potential and, above all, because it was easily defended. It attracted many refugees, but the population was predominantly Sotho; not only Swazi speech but Swazi culture was greatly modified. The political structure was much more democratic than that of, for instance, the Zulu kingdom, and the Swazi abandoned the Nguni insistence on exogamy in favour of preferred cross-cousin marriage.[41] The powers of the queen mother were so great that the kingdom was in effect a dual monarchy. Somnjalose Simelane is said to have built up this position to restrain Sobhuza's arbitrary use of power.[42]

When Sobhuza died, in 1839, he was succeeded by the 13-year-old Mswati, who survived as king largely as a result of the efforts of his mother, Thandile, a daughter of Zwide's. She strengthened the monarchy by ritual means, especially by developing the First Fruits ceremony, and created a network of age regiments and royal villages.[43] Mswati built on the foundations laid by his parents, protecting the state against white and Zulu aggression by diplomatic means, and developing Swaziland as a stable, unified society.

The Ndebele

The Khumalo were northern 'Nguni' speakers, whose leader, Mzilikaze, was a vassal of Shaka's; conflict broke out, apparently because he withheld cattle due as tribute, and in 1822 he escaped with some two or three hundred warriors, and fewer women and children, to the highveld.[44]

The local people called them maTebele; they adopted the ethonym, becoming the amaNdebele. Like the Kololo and Ngoni, they embarked on a long quest for security, following policies born of aggression and fear (the two of course are closely related). Like the other migrant warrior communities of the Mfecane, they incorporated large numbers of conquered peoples; by 1829, Mzilikaze may have had as many as 60 to 80 thousand subjects.[45]

The Ndebele may have overthrown the Pedi kingdom, leaving the area in 1823. They then settled, first on the middle Vaal, and then, in 1830, further north, on the Marico river. But security was not to be found here; they were still subject to Zulu attacks and were finally expelled by the Griqua, Afrikaners and Rolong – again, the deadly combination of firearms and horses.

In 1837, Mzilikazi led his people to what was to be a lasting home. They crossed the Zambezi, invading a Rozwi state already weakened by Ngoni attacks, and settled in what became Matabeleland, in the south-west of the modern nation of Zimbabwe, permanently modifying its ethnic composition and the shape of its future history. There was an unsuccessful Rozwi revolt against the Ndebele in the late 1840s and after this the Rozwi state came to an end.

An older historiography depicted the Ndebele as ruthless conquerors of a peaceful people, in part to justify European overrule. But unlike his Ngoni predecessors, Mzilikazi created a relatively peaceful and stable state, distributing cattle in return for allegiance, and collecting tribute in soldiers and grain.

The word 'Shona' was Ndebele in origin and first adopted by the people themselves from the 1890s on. Previously, they had no sense of common identity and called themselves Karanga, Manyika, Zezuru and so on. Many Shona 'became Ndebele' or, in the case of the Manyika, Shangaan. Some Shona communities avoided raids by the payment of tribute, and others remained untouched by Ndebele and Gaza alike. The Ndebele retained their original language, but their religious ideas and practice underwent an interesting change. In a sense, this was inevitable; having left their homeland, they could no longer, for instance, make rain at the royal graves. They came to worship the Shona supreme God, Mwari; missionary influence may have encouraged them towards monotheism, though Lobengula (*c.* 1836–94), the second and last Ndebele king, forbade his subjects to become Christians. A rainmaker whose prowess in this direction was acknowledged by Europeans, he was an articulate and self-aware advocate of religious pluralism: 'he believed in God, he believed God has made all things as he wanted them ... he believed God made the Amandebele as he wished them to be and it was wrong for anyone to seek to alter them'.[46]

Shangaan and the Ngoni

Defeated by the Zulu, some of the surviving Ndwandwe warriors fled to Mozambique, led by two of Zwide's generals, Zwangendaba and Soshangane.[47] Their choice of direction may well have been decided by the trade of Delagoa Bay. The Ngoni, as they are known, fought among themselves, and in 1831 Soshangane emerged victorious, founding a military kingdom which he named Gaza after his grandfather; its people are called Shangaan, Soshangane's people. As so often, the vanquished took the victor captive, and the language of the Gaza state was not Ngoni but Tsonga. They raided among the southern Shona, some of whom opted to become Shangaan; some Tsonga communities, however, moved away.

The defeated Ngoni continued onwards, led by Zwangendaba, and invaded modern Zimbabwe in 1832, weakening a Rozwi state already in decline. But they were defeated by other migrant warriors and moved on, crossing the Zambezi in 1835. They left behind several war leaders, one of them a woman, Nyamazuma, who is credited with killing the last ruling Rozwi Mambo in 1836,[48] and who married Mzilikazi. Like the other Mfecane warlords, Zwangendaba included large numbers of captives in his forces – Tsonga from Mozambique, Shona from Zimbabwe, Nsenga and Chewa from Malawi. In 1848, he died in southern Tanzania, at a place he called Dreams, having travelled over 3,000 kilometres from Natal.

When Zwangendaba died, his sons were still children. The succession was complicated by the fact that suspicions of witchcraft had led Zwangendaba to decimate his own Great House, which should have provided his heir, and different *indunas* espoused the cause of different princes. One section moved as far north as Lake Victoria Nyanza, and raided in Buzinza and Buha. They were few in number and have ceased to exist as a separate ethnic group. Several sections migrated to Songea, further east in southern Tanzania where, in about 1844, a separate Ngoni band, led by Mputa Maseko, had already settled. At first they paid allegiance to Mputa, but later overthrew him. Most of Zwangendaba's followers travelled south to modern Malawi, leaving Mapupo ('Dreams') deserted; their invasion of the area was facilitated by the decline of the old Chewa kingdoms. The followers of Mpezeni – the surviving prince of the Great House – settled on the frontiers of Mozambique, Malawi and Zambia, and gradually came to speak chiNsenga.

The followers of his brother founded what proved to be the largest Ngoni state in Malawi, in the north, and raided among the Tonga and Chewa and also among the Tumbuka, whose language they adopted. This prince was crowned as M'Mbelwa in 1857 and reigned until 1891, the year when a British protectorate was established over what was then Nyasaland. Yet another Ngoni kingdom was established among the Chewa by Chiwere, an *induna* of Senga, not Ngoni, stock. The Maseko Ngoni, displaced from Songea, found a lasting home in southern Malawi, coming to speak chiNyanja; like the other Malawi Ngoni, they retain a strong sense of ethnic identity.

The Ngoni had little interest in trade or agriculture; their lives were dominated by cattle and by war, and their raids caused great suffering, though within their states there was a strong respect for order. The Tonga lived in small communities west of Lake Malawi. They suffered from Ngoni depredations and were forced to grow cassava, because it was less palatable and more difficult to steal. 'The Angoni are men who believe more in love and war than in work ... so that if they are hungry they meet their needs from an Atonga garden. This causes the Atonga to grow a food which the Angoni do not like called "Chakow".'[49]

Some migrated away from the Ngoni, sometimes to an adverse environment. The Makonde moved from the Ruvuma valley to a waterless plateau. Others limited their hours in the fields for fear of attack; the Matengo left crops in the valley bottoms for the raiders and cultivated plots for their own needs on the hillsides.[50] Some peoples avoided Ngoni raids by paying tribute while others adopted the Ngoni lifestyle and became raiders in their turn, with varying degrees of success. Some Ndendeuli were assimilated by the Songea Ngoni; others fled to a new home and formed a militarised state, becoming the Mbunga.

Some peoples, notably the Bemba, were strong enough to resist the invaders, and in the late 1870s, the Tonga, Kamanga, Henga and Tumbuka rose against their masters. The Tonga, despite the small size of their polities, were the most successful. They settled in stockaded villages by the lake shore, enduring the disadvantages of the site. 'We saw the evil results of the terror of this tribe all along the coast ... all the people are collected into a few great towns close to the water's edge. They have chosen the most unhealthy situations, each town having a marsh or water behind it.'[51]

The missionaries of Livingstonia were valuable allies, and western education offered the Tonga and others a way into a new and more secure world.

The history of each of these Ngoni kingdoms reflects complex encounters with local cultures.[52] Among the Chewa, the ruler was the Owner of the Land, charged with its ritual care and with rain-making. Inevitably, after their long migrations, the Ngoni lacked the sense of a sacred landscape, and their attitude to the land was primarily utilitarian. They prayed to their ancestors, especially Zwangendaba. They dreaded witchcraft and adopted the *mwavi* ordeal to deal with witches, but employed it on a scale which the Chewa abhorred, believing it defiled the land. The Chewa, for their part, called the Ngoni *Msaviti* (red ants) or *Mafiti* (witches).[53] The Maseko Ngoni sacked the ritual centre of the High God, Chisumphi. The cult did not die out but changed from a state religion to an individual cult of affliction, manifested in spirit possession, and shared by both Chewa and Ngoni. The Nyau mask societies were among the core dimensions of Chewa identity; they were a secret male cult into which all youths were initiated, and were forbidden in areas under Ngoni rule. But the Nyau societies still flourish in Chewa villages.[54]

The Kololo

One of the most remarkable journeys was made by a Sotho people, the Fokeng, whose odyssey began when their herds were seized by the Tlokwa (again, the domino effect). Sebetswane, who became their king while still young, led his people to the west in a search for cattle and security. They adopted the name

Kololo after the clan of a captive who became Sebetswane's Great Wife. They sojourned for some years in Botswana, raiding for cattle far to the west, and in 1839/40 reached the Tonga plateau in Zambia. They went on to conquer the Lozi kingdom, on the Zambezi flood-plain, guided by a diviner called Tlapane. 'He said, looking eastward, "There, Sebitane, I behold a fire which will scorch you. The gods say, go not thither." Turning to the west, he said, "There I see a city and a nation of black men. Your tribe is perishing and will be consumed, but you will govern black men, men of the water. They must not be killed, they are your tribe." '[55]

The Kololo ruled the Lozi for twenty-four years. Sebetswane was conciliatory and accessible, in contrast with the secluded Lozi kings, but he died in 1851 from the effects of an old war wound. Bulozi attracted traders from the east and west, and in 1853 Livingstone 'met Arabs from Zanguebar, subjects of the Imaum of Muscat ... and Portuguese from the farthest trading station inland on the West'.[56]

Sebetswane had intended his daughter Mamochisane to succeed him, but she longed for ordinary family life and abdicated in favour of her brother Sekeletu. 'I have been a chief only because my father wished it. I always would have preferred to be married and have a family like other women.'[57]

The new king was a leper, his character distorted by this misfortune. His regime became increasingly hated, and in the end a Lozi prince returned from exile to lead a successful revolt. It was a victory for ecology, as the Kololo were already decimated by malaria, to which they had no inherited immunity.[58]

Modern Lozi tend to minimise the Kololo episode. But although their regime was soon over, their language became that of the Lozi people, whose original tongue, seLuyana, survived only as a court language. Why this happened – in contrast with the pattern in Gaza and in the Ngoni states – is something of a puzzle, especially since some core elements in Kololo culture – the circumcision of adolescent males, and the age grade – were not absorbed. Some attribute it to the influence of Kololo women, who survived the rising and became Lozi wives. Mission influence may have played a role, as missionaries, some of whom were themselves Sotho, came to Bulozi from Lesotho.[59]

Lewanika was originally called Lubosi, the Escaped One, a reference to exile. He came to the throne in 1878 and adopted the name Lewanika, Conqueror, in 1885, after defeating a rival for the throne. His attempt to recreate the earlier Lozi state on the brink of the imposition of colonial rule suggests comparisons with the experience of Bunyoro. At his court, the Lozi discussed the pros and cons of missionaries and modernity. 'Don't we hear tell of all the black nations, all the chiefs having their missionaries to teach the young people and the Kings the wisdom of the white nations ... Others said, "No we do not need these teachers unless they know and teach us to make powder and such like things." '[60]

The king ruled in the north but there was a twin capital in the south, which, after 1871, was ruled by a queen, the Mulena Mukwae. In 1895, the incumbent, Maibiba, epitomised half a century of history in words which were true of much of southern Africa: 'Ours is a land of blood; kings and chiefs succeed each other here like shadows, they never grow old.'[61]

Time of troubles

These tumultuous events caused an immense amount of suffering and loss of life. Many fled to mountainous areas, and some were forced by starvation to adopt cannibalism, the ultimate index of a society in collapse. Its victims included Moshoeshoe's grandfather. 'Hunger ... was the first cannibal, it devoured us ... Each one ate his dog, then the sandals he wore on his feet, then his old antelope kaross, finally his leather shield.'[62]

In Natal, particularly hard hit by the repercussions of Shaka's wars, large areas appeared depopulated, though in many cases the population was displaced or concealed.[63] The Sotho and Tswana suffered greatly from the depredations both of African warrior bands and of Griqua and Afrikaner frontiersmen. There was, noted the Tswana, a distinction. 'Mosilikatze was cruel to his enemies, and kind to those he conquered, but ... the Boers destroyed their enemies, and made slaves of their friends.'[64]

What later became Lesotho seems to have experienced a crisis of increased population and pressure on resources even before the advent of the warlords. Expansion was blocked in one direction by the great mountain mass of the Drakensbergs, where only the river valleys were cultivable, and in the other by increasing aridity. Famines became more frequent, and so did witchcraft accusations.[65] A memory of these troubles is fossilised in Leboqo, Dispute, which was the original name of the man history knows as Moshoeshoe.

Moshoeshoe of Lesotho

Moshoeshoe was the son of a Sotho village headman in the Caledon river valley, born in *c.* 1786. He chose the name soon after his initiation; it means Shearer, and refers to a successful cattle raid. Despite his youthful predilection for this exciting pursuit, he was, when possible, committed to peace. 'Peace is like the rain which makes the grass grow, while war is like the wind which dries it up.'[66]

Moshoeshoe seems to have been deeply influenced by a Sotho diviner and rainmaker called Mohlomi. During initiation he had a vision from God – 'Go, rule by love, and look on thy people as men and brothers.' He travelled far afield, urging his hosts to care for the poor, avoid war, and not to punish those accused of witchcraft.[67]

When Moshoeshoe was in his early thirties, his people were threatened by the first of many invasions, besieged by the Tlokwa, which induced Moshoeshoe to lead his followers to a new capital on the flat-topped mountain Thaba Bosiu, where he established a kingdom which came to include many refugees and dispossessed. He spared those who had turned to cannibalism and supplied them with cattle, saying they were the graves of his grandfather. He ruled largely by consent, and subject peoples had a large measure of self-government. He was hostile to both alcohol and tobacco. In later life, he virtually abandoned the death penalty and he strongly opposed the persecution of witches. He welcomed missionaries, though he did not part with his many wives, who cemented alliances with different parts of his state. 'It is enough for me to see your clothing, your arms, and the rolling houses in which you travel, to understand how much intelligence and strength you have. This country was full of inhabitants ... wars have devastated it ... I have been told that you can help us.'[68] In the 1830s and 1840s, the Sotho imported horses and guns and, like many of his subjects, Moshoeshoe learned to ride and shoot. He welcomed modernity and encouraged commercial agriculture. It was noted in the 1840s that he was anxious to introduce European vegetables and fruit trees,[69] and his son tried unsuccessfully to teach him to read. Sotho peasants exported grain to Cape Town, and adopted the horse-drawn wagon and plough. His kingdom was surrounded by enemies – he paid Shaka tribute, and spoke fluent Zulu. When necessary, he engaged in war, repelling an Ndebele invasion (but winning them over with diplomacy and gifts) and defeating the Tlokwa in 1853. His state reached its highest level of prosperity in the 1850s and 1860s.

Moshoeshoe was brilliantly successful in protecting his people from African warlords, but in time the remorselessly expanding frontier of white settlement engulfed him. Afrikaner voortrekkers founded Orange Free State and began to settle in the Caledon valley. They were driven back in 1858, but in a second war, in 1865–9, they burnt the standing grain in the fields, so that the people starved. Moshoeshoe invited the British to establish a protectorate, which seemed a lesser evil. In 1868, two years before he died, his kingdom became British Basutoland – destined to become the independent nation of Lesotho. But its most fertile area in the Caledon valley was lost to Orange Free State, and the Sotho still mourn its loss. Mid-nineteenth-century Lesotho exported grain to Cape Town. Twentieth-century Lesotho was forced by land shortages to export its people, as labour migrants.

Moshoeshoe was the friend of missionaries, and we see these events largely through missionary eyes. It is not impossible that this has led us to idealise Moshoeshoe himself; it has undoubtedly led us to overlook and marginalise his opponents, the Tlokwa.

Interpretations

Few areas of the African past have been the subject of as much controversy as the Mfecane. The impact of Cobbing's work is extraordinary, especially as much of his output remains unpublished, and his seminar papers are discussed in international journals. Many of the details of his argument seem clearly wrong – missionary involvement in slave raiding, the Delagoa Bay slave trade as a cause rather than consequence of the Mfecane. But his writings and those of others he has influenced have led to a much more qualified and nuanced picture, a careful re-examination of the sources on which, ultimately, all generalisations must rest.

Academic reputations are more readily created by denouncing or, in some cases, ignoring the work of one's predecessors than by endorsing it (from neither have the works of the present writer been immune!). But the ultimate wellsprings of the Cobbing critique are much deeper, and reflect the political tragedies of the present. He was reacting against a bowdlerised popularisation of history which was used to defend both Inkatha and white hegemony – which emphasised the violence of African warlords, a 'depopulation' of large areas, creating a vacuum which whites were therefore morally entitled to fill.

One must, of course, distinguish the work of academic historians from the distortions of propagandists. It is only on the pages of the latter that 'black societies ... self-sequestered themselves into proto-bantustans in the era of Shaka'.[70] But history must be true, and not simply politically appropriate. Cobbing replaced the 'Africanist' model with one where Africans are passive, their states 'reactive', events shaped almost wholly by Griqua and white slavers and marauders. Shaka, as the daemonic Other, has been replaced by the Griqua, who, like many other Africans of the time, were the victims of tragic injustices and struggled to pluck the flower, safety, from the nettle, danger.[71]

The Xhosa wars

The Xhosa bore the brunt of successive invasions by white pastoralists, whose economy and need for land and cattle were so much like their own. By the late eighteenth century the Xhosa had crossed the Great Fish River and occupied the Zuurveld. Expansion was built into Xhosa socio-political structures – a chief's sons left their father's kraal, to which they could never return, to found settlements of their own.

At first, like the Khoi, they welcomed the prospect of trade with white settlers; they had a robust confidence in the value of their own culture. When they visited Cape Town, in the early nineteenth century, 'They expressed surprise at many of the things which they saw, but never think the white men are more wise or skilful than themselves, for they suppose they could do all the white men do if they chose'.[72]

The first war between white settlers and the Xhosa was fought in 1779–81, the ninth and last in 1877–8, and some have called these conflicts a Hundred Years War. Many Khoi supported the Xhosa in the third war, 1799–1803. As Chungwa, the leader of the Gqunkhwebe pointed out in 1808, 'he was in this part of the country before the Christians and as proof asked me if I do not see as many of the remains of old cafree's kraals as the walls of old houses'.[73] Four years later, during the fourth war, during which some 22,000 Xhosa were expelled from the Zuurfeld, the British killed him as he lay helpless on his death bed.

The settler frontier advanced ever further. In 1819, the Xhosa were expelled from the region between the Fish and Keiskamma rivers, and the following year 5,000 British settlers were introduced in an attempt to create a buffer zone of smallholders. Most of them soon adopted other lifestyles, but their arrival added yet another strand to South Africa's ethnic and linguistic complexities. By 1835, the frontier had advanced to include the Ciskei. Wars with the colony were a form of total conflict unprecedented in Xhosa experience; in earlier struggles, combatants sought to win resources – women, children, cattle – rather than destroy them, and casualties were low. Now homes were destroyed, granaries emptied and cattle seized, so that the Xhosa were defeated by hunger. 'You sent a commando – you took our last cow – you left only a few calves which died for want, along with our children ... Without milk – our corn destroyed – we saw our wives and children perish – we saw that we must ourselves perish.'[74]

In 1829, a Xhosa asked soldiers why his house was being destroyed. 'It seemed to be difficult to make a reply: there was a general silence.'[75] When the Xhosa first met the Europeans, they called them People of Another House. Later, they called them Beasts of Prey.[76] In 1835, the British settled Mfengu on Xhosa land, and they fought on the colony's side.

Clearly, Xhosa armed resistance could not succeed. But the policy of collaborating with the colony often failed as well – Ngqika, who chose this alternative, lost much of his land, including his own birthplace. Where the traditional leadership of kings and chiefs seemed unable to halt the white advance, the political vacuum was filled by prophets.

Xhosa prophets

Nxele was a prophet who began as an orthodox Christian and came to adopt the lifestyle of a Xhosa diviner. By 1819, when he led the Xhosa to war, he had come to see the world as a battleground between the Gods of the blacks and of the whites. He was captured and sent to Robben Island, like so many political prisoners after him, and drowned while leading an escape.

His contemporary, Ntsikana, began as a traditional Xhosa mystic and then became a Christian. He opposed the war and composed a hymn which is still sung today:

> He is the one who brings together herds which oppose each other,
> He is the leader who has led us,
> He is the great blanket which we put on.[77]

When he felt death approaching, he asked to be buried in the Christian manner. When his family refused he took a spade and dug his own grave. By the 1850s, the Xhosa were impoverished, demoralised and dispossessed, much of their land alienated to white settlers or 'loyal' Africans. In 1856 a girl called Nongqawuse was given a message.[78] All the cattle should be killed, because those who had tended them were defiled by witchcraft. If this was done, the dead would return with great herds. The Xhosa were profoundly divided. Some widows urged their sons to kill their cattle, in the vain hope of restoring their husbands to life. 'It is all very well for you, Sandile. You have your wives and children, but I am solitary.'[79]

The sequel was catastrophic: some 400,000 cattle were killed and 40,000 Xhosa starved to death; many of the survivors were forced to look for work in Cape Colony. The Xhosa had inflicted on themselves the total defeat which the settlers had been unable to achieve, and the Cape government, under Sir George Grey, took full advantage of this situation. An earlier outbreak of bovine pleuropneumonia meant that most of the cattle were doomed anyway.[80]

Modern Xhosa believe – wrongly – that Grey was responsible for the prophecies; in the words of a Black Consciousness song of the 1970s:

> Sir George Grey took our country
> He entered in through Nongqawuse
> The cattle died, the sheep died
> The power of the black people was finished off.[81]

The Great Trek

The 'Great Trek' was invented by later Afrikaner nationalists; the underlying reality was one of a number of small separate migrations in the 1830s and 1840s, following leaders who were often bitterly divided. As we have seen, Cape Colony fell into British hands from 1806 on. The abolition of the slave trade – though not of slavery – a year later created a labour shortage which the Khoikhoi were too few in numbers to fill. One reaction to the situation was to restrict the Khoikhoi's freedom of movement, reducing them to virtual slavery – the notorious 1809 'Hottentot Codes', abolished, largely as a result of missionary agitation, in 1828. From 1808 to 1828, farmers were forbidden to employ 'free' black labour.[82] But in fact an ever-increasing number of 'Mantatees', victims of the Mfecane, sought work there to recoup their shattered fortunes.

In some ways, the Afrikaners benefited from the British presence. The volume of trade increased, and a standing army enforced settler interests more effectively than the earlier volunteer commandos. But their language and culture were marginalised, and, considering themselves 'religious', they bitterly resented attacks from missionaries. One of the leaders, Piet Retief, published a manifesto before his departure, in which he complained of vagrant Khoikhoi, the abolition of slavery, conflict with the Xhosa, and 'the unspeakable odium which has been cast upon us by interested and dishonest persons, under the cloak of religion'.[83]

Lacking land of their own, the former slaves, in the countryside at least, remained poor and less than free. The abolition of slavery caused serious financial loss to slave owners, since compensation was inadequate and largely siphoned off by the brokers handling claims in London. White expansion was blocked by increasing aridity to the north-west, and by the Xhosa to the north-east. Most of the voortrekkers came from the Eastern Cape, where land shortage was most acute. Whatever the brutality and exploitation intrinsic in their life-styles, they believed that they walked with God. Some believed their journeys were charted by the prophet Joel and would end in the discovery of a new Jerusalem. They were accompanied by a larger number of Khoi servants – the forgotten voortrekkers. Most were originally drawn to beautiful and fertile Natal; the initial party was almost wiped out by Dingane, Shaka's brother and successor. Later that year, the Afrikaners won a victory over the Zulu army – the victory which whites remembered as the battle of Blood River, and which later Afrikaner nationalists made, sadly, into a national celebration. A small number of armed men, with wagons lashed in the laager formation, could defeat a vast host armed only with spears. But although they could win individual battles, the white invaders were in the long run vastly outnumbered by Africans. This was to prove their enduring and insoluble dilemma.

Most Afrikaners left Natal when the British established a colony there in 1842. The white population, which numbered 14,000 in 1863, has been mainly British ever since. They were vastly outnumbered by Africans who emerged from hiding or returned from exile – often to find their land alienated by white farmers and land speculators. Theophilus Shepstone, in charge of 'native policy' from 1853 to 1875, maintained white hegemony by constructing a largely artificial mosaic of tribal jurisdictions – prototypes of later Bantustans. Africans who found themselves landless sometimes worked as tenants or squatters on what had suddenly become European land, and absentee landlords benefited from 'kaffir farming'. Some were attracted to the ample landholding of the mission stations.

White settlers found that coastal Natal was ideal for sugar cane. The pattern familiar in the Cape emerged again – the clamour of white farmers for cheap labour. From 1860 on, Indian workers were introduced to Natal, adding another strand to South Africa's ethnic mosaic. Much later, the young Gandhi began his political career in an endeavour to right their wrongs.

The Afrikaner republics

The pattern of Afrikaner migration was determined by the relative densities of African population, the intensity of African resistance. The voortrekkers settled on the highveld, in areas which appeared depopulated as a result of the Difaqane, displacing the Ndebele, who continued their migration to the north. In 1848, the British annexed the highveld, but three years later Moshoeshoe's followers defeated a British contingent. Imperial sentiment was still at a low ebb, and British sovereignty in the interior seemed more trouble and expense than it was worth. (All this was to change when diamonds and gold were discovered.) In 1852, the British recognised the independence of two Afrikaner states – South African Republic in the Transvaal (and usually known by that name) and Orange Free State, between the Orange and Vaal rivers. In 1868, as we have seen, the rump of Moshoeshoe's kingdom became British Basutoland. Some Afrikaners settled in the Soutpansberg, but were driven out by the Venda in 1867; thirty years were to elapse before the forces of the Transvaal conquered the area, and then it was with the help of African allies. The Venda were the last indigenous people of South Africa to lose their independence.

In the 1860s, the lifestyle of the voortrekkers was still very similar to that of their African neighbours. Tswana, Sotho, Griqua and Afrikaners combined pastoralism, cultivation, hunting, and sometimes raiding, in different permutations. Their exports – pelts, ivory and ostrich feathers – were marginal to the needs of industrial Europe, luxuries for middle-class consumers. The revenue of the Afrikaner republics, which had some 45,000 white settlers in 1870, was so small that their officials were paid, perforce, in land. They were often divided by internal conflicts, and they were surrounded by independent African states, which were obtaining guns both by the export of ivory and the labour of their migrant sons.

The inequality of black and white was enshrined in the Transvaal constitution. African children were often kidnapped as 'apprentices' for a life of virtual slavery; Africans could not own guns or horses and were expected to carry a pass in 'white' areas.

The Improvers

In the last years of his life, the founder of the Swazi state, Sobhuza, is said to have foretold the coming of Europeans, carrying a book and money, and advised his people to accept the first and reject the second.[84]

The modern missionary movement began in 1799, with the arrival of the first LMS representatives at the Cape. They founded Christian villages among the Khoi and were particularly successful among the Griqua, already divorced from their original cultures. Van der Kemp, and John Philip after him, embarked on a prophetic critique of settler injustice to indigenous peoples. It was Philip who said in 1833:

So far as my observation extends, it appears to me that the natural capacity of the African is nothing inferior to that of the European. At our schools the children of Hottentots, of Bushmen, of Caffres [Xhosa] and of the Bechuanas are in no respect behind the capacity of those of European parents; and the people at our missionary stations are in many instances superior in intelligence to those who look down on them as belonging to an inferior caste.[85]

When the British annexed Natal in 1842, a great influx of missionaries followed. Their appeal was largely to the poor and marginal, or to the landless, attracted by the missions' vast acreage. Christianity and western ways were often a package deal, and missionaries advocated the plough, literacy, western clothing and square, rather than round, houses. Despite the vast tracts of land alienated to white speculators, many Africans – Mfengu, Xhosa, Thembu and others – tackled commercial agriculture with enthusiasm and success.

In 1841, the Glasgow Missionary Society founded its famous college at Lovedale, where black and white studied and taught side by side. By 1887, it had educated over 2,000 Africans, a quarter of whom were women.[86]

Tiyo Soga (1829–71), the son of the first Xhosa to use the plough, was the archetypal Improver. He studied at Glasgow University, married a Scottish wife, and was ordained a United Presbyterian minister. When he returned to South Africa in 1857, he was suffering from tuberculosis. Despite this – and the pain of ostracism both by white Christians and most Xhosa – he worked devotedly for the mission until he died. Soga wrote in 1861:

The country of the Kaffirs is now forfeited and the greater part of it has been given out in grants to European farmers. I see plainly that unless the rising generation is trained to some of the useful arts, nothing else will raise our people ... But let your youth be taught trades, to earn money, and they will increase and purchase land.[87]

He translated the first part of *The Pilgrim's Progress* into Xhosa, and Thomas Mofolo paraphrased the same work in Sotho.[88] There is a profound symbolism in this, for Bunyan's Christian leaves his family and community in search of salvation, and Christianity often had precisely this divisive effect. Society was often polarised between School People (called *kholwa*, 'believers', in Natal) and Red People – traditionalists took ochre and the blanket as symbols of tradition, though both were obtained from foreign traders. They called School People 'those with a hole' (that is, who had allowed foreigners to gain an entrance).[89] School People and Red People were at first mainly Mfengu and Xhosa; later, the Xhosa were divided in the same way. As time went on, the proportion of Red People declined.

The most famous Tswana modernising kings belonged to a later period.[90] Kgama came to the Ngwato throne in 1875 (significantly, after a civil war with his father) and ruled until 1923. The Kwena king Sechele, a convert of Livingstone's, who was baptised in 1848 and died in 1891, welcomed missionaries – 'his reasons were a missionary could help him in sickness, mend his gun, teach him to read and "nthuta botlale" [teach me wisdom]'.[91]He studied reading and writing with such assiduity that he gained weight from lack of exercise.[92] He was expelled from church membership for many years, for resuming marital relations with one of his former wives.

Cape Colony obtained representative government in 1853, and responsible government in 1872; its franchise was colour blind, and the property qualification set low enough for some Cape Folk, and later, Africans, to qualify. Some built substantial houses with this end in view, but they tended to support white liberals rather than seek office themselves. Natal had a different franchise, and by 1903 only three Africans there had obtained the vote.

After the period covered by this book, in the late nineteenth and early twentieth centuries, men such as John Tengo Jabavu (1859–1921), Sol Plaatje (1875–1932) and Walter Rubusana (1858–1936) published vernacular newspapers. Rubusana was the only African to be elected to the Cape Provincial Council (in 1910). In 1889, John Dube founded Ohlange Institute, modelled on the work of Booker T. Washington; he tried to make his students 'Anglo-Saxons of Africa'.[93] The Improvers believed in the efficacy of petitions to London and were extravagant in their declarations of loyalty to the (British) crown – very much like their counterparts in West Africa. Some created a sphere of autonomy in founding independent churches, beginning with Nehemiah Tile's Thembu National Church in 1884.

Many of the Improvers were successful farmers, rather than urban workers. The late nineteenth century saw the rise and decline of a South African peasantry,[94] a brief Indian summer between a past when Africans were largely self-sufficient agro-pastoralists and a future when they became a rural proletariat on inadequate and eroding land. Some became teachers, clergy, or skilled artisans – there was a tradition of artisan skill among the 'Coloured' of Cape Town.

By the end of the nineteenth century, the position of the Improver was already threatened; successive laws limited the African franchise, and access to land was increasingly difficult. There was a great change for the worse after the Act of Union in 1910, and in 1920 John Jabavu's son, named after the missionary Davidson Don, described his fellow Africans as 'landless, voteless helots, pariahs, social outcasts in their fatherland with no future in any path of life'.[95]

The view in 1870

In 1870, all this lay in the future. In Natal, the whites were in a small minority – less than 6 per cent of the population, to which Indian labourers were now adding a further ethnic strand. By far the largest concentration of European population was in Cape Colony; the first official census, in 1865, reported 180,000 Europeans, 200,000 Khoi/'Coloured', and 100,000 'Kaffirs', black Africans. The European population was divided between Afrikaners, mainly farmers, concentrated in the west, and English speakers, who dominated commercial and professional life and lived mainly in the east. Despite the emigrations to the highveld, Afrikaners outnumbered English speakers in Cape Colony; their culture and language were often marginalised, reflected in the derogatory overtones of the ethonym 'Boer', farmer. In the 1870s, they embarked on a cultural revival, which was to have far reaching social and political consequences. The 'Coloured' population lived mainly in the west and in Cape Town. The size of the black population, which lived mainly in the Eastern Cape, reflected the extension of the colony's boundaries, and the immigration of 'Mantatees' in search of work. Slavery had been abolished in 1833, and in practice came to an end in 1838, but both black and 'Coloured' tended to be poor and marginalised, and successful Improvers were a tiny minority. A Masters and Servants Act, passed in 1856, imposed five-year contracts on workers, and imposed harsh penalties for disobedience or leaving an employer. *Plus ça change* . . .

In 1867, diamonds were discovered at what became Kimberley. (The last African to hold a mining claim at Dutoitspan, in 1883, was a Lovedale graduate and Free Church of Scotland minister.)[96] In 1879, British forces defeated the Zulu and the Pedi, the powerful African states the Afrikaners had been unable to subdue. In 1886, a vast goldfield was found south of Pretoria, on the Witwatersrand. The history of South Africa was changed forever.

23

East and East Central Africa

He who was my trusted friend died,
Let me cry for myself, no one will cry for me . . .
Death has taken all the people . . .
We were many but now I am alone . . .
Among many children there must be one very poor.

Soga song[1]

An introductory perspective

The dominant theme of the history of eastern Africa, from the eighteenth century on, is enlargement of scale. This took many forms – new caravan routes carried ivory and slaves to the coast; they were pioneered by Africans from the interior, first the Yao and later the Nyamwezi, and entrepreneurs from the coast and Zanzibar came to follow their example. These trade routes played a major role in the dissemination, not only of Islam and the Swahili language, but of many other cultural complexes as well. The ancient cleavage between the coast and the interior (the Other, *washenzi*, in Swahili thought) came to an end and new states were created by ambitious warlords. International trade had an immense impact on countless lives, but it is possible to exaggerate its importance, and from the viewpoint of the local community, the ultimate source or destination of trade goods made little difference. External trade impinged on the lives of inland peoples in different ways and to varying degrees and the entrepreneurs of caravan trade often generated their initial capital from local transactions.

Different communities made different choices, and Livingstone contrasted the Yao with the Mang'anja, who were 'much more fond of the home pursuits of spinning, weaving, smelting iron and cultivating the soil, than of foreign travel'.[2] The Chagga of Kilimanjaro would have been ideally situated to play a pivotal role in long-distance commerce; they did indeed trade with their neighbours, but they were far more interested in their banana groves and the complex irrigation systems which sustained them. The Nyakusa, who lived to the north of Lake Malawi, in villages organised around male age grades, were little affected by the convulsions of the world around them. A nineteenth-century visitor described their settlements, also set in luxuriant banana groves, as 'a perfect Arcadia, about which idyllic poets have sung, though few have seen it realised'.[3]

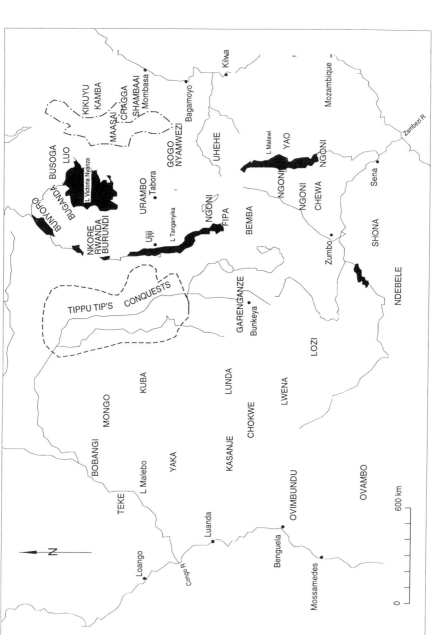

Map 16　East and Central Africa: the nineteenth century

Many of the written records, especially for the earlier period, were the work of visitors to the coast, and it is easy to see the whole history of this period from this perspective. But it is important to remember that some of the most dramatic events of the area's nineteenth-century history had nothing to do with a foreign presence or international trade – the southward thrust of the Masaai, the expansion of Rwanda. The impact of the Indian Ocean slave trade, though far-reaching, was far from universal – Rwanda and Burundi, for instance, remained unaffected.[4]

Many ethnic labels, such as 'Nyamwezi', date from the nineteenth century, and often a sense of ethnic consciousness developed then for the first time. 'Before the Ngoni wars the Ndendeuli did not know how to fight. The Ndendeuli did not know what tribe they were.'[5] Paradoxically, it was just at this time that secret societies, dance societies and witch-finding cults and other cultural complexes spread across different ethnic groups, and different languages, sometimes but not always Swahili, became a lingua franca. 'As cultures mingled, so, paradoxically, "tribes" became more distinct.'[6]

Indian Ocean trade

In the Atlantic zone, the external slave trade began on a small scale in the sixteenth century, expanded in the seventeenth, peaked in the eighteenth, and then declined. In the Indian Ocean zone, the export of slaves expanded during the eighteenth century and peaked in the nineteenth.

As in West and West Central Africa, historians have tended to interpret the pattern of change in one of two ways. An older Africanist model stressed Africans' creative innovation and entrepreneurship, while recognising the limits imposed on the choices available, and the human price which was paid. Thus Roberts wrote, 'there was a real element of significant economic growth in western Tanzania during the nineteenth century,' but noted that it was geared to 'certain needs of industrial and plantation economies far from Nyamweziland' and was explicit about the cruelty of Lozi, Bemba and Lunda kings.[7] Austen, in an interpretation similar to Miller's work on West Central Africa, stressed the predatory bent of the societies involved, the illusory character of the growth.[8]

Until the 1850s, cloth, beads and copper (this last, of African provenance) were the most favoured imports, valued by Big Men as a means of rewarding supporters, and by humbler individuals as a form of savings and a protection against famine. They delineated elite status – a Yao local historian listed the cloth styles which could only be worn by the aristocracy.[9] Maasai women sometimes wore thirty pounds' weight of copper wire – a burdensome distinction, like the ivory anklets which impeded the gait and chafed the skin of Igbo women married to titled men. Guns were imported on a very large scale from the late eighteenth century on, and often the success of a particular warlord such as Msiri is attributed to them. As we have noted in the context of West and Central Africa, this contrasts oddly with the evidence about their unreliability, and sometimes they were more of a danger to their owners than to anyone else – the third ruler of the (Yao) Makanjila dynasty lost his left arm when his gun exploded while he was hunting eland.[10]

Foreign presences: the Portuguese

It is one of the ironies of East Africa's past that Portugal and Oman – the foreign nations which influenced it most before the advent of colonialism – were both so small. In 1498, Vasco da Gama visited the Swahili coast, obtaining a pilot at Malindi, who guided him to India. It was always Asia, rather than eastern Africa, which was the focus of Portuguese imperial strategy. The administrative centre of its Indian Ocean empire was in Goa and many of the traders and clergy with Portuguese names who worked and died in Zambezia were Goans. Before the Portuguese arrived, the major Zambezi port was Sofala; in time, it was supplanted by Quelimane and Mozambique Island. Like African merchants before them, the Portuguese established trade posts on the Zambezi, first at Tete and Sena and later, further inland, at Zumbo, on the confluence of the Zambezi and the Luangwa. Here they obtained gold, ivory and copper, in return for cloth, first from India and later from the lower Zambezi.

Like twentieth-century colonial governments, the Portuguese were able to destroy individual settlements, but not to maintain a lasting and detailed control over people's lives. Mombasa, where the massive walls of Fort Jesus still stand, fought the Portuguese repeatedly, as did Pemba, while others allied with the foreigners to obtain advantages *vis-à-vis* their local rivals. Kilwa was polarised between pro- and anti-Portuguese factions. All this anticipated African divisions at the time when colonialism was imposed, and later.

The Shona kingdoms and Zambezi[11]

The Mutapa state was already in existence when the Portuguese arrived, and at first its ruler welcomed the prospect of direct trade. But in 1569 they made a signally unsuccessful attempt to conquer the Mutapa state and obtain direct access to its gold. The Portuguese weakened and destabilised Mutapa but they did not succeed in establishing direct rule over it.

The northern Shona did not build in stone, and the kingdom of the Mwene Mutapa is known not by its physical remains, which are as yet little studied,[12] but by historical records and oral tradition. (After the fall of the Zagwe, Ethiopia went through the same transition from monumental architecture in stone to a peripatetic court, building in thatch and clay.) The name Mwene Mutapa is spelt, and interpreted, in different ways. Mwene is probably cognate with Mane (Kongo) and Mwami (Rwanda) (though Beach, the foremost historian of the Shona, questions this),[13] and if so means Conqueror Lord – shedding some light on the ruler's relationship with his subjects. The Mutapa state was located in a gold-bearing region; it is likely that it was its foundation which, by intercepting its commerce, led to the abandonment of Ingombe Ilede. It survived into the late nineteenth century, but in a weakened and divided state.

A number of Portuguese, originally renegades from the garrisons, established what were in effect independent principalities on the Zambezi, called *prazos*, from the 1630s on. Soon, the *prazeiros* were Christian and Portuguese only in name; their revenues came, not from agriculture, but from their armed retainers who exacted tribute and hunted elephants. Their attacks on neighbouring peoples and each other caused immense suffering.[14] Each *prazeiro* had his own slave army, the Chikunda, who gradually developed their own culture and their own language, Nyungwe. They were often originally refugees from hunger: 'The greatest part came to be captives during the times of famines, pestilences and locusts.'[15] But in time, many escaped from the *prazeiros*, and in the nineteenth century there were Chikunda risings,[16] and warlords such as Kanyemba and Matakenya ('Jiggers') raided for slaves over a large area.[17]

In the late seventeenth century, a Shona general called Dombo Changamire led his followers and herds to found a new kingdom in a region called Butua, or Guruuswa. They were known as the Rozwi, Destroyers. This was the location of an earlier Shona kingdom, Torwa; its ruins reflect its tradition of dry-stone walling, often in elaborate herringbone and chevron patterns. Changamire conquered Torwa, and founded a new capital at Dhlodhlo. In the eighteenth century, the Rozwi state, at the zenith of its power, confined the Portuguese to the Zambezi. An earlier historiography telescoped these events, and credited the Rozwi with the building of Great Zimbabwe and the formation of the Mutapa state. The careful research of Beach established a succession of states; only the Rozwi kingdom covered a large area and it was in decline after 1750. Earlier works stressed the cult of the High God, Mwari, as a unifying ideology of empire. Beach stressed the military, indeed predatory, nature of the Rozwi state, its dependence on soldiers, cattle and gold, and interpreted the link with Mwari as a nineteenth-century invention – suggesting that after the Ndebele incursion the Shona transformed their past into a golden age, exaggerating its glories.[18] The closer their link with the supreme God, the more dramatic the reversal of their fortunes. But recent archaeological work at Great Zimbabwe has found considerable evidence of the role of spirit mediums.[19] Whereas in the fifteenth century there were several score miniature copies of Zimbabwe, by the early nineteenth, many Shona were rebelling against kingship and moving from the gold-bearing area towards the south; 'they built no more *Zimbabwe*'.[20]

Kilwa

Kilwa was a broker state, dealing in gold purchased at Sofala. It was sacked by the Portuguese in 1505, but its economic decline had begun earlier, a result of Sofala's independence and Mombasa's rise to economic dominance.

For many centuries, the Swahili coastal merchants had no direct knowledge of the interior and relied on products brought to the coast, apparently through a chain of intermediaries. The very predilection for island sites both symbolised and reinforced this sense of separateness, an orientation towards the sea, and in ibn Battuta's time the Kilwa people raided and plundered their neighbours. But in 1569, a Jesuit visited a Kilwa 'twice destroyed by our people' and found that its resilient merchants had developed a new trade with the interior in ivory, honey and wax.[21] (In the nineteenth century, the original Kilwa became a village, and a new Kilwa arose, Kisiwani.)

The rise of the Yao trading network

The trade route inland from Kilwa was the first of several which were to link the coast and the interior. From the early seventeenth century on, it was dominated by the Yao of northern Mozambique. Although long-distance trade often seems to have contributed to the growth of centralised states, it is noteworthy that the Yao, like the Nyamwezi, founded chieftaincies but not Great States.

The Yao were already involved in long-distance trade, based originally on their supplies of iron ore, their metallurgical skills, and their need for good salt. It was their intinerant blacksmiths, the Chisi, who came across cloth from the coast: 'the fame of this calico spread everywhere ... That was when the Yaos first began to trade and to penetrate as far as the coast.'[22] At first they traded in ivory; the slave trade developed in the late eighteenth century and was dominant by the mid-nineteenth. Yao tradition telescopes all this.

When they went to the coast they were told, 'Next year you must bring ivory and slaves from Yao-land, and you will make your fortune. You will get the powder you want so much and [guns] ... You will get anything you want if you bring these two things, ivory and slaves.'

And it was those words which suggested a new idea to our fathers of old; when they got home they spread the word, 'A new business has arisen in ivory and slaves.'[23]

The journey to the coast became a rite of passage for young men, a necessary dimension of adult identity. Although journeys were conducted in the dry season, when no farm work was done, the traders and porters often stayed on the coast for considerable periods. Their absence was possible only because women bore the primary burden of agricultural production. If a man suffered injury or death while away, it was blamed on the wife's presumed infidelity.[24] Caravan trade produced an increased social polarisation, and some imported cloth could only be worn by the elite. Those who succeeded are sometimes known by name in the historical records. The victims are usually anonymous. Sometimes there is an exception, like Swema.

Swema was a Yao, who was ten years old in 1865. Her father was killed in a lion hunt, and her mother borrowed two sacks of grain, one to eat and one to plant, but the harvest was destroyed by locusts. The creditor recompensed himself by selling Swema for three metres of cloth. Her mother chose to go with her child, but collapsed on the way to the coast, and was abandoned by the caravan. By the time she reached Zanzibar, Swema was apparently dead, and was buried, but she was rescued and taken to the Spiritan mission. She became a Sister of Mercy.[25]

Until the mid-nineteenth century, most Yao lived in what is now northern Mozambique. Then there was a great diaspora, when many Yao, Makonde and Makua crossed the Ruvuma, settling in what is now southern Tanzania. Some Yao settled in Malawi, where they lived in harmony with the Manganja, until, as so often, scarcity bred violence. 'When the provisions became scarce, the guests began to steal from the fields, quarrels arose in consequence.' Perhaps through their access to firearms, the Yao then succeeded in dominating or displacing their erstwhile hosts.[26]

The Bisa trading network

The Bisa live between two ecological zones – the Bemba plateau and the swamps of Lake Bangweulu – and this may have encouraged their entry into regional trade. In the eighteenth century, they began to develop trade links with the Kazembe kingdom, taking ivory to Lake Malawi, where it was sold to the Yao, and to the Zambezi, where it was sold to 'Portuguese'; later, like the Yao, they developed their own trade routes to the sea. In 1863, Livingstone compared their economic role with that of the Greeks in the Levant.[27] By that time their trade was already in decline, disrupted by Ngoni and Bemba warfare and undermined by the increasing number of Arab/Swahili traders who found their way to the Kazembe's court.

The Omani phase

Oman, with its port and capital at Muscat, is a small state on the south-eastern coast of Arabia. Its people were among the Arab and Persian seafarers who had traded for centuries on the Swahili coast. For a time, the Portuguese held Muscat, and after they were expelled the Omani continued the struggle in a wider arena, in 1698 joining forces with local people to defeat their old enemies at Mombasa. An increasing Omani involvement in African trade was aided by their adoption of western-style shipping, but they played little role in coastal commerce until the accession of the Saidi dynasty in 1741. Despite the bonds of Islam,[28] and Swahili cultural ideals of *ustaarabu* ('Arabness' – the Swahili word for civilisation),[29] the coastal elite often had as little enthusiasm for the Omani as for the Portuguese.[30]

So important did East African trade become in the long reign of Sayyid Said ibn Sultan (1804–56) that he spent much of his time in Zanzibar. He transferred his court and government there in 1840 and when he died, the island state became independent of Oman. Sayyid Said encouraged Indian financiers to settle in Zanzibar – they provided the capital for the Arab/Swahili caravan trade, and an Indian was Master of the Customs, the key role in government finance. Merchants from the western world, especially America, were also drawn to this cosmopolitan entrepot.

A chain of mainland ports – Tanga, Dar es Salaam, Bagamoyo – developed, which complemented Zanzibar rather than rivalling its role, for in many cases they lacked both harbour facilities and the economic infrastructure for international maritime commerce. When Sayyid Said died, there was an Omani governor in each coastal town, but the relationship was one of economic co-operation rather than political dominance. A few outward signs of allegiance were required – a Zanzibari flag, an Indian customs official.

Dar es Salaam means Land of Peace. But the flag of Zanzibar was blood red, and Bagamoyo was named by the enslaved. It means, Lay down your Hearts.

Ivory and slaves

The entrepreneurs of East and East Central Africa initially obtained imported goods in return for a product – ivory or gold – which was of marginal importance in their own cultures. Ivory was sometimes used in the insignia of rulers, but originally elephants were hunted for food[31] and to prevent their damaging the crops. It was said in 1609,

Throughout this Kaffraria there are many very large and wild elephants, that cause great damage to the plantations of millet and rice, which they eat and tread under foot to the loss of the Kaffirs. The principal reason why the Kaffirs hunt elephants and kill them is to obtain the flesh for food and secondly to sell the tusks, that is the ivory from which all the articles of taste and trinkets are made which come to Portugal from India.[32]

African ivory was whiter and less brittle than its Indian counterpart; ivory bracelets were an essential item for Hindu brides, and since they were broken when the husband died, they had to be perpetually replenished. In the nineteenth century, however, much East African ivory was destined for Europe, sometimes re-exported from India.[33] As we saw in an earlier chapter, it provided luxuries for the middle class – trinkets, billiard balls and piano keys.

The ivory frontier moved inland, as elephant populations near the coast were exterminated. In 1879, Thomson stated that during the previous twenty years they had almost disappeared between Lake Tanganyika and the coast.[34]

Local rulers obtained one tusk of every elephant killed; some obtained both, giving the hunter a payment in return. The claim both to control over specific areas of land and to sovereignty acquired new meaning and importance. In barren Ugogo, ivory was sometimes collected from elephants which died naturally or were trapped in pits, but often it was won at the risk of human lives. 'Was it not war to hunt such animals as the elephant?' asked a Kamba elder.[35] As Livingstone noted, 'The upper classes ... receive the lion's share of the profits from the elephant-hunt without undergoing much of the toil and danger.'[36]

Some slaves had long been exported to the Middle East and India – in an earlier chapter, we noted the revolt of the Zanj in ninth-century Iraq. In the nineteenth century, perhaps 300,000 slaves were exported from the Swahili coast to various destinations in India and the Middle East, where some became domestic servants or concubines, and others pearl divers, an occupation where few lived long.[37]

The large-scale import of slaves to the Mascarene Islands – Bourbon (later Réunion) and Ile de France (later Mauritius) – began in the 1730s, and by 1810 there were 160,000 slaves there, mainly from Madagascar and the East African mainland.[38] The introduction of large-scale sugar production there in the 1820s meant that the demand for slaves escalated just when the anti-slavery movement in England was largely triumphant. Radama, who became king of Madagascar in 1810, signed an anti-slavery treaty which took effect in 1820, and the Zanzibar slave trade with Christian nations was prohibited by a treaty signed in Muscat in 1822, but some 200,000 slaves were taken illegally to the Mascarenes in the nineteenth century – mainly from Madagascar, northern Mozambique and southern Tanzania.[39] The export of slaves to the Mascarenes finally came to an end when African slaves were replaced by Indian indentured labourers.[40] Some 386,000 slaves, most of them from Mozambique,[41] were exported across the Atlantic, mainly to Cuba and Brazil, between 1811 and 1867, reflecting the fact that the Indian Ocean was less stringently patrolled by anti-slave trade squadrons. The slaves paid a price, as the length of the journey increased their sufferings and mortality rates.

Domestic slavery

Here, as elsewhere in Africa, there was a clear connection between an external slave trade and the growth of domestic slavery. Slaves were often a by-product of wars fought for other reasons, but the prospect of reaping a profit from their capture and sale clearly encouraged conflict. From the viewpoint of the slaver, slaves were a 'free good', to be collected by the powerful. It seems clear that far more captives were absorbed locally than were exported abroad, and in the nineteenth century East Africa may have been the only place in the world where the institution of slavery expanded.

Many slaves were employed on the new clove plantations of Zanzibar and Pemba. Cloves were originally native to the Moluccas, and were introduced in Mauritius and Réunion in the eighteenth century and brought to Zanzibar in the second decade of the nineteenth, possibly by an Omani, Saleh bin Haramil al-Abry, who obtained them in Réunion.[42] Sayyid Said encouraged their cultivation – people were told to plant three clove trees for every coconut palm they owned – and by 1850 Zanzibar was the world's leading clove producer. He encouraged the caravan trade in order to avoid a perilous dependence on a single crop – on one occasion the clove plantations were almost destroyed in a hurricane. They depended on slave labour, and the slaves soon vastly outnumbered the free population.

Ironically, Madagascar, which had supplied so many slaves to Mauritius, Réunion and South Africa, became an importer of slaves from the 1820s on, and they may have comprised half of its population by the end of the nineteenth century. Arab and Swahili planters established slave plantations on the mainland, and produced grain and sesame for export to Arabia and Zanzibar.[43] Slaves also processed copra, dug up gum copal (used for varnish), and collected orchilia.[44] In many cases, they had been intended for the export market, but when demand fluctuated, their owners put them to other uses.

Domestic slavery also expanded far from the coast; the Gogo acquired slaves and cattle in return for ivory, and slaves filled labour shortages created by the long absences of Nyamwezi merchants and porters.[45] Yao tradition refers to their 'ill treatment and overworking'. 'A man who becomes a slave, becomes like a drum which one beats at one's pleasure.'[46]

There was a vast population of war captives, slaves and pawns in the interior. Often the boundaries between free and slave were fluid, and slavery sometimes seemed like a form of forced colonisation or of marriage. The use of the language of kinship often concealed the reality from the slaves themselves. 'The girls ... were shocked when, after one of their number was told to remain with the trader's "relatives" in Safwa country, they observed a new tusk of ivory.'[47]

Witchcraft accusations seem to have become more common in the nineteenth century, partly because of the profit to be obtained by the sale of witches. Some of those accused of witchcraft escaped and others were fined, or died in poison ordeals, but many were enslaved.[48] In some cases, enslavement saved the lives of those who would otherwise have been killed.

The slave trade distorted the social fabric, and sometimes the relatives of the accused were enslaved as well. Judicial processes were affected and people were enslaved for trivial offences; in Bondei a woman lost her freedom when she stole two vegetables. In some cases rulers preyed on their own people. Kidnapping became common, and one ruler sold his mother-in-law.[49]

There was an increasing militarisation of life – 'At this time every Kilindi needed to make war so that he could capture slaves to sell for gunpowder' – and professional soldiers tended to replace citizen levies. Often, they were recruited from the victims of social change – slaves, deserters or witches. The Chagga ruler, Rindi of Moshi, raised an army of fugitives and orphans.[50] The Pare king Mashombe, who died in the early 1870s, introduced a new technique for discerning witches, and instead of executing them, recruited them in his army![51]

Captives were not the only victims of social dislocation – there was also a vast floating population of refugees, fugitives and deserters. There was a great deal of migration, often along the caravan routes. Some Hehe moved to Ugogo, despite its aridity. People fled their burning villages, and abandoned homes in which it had become too dangerous to live. A few found refuge at mission stations; others joined one of a myriad of armies or settled down under a warlord's protection.

The Nyamwezi trade network

The Nyamwezi trade route ran inland from Bagamoyo, opposite Zanzibar. Like the caravan routes further north, it developed later than the Yao route inland from Kilwa, partly because of the physical difficulty and danger of the barren scrublands that had to be crossed – Burton wrote of the 'red glare of barren Ugogo'.[52] Nyamwezi tradition recalls how two disappointed contenders for office travelled east, and

when they were in Uzaramo they were told that further to the east there was a big lake. They asked to see it and went on as far as Bagamoyo ... Here they went to Bushiri and found beads and cloth ... They came back again and began looking for ivory. They carried this to Bagamoyo ... When the Arabs saw this, they wanted to go to the countries where the ivory was obtained.[53]

As among the Yao, long-distance trade became a male rite of passage; children at play carried miniature bundles, and anyone who failed to make such a journey was scorned. The newly appointed king of a Nyamwezi principality learnt of his elevation when he was away from home, carrying ivory. Nyamwezi traders generated the initial capital they needed, either by service as porters or by regional trade in iron hoes or salt from Uvinza.

Some ivory was transported by slaves, especially in the first Arab/Swahili caravans, and towards the end of the century,[54] but most was carried by contract porters, who were predominantly Nyamwezi. According to one late nineteenth-century estimate, 15–20,000 of them went to the coast each year.[55] Other figures are higher, comparable with those of labour migration in the colonial period, as were the wages paid.[56]

The ivory trade led easily to the slave trade. Elephant hunting and slave raiding both needed firearms and comparable skills and aptitudes, and when elephant herds declined, those involved in the ivory trade found themselves with nothing else to sell.

From the 1860s on, many Nyamwezi obtained guns and raided for slaves as far afield as the eastern Congo. Some went as far north as Bunyoro in search of ivory, or south-west to Shaba, to buy copper; there, they were called Yeke. In the second half of the nineteenth century, a Yeke adventurer, Msiri, established a powerful but short-lived state in Shaba, called Garenganze. Bunkeya, his cosmopolitan capital, attracted people from many different ethnic groups and it exported its products to both the Indian Ocean and the Atlantic, ruining the Kazembe kingdom in the process. Msiri's kingdom was soon swallowed up in a larger imperialism; in 1891 he died in a clash with an official of the Congo Free State, and Garenganze disintegrated.[57]

The Mijikenda and Kamba

The Mijikenda lived in hilltop settlements inland from the Kenya coast. From the beginning of the eighteenth century, they sold ivory, gum copal, honey, wax, grain and timber to the Swahili towns in return for salt, beads, cloth and iron hoes. But their immediate environment was barren, and their access to the products of the interior was limited by the presence of the warlike and hostile Boran Oromo to the north.[58] The Kamba lived to the south of the Tana river, in a still more difficult environment;[59] their mobility and hunting skills enabled them to overcome its obstacles and they turned eagerly to the ivory trade. By the mid-nineteenth century, they had wiped out most of the elephant population in their homeland. They built up trade networks with the Kikuyu and other peoples of the Mount Kenya area and founded many hunting and trading enclaves in what is now northern Tanzania. Famine was the dynamic behind at least some of these movements, and the migrants were called 'those who have followed the rain'.[60] The Kamba were skilled craftsmen, and much of their trade was in products for local markets – a particularly virulent arrow poison, and iron ornaments which reflected 'an artistic skill and taste far exceeding anything we had noticed elsewhere in Africa'.[61] Their economic role, like that of the Bisa, declined in the late nineteenth century, as the ivory frontier retreated, and as Swahili caravans developed direct contacts with their former inland trading partners.

Arab and Swahili traders in the interior

Although, for many centuries, the coastal states were brokers, their merchants did not travel inland in person. In *c.* 1777, the French slaver Morice was asked:

Do they trade in the interior? What is the nature of their trade? ... There are many posts on the mainland to which the Africans bring their slaves and ivory ... but only on the coast.
What Moorish [Swahili] or Arab traders have penetrated it? It is not possible to penetrate

it. There are Immense Rivers which the Africans call Sweet Water, and they state that no one crosses these rivers save Africans ... The interior is not known at all.[62]

Little had altered since Ptolemy wrote of the Mountains of the Moon. In the nineteenth century, Arab/Swahili merchants departed from the practice of centuries and began to send their own caravans to the interior. They were usually led by relatively poor men, who hoped to make their fortune and were often disappointed. Nyamwezi and Yao traditions suggest that they were consciously copying the initiatives of Africans from the interior. 'We Yaos became very rich ... the coast people began to realize what was happening and said "... Let us go ourselves to Yao-land".'[63]

Nineteenth-century sources tended to speak of 'Arabs' or 'Moors' but many of those concerned were Swahili speakers of at least part-African descent. 'In Central Africa we meet with three classes of Arabs – first the Muscat, or white Arab ... second the Mswahili, or coast Arab, who is black but strictly Muhammadan ... third any upcountry native who adopts the manners and customs of the Moslem.'[64]

The followers of coastal traders were well armed and equipped, but few in numbers compared with African populations. 'They are too strong to yield without fighting and are not strong enough to fight with success.'[65] The exception was the man of mixed Arab and Nyamwezi descent history knows as Tippu Tip, who raided for slaves and ivory amid the small polities of eastern Zaire from the 1870s on, and brought enormous wealth back to Zanzibar. He lived but did not perish by the sword, and retired to the coast in 1890.

Arab/Swahili traders began making regular journeys to Ukimbu in about 1825 and to Unyamwezi in about 1830,[66] and were present at the Kazembe's court in 1831.[67] They founded towns on their caravan routes – Tabora dated from 1852, 'a second Zanzibar without the sea'.[68] From Tabora, one route went west to Lake Tanganyika, where another cosmopolitan settlement was founded at Ujiji. Its buildings mirrored the encounter of cultures, for they 'represented almost every style of African architecture – the huge-roofed Indian bungalow, the flat-roofed tembe, the quadrangular hut of the Waswahili with baraza in front, and the beehive-shaped hut of most of the natives'.[69]

A Zanzibari, Salim b. Abdullah, founded a trade post, and later a principality, at Kota Kota, on the west shore of Lake Malawi, where the red flag of Zanzibar flew; a school there taught both Swahili and the Qur'an.[70] Kageyi, at the south end of Lake Victoria Nyanza, and Taveta in Kenya were flourishing commercial centres, which were, like Tabora, compared with Zanzibar.[71] The Bemba of Zambia kept the coastal merchants beyond their frontiers and, as a result, remained outside the Swahili language sphere.

Invaders from the north: the Maasai

In the nineteenth century, modern Tanzania was invaded by warlike pastoralists from the north and from the south. The invaders from the south, the Ngoni, have been analysed in the preceding chapter; their impact on peoples such as the

Hehe was incalculable, and the descendants of at least some of them still live in Songea.

The first European visitors saw the Maasai through the eyes of coastal middlemen, who stressed their ferocity to protect their own role as brokers. An image of the Maasai, as a warrior people devoted to pure pastoralism, developed which has shaped much subsequent historical writing – 'the Masai had two overriding passions – cattle and warfare'.[72] In a reaction against this, more recent studies have tended to stress other elements in Maasai life, such as commerce and cultural links with neighbours, and the flexibility with which they moved away from pure pastoralism in adverse circumstances. Maasai women traded with their neighbours, even in time of war, and Maasai men married Kikuyu and Chagga women, though the reverse was very rare. Taveta and some Kikuyu adopted Maasai age sets and circumcision techniques, and Maa often became a lingua franca.[73] But the traditions of the Kaguru of central Tanzania remind us of the suffering and dislocation Maasai attacks caused, telling of loss of life and of refugees escaping to the mountains. 'Even today if you climb Talagwe Mountain you will find their abandoned villages.'[74]

The original homeland of the Maasai was near Lake Turkana, in the barren near-desert of northern Kenya. By the 1830s, they had occupied a great swathe of central Kenya and Tanganyika. They reached Uhehe and Ugogo but could advance no further. Meanwhile, other pastoral peoples such as the Turkana and Suk were moving into Maasai territory from the north, and the Kamba and Kikuyu were becoming raiders rather than the raided.[75]

The need for more pasture for their expanding herds was the essential dynamic of Maasai expansion; it was built into their social structure, as the warrior age grade needed to obtain cattle by raiding as a precondition for economic independence. But expansion sometimes meant that they laid claim to more land than they could occupy effectively, and laid them open to invasion by others.[76]

If cattle raiding was the prime objective of war, it made more sense to attack other pastoralists, including other Maasai. By the mid-nineteenth century, pressure on resources and the internal dynamic of Maasai social structure drove them increasingly to prey upon each other. From the 1850s to the 1870s, there was a major and protracted conflict between the northern Masaai, the Ilaikipiak, and the southern 'Maasai proper', a cluster of clans which included the Purko and Kisongo.[77] It ended with the defeat of the Ilaikipiak and their absorption by the victors or by other clans. It has sometimes been understood as a conflict between pastoral and agricultural Maasai, but agriculture was an option into which Maasai were sometimes forced by adverse circumstances.

Maasai despised agriculture, hunting and fishing; their ideal diet was a purely pastoral one, of fresh and curdled milk and blood, but even prosperous pastoralists were often forced to supplement their diet by the purchase of grain or bananas in the dry season. Drought, defeat in war, or cattle disease could force pastoralists to adopt a different lifestyle in order to survive. The Arusha are Maa-speaking agriculturalists, and the Il Chamus practise fishing, among other avocations. The Parakuyu of central Tanzania are pastoralists, but they were defeated in the nineteenth century by the 'Maasai proper' and their herds were not large enough for a purely pastoral lifestyle. They made regular arrangements with neighbouring pastoralists such as the Kaguru, who planted grain for them.[78] By 1970, there were thought to be 226,000 'Maasai proper', 97,000 Arusha, 58,000 Samburu, 29,000 Parakuyu, and 7,000 Il Chamus.[79]

The Maasai remember their history in terms of named age grades and named prophets, *laibon*,[80] who guided them by means of dreams and divination. The 'Maasai proper' followed the Inkidongi prophetic family who lived near Mount Meru. Modern Maasai attribute the victories of the past to great prophetic figures such as Supeet (*c.* 1810 age set) who encouraged them to expand towards Mount Kilimanjaro and beyond, or Mbatiany, who united them against the Ilaikipiak. The following of a particular prophetic family is the essential factor which unites a Maasai clan cluster; the Parakuyu follow the Mtango family, and only the Samburu lack the *laibon* tradition.

The Nandi of Nyanza, in Kenya, have much in common with the Maasai; like them, they are Eastern Nilotic-speaking pastoralists, organised in age grades of youths, warriors and elders. They expanded dramatically in the nineteenth century, partly by moving into the territory of Maasai defeated by other Maasai, and by adopting the prophetic institutions which provided the Maasai with charismatic leadership in time of war. The first Nandi prophet was a mid-nineteenth-century Maasai *laibon*.[81]

Oromo and Somali

In an earlier chapter, we saw how the southern Oromo, the Boran and Orma, expanded southward into modern Kenya in the late sixteenth century. Unlike many of their counterparts in Ethiopia, they preserved their traditional religion, a pastoral lifestyle, and the *gado* age-grade system. By the late nineteenth century they were in decline, displaced both by Maasai migration from the east, and a southward thrust of the Somali from the east.

The Somali crossed the Juba in about 1850, establishing their hegemony as far south as the Tana. In 1865 they attacked the Orma, seized many of their cattle and absorbed many of their people, leaving them a small relict community. Later they defeated and displaced the Boran.

Caravan trade expanded among the Somali in the nineteenth century. There were two main networks – one ran north through Harar to Zeila and other ports in the Gulf of Aden, and one ran south from the upper Shabeelle river to ports on the Benadir coast such as Mogadishu.[82] The Somali exported slaves, ivory, pelts, ostrich feathers, aromatic woods and myrrh as well as meat, dairy products and hides. They also maintained regional trade networks in salt, natron and locally produced textiles.

These various Eastern Nilotic and Eastern Cushitic pastoralists were all subject to the same dynamic – the need to acquire more territory for expanding herds and population, the difficulty of maintaining control of it when famine and drought diminished their numbers. Certain explanations are conventionally given for expansion at particular times – prophetic leadership in the case of the Maasai and Nandi, other social mechanisms which favoured common action in the case of the Somali. But it is likely that the basic factors were demographic and ecological.

The interlacustrine kingdoms

On the island of Ukerewe, in Lake Victoria Nyanza, involvement in long-distance trade began in the reign of Mihigo II (*c.* 1780–*c.* 1820). Tradition personalises the danger and stress of that time of transition in the werelion Butamile, who preyed on the living.[83] Sinister beings, including witches, are often depicted as werepeople in African thought, and the lion, like the leopard, is a common symbol of political power; the Shambaa king was called Mwene Simba, Lion King.[84] Vansina has written perceptively of the political symbolism of Equatorial Africa – leopard, fish eagle and python – 'They were all carnivores, supreme in their respective realms, solitary predators.'[85] It is a chilling commentary on the exercise of political power.

We saw in an earlier chapter how the early history of the interlacustrine kingdoms, both large and small, must be seen through the mists of a rich and complex mythology. Bunyoro was the dominant power until the early eighteenth century but then declined, a process culminating in the secession of Toro in *c.* 1830. From the 1870s on, it was to experience a remarkable revival. Buganda was the dominant power of the area north of Lake Victoria Nyanza for perhaps 150 years, until, in the late 1880s, it was torn apart by wars of religion.

In much of the interlacustrine region, abundant rainfall and fertile soil supported a dense population, who produced a surplus which sustained courts and kings, and early European visitors wrote accounts of a land of plenty which attracted potential colonisers. It is easy to concentrate on the giants of the region – Buganda, Bunyoro, Rwanda, Burundi – to the neglect of their smaller neighbours, but there were over 200 polities in the region,[86] some of them very small, as in Buha and Buzinza. There were 68 states in Busoga alone.[87]

Many of the states of the interlacustrine region – but not Buganda – were linked by various versions of the Cwezi saga. In some – Rwanda, Burundi, Nkore, Bunyoro, Buha – there was a dominant caste of pastoralists; their power and demographic strength varied in different areas. Only in Rwanda was the premise of inequality at the heart of social and political relations, and even there it seems to have been an eighteenth-century development.

There was a flourishing network of regional trade based on the complementarity of resources.[88] The best salt came from near Lakes Edward and George; Buganda lacked good iron ore, but it was abundant in Bunyoro. Rwanda exported hides, Buganda bark cloth and dried bananas, often seized as tribute or plunder in Busoga, together with ivory, slaves and wives.[89] In general the policies of large states such as Buganda were geared less to commerce than to expansion and the exaction of tribute, but the pattern of expansion was motivated by economic considerations. Dissidents – including late eighteenth-century rebel Ganda princes – sought refuge in the forests and swamps to the east.[90] A Nyoro praise song for the Cwezi divinity, Ndahura, reflects an awareness of the human cost of the depredations of great kingdoms.

> Rwesakara the eagle, that place you have gone to,
> Do not kill the chicken belonging to someone else
> To bring me trouble; for this would be a great offence.

Eyi ... eyi ... you went away to wage war,
To crush them.[91]

The Ganda[92] were divided into thirty totemic clans headed by clan heads, *Bataka*, and into ten counties headed by lords, *Bakungu*; the latter positions were in the king's gift, as were those of the regional military commanders, *Batongole* – new posts introduced by Mutesa. Aristocratic youths were sent to court where they competed for advancement. The dangers of court life are illustrated by the fact that a holder of the highest office, the *Kattikiro*, asked missionaries for laudanum, to keep in case he should be tortured. Mutesa's praise names included Cause of Tears and a Ganda proverb runs, 'A prince is like a hippopotamus, which one does not wait for in the deep.'[93]

Foreign goods reached Buganda before foreign traders – the first cups and plates arrived in the late eighteenth century, the first 'Arab' traders from Tabora in the 1840s, during the reign of Suna (d. 1856). For a brief period, in the 1870s, ivory was carried in canoes but the main trade route ran west of the great lake and through Tabora. There was a more direct route to the coast through the Maasai plains, but its aridity and its warlike inhabitants discouraged its use. It was inauspicious in Ganda eyes, and an Anglican bishop who insisted on using it was put to death.

The leader of the 'Arabs' at the Ganda court, Ahmed bin Ibrahim, risked his life when he rebuked Suna in the name of Allah the Compassionate. The Kabaka expelled them after a time, but they returned under his successor, Mutesa (1856–84), who wore Muslim dress and kept Ramadan. But as some of his court pages and others became Muslims, he became anxious about an *imperium in imperio*, and in 1875–6, a thousand Muslims were martyred – ten times as many as the more famous Christian martyrs of 1886.[94] The advent of Anglican missionaries in 1877, and of Catholics in 1879, was to lead to prolonged and intense debate at the Ganda court and ultimately to wars of religion, in which Muslims, Catholics, Protestants and traditionalists fought, and which facilitated British conquest in 1890. Significantly, the Christian denominations were called Bafranza and Baingereza, the French and the English.

Mutesa and his heir, Mwanga, welcomed missionaries and coastal traders in part because of the threat from the north. As we saw in Chapter 15, Muhammad Ali carved out an empire in the Sudan; his grandson, the Khedive Ismail (1863–79), inherited his imperial aspirations, and poured financial resources into their realisation. Under the leadership of a succession of European officers, a short-lived Province of Equatoria was created, with its headquarters first at Gondokoro and later at Lado, both in what is now the southern Republic of Sudan. It was the first colonial presence in East Africa, but limited resources and manpower, and the vast distance from Cairo, made it both fragile and ephemeral. In 1872, a contingent led by Samuel Baker – big-game hunter turned explorer turned proconsul – burnt the thatched roofs of the Bunyoro capital with rockets, but was then forced to flee. In 1875 a small detachment raised the Egyptian flag briefly at Brava on the Somali coast. An attempt to conquer Buganda was equally unsuccessful, and Gordon wrote in his journal, 'Mutesa has annexed my soldiers; he has not been annexed himself.'[95] Ismail was deposed in 1879, and in 1882 the Mahdist rising swept away what was left of Egypt's African empire.

The military revival of Bunyoro began in the reign of Kamurasi; he allied with the Lango and traded with both Khartoumers and 'Arabs' from the coast. When he died, in 1869, his youthful heir Kabarega continued with these policies and acquired firearms – as did the Ganda. He built up an army, the *abarusura*, many of whose members were not Nyoro. They fought for plunder and reconquered Toro and defeated Buganda. Kamurasi wore Arab dress and spoke Arabic, but there was no indigenous Muslim or Christian community as in Buganda.

The real threat to these kingdoms was to come not from Egypt but from Britain – initially from the Imperial British East African Company – and the kings of Buganda and Bunyoro were destined to die in exile. These events had much significance for the future – their early enthusiasm for literacy and modernity stood the Ganda well in the colonial situation and the very name of Uganda reflected their dominance. The British tended to see Ugandan politics through Ganda eyes, and absorbed their hostility to Bunyoro. The 'Nubi' element in northern Uganda and in its army dates from the Province of Equatoria. Many years later, a Muslim Kakwa would seize power in Uganda, in the person of Idi Amin, and rule with 'Nubi' support.[96]

Rwanda

The history of Rwanda reminds us that in large areas of East Africa history cannot be explained by external factors. Rwanda held aloof from strangers, a policy which Stanley attributed to a fear of cattle diseases,[97] which time would show was only too well founded.

In nineteenth-century Rwanda, a military aristocracy of pastoralists, the Tutsi, who formed 10 per cent of the population, ruled the farmers, the Hutu, who formed the vast majority of the population, as well as a small body of Twa, hunter-gatherers who filled despised or marginalised roles as potters, jesters or executioners. The Tutsi controlled the cattle, the main form of wealth, and distributed them to farmer families in return for their allegiance. Inequality was justified by a mythological charter, where Kigwa descended from heaven and gave each of his three sons a calabash of milk to guard. Gatwa drank his milk and Gahutu knocked over his calabash. Gatutsi did as his father had commanded, and earned the right to rule. Pastoral values were dominant – each beast had its own name (as among the Nuer and Dinka) and regiments were named after herds.

Rwanda court traditions were recorded in great detail by a Tutsi Catholic priest, Alexis Kagame, who welcomed the colonial identification of Tutsi and 'Hamites', and believed that both the geographic boundaries of nineteenth-century Rwanda and its social stratification were a thousand years old. More recent research has established that both the boundaries of late nineteenth-century Rwanda and its extreme inequalities were of recent growth.[98] Both were to be fossilised by colonial rule, and to lead to recurrent inter-ethnic bloodshed in independent Rwanda, as in Burundi.

Originally, there were a number of small independent Hutu kingdoms, the source of the most characteristic institutions of the later Rwanda state, such as the ritual fire and the royal drums. The sacred Hutu king lived in seclusion until his heir was seven years old, and lived in seclusion in his turn. He ruled in conjunction with a Queen Mother, and his authority rested on his control of rain. At an unknown date, the ancestors of the Tutsi moved into central Rwanda, possibly from Karagwe. They were pastoralists, living on the hilltops which were unsuitable for farming. Gradually, through their military prowess, they became a ruling class, though the great ritual specialists, *abiru*, were originally Hutu. It was only in the eighteenth century that Rwanda became a unified state and that the position of the Tutsi hardened into one of hereditary power and privilege, perhaps because, as the population expanded, land was increasingly at a premium. These demographic pressures led, in the reign of Kigeri Rwabugeri (1860–95), to wars of expansion to the north, where few Tutsi had lived. This meant that the premise of inequality was extended over a wider area. These political changes were mirrored in the cognitive sphere in the growth of the cult of the hero Ryangombe. It is possible that the historical prototype was a Hutu king. Transmuted to myth, he offered an eternity of plenty to his initiates on Mount Muhavera, a volcano in north-western Rwanda. The lobelias which grow round the crater rim are tobacco plantations, guarded by his sacred sheep and cow. He and his son Binego challenge the values of Tutsi societies and he is remembered as the enemy of Ruganzu II, one of the great Rwanda kings. Significantly, he is a hunter not a pastoralist, and Binego declares, through his medium, 'No one commands me and I heed no one. I walk behind no lord and no vassal follows me.'[99]

The cult of the goddess Nyabingi, in southern Uganda and northern Rwanda, which became more powerful in the nineteenth century, is often interpreted as a vehicle of Hutu protest.[100]

New states

Long-distance trade impinged on political history in many different ways. Sometimes Arab/Swahili merchants weakened and destabilised African polities, supporting one side in internal power struggles. This happened in the Nyamwezi state of Unyanyembe, from the 1860s on.

The Kazembe kingdom declined when Garenganze cut it off from both the Lunda heartland and the resources of Shaba, and when Bemba and Ngoni raids disrupted its eastern trade routes. 'Arab' intervention in local affairs was largely responsible for the deposition of two Kazembe in rapid succession in the early 1870s.

Nineteenth-century European observers stressed the cruelty of the new regimes, the arbitrary power of their rulers, often in order to justify their own role as agents of change, whether as missionaries or as agents of colonial governments. Africanist historians of the 1970s reacted against this and stressed the courage and ability of the New Men. Sometimes they wrote as if the merits of enlargement of scale were self-evident. Bennett said of Mirambo, whose self-chosen name means Corpses, 'one can argue that Mirambo was one of the most successful of the rulers of east central Africa – A large part of [his] greatness came from his receptivity to the new objects and ideas.'[101] Omer-Cooper called

Zwangendaba 'one of the most remarkable leaders in African history'.[102] Shorter spoke of the notoriously cruel Nyungu-ya-Mawe's activities as 'the only realistic attempt made to reform the Kimbu tribe and halt the process of proliferation and decline'.[103] Others laid more stress on the cruelty of their regimes, the burning villages, the pain of the enslaved.[104] Historians are now more likely to realise that the interests of kings and of their subjects were not necessarily the same. The subjects always knew this.

> War came into being because of the chiefs –
> it is not a new thing . . .
> the pounding today is not the pounding of millet,
> this pounding is war
> these are the men who scoop up and devour from their hands
> the blood of enemies.[105]

Aristocrats were not immune to the pain and suffering caused by nineteenth-century wars. Mkwawa's mother drowned herself while fleeing from an enemy and Nyungu's daughter and heir committed suicide ten years after she succeeded to his kingdom. Isike blew up himself and his fortress. Mkwawa shot himself, after years as a fugitive.

The warlords were often – not always – loyal and generous to their supporters. Loyalty – and fear – preserved Mkwawa in his fugitive years, when it was said that the character of his country and people protected him like a wall.

Long-distance trade encouraged social polarisation and enabled a successful merchant to amass dependants. In a matrilineal society, only the progeny of slave wives belonged to the father's lineage. The Yao warlord, Mataka I (*c.* 1800– *c.* 1879), is said to have had 600 wives. He was the grandson of a woman called Syunguli, 'a powerful and fully recognised chief, and a successful',[106] and began his career by migrating away from her sphere of influence. He and his brothers built up capital by making baskets, which they traded for hoes. With the hoes they bought slaves, and Mataka 'no longer made baskets; he robbed the villages of his fellow Yaos . . . If a cock crowed in a village, he brought a case against them on the grounds that the bird had sworn against him, and the penalty was thirty slaves.' When he died, he was buried with sixty living children.

The New Men of the nineteenth century had a number of things in common. Typically, they belonged to a royal family, like Mkwawa, or married into one, like Mwambambe, but their power rested essentially on leadership qualities and especially a talent for war.

One of the most striking case studies of the impact of long-distance trade can be found in the nineteenth-century history of the Kilindi kingdom in Shambaai. It was not of great antiquity – Kimweri, who reigned from *c.* 1815 to 1862, was the great-grandson of its founder.[107] He was a sacred king, living in the mountain capital of Vugha; his son, Semboja, became the chief of Mazinde, a cosmopolitan centre in the plains, where both Zigua and Swahili were spoken. Semboja acquired guns, built a house in the coastal style, and wore Arab dress. When Kimweri died, he was succeeded by his grandson, Shekulwavu; a civil war with Semboja ended with the young king's defeat and death. Semboja placed his own son on the throne at Vugha, and continued to live in the plains.

Mkwawa and the Hehe

The Hehe were a striking example of a people which absorbed military techniques from the Ngoni and used them successfully against them. In 1800, fifteen small communities lived in the uplands of what is now Uhehe, in Iringa district. Their language and culture were close to that of their lowland neighbours, the Bena and the Sanga – another case where ethnic consciousness was formed partly by the physical environment. The Sanga were the first to bear the brunt of the Ngoni invasion, adopting their weapons and tactics and founding a state which lasted until 1860, when they were defeated by the forces of a Hehe leader, Munyigumba (d. 1879). The Sanga king retreated to Usafwa and built a stone fortress near Mbeya, one of a number of nineteenth-century East African rulers who sought security in monumental architecture. The Hehe fought the Ngoni from 1878 until 1881, when the losses on both sides forced them to make peace until their children had grown up.

When Munyigumba died, he was succeeded by his son Mkwawa, who began his career by defeating a rival at Ilundamatwe, 'the place where many heads are piled up'.[108] Mkwawa's Hehe stemmed the advance of the Maasai, as well as of the Ngoni, after a devastating struggle which led to the abandonment of many villages. In 1891, they won a Pyrrhic victory over the Germans, with so many losses that Mkwawa forbade mourning. He fought on, with an ever diminishing band of followers, who were defeated less by the invaders than by hunger, disease and exhaustion. In 1898, he shot himself to avoid capture. He may have been, like Shaka, mentally unstable – his praise names included 'the madness of the year' – but he was the architect of a sense of Hehe identity which still endures. The Hehe won the reluctant admiration of the Germans, who educated Mkwawa's son in Europe and made him an *akida*.[109]

Nyamwezi warlords

Several nineteenth-century Nyamwezi founded kingdoms – we have noted Msiri's Garenganze. The man history knows as Mirambo (c. 1840–84) was the son of a sacred king, *ntemi*, but since succession was matrilineal, he was not the heir.[110] Ngoni warriors reached Unyamwezi in the 1850s; Mirambo learnt their language and adopted their military techniques, and founded a kingdom which he named after himself, Urambo. He built up an army of men from many different ethnic groups, absorbing large numbers of war captives and offering local kings a choice of submission or war. One was sent a hundred bullets and a hundred hoes. He prudently opted for the hoes, and acquired the nickname Majembe Gana.

From 1871 to 1875, Mirambo fought the Arab/Swahili enclave at Tabora. Stanley took part in one of the battles, on the Arab side, and narrowly escaped with his life. In his last years, Mirambo fought the Ngoni. He died in 1884, of a disease of the throat, and the state he had created died with him.

Isike, who became *ntemi* of Unyanyembe in 1876, was Mirambo's mortal enemy. At first he ruled with the support of Tabora, but later became independent. In 1892, the Germans stormed his fortress, and he blew himself up rather than surrender. He was not quite dead, so they hanged him. Brutality was not confined to African warlords. Nyungu ya Mawe ('pot of stone', that is, Indestructable) was a member of the Unyanyembe royal family who had carved out a state in Ukimbu by 1871. Like Mirambo, he relied on *rugaruga*, a private army of captives, caravan deserters and escaped slaves, whose ferocity was intensified, like that of some modern African guerrillas, by the practice of smoking hemp.[111] Nyungu roasted his prisoners alive and Kimbu tradition remembers him as Ili-Nyungu, Nyungu the Terrible. He died in 1884, the same year as Mutesa of Buganda and Mirambo.

Comoro, a notable of the Gondokoro region, gave Baker his own exegesis of the interface between morality and power. He said, 'only the weak are good; they are good because they are not strong enough to be bad.'[112]

Cultural change

Ideas as well as ivory, travelled along the trade routes. The language of kinship not only softened the reality of enslavement but also often provided a model for inter-group relations. A joking relationship of affection and banter often bonded grandparents and grandchildren. Called *utani*, it bonded long-distance traders with their hosts, as did marriages and blood brotherhood. Sometimes trade was in the hands of women and continued undisturbed when the men were at war – this was the case among the Maasai, Kikuyu and Chagga.[113]

Africans were keenly aware of the need for new knowledge to equip them to deal with the challenges of a new age. Often this was conceptualised in traditional terms as *dawa*, [supernatural] medicine. In 1890, a Kerebe king sent representatives to Zaire, to exchange ivory for *dawa*.[114] Chileshya was a famous Bemba king, who died in 1860. When he visited one of his fellow rulers, the gifts he received included magic and new technology for divination.[115]

As these examples show, a stranger's religion often appeared more powerful and efficacious than the home-grown variety. The spread of spirit possession cults, so evident in twentieth-century Africa, was also typical of the nineteenth – they were first introduced to Upare by visiting Shambaa traders,[116] and the Cwezi cult spread to Usukuma, Unyamwezi and the eastern Congo.[117] The ivory trade led to the spread of hunters' guilds;[118] secret societies, including dance societies, provided another way of linking trading partners from different ethnolinguistic groups. Some peoples, such as the Sukuma, were particularly known for their magical powers.

... secret societies of snake charmers, porcupine hunters, elephant hunters and societies concerned with ancestor worship and divination had thriven in Sukumaland besides a great number of dance societies. As porters on the old trade routes to the coast and as twentieth century migrant workers they came into contact with many other tribes who soon began to be impressed by their skill in divination and other magic vocations.[119]

We have noted the increase in witchcraft accusations, which were not always caused by considerations of profit. The dangers of the nineteenth century encouraged resettlement into stockaded villages and may have made access to farmland more difficult; this was another potential source of tension. In the colonial period, in East Africa as elsewhere in Africa, people were able to move away from settlements created for defensive purposes. 'Even cowards want their own space,' say the Luo of western Kenya.[120]

Most of all, perhaps, the repeated scourges of new and unfamiliar diseases cried out for an explanation. 'When diseases came and many people died, then people started to say that someone was a sorcerer because he could make a certain medicine to kill a person ... sorcerers, drinking medicines [and] taboos ... appeared when diseases came during Ibanda's time [c. 1830–5].'[121]

In Ukerewe, the king's sacred role was undermined by his inability to protect his subjects from the new diseases, and diviners became more powerful.[122] But where the king controlled poison ordeals, the increase in witchcraft accusations had the effect of increasing his power. The *mwavi* ordeal seems to have originated in Malawi; it was adopted by the Ngoni and spread rapidly in nineteenth-century Tanganyika.[123] Islam, Swahili, coastal crops and building styles percolated inland from the coast. Rindi of Moshi learnt Swahili and employed a Swahili secretary.[124] 'They [the Yao] built dhows copied from those of the Arabs; also they planted cocoanuts with the object of making the Lake-shore resemble the Coast.'[125] Mataka planted mangoes and said, 'Ah! now I have changed Yao so that it resembles the coast.'[126] In the late nineteenth century, most Yao became Muslims.

In Buganda and Madagascar, Christianity made many converts among the elite. Elsewhere, it appealed mainly to the poor and marginalised. By 1870, there was no equivalent in East Africa to the large numbers of educated Christians in the Cape, Natal, Lagos, Sierra Leone and Liberia. Johann Krapf worked as a Church Missionary Society missionary near Mombasa from 1844 on. He would pray that his life be preserved until he should have made at least one convert;[127] his first Christian, Mrenge of Rabai, was disabled.

David Livingstone began his missionary career among the Tswana. He had little success, and turned to exploration; between 1853 and 1856 he and his Kololo bearers crossed Africa to the coast of Angola, and recrossed it to the Zambezi Delta. It was a 'discovery' of routes well known to Africans,[128] but it made him a national hero in Britain where the government financed an expedition to the Zambezi under his leadership in 1866.[129] A missionary party went with him, but the venture was a failure and its members retreated to Zanzibar, where they concentrated on work among freed slaves. The CMS also ran freed slaves settlements, near Mombasa, in the last quarter of the century. But by 1870, most of East and East Central Africa had never seen a European or a missionary.

Agrarian change

Wider trade contacts often led to the adoption of new crops. Kerebe, who left home as porters, collected seeds, which were then cultivated under the king's supervision. This led to the introduction of maize and cassava, and of new varieties of sorghum and millet which gradually replaced those previously planted.[130] Rice, maize and cassava spread in western Tanzania in the nineteenth century; cassava offered some protection against famine, and rice was grown on land hitherto unused – river margins which flooded in the rainy season.[131]

Gender

Women were peculiarly vulnerable in the dislocations of the nineteenth century, as the story of Swema and her mother reminds us. Often they spent their lives in a fruitless quest for security. Chisi, born in 1870, was a Bisa, capured by Bemba raiders, who escaped to a Safwa village but remained a marginal refugee. At one stage she fostered two youths; when one committed adultery, she was liable for the fine, and moved away. 'I was afraid that the Zambe people would kill me, for I was poor, and had nothing to give to atone for this crime.'[132]

In agricultural societies, women were primarily responsible for food production; in pastoral ones, they tended to be kept at a distance from the herds. The advantages of class often outweighed the disadvantages of gender; two of the three people hailed as Kabaka in Buganda were women, and the Queen Mother and Queen Sister had their own courts, chiefs and revenues. But in Buganda as a whole, women were supposed to speak to men on their knees.[133]

Women were often mediums of the Cwezi. Speke described them in Karagwe: 'Many mendicant women called by some Wichwezi, by others Mbandwa ... some called them devil-drivers, others evil-eye averters. But whatever, they imposed a tax on the people.'[134] One version of Ryangombe's dying words is, 'I will help women in their confinements and I will give children to barren women.' When missionaries and colonial officials showed hostility to the spirit possession cults, it was believed in Bunyoro that they wanted the population to disappear.[135]

Some women – Chisi among them – were among the pioneer Christians. Fiambarema was the first convert at the Moravian mission in Rungwe.[136] Titled women were sometimes implacably hostile to the new religion. Ranavalona, who seized the Madagascar throne after the death of Radama in 1828, and reigned until 1861, persecuted Christians – 'They hold assemblies in the night and deliver speeches without permission from the Queen.'[137] Mutesa's mother, Muganzirwaza, who played an active role in public affairs, was hostile to Christianity, and so was Kanjogera, who became Rwanda Queen Mother in 1889.

Famine and disease

In the Cwezi pantheon in Nkore, Ndahura is held responsible for plague and smallpox. 'He is always the most feared of the Abacwezi because of the fear of his anger.'[138]

The contacts which sprang from trade led to the spread of new diseases, and smallpox and cholera had a catastrophic impact on inland communities where they were previously unknown. In Karagwe and Unyakusa, people were decimated by plague at the time the Arabs first arrived – clearly cause and effect – but according to Burton, 'The most dangerous epidemic is ... smallpox, which ... sweeps at times like a storm of death over the land.'[139]

Smallpox and cholera reached Ukerewe in the late eighteenth or early nineteenth century. Tradition claims that they were deliberately introduced by the king, who obtained them from the Dadog, an interesting example of the way in which oral tradition personalises patterns of historical change. Syphilis was brought to Ukerewe by coastal traders, and may have caused a decline in the island's population. Royals were the most likely to be affected, because they had the largest number of sexual partners.[140] The decline in population led to an expansion of domestic slavery.

Cholera evolved in India and was confined to Asia until the nineteenth century, when four world pandemics afflicted much of the globe, their impact greatly worsened by inappropriate means of treatment.[141] All four pandemics reached Zanzibar – in 1821, 1836–7, 1858–9 and 1869–70. The third of these, which killed 20,000 in Zanzibar in four months, may have penetrated as far as Buganda, and Mutesa asked, 'What brought the scourge? What could cure it?' It wrought particular havoc among the Maasai and Oromo and their neighbours.[142]

The jigger flea is a native of South America. It burrows into human feet and lays its eggs under the skin; if they are left there, they cause abscesses and sometimes death by blood poisoning. They were established in West Africa by 1700 but reached Central and then East Africa after 1872, when a British ship brought them in ballast to Angola from Rio de Janeiro. Jiggers crossed the continent with lightning rapidity and had a catastrophic effect on peoples unfamiliar with them. Many lost their feet, and even their lives, and the impact on agricultural production was disastrous; this carries us, however, beyond the time span of this book.

It is generally agreed that the population of Tanganyika declined between the 1890s and the 1920s; in some localised areas, this may have happened earlier. The tsetse fly (*Glossina*) causes trypanosomiasis in cattle and sleeping sickness in people. The former, but not the latter, is documented in East Africa in the nineteenth century. Pastoralists were well aware of the dangers and avoided tsetse-infected areas. There were great outbreaks of sleeping sickness from 1901 on, and in vast areas where cattle once flourished they could survive no longer. This seems to reflect a major reversal of the relations between humanity and environment. Tsetse flies flourish in the bush, finding a host among game. The clearing of the bush – a process which began, as we have seen, in the Early Iron Age – was reversed by a large number of factors, including deaths of people in famines, epidemics and war, migration, and the forced migration of enslavement. The insecurity of the nineteenth century meant that in some areas, such as Ukimbu and Unyamwezi, scattered hamlets were replaced by stockaded villages for defensive purposes. It is possible that this change reduced the area under cultivation and encouraged the spread of tsetse fly. The Kimbu kept cattle for a century, and then it became impossible.[143] In Karagwe, 'No longer could a depleted population, with few cattle, maintain the open grasslands. The bush grew away from them and created a habitat favorable to invasion by the tsetse fly.'[144]

The adoption of new crops did not prevent famine. It was no novelty in eastern Africa – in many areas rainfall was so low that a relatively small fluctuation could mean the difference between life and death. There was a well-documented and widespread famine caused by drought in *c.* 1836. In Ukerewe it caused the deposition of a king and it forced many Kamba to leave their homes for new settlements among the Mijikenda.[145] In Ukimbu, the population of each principality was reduced to that of a village.

> We are wiped out ...
> Let us flee to those who have grain.[146]

In Ugogo, eight named famines are remembered from the nineteenth century, the worst of which, caused by drought, predated 1850. A famine in 1850 is remembered as 'Hobble' (the weakness of the starving), of 1870 as 'bursting of the intestines'.[147]

The famine of 1897–1901 is remembered in central Kenya as the Great Famine.[148] It was caused largely by drought, and a detailed history of it sheds light on the way in which social patterns must have been distorted in earlier famines. People retreated from their obligations, first to the extended family and clients, then to spouses and children.[149] Women were given as debt pawns and often not recovered, creating an abiding sense of grievance that Kamba women had become Kikuyu wives. Some turned to robbery and violence – bands of outlaws were formed, called *muthakethe*. Even when the rains returned, the starving had eaten their seeds and lacked the strength to plant and weed. Famine increased the distance between rich and poor – 'The poor people simply died and the rich survived.'

Understandings of change

In many different parts of nineteenth-century Africa, prophets arose who seemed to have a remarkable understanding of the patterns of change. In some cases, their notably accurate predictions may be later inventions, attributed to past individuals in an attempt to own or control the changes so evident in their own times. Sometimes, of course, the prediction was enigmatic, and those who came later interpreted it with the benefit of hindsight. In Shambaa 'Kighobo foretold that the Wataita will no longer come to fight the Washambaa – this came to be true. He also said that all places which had forests would become villages ... and that there would be houses along the roads ... He had already foretold that there would come white people.'[150]

In Ufipa, there was a late nineteenth-century prophet called Kaswa.

> He said: 'There are monstrous strangers coming,
> Bringing war, striking you unawares relentlessly
> O you people, you're going to be robbed of your country ...
> Everything will have its price: grass and the very earth itself.'[151]

Notes

PERIMETERS

1 Mupun oral testimonies, Muhammad Dabal Gupa of Abwor Dyis, July 1977, and others.
2 T. S. Eliot, *Four Quartets*, Little Gidding, V (London, 1944), p. 43.
3 A. Hopkins, 'African economic history: the first twenty-five years', *Journal of African History*, 1989, p. 157. See his *An Economic History of West Africa* (London, 1973).
4 See p. 402 below.
5 See p. 96 below.
6 P. Geschiere, 'Witchcraft, kinship and the moral economy of ethnicity', (Conference on Ethnicity in Africa, Edinburgh, May 1995). See pp. 84–5, 100 below.
7 J. Miller, *Equatorial Africa* (American Historical Association, 1976), pp. 5–6.
8 Ibid., p. 6.
9 C. Geertz, *Islam Observed: Religious Development in Morocco and Indonesia* (New Haven and London, 1968), p. 71.
10 On this, see, for instance, P. Chabal, 'Africans, Africanists and the African crisis', *Africa*, 1991, pp. 530ff.
11 Quoted in D. Levine, *Greater Ethiopia: The Evolution of a Multiethnic Society* (Chicago, 1974), p. 102.

I PRELUDE: AFRICA AND THE HISTORIANS

1 Quoted in J. Vansina, *Children of Woot: A History of the Kuba Peoples* (Madison, 1978), p. 19.
2 A. F. C. Ryder, *Benin and the Europeans, 1485–1897* (London, 1969). He also made use of the pioneering work of a Bini historian, J. Egharevba, *A Short History of Benin* (3rd edn, Ibadan, 1960).
3 Tradition claims that Arabic characters were first used to write Hausa by a son of Uthman dan Fodio, in the first half of the nineteenth century. The earliest surviving Swahili manuscript is from the early eighteenth century; this does not mean, of course, that Swahili was not written earlier. Fulfulde was written in Arabic in Futa Jallon and elsewhere, in the early nineteenth century. (D. Robinson, 'Fulfulde literature in Arabic script', *History in Africa*, 1982, pp. 251–61). The general reader does best to approach source material through historical anthologies. These include B. Davidson, *The African Past* (London, 1964); T. Hodgkin, *Nigerian Perspectives: A Historical Anthology* (2nd edn, London, 1975); F. Wolfson (ed.), *Pageant of Ghana* (London, 1958); C. Fyfe, *Sierra Leone Inheritance* (London, 1964); E. Isichei, *Igbo Worlds: An Anthology of*

Oral Histories and Historical Descriptions (London, 1977); N. Levtzion and J. F. P. Hopkins, *Corpus of Early Arabic Sources for West African History* (Cambridge, 1981); G. S. P. Freeman-Grenville, *The East African Coast: Select Documents from the First to the Earlier Nineteenth Century* (2nd edn, London, 1975). This list is only a selection. Many classics of African exploration were reprinted in the 1960s and 1970s, often by Frank Cass.

4   See R. Hackett, 'African religions: images and I-glasses', *Religion*, 1990, pp. 303ff.

5   W. Allen and T. R. H. Thomson, *A Narrative of the Expedition to the River Niger* (London, 1848), I, p. 294 and engraving facing p. 293.

6   P. Edwards, Introduction to his abridged edition of *The Life of Olaudah Equiano* (Harlow, 1988).

7   And particularly of Jan Vansina. He is, for instance, cited five times in P. Burke (ed.), *New Perspectives on Historical Writing* (Cambridge, 1991). His book, *Oral Tradition: A Study in Historical Methodology* (London, 1972 reprint) was enormously influential; his *Oral Tradition as History* (Madison, 1985) is a more recent study.

8   For a notable discussion of this and allied issues, see C. C. Wrigley, 'Historicism in Africa: slavery and state formation', *African Affairs*, 1971, pp. 113–24. My own oral history collection has been made exclusively among peoples organised in small communities.

9   My own work is an exception; in 1983–5, I carried out an oral and archival research project on the history of the Anaguta, who number about 5,000.

10 R. Horton, 'Stateless societies in the history of West Africa', in J. F. A. Ajayi and M. Crowder (eds.), *History of West Africa* I (3rd edn, Harlow, 1985), pp. 87ff.

11 A. E. Afigbo, 'Oral tradition and the history of segmentary societies', *History in Africa*, 1985, pp. 1ff., makes no mention of my three books on the Igbo – his own research field, nor of D. Northrup, *Trade without Rulers: Pre-Colonial Economic Development in South-Eastern Nigeria* (Oxford, 1978), nor of the historical sections of R. Henderson's excellent and underused study of Onitsha, *The King in Every Man* (New Haven and London, 1972). A recent article by F. Fuglestad makes a plea for the study of societies which were 'non-literate, acephalous and strongly religiously oriented'. It makes no mention of these works – nor of E. Isichei (ed.), *Studies in the History of Plateau State, Nigeria* (London, 1982): F. Fuglestad, 'The Trevor-Roper trap or the imperialism of history, an essay', *History in Africa*, 1992, p. 317.

12 Mamdou Diawara, 'Women, servitude and history', in K. Barber and P. de Moraes Farias (eds.) *Discourse and Its Disguises* (Birmingham, 1989), pp. 109ff.

13 Or when I lent all my own notes, translations and transcripts from the Society of African Missions archives in Rome to a Nigerian historian who had funding to visit Rome, but had no French, the language in which all the relevant material was written. He took them all to Rome, and brought them back safely!

14 When I solicited material for Jos Oral History and Literature Texts, it became obvious that some historians and scholars in related disciplines who had worked in the field had substantial collections of material, but that others did not. To particularise only the former – Polly Hill, Samson Amali and E. J. Alagoa did have large collections, which they were anxious to share with the scholarly community. It is significant that two of the three were Africans, working in their

own languages, and that the third offered, not oral texts, but field notes. Any of the three could have provided a whole series of volumes. In retrospect, I should have given them the chance to do so.

15 E. Isichei, *Igbo Worlds: An Anthology of Oral Histories and Historical Descriptions* (London, 1981); six volumes of Jos Oral History and Literature Texts were published by the Department of History, University of Jos, between 1981 and 1986.

16 See R. Law, *The Slave Coast of West Africa* (Oxford, 1991), pp. 4–5.

17 D. Robinson, *The Holy War of Al-Hajj Umar* (Oxford, 1985), p. 36.

18 J. D. Y. Peel, *Ijeshas and Nigerians* (Cambridge, 1982); J. Janzen, *Lemba, 1650–1930: A Drum of Affliction in Africa and the New World* (New York and London, 1982); R. Horton, 'A hundred years of change in Kalabari religion', in J. Middleton (ed.), *Black Africa, Its Peoples and Their Cultures Today* (London, 1970), pp. 192ff. My admiration for this and his other articles on the Kalabari is not inconsistent with p. 9 above!

19 J. Fabian, *Time and the Other: How Anthropology Makes Its Object* (New York, 1983).

20 J. Vansina, *Paths in the Rainforests: Towards a History of Political Tradition in Equatorial Africa* (Madison, 1990), p. 27.

21 C. Wrigley, 'The story of Rukidi', *Africa*, 1973, pp. 219–35. His earlier assessment of L. de Heusch's classic structuralist study *Le roi ivre* was probably the most influential review ever to appear in *The Journal of African History* ('Myths of the savanna', *Journal of African History*, 1974, pp. 131–5).

22 J. B. Webster (ed.), *Chronology, Migration and Drought in Interlacustrine Africa* (London, 1979). See Chapter 8 below.

23 An outstanding example is J. Miller (ed.), *The African Past Speaks: Essays on Oral Tradition and History* (Folkestone, 1980).

24 J. Vansina, 'Deep-down time: political tradition in Central Africa', *History in Africa*, 1989, p. 348.

25 D. Henige, *The Chronology of Oral Tradition* (Oxford, 1974), pp. 105–14. On Buganda, see his later piece, '"The Disease of Writing": Ganda and Nyoro kinglists in a newly literate world', in Miller, *The African Past Speaks*, pp. 240–61.

26 J. Goody, 'What's in a list?', *The Domestication of the Savage Mind* (Cambridge, 1977), pp. 74–111.

27 This is true of Asaba, and of Arochukwu, for instance. I have grappled with the thorny question of their chronology in various writings. E. Isichei, 'Historical change in an Ibo polity: Asaba to 1885', *Journal of African History*, 1969, pp. 421–38; *The Ibo People and the Europeans: The Genesis of a Relationship – to 1906* (London, 1973), pp. 34–5; for a recent article endorsing a seventeenth-century date for Arochukwu, see A. Nwauwa, 'The dating of the Aro chiefdom: a synthesis of correlated genealogies', *History in Africa*, 1990, pp. 227–45.

28 For a striking instance, see J. Miller, 'Kings, lists and history in Kasanje', *History in Africa*, 1979, pp. 51–96. Two classic studies which collate an early version of written oral tradition and a meticulous collection of written data to produce a detailed and accurate history are Ryder's study of Benin (n. 2 above) and R. C. C. Law, *The Oyo Empire, c.1600–1836: A West African Imperialism in the Era of the Atlantic Slave Trade* (Oxford, 1977).

29 W. G. Clarence-Smith, 'For Braudel: a note on the "Ecole des *Annales*" and the historiography of Africa', *History in Africa*, 1977, pp. 276–81; cf. the reply by

J. Vansina, 'For oral tradition (but not against Braudel)', *History in Africa*, 1978, pp. 351–6.

30 Vansina, *The Children of Woot*, pp. 24–5.

31 J. C. Miller, *Kings and Kinsmen – Early Mbundu States in Angola* (Oxford, 1978); see W. MacGaffey, 'Oral traditions in Central Africa', *International Journal of African Historical Studies*, 1974, pp. 417–26.

32 R. Oliver, 'The traditional histories of Buganda, Bunyoro and Ankole', *Journal of the Royal Anthropological Institute*, 1955, pp. 111–12.

33 M. Hall, *The Changing Past: Farmers, Kings and Traders in Southern Africa, 200–1860* (Cape Town and Johannesburg, 1987), pp. 5–7.

34 See for instance, C. K. Meek, *A Sudanese Kingdom* (London, 1931); M. D. W. Jeffries, 'Circumcision: its diffusion from Egypt among the Bantu', *Criteria* (Johannesburg), 1949, pp. 73–84; E. Meyerowitz, *The Divine Kingship in Ghana and Ancient Egypt* (London, 1960).

35 'Hamitic', a term no longer used, referred to all the branches of Afroasiatic except Semitic. See E. R. Sanders, 'The Hamitic hypothesis: its origin and functions in time perspective', *Journal of African History*, 1969, pp. 521–32.

36 See Abdullahi Smith, 'Some considerations relating to the formation of states in Hausaland', *Journal of the Historical Society of Nigeria*, 1970, pp. 329–46 for an influential rebuttal.

37 S. Johnson, *History of the Yorubas* (London, 1921); J. O. Lucas, *The Religion of the Yorubas in Relation to the Religion of Ancient Egypt* (Lagos, 1948); Cheikh Anta Diop, *L'Afrique noire précoloniale* (Paris, 1960).

38 J. Despois, *L'Afrique du nord* (Paris, 1958), p. 543, quoted in J. Abun-Nasr, *A History of the Maghrib in the Islamic Period* (Cambridge, 1987), p. 1.

39 J. Vansina, *Art History in Africa* (London, 1984), p. 119, Fig. 6.4.

40 Some outstanding Africanists were drawn into the field by circumstances, usually as a result of taking up a university appointment there, though of course those unsympathetic to African aspirations would be less likely to take such a step. Some Americans were drawn to the field through their involvement in the civil rights movement.

41 H. Trevor-Roper, 'The rise of Christian Europe', *The Listener*, November 28 1963, p. 871. He also said, in words which in a sense encapsulate the history of African historiography from 1962 on, 'Perhaps in the future, there will be some African history to teach. But at present there is none; there is only the history of the Europeans in Africa.'

42 P. Veyne, *Writing History: An Essay on Epistemology* (Eng. trans. Middletown, Conn., 1984), p. 62.

43 R. Fry, *Vision and Design*, quoted in V. Mudimbe, *The Invention of Africa* (Bloomington, 1988), p. 11.

44 The literature on resistance is too vast to outline here. A seminal figure was Terence Ranger. His *Revolt in Southern Rhodesia* (London, 1967) has been much criticised in detail, but was immensely influential. See too his 'Primary resistance movements and modern mass nationalism in East and Central Africa', *Journal of African History*, 1968, pp. 473–53. Outstanding among more recent work is A. Isaacman with B. Isaacman, *The Tradition of Resistance in Mozambique* (London, 1976); see also A. and B. Isaacman, 'Resistance and collaboration in southern and central Africa, *c*.1850–1920', *The International Journal of African Historical Studies*, 1977, pp. 31–62.

45 Examples include A. G. Hopkins, *An Economic History of West Africa* (London, 1973); R. Gray and D. Birmingham (eds.), *Pre-Colonial African Trade* (London, 1970).

46 A notable pioneering attempt to come to grips with the historiographic implications of this is C. Fyfe (ed.), *African Studies since 1945: A Tribute to Basil Davidson* (London, 1976).

47 See J. D. Fage, 'Slavery and the slave trade in the context of West African history', *Journal of African History*, 1969, pp. 394–404, and the critique by C. Wrigley, 'Historicism in Africa, slavery and state formation', *African Affairs*, 1971, pp. 113–24. It is noteworthy that two ameliorationist studies of the slave trade deal with south-eastern Nigeria, where its impact was especially severe. See Northrup, *Trade without Rulers*, and A. J. H. Latham, *Old Calabar, 1600–1891* (Oxford, 1971); the latter study is positive about its impact on the Efik, and agnostic about its impact on the hinterland.

48 J. D. Omer-Cooper, *The Zulu Aftermath: A Nineteenth Century Revolution in Bantu Africa* (London, 1966). See the comment of C. Wrigley in 'Historicism in Africa', p. 119: 'On the author's own showing, Shaka was a raging pyschopath, who would have been placed under restraint in any society in which he himself would willingly live.'

49 J. Barbot, *A Description of the Coasts of North and South Guinea* (London, 1746), p. 270.

50 Elizabeth Isichei, *The Ibo People and the Europeans* (London, 1973); *A History of the Igbo People* (London, 1976); *Igbo Worlds* (London, 1977); Isichei (ed.), *Studies in the History of Plateau State, Nigeria* (London, 1982); Isichei, 'On being invisible: an historical perspective of the Anaguta and their neighbours', *The International Journal of African Historical Studies*, 1991, pp. 513ff. and other articles on the Anaguta.

51 I. Wilks, *Asante in the Nineteenth Century* (Cambridge, 1975).

52 T. McCaskie, 'Komfo Anokye of Asante: meaning, history and philosophy in an African society', *Journal of African History*, 1986, pp. 315ff. and his 'Empire state: Asante and the historians', *Journal of African History*, 1992, pp. 467ff.

53 Isichei, *The Ibo People and the Europeans*, p. 17.

54 J. F. Ade Ajayi, *Christian Missions in Nigeria 1841–1891: The Making of a New Elite* (London, 1965); E. A. Ayandele, *The Missionary Impact on Modern Nigeria* (London, 1966).

55 E. A. Ayandele, *The Educated Elite in the Nigerian Society* (Ibadan, 1974).

56 See an interesting evaluation in Peel, *Ijeshas and Nigerians*, pp. 11–123.

57 See A. Temu and B. Swai, *Historians and Africanist History: A Critique* (London, 1981). This work, incidentally, quotes Ho Chi Minh as an authority on the Congo (p. 34).

58 D. Denoon and A. Kuper, 'Nationalist historians in search of a nation: the "New Historiography" in Dar es Salaam', *African Affairs*, 1970, pp. 329–49; T. Ranger, 'The "New Historiography" in Dar es Salaam: an answer', *African Affairs,* 1971, pp. 50–61.

59 J. Iliffe's, *The Emergence of African Capitalism* (London, 1983). See also J. Goody, *Production and Reproduction: A Comparative Study of the Domestic Domain* (Cambridge, 1976), an excellent example of a major book by a non-Marxist which embodies Marxist insights.

60 See for instance, E. Terray, 'Long-distance exchange and the formation of the

state: the case of the Abron kingdom of Gyaman', *Economy and Society*, 1974, pp. 315ff.

61 B. Hindess and P. Q. Hirst, *Pre-Capitalist Modes of Production* (London, 1977 reprint), p. 321. It is quoted in R. Law, 'In search of a Marxist perspective on pre-colonial tropical Africa', *Journal of African History*, 1978, p. 443; in R. Austen, *African Economic History* (London, 1987), p. 6 n. 17, in J. Lonsdale, 'States and social processes in Africa: a historiographic survey', *African Studies Review*, p. 207, n. 4, and elsewhere.

62 E. P. Thompson, *The Poverty of Theory and Other Essays* (New York, 1978). He ends with a quotation from Dickens' *Hard Times*, replacing Gradgrind's name with that of Althusser.

63 M. Turshen, *The Political Ecology of Disease in Tanzania*, quoted in B. Fetter, 'Pitfalls in the application of demographic insights to African history', *History in Africa*, 1992, pp. 299ff.

64 C. Meillassoux, 'From reproduction to production: a Marxist approach to economic anthropology', *Economy and Society*, 1972, pp. 93ff; C. Meillassoux, *Maidens, Meal and Money* (Cambridge, 1981).

65 Cf. the articles by Law (n. 61 above) and Foster-Carter (n. 78 below).

66 I explore the lineage mode of production further in Chapter 6.

67 T. McCaskie, 'Empire state: Asante and the historians', *Journal of African History*, 1992, p. 471.

68 C. Coquery-Vidrovitch, 'The process of urbanization in Africa (from the origins to the beginning of independence)', *African Studies Review*, 1991, p. 3.

69 M. Klein, 'The use of mode of production in historical analysis', *Canadian Journal of African Studies*, 1985, p. 9. This issue contains seven valuable short papers on this subject.

70 E. Alpers, 'Saving baby from the bath water', *Canadian Journal of African Studies*, 1985, p. 17.

71 C. Clarence-Smith, 'Thou shalt not articulate modes of production', *Canadian Journal of African Studies*, 1985, p. 20.

72 Such as Hall, *The Changing Past* (n. 33 above).

73 R. Kea, *Settlements, Trade and Politics in the Seventeenth Century Gold Coast* (Baltimore, 1982).

74 Clarence-Smith, 'Thou shalt not articulate', p. 19.

75 K. Marx, 'Preface to a *Critique of Political Economy*', in Marx, *Selected Writings* (London, 1977), p. 389.

76 M. Rader, *Marx's Interpretation of History* (New York, 1979), p. 185. Rader quotes Harrington to the effect that 'Marx and the Marxists made a major contribution to the misunderstanding of Marxism'.

77 See for instance, Klein, 'The use of mode of production', p. 10 and references cited there.

78 There is a useful survey of Marxist thought on underdevelopment in A. Foster-Carter, 'The modes of production controversy', *New Left Review*, 1978, pp. 47–77.

79 W. Rodney, *How Europe Underdeveloped Africa* (London and Dar es Salaam, 1972); this was widely read by African students; Samir Amin, *Neo-Colonialism in West Africa* (Eng. trans., Harmondsworth, 1973). Amin is an Egyptian; the initial impact of his work on Anglophone Africa was diminished by the fact that it first appeared in French.

80 I explore this theme in 'On being invisible', (n. 50 above).
81 The phrase comes from an article by E. P. Thompson in the *Times Literary Supplement*, 7 April 1966, pp. 252–3.
82 E. J. Hobsbawm, *Bandits* (London, 1969); D. Crummey (ed.), *Banditry, Rebellion and Social Protest in Africa* (London, 1986).
83 E. Isichei, 'African patterns of thought', *The African Review*, 1970, pp. 148–54.
84 F. Braudel, *The Mediterranean and the Mediterranean World* (2 vols., Eng. trans. New York, 1972).
85 See for instance, his 'History and sociology', in F. Braudel, *On History* (Chicago and London, 1980), pp. 64ff.
86 Braudel, Preface to the 1st edition, p. 21.
87 L. Stone, 'The revival of narrative', *Past and Present*, 1979, pp. 3ff. Cf. P. Burke, 'History and the revival of narrative', in Burke, *New Perspectives*, pp. 233ff.
88 P. Burke, 'Overture: the New History', in *New Perspectives*, p. 9.
89 But see W. G. Clarence-Smith, 'For Braudel: a note on the 'Ecole des *Annales*' and the historiography of Africa', pp. 275ff. John Lonsdale's insightful survey, 'States and social processes', lists three major works influenced by Braudel. All indeed are richly textured, with a strong emphasis on the environment. Of the three, J. Iliffe, *A Modern History of Tanganyika* (Cambridge, 1979), does not mention Braudel; G. Prins, *The Hidden Hippopotamus* (Cambridge, 1980), p. 8, does cite Braudel, and employs a structure similar to *The Mediterranean*, with the narrative at the end. J. Vansina, *The Children of Woot*, cites Braudel on p. 11 and elsewhere.
90 Cf. A. Hess, *The Forgotten Frontier: A History of the Sixteenth-Century Ibero–African Frontier* (Chicago and London, 1978), and a ground-breaking study of the rural poor, L. Valensi, *Tunisian Peasants in the Eighteenth and Nineteenth Centuries* (1977, Eng. trans. Cambridge, 1985).
91 Isichei, *The Ibo People and the Europeans*, Ch. 5; D. Johnson and D. Anderson (eds.), *The Ecology of Survival: Case Studies from Northeast African History* (London, 1988).
92 D. W. Cohen and E. Atieno-Odhiambo, *Siaya: The Historical Anthropology of an African Landscape* (London, 1989).
93 Extract in Hodgkin, *Nigerian Perspectives*, p. 115.
94 A. Millson, 'The Yoruba country, West Africa', *Proceedings of the Royal Geographical Society*, 1891, p. 584. He notes the exception – deep river valleys.
95 J. R Ford, *The Role of the Trypanosomiases in African Ecology: A Study of the Tsetse Fly Problem* (Oxford, 1971).
96 I. Kopytoff, 'The internal African frontier: the making of African political culture', in Kopytoff, (ed.), *The African Frontier: The Reproduction of Traditional African Societies* (Bloomington and Indianapolis, 1987).
97 R. O'Fahey, 'Fur and Fartit: the history of a frontier', in J. Mack and P. Robertshaw (eds.), *Culture History in the Southern Sudan: Archaeology, Linguistics and Ethnohistory* (Nairobi, 1982).
98 W. van Binsbergen, '*Likota lya Bakoya*: memory, myth and history', *Cahiers d'études africaines*, 1987, p. 360. This model has been questioned, and may well be wrong.
99 A. G. Hopkins, 'Africa's age of improvement', *History in Africa*, 1980, p. 151.

100 N. H. Ngada et al., *Speaking for Ourselves* (Braamfontein, 1985), p. 5. They gained access to this literature through an educated member of the group – Ngada – and through a facilitator from the Institute of Contextual Theology.

101 V. Mudimbe, *The Invention of Africa: Gnosis, Philosophy and the Order of Knowledge* (London, 1988).

102 T. McCaskie, 'Komfo Anokye of Asante: meaning, history and philosophy in an African society', *Journal of African History*, 1986, p. 321. For more on these issues, see pp. 345–7 below.

103 Notably in Placide Tempels, *Bantu Philosophy*, but also in various attempts to delineate 'African religion'. (See G. Parrinder, *African Traditional Religion* (2nd edn, London, 1962); J. Mbiti, *African Religions and Philosophy* (London, 1969); E. B. Idowu, *African Traditional Religion: A Definition* (London, 1973).)

104 A notable instance of the application of these insights to historical writing in Africa is to be found in the work of T. McCaskie (n. 52 above).

105 For instance, on both penology and the fragmentation of knowledge into 'disciplines', see *Discipline and Punish* (Eng. trans. London, 1977); on insanity, see *Madness and Civilisation* (Eng. trans. New York, 1973); on sexual 'deviance', *The History of Sexuality*, vol . I, *An Introduction* (Eng. trans. New York, 1980).

106 Edward Said, *Orientalism* (New York, 1979).

107 See especially J. Fabian, *Time and the Other*, and J. Clifford and G. Marcus, *Writing Cultures: The Poetics and Politics of Ethnography* (Berkeley, 1986). M. Izard and P. Smith, *Between Belief and Transgression: Structuralist Essays in Religion, History and Myth* (Chicago, 1982). These works are not exclusively concerned with Africa. Uche Isichei, an architect, is exploring these themes in the context of traditional African architecture.

108 M. Douglas, *Purity and Danger* (London, 1966), pp. 173–4.

109 S. Marks and R. Rathbone (eds.), *Industrialisation and Social Change in South Africa* (Harlow, 1982). My emphasis.

110 Jean Comaroff, *Body of Power, Spirit of Resistance* (Chicago, 1985).

111 J. Fernandez, 'African religious movements', *Annual Review of Anthropology*, 1978, p. 215.

112 R. Wagner, *The Invention of Culture* (Chicago, 1980); Mudimbe, *The Invention of Africa*.

113 See, for instance, S. Hutchinson, 'Relations between the sexes among the Nuer: 1930', *Africa*, 1980, pp. 371ff.; J. Burton, 'The wave is my mother's husband: a piscatorial theme in pastoral Nilotic ethnology', *Cahiers d'études africaines*, 1982, p. 469.

114 D. Moore and R. Roberts, 'Listening for silences', *History in Africa*, 1990, pp. 319ff.

115 Quoted in D. Conrad, 'Searching for history in the Sunjata epic: the case of Fakoli', *History in Africa*, 1992, p. 147.

116 J. Dupuis, *Journal of a Residence in Ashantee* (1824, 2nd edn. London, 1966), p. 45.

117 W. G. Clarence-Smith, 'For Braudel', p. 277.

118 The title of a collection of essays on comparative religion by Jonathan Z. Smith.

2 OUT OF AFRICA: THE PRECURSORS

1 I am extremely grateful to Michael Green for his detailed comments on this chapter.

2 The epigraph to E. Herbert, *Red Gold of Africa* (Madison, 1984). I have changed the order of the first sentence.

3 Quoted in P. Veyne, *Writing History* (Eng. trans. Middletown, 1984), p. 15.

4 For which see p. 29 below.

5 Or kya, thousand years ago.

6 Mary Leakey's initial find in the Olduvai Gorge was first called *Zinjanthropus*. It is now categorised as *Anthropithecus* (or *Paranthropus*) *boisei*, but 'Zinj' has stuck.

7 L. Binford, *Bones: Ancient Men and Modern Myths* (New York, 1981), p. 295. For his own views, see p. 33 below. For Lee on the San ('Bushmen') see p. 67 below.

8 This belongs to a period much later than that covered in this chapter, from *c.* 500 BCE to *c.* 500 CE.

9 A paper by P. Williamson et al. on fossil molluscs in Lake Turkana, published in *Nature*, 1981, pp. 437–43, claimed to substantiate this, and instantly became the focus of international attention. There is a vast literature on evolution. An up-to-date survey is O. Mayo, *Natural Selection: Its Constraints* (London, 1983); G. R. Taylor, *The Great Evolution Mystery* (London, 1983), is a more popular version.

10 J. S. Jones and S. Rouhani, 'How small was the bottleneck?', *Nature*, 1986, p. 449.

11 T. H. Huxley, *Lay Sermons, Addresses and Reviews* (London, 1870), p. 297, quoted here from R. J. Berry, *'Natura non fecit saltum'*, *Biological Journal of the Linnaean Society*, 1985, pp. 301–5.

12 Richard Walter, personal communication. See R. Berger, 'Radiocarbon dating with accelerators', *Journal of Archaeological Science*, 1979, pp. 101ff.

13 But it can only be used to compare bones from the same location, and many areas lack natural fluorine.

14 On dating technology see R. Jurmain and H. Nelson, *Introduction to Physical Anthropology* (6th edn, Minneapolis, 1994), pp. 335–44. I am much indebted to this excellent survey. See also R. Foley and M. Lahr, 'Beyond "Out of Africa": reassessing the origins of *Homo sapiens*,' *Journal of Human Evolution*, 1992, pp. 523ff. (This paper begins with the point, 'These new techniques must become comprehensible to, and scrutinized by, the palaeoanthropological community'[!])

15 Such as amino-acid racemisation, which works best on eggshells, but has the drawback that it is influenced by temperature (hence climate) changes. It has been applied to finds from Klasies River Mouth and Border Cave (p. 36 below).

16 Humanity, chimps, gorillas, and their Asian cousins, the orangs, together form the large-bodied homin*oid* family – not to be confused with protohumans, or homin*ids*. It is because of this close relationship that Louis Leakey not only hunted for fossils, but encouraged the famous research of Dian Fossey into the mountain gorillas of Rwanda, and of Jane Goodall into chimpanzees.

17 T. Radford, 'Four million year old find', *Guardian Weekly*, 2 Oct. 1994, p. 4.

18 Probably found only in Asia.

19 Elaine Morgan, *The Aquatic Ape: A Theory of Human Evolution* (London, 1982).

This theory would explain hairlessness and the ready achievement of bipedalism. It rests upon evidence such as the aquatic propensities of human infants and the sexual habits of aquatic mammals.

20 G. Conroy et al., '*Otavipithecus namibiensis*, first Miocene hominoid from southern Africa', *Nature*, 12 March 1992, pp. 144–7; P. Andrews, 'An ape from the south', *Nature*, 12 March 1992, p. 106; R. and M. Leakey, 'A new Miocene hominoid from Kenya', *Nature*, 13 March 1986, p. 143; R. and M. Leakey, 'A second new Miocene hominoid from Kenya', *Nature*, 13 Nov. 1986, pp. 146–8.

21 F. Chideya, 'Finding the missing link', *Newsweek*, 8 July 1991, p. 49.

22 Conroy et al., '*Otavipithecus*', p. 147.

23 Lucy's skull was missing; these data come from other examples of the same species.

24 Jurmain and Nelson, *Introduction to Physical Anthropology*, p. 362. The uncertainty stems from the fact that these are incomplete remains and it is often not clear which bone belongs to which skeleton.

25 See for instance, B. Wood, 'A remote sense for fossils', *Nature*, 30 Jan. 1992, p. 398.

26 Radford, 'Four million year old find', p. 4.

27 No hip, knee or foot bones were found, but the location of the hole for the spinal cord in the base of the skull sheds light on this question.

28 The Inuit are usually cited as the modern exception to the predominance of plant food. This clearly reflects their extreme modern habitat in the Arctic. It is claimed, however, that the Okiek of Kenya have a 50 per cent meat diet, and that only children eat large quantities of nuts, berries, etc.

29 The account which follows is based on C. Gabel, 'Demographic perspectives on the African Pleistocene', in C. Fyfe (ed.), *African Historical Demography* (Edinburgh, 1977), pp. 71–104.

30 A. Hill et al., 'Earliest *Homo*', *Nature*, 20 Feb. 1992, pp. 719–22. The specimen they dated may be the oldest exemplar of the genus *Homo* in the world. B. Wood, 'Old bones match old stones', *Nature*, 20 Feb. 1992, p. 678. It had always been generally assumed that *Homo* was the first toolmaker. Until this discovery, the oldest known stone tools were significantly older than the first remains of *Homo* (Hill et al., p. 720). See also R. Leakey, 'Evidence for an advanced Plio-Pleistocene hominid from East Rudolf, Kenya', *Nature*, 13 April 1973, pp. 447ff. This describes a skull, closer to *Homo* than to australopithecines, thought to be 2.9 million years old.

31 Hill et al., 'Earliest *Homo*', p. 719.

32 Jurmain and Nelson, *Introduction to Physical Anthropology*, p. 397.

33 It should be noted that absolute brain size is not the only citerion; the size of the brain is also proportionate to the total body size. This relationship is called encephalisation.

34 N. Toth, 'The Oldowan reassessed: a close look at early stone artefacts', *Journal of Archaeological Science*, 1985, pp. 109–13, 118. Toth made thousands of these tools in the course of his research, and he also got Berkeley students to make stone tools.

35 C. Brain, *The Hunters or the Hunted? An Introduction to African Cave Taphonomy*, (Chicago, 1981); cf. L. Binford, 'Man the mighty hunter?' in his *In Pursuit of the Past: Decoding the Archaeological Record* (London, 1983), pp. 33ff. Porcupines need to chew on bones as their teeth continue growing; they accumulate a large

supply for this purpose. Leopards eat their prey in trees; the water which sustains the trees frequently carves out caves.

36 This is argued by Binford, *Ancient Bones*, p. 294; Marie-Antoinette de Lumley rejects the scavenger theory, pointing out that in the area of her own research, in France, the bones were largely those of young animals (tender, and easier to catch).

37 Binford, *In Pursuit of the Past*, p. 58.

38 A. Dorfman, 'How man began', *Time*, 14 March 1994, p. 50. This article is an excellent survey of very recent research findings.

39 There is little of the hands, feet and forearms, and no neck vertebrae.

40 B. Wood, 'Old boy', *Nature*, 17 March 1994, pp. 201–2.

41 Jurmain and Nelson, *Introduction to Physical Anthropology*, p. 426; T. Shaw, *Nigeria: Its Archaeology and Early History* (London, 1978), p. 24, citing the research of Yves Coppens.

42 It is usually said that they have not been found in the heavily forested areas of Central and West Africa. A major find of bifaces at Okigwe in south-eastern Nigeria suggests otherwise.

43 L. R. Binford, 'Isolating the transition to cultural adaptations: an organizational approach', in E. Trinkaus (ed.), *The Emergence of Modern Humans: Biocultural Adaptations in the Later Pleistocene* (Cambridge, 1989), pp. 28–9: 'we have a technologically aided, biologically based, panspecific form of adaptation.'

44 Java Man was discovered in the 1890s. The dating was recalculated using a mass spectrometer (C. Swisher et al., 'Age of the earliest known hominids in Java, Indonesia', *Science*, 25 Feb. 1994, pp. 1118–21).

45 *Time*, 14 March 1994, p. 53.

46 T. Wynn, 'The intelligence of later Acheulian hominids', *Man*, 1979, pp. 379ff.

47 W. Goodenough, 'Evolution of the human capacity for beliefs', *American Anthropologist*, 1990, p. 600.

48 The two are not necessarily the same – it would be possible to use fire (from, for instance, lightning), without knowing how to make it, in ways such as striking rocks together.

49 Walker in Jurmain and Nelson, *Introduction to Physical Anthropology*, p. 425; there is no extant adult female *H. erectus* pelvis – this is based on a male exemplar.

50 G. P. Rightmire, *The Evolution of Homo Erectus: Comparative and Anatomical Studies of an Extinct Human Species* (Cambridge, 1990), pp. 226–9.

51 *Homo sapiens Neanderthalensis*. 'Tal' is modern German for valley, and 'Thal', an older form, is preserved in the scientific name.

52 This is thought to reflect an adaptation to the cold; the modern Inuit also have unusually large brains.

53 M. H. Wolpoff, 'The place of the Neandertals in human evolution', in Trinkaus, *Emergence*, p. 121.

54 See J.-P. Dufour, 'Behind the ancient bones of contention', *Guardian Weekly [Le Monde]*, 3 July 1994, p. 16, reporting the view of Yves Coppens.

55 R. Cann et al., 'Mitochondrial DNA and human evolution', *Nature*, 1987, pp. 31ff. Mitochondrial DNA was preferred for this research because it evolves ten times as fast as nuclear DNA and is transmitted only through the female line, thus bypassing the complications of the recombination of two lines of genes in

each reproduction. Mitochondria are minute organelles in the cell, outside the nucleus, and are the source of its energy.

56 Called a phylogeny.

57 Cann et al., 'Mitochondrial DNA', p. 31.

58 Foley and Lahr, 'Beyond "Out of Africa"', p. 527. They compare this date with *H. sapiens sapiens* dates elsewhere (such as 55 kya in Australia).

59 The reader of a general book such as this is unlikely to pursue this matter through detailed articles and monographs. C. B. Stringer, 'Documenting the origin of modern humans', in Trinkaus, *Emergence*, provides a good guide to the literature. For the objections, see M. Wolpoff, 'Multiregional evolution: the fossil alternative to Eden', in P. Mellars and C. Stringer (eds.), *The Human Revolution* (Edinburgh, 1989), pp. 64–6.

60 This is intrinsic to the definition of a species. Animals belong to a single species if they can interbreed naturally and produce fertile offspring. Problems such as those we are now considering have led scholars to distinguish between morphological and biological species.

61 Wolpoff, 'Multiregional evolution', pp. 70, 97.

62 Ibid., pp. 66, 92.

63 See for instance, M. Barinaga, ' "African Eve" backers beat a retreat', *Science*, 7 Feb. 1992, pp. 686–7.

64 J. Wainscott, 'Out of the garden of Eden', *Nature*, 1987, 325, p. 13, pointed out that this assumes that mtDNA in the past was as heterogeneous as it is today, citing a recent study of mtDNA in the fruit fly. Studies tracing descent through the female line are bound to conclude with a woman ancestor.

65 Barinaga, ' "African Eve"', p. 687; A. Gibbons, 'Mitochondrial Eve: wounded, but not dead yet', *Science*, 14 Aug. 1992, pp. 873–5.

66 Stoneking (one of Cann's two original co-authors) now suggests a range between 350 and 64 thousand years ago. Cf. Foley and Lahr, 'Beyond "Out of Africa"', p. 526.

67 J. S. Jones and S. Rouhani, 'Mankind's genetic bottleneck', *Nature*, 1986, pp. 599–600.

68 For instance, a study of the mtDNA of 186 people from Senegal (Gibbons, 'Mitochondrial Eve', p. 874).

69 L. Cavalli-Sforza, et al., 'Reconstruction of human evolution, bringing together genetic, archaeological and linguistic data', *Proceedings of the National Academy of Science, USA*, 1988, pp. 6002–6. This paper also makes an interesting attempt to correlate world genetic and linguistic data.

70 The relationships between body mass, body surface area, and climate were formulated in the nineteenth century, as Bergmann's rule and Allen's rule; the larger the body's surface, the greater the loss of heat by sweating – essential at high temperatures (D. F. Roberts, *Climate and Human Variability*, 2nd edn, Menlo Park, Calif., 1978), pp. 29–33.

71 Quoted in Dufour, 'Behind the ancient bones', p. 16. This was in 1994.

72 'Richard Eden's account of John Lok's voyage to Mina, 1554–5', in J. W. Blake (ed.), *Europeans in West Africa 1450–1560* (Hakluyt, 2nd ser. LXXXVII, 1942), pp. 338–9.

73 Ammianus Marcellinus, quoted in A. K. Bowman, *Egypt after the Pharaohs* (Berkeley, 1986), p. 16.

74 This has led the Senegalese Cheikh Anta Diop and some others to claim ancient

Egypt as a 'black' civilisation. Egypt, like the rest of the Mediterranean world, had an admixture of different populations.

75 Foley and Lahr, 'Beyond "Out of Africa" ', p. 528.

76 L. Vigilant et al., 'Mitochondrial DNA sequences in single hairs from a southern African population', *Proceedings of the National Academy of Science* (USA), 1989, p. 9353.

77 J. Vansina, *Paths in the Rainforests* (Madison, 1990), p. 29.

78 S. Bahuchet, 'L'invention des Pygmées', *Cahiers d'études africaines*, 1993, p. 175.

79 J. S. Jones, 'How different are human races?', *Nature*, 1981, pp. 188–9.

80 J. Hiernaux, *The People of Africa* (London, 1974).

81 H. L. Dibble, 'The implications of stone tool types for the presence of language during the Middle Pleistocene', in Mellars and Stringer, *Human Revolution*, pp. 415–32, esp. p. 421.

82 P. Vinnicombe, 'Myth, motive and selection in southern African rock art', *Africa*, 1972, p. 202.

3 ENVIRONMENT, LANGUAGE AND ART (*c.* 10,000 – *c.* 500 BCE)

1 J. Vansina, *Kingdoms of the Savanna* (Madison, 1966), p. 85. It is not intended to imply that this tradition embodies a memory of the aqualithic age.

2 C. Ehret, for instance, believes that Afroasiatic has a time depth of 15,000 or more years ('On the antiquity of agriculture in Ethiopia', *The Journal of African History*, 1980, p. 164).

3 J. Gowlett, 'Human adaptation and long-term climatic change in northeast Africa', in D. Johnson and D. Anderson (eds.), *The Ecology of Survival: Case Studies from Northeast African History* (London, 1988), p. 32.

4 S. K. McIntosh and R. J. McIntosh, 'West African prehistory', *American Scientist*, 1981, p. 604.

5 The account which follows is based on an enormously influential article by J. E. G. Sutton, 'The aquatic civilisation of Middle Africa', *Journal of African History*, 1974, pp. 529ff. Some of the details on which it was based have been challenged, and it seems better to regard this complex, not as a single civilisation, but as a cluster of similar but independent responses to the same environmental conditions. More is now known about the chronology of climate; the basic theory, however, remains of arresting interest.

6 T. Shaw, *Nigeria: Its Archaeology and Early History* (London, 1978), pp. 20–1, and Map 5, p. 21.

7 C. P. D. Harvey, 'The archaeology of the southern Sudan: environmental context', in J. Mack and P. Robertshaw (eds.) *Culture History in the Southern Sudan* (Nairobi, 1982), pp. 11–13.

8 S. K. and R. J. McIntosh, 'Recent archaeological research and dates from West Africa', *Journal of African History*, 1986, p. 417. The dating of this mid-Holocene dry phase has far-reaching implications. For instance, it affects our dating of rock art. For alternative views, see n. 14 below.

9 Harpoons were not necessarily only used for fishing. In north-eastern Nigeria, one was found embedded in a human skeleton. The catfish spine decoration has been duplicated in modern experiments.

10 H. Lhote, *The Search for the Tassili Frescoes* (Eng. trans. 2nd edn, London, 1973), p. 17.

11 McIntosh and McIntosh, 'Recent archaeological research', p. 419.

12 Cultures without pottery develop other characteristic cooking styles; the New Zealand Maori perfected the earth oven, or *hangi*. The present writer has first-hand expertise in the cooking of Nigerian 'soup', which is, perhaps, rare among professional historians!

13 See N. David, 'Prehistory and historical linguistics in central Africa: points of contact', in C. Ehret and M. Posnansky, *The Archaeological and Linguistic Reconstruction of African History* (Berkeley and Los Angeles, 1982), p. 79.

14 Authorities agree about the general pattern, disagree about the details. Muzzolini describes 'Le "grand aride mi-holocène" vers 5500–4500 B.C.' (A. Muzzolini, *L'art rupestre préhistorique des massifs centraux sahariens* (Oxford, 1986), p. 316). G. E. Brooks refers to 'The Atlantic wet phase ca. 5500–ca. 2500 B.C.', 'Ecological perspectives on Mande population movements, commercial networks, and settlement patterns from the Atlantic wet phase (ca. 5500 B.C.) to the present', *History in Africa*, 1989, p. 26.

15 Gowlett, 'Human adaptation', p. 39.

16 Quoted in Sutton, 'Aquatic civilisation', p. 544, n. 55.

17 R. Inskeep, *The Peopling of Southern Africa* (Claremont, 1978), pp. 112–14.

18 This is in fact a nineteenth-century name, which has been changed twice since, but its use has become conventional in Saharan studies.

19 Lhote, *Search*, p. 81. Cf. F. Willett, *African Art: An Introduction* (London, 1971), p. 62.

20 Muzzolini, *L'art rupestre*, p. 123. The analysis above rests heavily on his admirable analysis. Lhote's work, *The Search for the Tassili Frescoes*, is an account of his expedition, and has excellent illustrations. He has also written many specialised articles in French. Mori's work is mainly in Italian. In English, see his 'The earliest Saharan rock engravings', *Antiquity*, 1974, pp. 87–92.

21 Herodotus, *The Histories* (trans. E. de Selincourt, Harmondsworth, 1954), II, 32. This passage makes no reference to chariots – but see IV, 170 and 183.

22 Quoted in J. D. Lewis-Williams, *Believing and Seeing* (London, 1981), p. 31.

23 B. Fetter, 'Pitfalls in the application of demographic insights to African history', *History in Africa*, 1992, p. 304.

24 G. Prins, *The Hidden Hippopotamus* (Cambridge, 1980), p. 94.

25 C. D. Darlington, quoted in K. Kiple and V. H. King, *Another Dimension to the Black Diaspora: Diet, Disease, and Racism* (Cambridge, 1981), p. 4.

26 Sickle-cell disease is deadly; those who transmit the gene, but do not have the disease, have some immunity from malaria, and it is likely that other abnormal blood haemoglobins have the same effect (Kiple and King, *Another Dimension*, pp. 16ff.).

27 K. D. Patterson, 'River blindness in northern Ghana, 1900–50', in G. Hartwig and K. D. Patterson (eds.), *Disease in African History* (Durham, N.C., 1978), p. 88. This chapter, like most of those in this volume, concentrates on the modern period; these diseases are, of course, part of a much more ancient history.

28 N. David, '*Tazunu*: megalithic monuments of central Africa', *Azania*, 1982, pp. 43–77. For the megaliths of the Senegambia, see pp. 216–17 below.

29 See for instance, C. Ehret, 'The first spread of food production to southern Africa', in Ehret and Posnansky, *Archaeological and Linguistic Reconstruction*, p. 162. 'However ill formulated and, to some, improbable sounding glottochronology may be, it responds to a real phenomenon of lexical change in languages ... the dates it gives are ... center points along ranges of possible dates.' See also

J. Vansina, 'Glottochronology', in his *Paths in the Rainforests* (Madison, 1990), p. 16.

30 J. Vansina, 'Bantu in the crystal ball, II', *History in Africa*, 1980, p. 311.

31 H. Meredith, cited from *Parliamentary Papers* in M. McCarthy, *Social Change and the Growth of British Power in the Gold Coast* (Lanham, 1983), p. 23.

32 The term 'Afroasiatic' was coined by J. Greenberg. Other names, less often used, are 'part of the dialect geography of linguistic terminology'. They include Erythraic, Afro-Asian and Lismaric. See C. F. Hodge, 'Lismaric (Afroasiatic): an overview', in M. L. Bender (ed.), *The Non-Semitic Languages of Ethiopia* (East Lansing, 1976), p. 43. Hodge himself is the only advocate of 'Lismaric'.

33 B. G. Trigger, 'The rise of civilisation in Egypt', in J. D. Clark, *The Cambridge History of Africa*, I, 488 (based on information from J. Greenberg).

34 J. Bynon, 'The contribution of linguistics to history in the field of Berber studies', in D. Dalby (ed.) *Language and History in Africa* (London, 1970), p. 67.

35 A. Zaborski, 'Cushitic overview', in Bender, *Non-Semitic Languages*, pp. 67ff.

36 The study of Omotic as a separate language family was pioneered by H. Fleming. See his 'Omotic overview', in Bender, *Non-Semitic Languages*, pp. 299ff. See also M. L. Bender, *Omotic: A New Afroasiatic Language Family* (Carbondale, 1975).

37 It should be noted that some scholars disagree with the grouping together of Khoikhoi and San, and others oppose the inclusion of Sandawe and Hadza.

38 C. Ehret, 'Population movement and culture contact in the southern Sudan, c. 3000 BC to AD 1000, a preliminary linguistic overview', in Mack and Robertshaw, *Culture History*, pp. 37–8. The word, preserved in a Nilo-Saharan language, is one for sausage-tree, an ingredient in mead, popular among contemporary East African hunter-gatherers.

39 Bender, 'Nilo-Saharan overview', p. 464. The utility of this generalisation is reduced by the fact that specialists disagree about the age of Indo-European.

40 Ibid., p. 457.

41 There is an excellent survey of the changing analysis of this subject in J. Vansina, 'Bantu in the crystal ball', *History in Africa*, 1979, pp. 321–5 and 1980, pp. 293–325.

42 The reason why they paid such deference to his views was that he was an outstanding scholar, who based his conclusions on a lifetime of research. He studied 200 languages in general and 28 in detail. The revised picture has been obtained in part by applying lexico-statistical methods to his data. The error he made was to misinterpret the phenomenon of convergence (borrowing).

43 It is worth noting that proto-Bantu reconstructions are customarily cited from Guthrie's work.

44 C. Ehret, 'Linguistic inferences about early Bantu history', in Ehret and Posnansky, *Archaeological and Linguistic Reconstruction*, p. 61.

45 There is less direct evidence on this point, but it is deduced from the existence of larger settlements and from iron working.

46 Inskeep, *Peopling*, p. 124.

47 M. Hall, *The Changing Past: Farmers, Kings and Traders in Southern Africa, 200–1860* (Claremont, South Africa, 1987), p. 31.

48 The names of these languages should also be written with the appropriate prefix (luGanda, giKikuyu, ciChewa and so on). They are omitted in the interests of general intelligibility, because of the general nature of this book. Some scholars question the East/West Bantu distinction.

49 J. Vansina, *Paths in the Rainforests*, p. 49.

50 D. Phillipson, *African Archaeology* (revised edn, Cambridge, 1990), pp. 172ff. He suggests renaming the Early Iron Age pottery style, but the new name, Chifumbaze, has not won general acceptance. Huffman distinguishes a third, Central Stream (T. Huffman, 'Archaeology and ethnohistory of the African Iron Age', *Annual Review of Anthropology*, 1982, pp. 134ff.). Underlying this debate are interesting issues of methodology: can a pottery style be defined by what is distinctive (such as rouletting or comb-stamping) or is multivariate analysis the only correct approach?

51 There are other difficulties with this theory. Bananas do not grow in many of the areas where the Bantu spread. And botanical studies suggest that their presence in Africa is of great antiquity.

52 Quoted in R. Ross, 'Ethnic identity, demographic crises and Xhosa–Khoikhoi interaction', *History in Africa*, 1980, pp. 260–1.

53 C. Ehret, 'Linguistic inferences', p. 63.

54 Ibid., p. 58.

55 H. Kuper, *An African Aristocracy* (2nd edn, New York, 1980), p. 18. For more on these events, see pp. 417–18 below.

56 G. Barker, communication in *Current Anthropology*, 1988, pp. 448–9.

4 PRODUCING MORE FOOD *c.* 10,000 – *c.* 500 BCE

1 Quoted in L. V. Cassanelli, *The Shaping of Somali Society: Reconstructing the History of a Pastoral People, 1600–1900* (Philadelphia, 1982), p. 9.

2 Yohanna Abdallah, *The Yaos* (trans. M. Sanderson, Zomba, 1919), p. 11.

3 Ibn Battuta, extract in G. S. P. Freeman-Grenville, *The East African Coast: Select Documents* (London, 1975 reprint), p. 29.

4 It is only fair to add that ibn Battuta is describing the diet of the court and the merchant class.

5 L. Valensi, *Tunisian Peasants in the Eighteenth and Nineteenth Centuries* (1977, Eng. trans. Cambridge, 1985), p. 167.

6 R. L. Desfontaines, *Flora atlantica* (1798), extract in Valensi, *Tunisian Peasants*, p. 120.

7 P. Curtin, *Economic Change in Precolonial Africa* (Madison, 1975), pp. 23–5.

8 See p. 67 below.

9 M. N. Cohen, *The Food Crisis in Prehistory: Overpopulation and the Origins of Agriculture* (New Haven and London, 1977).

10 This paragraph is based on P. Bonte and J. Galaty's Introduction to their *Herders, Warriors and Traders: Pastoralism in Africa* (Boulder, 1991), pp. 3–32; the quotation is from p. 10.

11 D. McMaster, 'Speculations on the coming of the banana to Uganda', *The Journal of Tropical Geography*, 1962, p. 61.

12 J. W. Burton, 'The wave is my mother's husband: a piscatorial theme in pastoral Nilotic ethnology', *Cahiers d'études africaines*, 1982, p. 465.

13 There are few parallels to the robust and admirable agnosticism of Daniel Livingstone about his own research. He states that identification of plants other than maize by pollen 'should be treated with something between skepticism and credulity ... In 18 years of looking for the pollen of cultivated plants in African deposits, the present writer has found a single grain' (D. Livingstone, 'Interactions of food production and changing vegetation in Africa', in J. D. Clark and

S. A. Brandt, *From Hunters to Farmers: The Causes and Consequences of Food Production in Africa* (Berkeley, 1984), p. 24).

14 F. Wendorf and R. Schild, 'The emergence of food production in the Egyptian Sahara', in *ibid.*, pp. 99 and 101 and see p. 12.

15 L. Kryzaniak, 'New light on early food-production in the central Sudan', *Journal of African History*, 1978, pp. 159–72.

16 F. J. Simoons, 'The determinants of dairying and milk use in the Old World: ecological, physiological and cultural', in J. R. K. Robson, *Food, Ecology and Culture: Readings in the Anthropology of Dietary Practices* (New York and London, 1980), p. 83, n.

17 S. K. McIntosh and R. J. McIntosh, 'West African prehistory', *American Scientist*, 1981, p. 607.

18 R. Bulliet, *The Camel and the Wheel* (Cambridge, Mass., 1975), p. 44. On Punt, see p. 154 below.

19 Experts state that the Barbary sheep is not a possible progenitor.

20 There are a number of radiocarbon dates from *c.* 5000 BP; the paper by Robertshaw and Collett cited below questions their validity on technical grounds.

21 S. H. Ambrose, 'Archaeology and linguistic reconstructions of history in East Africa', in C. Ehret and M. Posnansky, *The Archaeological and Linguistic Reconstruction of African History* (Berkeley and Los Angeles, 1982), pp. 104–57, distinguishes the Lowland Savanna Pastoral Neolithic Complex, Highland Savanna PNC (both thought to be Southern Cushites) and the Elmenteitan, identified with Southern Nilotes. These equations are rejected, and the cultures redefined, in P. Robertshaw and D. Collett, 'A new framework for the study of early pastoral communities in East Africa', *Journal of African History*, 1983, pp. 289–301.

22 A. Sherratt, 'Plough pastoralism, aspects of the secondary products revolution', in I. Hodder, G. Isaac and N. Hammond (eds.), *Pattern of the Past* (Cambridge, 1981).

23 In southern Nigeria, for instance, dwarf shorthorn and goats were kept for meat, but not milked, and the incidence of adult lactose intolerance is very high. The latter is likely to be consequence rather than cause of the former phenomenon. The study of animals suggests that adult lactose intolerance is the norm, and tolerance an acquired adaptation in dairying peoples. See F. J. Simoons, 'The determinants of dairying', pp. 83–92.

24 Tuan Ch'eng-Shih (d. 863), extract in G. S. P. Freeman-Grenville, *The East African Coast*, p. 8.

25 C. Ehret, 'Cattle-keeping and milking in eastern and southern African history: the linguistic evidence', *Journal of African History*, 1967, pp. 1–17.

26 C. Aldred, *The Egyptians* (rev. edn, London, 1984), p. 57.

27 This account is based on J. Harlan and A. Stemler, 'The races of sorghum in Africa', and T. Shaw, 'Early crops in Africa: a review of the evidence', both in J. Harlan, J. de Wet and A. Stemler (eds.), *Origins of African Plant Domestication* (The Hague, 1976), pp. 107ff. and 465ff.

28 D. Coursey, 'The origins and domestication of yams in Africa', in Harlan et al., *Origins of African Plant Domestication*, pp. 383ff. J. Alexander and D. Coursey, 'The origins of yam cultivation', in P. Ucko and G. W. Dimbleby (eds.), *The Domestication and Exploitation of Plants and Animals* (London, 1969), pp. 405ff.

29 M. D. W. Jeffries, 'The Umundri tradition of origin', *African Studies*, 1956, pp. 122–3.

30 Valensi, *Tunisian Peasants*, p. 121.

31 C. Ehret, 'On the antiquity of agriculture in Ethiopia', *Journal of African History*, 1979, pp. 174–5; F. J. Simoons, 'Some questions on the economic prehistory of Ethiopia', *Journal of African History*, 1965, pp. 10–12. Both accept that the Semites had previous knowledge of all three.

32 A. Watson, *Agricultural Innovation in the Early Islamic World* (Cambridge, 1983), p. 20.

33 McIntosh and McIntosh, 'West African prehistory', p. 607. See p. 59 above.

34 Ibid., p. 609.

35 On this, see ibid., p. 609.

36 Ibid., p. 609; S. K. and R. J. McIntosh, 'Current directions in West African prehistory', *Annual Review of Anthropology*, 1983, pp. 238–9.

37 Ibn Battuta, extract in N. Levtzion and J. F. P. Hopkins (eds.), *Corpus of Early Arabic Sources for West African History* (Cambridge, 1981), pp. 288–9.

38 And earlier, in the former case (Watson, *Agricultural Innovation*, p. 46).

39 McMaster, 'Speculations', p. 61. This article is the main source for my account.

40 Watson, *Agricultural Innovation*, pp. 28–30.

41 Ibid., pp. 32–41, 72.

42 Al-Masudi, in G. S. P. Freeman-Grenville, *The East African Coast*, p. 17.

43 See p. 154 below.

44 Ibn Said, in Levtzion and Hopkins, *Corpus*, p. 188.

45 S. Johnson, *The History of the Yorubas* (Lagos, 1973 reprint), pp. 73, 283.

46 Watson, *Agricultural Innovation*, p. 83.

47 C. Ehret, 'Cattle-keeping and milking in eastern and southern African history: the linguistic evidence', and his more recent paper, 'The first spread of food production to southern Africa', in Ehret and Posnansky, *Archaeological and Linguistic Reconstruction*, pp. 158–81. Ehret spans the disciplines of linguistics and history, and his work is immensely influential. Archaeologists, however, find no evidence to support the southern thrust he postulates for Central Sudanic peoples.

48 G. Harinck, 'Interaction between Xhosa and Khoi: emphasis on the period 1620–1750', in L. Thompson (ed.), *African Societies in Southern Africa* (London, 1978 reprint), p. 151.

49 E. E. Evans-Pritchard, *The Nuer* (Oxford, 1940), p. 49.

50 Quoted in P. R. Schmidt, *Historical Archaeology: A Structural Approach in an African Culture* (Westport, 1978), p. 305.

51 See M. Ehrenberg, *Women in Prehistory* (London, 1989), Ch. 3. It should be noted that this book is not by an Africanist, so shows a lack of familiarity with African plant domestication.

52 But see Burton, 'The wave is my mother's husband', pp. 459ff.

53 P. Rigby, 'Some Gogo rituals of "Purification": an essay on social and moral categories', in E. Leach (ed.), *Dialectic in Practical Religion* (Cambridge, 1968), pp. 159ff.

54 R. B. Lee and I. DeVore, 'Problems in the study of hunters and gatherers', in R. Lee and I. DeVore (eds.), *Man the Hunter* (Chicago, 1968), p. 3.

55 R. B. Lee, *The !Kung San: Men, Women and Work in a Foraging Society* (Cambridge, 1979).

56　Marshall D. Sahlins, 'Notes on the original affluent society', in Lee and DeVore, *Man the Hunter*, pp. 85–9.

57　K. Hawkes and J. O'Connell, 'Affluent hunters? Some comments in the light of the Alyawara case', *American Anthropologist*, 1983, pp. 622–5. For a critique from a different viewpoint, see p. 144 below.

58　Two papers by F. J. Bennett et al., summarised in C. Gabel, 'Demographic perspectives on the African Pleistocene', in C. Fyfe (ed.), *African Historical Demography* (Edinburgh, 1977), p. 87.

59　Colin Turnbull, *The Mountain People* (London, 1973). The Ik are food-producers, who are often forced by want to rely largely on gathered foods.

5　COPPER AND IRON *c.* 600 BCE TO *c.* 1000 CE

1　Extract in G. S. P. Freeman-Grenville, *The East African Coast* (Oxford, 1962), p. 19.

2　C. Stanley, quoted in E. Herbert, *Red Gold of Africa* (Madison, 1984), p. 3. This is the main source for this paragraph.

3　Ibid., p. 9.

4　Ibid., p. 5.

5　K. McIntosh and R. J. McIntosh, 'Recent archaeological research and dates from West Africa', *Journal of African History*, 1986, pp. 424–7. J. E. G. Sutton, 'Archaeology in West Africa: a review of recent work and a further list of radiocarbon dates', *Journal of African History*, 1982, pp. 296–7.

6　Sutton, 'Archaeology in West Africa', p. 297.

7　Herbert, *Red Gold*, pp. 16–18.

8　F. J. Kense, 'The initial diffusion of iron to Africa', in R. Haaland and P. Shinnie (eds.), *African Iron Working: Ancient and Traditional* (Oslo, 1985), p. 15, citing an unpublished 1971 thesis by J. Dombrowki. N. J. van der Merwe ('The advent of iron in Africa', in T. A. Wertime and J. D. Muhly (eds.), *The Coming of the Age of Iron* (New Haven, 1980), p. 475) points out that iron working was known in southern Arabia from the beginning of the first millennium BCE. Aksum iron working may therefore well be older.

9　Van der Merwe, 'Advent of iron', pp. 476–8. There is indirect evidence, such as references on stelae, of their close connections with the Etruscans, and their military successes against Greeks, Iberians and Romans.

10　D. Calvocoressi and N. David, 'A new survey of radiocarbon and thermoluminescence dates for West Africa', *Journal of African History*, 1979, p. 11.

11　Ibid., p. 10. The main possible source of error here – and in other cases which date charcoal – is that the wood may have already been old when used. Calvocoressi and David also cite dates elsewhere in the Sahara from the last three centuries BCE.

12　P. R. Schmidt, *Historical Archaeology: A Structural Approach in an African Culture* (Westport, 1978).

13　See N. David, 'Prehistory and historical linguistics in central Africa: points of contact', in C. Ehret and M. Posnansky, *The Archaeological and Linguistic Reconstruction of African History* (Berkeley and Los Angeles, 1982), p. 93.

14　P. de Maret, 'Recent archaeological research and dates from Central Africa', *Journal of African History*, 1985, p. 139.

15　Ibid., p. 135; B. Clist, 'Early Bantu settlements in west-central Africa: a review of recent research', *Current Anthropology*, 1987, pp. 381–2.

16 C. Ehret, *Southern Nilotic History: Linguistic Approaches to the Study of the Past* (Evanston, 1971), pp. 28–9. On the Southern Nilotic role in East African history, see p. 125 below.

17 J. Vansina, *Paths in the Rainforests: Towards a History of Political Tradition in Equatorial Africa* (Madison, 1990), pp. 58–60.

18 The Berg-Dama of Namibia, who cut across many cultural categories, are an exception. See p. 143 below.

19 Vansina, *Paths in the Rainforests* pp. 137ff.

20 P. Bellwood, *The Polynesians: Prehistory of an Island People* (revised edn, London, 1987), pp. 45ff.

21 B. Trigger, 'The myth of Meroe and the Iron Age', *African Historical Studies*, 1969, pp. 23–50.

22 See N. David, 'The BIEA Southern Sudan Expedition of 1979: interpretation of the archaeological data', in J. Mack and P. Robertshaw (eds.), *Culture History in the Southern Sudan* (Nairobi, 1972), p. 55; also R. Oliver, 'Reflections on the British Institute's expeditions to the Southern Sudan 1977–81', in ibid., p. 167.

23 Linguistic evidence suggests that the intermediaries to eastern Africa were Central Sudanic speakers – though there are some problems here (C. Ehret, 'Population movement and culture contact in the Southern Sudan, *c.* 3000 BC to AD 1000: a preliminary overview', in Mack and Robertshaw, *Culture History*, p. 35. Cf. Oliver, 'Reflections', p. 167. There has always been a problem in correlating the importance he gives to Central Sudanic speakers, in this and other contexts, with other evidence. To complicate matters further, Central Sudanic as a language family has been questioned.

24 N. David supports the former view, and Schmidt the latter, partly on the grounds of similarities in furnace design.

25 Van der Merwe distinguishes four furnace types, all of which are widely distributed. But cf. J. E. G. Sutton, 'Temporal and spatial variability in African iron furnaces', in Haaland and Shinnie, *African Iron Working*, pp. 164–96.

26 Van der Merwe, 'Advent of iron', pp. 485ff.

27 R. Haaland, 'Iron production, its socio-cultural context and ecological implications', in Haaland and Shinnie, *African Iron Working*, p. 61.

28 Roland Oliver states that 80 tons of wood are needed for one ton of smelted iron ('The earliest Iron Age?' *Journal of African History*, 1979, p. 290).

29 Haaland, 'Iron production', p. 67.

30 C. L. Goucher, 'Iron is iron 'til it is rust: trade and ecology in the decline of West African iron smelting', *Journal of African History*, 1981, pp. 179–89. She cites a study which states that there can be as few as 225 trees of all types per acre of derived savanna.

31 Van der Merwe, 'Iron production', p. 486.

32 See for instance, G. Prins, *The Hidden Hippopotamus* (Cambridge, 1980), p. 108.

33 Quoted from E. Isichei, *A History of Nigeria* (Harlow, 1983), p. 45.

34 This point is made in Vansina, *Paths in the Rainforest*, p. 60 but ring-barking is easier with metal implements.

35 D. A. Low, 'The northern interior 1840–1884', in R. Oliver and G. Mathew (eds.), *History of East Africa*, I (London, 1963), p. 327.

36 See E. Isichei, *A History of Nigeria* (Harlow, 1983), p. 375; E. Isichei, 'Coloni-

alism resisted', in Isichei (ed.), *Studies in the History of Plateau State, Nigeria* (London, 1982), p. 208.

37 S. Johnson, *The History of the Yorubas* (Lagos, 1921, 1973 reprint), p. 126.
38 H. Courlander, *Tales of Yoruba Gods and Heroes* (New York, 1973) pp. 18 and 33ff.
39 J. Barbot, *A Description of the Coasts of North and South Guinea* (London, 1746), p. 380; G. T. Basden, *Niger Ibos* (1938, London, 1966), p. 339.
40 The main sources for what follows are E. Herbert, *Red Gold*, and M. Bisson, 'Copper currency in Central Africa: the archaeological evidence', *World Archaeology*, Feb. 1975, pp. 276–93.
41 Quoted in A. Roberts, *A History of Zambia* (London, 1976), p. 105.
42 Herbert, *Red Gold*, pp. 23–30.
43 Ancient copper, lead and zinc mines were recently discovered near Abakalili, which may have provided the raw materials for Igbo-Ukwu. The research of V. Chikwendu and P. Craddock, reported in *New Scientist*, 10 June 1989, p. 15.
44 See pp. 251, 352 below.
45 A. Hilton, *The Kingdom of Kongo* (Oxford, 1985), pp. 54–5.
46 P. Martin, *The External Trade of the Loango Coast, 1576–1870* (Oxford, 1972), pp. 42, 59.
47 Quoted in Herbert, *Red Gold*, p. 20.
48 Gold mining was of much more localised importance than copper and iron working, and is dealt with later in this study. The alluvial gold was collected by peasants in the farming off-season.
49 Ibn Battuta, in *Corpus*, p. 302.
50 E. Terray, 'Long distance exchange and the formation of the state', *Economy and Society*, 1974, pp. 315ff.; R. Dumett, 'Precolonial goldmining and the state in the Akan region, with a critique of the Terray hypothesis', in *Research in Economic Anthropology*, 2, 1979, pp. 37ff.; E. Terray, 'Gold Production, slave labor, and state intervention in precolonial Akan societies: a reply to Raymond Dumett', *Research in Economic Anthropology*, 1983, pp. 95ff.
51 Herbert, *Red Gold*, p. 45.
52 Ibid., p. 181.
53 Herbert, 'Aspects', p. 184.
54 The account which follows is based on Herbert, *Red Gold*, pp. 186ff. and Bisson, 'Copper currency', pp. 276ff.
55 J. Vansina, *The Tio Kingdom of the Middle Congo* (London, 1973), p. 285. For the shrinkage of salt blocks and raffia cloth, used as currency, see J. Miller, *Way of Death: Merchant Capitalism and the Angolan Slave Trade 1730–1830* (London, 1988), p. 64. For a shrinking iron currency, see p. 74 above.
56 Ehret, *Southern Nilotic History*, p. 29. For an interesting re-evaluation of the Nilotic presence, see R. Oliver, 'The Nilotic contribution to Bantu Africa', *Journal of African History*, 1982, pp. 433–42.
57 D. Phillipson, 'Iron Age history and archaeology in Zambia', *Journal of African History*, 1974, pp. 20–2.
58 M. Hall, *The Changing Past: Farmers, Kings and Traders in Southern Africa* (Cape Town, 1987), p. 71.
59 P. de Maret, 'New survey of archaeological research and dates for west-central and north-central Africa', *Journal of African History*, 1982, p. 6; on the general trend, see Oliver, 'The Nilotic contribution to Bantu Africa', pp. 435–6.

6 MODELS: PRODUCTION, POWER AND GENDER

1 The Voyages of Cadamosto ... (trans. G. R. Crone, Hakluyt, 2nd series, 80, 1937), p. 37.

2 Muhammadu Na Birnin Gwari, *flor. c.* 1850 quoted in M Hiskett, *The Sword of Truth: The Life and Times of the Shehu Usuman dan Fodio* (London, 1973), p. 155.

3 These could include intensive perpetual cultivation by manuring (as among the Hausa of northern Nigeria, or the Fipa of Tanzania); sometimes the village was sustained by trade or scarce resources, such as salt pans. Commonly, shifting cultivation took place in the area round the village.

4 Lele figures from M. Douglas, *The Lele of the Kasai* (London, 1963), p. 28. She cites figures suggesting that Bemba, Tonga, Yao and Chewa villages (in Zambia and Malawi) are smaller. For Kongo, see J. Thornton, *The Kingdom of Kongo* (Madison, 1983), p. 28. For Ufipa, see R. Willis, *A State in the Making: Myth, History, and Social Transformation in Pre-Colonial Ufipa* (Bloomington, 1981), p. 115. As Willis points out (p. 267, n. 12), many villages expanded in colonial and post-colonial times, and settlement patterns in Tanzania were dramatically changed by government policy in the 1970s.

5 D. Forde and G. I. Jones, *The Ibo and Ibibio-Speaking Peoples of South-Eastern Nigeria* (Ethnographic Survey of Africa, 1950), p. 17.

6 P. de Maret, 'Recent archaeological research and dates from Central Africa', *Journal of African History*, 1985, p. 143.

7 I have explored this myth in two contexts: 'Historical change in an Ibo polity: Asaba to 1885', *Journal of African History* 1969, pp. 421–38, and 'Myth, gender and society in pre-colonial Asaba', *Africa*, 1991, pp. 513ff.

8 R. S. Rattray, *Asanti Law and Constitution* (1929, London, 1956 reprint), pp. 23ff.

9 Mary Douglas, 'Is matriliny doomed in Africa?', in M. Douglas and P. Kaberry (eds.), *Man in Africa* (London, 1969), pp. 121–36. The issue is discussed by J. Goody, in his studies of matrilineal peoples in Ghana, and recently by the present writer, in the central Nigerian context, in 'Does Christianity empower women? The case of the Anaguta of central Nigeria', in S. Ardener et al. (eds.), *Women and Missions* (Oxford, 1993), pp. 209ff.

10 A. N. Klein, 'The two Asantes: competing interpretations of "Slavery" in Akan-Asante culture and society', in P. Lovejoy (ed.), *The Ideology of Slavery in Africa* (Beverly Hills, 1981), p. 162.

11 J. Goody, *Death, Property and the Ancestors: A Study of the Mortuary Customs of the LoDagaa of West Africa* (London, 1962), p. 373. It is possible these eschatological rewards and punishments reflect mission teachings. In other cultures, rewards and punishments appear indirectly. Thus among the Igbo, a second burial is the necessary gateway to the world of ancestors; those denied it become malicious homeless ghosts. One can be denied it for one's faults, as in the case of a murderer, or for sheer mischance, as with a leper or victim of dropsy.

12 R. Harms, *River of Wealth, River of Sorrow* (New Haven and London, 1981), pp. 38–9.

13 J. Vansina, *The Tio Kingdom of the Middle Congo 1880–1892* (London, 1973), p. 440.

14 R. Law, *The Slave Coast of Africa 1550–1750* (Oxford, 1991), p. 70.

15 Quoted in J. Vansina, *The Children of Woot: A History of the Kuba Peoples* (Madison, 1978), p. 121.

16   F. Forbes, *Dahomey and the Dahomans* II (London, 1851), p. 90.
17   See Chapter 8, p. 123 below, and R. Waller, 'Ecology, migration and expansion in East Africa', *African Affairs*, 1985, p. 350.
18   See pp. 255–6 below.
19   D. Gaitskell, citing the research of Jeanne Jenn, in a review in *Journal of African History*, 1990, pp. 336–7.
20   S. Feierman, *The Shambaa Kingdom: A History* (London, 1974), pp. 33–4.
21   A Hausa women's grinding song (a socially sanctioned form of complaint), collected and translated by Fatima Othman, *West Africa*, 26 Sept. 1983, p. 2242.
22   J. Vansina, *Art History in Africa* (Harlow, 1984), p. 205.
23   J. Boddy, 'Womb as oasis: the symbolic context of Pharaonic circumcision in rural Northern Sudan,' *American Ethnologist*, 1982, p. 687.
24   D. O'Connor, 'Egypt, 1552–664 BC', in J. D. Clark (ed.), *Cambridge History of Africa*, I, p. 866.
25   See p. 399 below.
26   B. Cooper, 'Cloth, commodity production and social capital: women in Maradi, Niger 1890–1989', *African Economic History*, 1993, pp. 51ff.; B. Frank, 'Reconstructing the history of an African ceramic tradition', *Cahiers d'études africaines*, 1993, pp. 381ff.
27   C. Monteil, *Les Bambara du Segou* (1924), quoted in R. L. Roberts, *Warriors, Merchants and Slaves* (Stanford, 1987), p. 33.
28   R. Armstrong, S. Amali et al., Idoma *ichicha* song, sung by Ediigwu, transcribed and translated texts accompanying Asch Records, Album AHM 4221.
29   J. Lonsdale, 'When did the Gusii (or any other group) become a tribe?', *Kenya Historical Review*, 1977, p. 124.
30   J. H. Nketia, *Funeral Dirges of the Akan People* (1955, New York, 1969 reprint), p. 142.
31   Douglas, *The Lele of the Kasai*, p. 74.
32   P. Curtin, *Economic Change in Precolonial Africa* (Madison, 1975), p. 36.
33   A. Legesse, *Gada: Three Approaches to the Study of African Society* (New York, 1973). For Gada, see also p. 276 below.
34   A song of uninitiated boys in the Igbo town of Onitsha (R. N. Henderson, *The King in Every Man: Evolutionary Trends in Onitsha Ibo Society and Culture* (New Haven and London, 1972), p. 355).
35   See p. 259 below.
36   O. and C. L. Temple, *Notes on the Tribes, Provinces, Emirates and States of the Northern Provinces* (1919, 2nd edn London, 1965), p. 182.
37   A Ham informant, quoted in E. Isichei, 'On masks and audible ghosts: some secret male cults in central Nigeria', *Journal of Religion in Africa*, 1988, p. 60.
38   C. K. Omari, 'God and worship in traditional Asu society' (University of East Africa Ph.D., 1970), quoted in J. Iliffe, *A Modern History of Tanganyika* (Cambridge, 1979), p. 11.
39   J. Murphy, 'Oshun the Dancer', in C. Olson (ed.), *The Book of the Goddess Past and Present* (New York, 1983), pp. 190ff.; C. N. Ubah, 'The Supreme Being, divinities and ancestors in Igbo traditional religion: evidence from Otanchara and Otanzu', *Africa*, 1982, pp. 96–7. There is a growing literature on Mammy Wata; see H. J. Drewal, 'Performing the Other; Mami Wata worship in West Africa', *TDR (The Drama Review, a Journal of Performance)*, 1988, pp. 160ff.

40 Quoted in R. LeVine, 'Sex roles and economic change in Africa', in J. Middleton (ed.), *Black Africa: Its Peoples and Their Cultures Today* (New York, 1970), p. 180, n. 5.

41 J. Picton, 'Masks and the Igbirra', *African Arts*, 1974, p. 38.

42 National Archives, Ibadan, Nigeria, CSO 1/26, vol. 154, encl. in Lugard to Harcourt, 29 Jan. 1913.

43 M. Wilson, *Communal Rituals of the Nyakusa* (London, 1959), pp. 157–9.

44 R. Horton, 'African conversion', *Africa*, 1971, pp. 85ff.

45 J.-C. Muller, 'Quelques réflexions sur l'auto-restriction technologique et la dépendance economique dans les sociétés d'auto-subsistance', *Cahiers d'études africaines*, 1972, pp. 659ff.

46 M. Kenny, 'Pre-colonial trade in eastern Lake Victoria', *Azania*, 1979, pp. 97–107.

47 J. Guyer, 'Wealth in people and self-realisation in Equatorial Africa', *Man*, 1993, p. 243.

48 J. Vansina, *Paths in the Rainforest: Towards a History of Political Tradition in Equatorial Africa* (Madison, 1990), pp. 73–9.

49 J. L. Krapf, *Travels, Researches and Missionary Labours during an Eighteen Years' Residence in Eastern Africa* (1860, London, 1968 reprint), p. 355.

50 Al-Umari (d. 1349) in N. Levtzion and J. F. P. Hopkins (eds.), *Corpus of Early Arabic Sources for West African History* (Cambridge, 1981), p. 260.

51 T. Q. Reefe, *The Rainbow and the Kings: A History of the Luba Empire to 1891* (Berkeley, 1981), p. 186.

52 M. Hiskett (trans.), 'The "Song of Bagauda", a Hausa king list and homily in verse', *Bulletin of the School of Oriental and African Studies*, 1965, pp. 114–15.

53 Quoted in D. W. Cohen, *The Historical Tradition of Busoga* (Oxford, 1972), p. 166.

54 J. Miller, 'Lineages, ideology and the history of slavery in western central Africa', in P. Lovejoy (ed.), *The Ideology of Slavery in Africa* (Beverly Hills, 1981), pp. 47ff. and also his 'The significance of drought, disease and famine in the agriculturally marginal zone of West Central Africa', *Journal of African History*, 1982, pp. 17ff.

55 J. C. Taylor, journal entry for 27 May 1865 in *The Church Missionary Record*, 1866, p. 205.

56 See M. Eliade, *Forgerons et alchimistes* (Paris, 1977).

57 Quoted in Iris Berger, 'Deities, dynasties, and oral tradition: the history and legend of the Abacwezi', in J. Miller (ed.), *The African Past Speaks: Essays on Oral Tradition and History* (Folkestone, 1980), p. 67.

58 Vansina, *Paths in the Rainforests*, p. 60.

59 There is a considerable literature, mainly in French, on this theme. P. de Maret, 'The smith's myth and the origin of leadership in Central Africa', in Haaland and Shinnie, *African Iron Working*, pp. 73–87, is the main source for the account here.

60 Herbert, *Red Gold*, p. 41.

61 Chapter 8, p. 130 below.

62 For the Tio, see J. Vansina, *The Tio Kingdom of the Middle Congo 1880–1892* (London, 1973), p. 440.

63 Vansina, *The Children of Woot*, p. 67.

64 Quoted in Kenny, 'Pre-colonial trade', p. 97.

65 Pero Rodrigues, *Historia* (1594), quoted in B. Heintze, 'Historical notes on the Kisama of Angola', *Journal of African History*, 1972, p. 411.

66 Thornton, *The Kingdom of Kongo*, p. 34.

67 E.g. in Ngola a Kiluanje (A. Hilton, *The Kingdom of Kongo* (Oxford, 1985)) and in Shaba (Reefe, *The Rainbow and the Kings*, p. 95). The use of salt as a currency is also recorded among the northern Igbo.

68 J. Goody, *Technology, Tradition and the State in Africa* (London, 1971). See R. Law, 'Horses, firearms and political power in pre-colonial West Africa', *Past and Present*, 1976, pp. 112ff., and his longer study, *The Horse in West African History* (London, 1980).

69 Goody, *Technology, Tradition*, p. 43, n. 2.

70 Al-Baladhuri, quoted in P. L. Shinnie, 'The Nilotic Sudan and Ethiopia, *c.* 660 BC to AD 600', *The Cambridge History of Africa: From c. 500 BC to AD 1050*, II, ed. J. D. Fage, p. 564.

71 This paragraph is based on Law, 'Horses, firearms'.

72 J. Clutton-Brock, 'The Buhen horse', *Journal of Archaeological Science*, 1974, pp. 89ff.

73 See p. 59 above.

74 T. M. Baker, 'The social organisation of the Birom' (University of London, Ph.D. thesis, 1954), p. 180.

75 See pp. 222–3 below.

76 For whom see p. 186 below.

77 As was pointed out in the pioneering study of this subject, R. Gray and D. Birmingham, 'Some economic and political consequences of trade in central and eastern Africa in the pre-colonial period', in Gray and Birmingham (eds.), *Pre-Colonial African Trade* (London, 1970), p. 16.

78 'The Kano Chronicle', in H. R. Palmer, *Sudanese Memoirs* (1-volume edition, London, 1967), p. 97.

79 'Song of Bagauda', p. 113.

80 P. G. Harris, 'Notes on Yauri (Sokoto Province), Nigeria', *Journal of the Royal Anthropological Institute*, 1930, p. 287.

81 J. Thornton, 'The state in African historiography: a reassessment', *Ufahamu*, 1973, p. 117.

82 G. Prins, *The Hidden Hippopotamus* (Cambridge, 1980), p. 118.

83 J. Miller, *Way of Death, Merchant Capitalism and the Angolan Slave Trade 1730–1830* (London, 1988), p. 47.

84 Roberts, *Warriors*, p. 20.

85 For some detailed comparative data on royal income and expenditure, see E. Isichei, *A History of Nigeria* (Harlow, 1983), pp. 192ff.

86 S. Crowther, letter, 4 Dec. 1871, in *Church Missionary Intelligencer*, 1871, p. 219.

87 'D. R.', extract in T. Hodgkin, *Nigerian Perspectives* (London, 1975), pp. 156–7.

88 Al-Yaqubi, in *Corpus*, p. 21.

89 *The Voyages of . . . Cadamosto . . .*, p. 37. See the passage which is the epigraph of this chapter.

90 J. D. Fage, 'Slaves and society in western Africa, *c.* 1445–1700', *Journal of African History*, 1980, pp. 289–310.

91 S. Miers and I. Kopytoff, *Slavery in Africa: Historical and Anthropological Perspectives* (Madison, 1977).

92 For the first view, see I. Kopytoff and S. Miers, 'African "slavery" as an institution of marginality', in S. Miers and I. Kopytoff (eds.), *Slavery in Africa*, pp. 3–81; for the second, see P. Lovejoy, *Transformations in Slavery: A History of Slavery in Africa* (Cambridge, 1983), Ch. 1.

93 P. Manning, *Slavery and African Life* (Cambridge, 1990), p. 106 and *passim*.

94 *The Life and Travels of Mungo Park* (Edinburgh, 1896), p. 235.

95 Park, *Travels*, p. 234.

96 This paragraph is based on C. Robertson and M. Klein, *Women and Slavery in Africa* (Madison, 1983), 'Introduction', pp. 3ff.

97 I exclude the Mamluks of Egypt who, although acquired by purchase as children, lived their adult lives as free – and privileged – men.

98 Quoted in R. S. O'Fahey and J. L. Spaulding, *Kingdoms of the Sudan* (London, 1974), p. 45.

99 Haaland, 'Iron production', in Haaland and Shinnie, *African Iron Working*, pp. 56–61; also J. Todd, 'Iron production by the Dimi of Ethiopia' in the same volume, pp. 88–101.

100 Curtin, *Economic Change*, p. 4.

101 Henderson, *The King in Every Man*, pp. 272–4. Some observers 'found it difficult to accept ... that such mediators between men and their gods could be so despised ... In Onitsha ... only one kind of person approximates the condition of a cult slave, and that is a king.'

102 K. Daaku, 'Trade and trading patterns of the Akan in the seventeenth and eighteenth centuries', in C. Meillassoux, *The Development of Indigenous Trade and Markets in West Africa* (London, 1971), p. 177.

103 A. Jones, ' "My arse for Akou": a wartime ritual of women on the nineteenth-century Gold Coast', *Cahiers d'études africaines*, 1993, p. 546.

104 T. O. Ranger, *Dance and Society in Eastern Africa* (Berkeley, and Los Angeles, 1975).

105 Jones, ' "My arse for Akou" ', pp. 545ff.

106 S. F. Nadel, *A Black Byzantium: The Kingdom of Nupe in Nigeria* (London, 1972), p. 16.

107 A. Kuper and P. van Leynseele, 'Social anthropology and the "Bantu Expansion" ', *Africa*, 1978, pp. 339ff., point this out and suggest another typology for 'Southern Bantu'.

108 Vansina, *Paths in the Rainforests*, p. 20.

109 Law, *Slave Coast*, pp. 189–90.

110 Duarte Pacheco Pereira, *Esmeraldo de Situ Orbis* (Hakluyt, 1937, 2nd series, LXXIX), p. 120.

111 Vansina, *Art History in Africa*, pp. 161–8.

112 J. Lonsdale, 'States and social processes in Africa: a historiographic survey', *African Studies Review*, 1981, p. 173.

113 See R. Werbner (ed.), *Regional Cults* (London and New York, 1977).

114 J. Janzen, *Lemba. 1650–1930: A Drum of Affliction in Africa and the New World* (New York, 1982).

115 I. Kopytoff, 'The internal African frontier', in I. Kopytoff (ed.), *The African Frontier* (Bloomington, 1987), p. 34.

116 See E. Isichei, *A History of Christianity in Africa* (London, 1995), p. 83.

117 D. Crawford, *Thinking Black* (London, 1913), p. 114. Crawford worked as a Brethren missionary, first in coastal Angola, then in Shaba.

118 M. Griaule, *Conversations with Ogotemmili* (London, 1965); see also S. Pern, *Masked Dancers of West Africa: The Dogon* (Amsterdam, 1982), p. 28.
119 Vansina, *Children of Woot*, p. 209.
120 Harms, *River of Wealth*, pp. 198ff.
121 Goody, *Death, Property and the Ancestors*, p. 373.
122 Guyer, 'Wealth in people', p. 261.

7 CENTRAL AFRICA

1 The area covered by this chapter is now divided among the modern nations of Cameroon, Central African Republic, Gabon, Congo, Zaire, Angola, Zambia, Mozambique and Zimbabwe, or adjacent areas, such as northern Transvaal.
2 Quoted in G. Prins, *The Hidden Hippopotamus* (Cambridge, 1980), p. 119.
3 J. Vansina, *Paths in the Rainforests: Towards a History of Political Tradition in Equatorial Africa* (Madison, 1990), pp. 106 and 329 n. 13; on the cataracts, see R. Harms, *River of Wealth, River of Sorrow* (New Haven and London, 1981), p. 1.
4 D. Crawford, *Thinking Black* (London, 1913), p. 152.
5 B. Heintze, 'Historical notes on the Kisama of Angola', *Journal of African History*, 1972, pp. 407ff.
6 But see, for a valuable survey, D. C. Cordell, 'The savanna belt of north-central Africa', in D. Birmingham and P. M. Martin (eds.), *History of Central Africa* (Harlow, 1986 reprint), I, pp. 30–74.
7 I collected texts in central Nigeria which suggested a much longer period, but this has been questioned.
8 As is argued in J. Miller, *Way of Death: Merchant Capitalism and the Angolan Slave Trade 1730–1830* (London, 1988), pp. 40ff. We revert to this question below (pp. 334ff.).
9 T. Q. Reefe, *The Rainbow and the Kings: A History of the Luba Empire to 1891* (Berkeley and Los Angeles, 1981) pp. 30–1.
10 J. Vansina, *The Children of Woot: A History of the Kuba Peoples* (Madison, 1978), *passim*.
11 G. Merolla, quoted in J. Thornton, *The Kingdom of Kongo: Civil War and Transition 1641–1718* (Wisconsin, 1983), p. 29.
12 Pigafetta, *A Report of the Kingdom of Congo* (based on information from Duarte Lopez) (1591, London, 1981 reprint), pp. 30–1.
13 Thornton, *The Kingdom of Kongo*, pp. 29ff.; A. Hilton, *The Kingdom of Kongo* (Oxford, 1985), pp. 6–7.
14 Pigafetta, *A Report*, p. 18.
15 E. Alpers, *Ivory and Slaves in East Central Africa* (London, 1975), pp. 22–5.
16 Vansina, *Children of Woot*, pp. 170–1.
17 Quoted in J. Miller, *Kings and Kinsmen* (London, 1976), p. 66. For *ngola*, see p. 109 below.
18 Vansina, *Children of Woot*, pp. 41–5.
19 W. MacGaffey, 'Oral tradition in Central Africa', *International Journal of African Historical Studies*, 1974, pp. 418–21. See M. Orbell's interpretation of Maori traditions of Kupe's migration from Hawaiiki in the east. Both Hawaiiki and the east are symbols of life. M. Orbell, *Hawaiki: A New Approach to Maori Tradition* (Christchurch, 1985).
20 The various contributors to D. Birmingham and P. Martin (eds.), *History of Central Africa*, I (Harlow, 1983) make a conscious effort to include small-scale

societies, notably J. Vansina, 'The peoples of the forest', pp. 83–91, but this discussion is ethnographic rather than historical, because of lack of data.

21 M. Douglas, 'Lele economy compared with the Bushong: a study in "economic backwardness"', in P. Bohannan and G. Dalton (eds.), *Markets in Africa* (Evanston, 1962), Ch. 8, and her classic study, *The Lele of the Kasai* (London, 1963), pp. 49ff.

22 Mary Douglas on the Lele and J. Vansina on the Kuba.

23 See pp. 79–80 above.

24 Hilton, *The Kingdom of Kongo*, p. 87.

25 Reefe, *The Rainbow and the Kings*, pp. 72–3.

26 J. Vansina, 'Deep down time: political tradition in Central Africa', *History in Africa*, 1989, p. 358.

27 Al-Masudi, extract in G. S. P. Freeman-Grenville, *The East African Coast* (London, 1975), p. 18 (plural form, *wafalme*).

28 Just to complicate matters, king lists, etc. can also be artificially elongated. For an example see Vansina, *Children of Woot*, p. 39. 'There are strong presumptions that informants attempted to make their lists as long as possible to bask in the admiration of their audience.'

29 P. de Maret, 'Sanga: new excavations, more data, and some related problems', *Journal of African History*, 1977, pp. 321–37. The ingots unearthed at Sanga are discussed in Chapter 5 above, in the context of the history of copper working.

30 J. Vansina, 'The bells of kings', *Journal of African History*, 1969, pp. 187–97. See also p. 98 above. A clapperless bell is perhaps a contradiction in terms.

31 T. Q. Reefe, 'Traditions of genesis and the Luba diaspora', *History in Africa*, 1977, p. 192.

32 See R. Needham, *Symbolic Classification* (Santa Monica, 1979), Ch. 5, 'Transformations'.

33 Miller, *Kings and Kinsmen*, p. 147. On *lukano*, see p. 76 above.

34 Vansina, *Children of Woot*, p. 56. J. C. Yoder, 'The historical study of a Kanyok genesis myth: the tale of Citend a Mfumu', in J. Miller (ed.), *The African Past Speaks: Essays on Oral Tradition and History* (Folkestone, 1980), p. 93. The Kanyok, who number about 75,000, live in the Kasai.

35 Vansina, *Children of Woot*, p. 121. See p. 80 above.

36 R. E. Schecter, 'A propos the Drunken King: cosmology and history', in Miller (ed.), *The African Past Speaks*, p. 114.

37 Miller, *Kings and Kinsmen*, pp. 80–1.

38 The account which follows is based on Hilton's admirable study, *The Kingdom of Kongo*.

39 Yoder, 'Historical study of a Kanyok genesis myth', p. 92; Vansina, *Children of Woot*, pp. 49–51; Cavazzi, cited in Miller, *Kings and Kinsmen*, p. 74.

40 Hilton, *The Kingdom of Kongo*, pp. 32–3.

41 See Vansina, 'People of the forest', pp. 93–4. White clay and leopard skins are symbols which are found very widely, and undoubtedly evolved independently in different areas. For instance, white clay is a symbol of ritual purity among the Igbo, who use it to anoint titled men.

42 See T. Q. Reefe, *The Rainbow and the Kings*, p. 6. 'The erection of an exploitive and territorially extensive tribute-gathering system must be judged both as one of the [Luba] Empire's historical achievements and as a symbol of its political life.'

43 Thornton, *The Kingdom of Kongo*, p. 19. This study and Hilton's (n. 13 above) use much the same sources, but ask different questions of the material, and hence complement each other.

44 Quoted in Douglas, *The Lele of the Kasai*, p. 36.

45 A. Roberts, *A History of Zambia* (London, 1976), pp. 75–6. For masking societies in West Africa, see p. 259.

46 Reefe, *The Rainbow and the Kings*, pp. 81–2. This study is, of course, the source of the subheading.

47 See J. Vansina, *Kingdoms of the Savanna* (Madison, 1966), p. 71. See the analysis of this myth and its meaning in Reefe, *The Rainbow and the Kings*, pp. 23–40.

48 A number of alternative names are given for this figure.

49 C. C. Wrigley, 'Myths of the savanna', *Journal of African History*, 1974, pp. 131–5. See Luc de Heusch, *The Drunken King or the Origin of the State* (Eng. edition, Bloomington, 1982). There is a brief introduction to de Heusch's ideas in his, 'What shall we do with the Drunken King?', *Africa*, 1975, pp. 363–72.

50 J. Miller, *Kings and Kinsmen*, applies this model to both the Mbundu and the Lunda. Positional inheritance and perpetual kinship relations are also character-istic of the eastern savannas, and Zambia. The underlying ethnographic model was first described in I. Cunnison, 'Perpetual kinship: a political institution of the Luapula peoples', *Rhodes-Livingstone Journal*, 1956, pp. 28–48. Vansina, *Kingdoms of the Savanna*, p. 27, draws attention to the phenomenon. For Miller's more recent analysis of the Kinguri, see pp. 398–9 below.

51 Miller, *Kings and Kinsmen*, p. 126.

52 Reefe, *The Rainbow and the Kings*, pp. 81–2.

53 T. Q. Reefe, 'Lukasa: a Luba memory device', *African Arts*, 1977, pp. 48–50.

54 M. G. Marwick, 'History and tradition in East Central Africa through the eyes of the northern Rhodesian Cewa', *Journal of African History*, 1963, pp. 375–7.

55 E. Alpers, *Ivory and Slaves in East Central Africa*, pp. 46ff.; E. Alpers and C. Ehret, 'Eastern Africa', *Cambridge History of Africa*, IV: *From c. 1600 to c. 1790*, ed. R. Gray, p. 516. This has been questioned by both Newitt and Schoffeleers, (see n. 61 below).

56 For a caveat on the problems of extrapolating 'the Tumbuka' (or Chewa) into the past, as historical entities, see H. Leroy Vail, 'Suggestions towards a reinterpreted Tumbuka history', in B. Pachai, *The Early History of Malawi* (London, 1972), pp. 148ff.

57 T. Ranger, 'Territorial cults in the history of Central Africa', *Journal of African History*, 1973, pp. 581ff.

58 M. Schoffeleers, 'The history and political role of the M'Bona cult among the Mang'anja', in T. Ranger and I. Kimambo (eds.), *The Historical Study of African Religion* (London, 1972), pp. 73ff. W. H. J. Rangeley, 'Mbona – the rain maker', *The Nyasaland Journal*, 1953, pp. 8ff.

59 J. M. Schoffeleers, 'The meaning and use of the name *Malawi* in oral traditions and precolonial documents', in B. Pachai (ed.), *The Early History of Malawi*, p. 99.

60 Schoffeleers, 'The name *Malawi*', p. 98.

61 M. D. Newitt, 'The early history of the Maravi', *Journal of African History*, 1982, pp. 145ff. His findings are criticised by M. Schoffeleers, 'The Zimba and the Lundu state in the late sixteenth and early seventeenth centuries', *Journal of Africa History*, 1987, pp. 337ff.

62 In an early paper, J. Miller suggested that the 'Jaga', 'Mane' and 'Zimba' are all

non-historic stereotypes of the Other ('Requiem for the Jaga', *Cahiers d'études africaines*, 1973, pp. 121ff., but this has not won general acceptance. The historicity of the Jaga is supported by Thornton and Hilton, and the historicity of the Zimba by Alpers, Schoffeleers and Newitt.

63 Quoted in Newitt, 'Early history of the Maravi', p. 156.

64 Schoffeleers, 'The Zimba', pp. 347–8.

65 Ibid., p. 344.

66 It is generally thought that he was a Kalonga (See Alpers, *Ivory and Slaves in East Central Africa*, p. 53). Schoffeleers ('The Zimba', pp. 344ff.) believes he founded a separate state.

67 Schoffeleers, 'The Zimba', pp. 345–6. He believes Muzora's state was swallowed up in that of the Kalonga.

68 E. Herbert, *Red Gold of Africa* (Madison, 1984), p. 45.

69 D. N. Beach, *The Shona and Zimbabwe 900–1850* (London, 1980), pp. 26, 100–1.

70 A. Kuper, 'Symbolic dimensions of the Southern Bantu homestead', *Africa*, 1980, pp. 8ff.; also his *Wives for Cattle: Bridewealth and Marriage in Southern Africa* (London, 1982).

71 There is a large and rapidly growing literature on this theme. See T. Huffman, 'Archaeology and ethnohistory of the African Iron Age', *Annual Review of Anthropology*, 1982, pp. 140–1; T. M. Evers, 'Sotho-Tswana and Moloko settlement patterns and the Bantu cattle pattern', in M. Hall et al., *Frontiers: Southern African Archaeology Today* (Oxford 1984), pp. 236ff. For a caveat, see M. Hall, 'The role of cattle in southern African agropastoral societies: more than bones alone can tell', in *Prehistoric Pastoralism* (The South African Archaeological Society, Goodwin Series, 1986), p. 83. It is striking that Kuper's original model was based mainly on Nguni data; it has been applied very extensively to the ethnoarchaeology of the Sotho-Tswana.

72 A. Kuper, 'Symbolic dimensions', pp. 8ff. These ideas are applied to archaeological sites in T. Huffman, 'Archaeology and ethnohistory' pp. 140–1.

73 J. R. Denbow, 'Cows and kings: a spatial and economic analysis of a hierarchical Early Iron Age settlement system', in Hall, *Frontiers*, pp. 24ff.

74 Hall, *The Changing Past*, pp. 75ff., 88.

75 This is the generally accepted picture; however, fragments of sixteenth-century Chinese porcelain were recently found in Great Zimbabwe (P. Sinclair, 'Archaeology in eastern Africa', *Journal of African History*, 1991, p. 210).

76 T. Huffman, 'Where you are the girls gather to play', in Hall, *Frontiers*, p. 257.

77 T. Huffman, 'The soapstone birds from Great Zimbabwe', *African Arts*, 1985, pp. 68–71; 'Snakes and birds, expressive space at Great Zimbabwe', *African Studies*, 1981, pp. 131–50; 'Where you are the girls gather to play', pp. 252ff.

78 P. S. Garlake, 'Pastoralism and Zimbabwe', *Journal of African History*, 1978, pp. 479ff.

79 Hall, *The Changing Past*, pp. 134–6.

80 This account is based on the classic study by C. Turnbull, *The Forest People* (New York, 1961). The Baka are the subject of a fine ethnographic film by Phil Agland (DJA Rivers Films, for Channel 4).

81 See J. Vansina, *Paths in the Rainforests*, p. 311 n. 23, citing an unpublished study by R. C. Bailey.

82 See p. 38 above.

83 Vansina, *Paths in the Rainforests*, p. 56.

8 EASTERN AFRICA

1 C. S. Nason, 'Proverbs of the Baganda', *Uganda Journal*, 1936, pp. 251–2.
2 Shambaa song, quoted in S. Feierman, *The Shambaa Kingdom: A History* (Madison, 1974), p. 20.
3 Yao tradition, quoted in E. Alpers, *Ivory and Slaves in East Central Africa* (London, 1975), p. 15. This is not to be confused with nineteenth-century Yao movements to what later became southern Tanzania.
4 G. Hartwig, *The Art of Survival in East Africa: The Kerebe and Long Distance Trade, 1800–1895* (New York, 1976), p. 82.
5 J. Sutton, 'Irrigation and soil conservation in African agricultural history', *Journal of African History*, 1984, pp. 2–41. D. Anderson, ' "Cultivating pastoralists": ecology and economy among the Il Chamus of Baringo 1840–1980', in D. Johnson and D. Anderson (eds.), *The Ecology of Survival: Case Studies from Northeast African History* (London, 1988), pp. 241–60.
6 J. Iliffe, *A Modern History of Tanzania* (Cambridge, 1979), p. 28. The first chapter of this superb national history is full of insights into 'traditional' livelihood, ecology and religion. See also R. Waller, 'Ecology, migration and expansion in East Africa', *African Affairs*, 1985, pp. 347–70.
7 Waller, 'Ecology, migration', pp. 354–5.
8 Hartwig, *Art of Survival*, p. 162.
9 *The Africa Review* (11th edn, Saffron Waldron, 1987), pp. 171 and 233.
10 A. Roberts (ed.), *Tanzania before 1900* (Nairobi, 1966); B. A. Ogot, *Kenya before 1900. Eight Regional Studies* (Nairobi, 1986 reprint).
11 *The Periplus of the Erythraean Sea* (trans. G. W. B. Huntingdon, Hakluyt Society, (2nd series, 151, London, 1980) (a marine guide from early in the Christian era).
12 Feierman, *The Shambaa Kingdom*, p. 133.
13 A. Shorter, *Chiefship in Western Tanzania: A Political History of the Kimbu* (Oxford, 1972), pp. 99–106 and 186–9.
14 A. Redmayne, 'The Hehe', in Roberts (ed.), *Tanzania before 1900*, p. 37.
15 Roberts in *Tanzania before 1900*, p. 117.
16 T. Spear, *Kenya's Past: An Introduction to Historical Method in Africa* (Harlow, 1981), pp. 56 and 101. A great strength of this study is the author's command of linguistic data.
17 Waller, 'Ecology, migration', p. 350.
18 Roberts' collection includes a chapter on the Nyiha; Fipa tradition tells how Twa women married Nyika hunters; Nyika is a less acceptable name for the Mijikenda.
19 G. Muriuki, 'The Kikuyu in the pre-colonial period', in Ogot (ed.), *Kenya before 1900*, pp. 108–9. For a Maasai version of the same story, see J. Bernsten, 'The Maasai and their neighbours: variables of interraction', *African Economic History*, 1976, p. 3.
20 Yohanna Abdallah, *The Yaos* (trans. M. Sanderson, (Zomba, 1919), p. 7.
21 Feierman, *The Shambaa Kingdom*, p. 19.
22 J. Lonsdale, 'When did the Gusii (or any other group) become a tribe?', *Kenya Historical Review*, 1977, p. 125.
23 The historical significance of the Southern Cushites and Southern Nilotes was demonstrated, on linguistic grounds, by C. Ehret, *Ethiopians and East Africans* (Nairobi, 1974) and *Southern Nilotic History Linguistic Approaches to the Study of the Past* (Evanston, 1971).

24 Ehret, *Southern Nilotic History*, pp. 28–9.

25 R. Oliver, 'The Nilotic contribution to Bantu Africa', *Journal of African History*, 1982, pp. 433–42.

26 On this see R. Blackburn, 'Okiek history', in Ogot, *Kenya before 1900*, pp. 63–4, citing, among other evidence of physical descent from Khoisan-type predecessors, their distinctive physical characteristics: light complexion, short stature (interestingly the Okiek themselves stress the importance of eyes in telling an Okiek).

27 There is a considerable literature on the Okiek/'Dorobo'. See J. A. Distefano, 'Hunters or hunted? Towards a history of the Okiek of Kenya', *History in Africa*, 1990, pp. 41–57; J. L. Berntsen, 'The Maasai and their neighbours: variables of interaction', *African Economic History*, 1976, pp. 1–11; M. Kenny, 'Mirror in the forest: the Dorobo hunter-gatherers as an image of the Other', *Africa*, 1981, pp. 477ff.

28 N. Sobania, 'Fishermen herders: subsistence, survival and cultural change in northern Kenya', *Journal of African History*, 1988, pp. 41–56.

29 See J. Vansina, *The Children of Woot: A History of the Kuba Peoples* (Madison, 1978), pp. 56–7 on comparable attributions to the pygmoid Cwa.

30 See W. MacGaffey, *Custom and Government in the Lower Congo* (Berkeley, 1970), p. 30.

31 Both explanations are to be found in a single volume, Ogot, *Kenya before 1900*, pp. 75–6 (Blackburn) and pp. 48–51 (Sutton). Sutton, the acknowledged authority on the archaeology of western Kenya, is probably right.

32 There is a rich literature on Singwaya. F. Morton, 'The Shungwaya myth of Mijikenda origins: a problem of late nineteenth century Kenya coastal history', *International Journal of African Historical Studies*, 1973, pp. 397–423; T. Spear, 'Traditional myths and historians' myths: variations on the Singwaya theme of Mijikenda origins', *History in Africa*, 1974, pp. 67–84, and T. Spear, 'Traditional myths and linguistic analysis: Singwaya revisited', *History in Africa*, 1976, pp. 229–46.

33 The account which follows is based mainly on D. Nurse and T. Spear, *The Swahili: Reconstructing the History and Language of an African Society 800–1500* (Philadelphia, 1985).

34 Ibn Battuta, extract in G. S. P. Freeman-Grenville, *The East African Coast: Select Documents from the First to the Earlier Nineteenth Century* (Oxford, 1966 reprint), p. 31.

35 *The Periplus*, xvi.

36 R. Austen, *African Economic History* (London, 1987), p. 58.

37 *The Periplus*, xvii.

38 Al-Masudi (d. *c.* 945), extract in Freeman-Grenville, *Documents*, p. 15.

39 Al-Idrisi, extract in Freeman-Grenville, *Documents*, p. 20. Abu al-Fida (d. 1331) wrote that gold and iron mining are 'their chief means of existence' (*Documents*, p. 24).

40 Extract in Freeman-Grenville, *Documents*, p. 31.

41 Ibid., pp. 14–17.

42 Ibid., p. 31.

43 J. Knappert, *Four Centuries of Swahili Verse* (London, 1979), pp. 192–3 and 144.

44 Ibid., pp. 132–3.

45 Alpers, *Ivory and Slaves*, p. 235.

46 Ibid., pp. 42–6.
47 The historiography of this is complex. Colonial writers assumed that they were 'Hamites' from Rwanda or Ankole, which has now influenced oral tradition. The current unacceptability of the Hamitic hypothesis does not, however, necessarily imply that these connections were not real (R. Willis, *A State in the Making: Myth, History and Social Transformation in Pre-colonial Ufipa* (Bloomington, 1981), pp 14, 29–35, 150).
48 The account which follows is based on Willis, *Precolonial Ufipa*. For queen mothers in general, see R. Cohen, 'Oedipus Rex and Regina', *Africa*, 1977, pp. 14–30.
49 R. Austen, 'Ntemiship, trade and statebuilding: political development among the Western Bantu of Tanzania', in D. McCall et al. (eds.), *Eastern African History: Boston University Papers in African History* (New York, 1969), pp. 133ff; I. N. Kimambo, 'The interior before 1800', in I. N. Kimambo and A. J .Temu (eds.), *A History of Tanzania* (Nairobi, 1969), pp. 22–6.
50 Ntemi/Mtemi is found among the Nyamwezi, Sukuma, Gogo and Bena, Mutwa/ Ntwa among the Hehe and Nyakusa (R. Oliver, 'Discernible developments in the interior *c.* 1500–1840', pp. 191 and 197; Austen, 'Ntemiship', pp. 133ff.).
51 Aylward Shorter, personal communication, 20 April 1995.
52 Quoted in A. Shorter, *Chiefship in Western Tanzania: A Political History of the Kimbu* (Oxford, 1972), p. 392.
53 Ibid., pp. 154–6 and 180–2. See also his 'Religious values in Kimbu historical charters', *Africa*, 1969, pp. 227–37. There are many parallels to this account of the king's descent into the earth, possibly based on the widespread practice of royal suicide.
54 Shorter, *Chiefship*, p. 60.
55 I. Kimambo, 'The Pare', in A. Roberts (ed.), *Tanzania before 1800*; there is a more detailed account in his *A Political History of the Pare of Tanzania c. 1500–1900* (Nairobi, 1969).
56 Feierman, *The Shambaa Kingdom*, pp. 40ff. His detailed analysis of the myth, like Willis' comparable analysis of Fipa myth, cannot be adequately summarised in a study of this kind.
57 M. Kenny, 'The stranger from the lake: a theme in the history of the Lake Victoria shorelands', *Azania*, 1982, p. 13.
58 Quoted in Feierman, *The Shambaa Kingdom*, p. 103.
59 Their findings are conveniently summarised in their respective contributions to Ogot, *Kenya before 1900*: G. Muriuki, 'The Kikuyu in the pre-colonial period', pp. 106–38; J. Fadiman, 'The Meru peoples', pp. 139–73; and K. Jackson, 'The dimensions of Kamba pre-colonial history', pp. 174–261. The interpretation given here is indebted to Spear, *Kenya's Past*, pp. 58–61.
60 Spear, *Kenya's Past*, p. 60, citing the work of J. Mahner.
61 Muriuki, 'The Kikuyu', p. 130.
62 R. Waller, 'Emutai: crisis and response in Maasailand 1883–1902', in Johnson and Anderson, *The Ecology of Survival*, p. 97. See W. Lawren, 'Masai and Kikuyu: an historical analysis of culture transmission', *Journal of African History*, 1968, pp. 571–83.
63 D. W. Cohen, 'A survey of interlacustrine chronology', *Journal of African History*, 1970, pp. 177–94; R. Gray, 'Eclipse maps', *Journal of African History*, 1965, pp. 251–62.

64 D. Henige, 'Reflections on early interlacustrine chronology', *Journal of African History*, 1974, pp. 27–46; *The Chronology of Oral Tradition: Quest for a Chimera* (Oxford, 1974). At first he accepted the authenticity of the Buganda king list but later came to question this as well.

65 J. B. Webster, 'The reign of the gods', in *Chronology, Migration and Drought* (New York, 1979), pp. 125–44. It is noteworthy that Cohen's widely cited work on Busoga, published seven years earlier, also cites the Batembuzi as Madi kings, and makes both the Bacwezi and Kintu historic figures (D. W. Cohen, *The Historical Tradition of Busoga* (Oxford, 1972), pp. 80, 106). This reflects the state of African historiography when this book was written; his later studies abandon this literalism.

66 The standard study is I. Berger, *Religion and Resistance: East African Kingdoms in the Precolonial Period* (Tervuren, 1981).

67 C. Wrigley, 'The story of Rukidi', *Africa*, 1973, pp. 219–35. His pupil, Caroline Neale, ended her lively survey of contemporary African historiography with 'The hairy bridegroom' (Rukidi) (Caroline Neale, *Writing 'Independent' History: African Historiography 1960–1980* (Westport, 1985), pp. 185–96). See p. 11 above.

68 Iris Berger, 'Deities, dynasties and oral tradition: the history and legend of the Abacwezi', in J. C. Miller (ed.), *The African Past Speaks: Essays on Oral Tradition and History* (Folkestone, 1980), p. 67.

69 C. Wrigley, 'The kinglists of Buganda', *History in Africa*, 1974, p. 134.

70 Kenny, 'The stranger from the lake', p. 20. An alternative view is that centre of gravity of the kingdom shifted, during its expansion, from inland Busiro to the shore and Ssese islands, and that the latter's canoemen played a role in it (C. Wrigley, 'The kinglists of Buganda', *History in Africa*, 1974, pp. 135–6).

71 C. Wrigley, 'The Christian revolution in Buganda', in M. Klein and G. W. Johnson (eds.), *Perspectives on the African Past* (Boston, 1972), p. 253.

72 D. Low, *Religion and Society in Buganda 1875–1900* (Kampala, 1957), quoting J. Roscoe, *The Baganda* (London, 1911), p. 220. This begs the question of when, if ever, Ndaula (Ndawula, the Ganda form of Ndahuru) existed.

73 Nason, 'Proverbs of the Baganda', p. 250.

74 Among the riverain Igbo of Nigeria, the feathers of the fish-eagle, *ugo*, are among the insignia of a titled man.

75 This paragraph is based on Kenny's admirable paper, 'The stranger from the lake', pp. 1–26.

76 D. W. Cohen, *The Historical Tradition of Busoga, Mukama and Kintu* (Oxford, 1972), pp. 104–5. Despite his own caution (citing the lack of tie-ins for the earliest period), this schema is widely cited and accepted – an interesting contrast to the scepticism about the Webster group's interlacustrine chronology.

77 Cohen, *The Historical Tradition of Busoga*, pp. 70–7 and 84–5.

78 J. Beattie, *The Nyoro State* (Oxford, 1971), p. 6. See Neale, *Writing 'Independent' History*, p. 192.

79 Quoted in Cohen, *The Historical Tradition of Busoga*, p. 151.

80 R. Herring, 'Hydrology and chronology', in J. B. Webster (ed.), *Chronology, Migration and Drought in Interlacustrine Africa* (London, 1979), Ch. 2. See F. Hassan, 'Historic Nile floods and their importance for climatic change', *Science*, 1981, pp. 1142–8. The problem lies in the fact that the scale and method of measurement of the Roda Nilometer changed.

81 J. B. Webster, 'Noi! Noi! Famines as an aid to interlacustrine chronology', in *Chronology, Migration and Drought*, pp. 10–12.

82 R. [Mrs A. B.] Fisher, *Twilight Tales of the Black Baganda* (London, 1911); see Neale, *Writing 'Independent History'*, pp. 194–5.

83 Quoted in P. Robertshaw, 'Prehistory in the upper Nile basin', *Journal of African History*, 1987, p. 185.

84 C. Wrigley, 'The problem of the Luo', *History in Africa*, 1981, pp. 219–45.

85 Ibid., pp. 232–4.

86 D. W. Cohen, 'The political transformation of northern Busoga, 1600–1900', *Cahiers d'études africaines*, 1982, pp. 465–88.

87 B. Ogot, *History of the Southern Luo* (Nairobi, 1976).

88 S. Karugire, *A History of the Kingdom of Nkore in Western Uganda to 1896* (Oxford, 1971).

89 S. Ambrose, 'Archaeology and linguistic reconstruction of history in East Africa', in C. Ehret and M. Posnansky (eds.), *The Archaeological and Linguistic Reconstruction of African History* (Berkeley, 1982).

90 P. Robertshaw and D. Collett, 'A new framework for the study of early pastoral communities in East Africa', *Journal of African History*, 1983, pp. 289–301.

91 A. Jacobs, 'Maasai pastoralism in historical perspective', in T. Monod (ed.), *Pastoralism in Tropical Africa* (London 1975), p. 406. Here, as elsewhere in this book, demographic data are very approximate, but they serve to establish a relative order of magnitude.

92 Their population was estimated in 1948 as Karimojong 54,696, Jie 18,211 and Dodos 20,155. Gulliver's estimate, cited in B. Gartrell, 'Prelude to disaster: the case of Karamoja', in Johnson and Anderson, *The Ecology of Survival*, p. 197 n. 8.

93 Jacobs, 'Maasai pastoralism', p. 411.

94 Ibid., pp. 408–9.

95 On this see Waller, 'Ecology, migration', p. 361.

96 J. Bernsten, 'The Maasai and their neighbours', p. 4.

97 N. Sobaania, 'Fishermen herders: subsistence, survival and cultural change in northern Kenya', *Journal of African History*, 1988, pp. 41–56. Cf. p. 126 above.

98 Bernsten, 'The Maasai and their neighbours', pp. 6–8; see also his 'The enemy is us: eponymy in the historiography of the Maasai', *History in Africa*, 1980, p. 10.

9 AFRICA SOUTH OF THE LIMPOPO

1 Quoted in G. Harinck, 'Interaction between Khosa and Khoi: emphasis on the period 1620–1750', in L. Thompson (ed.), *African Societies in Southern Africa* (London, 1969), p. 166. It should be noted that the passage begins by excepting three groups from this generalisation – 'the Damaqua, Damasonqua, and Hoengeiqua'. The early history of the area now covered by Malawi, Zambia and Zimbabwe is included in Chapter 7.

2 J. B. Peires, *The House of Phalo: A History of the Xhosa People in the Days of Their Independence* (Berkeley, 1982), p. 2.

3 R. Lee and M. Guenther, 'Problems in Kalahari historical ethnography and the tolerance of error', *History in Africa*, 1993, p. 190. The dividing line runs through Maun, in Botswana.

4 See Jean and John Comaroff, *Of Revelation and Revolution: Christianity, Colonialism and Consciousness in South Africa* (Chicago, 1991), p. 42.

5   M. Hall, 'The role of cattle in southern African agropastoral societies', in
    M. Hall and A. Smith (eds.), *Prehistoric Pastoralism in Southern Africa* (South
    African Archaeological Society, Goodwin Series, 1986), p. 85; for a different
    view, cf. T. Maggs and G. Whitelaw, 'A review of recent archaeological research
    on food-producing communities in southern Africa', *Journal of African History*,
    1991, p. 19, citing the work of J. Feeley.

6   E. Wilmsen, 'A myth and its measure', *Current Anthropology*, 1992, p. 612.

7   The account which follows is based on R. Elphick, 'The Khoisan', in R. Elphick
    and H. Gilomee, *The Shaping of South African Society 1652–1820* (Cape Town
    and London, 1979), pp. 3ff. and R. Elphick, *Khoikhoi and the Peopling of White
    South Africa* (Johannesburg, 1985).

8   M. Hall, *The Changing Past: Farmers Kings and Traders in Southern Africa 200–
    1860* (Cape Town, 1987), p. 34.

9   C. Schrire, 'An inquiry into the evolutionary status and apparent identity of San
    hunter-gatherers', *Human Ecology*, 1980, pp. 20ff. This view is not universally
    held; see A. Smith, 'Competition, conflict and clientship: Khoi and San relation-
    ships in the Western Cape', in Hall and Smith, *Prehistoric Pastoralism*, pp. 36ff.

10 Lee and Guenther, 'Problems in Kalahari historical ethnography', p. 193.

11 Quoted in R. J. Gordon, 'The making of the "Bushmen"', *Anthropologica*, 1992,
    p. 191.

12 N. Parsons, *A New History of Southern Africa* (London, 1982), p. 54.

13 J. D. Lewis-Williams, 'Ideological continuities in prehistoric southern Africa: the
    evidence of rock art', in C. Schrire (ed.), *Past and Present in Hunter–gatherer
    Studies* (Orlando, 1984), pp. 225ff. The art on rock faces has not been dated; the
    dates refer to the 'art mobilier' on flat stones.

14 P. Vinnicombe, 'Myth, motive and selection in southern African rock art',
    Africa, 1972 , pp. 195–8 and her *People of the Eland* (Pietermaritzburg, 1976).

15 The major books are R. Lee, *The !Kung San: Men, Women and Work in a
    Foraging Society* (Cambridge, 1979) and E. Wilmsen, *Land Filled with Flies: A
    Political Economy of the Kalahari* (Chicago, 1989); there is a large and notably
    polemical literature; see Lee and Guenther, 'Problems in Kalahari historical
    ethnography'; also E. Wilmsen, 'The ecology of illusion: anthropological fora-
    ging in the Kalahari', *Reviews in Anthropology*, 1983, pp. 9ff.; and 'A myth and its
    measure', pp. 611ff.

16 See p. 97 above. Nguni and Sotho-Tswana, although ultimately related, are not
    mutually intelligible.

17 T. Wright, 'Politics, ideology, and the invention of the "Nguni"', in T. Lodge
    (ed.), *Resistance and Ideology in Settler Societies* (Johannesburg, 1986), pp. 96ff.

18 But see pp. 72–3 above.

19 T. Maggs, quoted in Hall, *The Changing Past*, p. 48.

20 T. Maggs and P. Davison, 'The Lydenburg heads', *African Arts*, 1881, pp.
    28ff.

21 See L. Thompson, *A History of South Africa* (New Haven, 1990), p. 14.

22 A. Kuper, 'The social structure of the Sotho-speaking peoples of southern
    Africa', *Africa*, 1975, pp. 145–7.

23 Hall, *The Changing Past*, pp. 47–53, 65, citing the research of T. Maggs.

24 Quoted in M. Legassick, 'The Sotho-Tswana peoples before 1800', in
    L. Thompson, *African Societies*, pp. 96–7.

25 Quoted in J. Guy, *The Destruction of the Zulu Kingdom* (London, 1979), p. 3.

26 W. Fehr (trans.), *Ludwig Alberti's Account of the Tribal Life and Customs of the Xhosa* (Cape Town, 1968), p. 54. Kaffir is another long-discarded European ethonym (for the Xhosa).

27 Bantu proverb, quoted in A. Kuper, *Wives for Cattle: Bridewealth and Marriage in Southern Africa* (London, 1982), p. 21.

28 Peires, *House of Phalo*, p. 41.

29 Circumcision song quoted in M. Wilson, 'The Sotho, Venda and Tsonga', in M. Wilson and L. Thompson, *The Oxford History of South Africa* (Oxford, 1969), p. 167.

30 Quoted in R. Ross, 'Ethnic identity, demographic crises, and Xhosa–Khoikhoi interaction', *History in Africa*, 1980, p. 265.

31 R. Moffat, *Missionary Labours and Scenes in Southern Africa* (London, 1842), p. 250.

32 A. T. Bryant, *Olden Times in Zululand and Natal* (London, 1929), p. 74. Bryant reached Natal as a missionary in 1883 and worked there for 45 years.

33 J. Guy, 'Analysing pre-capitalist societies in southern Africa', *Journal of Southern African Studies*, 1987, p. 25.

34 D. Golan, 'The life story of King Shaka and gender tensions in the Zulu state', *History in Africa*, 1990, p. 104.

35 J. Guy, 'Analysing pre-capitalist societies', pp. 18ff.

36 Bryant, *Olden Times*, p. 75.

37 Ibid., p. 74.

38 Hall, *The Changing Past*, p. 68. See pp. 72–3 above for more on the ecological implications of iron smelting.

39 Kuper, *Wives for Cattle*, p. 23.

40 Hall, *The Changing Past*, pp. 65–6.

41 A nineteenth-century Xhosa, quoted in Peires, *House of Phalo*, p. 15.

42 H. Langworthy, 'Chewa or Malawi political organization in the precolonial era', in B. Pachai, *The Early History of Malawi* (Evanston, 1972), p. 106.

43 Many historians of Africa, the present writer included, dislike 'chief' for the same reason that they avoid 'tribe' or 'hut', a use of (?derogatory) words for the Other. But 'chief' is not derogatory in the Highlands of Scotland, and 'tribe' is used without hesitation in New Zealand. In West African studies, scholars, myself among them, do not hesitate to describe the sacred ruler of a single town or cluster of hamlets as a 'king'.

44 Peires, *House of Phalo*, p. 13, points out that the ethonym was probably in fact derived from Khoi //*kosa*, angry men.

45 Maggs and Whitelaw, 'A review of recent archaeological research', p. 22.

46 M. Legassick, 'The northern frontier to 1820: the emergence of the Griqua people', in Elphick and Giliomee, *The Shaping*, p. 254.

47 See, for instance, D. Livingstone, *A Popular Account of Missionary Travels and Researches in South Africa* (London, 1875), p. 62.

48 This account is based on M. Legassick, 'The Sotho-Tswana peoples before 1800', in Thompson (ed.), *African Societies*, pp. 98ff. It reflects, of course, the approach to the interpretation of oral history current when it was written. It is surprising that more recent work on this important theme is lacking. Overlain by the events of the Mfecane, in which some communities were displaced or fragmented, it is a difficult past to recover.

49 Legassick, 'The Sotho-Tswana peoples', pp. 115–16.

50 P. Delius, *The Land Belongs to Us: The Pedi Polity, the Boers and the British in the Nineteenth Century Transvaal* (London, 1984), p. 13.

51 Ibid., p. 14.

52 Legassick, 'The northern frontier', p. 234. Korana is the plural form.

53 Quoted in Peires, *House of Phalo*, p. 23.

54 Ibid., p. 24.

55 M. Wilson, 'Changes in social structure in southern Africa', in Thompson (ed.), *African Societies*, p. 78.

56 P. Bonner, *Kings, Commoners and Concessionaires* (Cambridge, 1983), p. 36.

57 Peires, *House of Phalo*, pp. 39–40.

58 Bryant, *Olden Times*, p. 74.

59 Van der Kemp in 1804, quoted in Peires, *House of Phalo*, pp. 35–6.

60 Peires, *House of Phalo*, pp. 25, 67.

61 R. Inskeep, *The Peopling of Southern Africa* (Claremont, 1978), p. 135.

IO   NORTHERN AFRICA TO THE SEVENTH CENTURY CE

1 R. Jobson, *The Golden Trade* (London, 1623), p. 3. I am grateful to Chris Ehrhardt, who read and criticised this chapter for me.

2 B. Bell, 'The oldest records of Nile floods', *Geographical Journal*, 1970, pp. 569–73.

3 B. G. Trigger, 'The rise of civilization in Egypt', in *The Cambridge History of Africa*, I: *From the Earliest Times to c. 500 BC*, ed. J. D. Clark, pp. 485–7.

4 A. K. Bowman, *Egypt after the Pharaohs* (Berkeley, 1986), p. 13; Trigger, 'The rise of civilisation', p. 487.

5 One confusing aspect of the literature on this early period is the existence of alternative names for the same culture; the older terminology of Amratian and Gerzean, the more recent one of Naqada I, II and III. There was also a Badarian culture in Upper Egypt, which followed the Amratian.

6 Herodotus, II, 4 and 99. It is easy to forget that Herodotus lived in the fifth century BCE and was therefore approximately as remote from these events as we are from him.

7 A. J. Spencer, *Early Egypt: The Rise of Civilisation in the Nile Valley* (London, 1993), p. 63.

8 There is an engraving and description in F. L. Norden, *Travels in Egypt and Nubia* (Eng. trans. London, 1757); reproduction and extract in P. M. Holt, *Egypt and the Fertile Crescent 1526–1922: A Political History* (London, 1966), p. xi and facing p. 148.

9 Spencer, *Early Egypt*, p. 57. It is important to remember, as Spencer points out, that the meaning of this and other symbols may well have changed over time.

10 Ibid., p. 63.

11 C. Aldred, *The Egyptians* (rev. edn, London, 1984), p. 87. This is the garb shown on the Narmer palette and elsewhere (for instance the picture of King Djoser, *c.* 2680 BCE, in Spencer, *Early Egypt*, p. 100).

12 Spencer, *Early Egypt*, p. 61.

13 Trigger, 'The rise of civilisation in Egypt', p. 514.

14 Ibid., p. 528.

15 R. Oliver, *The African Experience* (London, 1991), p. 57.

16 Aldred, *The Egyptians*, p. 59.

17 Ammianus Marcellinus, quoted in Bowman, *Egypt after the Pharaohs*, pp. 14–15.

18 E. Naville, *The Temple of Deir el Bahari*, III (London, 1898). It should be noted that Punt (often equated with the Biblical Ophir) may not have been on the African side of the Red Sea at all.

19 Herodotus, II, 35.

20 Aldred, *The Egyptians*, p. 65.

21 J. L. Angel, 'Ecology and population in the eastern Mediterranean', *World Archaeology*, 1972, p. 101, citing data from tombstones which suggest a life expectancy of 35.8 for males and 30.5 for females.

22 Aldred, *The Egyptians*, pp. 91–2, 137–8.

23 W. Y. Adams, *Nubia, Corridor to Africa* (Princeton, 1977), pp. 137–8.

24 Yahya Haqqi, quoted in M. Morsy, *North Africa 1800–1900: A Survey from the Nile Valley to the Atlantic* (London and New York, 1984), p. 10.

25 W. Stevenson Smith, *The Art and Architecture of Ancient Egypt* (Harmondsworth, 1958,) Plate 48B. This dates from the Fifth Dynasty (*c.* 2565–2420 BCE).

26 This is argued by B. Bell, 'The Dark Ages in ancient history', *American Journal of Archaeology*, 1971, pp. 1ff. For plague and famine in Israel in the Late Bronze Age, see C. Meyers, 'The roots of restriction: women in early Israel', *Biblical Archaeologist*, 1978, pp. 93ff.

27 Quoted in Bell, 'Dark Ages', p. 9.

28 D. O'Connor, 'Egypt, 1552–664 BC', in *Cambridge History of Africa*, I, p. 842.

29 Herodotus, II, 3.

30 This is claimed by J. Vansina, *Art History in Africa: An Introduction to Method* (London, 1984), p. 117. The motif is in fact still more widespread (Marduk slays the female water-dragon, Tiamit), but I am unconvinced about the connections.

31 Herodotus, II, 35.

32 The major text on Nubian history in general, and the main source for what follows, is Adams, *Nubia*. See also W. Y. Adams, 'The coming of Nubian speakers to the Nile valley', and R. Thelwall, 'Linguistic aspects of Greater Nubian history', in C. Ehret and M. Posnansky (eds.), *The Archaeological and Linguistic Reconstruction of African History* (Berkeley and Los Angeles, 1982), pp. 11–38 and 39–56. On the Meroitic period, see P. L. Shinnie, *Meroe: A Civilisation of the Sudan* (London, 1967).

33 T. Krump, *Hoher und Fruchtbarer Palm-Baum des heiligen Evangelj* (1710), quoted in R. S. O'Fahey and J. L. Spaulding, *Kingdoms of the Sudan* (London, 1974), p. 3.

34 D. Anderson and D. Johnson, 'Introduction, ecology and society in northeast African history', D. Johnson and D. Anderson (eds.), *The Ecology of Survival* (London, 1988), p. 20.

35 Quoted in O'Fahey and Spaulding, *Kingdoms of the Sudan*, p. 4.

36 Adams, *Nubia*, pp. 136–7.

37 The significance of Napata is debated, and it is possible that it was a necropolis, not a capital.

38 For which see P. E. Cleator, *Lost Languages* (London, 1973 reprint).

39 Adams, 'The coming of Nubian speakers', pp. 11ff.

40 On this, and Meroe in general, see P. L. Shinnie, 'The Nilotic Sudan and Ethiopia, *c.* 660 BC to AD 600', in *The Cambridge History of Africa*, II: *From c. 500 BC to AD 1050*, ed. J. D. Fage (Cambridge, 1978), pp. 210–59.

41 Strabo, XVII, 1, 53–4. The relevant extract is given in full in Shinnie, 'The Nilotic Sudan', pp. 246–7.

42 Herodotus, IV, 183.
43 Herodotus, IV, 168ff.
44 See, for instance, P. MacKendrick, *The North African Stones Speak* (Chapel Hill, 1980), p. 8.
45 Bowman, *Egypt after the Pharaohs*, pp. 17–19.
46 Cyprus was ruled by the Ptolemies from 312 to 30 BCE, except for 58–48 BCE, Cyrenaica from 322 to 96 BCE, and areas of Asia Minor in the third century BCE (ibid., p. 29).
47 Zoscales is mentioned in *The Periplus of the Erythraean Sea* (trans. G. W. B. Huntingdon, Hakluyt Society, 2nd series, CLI, London, 1980), p. v. The account of Ergamenes in Diodorus Siculus is given *in extenso* in P. L. Shinnie, 'The Nilotic Sudan and Ethiopia', p. 229. See also p. 159 above.
48 His estimate was 252,000 stadia (46, 695 kilometres); the actual figure is 40,008 kilometres (H. Riad with J. Devisse, 'Egypt in the Hellenistic era', in G. Mokhtar (ed.), *General History of Africa*, II (London and Paris, 1981), p. 193).
49 Quoted in Bowman, *Egypt after the Pharaohs*, p. 31.
50 There is an excellent account of the Libyan kingdoms in R. Law, 'North Africa in the Hellenistic and Roman periods, 323 BC to AD 305', in *Cambridge History of Africa*, II, pp. 176ff. Ancient Mauretania lay in northern Morocco and western Algeria, Numidia in eastern Algeria.
51 Diodorus Siculus, III, 53ff. See O. Bates, *The Eastern Libyans: An Essay* (London, 1914), p. 113: 'the very existence of a nation of fighting women and spinning men is in itself an absurdity'.
52 Herodotus, IV, 162. She obtained revenge for her son's death with the help of a Persian army (IV, 200–2; see IV, 205: 'A fitting conclusion to this story is the manner of Pheritima's death . . . she died a horrible death.'
53 In *Cambridge History of Africa*, II, the period between 305 CE (when Chapter 3 ends) and the Arab conquest (when Chapter 8 begins) the history of Egypt and the Maghrib is dealt with exclusively in terms of church history (Ch. 7, W. H. C. Frend, 'The Christian period . . .', pp. 410ff.).
54 For an admirable survey, see R. Law, 'North Africa in the Hellenistic and Roman periods', pp. 191ff.
55 Josephus, *The Jewish War*, II, 383, 386.
56 Tacitus, *Annals*, II, 59, 4.
57 Quoted in Frend, 'The Christian period', p. 423.
58 Bowman, *Egypt after the Pharaohs*, p. 19.
59 Ibid., p. 157.
60 Quoted in ibid., p. 132.
61 Some place this in the reign of Diocletian.
62 There is a magisterial account in W. H. C. Frend, 'The Christian period in Mediterranean Africa *c*. AD 200 to 700', *Cambridge History of Africa*, II, pp. 410ff. See also E. Isichei, *A History of Christianity in Africa from Antiquity to the Present* (London, 1995), pp. 13ff.
63 The see of Jerusalem fell into abeyance when Titus sacked the city in 70; Constantinople was founded in 330 and recognised as the second see of Christendom at councils in 381 and 451.
64 Porphyry, *Life of Plotinus*, I, quoted in Bowman, *Egypt after the Pharaohs*, p. 140.
65 Tertullian, *Apology*, 40.
66 The others were the Armenian church and the Jacobite church in Syria. For a

definitive study of the movement, see W. H. C. Frend, *The Rise of the Monophysite Movement* (Cambridge, 1972).
67 A. Badawy, *Coptic Art and Archaeology* (London, 1978), p. 1.
68 Quoted in ibid., p. 1.
69 Quoted in P. Brown, *Augustine of Hippo: A Biography* (London, 1967), p. 20.
70 T. R. S. Broughton, *The Romanization of Africa Proconsularis* (1929, reprint New York, 1968), p. 6.
71 Ibid., pp. 91ff.
72 W. H. C. Frend, *The Donatist Church* (2nd edn, Oxford, 1971). Both the nationalist and socio-economic aspects of the theory have been much criticised. See A. H. M. Jones, 'Were ancient heresies national or social movements in disguise?', *Journal of Theological Studies*, 1959, pp. 280–98; and Brown, 'Christianity and local culture in the late Roman empire', *Journal of Roman Studies*, 1968, pp. 85ff. For a postscript by Frend, see his 'The Donatist church – forty years on', in C. Landman and D. Whitelaw (eds.), *Windows on Origins* (Pretoria, 1985), pp. 71ff.
73 Optatus of Milevis, quoted in W. H. Frend, *The Rise of Christianity* (London, 1986), pp. 572–3.
74 Augustine, Ep. 185 in Frend, *The Rise of Christianity*, p. 723.
75 Adams, *Nubia*, pp. 433ff. is an exhaustive account.
76 Quoted in ibid., p. 461.

II NORTHERN AFRICA FROM THE SEVENTH CENTURY CE

1 Quoted in M. Brett, 'Arab conquest and the rise of Islam in North Africa', in *Cambridge History of Africa*, II: *From c. 500 to AD 1050*, ed. J. D. Fage, p. 542.
2 Ibn Qunfudh, in the fourteenth century, quoted in J. M. Abun-Nasr, *A History of the Maghrib in the Islamic Period* (Cambridge, 1987), p. 24.
3 M. Brett and W. Forman, *The Moors: Islam in the West* (London, 1980), p. 70. This superbly illustrated book, which also covers al-Andalus, sheds much light on the cultural achievements of Muslims in the Maghrib.
4 Abu Zakariyya, quoted in Abun-Nasr, *History of the Maghrib*, p. 27. (Hadith are Sayings attributed to the Prophet.) A different Hadith called Ifriqiya a gate to hell (E. Savage, 'Berbers and blacks: Ibadi slave traffic in eighth-century North Africa', *Journal of African History*, 1992, p. 356 n. 38).
5 See, for instance, ibn Hawqal, in N. Levtzion and J. F. P. Hopkins, *Corpus of Early Arabic Sources for West African History* (Cambridge, 1981), p. 48.
6 Ibn Abi Zar, in *Corpus*, p. 235.
7 A. K. Bowman, *Egypt after the Pharaohs* (Berkeley, 1986), p. 40.
8 The Egyptian, ibn Abd al-Hakam. My interpretation follows various studies by M. Brett, and especially his 'Arab conquest', pp. 490ff.
9 On this, and the other elements in the equation, see M. Brett, 'The spread of Islam in Egypt and North Africa', in M. Brett (ed.), *Northern Africa: Islam and Modernization* (London, 1973), pp. 2–4.
10 On the relationship between Ancient Libyan and modern Berber, see J. Bynon, 'The contribution of linguistics to history in the field of Berber studies', in D. Dalby (ed.), *Language and History in Africa* (London, 1970), pp. 64ff.
11 For more on Berber social organisation, see pp. 264–5 below.
12 E. Gellner, *Saints of the Atlas* (London, 1969), pp. 16–17.
13 W. Y. Adams, *Nubia: Corridor to Africa* (Princeton, 1977), p. 505.

14 Savage, 'Berbers and blacks', p. 357, nn. 41 and 42.

15 Brett and Forman, *The Moors*, p. 39.

16 Brett, 'Arab conquest', p. 509.

17 Brett and Forman, *The Moors*, p. 18.

18 For an excellent recent survey, see Yann Richard, *Shi'ite Islam: Polity, Ideology and Creed* (Oxford, 1994).

19 Sharifs are those who claim descent from Muhammad.

20 E. Alport, 'The Mzab', in E. Gellner and C. Micaud, *Arabs and Berbers* (London, 1972), pp. 142–3. This represents not Berber patriotism but their self-imposed isolation from the wider society.

21 Brett, 'Arab conquest', p. 551.

22 M. Brett, 'The Fatimid revolution (861–973) and its aftermath in North Africa', *Cambridge History of Africa*, II, p. 595.

23 Savage, 'Berbers and blacks', pp. 353, n. 6, 360.

24 Both wine and olive oil, of course, involved some processing.

25 M. Morsy, *North Africa 1800–1900: A Survey from the Nile Valley to the Atlantic* (Harlow, 1984), p. 45. No date is given for this figure.

26 L. Valensi, *Tunisian Peasants in the Eighteenth and Nineteenth Centuries* (1977, Eng. trans. Cambridge, 1985), p. 158.

27 A. Laroui, *The History of the Maghrib: An Interpretive Essay* (Eng. trans. Princeton, 1977), pp. 123ff. and 144ff. See Brett, 'The Fatimid revolution', pp. 615ff.

28 T. Garrard, 'Myth and metrology: the early trans-Saharan gold trade', *Journal of African History*, 1982, pp. 446–7.

29 R. Austen, *African Economic History* (London, 1987), p. 36.

30 R. Le Tourneau, *Fez in the Age of the Marinides* (Norman, Okla., 1961), pp. 137–9.

31 Le Tourneau, *Fez in the Age of the Marinides*, p. 8.

32 Quoted in P. Brown, *Augustine of Hippo* (London, 1967), p. 190.

33 H. Z. Hirschberg, 'The problem of the Judaised Berbers', *Journal of African History*, 1963, p. 323.

34 N. R. Keddie, 'Introduction: deciphering Middle Eastern women's history', in N. R. Keddie and B. Baron (eds.), *Women in Middle Eastern History: Shifting Boundaries in Sex and Gender* (New Haven and London, 1991), pp. 1–2.

35 H. Lutfi, 'Manners and customs of fourteenth-century Cairene women', in Keddie and Baron, *Women in Middle Eastern History*, pp. 101–2.

36 Ibid., pp. 101, 119.

37 Ibid., pp. 105, 116–17.

38 H. T. Norris, 'Znaga Islam during the seventeenth and eighteenth centuries', *Bulletin of SOAS*, 1969, p. 497, re the mother of Al Fahga Musa.

39 Quoted in Valensi, *Tunisian Peasants*, p. 166.

40 Ibid., pp. 152–7; the Hamama, whose men made rugs on a commercial scale, were an exception.

41 Ibn Iyas, quoted in C. Petry, 'Class solidarity versus gender gain: women as custodians of property in later medieval Egypt', in Keddie and Baron, *Women in Middle Eastern History*, p. 12.

42 Petry, 'Women as custodians of property', pp. 131–2.

43 Brett, 'Fatimid revolution', p. 590. These sources were not independent, and Brett calls the figures unreliable.

44 Brett, 'Arab conquest', p. 550.
45 Savage, 'Berbers and blacks', p. 355. 'Zanj' originally referred to slaves from East Africa; it seems likely that some came from other parts of sub-Saharan Africa.
46 Adams, *Nubia*, pp. 551ff.
47 Ibid., p. 553.
48 There was initially a ban on Muslims owning land, to ensure their availability for the army; this soon came to an end (M. Brett, personal communication).
49 I. M. Lapidus, *A History of Islamic Societies* (Cambridge, 1993 reprint), p. 345.
50 Alfred Bel, cited in C. Geertz, *Islam Observed: Religious Development in Morocco and Indonesia* (New Haven and London, 1968), p. 46.
51 Geertz, *Islam Observed*, p. 5.
52 See Brett, 'Fatimid revolution', pp. 589ff.
53 R. le Tourneau, *The Almohad Movement in North Africa in the Twelfth and Thirteenth Centuries* (Princeton, 1969), p. 45.
54 See p. 268 below.
55 M. Brett, 'Ibn Khaldun and the Arabisation of North Africa', *The Maghrib Review*, 1979, pp. 12–13.
56 E. W. Bovill, *The Golden Trade of the Moors* (2nd edn, London, 1968), p. 5.
57 J. Poncet, 'Le mythe de la "catastrophe" hilalienne', *Annales: économies, sociétés, civilisations*, 1967, pp. 1099–1120; there is a rejoinder in H. R. Idris, 'De la réalité de la catastrophe hilalienne', *Annales*, 1968, pp. 390–4.
58 Valensi, *Tunisian Peasants*, pp. 140–1.
59 Brett, 'Ibn Khaldun', p. 13.
60 Al-Yaqubi, in *Corpus*, p. 22. It is unlikely that this desert aristocrat lived in Awdaghust.
61 Ibn Hawqal, in *Corpus*, pp. 49–50.
62 H. Fisher stresses the role of clerics and also of Sharifs ('The eastern Maghrib and the Central Sudan', *Cambridge History of Africa*, III, pp. 312ff.).
63 M. Brett, 'Islam and trade in the Bilad al-Sudan', *Journal of African History*, 1983, pp. 431ff. See p. 178 above.
64 Al-Muhallabi, in a lost work cited in Yaqut, in *Corpus*, p. 168.
65 Al-Bakri, in *Corpus*, p. 70; also Ibn Abi Zar (d. 1315), in *Corpus*, p. 238.
66 See p. 306 below.
67 Al-Bakri, in *Corpus*, p. 241.
68 Some later sources refer to an island, and considerable efforts have been made to identify it; it now seems more likely that he returned to his own teacher in the Atlas mountains. See H. Fisher, 'What's in a name? The Almoravids of the eleventh century in the western Sahara', *Journal of Religion in Africa*, 1992, pp. 291ff. There is a large body of literature on the Almoravid movement; see N. Levtzion, ''Abd Allah b. Yasin and the Almoravids', in J. R. Willis (ed.), *Studies in West African Islamic History* I: *The Cultivators of Islam* (London, 1979), pp. 78ff.; D. Conrad and H. Fisher, 'The conquest that never was: Ghana and the Almoravids, 1076', *History in Africa*, 1982, pp. 21ff. and 1983, pp. 53ff.; S. Burckhalter, 'Listening for silences in Almoravid history: another reading of 'The conquest that never was', *History in Africa*, 1992, pp. 103ff.
69 Fisher, 'What's in a name?' pp. 303ff.; an alternative translation is 'holy war'. See *Corpus*, p. 70 and elsewhere.
70 The Andalusian al-Bakri (d. 1094), in *Corpus*, pp. 73, 77.
71 Al-Bakri; al-Zuhri, in *Corpus*, p. 99.

72 Ibn al-Athir (1160–1233), in *Corpus*, p. 160.

73 Ibn Abi Zar, in *Corpus*, p. 243.

74 Conrad and Fisher, 'The conquest that never was', pp. 53ff.; their conclusions are not universally accepted. See for instance D. Lange, 'Les rois de Gao-Sané et les Almoravides', *Journal of African History*, 1991, p. 251 n. 3.

75 Burckhalter, 'Listening for silences', pp. 103ff.

76 Al-Zuhri, in *Corpus*, p. 99.

77 Yaqut, in *Corpus*, pp. 170–1.

78 N. Levtzion, 'The Sahara and the Sudan from the Arab conquest', *Cambridge History of Africa*, II, p. 664.

79 Al-Bakri, in *Corpus*, p. 70.

80 Lange, 'Les rois de Gao-Sané', p. 252.

81 Conrad and Fisher, 'The conquest that never was', p. 45.

82 N. Levtzion, 'The western Maghrib and Sudan', in *Cambridge History of Africa*, III: *From c. 1050 to c. 1600*, ed. R. Oliver, p. 336.

83 Al-Idrisi (*c.* 1154), in *Corpus*, p. 128.

84 On the Almohads, see le Tourneau, *The Almohad Movement*.

85 Whether he was a sufi himself is debatable; like many other *turuq*, the Qadiriyya (see pp. 293–4 below) seems to have developed centuries after the life of its founder. See A. J. Arberry, 'Mysticism', in P. Holt et al. (eds.), *The Cambridge History of Islam*, II, p. 621 and R. Jenkins, 'The evolution of religious brotherhoods in North and northwest Africa', in Willis (ed.), *The Cultivators of Islam*, p. 47.

86 Le Tourneau, *The Almohad Movement*, pp. 28–9.

87 Levtzion, 'The western Maghrib and Sudan', p. 344.

88 A. MacKay, *Spain in the Middle Ages: From Frontier to Empire 1000–1500* (London, 1977), pp. 83–5.

89 Al-Nasiri (1835–97), extract in T. Hodgkin, *Nigerian Perspectives* (2nd edn, London, 1975), p. 93; there is a contemporary reference in Yaqut (1179–1229), in *Corpus*, p. 173. Abu Ishaq lived at Marrakesh in the reign of Abu Yusuf al-Mansur (1184–99). Averroes died at Marrakesh in 1198.

90 Le Tourneau, *The Almohad Movement*, p. 77.

91 For contrasting views, see Levtzion, 'The western Maghrib and Sudan', p. 346 and Jenkins, 'The evolution of religious brotherhoods', p. 44.

92 The title of a well-known book by E. Gellner. For more on this, see pp. 264–5 below.

93 Boumédienne was the head of independent Algeria from 1965 until his death in 1978; he was succeeded by Chedli Boudjedid.

94 F. Braudel, *The Mediterranean and the Mediterranean World in the Age of Philip II* (Eng. trans. New York, 1972), I, p. 96.

95 Ibid., I, p. 97.

96 R. Irwin, *The Middle East in the Middle Ages: The Early Mamluk Sultanate 1250–1382* (Carbondale, 1986), p. 2.

97 This picture has, however, been questioned; see the biography by A. Ehrenkreuz, *Saladin* (Albany, 1972), which is much more critical of Saladin, and considers the idealised portrait the work of Muslim propaganda.

98 Fisher, 'The eastern Maghrib', p. 269.

99 Levtzion, 'The western Maghrib and Sudan', p. 338.

100 Ibid., p. 364.

101 See Irwin, *The Middle East in the Middle Ages*, for the account which follows.
102 In the Muslim sources of the period, 'Slav' refers to Europeans in general from north of the Pyrenees. See p. 188 above.
103 J. L. Angel, 'Ecology and population in the eastern Mediterranean', *World Archaeology*, 1972, p. 91.
104 On the impact of the Black Death, see I. Hrbek, 'Egypt, Nubia and the eastern deserts', *Cambridge History of Africa*, III, p. 53.
105 Quoted in Adams, *Nubia*, p. 508.
106 Ibid., p 521.
107 Ibid., p. 539.
108 B. Rosenberger and H. Triki, 'Famines et épidémies au Maroc aux xvie et xviie siècles', *Hesperis-Tamuda*, 1973/4, p. 113.
109 Al-Qairawani on Morocco, cited in ibid., p. 113.
110 See p. 264 below.

12   THE NORTH-EAST

1 J. Gold (ed.), *A Voyage to Abyssinia* (trans. Samuel Johnson, New Haven and London, 1985), p. 40.
2 Particularly welcome beginnings in overcoming the traditional dichotomy between the history of Ethiopia and the rest of north-east Africa are to be found in two recent books: D. Johnson and D. Anderson (eds.), *The Ecology of Survival: Case Studies from Northeast African History* (London and Colorado, 1988) and D. Donham and W. James, *The Southern Marches of Imperial Ethiopia: Essays in History and Social Anthropology* (Cambridge, 1986).
3 D. Crummey, 'Abyssinian feudalism', *Past and Present*, 1980, pp. 115–38. See also D. Donham, 'Old Abyssinia and the new Ethiopian empire: themes in social history', in Donham and James, *The Southern Marches of Ethiopia*, pp. 3–50.
4 Seneca, *Naturales quaestiones*, 6, 8, quoted here from the translation in M. Cary and E. H. Warmington, *Ancient Explorers* (London, 1963), p. 211.
5 C. Hallpike, quoted in D. Levine, *Greater Ethiopia: The Evolution of a Multiethnic Society* (Chicago, 1974), p. 178.
6 M. L. Bender (ed.), *The Non-Semitic Languages of Ethiopia* (East Lansing, 1976), pp. 12, 13 and 304; see p. 7 for 'Beja'.
7 W. James, 'Lifelines: exchange marriage among the Gumuz', in Donham and James, *The Southern Marches of Ethiopia*, p. 119.
8 Donham, 'Old Abyssinia', pp. 12–13. This chapter is greatly indebted to this seminal essay.
9 L. Cassanelli, *The Shaping of Somali Society: Reconstructing the History of a Pastoral People 1600–1900* (Philadelphia, 1982), pp. 15–16. The account of Somalia which follows is based on this excellent study.
10 Including Ethiopia's occupation of the Ogaden.
11 Extract in G. S. P. Freeman-Grenville, *The East African Coast: Select Documents* (Oxford, 1962), p. 6.
12 Extract in Freeman-Grenville, *Documents*, n.p. but p. 8.
13 This quotation cannot be identified with the ancestors of any modern people (Cassanelli, *The Shaping of Somali Society*, p. 11: 'Somalis have not been known in recent times to drink the blood of their cattle'). But see H. Lewis, 'The origins of the Galla and Somali', *Journal of African History*, 1966, p. 30 n. 11, to the effect that the practice is found among some Somali and Oromo.

14 H. S. Lewis, 'The origins', p. 39. M. Bender, 'The languages of Ethiopia: a new lexico-statistical classification and some problems of diffusion', *Anthropological Linguistics*, 1971, pp. 184ff.

15 R. Bulliet, *The Camel and the Wheel* (Cambridge, Mass., 1975), pp. 39–42.

16 D. Johnson, quoted in Cassanelli, *The Shaping of Somali Society*, p. 83.

17 B. Lynch and L. Robbins, 'Cushitic and Nilotic prehistory: new archaeological evidence from north-west Kenya', *Journal of African History*, 1979, pp. 320–3.

18 T. Tamrat, 'Ethiopia, the Red Sea and the Horn', *Cambridge History of Africa*, III: *From c. 1050 to c. 1600*, ed. R. Oliver (1977), p. 156. The way in which these sultanates are analysed in terms of their relationship to the Christian kingdom is a good example of an 'Ethiopianist' viewpoint.

19 Ibid., p. 142.

20 I. Lewis, *Peoples of the Horn of Africa* (London, 1969 reprint), p. 135. For a sympathetic account, with grim details, see J. Boddy, 'Womb as oasis: the symbolic context of Pharaonic circumcision in rural Northern Sudan', *American Ethnologist*, 1982, pp. 682ff.

21 I. Lewis, *Ecstatic Religion* (Harmondsworth, 1971). See especially pp. 72–8.

22 J. Boddy, *Wombs and Alien Spirits: Women and the Zar Cult in Northern Sudan* (Madison, 1989).

23 The concentration on Ethiosemitic peoples is evident in E. Ullendorff, *The Ethiopians* (London, 1960); for a wider perspective, see Levine, *Greater Ethiopia*.

24 As is pointed out by Tamrat, 'Ethiopia, the Red Sea', pp. 127–8, citing the research of H. Fleming and M. Bender.

25 T. Tamrat, 'Processes of ethnic interaction and integration in Ethiopian history: the case of the Agaw', *Journal of African History*, 1988, p. 8.

26 Y. M. Kobishanov, 'Aksum: political system, economics and culture, first to fourth century', in G. Mokhtar, *General History of Africa*, II: *Ancient Civilisations of Africa* (London, 1981), pp. 398–9.

27 M. Bender, 'The languages of Ethiopia', p. 217. Other authorities suggest sixty. Statistics of this kind are unsatisfactory, as much depends on whether the speech of a given people is considered a separate language, part of a language cluster, or a dialect.

28 A. Zaborski, 'Cushitic overview', in M. Bender, *Non-Semitic Languages*, p. 82. For the numbers of speakers of different languages, see Bender, pp. 5ff., 'Brief directory of Ethiopian languages'.

29 H. Fleming, 'Omotic overview', in Bender, *Non-Semitic Languages*, p. 357.

30 Bender, 'The languages of Ethiopia', p. 182.

31 Bender, cited by Levine, *Greater Ethiopia*, p. 72.

32 Bender, 'The languages of Ethiopia', pp. 179–82. This is a good example of the lack of appropriate terminology for religions other than Christianity and Islam. Christianity is extremely 'traditional' in Tigre and Amhara.

33 Levine, *Greater Ethiopia*, p. 29.

34 S. Kaplan, 'Ezana's conversion reconsidered', *Journal of Religion in Africa*, 1982, pp. 101–9.

35 Ibid., p. 102. See pp. 85–6 above.

36 J. Goody, *Technology, Tradition and the State in Africa* (Oxford, 1971) and *Production and Reproduction: A Comparative Study of the Domestic Terrain* (Cambridge, 1976). Ethiopianists refer to the framework of his analysis but dispute his specific interpretation of Ethiopia (Donham, 'Old Abyssinia',

p. 251, n. 8). I. Wallerstein and P. Curtin are also writers on Africa with a global perspective.
37 Donham, 'Old Abyssinia,' pp. 4ff.; see also D. Crummey, 'Abyssinian feudalism', pp. 115–38 and the various works of Jack Goody, including *Technology, Tradition and the State in Africa*.
38 Levine, *Greater Ethiopia*, p. 54. He also cites Kefa, Konso and Gurage examples.
39 Quoted in Donham, 'Old Abyssinia', pp. 14–15.
40 D. Anderson and D. Johnson, 'Introduction: ecology and society in northeast African history', and J. McCann, 'History, drought and reproduction: dynamics of society and ecology in northeast Ethiopia', in Johnson and Anderson, *The Ecology of Survival*, pp. 19 and 286.
41 Anderson and Johnson, 'Introduction', p. 21.
42 See D. Crummey, 'Banditry and resistance: noble and peasant in nineteenth century Ethiopia' and T. Fernhough, 'Social mobility and dissident elites in northern Ethiopia: the role of banditry, 1900–69', in D. Crummey (ed.), *Banditry, Rebellion and Social Protest in Africa* (London, 1986), pp. 133ff. and 151ff.
43 Tamrat, 'Ethiopia, the Red Sea', pp. 102–3.
44 The manifestations of this are listed in E. Ullendorff, 'Hebraic–Jewish elements in Abyssinian (Monophysite) Christianity', *Journal of Semitic Studies*, 1955, pp. 216–15.
45 J. Iliffe, *The African Poor: A History* (Cambridge, 1987), p. 10. His chapter on 'Christian Ethiopia', reflecting a breadth of reading extraordinary in a general text, is a notable chapter in a remarkable book.
46 Quoted in ibid., p. 15.
47 Tewodros, quoted in ibid., p. 15.
48 Quoted in ibid., p. 28.
49 This account is based on J. Quirin, 'The process of caste formation in Ethiopia: a study of the Beta Israel (Felasha), 1270–1868', *International Journal of African Historical Studies*, 1979, pp. 235–58.
50 W. Shack, 'Notes on occupational castes among the Gurage of south-west Ethiopia', *Man*, 1964, pp. 50–2; C. Hallpike, 'The status of craftsmen among the Konso of south-west Ethiopia', *Africa*, 1968, pp. 258–69.
51 Camera Laye, *The Dark Child* (Eng. trans. London, 1955); P. McNaughton, *The Mande Blacksmiths: Knowledge, Power and Art in West Africa* (Bloomington and Indianapolis, 1988). (McNaughton is an American who apprenticed himself to a Mande smith.)
52 Dinka song, quoted in F. M. Deng, 'Development in context', in M. Daly (ed.), *Modernization in the Sudan* (New York, 1985), p. 148.
53 A. Southall, 'Nuer and Dinka are people: ecology, ethnicity and logical possibility', *Man*, 1976, p. 489 n. 10.
54 Atuot appears to be a dialect of Nuer.
55 E. E. Evans-Pritchard, *The Nuer: A Description of the Modes of Livelihood and Political Institutions of a Nilotic People* (Oxford, 1940), p. 126.
56 C. Ehret, 'Population movement and culture contact in the southern Sudan, *c.* 3000 BC to AD 1000: a preliminary linguistic overview', in J. Mack and P. Robertshaw (eds.), *Culture History in the Southern Sudan* (Nairobi, 1982), p. 27. The earlier date refers to the separation of the divergent Burun languages. He does not give a date for the (relatively recent) separation of Nuer and Dinka.

57 S. Baker, 'The races of the Nile basin', *Transactions of the Ethnological Society of London*, 1867, pp. 228–39.

58 Evans-Pritchard, quoted in Southall, 'The Nuer and Dinka are people', p. 463. The historical study of these peoples has been pioneered in a number of important papers by Douglas Johnston; they concentrate, however, on the nineteenth and twentieth centuries. See his, 'The fighting Nuer: primary sources and the origins of a stereotype', *Africa*, 1981, pp. 508–27; also R. Kelly, *The Nuer Conquest* (Ann Arbor, 1985).

59 See J. Burton, ' "The wave is my mother's husband": a piscatorial theme in pastoral Nilotic ethnology', *Cahiers d'études africaines*, 1982, pp. 459–77. As Burton points out (p. 465), Evans-Pritchard makes a passing reference to the centrality of fish in the diet.

60 Burton, 'The wave', p. 472.

61 P. Robertshaw, 'Prehistory in the upper Nile basin', *Journal of African History*, 1987, pp. 182ff.

62 P. Newcomer, 'The Nuer are Dinka: an essay on origins and environmental determinism', *Man*, 1972, pp. 5–11; Southall, 'The Nuer and Dinka are people', pp. 463–91; Kelly, *The Nuer Conquest*.

63 M. Sahlins, 'The segmentary lineage: an organisation of predatory expansion', *American Anthropologist*, 1961, pp. 322–44.

64 For a discussion of this, in the Berber/Arabised Berber context in the Maghrib, see pp. 264–5 below.

65 D. Johnson, 'On the Nilotic frontier: imperial Ethiopia in the southern Sudan, 1898–1936', in Donham and James, *The Southern Marches of Ethiopia*, p. 244. This quotation reverses his original order.

66 Southall, 'Nuer and Dinka are people', pp. 466–7.

67 The main source for what follows is G. Lienhardt, 'Getting your own back: themes in Nilotic myth', in J. Beattie and G. Lienhardt (eds.), *Studies in Social Anthropology* (Oxford, 1975), pp. 213ff.

68 These interpretations come from Lienhardt, 'Getting your own back', pp. 226ff.

69 A. Southall, *Alur Society: A Study in Processes and Types of Domination* (Cambridge, 1956), p. 359. As this example makes clear, the names of the brothers vary with the ethnic contexts, but one always bears some relation to 'Nyikang'.

70 Quoted in Lienhardt, 'Getting your own back', p. 221 n. 15.

71 J. Lamphear, 'The People of the Grey Bull: the origin and expansion of the Turkana', *Journal of African History*, 1988, pp. 27–39; T. Beidelman, 'Myth, legend and oral history: a Kaguru traditional text', *Anthropos*, 1970, pp. 74ff.

72 J. Janzen, *Lemba, 1650–1930: A Drum of Affliction in Africa and the New World* (New York, 1982), pp. 210–19. Janzen's exegesis is on completely different lines, which we cannot explore here.

13 THE WESTERN SUDAN

1 *Infaq al-Maysur*, trans. F. J. Arnett as *The Rise of the Sokoto Fulani* (Kano, 1922), p. 10.

2 S. K. and R. J. McIntosh, 'West African prehistory', *American Scientist* 1981, pp. 602–13.

3 G. Brooks, 'Ecological perspectives on Mande population movements, commercial networks, and settlement patterns from the Atlantic wet phase (ca. 5500–2500 BC) to the present', *History in Africa* 1989, pp. 30ff.

4 See M. Last, 'The early kingdoms of the Nigerian savanna', in J. F. A. Ajayi and M. Crowder, *History of West Africa* I (3rd edn, Harlow, 1985), p. 212.

5 N. Levtzion, 'North-west Africa: from the Maghrib to the fringes of the forest', *Cambridge History of Africa* IV: *From c. 1600 to c. 1790*, ed. R. Gray (1977), p. 167.

6 Al-Hajj Umar, quoted in B. G. Martin, *Muslim Brotherhoods in Nineteenth-Century Africa* (Cambridge, 1976), p. 74.

7 R. Bulliet, *The Camel and the Wheel* (Cambridge, Mass., 1975), p. 9; my account of the camel is based on this fascinating study.

8 In a lost work by al-Fazari (N. Levtzion and J. F. P. Hopkins, *Corpus of Early Arabic Sources for West African History* (Cambridge, 1981), p. 32).

9 See p. 63 above.

10 P. J. Munson, 'Archaeology and the prehistoric origins of the Ghana empire', *Journal of African History* 1980, pp. 457–66; also his 'Archaeological data on the origins of cultivation in the southwestern Sahara and their implications for West Africa', in J. Harlan et. al, *Origins of African Plant Domestication* (The Hague, 1976), pp. 187ff. His work has been very widely cited, though there are suggestions that later researchers in the area have questioned the precision of his successive phases.

11 R. McIntosh, 'The pulse model: genesis and accommodation of specialization in the middle Niger', *Journal of African History*, 1993, pp. 181ff.

12 Al-Sa'di, *Tarikh al-Sudan*, cited in N. Levtzion, 'The early states of the Western Sudan to 1500', in Ajayi and Crowder, *History of West Africa*, I, p. 149.

13 Al-Sadi, *Tarikh al-Sudan*, quoted in N. Levtzion, *Ancient Ghana and Mali* (London, 1973), pp. 156–7.

14 S. K. McIntosh and R. J. McIntosh, 'Current directions in West African prehistory', *Annual Review of Anthropology*, 1983, pp. 245–9. On dating, cf. M. Hill, 'Dating of Senegambian megaliths: a correction', *Current Anthropology*, 1978, pp. 604–5.

15 *Corpus*, pp. 80–1.

16 See p. 46 above.

17 M. Last, 'Before Zaria: evidence for Kankuma (Kangoma and its successor states)', in A. Mahadi (ed.), *Facts, Values and Nigerian Historiography* (Zaria 1980), pp. 157ff.; this is much more satisfactory than his highly speculative 'Early kingdoms'.

18 Last, 'Early kingdoms', pp. 200–1, suggests various identifications.

19 E. F. Wilson, 'More about the Bassas', *Western Equatorial Africa Diocesan Magazine*, 1898, p. 29. There is, of course, no reason to accept this dating.

20 Al-Hamdani, in *Corpus*, p. 29.

21 R. Dumett, 'Precolonial gold mining and the state in the Akan religion: with a critique of the Terray hypothesis', *Research in Economic Anthropology*, 1979, p. 43.

22 Duarte Pacheco Pereira, *Esmeraldo de situ oribis* (Hakluyt, 2nd series, LXXIX, 1937), p. 89. On the market town of Bitu or Beghu, see pp. 256–7 below. He adds exotic details about silent trade and dog-featured inhabitants, which may have been part of Dyula propaganda to discourage potential trade rivals. He lists two other towns, which have not been certainly identified.

23 Ivor Wilks, 'The Mossi and the Akan states, 1400 to 1800', in Ajayi and Crowder, *History of West Africa*, I, p. 480.

24 C. Meillassoux, 'The role of slavery in the economic and social history of

Sahelo-Sudanic Africa', in J. Inikori, *Forced Migrations* (London, 1982), pp. 80–1.

25 See p. 329 below. R. Austen, *African Economic History* (London, 1987), p. 36. Cf. his earlier paper, 'The trans-Saharan slave trade: a tentative census', in H. Gemery and J. Hogendorn, *The Uncommon Market: Essays in the Economic History of the Atlantic Slave Trade* (New York, 1979), pp. 23–76.

26 *Corpus*, p. 303.

27 Al-Sa'di, *Tarikh al-Sudan* (c. 1655), extract in N. Levtzion, *Ancient Ghana and Mali* (London, 1973), p. 157.

28 C. Meillassoux, 'The role of slavery', p. 83.

29 E. A. McDougall, 'Salts of the western Sahara: myths, mysteries, and historical significance', *The International Journal of African Historical Studies*, 1990, p. 242.

30 B. Barry, 'The subordination of power and the mercantile economy', in R. Cruise O'Brien (ed.), *The Political Economy of Underdevelopment: Dependence in Senegal* (Beverly Hills, 1979), p. 43.

31 P. Lovejoy and S. Baier, 'The desert-side economy of the central Sudan', *The International Journal of African Historical Studies*, 1975, pp. 555–6.

32 'Leo Africanus' (al-Hassan ibn Muhammad), *The History and Description of Africa* (trans. John Pory, 1600, Hakluyt, 1st series, XCIV, 1896), III, p. 833.

33 *Infaq al-Maysur*, p. 3.

34 Al-Sa'di, *Tarikh al-Sudan*, quoted in Levtzion, *Ancient Ghana and Mali*, p. 157.

35 See p. 189 above. Al-Umari (d. 1349), in *Corpus*, p. 260; also p. 462.

36 B. Barkindo, 'The early states of the Central Sudan', in Ajayi and Crowder, *History of West Africa*, I, p. 230, citing a study by T. Lewicki.

37 J. Hunwick, 'Al-Mahili and the Jews of Tuwat; the demise of a community', *Studia Islamica*, 1985, pp. 155ff.

38 N. Levtzion, 'The eighteenth century background to the Islamic revolutions in West Africa', in N. Levtzion and J. Voll, *Eighteenth Century Renewal and Reform in Islam* (Syracuse, N.Y., 1987), p. 21.

39 Malal is widely thought to be Mali or another Mande state, but one source places it near Kanem. Al-Ya'qubi (d. 897, *Corpus*, p. 21 and n. 2): 'another kingdom called Malal, who hate the king of Kanim. Their king is called MYWSY [Mai?].' The Italian writer Anania, in 1571, places 'Mele' in Mandara, that is, south of Borno.

40 Al-Shammakhi (d. 1522) in a compilation of earlier sources (*Corpus*, pp. 368–9). There is no way of knowing whether the incident described by al-Bakri is the same, but it seems unlikely.

41 This is explored, in a different context, in R. O'Fahey, 'Fur and Fartit: the history of a frontier', in J. Mack and P. Robertshaw (eds.), *Culture History in the Southern Sudan* (Nairobi, 1982), pp. 75–89.

42 Ibid., p. 75.

43 *Akhbar al-zaman* (c. 1000), in *Corpus*, p. 37 and p. 380 n. 11.

44 Al-Umari, in *Corpus*, p. 262.

45 J. H. Greenberg, *The Influence of Islam on a Sudanese Religion* (New York, 1946); G. Dieterlen, *Essai sur la religion Bambara* (Paris, 1951); D. Zahan, *Sociétés d'initiation Bambara* (Paris, 1960).

46 D. Conrad, 'Islam in the oral traditions of Mali: Bilali and Surakata', *Journal of African History*, 1985, pp. 36–9.

47 Ibn Said, in *Corpus*, p. 188.

48 H. T. Morris, *Saharan Myth and Saga* (Oxford, 1972), pp. 26ff.

49 *Infaq al-Maysur*, p. 9. Dhu al-Qarnayn is thought to be Alexander the Great. See *Qur'an*, 18: 95ff. and 22:96.

50 *Ifaq al-Maysur*, p. 16.

51 P. Stevens, 'The Kisra legend and the distortion of historical tradition', *Journal of African History*, 1975, pp. 185–200.

52 For an exhaustive survey of the evidence (including archaeological and linguistic), see R. Law, *The Horse in West African History* (London, 1980), pp. 1ff.

53 'The Kano Chronicle', in H. R. Palmer, *Sudanese Memoirs* (one-vol. edn, London, 1967), p. 107. The role of firearms is discussed later in this study.

54 Brooks, 'Ecological perspectives', p. 32; C. Bird, 'The development of Mandekan', in D. Dalby (ed.), *Language and History in Africa* (London, 1970), pp. 146ff.

55 R. L. Roberts, *Warriors Merchants and Slaves: The State and the Economy in the Middle Niger Valley, 1700–1914* (Stanford, 1987), p. 7. He adopts the more accurate but less familiar FulBe and Maraka for Fulbe and Marka. Pulo is the singular of Fulbe, but is not used in this study in the interests of clarity.

56 *Infaq al-Maysur*, p. 10.

57 *Corpus*, p. 78 and p. 386 n. 36. Levtzion believes the Zafun were Soninke.

58 Al-Bakri, in *Corpus*, pp. 79–81 and for what follows.

59 Ibn Khaldun, in *Corpus*, p. 333.

60 See p. 187 above.

61 Al-Idrisi, in a work completed in 1154; *Corpus*, p. 120.

62 Levtzion, *Ancient Ghana and Mali*, p. 59.

63 There are a number of published versions of these epics. The most accessible – albeit a popular one – is D. T. Niane, *Sundiata: An Epic of Old Mali* (London, 1965).

64 C. Bird and M. Kendall, 'The Mande hero, text and context', in I. Karp and C. Bird (eds.), *Explorations in African Systems of Thought* (Washington, 1987), pp. 13–26.

65 Levtzion, *Ancient Ghana and Mali*, p. 58.

66 *Corpus*, pp. 294–5. Significantly, the coup did not seek to gain her the throne, but was on behalf of a male candidate.

67 Valentim Fernandes, quoted in P. Lovejoy, *Transformations in Slavery* (Cambridge, 1983), p. 32.

68 P. Curtin, 'The lure of Bambuk gold', *Journal of African History*, 1973, pp. 628–30. There were more women in a team than men, so individual women obtained less than their male counterparts. On Akan gold mining, see pp. 344–5 below.

69 *Corpus*, p. 282.

70 See Levtzion, 'North-west Africa', p. 182.

71 P. Lovejoy, 'The internal trade of West Africa to 1800', in Ajayi and Crowder, *History of West Africa*, I, pp. 667–8.

72 As is Kanem ('Zaghawa'); al-Khuwarizmi (d. after 846–7), in *Corpus*, p. 7.

73 Al-Yaqubi, in a work completed in 889–90, *Corpus*, p. 21.

74 Al-Bakri, in *Corpus*, p 87.

75 He kept Ramadan, however, and his 'pagan' image was partly created during the reign of Askia Muhammad, to justify his own regime.

76 J. Hunwick, 'Songhay, Borno and the Hausa states, 1450–1600', in Ajayi and Crowder, *History of West Africa*, I, p. 368; this account, and that by Levtzion in the same volume, are the main sources for my account of Songhai.

77 Al-Sadi, *Tarikh al-Sudan*, in Hunwick, 'Songhay, Borno', p. 368.

78 J. R. Willis, 'The western Sudan from the Moroccan invasion . . .', in Ajayi and Crowder, *History of West Africa*, I, pp. 558ff and 565ff.

79 D. Robinson, 'The Islamic revolution of Futa Toro', *International Journal of African Historical Studies*, 1975, p. 185.

80 Tukulor proverb, referring to highland and flood-plain cultivation, quoted in D. Robinson, *Chiefs and Clerics* (Oxford, 1975), p. 1.

81 P. D. Curtin, *Economic Change in Precolonial Africa: Senegambia in the Era of the Slave Trade* (Madison, 1975), pp. 17–18.

82 Ibn Said, in *Corpus*, p. 184.

83 Levtzion, *Ancient Ghana and Mali*, p. 149.

84 Valentim Fernandes, quoted in Levtzion, *Ancient Ghana and Mali*, p. 95.

85 L. G. Colvin, 'Islam and the state of Kajoor: a case of successful resistance to jihad', *Journal of African History*, 1974, p. 592. Some sources suggest the twelfth century. These later traditions are not necessarily, of course, objectively true. They shed light on later Wolof perceptions of their own past. Spelling is a particular problem in dealing with francophone Africa; French books – and many English ones, mirroring their usage – call him Ndiadian N'Diaye.

86 J. Webb, 'The horse and slave trade between the western Sahara and the Senegambia', *Journal of African History*, 1993, pp. 221ff.

87 M. Klein, 'Social and economic factors in the Muslim revolution in Senegambia', *Journal of African History*, 1972, p. 421.

88 Ibn al-Mukhtar, *Tarikh al-Fattash* (*c.* 1665), quoted in Levtzion, *Ancient Ghana and Mali*, p. 165.

89 R. Jobson, *The Golden Trade* (London, 1623), p. 116.

90 Ibid., pp. 97–9.

91 Fernandes (1506–10), quoted in Levtzion, *Ancient Ghana and Mali*, p. 165.

92 L. Sanneh, 'The origins of clericalism in West African Islam', *Journal of African History*, 1976, pp. 59–68; the quotation, from ibn al-Mukhtar, *Tarikh al-Fattash*, is on p. 68.

93 This paragraph is based on Sanneh, 'The origins of clericalism', pp. 49ff.

94 Ibn Hawqal, in *Corpus*, p. 44.

95 On which see P. de Farias, 'Silent trade: myth and historical evidence', *History in Africa*, 1974, pp. 9–24. One of the commonest of these myths, that gold grew in the ground like carrots, cannot have served this function.

96 Levtzion, 'North-west Africa', p. 194.

97 Wilks, 'The Mossi and the Akan states', p. 466. This is the source for the account which follows.

98 J. Goody, *Technology, Tradition and the State in Africa* (London, 1971), pp. 57ff.

99 Meillassoux, 'The role of slavery', pp. 79–80.

100 I. Wilks, 'Wangara, Akan and Portuguese in the fifteenth and sixteenth centuries. II The struggle for trade', *Journal of African History*, 1982, pp. 468–70.

101 Goody, *Technology, Tradition*, pp. 57ff.

102 O. Davies, quoted in Wilks, 'Land, labour', p. 519.

103 This seems to have been the culmination of a process which began in the first

half of the thirteenth century. See D. Lange, 'L'éviction des Sefuwa du Kanem et l'origine des Bulala', *Journal of African History*, 1982, pp. 315–32.

104 Al-Yaqubi, in *Corpus*, p. 21.

105 Ibid. Al-Masudi (d. 956) lists Kanem and the Zaghawa as having separate kings and capitals (*Corpus*, p. 31). This may be an error or may reflect political complexity.

106 A lost work by al-Muhallabi (late tenth century), extract in Yaqut, in *Corpus*, p. 171.

107 Al-Umari (1301–49), in *Corpus*, pp. 260–1.

108 *Kano Chronicle*, in Palmer, *Sudanese Memoirs*, p. 82.

109 Quoted in A. Smith, 'The early states of the Central Sudan', in Ajayi and Crowder, *History of West Africa*, I (2nd edn), p. 173. Although replaced in the 3rd edition of this book, this study is of enduring value.

110 A letter of 1391/2 in al-Qalqashandi, in *Corpus*, p. 347. The Shuwa Arabs are among the modern descendants of these migrants.

111 Lange, 'L'éviction des Sefuwa', p. 327.

112 D. Lange, 'Préliminaires pour une histoire des Sao', *Journal of African History*, 1989, pp. 189–210.

113 Ahmad ibn Fartuwa, *History of the First Twelve Years of the Reign of Mai Idrisa Alooma of Bornu* (trans. H. R. Palmer, London 1970 reprint), pp. 45–6.

114 For more detail on this, see E. Isichei, *A History of Nigeria* (Harlow, 1983), p. 156.

115 S. Maceachern, 'Selling the iron for their shackles: Wandala *montagnard* interactions in northern Cameroon', *Journal of African History*, 1993, p. 254.

116 D. Lange and S. Berthoud, 'L'intérieur de l'Afrique Occidentale d'après ... Anania (XVIe siècle)', *Journal of World History*, 1972, p. 351.

117 Maceachern, 'Selling the iron', pp. 247ff.

118 The account which follows is indebted to Last, 'Early kingdoms', pp. 190–202; much of this chapter, however, is controversial, especially the claim that there is a relationship between widely scattered (and markedly divergent) place-names and titles.

119 Last, 'Early kingdoms', pp. 167ff.

120 On this, see J. E. G. Sutton, 'Towards a less orthodox history of Hausaland', *Journal of African History*, 1979, pp. 179–202.

121 *Infaq al-Maysur*, p. 12. There are many different versions of the Bayajida legend; see the Daura *Girgam*, in Palmer, *Sudanese Memoirs*, III, pp. 132–4. Cf. also W. K. R. Hallam, 'The Bayajida legend in Hausa folklore', *Journal of African History*, 1966, pp. 47–60. The reference to the mai's slave comes from *Infaq al-Maysur*, p. 12.

122 A. Smith, 'Some considerations relating to the formation of states in Hausaland', *Journal of the Historical Society of Nigeria*, 1971, p. 337.

123 The turning point was Smith's paper (n. 122 above). It is noteworthy that Borno traditional history claims that Salma (d. 1210) was the first black Mai and that Lange believes Umme Jilme was a Berber – though this has not won general acceptance (see D. Lange, 'Progrès de l'Islam et changement politique au Kanem du XIe au XIIIe siècle: un essai d'interpretation', *Journal of African History*, 1978, pp. 507–8).

124 'Kano Chronicle', in Palmer, *Sudanese Memoirs*, III, p. 97. See vol. II, p. 64, 'The So': 'Among their characteristics was that one of them could hunt an

elephant and carry it on his head.' As Last points out, Barbushe probably refers to ethnic identity – Ba Buce.

125 'Kano Chronicle', p. 99.

126 M. Hiskett, 'The Song of Bagauda: a Hausa king list and homily in verse', *Bulletin SOAS*, 1965, pp. 114–15.

127 'Kano Chronicle', p. 111.

128 Ibid., p. 75; *Infaq al-Maysur*, p. 12.

129 Palmer, *Sudanese Memoirs*, III, pp. 145–6.

130 R. Needham, *Symbolic Classification* (Santa Monica, 1979), Ch. 5, 'Relational constants'.

131 H. R. Palmer, intro. to C. K. Meek, *A Sudanese Kingdom* (London, 1931), p. xiv.

132 R. Armstrong, et. al., 'Music of the Idoma of central Nigeria', transcribed and translated texts accompanying Asch Records, Album AHM 4221; E. O. Erim, *Idoma Nationality 1600–1900* (Enugu, 1981), pp. 14–20. Ancestral masks sing of a home in the Ebirra kingdom of Panda, also in the Benue valley.

133 Isichei, *History of Nigeria*, p. 288.

134 E. Isichei, 'On masks and audible ghosts: some secret male cults in central Nigeria', *Journal of Religion in Africa*, 1988, pp. 42ff.

135 For more on Jankai, see E. Isichei, 'Change in Anaguta traditional religion', *Canadian Journal of African Studies*, 1991, pp. 34ff.

136 C. L. Temple, *Notes on the Tribes, Provinces, Emirates and States of Northern Nigeria* (Lagos, 1922), pp. 182–3. 'Dodo' is Hausa for masked spirit.

137 S. F. Nadel, *Nupe Religion* (London, 1954), pp. 172–3 and 200.

138 J. Picton, 'Masks and the Igbirra', *African Arts*, 1974, p. 38. See pp. 254–5 below.

139 See pp. 95–6 above.

140 J. Vaughan, 'Caste systems in the Western Sudan', in A. Tuden and L. Plotnicov (eds.), *Social Stratification in Africa* (New York, 1970), pp. 59–92.

141 T. Tamari, 'The development of caste systems in West Africa', *Journal of African History*, 1991, pp. 221–50, the major source for what follows.

142 W. Shack, 'Notes on occupational castes among the Gurage of south-west Ethiopia', *Man*, 1964, p. 51. This society is similar to Sande, among the Mende (p. 259 below).

143 Ibn Battuta, in *Corpus*, pp. 290–3.

144 Bird and Kendall, 'The Mande hero', pp. 16–17. See also the magnificent analysis in P. McNaughton, *The Mande Blacksmiths: Knowledge, Power and Art in West Africa* (Bloomington, 1988), pp. 40–100, 'Smiths and the shape of civilised space'.

145 On this see Tamari, 'Development of caste systems', pp. 238ff. He suggests plausibly that Sumanguru was not a casted smith, but was linked with the same mystical forces. See also Conrad, 'Islam in the oral traditions of Mali', pp. 36–9.

14 WEST AFRICA: FROM THE SAVANNA TO THE SEA

1 Quoted in P. Ben-Amos, *The Art of Benin* (London, 1980), p. 11.

2 Cognitive history as reflected in language change, explored by Vansina in West Central Africa and by Ehret in East Africa, remains unstudied in West Africa.

3 A good example of this can be found in the present study – Nupe and Kwararafa are in much the same latitude but (for good reason) discussed in different chapters.

4   F. O. 2/63, Casement to MacDonald, 10 April 1894 (near Arochukwu).
5   I. Wilks, 'Land, labour, capital and the forest kingdom of Asante', in J. Friedman and M. Rowlands, *The Evolution of Social Systems* (London, 1977), p. 501.
6   R. S. Rattray, *Ashanti Law and Constitution* (1929, London, 1956 reprint), p. 348.
7   Wilks, 'Land, labour, capital'. This model is endorsed by McCaskie, in general critical of Wilks; see, for instance, T. McCaskie, 'Accumulation, wealth and belief in Asante history', *Africa*, 1983, pp. 26–7; see also L. Yarak, *Asante and the Dutch 1744–1873* (Oxford, 1990), pp. 5–7.
8   R. Law, *The Slave Coast of West Africa 1550–1750* (Oxford, 1991), p. 42.
9   John Barbot, *A Description of the Coasts of North and South Guinea* (1746), p. 156. I have used the original version of this work, as the new Hakluyt edition became available to me too late to use in this study. In a general work of this kind, sources are cited for illustrative purposes, and it is not a matter of great moment if a passage originated with Barbot or was borrowed from Bosman!
10 R. Smith, 'The canoe in West African history', *Journal of African History*, 1970, p. 522. The reference may be to Loango.
11 See J. D. Y. Peel, *Ijeshas and Nigerians: The Incorporation of a Yoruba Kingdom, 1890s–1970s* (Cambridge, 1983), p. 28.
12 E. B. Idowu, *Oludumare: God in Yoruba Belief* (London, 1962), p. 153.
13 See p. 334 below.
14 Barbot, *Description*, p. 33 (on the late seventeenth century in the Senegambia).
15 F. Willett, *Ife in the History of West African Sculpture* (London, 1967), pp. 61–3; R. F. Thompson, 'Icons of the mind', *African Arts*, Spring, 1975, pp. 52ff.
16 E. Isichei, *A History of Nigeria* (Harlow, 1983), pp. 296–7; E. Herbert, 'Smallpox inoculation in Africa', *Journal of African History*, 1975, pp. 539ff. For jiggers, see p. 454 below. They were not indigenous to West Africa.
17 W. Bosman, *A New and Accurate Description of the Coast of Guinea* (first pub. in Dutch, 1704; London, 1967 edition), pp. 108–9; also p. 43.
18 Ibid., p. 109; K. Kiple and V. H. King, *Another Dimension to the Black Diaspora: Diet, Disease, and Racism* (Cambridge, 1981), pp. 119ff.; it may reflect nutritional deficiencies.
19 H. M. Waddell, *Twenty Nine Years in the West Indies and Central Africa* (London, 1863), p. 459.
20 K. D. Patterson, 'River blindness in northern Ghana, 1900–50', in G. Hartwig and K. D. Patterson (eds.), *Disease in African History* (Durham, N.C., 1978), pp. 88ff.
21 A. Mabogunje and P. Richards, 'The land and peoples of West Africa', in J. F. A. Ajayi and M. Crowder (eds.), *History of West Africa* (3rd edn, Harlow, 1985), p. 45.
22 S. Johnson, *The History of the Yorubas* (1921, Lagos, 1973 reprint), p. 18.
23 J. Egharevba, *A Short History of Benin* (1934, 4th edn, Ibadan, 1968), pp. 6–7. See p. 92 above for other examples.
24 A. Obayemi, 'The Yoruba and Edo-speaking peoples and their neighbours before 1600', in Ajayi and Crowder, *History of West Africa*, I, pp. 255ff.
25 J. Miller, *Way of Death: Merchant Capitalism and the Angolan Slave Trade 1730–1830* (London, 1988), p. 27.
26 See Peel, *Ijeshas and Nigerians*, p. 26.
27 Johnson, *History of the Yorubas*, p. 21.
28 J.-C. Muller, 'Quelques réflexions sur l'auto-restriction technologique et la

dépendance économique dans les sociétés d' auto-subsistance', *Cahiers d'études africaines*, 1972, pp. 659ff.

29 Quoted in E. Isichei, 'Colonialism resisted', in E. Isichei (ed.), *Studies in the History of Plateau State, Nigeria* (London, 1982), p. 214.

30 Obayemi, 'The Yoruba and Edo-speaking peoples', p. 313, citing G. J. Ojo. For a consideration of this question, see R. Law, 'Towards a history of urbanisation in pre-colonial Yorubaland', in C. Fyfe (ed.), *African Historical Demography* (Edinburgh, 1977), pp. 260–71.

31 See p. 216 above.

32 P. J. Darling, 'Questions concerning the linear earth boundaries (Iya) of the Benin empire' (mimeo, University of Benin, 1975); R. Bradbury, 'The kingdom of Benin', in D. Forde and P. Kaberry (eds.), *West African Kingdoms in the Nineteenth Century* (London, 1969 reprint), p. 15.

33 T. J. Dennis, 'From Oyo to the Niger (3 February – 20 March, 1902)', *Niger and Yoruba Notes*, 1903, p. 13.

34 R. E. Bradbury, 'The historical uses of comparative ethnography, with special reference to Benin and the Yoruba', in J. Vansina, R. Mauny and L. V. Thomas (eds.), *The Historian in Tropical Africa* (London, 1964), p. 150. 'Ibo' is an older and now obsolete spelling of 'Igbo'. In the same volume, R. Armstrong suggested a time depth of 2,000 years for Yoruba/Igala and 6,000 for Yoruba/Idoma.

35 P. E. H. Hair, 'An ethnolinguistic inventory on the Guinea coast before 1700', *African Language Review*, 1968, p. 249.

36 Duarte Pacheco Pereira, *Esmeraldo de situ orbis* (written *c.* 1505–8, Hakluyt, 2nd series, LXXIX, 1937), pp. 124–5, 129.

37 T. Weiskel, 'The precolonial Baule: a reconstruction', *Cahiers d'études africaines*, 1978, p. 507.

38 W. Towerson, *First Voyage to Guinea, 1555–6*, extract in F. Wolfson, *Pageant of Ghana* (London, 1958), p. 47.

39 Barbot, *Description*, p. 168. By this time, life in the southern Gold Coast was modified by the European presence – but this description undoubtedly holds true of an earlier time, with the probable exception of the population density.

40 M. Onwuejeogwu, in *Odinani*, 1972, pp. 39–40; R. Henderson, *The King in Every Man* (New Haven and London, 1972); M. Green, *Igbo Village Affairs* (2nd edn, London, 1964), p. 7.

41 E. Isichei, *A History of the Igbo People* (London, 1976), p. 3. This is still the standard account.

42 A. G. Leonard, *The Lower Niger and Its Tribes* (London, 1906), pp. 36–7.

43 As were some other Igbo priest-kings in the Nri culture area. See P. M. Friedrich, 'Description de l'enterrement d'un chef à Ibouzo', *Anthropos*, 1907, pp. 100–6.

44 M. D. W. Jeffries, 'The Umundri tradition of origin', *African Studies*, 1956, p. 122.

45 A. E. Afigbo, 'Traditions of Igbo origins: a comment', *History in Africa*, 1983, p. 9.

46 Nwaokoye Odenigbo, in E. Isichei (ed.), *Igbo Worlds* (London, 1978), p. 28.

47 See Map 2 in Isichei, *A History of the Igbo People*, p. 11. This is based on various studies by M. A. Onwuejeogwu. See his *A Brief History of an Anambra Civilisation* (Onitsha, n.d.).

48 Isichei, *Igbo Worlds*, pp. 21–67. Significantly, a journal published at the University of Nigeria, Nsukka, was called *Ikenga*.
49 Jeffries, 'The Umundri tradition', p. 123.
50 Ibid., p. 125.
51 Pereira, *Esmeraldo de situ orbis*, p. 132 (an early sixteenth-century account of this trade). See p. 355 below.
52 N. W. Thomas, *Law and Custom of the Ibo of the Awka Neighbourhood* (London, 1913), pp. 49–50. It is noteworthy that more recent compilations list ten named and two unnamed Eze Nri – researchers explain the discrepancy by claiming that the earlier list included unsuccessful contenders (M. Onwuejeogwu, 'An outline account of the dawn of Igbo civilisation in the Igbo culture area', *Odinani*, 1972).
53 T. Shaw, *Igbo-Ukwu: An Account of Archaeological Discoveries in Eastern Nigeria* (London, 1970, 2 vols.). For the debate about dating, see B. Lawal, 'Dating problems at Igbo-Ukwu', *Journal of African History*, 1973, pp. 1–8; T. Shaw, 'Those Igbo-Ukwu radiocarbon dates: facts, fictions and probabilities', *Journal of African History*, 1975, pp. 503–18.
54 Quoted in A. E. Afigbo, 'Oral tradition and the history of segmentary societies', *History in Africa*, 1985, p. 6 (re Aba Division).
55 The research of V. Chikwendu and A. Umeji, reported in *New Scientist*, 10 June 1989, p. 15. 'Bronze' is used in the present study as a general term for sculptures in copper alloys.
56 The position is complicated by the fact that the tsetse belt shifts in response to climate change and other factors. In the nineteenth century, Igbo on the extreme northern edge of Igboland obtained horses for sacrifice to obtain a rare and prestigious title.
57 D. Hartle, 'Bronze objects from Ezira, eastern Nigeria', *West African Archaeological Newsletter*, 1966. These objects disappeared during the Nigerian civil war. The swords are depicted in James Barbot, 'An abstract of a voyage to New Calabar river ... in 1699', in Churchill's *Voyages*, V (London, 1746), and reproduced in Isichei, *A History of the Igbo People*, Plate 3. Throughout this study, 'Barbot', unqualified, refers to John (Jean) Barbot.
58 H. Cole, 'Mbari is life', *African Arts/Arts d'Afrique*, Spring 1969, pp. 8ff.
59 For more on this Niger Igbo town, see p. 79 above.
60 J. Spencer, 'The history of Asaba and its kings', *Niger and Yoruba Notes*, September 1901, p. 21; Church Missionary Society Archives, Birmingham, CA3/02, Isaac Spencer, 'Araba and the Arabans', 10 September 1879.
61 Isichei, *Igbo Worlds*, pp. 57–67.
62 Ibid., pp. 179–83 and 192–6.
63 C. Ubah, 'The Supreme Being, divinities and ancestors in Igbo traditional religion: evidence from Otanchara and Otazu', *Africa*, 1982, pp. 96–8.
64 R. Horton, 'A hundred years of change in Kalabari religion', in J. Middleton (ed.), *Black Africa: Its Peoples and Their Cultures Today* (London, 1970), pp. 192ff.; 'The Kalabari *ekine* society: a borderland of religion and art', *Africa*, 1963, pp. 94ff.
65 E. Ardener, 'Belief and the problem of women', in S. Ardener (ed.), *Perceiving Women* (London, 1975), pp. 7ff.
66 Johnson, *History of the Yorubas*, p. 19.
67 W. H. Clarke, *Travels and Explorations in Yorubaland 1854–1856* (Ibadan, 1972), p. 125.

68   *The Church Missionary Intelligencer*, 1854, p. 58.
69   A. Apter, 'The historiography of Yoruba myth and ritual', *History in Africa*, 1987, p. 12. See p. 249 above for the Sixteen Kings of Ekiti.
70   Apter, 'The historiography', pp. 1–25.
71   Quoted in B. A. Agiri, 'Early Oyo history reconsidered', *History in Africa*, 1975, p. 1.
72   E. A. Oroge, 'The institution of slavery in Yorubaland, with particular reference to the nineteenth century' (University of Birmingham, Ph.D. thesis, 1971), p. 6; E. B. Idowu, *Oludumare God in Yoruba Belief* (London, 1975), p. 24.
73   J. Peel, *Ijeshas and Nigerians* (Cambridge, 1982), pp. 21–2, 275–6.
74   Agiri, 'Early Oyo history', p. 7, citing the Oba Alaye, Oba Loron and Ompetu.
75   R. C. C. Law, 'Traditional history', in S. O. Biobaku (ed.), *Sources of Yoruba History* (Oxford, 1973), p. 38. Law calls the story 'a pure fabrication'.
76   Thompson, 'Icons of the mind', p. 54.
77   Theodore Monot discovered the copper carried by such a caravan, in Mauritania, in 1964 (E. Herbert, *The Red Gold of Africa* (Madison, 1984), pp. 114 and 120).
78   Peel, *Ijeshas and Nigerians*.
79   The standard account is R. Law, *The Oyo Empire, 1600–1836: A West African Imperialism in the Era of the Atlantic Slave Trade* (Oxford, 1977). The history of the other Yoruba kingdoms is summarised in R. Smith, *Kingdoms of the Yoruba* (London, 1976).
80   Agiri, 'Early Oyo history', p. 9.
81   N. Calvocoressi and N. David, 'A new survey of radiocarbon and thermoluminescence dates for West Africa', *Journal of African History*, 1979, pp. 19–20.
82   The subsequent fortunes of Oyo are analysed later in this study.
83   Johnson, *The History of the Yorubas*, p. 156.
84   J. Peel, 'Kings, titles and quarters: a conjectural history of Ilesa', *History in Africa*, 1979, pp. 125–7.
85   The ruler is described as Ogane, the modern Benin name for the Ooni of Ife, but the kingdom is described as north or east of Benin, and Ife is to the west. See A. Ryder, 'A reconsideration of the Ife–Benin relationship', *Journal of African History*, 1965, pp. 25–37 and J. Thornton, 'Traditions, documents, and the Ife–Benin relationship', *History in Africa*, 1988, pp. 351–62.
86   See p. 242 above.
87   J. Boston, 'Oral tradition and the history of Igala', *Journal of African History*, 1969, pp. 29ff.
88   R. Sargent, 'On the methodology of chronology: the Igala core dating progression', *History in Africa*, 1984, pp. 269–89.
89   The view of Obayemi, 'The Yoruba and Edo-speaking peoples', p. 294.
90   S. F. Nadel, *A Black Byzantium: The Kingdom of Nupe in Nigeria* (London, 1942), p. 75.
91   The view of M. Mason, 'The Tsoede myth and the Nupe kinglists: more political propaganda', *History in Africa*, 1975, pp. 101–12.
92   Art historians have written superb studies of these symbolic complexes. See D. Fraser, 'The Tsoede bronzes and Owo Yoruba art', *African Arts*, Spring 1975, pp. 30–55; R. F. Thompson, 'The sign of the divine king: Yoruba bead-embroidered crowns with veil and bird decorations', *African Arts*, Spring, 1970, pp. 8ff.; reprinted in D. Fraser and H. M. Cole (eds.), *African Art and Leadership* (Madison, 1972).

93 See Denis Williams, *Icon and Image: A Study of Sacred and Secular Forms of African Classical Art* (London, 1974).

94 Thompson, 'The sign of the divine king', in Fraser and Cole, *African Art and Leadership*, p. 256, n. 22.

95 J. Picton, 'Masks and the Igbirra', *African Arts*, 1974, p. 38. See p. 236 above

96 Extract in W. Abimbola, *Ifa: An Exposition of Ifa Literary Corpus* (Ibadan, 1976), p. 167.

97 R. F. Thompson, *African Art in Motion* (Los Angeles, 1974), p. 219.

98 Barbot, *Description*, p. 340.

99 H. C. Capo, 'Le Gbe est une langue unique', *Africa*, 1983, pp. 321ff.

100 Law, *The Slave Coast*, p. 28. See p. 92 for other anti-royal myths.

101 Ibid., p. 70.

102 S. Greene, 'Land, lineage and clan in early Anlo', *Africa*, 1981, pp. 451ff.

103 M. E. Kropp Dakubu, 'The peopling of southern Ghana: a linguistic viewpoint', in C. Ehret and M. Posnansky, *The Archaeological and Linguistic Reconstruction of African History* (Berkeley and Los Angeles, 1982), pp. 245ff.

104 It is the subject of a fine monograph by M. Kropp Dakubu, *One Voice* (Leiden, 1981).

105 Kropp Dakubu, 'The peopling', p. 248.

106 D. Kiyaga-Mulindwa, 'The "Akan" Problem', *Current Anthropology*, 1980, pp. 503ff.

107 I. Wilks, 'The state of the Akan and the Akan states: a discursion', *Cahiers d'études africaines*, 1982, p. 231.

108 Boahen suggests Akim Abuakwa, Assim and Akim Kotuku, but Kiyaga-Mulindwa questions this, and these polities, were, of course in a state of change and development (A. Boahen, 'Arcany or Accany or Arcania ...', *Transactions of the Historical Society of Ghana*, 1973, pp. 105ff.).

109 See p. 218 above.

110 Posnansky, 'Archaeological and linguistic reconstruction in Ghana', in Ehret and Posnansky, *Archaeological and Linguistic Reconstruction*, p. 260.

111 Quoted in Wilks, 'Land, labour, capital', p. 509.

112 Here I follow Wilks, 'Land, labour, capital' and 'The state of the Akan'. It is puzzling that the Akan cleared the forest so much later than, for instance, the Igbo.

113 The account which follows is based on Wilks, 'Land, labour, capital', pp. 508ff.

114 R. S. Rattray, *Ashanti Law and Constitution* (1929, London, 1956 reprint), p. 132.

115 R. Dumett, 'Precolonial gold mining and the state in the Akan region', *Research in Economic Anthropology*, 1979, pp. 44–6; there is also considerable evidence of gold mining by slaves, for which see E. Terray, 'Gold production, slave labor and state intervention in precolonial Akan societies', *Research in Economic Anthropology*, 1983, pp. 95ff.

116 Wilks, 'Land, labour, capital', p. 522.

117 P. Allison, *Cross River Monoliths* (Lagos, 1968).

118 P. Allison, *African Stone Sculptures* (New York, 1968), pp. 11ff.

119 Earlier literature is summarised and critiqued in W. Hart and C. Fyfe, 'The stone sculptures of the Upper Guinea coast', *History in Africa*, 1993, pp. 71ff. Nomoli is the best known name, but they fall into three groups, one of which is called *pomta*.

120 Ibid., p. 85 n. 33.

121 Andre d'Almada, extract in C. Fyfe, *Sierra Leone Inheritance* (London, 1964), p. 44.

122 Andre Donelha, quoted [as 'Dornelas'] in W. Rodney, 'A reconsideration of the Mane invasions of Sierra Leone', *Journal of African History*, 1967, p. 219.

123 A. Jones, 'Who were the Vai?', *Journal of African History*, 1981, pp. 171ff.

124 Andre Alvares d'Almada, in a work published in 1594, extract in Fyfe, *Sierra Leone Inheritance*, p. 45.

125 Pereira, *Esmeraldo*, p. 98. Fyfe believes that Rodney – and the Portuguese sources he worked from – exaggerated the Mane impact, and argues for continuity (C. Fyfe, 'From language to culture: some problems in the systematic analysis of the ethnohistorical records of the Sierra Leone region', in R. P. Moss and R. Rathbone, *The Population Factor in African Studies* (London, 1975), pp. 71ff.).

126 Valentim Fernandes, in *c.* 1506–10, extract in Fyfe, *Sierra Leone Inheritance*, p. 30.

127 Manuel Alvares, quoted in Rodney, 'A reconsideration', p. 240.

128 C. Bird, 'The development of Mandekan (Manding): a study of the role of extra-linguistic factors in linguistic change', in D. Dalby (ed.), *Language and History in Africa* (London, 1970), pp. 155ff. Manding dialects include Bambara, Mandinka, Dyula, Marka and Vai, but not Mende.

129 G. Brooks, 'Ecological perspectives on Mande population movements', *History in Africa*, 1989, p. 35. See K. C. Wylie, *The Political Kingdoms of the Temne* (New York, 1977), p. 22.

130 E. Tonkin, 'Women excluded? Masking and masquerading in West Africa', in P. Holden (ed.), *Women's Religious Experience: Cross-Cultural Perspectives* (Beckenham, 1983), p. 168, citing articles by W. d'Azevedo.

131 Extracts in Fyfe, *Sierra Leone Inheritance*, pp. 27 and 32. Some spirits manifest themselves as masked figures, while others speak through a voice disguiser; the identical phenomenon is well documented in modern Nigeria.

132 O. Dapper, extract in ibid., pp. 35–6, 39.

133 F. W. H. Migeod, 'The Poro society: the building of the Poro house and making of the image', *Man*, 1916, 61, pp. 102–8; H. G. Warren, 'Secret societies', *Sierra Leone Studies*, 1926, pp. 82ff.; G. W. Harley, *Notes on the Poro in Liberia* (Cambridge, Mass., 1941); K. Little, 'The political function of the Poro', *Africa*, 1965, pp. 349–65, and 1966, pp. 62–71.

134 D. Rosen, 'Dangerous women: "ideology", "knowledge" and "ritual" among the Kono of Eastern Sierra Leone', *Dialectical Anthropology*, 1981, pp. 151–83.

15   NORTHERN AFRICA

1 Quoted in P. Rabinow, *Symbolic Domination, Cultural Form and Historical Change in Morocco* (Chicago, 1975), p. 16.

2 Quoted in A. Hourani, *Arabic Thought in the Liberal Age 1798–1939* (London, 1962), p. 52.

3 See also pp. 271–2 below.

4 E. Gellner, *Saints of the Atlas* (London, 1969), p. 3.

5 J. Abun-Nasr, *A History of the Maghrib in the Islamic Period* (rev. edn, Cambridge, 1987), p. 213.

6 The chronicler al-Zayyani, extract in Abdelaziz K. Temsamani, 'The Jebala region: Makhzan, bandits and saints', in E. G. H. Joffe and C. R. Pennell (eds.),

Tribe and state: Essays in Honour of David Montgomery Hart (Wisbech, 1991), p. 31.

7 Quoted in F. V. Parsons, *The Origins of the Morocco Question 1880–1900* (London, 1976), p. 8.

8 D. Rosenberger and H. Triki, 'Famines et épidémies au Maroc aux xvie et xviie siècles', *Hesperis-Tamuda*, 1974, pp. 114–15.

9 Ibid., p. 109.

10 Ibid., p. 119.

11 Temsamani, 'The Jebala region', p. 29.

12 Rosenberger and Triki, 'Famines et épidémies', p. 40.

13 E. Gellner, 'Patterns of rural rebellion in Morocco: tribes as minorities', *European Journal of Sociology*, 1962, p. 300.

14 C. Geertz, *Islam Observed: Religious Development in Morocco and Indonesia* (New Haven and London, 1968), p. 5.

15 See C. Pennell, 'Makhzan and Siba in Morocco: an examination of early modern attitudes', in Joffe and Pennell, *Tribe and State*, pp. 158–62.

16 See H. Munson, Jr, 'The segmentary lineage model in the Jbalan highlands of Morocco', in Joffe and Pennell, *Tribe and State*, p. 68: 'Pre-colonial Jebalan society was in no way segmentary.'

17 'Clan' is used here as synonymous with 'tribe'; it is often used to refer to a smaller unit – usage varies (on this, see Munson, 'The segmentary lineage model', in Joffe and Pennell, *Tribe and State*, p. 50).

18 J. Waterbury, 'Bargaining for segmentarity', in Joffe and Pennell, *Tribe and State*, p. 7.

19 Ibid., p. 10, on Hart and Gellner.

20 Temsamani, 'The Jebala region', p. 20 n. 30.

21 Waterbury, 'Bargaining for segmentarity,' p. 9.

22 M. Brett, 'Ibn Khaldun and the Arabisation of North Africa', *The Maghrib Review*, 1979, p. 14; his source is al-Tijani, writing at the beginning of the fourteenth century.

23 Munson, 'The segmentary lineage model', p. 56.

24 See for instance, ibid., p. 51 n. 13.

25 L. Valensi, *Tunisian Peasants in the Eighteenth and Nineteenth Centuries* (1977, Eng. trans. Cambridge, 1985), pp. 124–5.

26 Temsamani, 'The Jebala region', pp. 16–17.

27 Gellner's picture of the pacificist saint has, however, been criticised as idealised. Cf. A. Hammoudi, 'Segmentarité, stratification sociale, pouvoir politique et sainteté: réflexions sur les thèses de Gellner', *Hesperis-Tamuda*, 1974, pp. 147ff.

28 Hart, quoted in Waterbury, 'Bargaining for segmentarity', p. 9.

29 C.-R. Ageron, *Modern Algeria: A History from 1830 to the Present* (Eng. trans. London, 1991), pp. 3–4.

30 On the role played by al-Maghili, see J. Hunwick, 'Al-Mahili and the Jews of Tuwat; the demise of a community', *Studia Islamica*, 1985, pp. 155ff. The reference to the Jews of the Mzab is on p. 181. An additional factor was their association with an epidemic (for which see p. 264 above.).

31 Quoted in Geertz, *Islam Observed*, p. 31. For a detailed study of this saint and his descendants, see Rabinow, *Symbolic Domination*. Lyussi lived during the rise of the Alawites, and, on occasion, challenged their authority.

32 R. Hess, *The Forgotten Frontier: A History of the Sixteenth-Century Ibero-African Frontier* (Chicago and London, 1978), p. 15.

33 R. Austen, *Africa in Economic History* (London, 1987), pp. 37–8.

34 M. Morsy, *North Africa 1800–1900: A Survey from the Nile Valley to the Atlantic* (London and New York, 1984), p. 34.

35 C. Issawi, *An Economic History of the Middle East and North Africa* (London, 1982), p. 27.

36 W. Spencer, *Algiers in the Age of the Corsairs* (Norman, Okla., 1976), p. 10.

37 Ibid., pp. 12–13. His account refers to the period before the Regencies; he also refers to the Maghrib's imports of precious metals from Europe for currency and jewellery; this contrasts oddly with the usual picture of gold exports from the Western Sudan.

38 V. Cornell, 'Socioeconomic dimensions of reconquista and jihad in Morocco: Portuguese Dukkala and the Sa'did Sus. 1450–1557', *International Journal of Middle East Studies*, 1990, pp. 381–90, 403.

39 A. Laroui, *The History of the Maghrib: An Interpretative Essay* (Princeton, 1977), pp. 258, 260.

40 Gellner, *Saints of the Atlas*, p. 137.

41 Laroui, *The History of the Maghrib*, pp. 244–5.

42 For this distinction on the Senegambia, see p. 37 above.

43 M. Brett and W. Forman, *The Moors: Islam in the West* (London, 1980), p. 25.

44 Gellner, *Saints of the Atlas*, p. 70.

45 Geertz, *Islam Observed*, p. 51.

46 Laroui, *The History of the Maghrib*, p. 261, and n. 35.

47 M. Gracia-Arenal, 'Mahdi, Murabit, Sharif: l'avènement de la dynastie Sa'dienne', *Studia Islamica*, 1990, p. 83.

48 Cordell, 'Socioeconomic dimensions of reconquista', p. 414 n. 67.

49 E. Evans-Pritchard, *The Sanusi of Cyrenaica* (Oxford, 1949), pp. 51–3.

50 Al-Qa'im bi'llah. See p. 184 above.

51 V. Cornell, 'The logic of analogy and the role of the Sufi shaykh in post-Marinid Morocco', *International Journal of Middle Eastern Studies*, 1983, p. 73; D. Yahya, *Morocco in the Sixteenth Century* (Harlow, 1981), p. 3.

52 Gracia-Arenal, 'Mahdi, Murabit, Sharif', pp. 77ff.

53 Laroui, *The History of the Maghrib*, pp. 256–7.

54 Cordell, 'Socioeconomic dimensions, pp. 407 and 416 n. 83.

55 For the impact on Songhai, see p. 227 above.

56 In an age when historians of Africa avoid words such as 'tribe', it is odd that they still write of 'renegades'.

57 Laroui, *The History of the Maghrib*, p. 258.

58 Rabinow, *Symbolic Domination*, p. 19.

59 See p. 300 below.

60 Spencer, *Algiers*, pp. 15, 47–8.

61 Hess, *The Forgotten Frontier*, pp. 137–8.

62 Al-Bakri, quoted in Spencer, *Algiers*, p. 15 – the source of this paragraph.

63 A. MacKay, *Spain in the Middle Ages: From Frontier to Empire 1000–1500* (London, 1977).

64 A French visitor in 1619, quoted in Spencer, *Algiers*, p. xi.

65 Hess, *The Forgotten Frontier*, p. 165.

66 Ageron, *Modern Algeria*, p. 5.

67 Spain lost Oran between 1708 and 1732.
68 This is very widely accepted; for a stimulating rethinking, cf. p. 275 below.
69 Valensi, *Tunisian Peasants*, p. 219; she states that knowledge of Turkish was limited to recent recruits.
70 A seventeenth-century observer, quoted in Ageron, *Modern Algeria*, p. 4.
71 Morsy, *North Africa 1800–1900*, p. 43.
72 Or of Ottoman rule, in the case of Tripoli.
73 Quoted in P. J. Vatikiotis, *The History of Egypt from Muhammad Ali to Sadat*, (2nd edn, London, 1980), p. 35.
74 This type of generalisation (where the Hausa were martial, and the Igbo non-martial) was greatly undermined by the Nigerian civil war!
75 Cited in Ageron, *Modern Algeria*, p. 4, n. 10.
76 Hess, *The Forgotten Frontier*, p. 177. On women spirit mediumship in Somalia and elsewhere, see p. 202 above.
77 Laroui, *The History of the Maghrib*, p. 268. The economic and political significance of the rise and fall of corsairing is not always clear. See the passage cited on p. 267 above. D. Johnson ('The Maghrib', in J. Flint (ed.), *Cambridge History of Africa: From c. 1790 to c. 1870* (1976), V, p. 103) states that 'piracy was a small entirely marginal activity'. On p. 123 he states, with reference to Tripoli, 'The loss of the pirate trade led to a financial crisis'.
78 B. G. Martin, *Muslim Brotherhoods in the Nineteenth Century* (Cambridge, 1976), pp. 43ff.; Laroui, *The History of the Maghrib*, p. 269.
79 Afaf Lutfi al-Sayyid Marsot, *Egypt in the Reign of Muhammad Ali* (Cambridge, 1984), p. 5.
80 Issawi, *An Economic History*, pp. 213–14; there are many problems with comparisons of this kind.
81 Marsot, *Muhammad Ali*. pp. 2–3.
82 C. H. Robinson, *Hausaland* (London, 1986), p. 62; A. Schultze, *The Sultanate of Bornu* (Eng. trans. London, 1913), p. 215.
83 Quoted in Morsy, *North Africa 1800–1900*, p. 73.
84 Extract in P. M. Holt, 'Egypt, the Funj and Darfur', in *The Cambridge History of Africa: From c. 1600 to c. 1790*, ed. R. Gray (1975), IV, pp. 36–7.
85 Nicolas Turc, quoted in Marsot, *Muhammad Ali*, p. 70.
86 Quoted in Valensi, *Tunisian Peasants*, p. 220.
87 Ibid., pp. 183ff., pp. 195, 223ff.
88 R. Owen, 'The Middle East in the eighteenth century – an "Islamic" society in decline?' *Bulletin, Society for Middle Eastern Studies*, 1976, pp. 110ff.; see p. 114.
89 H. Lewis, 'The origins of the Galla and Somali', *Journal of African History*, 1966, pp. 32–5.
90 P. Spencer, *Nomads in Alliance, Symbiosis and Growth among the Rendille* (London, 1973), p. 113.
91 M. L. Bende, 'The languages of Ethiopia', *Anthropological Linguistics*, 1971, p. 185.
92 D. Levine, *Greater Ethiopia: The Evolution of a Multiethnic Society* (Chicago, 1974), Ch. 9, 'The Oromo system'; P. Baxter, 'Repetition in certain Boran ceremonies', in M. Fortes and P. Dieterlen (eds.), *African Systems of Thought* (London, 1965), pp. 64–76; K. Knutsson, *Authority and Change: A Study of the Kalla Institution among the Macha Galla of Ethiopia* (Goteborg, 1967); Asmarom Legesse, *Gada: Three Approaches to the Study of African Society* (New York, 1973).

93 C. Ehret, *Ethiopians and East Africans: The Problem of Contacts* (Nairobi, 1974), p. 48.

94 Levine, *Greater Ethiopia*, p. 145.

95 T. Tamrat, 'Processes of ethnic interaction and integration in Ethiopian history: the case of the Agaw', *Journal of African History*, 1988, p. 6. The account which follows is based on this article.

96 Ibid., p. 12.

97 A contemporary chronicler in 1669, quoted in ibid., p. 14.

98 M. Brett, 'Modernisation in 19th century North Africa', *The Maghrib Review*, 1982, p. 19.

99 Quoted in Valensi, *Tunisian Peasants*, pp. 165–6.

100 See J. Clancy-Smith, 'The house of Zainab: female authority and saintly succession in colonial Algeria', in N. Keddie and B. Baron (eds.), *Women in Middle Eastern History* (New Haven and London, 1991), pp. 254ff.

101 See A. Hourani, *Arabic Thought in the Liberal Age 1798–1939* (London, 1962), pp. 41 and 67ff.

102 Quoted in ibid., p. 79.

103 Morsy, *North Africa 1800–1900*, p. 93.

104 Brett, 'Modernisation', pp. 16ff.

105 Hourani, *Arabic Thought*, p. 51.

106 The scale of this has often been exaggerated. twenty-four beys and 40 others were killed, at a time when there were 1,200 mamluks – their numbers had declined through war and plague (Marsot, *Muhammad Ali*, p. 72).

107 Ibid., p. 21. See pp. 193–4 above.

108 L. C. Brown, *The Tunisia of Ahmad Bey 1837–1855* (Princeton, 1974), pp. 46–7.

109 Issawi, *An Economic History*, p. 31.

110 Ibid., p. 120.

111 Yahya Haqqi in the 1920s, quoted in Morsy, *North Africa 1800–1900*, p. 10.

112 Marsot, *Muhammad Ali*, p. 122.

113 See Afaf Lutfi al-Sayyid Marsot, 'The Ulama of Cairo in the eighteenth and nineteenth centuries', in N. Keddie (ed.), *Scholars, Saints and Sufis* (1972, Berkeley, 1978 edition) p. 163.

114 Marsot, *Muhammad Ali*, p. 90.

115 R. Gray, *A History of the Southern Sudan 1839– 1899* (Oxford, 1961), pp. 1ff.

116 Ibid., pp. 32–3.

117 Morsy, *North Africa 1800–1900*, p. 114.

118 Marsot, *Muhammad Ali*, pp. 133–4.

119 Ibid., pp. 118–19. She attributes the growth to improved public security. There seems to have been a local decline of population in the Nile Delta.

120 Brett, 'Modernisation', p. 16. This article provides a valuable bird's-eye view of the period.

121 Vatikiotis, *The History of Egypt*, pp. 127–8.

122 Holt, 'Egypt and the Nile valley,' in *Cambridge History of Africa*, V, p. 41.

123 Ibid., p. 41.

124 P. Holt, *The Mahdist State in the Sudan* (London, 1958).

125 For contrasting perspectives on Tunisian history, cf. Valensi's study, which ends with the 1864 revolt, and L. C. Brown, *The Tunisia of Ahmad Bey 1837–1855* (Princeton, 1974). A newcomer to North African history could be forgiven for thinking that they were writing about two different countries!.

126 Hourani, *Arabic Thought*, pp. 84ff.
127 Quoted in Ageron, *Modern Algeria*, p. 5.
128 Morsy, *North Africa 1800–1900*, pp. 133–4.
129 Ibid., p. 143.
130 Laroui, *The History of the Maghrib*, p. 303; Johnson, 'The Maghrib', pp. 112–13, 117.
131 Johnson, 'The Maghrib', p. 118.
132 Issawi, *An Economic History*, p. 33.
133 Quoted in Parsons, *The Origins of the Morocco Question*, p. 3. The first chapter of this study contains much detail on European attitudes to Morocco in the nineteenth century.
134 Ibid., p. 4.
135 Quoted in Pennell, 'Makhzan and Siba in Morocco', p. 164.
136 A letter of 1894, quoted in Parsons, *The Origins of the Morocco Question*, p. 16.
137 E. W. Bovill (ed.), *Missions to the Niger: The Bornu Mission, 1822–25* (Hakluyt, 2nd series, CXXX), Part 3, Denham's narrative, p. 478.
138 Mawlay Hassan in 1892, quoted in Parsons, *The Origins of the Morocco Question*, p. 20.
139 J. MacGregor, *Commercial Statistics* (1844), quoted in Issawi, *An Economic History*, p. 17.
140 Brett, 'Modernisation', p. 19. My account of nineteenth-century Morocco follows his analysis closely.
141 Ibid., p. 19.
142 J. Berque, cited in ibid., p. 20.
143 Parsons, *The Origins of the Morocco Question*, p. 22.
144 Ibid., p. 22.
145 Sir John Drummond Hay, British representative at Tangier from 1845 to 1886, in 1877, quoted in Parsons, *The Origins of the Morocco Question*, p. 63.
146 Temsamani, 'The Jebala region', p. 31.
147 Ibid., p. 28.
148 Evans-Pritchard, *The Sanusi of Cyrenaica*.
149 Quoted in S. Rubenson, 'Ethiopia and the Horn', in *The Cambridge History of Africa*, V, p. 72. See also his *King of Kings: Tewodros of Ethiopia* (Addis Ababa, 1966).
150 P. Verghese, 'The Ethiopian and Syrian Orthodox churches', in A. Arberry (ed.), *Religion in the Middle East* (Cambridge, 1969), I, p. 462.

16   THE WESTERN SUDAN IN A TIME OF JIHAD

1 Quoted in B. Barry, 'The subordination of power and the mercantile economy', in R. Cruise O'Brien (ed.), *The Political Economy of Underdevelopment: Dependence in Senegal* (London, 1979), pp. 49–50.
2 D. Robinson, *Chiefs and Clerics: The History of Abdul Bokar Kan and Futa Toro 1853–1891* (Oxford, 1975), p. 13. This chapter is greatly indebted to this fine scholar, and to the work of D. M. Last and N. Levtzion.
3 E. Isichei, *History of West Africa since 1800* (London and Basingstoke, 1977), esp. Ch. 2, 'Building new societies: the Islamic model'.
4 See p. 298 below.
5 Extracts in T. Hodgkin, *Nigerian Perspectives* (London, 1975), p. 249, and

M. Hiskett, *Sword of Truth: The Life and Times of the Shehu Usuman dan Fodio* (New York, 1973), p. 106.

6 For whom see p. 220 above.

7 J. O. Hunwick, 'Salih al-Fullani of Futa Jallon: an eighteenth century scholar and *Mujaddid*', *Bulletin IFAN*, 1978, pp. 879ff.

8 J. Spencer Trimingham, *The Sufi Orders in Islam* (Oxford, 1971), p. 103.

9 Ibid., p. 106.

10 M. Last, 'Reform in West Africa: the Jihad movements of the nineteenth century', in J. F. A. Ajayi and M. Crowder (eds.), *History of West Africa* (London, 1974), II, p. 26.

11 See J. R. Willis, 'The writings of Al-Hajj Umar al-Futi', in Willis (ed.), *Studies in West African Islamic History: The Cultivators of Islam* (London, 1979), p. 184.

12 C. Stewart with E. Stewart, *Islam and Social Order in Mauretania* (Oxford, 1973), p. 2.

13 The word is unsatisfactory since they were not, of course, ordained clergy. In Francophone West Africa they are called marabouts, in Anglophone West Africa mallams (Hausa). The words have different derivations and meanings (from *murabit* and *ulama*).

14 D. Robinson, 'The Islamic revolution of Futa Toro', *The International Journal of African Historical Studies*, 1975, p. 192. He notes that Sulaiman Bal and Abdul Kader had a higher level of learning.

15 Imam Mahmud, *Tarikh Umara Bauchi*, fos, 239, 141–2 (an Arabic MS written in the 1950s, cited here from a translation made for me by G. Ibrahim). A. Fika, *The Kano Civil War and British Over-rule* (Ibadan, 1978), p. 18.

16 D. Robinson, *The Holy War of Umar Tal* (Oxford, 1985), p. 136; see also pp. 189, 191, 308.

17 R. Roberts, *Warriors, Merchants and Slaves* (Stanford, 1987). He finds many parallels, too, with the early French colonial state.

18 This was the theme of a pioneering article by the late W. Rodney, 'Jihad and social revolution in Futa Djalon in the eighteenth century', *Journal of the Historical Society of Nigeria*, 1968, pp. 269ff. I pay tribute to a former colleague and friend.

19 D. Cruise O'Brien, 'Introduction', in O'Brien and C. Coulson (eds.), *Charisma and Brotherhood in African Islam* (Oxford, 1988), pp. 7–9; this account cites an unpublished paper by H. Fisher entitled 'A Muslim William Wilberforce? The Fulani *jihad* as anti-slavery crusade'.

20 M. al-Hajj, cited in L. Brenner, 'Muslim thought in eighteenth-century West Africa: the case of Shaykh Uthman b. Fudi', in N. Levtzion and J. Voll, *Eighteenth-Century Renewal and Reform in Islam* (Syracuse, N.Y., 1987), p. 44.

21 J. Barbot, *A Description of the Coasts of North and South Guinea* (London, 1746), p. 33.

22 P. Lovejoy and S. Baier, 'The desert-side economy of the Central Sudan', *International Journal of African Historical Studies*, 1975, pp. 573–4.

23 P. D. Curtin, *Economic Change in precolonial Africa: Senegambia in the Era of the Slave Trade* (Madison, 1975), p. 111.

24 This can be documented a hundred years later, during the Senegambia cholera epidemic; see D. Robinson, 'French "Islamic" policy and practice in late nineteenth century Senegal', *Journal of African History*, 1988, p. 424.

25 The exception is Futa Toro under the Denianke, and presumably ancient Takrur.
26 Robinson, *Chiefs and Clerics*, p. 26 n. 1.
27 A French study published in 1864, quoted in ibid., p. 8.
28 C. Quinn, 'A nineteenth century Fulbe state', *Journal of African History*, 1971, p. 428.
29 R. Jobson, *The Golden Trade* (London, 1623), p. 44.
30 Robinson, *Holy War*, p. 47.
31 S. Abubakar, *The Lamibe of Fombina: A Political History of Adamawa 1809–1901* (Zaria, 1977), p. 37.
32 L. Brenner and M. Last, 'The role of language in West African Islam', *Africa*, 1985, pp. 432ff.
33 Mamadu Samba of Futa Jallon (*c.* 1765–1852), quoted in Robinson, *Holy War*, p. 59.
34 Muhammad Bello, *Infaq al-Maysur* (*c.* 1812, trans. E. J. Arnett, *The Rise of the Sokoto Fulani* (Kano, 1922), pp. 137–8). Different sources give different identities to Uqba, and, as Robinson points out (*Holy War*, p. 84), Bello mentions three.
35 Quoted in P. Lovejoy, *Transformations in Slavery: A History of Slavery in Africa* (Cambridge, 1983), p. 30.
36 H. Fisher, 'Prayer and military activity in the history of Muslim activity south of the Sahara', *Journal of African History*, 1971, p. 403.
37 Quoted in L. G. Colvin, 'Islam and the state of Kajoor: a case of successful resistance to jihad', *Journal of African History*, 1974, p. 603.
38 Extract in Hodgkin, *Nigerian Perspectives*, p. 263.
39 Quoted in Brenner, 'Muslim thought', p. 44.
40 Colvin, 'Islam and the state of Kajoor', p. 590.
41 Levtzion, 'Islamic revolutions', in Levtzion and Voll, *Eighteenth-Century Renewal and Reform*, p. 24.
42 Dan Fodio was, for a time, the tutor of a Gobir prince, Yunfa, but did not, it seems, frequent the court.
43 M. Johnson, 'The economic foundations of an Islamic theocracy – the case of Masina', *Journal of African History*, 1976, p. 484.
44 Quoted in L. Sanneh, 'Field work among the Jakhanke of Senegambia', *Présence africaine*, 1975, p. 100.
45 C. Stewart, 'Southern Saharan scholarship and the *Bilad al-Sudan*', *Journal of African History*, 1976, p. 84.
46 Ahmad Al-Bekkay, quoted in Robinson, *Holy War*, p. 44.
47 Quoted in L. Brenner, 'Concepts of *tariqa* in West Africa: the case of the Qadiriyya', in Cruise O'Brien and Coulson, *Charisma and Brotherhood in African Islam* p. 39. See also A. Batran, 'The Kunta, Sidi al-Mukhtar al Kunti …', in J. R. Willis (ed.), *The Cultivators of Islam*, pp. 113ff.
48 Quoted in V. Monteuil, 'The Wolof kingdom of Kayor', in D. Forde and P. Kaberry (eds.), *West African Kingdoms in the Nineteenth Century* (London, 1967), p. 41.
49 *The Life and Travels of Mungo Park* (Edinburgh, 1896), p. 233.
50 Curtin, *Economic Change*, pp. 35–6.
51 'Cahiers de Yoro Dyao', 1933, quoted in M. Klein, 'Social and economic factors in the Muslim revolution in Senegambia', *Journal of African History*, 1972, p. 423.

52 Barry, 'The subordination of power', pp. 49–50. His analysis contrasts with that of Colvin, to whom the area was already Muslim. To Barry, the jihads marked a change from a situation where Islam was a merchant/clerical faith to where it became a popular ideology.

53 Barry, 'The subordination of power', pp. 59–60.

54 This account is based on C. Stewart with E. Stewart, *Islam and Social Order*, pp. 12ff. See also H. T. Norris, 'Znaga Islam during the seventeenth and eighteenth centuries', *Bulletin SOAS*, 1969, pp. 512ff.

55 N. Levtzion, 'The eighteenth century', in Levtzion and Voll, *Eighteenth Century Renewal and Reform*, p. 31

56 On its meaning, see Colvin, 'Islam and the state of Kajoor', p. 596.

57 Barbot, *Description*. p. 62.

58 Stewart, 'Southern Saharan scholarship', pp. 73ff.

59 M. Gomez, *Pragmatism in the Age of Jihad: The Precolonial State of Bundu* (Cambridge, 1992).

60 W. Rodney, 'Jihad and social revolution in Futa Djalon', pp. 269ff. Slave raiding, however, seems to have been a consequence rather than a cause of the jihad.

61 R. Botte, 'Révolte, pouvoir, religion: les Hubbu du Futa-Jalon (Guinée)', *Journal of African History* 1988, pp. 391ff.

62 Cerno Sadu Ibrahim, quoted in Robinson, *Holy War*, p. 119.

63 Especially in the late sixteenth and early seventeenth centuries. Robinson, 'The Islamic revolution', p. 189 n. 11.

64 Robinson, *Holy War*, p. 48; see pp. 221–2, 225 above.

65 J. Boyd and M. Last, 'The role of women as *"agents religieux"* in Sokoto', *Canadian Journal of African Studies*, 1985, p. 286.

66 Fisher, 'Prayer and military activity', p. 405 n 84.

67 Boyd and Last, 'The role of women', p. 285.

68 J. Lavers, 'Islam in the Bornu caliphate: a survey,' *Odu*, 1971, p. 29.

69 The Hausa form of Shaykh, the usual term for a Sufi master.

70 A. D. H. Bivar, 'The Wathiqat ahl al-Sudan: a manifesto of the jihad', *Journal of African History*, 1961, p. 240.

71 Hiskett, *The Sword of Truth*, p. 66; this is the main source for my account of dan Fodio.

72 F. de F. Daniel, 'A history of Katsina' (mimeo), fo. 16.

73 Muhammad na Birnin Gwari, extract in Hiskett, *Sword of Truth*, p. 155.

74 M. Hiskett, 'The nineteenth century jihads in West Africa', *Cambridge History of Africa*, V, p. 150.

75 Extract in Hodgkin, *Nigerian Perspectives*, p. 254.

76 Boyd and Last, 'The role of women', pp. 290–5.

77 On this, see Johnson, 'Masina', pp. 481–2.

78 *The Life and Travels of Mungo Park*, pp. 153, 154.

79 Roberts, *Warriors, Merchants*, pp. 21ff.

80 C. Stewart, 'Frontier disputes and problems of legitimation: Sokoto–Masina relations, 1817–1837', *Journal of African History*, 1976, p. 500. It seems Ahmadu offered allegiance to dan Fodio, but withdrew it during the succession dispute which followed the latter's death.

81 This account is based on Johnson, 'Masina', pp. 481ff.; Hiskett, 'Nineteenth century jihads', pp. 151–5, and on A. Hampate-Ba and J. Daget, *L'empire peul du Macina* (Paris, 1962).

82 There was an element of clan conflict – Ahmadu and his supporters belonged on the whole to the Bari clan, the *ardoen* to the Dikko branch of the Diallo clan (V. Azarya, 'Traders and the center in Massina, Kong, and Samori's state', *International Journal of African Historical Studies*, 1980, pp. 420ff.).

83 N. Levtzion, 'North-west Africa: from the Maghrib to the fringes of the forest', *Cambridge History of Africa*, IV: *From c. 1600 to c. 1790*, ed. R. Gray (1975), p. 198.

84 Roberts, *Warriors, Merchants*, p. 26. The expression Bambara Segu is used to distinguish it from al-Hajj Umar's later (Tukulor) state.

85 Azarya, 'Traders and the center', p. 431.

86 There is a substantial literature on Umar and the empire he founded. The most recent and authoritative study is Robinson, *Holy War*. R. Roberts, *Warriors, Merchants*, Ch. 3, is a study of political economy. See also J. M. Abun Nasr, *The Tijaniyya* (London, 1965).

87 Robinson, *Holy War*, p. 71.

88 Ibid., pp. 4 and 137.

89 He also visited Borno and Segu.

90 Willis, 'The writings of al-Hajj Umar al Futi', p. 179.

91 General Louis Faidherbe (1818–89) was Governor of Senegal from 1854 to 1861, and followed a policy of rapid expansion.

92 Robinson, *Chiefs and Clerics*, p. 43.

93 Quoted in ibid., p. 48.

94 Ibid., pp. 36–7.

95 Robinson, 'French "Islamic" policy', pp. 415ff.

96 D. Robinson, 'The "Chronicle of the Succession"': an important document for the Umarian state', *Journal of African History*, 1990, pp. 250ff.

97 J. D. Hargreaves, 'The Tokolor empire of Sègou and its relations with the French', in J. Butler (ed.), *Boston University Papers on African History*, II (Boston, 1966), p. 138.

98 Roberts, *Warriors, Merchants*, p. 119.

99 Ibid., p. 8.

100 Quoted in ibid., p. 134.

101 Quoted in M. Crowder, *West Africa under Colonial Rule* (London, 1968), p. 86.

102 C. Quinn, *Mandingo Kingdoms of the Senegambia* (Evanston, 1972); for a shorter account, see her 'Maba Diakhou and the Gambian jihad 1850–1890', in Willis, *Cultivators of Islam*, pp. 233ff.

103 Soninke refers to a linguistic subgroup of Mande; the Jakhanké are Soninke speakers. Because in the context of the nineteenth-century Gambia, Soninke means pagan, some prefer to use some form of Sarakollé for the linguistic group.

104 He carried no arms in person, but prepared amulets for the soldiers, and prayed on the battle field with an entourage of blind marabouts.

105 Quinn, 'Maba Diakhou', pp. 251–2.

106 Ibid., p. 254.

107 Y. Person is the leading authority on Samori; he is the author of a magisterial three-volume study, *Samori: une révolution Dyula* (3 vols., Dakar, 1968–75); see also his 'Samori and resistance to the French', in R. Rotberg and A. Mazrui, *Protest and Power in Black Africa* (New York, 1970), pp. 80ff.

108 Y. Person, 'Guinea-Samori', in M. Crowder (ed.) *West African Resistance* (London, 1971), p. 112.

109 Azarya, 'Traders and the center', p. 434.

110 Y. Person, 'Samori and Islam', in Willis, *Cultivators of Islam*, p. 261.

111 Person, 'Samori and resistance', p. 82.

112 M. Legassick, 'Firearms, horses and Samorian army organisation 1870–1898', *Journal of African History*, 1966, p. 105.

113 Ruth Schachter Morgenthau, *Political Parties in French-Speaking West Africa* (Oxford, 1964), pp. 324–5.

114 J. Thompson, 'Niger and Central Sudan sketches', *Scottish Geographical Magazine*, 1886, p. 592.

115 Robinson, *Al Hajj Umar*, pp. 85, 89, 134.

116 Brenner and Last, 'The role of language', pp. 432ff.

117 Quoted in M. Mason, 'The Nupe kingdom in the nineteenth century: a political history' (University of Birmingham, Ph.D. thesis, 1970), p. 466.

118 S. Crowther, *Journal of an Expedition up the Niger and Tsadda Rivers ... in 1854* (London, 1855), pp 157–8.

119 Mada oral history, quoted in E. Isichei, 'Introduction', *Studies in the History of Plateau State, Nigeria* (London, 1982), p. 46.

120 J. Hogendorn, 'Slave acquisition and delivery in precolonial Hausaland', in B. K. Swartz and R. Dumett, *West African Culture Dynamics* (The Hague, 1980), p. 480. This study (pp. 477ff.) analyses Zaria's systematic slave raiding as a major source of revenue and tribute.

121 A. Paton, 'An Islamic frontier polity: the Ningi mountains of northern Nigeria, 1846–1902', in I. Kopytoff (ed.), *The African Frontier* (Bloomington, 1987), pp. 195ff.

122 P. Staudinger, *Im Herzen der Hausaländer* (1891), quoted in P. Lovejoy, 'Slavery in the Sokoto caliphate', in Lovejoy (ed.), *The Ideology of Slavery in Africa* (Beverly Hills and London, 1981), p. 230.

123 E. Isichei, 'On being invisible: an historical perspective of the Anaguta and their neighbours', *The International Journal of African Historical Studies*, 1991, p. 538. The date is estimated from an archival account collected from a Bauchi participant in the raid in 1915.

124 Ibid., p. 524.

125 T. M. Baker, 'The social organisation of the Birom' (University of London, Ph.D. thesis, 1965), p. 119.

17 THE EASTERN AND CENTRAL SUDAN

1 H. Barth, *Travels and Discoveries in North and Central Africa* (New York, 1857–9, London, 1965 reprint), II, p. 544.

2 See D. Cordell, 'The savanna belt of North-Central Africa', in D. Birmingham and P. M. Martin (eds.), *History of Central Africa* (London, 1983), I, pp. 30ff., for an exception; also H. Fisher, 'The central Sahara and Sudan', in *Cambridge History of Africa*, IV: *From c. 1600 to c. 1790*, ed. R. Gray (1975), pp. 58ff. Fisher's 'Central Sudan' extends still further west, including Hausaland and Kwararafa.

3 Cordell, 'The savanna belt', pp. 43–4.

4 But cf. p. 50 above.

5 N. David, 'Prehistory and historical linguistics in Central Africa: points of contact', in C. Ehret and M. Posnansky (eds.), *The Archaeological and Linguistic Reconstruction of African History* (Berkeley and Los Angeles, 1982), p. 80.

6 Here I follow David, 'Prehistory', p. 88; see D. E. Saxon, 'Linguistic evidence

for the eastward spread of the Ubangian peoples', in Ehret and Posnansky, *Archaeological and Linguistic Reconstruction*, pp. 66–77.

7 To be consistent, one should refer to them without the prefix, as Zande; Azande is more familiar, because of the writings of Evans-Pritchard.

8 W. Y. Adams, *Nubia Corridor to Africa* (Princeton, 1977), p. 548.

9 Quoted in P. M. Holt, 'The Islamization of the Nilotic Sudan', in M. Brett (ed.), *Northern Africa: Islam and Modernization* (London, 1973), p. 15.

10 Burckhardt, in 1813, quoted in Adams, *Nubia*, p. 563.

11 Adams, *Nubia*, pp. 557–8.

12 Ibid., pp. 567, 575. *Baraka* is a transmittable blessing emanating from the holy.

13 R. S. O'Fahey and J. L. Spaulding, *Kingdoms of the Sudan* (London, 1974), pp. 30–1, summarising data in F. Caillaud, *Voyage à Meroé* (1823). O'Fahey and Spaulding's joint study is my main source for the account which follows.

14 O'Fahey and Spaulding, *Kingdoms of the Sudan*, p. 23.

15 James Bruce, who visited Nubia in 1772, quoted in Adams, *Nubia*, p. 601.

16 Bruce, quoted in O'Fahey and Spaulding, *Kingdoms of the Sudan*, p. 26.

17 Ibid., pp. 29 and 33. See Adams, *Nubia*, p. 600: 'there is no such thing as a Funj tribe or language. They were, rather, a hereditary ruling caste.'

18 Ibid., pp. 61–3.

19 Ibid., pp. 68–9.

20 'Leo Africanus' [al-Hassan ibn Muhammad], *The History and Description of Africa* (trans. John Pory, 1600; Hakluyt, 1st series, XCIV, 1896), III, p. 835.

21 Barth, II, p. 545. See p. 232 above.

22 P. Kalck, 'Pour une localisation du royaume de Gaoga', *Journal of African History*, 1972, pp. 529ff.; see the discussion by H. Fisher, 'The eastern Maghrib and the Central Sudan', *Cambridge History of Africa*, III: *From c. 1050 to c. 1600*, ed. R. Oliver (1977), p. 304.

23 The main source for the account which follows is R. S. O'Fahey, 'Dar Fur', in O'Fahey and Spaulding, *Kingdoms of the Sudan*, pp. 107–86.

24 A Keira prince was restored from 1898 to 1916.

25 Quoted in O'Fahey, 'Dar Fur', p. 121.

26 Quoted in R. S. O'Fahey, 'Fur and Fartit: the history of a frontier', in J. Mack and P. Robertshaw (eds.), *Culture History in the Southern Sudan: Archaeology, Linguistics, and Ethnohistory* (Nairobi, 1982), p. 78.

27 Ibid., pp. 153–4.

28 This account is based on Fisher, 'The central Sahara and Sudan', pp. 137ff. The Tunjur were dominant in the area at the time.

29 Barth, II, p. 643.

30 Quoted in Fisher, 'The central Sahara and Sudan', p. 138.

31 S. W. Koelle, *Polyglotta Africana* (London, 1854), p. 21.

32 Barth, II, p. 643.

33 Fisher, 'The central Sahara and Sudan', p. 132.

34 Barth, II, pp. 549–50.

35 Ibid., II, p. 557.

36 Ibid., II, p. 555.

37 Ibid., II, pp. 557, 644–5.

38 Ibid., II, p. 560.

39 L. Brenner, *The Shehus of Kukawa* (London, 1973), is the standard account.

40 Quoted in ibid., pp. 30–1.

41 E. Bovill, *Missions to the Niger* (Hakluyt, London, 1966), p. 113 (Denham's narrative).
42 L. Brenner, 'Muhammad al-Amin al-Kanemi and religion and politics in Borno', in J. R. Willis (ed.), *Studies in West African Islamic History: The Cultivators of Islam* (London, 1979), p. 170.
43 Barth, *Travels and Discoveries*, II, p. 599.
44 Better known by its Kanuri name, Mandara; this appears, with other local ethonyms, on a European map of 1459.
45 Barth, *Travels and Discoveries*, III, p. 51.
46 Ibid., II, p. 599.
47 'Leo Africanus' (al-Hassan ibn Muhammad), *History*, pp. 833–4.
48 Barth, *Travels and Discoveries*, II, p. 316.
49 Brenner, *The Shehus*, p. 104.
50 Ibid., p. 87.
51 C. Keim, 'Long distance trade and the Mangbetu', *Journal of African History*, 1983, pp. 1ff.
52 E. Evans-Pritchard, 'A contribution to the study of Zande culture', *Africa*, 1960, p. 309.
53 E. E. Evans-Pritchard, *Witchcraft, Oracles and Magic among the Azande* (Oxford, 1937), pp. 13–20; A Singer and B. Street (eds.), *Zande Themes* (Oxford, 1972).
54 M. Johnson, 'Calico caravans: the Tripoli–Kano trade after 1880', *Journal of African History*, 1976, pp. 95ff.
55 D. Cordell, 'Eastern Libya, Wadai and the Sanusiya: a tariqa and a trade route', *Journal of African History*, 1977, pp. 21ff.
56 R. Collins, 'Sudanese factors in the history of the Congo', in Yusuf Fadl Hasan (ed.), *Sudan in Africa* (Khartoum, 1971), pp. 156ff.
57 Cordell, 'The savanna belt', pp. 68–70.
58 'Narrative of the Travels of Ali Eisami', in P. Curtin (ed.), *Africa Remembered* (Madison, 1967), pp 207–8.
59 Barth, *Travels and Discoveries*, II, p. 646.

18   THE ATLANTIC SLAVE TRADE

1 Quoted in M. Jackson, *The Kuranko: Dimensions of Social Reality in a West African Society* (London, 1977), p. 237.
2 This expression was once used by Marion Johnson.
3 R. Harms, *River of Wealth, River of Sorrow* (New Haven and London, 1981), p. 2.
4 W. Smith, *A New Voyage to Guinea* (London, 1744), p. 266, citing Charles Wheeler, on the Gold Coast.
5 Y. Abdallah, *The Yaos* (Zomba, 1919), p. 10. See p. 436 below.
6 R. Kea, ' "I am here to plunder on the general road": bandits and banditry in the pre-nineteenth century Gold Coast', in D. Crummey (ed.), *Banditry, Rebellion and Social Protest in Africa* (London, 1986), p. 111, quoting traditions collected in the 1740s by Ludwig Roemer.
7 Pede Mangdar of Njak, in August 1979, text in E. Isichei (ed.), *Jos Oral History and Literature Texts* I (Jos, 1981), p. 719. Nigeria National Archives, Kaduna, SNP K 3328; H. D. Foulkes, 'Some preliminary notes on the Angass', 1907. For Benin and north Togo versions, see A. F. Iroko, 'Cauris et esclaves en Afrique occidentale entre le xvie et le xixe siècles', in S. Daget (ed.), *Colloque internationale sur la traite des noirs* (Nantes, 1985), I, pp. 199ff.

8   Paul Edwards (ed.), *The Life of Olaudah Equiano* (London, 1988), pp. 22, 30, 32. There is much other evidence of this.

9   *The Life and Travels of Mungo Park* (Edinburgh, 1896), p. 262.

10 See p. 390 below.

11 W. H. Bentley, *Pioneering on the Congo* (London, 1900), I, p. 252.

12 W. MacGaffey, *Modern Kongo Prophets* (Bloomington, 1983), p. 135. This study contains other modern examples of this kind.

13 J. M. Janzen, *Lemba 1650–1930: A Drum of Affliction in Africa and the New World* (New York and London, 1982), pp. 223–8, also xiii.

14 Harms, *River of Wealth*, pp. 38–9.

15 A review of W. E. F. Ward, *The Royal Navy and the Slavers* in *West Africa*, 15 March 1969, referring to the British anti-slavery squadron.

16 Eric Williams, *Capitalism and Slavery* (Durham, N.C., 1945).

17 See S. Engerman, 'The slave trade and British capital formation in the eighteenth century: a comment on the Williams thesis', *Business History Review*, 1972, pp. 430ff.; S. Engerman and D. Eltis, 'Economic aspects of the abolition debate', in C. Bolt and S. Drescher (eds.), *Anti-Slavery, Religion and Reform* (Folkestone, 1980), pp. 272ff.

18 W. Rodney, *How Europe Underdeveloped Africa* (London, 1972). For a succinct statement, see I. Wallerstein, 'The three stages of African involvement in the world economy, in P. Gutkind and I. Wallerstein (eds.), *The Political Economy of Contemporary Africa* (London, 1976), pp. 30ff.

19 P. O'Brien, 'European economic development: the contribution of the periphery', *Economic History Review*, 1982, pp. 1ff. See also I. Wallerstein, 'European economic development: a comment on O'Brien', *Economic History Review*, 1983, pp. 580ff.

20 Basil Davidson, *Black Mother Africa: The Years of Trial* (London, 1972); Rodney, *How Europe Underdeveloped Africa* and 'African slavery and other forms of social oppression on the Upper Guinea coast in the context of the Atlantic slave trade', *Journal of African History*, 1966, pp. 431ff., reprinted in J. Inikori (ed.), *Forced Migrations* (London, 1982), pp. 61ff.

21 Davidson, *Black Mother*, pp. 205–6. See E. Isichei, *The Ibo People and the Europeans: The Genesis of a Relationship to 1906* (London, 1973), p. 47.

22 J. D. Fage, 'Slavery and the slave trade in the context of West African history', *Journal of African History*, 1969, p. 397. This model was criticised by C. Wrigley, 'Historicism in Africa: slavery and state formation', *African Affairs*, 1971, pp. 113–24.

23 Isichei, *The Ibo People and the Europeans* and *A History of Nigeria* (Harlow, 1983), pp. 93ff. See R. Law, 'Human sacrifice in colonial West Africa', *African Affairs*, 1985, p. 56.

24 D. Northrup, *Trade without Rulers* (Oxford, 1978); see also A. J. H. Latham, *Old Calabar 1600–1891* (Oxford, 1973). Igbo scholars, for different reasons, sometimes avoided acknowledging my work. A notable instance is A. E. Afigbo, 'Igboland before 1800', in O. Ikime (ed.), *Groundwork of Nigerian History* (Ibadan, 1980) which makes no reference to the three books on Igbo history I published between 1973 and 1977, but uses (with due acknowledgement) one of my maps!

25 See, for instance, P. Lovejoy, *Transformations in Slavery: A History of Slavery in Africa* (Cambridge, 1983) and P. Manning, *Slavery and African Life* (Cambridge, 1990); Miller, *Way of Death* and other works by these remarkable scholars.

26 D. Eltis, *Economic Growth and the Ending of the Transatlantic Slave Trade* (New York, 1987), p. 72; see p. 183 – 'The slave and commodity-export trades together formed such a small percentage of total African economic activity' that the expansion of one would not affect the growth of the other.

27 Ibid., p. 67. The European emigration figures are for 1846–1932.

28 Manning, *Slavery and African Life*, p. 71.

29 Ibid., p. 85.

30 Lovejoy, *Transformations*, pp. 8–11; Manning, *Slavery and African Life*, pp. 126ff.

31 P. D. Curtin, *The Atlantic Slave Trade: A Census* (Madison, Wis., 1969).

32 P. Lovejoy, 'The impact of the Atlantic slave trade on Africa: a review of the literature', *Journal of African History*, 1989, p. 373.

33 An interloper was, for instance, a British merchant trading in a part of Africa where the Portuguese claimed exclusive rights. On smuggling and 'tightpacking' see Miller, *Way of Death*, pp. 336–51. But cf. Lovejoy, 'The impact of the Atlantic slave trade', p. 373 n. 43, for the suggestion that 'there may be less missing data than some scholars might like to think'.

34 D. Henige, 'Measuring the immeasurable: the Atlantic slave trade, West African population and the Pyrrhonian critic', *Journal of African History*, 1986, pp. 295ff.

35 See J. E. Inikori, 'Measuring the Atlantic slave trade: an assessment of Curtin and Anstey', *Journal of African History*, 1976, pp. 197ff.

36 Lovejoy, *Transformations*, p. 61.

37 Miller, *Way of Death*, p. 384.

38 Lovejoy, 'The impact of the Atlantic slave trade', pp. 381ff.; D. Geggus, 'Sex ratio, age and ethnicity in the Atlantic slave trade: data from French shipping', *Journal of African History*, 1989, pp. 23ff. and 'Sex ratio and ethnicity: a reply to Paul Lovejoy', *Journal of African History*, 1989, pp. 395ff. Eltis, *Economic Growth*, pp. 256–8, tabulates a great deal of data for the period after 1810.

39 Instructions to Captain William Barry, 7 Oct. 1725, in E. Donnan (ed.), *Documents Illustrative of the History of the Slave Trade* (Washington, 1930–5), II, p. 327.

40 There is an interesting analysis of this census in J. Thornton, 'The slave trade in eighteenth century Angola: effects on demographic structures', *Canadian Journal of African Studies*, 1980, pp. 417ff.

41 Manning, *Slavery and African Life*, p. 120.

42 H. Barth, *Travels and Discoveries in North and Central Africa* (New York, 1857–9, London, 1965 reprint), I, p. 527.

43 Des Marchais, quoted in R. Law, *The Slave Coast of West Africa 1550–1750*, (Oxford, 1991), p. 64. He cites other evidence to the same effect; but Bosman, as he points out, states that 'Men as well as women ... are vigorously industrious' (W. Bosman, *A New and Accurate Description of the Coast of Guinea* (1704, London, 1967 reprint), p. 342).

44 My account here is based on J. Thornton, 'Sexual demography: the impact of the slave trade on family structure', in C. Robertson and M. Klein (eds.), *Women and Slavery in Africa* (Madison, 1983), esp. pp. 41ff. Women were never involved in hunting, but did catch fish, especially with nets and traps, in some societies.

45 Lemos Coelho, quoted in Thornton, 'Sexual demography', p. 44.

46 Manuel Alvares, quoted in Thornton, 'Sexual demography', p. 44. See also the extracts in J. Fage, 'Slaves and society in western Africa *c.* 1445–1700', *Journal of African History*, 1980, pp. 304–5.

47 Bosman, *A New and Accurate Description*, p. 344.
48 Manning, *Slavery and African Life*, p. 99. The reasons for this are complex: in part it reflects the very high prices of adult slaves in the Americas (encouraging the purchase of children, who were cheaper). It was often an attempt to circumvent Portuguese regulations on the number of slaves a ship could carry (Miller, *Way of Death*, pp. 346–8).
49 Lovejoy, 'The impact of the Atlantic slave trade', p. 385.
50 Quoted in ibid., p. 387.
51 Miller, *Way of Death*, pp. 153ff.; his views are particularly instructive, since he devotes so much detailed atention to the various forms of suffering and mortality the slave trade caused.
52 Ibid., pp. 195 and 382ff.
53 Ibid., pp. 390–1.
54 Ibid., p. 410.
55 S. W. Koelle, *Polyglotta Africana* (London, 1854), p. 18.
56 Law, *Slave Coast*, p. 69. See pp. 199–200 for the importance of cowries.
57 Bosman, *A New and Accurate Description*, p. 354.
58 Lovejoy, *Transformations*, p. 19. The total was later revised to 11,863,000 in the light of research by David Richardson.
59 P. Curtin, 'Epidemiology and the slave trade', *Political Science Quarterly*, 1968, pp. 190ff.
60 Figures quoted in Manning, *Slavery and African Life*, p. 31; they have been challenged.
61 Quoted in A. W. Crosby, *The Columban Exchange: Biological and Cultural Consequences of 1492* (Westport, Conn., 1973 edition), p. 36. The general effects of smallpox are described in Ch. 2, pp. 35ff. *passim.*
62 Quoted in B. Barry, 'The subordination of power and the mercantile economy: the kingdom of Waalo, 1600–1831', in R. Cruise O'Brien (ed.), *The Political Economy of Underdevelopment* (Beverly Hills, 1979), pp. 47–8.
63 P. D. Curtin, *Economic Change in Precolonial Africa: Senegambia in the Era of the Slave Trade* (Madison, 1975), p. 169.
64 R. P. Thomas and R. N. Bean, 'The fishers of men: the profits of the slave trade', *The Journal of Economic History*, 1974, pp. 908ff. Firearms, where used, were an economic input; there is also the value of the slave's services if retained in the captor society.
65 Law, *Slave Coast*, p. 175. It is relevant in other ways – it was because they were 'cheap' that slaves were bought at all.
66 Lovejoy, 'The impact of the Atlantic slave trade', p. 374.
67 Curtin, *The Atlantic Trade*, p. 100.
68 P. D. Curtin, 'The external trade of West Africa to 1800', in J. F. A. Ajayi and M. Crowder (eds.), *History of West Africa*, I (3rd edn, Harlow, 1985), pp. 644–5.
69 J. Barbot, *A Description of the Coasts of North and South Guinea* (vol. V in Churchill's *Voyages and Travels*, London, 1746), p. 381. The citation of this type of impressionistic evidence is now unfashionable; the counting of heads is preferred, but when the evidence is incomplete, the opinions of participants are not to be despised. In my 1973 study (*The Ibo People and the Europeans*, pp. 45–6) I cited this and other passages in support of 'a substantial number' of slaves from the Delta in the late seventeenth century. In 1989, Lovejoy writes, 'Perhaps Richardson's most important discovery concerns the trade of the Bight

of Biafra, which he shows to have been substantial from at least the beginning of the eighteenth century ... Richardson's data show a ... gradual but nonetheless significant expansion that began before 1700 [rather than from the 1730s on]' (Lovejoy, 'The impact of the Atlantic slave trade', pp. 373–4).

70 Lovejoy, *Transformations*, p. 58. His 'The impact of the Atlantic slave trade', p. 374, implies an upward modification.

71 J. Adams, *Remarks on the Country Extending from Cape Palmas to the River Congo* (London, 1823, 1966 reprint), p. 129. (This is cited in Isichei, *The Ibo People and the Europeans*, p. 46.) The comparability of the contemporary estimate and the results attained by later research is striking; the difference *may* reflect unrecorded voyages. Old Calabar is modern Calabar, and New Calabar is Elim Kalabari. The two were unrelated, speaking Efik and Ijo respectively.

72 W. Rodney, *A History of the Upper Guinea Coast 1545–1800* (Oxford, 1969), pp. 181ff.

73 P. Martin, 'The trade of Loango in the seventeenth and eighteenth centuries', in R. Gray and D. Birmingham (eds.), *Pre-Colonial African Trade* (London, 1970), p. 139. The hairs from elephants' tails were a component in jewellery.

74 Duarte Pacheco Pereira, *Esmeraldo de situ orbis* (trans. G. H. T. Kimble, 1937, Hakluyt, 2nd series, pp. 126, 128–9).

75 J. Welsh, 'A voyage to Benin beyond the countrey of Guinea', extract in T. Hodgkin, *Nigerian Perspectives* (2nd edn, London, 1975, first pub. 1960), p. 143.

76 R. Jobson, *The Golden Trade* (London, 1932, first pub. 1623), p. 112.

77 Quoted in Law, *The Slave Coast*, p. 194.

78 P. Martin, *The External Trade of the Loango Coast 1576–1870* (Oxford, 1972), pp. 52ff.

79 Barbot, *A Description of the Coasts*, pp. 345–6.

80 Instructions to Captain William Barry, 7 Oct. 1725, in Donnan, *Documents*, II, p. 327.

81 Barbot, *A Description of the Coasts*, p. 45.

82 R. Bean, 'A note on the relative importance of slaves and gold in West African exports', *Journal of African History*, 1974, pp. 351ff. See E. van den Boogaart, 'The trade between western Africa and the Atlantic world 1600–90', *Journal of African History*, 1992, Table 4, p. 378 and p. 382.

83 Harms, *River of Wealth*, pp. 5, 50–1.

84 Laws, *The Slave Coast*, p. 149.

85 Harms, *River of Wealth*, p. 70.

86 Quoted in Fage, 'Slaves and society', p. 306.

87 Barbot, *A Description of the Coasts*, pp. 47–8.

88 P. E. H. Hair, 'The enslavement of Koelle's informants', *Journal of African History*, 1965, pp. 196ff.

89 Bosman, *A New and Accurate Description*, p. 364.

90 A. Dalzel, *The History of Dahomy, An Inland Kingdom of Africa* (London 1793, 1967 reprint), pp. 218–19. Dalzel was a slave trader, concerned to show that the slave trade did not lead to an increase in war.

91 Report of the Lords of the Council, I, William James' Evidence; cf. also Falconbridge's Evidence.

92 *The Life of Olaudah Equiano ... Written by Himself* (1789, Harlow, 1988 edition), pp. 2, 7, 15–16.

93 Zachary Macaulay, Journal, 18 Nov. 1793, extract in C. Fyfe, *Sierra Leone Inheritance* (London, 1964), p. 75. The reference is to individuals accused of witchcraft or adultery being given a choice between enslavement or the poison ordeal; he goes on to describe the enslavement of whole villages by a local ruler when a child was taken by alligators or wild animals.

94 T. Clarkson, *The Substance of the Evidence* (London, 1789), p. 120, Baggs' Evidence; see Rodney, *A History of the Upper Guinea Coast*, pp. 106–8 and 114–15. See also p. 393 below.

95 F. Moore, *Travels into the Inland Parts of Africa* (1738) quoted in Lovejoy, *Transformations*, p. 87.

96 Law, *Slave Coast*, p. 184.

97 See p. 436 below. The phrase 'texts of terror' is the title of a book by Phyllis Trible – an exegesis, from a feminist viewpoint, of certain stories in the Hebrew Bible.

98 Letter from Afonso in B. Davidson, *The African Past: Chronicles from Antiquity to Modern Times* (Harmondsworth, 1964), pp. 194–7.

99 P. Curtin, *Economic Change*, p. 183. D. Robinson, *The Holy War of Umar Tal* (Oxford, 1985), p. 63, points out that the rulers of the Futas prohibited the enslavement of Muslims, especially local Muslims, but profited by trade in slaves from further afield.

100 I. Wilks, *Asante in the Nineteenth Century* (1975, Cambridge, 1989 edition), p. 673.

101 Miller, *Way of Death*, pp. 40ff.

102 S. Johnson, *History of the Yorubas* (1921, Lagos, 1973 reprint), p. 321.

103 See p. 349 below.

104 Rodney found no evidence of domestic slavery in Upper Guinea in the late sixteenth century; it was a dominant feature by the late eighteenth, especially in Mande and Fulbe communities involved in slave trading (W. Rodney, 'African slavery and other forms of social oppression on the Upper Guinea coast in the context of the Atlantic slave trade', reprinted in Inikori, *Forced Migration*, pp. 61ff. But see Fage, 'Slaves and society in western Africa', pp. 289ff.

105 Manning, *Slavery and African Life*, p. 23; Lovejoy, *Transformations*, pp. 9–11.

106 E. Isichei, *Igbo Worlds* (London and Basingstoke, 1978), p. 289.

107 This is questioned in R. Law, 'Human sacrifice in pre-colonial West Africa', *African Affairs*, 1985, pp. 53ff.

108 P. de Marees, quoted in Fage, 'Slaves and society', p. 308.

109 Bosman, *A New and Accurate Description*, p. 231.

110 A Dutch trader in 1718, quoted in Law, *Slave Coast*, p. 212.

111 Quoted in Law, *Slave Coast*, p. 289.

112 A. F. C. Ryder, *Benin and the Europeans 1485–1897* (Harlow, 1969), p. 40.

113 D. Richardson, 'West Africa consumption patterns and their influence on the eighteenth-century English slave trade', in H. Gemery and J. Hogendorn (eds.), *The Uncommon Market* (New York, 1979), p. 316.

114 F. Pigafetta, *A Report of the Kingdom of Congo* (based on information from Duarte Lopez) (1591, London, 1981 reprint), pp. 30–1.

115 Ryder, *Benin and the Europeans*, pp. 88, 93–5. Adams, *Remarks on the Country*, pp. 97 and 108.

116 Traditional cloths were still made for ceremonial – and sometimes elite – wear.

117 Bentley, *Pioneering on the Congo* , I, p. 253.

118 Miller, *Way of Death*, p. 75.

119 F. O. 2/64, Mills to MacDonald (copy), 7 June 1894.

120 Law, *Slave Coast*, pp. 199–204.

121 J. Atkins, *A Voyage to Guinea, Brasil and the West Indies* (London, 1735), p. 159.

122 Adams, *Remarks on the Country*, p. 252.

123 G. White, 'Firearms in Africa: an introduction', *Journal of African History*, 1971, p. 180.

124 J. Inikori, 'The import of firearms into West Africa, 1750 to 1807: a quantitative analysis', in Inikori, *Forced Migrations*, p. 147.

125 Miller, *Way of Death*, pp. 87–8.

126 J. Hogendorn and M. Johnson, *The Shell Money of the Slave Trade* (Cambridge, 1986), pp. 148ff.

127 W. Ofonagoro, quoted in ibid., p. 154.

128 H. Crow, *Memoirs of Captain Hugh Crow* (London, 1830), pp. 272–3; see p. 356 below for the comparable case of Perekule of Bonny.

129 T. McCaskie, 'Accumulation, wealth and belief in Asante history. Part 1: To the close of the nineteenth century', *Africa*, 1983, p. 38.

130 Isichei, *The Ibo People and the Europeans*, pp. 50–1.

131 See pp. 72–3 above.

132 J. Thornton, *Africa and Africans in the Making of the Atlantic World, 1400–1680*, (Cambridge, 1992), pp. 44–53.

133 F. Coillard, *On the Threshold of Central Africa* (London, 1897), p. 222. For a comparable case, see p. 367 below.

134 J. Vansina, *The Children of Woot: A History of the Kuba Peoples* (Madison, Wis., 1978), p. 59.

135 Quoted in D. Crawford, *Thinking Black* (London, 1913), p. 413. The reference is to Christianity.

136 Quoted in J. Vansina, 'Finding food and the history of precolonial Equatorial Africa: a plea', *African Economic History*, 1979, p. 12.

137 J. Thornton, *The Kingdom of Kongo: Civil War and Transition 1614–1718* (Madison, 1983), p. 23.

138 Vansina, *The Children of Woot*, p. 348 n. 15.

139 T. Q. Reefe, *The Rainbow and the Kings: A History of the Luba Empire to 1891* (Berkeley, 1981), p. 59.

140 Ibid., p. 59. The text reads 'manioc', not 'cassava'.

141 Curtin, *Economic Change*, p. 24.

142 See J. Vansina, 'The peoples of the forest', in D. Birmingham and P. Martin (eds.), *History of Central Africa*, I (Harlow, 1983), p. 109.

143 K. D. Patterson and G. Hartwig, 'The disease factor: an introductory overview', in G. Hartwig and K. Patterson, *Disease in African History* (Durham, N.C., 1978), p. 9.

144 K. Kiple and V. H. King, *Another Dimension to the Black Diaspora Diet Disease and Racism* (Cambridge, 1981), Chs. 2–4. See p. 74.

145 K. D. Patterson, 'River blindness in northern Ghana 1900–1950', in Hartwig and Patterson, *Disease in African History*, p. 88.

146 They were established earlier in West Africa; either their impact was less dramatic, because local people developed efficient means of dealing with the problem, or it has not been recorded.

147 This is overwhelmingly probable, but has been disputed. See A. W. Crosby,

'The early history of syphilis: a reappraisal', in his *The Columban Exchange*, pp. 122ff.

148 O. Dapper, *Description de l'Afrique* (Fr. trans. 1786), p. 118. On the identity of the Quoja, see P. E. H. Hair, 'Ethnolinguistic continuity on the Guinea coast', *Journal of African History*, 1967, p. 257.

149 Eltis, *Economic Growth*, pp. 72–3; see Manning, *Slavery and African Life*, p. 126.

150 See p. 409 below.

19 WEST AFRICA TO 1800

1 J. Barbot, *A Description of the Coasts of North and South Guinea* (London, 1746), p. 270.

2 P. Curtin, 'The external trade of West Africa', in J. F. A. Ajayi and M. Crowder (eds.), *History of West Africa*, I (3rd edn, Harlow, 1985), p. 629. See p. 218 above.

3 I. Wilks, *Asante in the Nineteenth Century* (Cambridge, 2nd edn, 1989), pp. 127–9.

4 S. Johnson, *The History of the Yorubas* (Lagos, 1921, 1971 reprint), p. 50; J. Spencer, 'The history of Asaba and its kings', *Niger and Yoruba Notes*, 1901, p. 21.

5 R. Law, *The Oyo Empire c. 1600–c. 1836*, (Oxford, 1977), pp. 99, 100, 165.

6 See p. 344 below.

7 A. G. Leonard, 'Notes of a journey to Bende', *Journal of the Manchester Geographical Society*, 1898, p. 198.

8 See pp. 257–8 above.

9 M. Jackson, *The Kuranko: Dimensions of Social Reality in a West African Society* (London, 1977), p. 4.

10 K. Wylie, *The Political Kingdoms of the Temne: Temne Government in Sierra Leone, 1825–1910* (New York, 1977), p. 3: a literal migration would mean that all their linguistic relatives migrated too. They are described in modern Sierra Leone in the earliest European accounts.

11 E. F. Sayers in 1927, quoted in ibid., pp. 6–7.

12 Ibid., p. 21.

13 J. Atkins, *A Voyage to Guinea, Brasil and the West-Indies* (2nd edn, London, 1737), pp. 41–2.

14 T. Winterbottom, *An Account of the Native Africans in the Neighbourhood of Sierra Leone* (London, 1803), I, p. 6.

15 R. Kea, *Settlements, Trade and Politics in the Seventeenth-Century Gold Coast* (Baltimore and London, 1982), pp. 169ff.

16 J. E. Casely Hayford, *Gold Coast Native Institutions*, quoted in D. Kimble, *A Political History of Ghana: The Rise of Gold Coast Nationalism 1850–1928* (Oxford, 1963), p. 6 n. 2.

17 R. Kea, ' "I am here to plunder on the general road": bandits and banditry in the pre-nineteenth century Gold Coast', in D. Crummey (ed.), *Banditry, Rebellion and Social Protest in Africa* (London, 1986), p. 116.

18 Kea, *Settlements, Trade*, p. 19. For a different interpretation, cf. K. Daaku, 'Trade and trading patterns of the Akan in the seventeenth and eighteenth centuries', in C. Meillassoux (ed.), *The Development of Indigenous Trade and Markets in West Africa* (London, 1971), pp. 174–9 – on the popularity of long-distance trading journeys as a rite of passage, and the 'easy social mobility' trade afforded.

19 Quoted in Kea, *Settlements, Trade*, p. 179.
20 Kea, 'Bandits and banditry', pp. 109ff.
21 Barbot, *A Description*, p. 321. See W. Bosman, *A New and Accurate Description of the Coast of Guinea* (London, 1705, 1967 reprint), pp 330–1.
22 Kea, *Settlements, Trade*, pp. 286–7.
23 Barbot, *A Description*, p. 189.
24 Du Cassé in 1688, quoted in R. Kea, 'Administration and trade in the Akwamu empire', in B. Swartz and R. Dumett (eds.), *West African Culture Dynamics: Archaeological and Historical Perspectives* (The Hague, 1980), p. 374.
25 Bosman, *A New and Accurate Description*, p. 70.
26 L. Roemer, quoted in R. Atkinson, 'Old Akyem and the origins of Akyems Abuakwa and Kotoku', in Swartz and Dumett, *West African Culture Dynamics*, p. 355.
27 R. Kea, 'Firearms and warfare on the Gold and Slave Coasts from the sixteenth to the nineteenth centuries', *Journal of African History*, 1971, pp. 185ff.
28 Kea, 'Bandits and banditry', pp. 126–7. This point was also made in a study by W. Rodney, 'Gold and slaves on the Gold Coast', *Transactions of the Historical Society of Ghana*, 1969, p. 25.
29 Kea, *Settlements, Trade*, p. 140.
30 Rodney, 'Gold and slaves on the Gold Coast', p. 17.
31 I. Wilks, 'The Mossi and Akan states, 1400 to 1800', in Ajayi and Crowder, *History of West Africa*, p. 502.
32 A. N. Klein, 'The two Asantes: competing interpretations of "slavery" in Akan–Asante culture and society', in P. Lovejoy (ed.), *The Ideology of Slavery in Africa* (Beverly Hills, 1981), p. 164. T. McCaskie has made this point in a number of papers.
33 E. Isichei, *History of West Africa since 1800* (London and Basingstoke, 1977), Ch. 3, 'Innovation and reform in the States of Guinea'.
34 R. Law, 'Human sacrifice in pre-colonial West Africa', *African Affairs*, 1985, pp. 53ff.; I discussed human sacrifice in E. Isichei, 'The quest for social reform in the context of traditional religion', *African Affairs*, 1977, p. 469, and elsewhere, in work which Law analysed in some detail. The theme was explored more fully in two seminal papers which appeared later: R. Law, ' "My head belongs to the king": on the political and ritual significance of decapitation in pre-colonial Dahomey', *Journal of African History*, 1989, pp. 399ff. and T. McCaskie, 'Death and the Asantehene: a historical meditation', *Journal of African History*, 1989, pp. 417ff. Witchcraft persecution has also been treated in the 'rationalist' way – primarily by social anthropologists. For an analysis by a historian in this vein, cf. A. J. H. Latham, 'Witchcraft accusations and economic tensions in precolonial Old Calabar', *Journal of African History*, 1972, pp. 249ff.
35 This point has been elaborated by T. McCaskie; see for instance, 'Komfo Anokye of Asante: meaning, history and philosophy in an African society', *Journal of African History*, 1986, p. 329.
36 J. Yoder, 'Fly and elephant parties: political polarisation in Dahomey, 1840–1870', *Journal of African History*, 1974, pp. 417ff.
37 Because of matrilineally based claim to office, Opuku Ware was Osei Tutu's sister's daughter's son.
38 Quoted in Wilks, 'Mossi and Akan states', p. 499.
39 L. F. Roemer, cited in Wilks, *Asante in the Nineteenth Century*, p. 26 n. 136.

40   Wilks, 'Mossi and Akan states', p. 501.

41   T. McCaskie, 'Accumulation, wealth and belief in Asante history', *Africa*, 1983, pp. 23ff. My account here is based on this remarkable paper.

42   This is elaborated by McCaskie; see for instance, his 'Death and the Asantehene', pp. 417ff.

43   Here I follow McCaskie; there are other ways of looking at large trees, which are also (?primarily) valued for their shade!

44   Quoted in McCaskie, 'Death and the Asantehene', p. 426.

45   M. E. Kropp Dakubu, 'The peopling of southern Ghana: a linguistic viewpoint', in C. Ehret and M. Posnansky, *The Archaeological and Linguistic Reconstruction of African History* (Berkeley and Los Angeles, 1982), p. 254.

46   M. McCarthy, *Social Change and the Growth of British Power in the Gold Coast* (Lanham, 1983), p. 55, for an example of the oracle's adjudication in 1811.

47   See the (undated, *c.* 1800?) map in A. Boahen, 'Politics in Ghana, 1800–1874', in Ajayi and Crowder, *History of West Africa*, II, p. 173.

48   Bosman, *A New and Accurate Description*, p. 57.

49   The British Governor of Cape Coast Castle, in 1772, quoted in McCarthy, *Social Change*, p. 7.

50   But see T. Weskel, 'The precolonial Baule: a reconstruction', *Cahiers d'études africaines*, 1978, pp. 503ff. – the source for what follows.

51   Kropp Dakubu, 'The peopling', p. 249.

52   H. Clapperton, *Journal of a Second Expedition into the Interior of Africa* (London, 1829), p. 68. The standard study of the kola trade is P. Lovejoy, *Caravans of Kola: The Hausa Kola Trade 1700–1900* (Zaria, 1980).

53   R. Law, *The Slave Coast of West Africa, 1550–1750* (Oxford, 1991), p. 30. Akinjogbin suggested 1575 – a date widely cited in secondary literature (including that written by the present writer!). It is a good example of the way in which apparently precise information tends to be accepted without question (I. A. Akinjogbin, *Dahomey and Its Neighbours 1708–1818* (Cambridge, 1967), p. 11).

54   See pp. 326ff. above

55   Jonathan Swift, *On Poetry*; see also Law, *The Slave Coast* pp. 222–3. This superbly researched study is the main source for the account which follows. There is a vast secondary literature on Dahomey, much of it now out of date.

56   R. Law, 'Dahomey and the slave trade: reflections on the historiography of the rise of Dahomey', *Journal of African History*, 1986, p. 253.

57   Law, *Slave Coast*, p. 332.

58   Ibid., pp. 300 ff.

59   Law, ' "My head belongs to the king" ' pp. 407–8.

60   Akinjogbin, *Dahomey and Its Neighbours*, pp. 14–17, 24–6.

61   Law, *Slave Coast*, pp. 72–3; see also Akinjogbin, *Dahomey and Its Neighbours*, p. 15.

62   Law, *Slave Coast*, p. 271.

63   Quoted in ibid., p. 277.

64   Ibid., pp. 272–3.

65   Johnson, *The History of the Yorubas*, pp. 159–60.

66   The account which follows is based on Law, *The Oyo Empire*.

67   Johnson, *The History of the Yorubas*, p. 168.

68   J. Goody, *Technology, Tradition and the State in Africa* (London, 1971), pp. 47ff.

69 Johnson, *The History of the Yorubas*, pp. 168–84. To describe Johnson's late nineteenth-century text as 'traditional' is a useful shorthand but begs many questions.

70 P. Morton-Williams, 'The Yoruba kingdom of Oyo', in D. Forde and P. M. Kaberry (eds.), *West African Kingdoms in the Nineteenth Century* (London, 1967), pp. 40–1.

71 Paraphrased from Johnson, *The History of the Yorubas*, p. 188.

72 Law, *The Oyo Empire*, pp. 251–2; my account is based primarily on his thoroughly researched analysis of these events.

73 Ali Eisami in P. D. Curtin (ed.), *Africa Remembered: Narratives by West Africans from the Era of the Slave Trade* (Madison, 1967), p. 212.

74 A situation reflecting the fact that it was cheaper to buy a new slave in Africa than to rear infants in a state of slavery. The reproductive rates of slaves in the Americas were low, reflecting both slave women's living conditions and diet, and conscious decisions they made.

75 A. F. C. Ryder, *Benin and the Europeans 1485–1897* (London, 1969), pp. 45, 168, 173.

76 P. Ben-Amos, *The Art of Benin* (London, 1980) p. 10.

77 See E. Isichei, *The Ibo People and the Europeans* (London, 1973), p. 27.

78 E. Isichei, *A History of the Igbo People* (London and Basingstoke, 1976), p. 58; this account gives a fuller and more amply documented account of these events.

79 This is argued by A. E. Afigbo in a number of papers, including, 'The Aro of southeastern Nigeria: a socio-historical analysis of legends of their origin', *African Notes*, 1971, pp. 31ff. and 1972, pp. 91ff. There is a more accessible version in his 'Traditions of Igbo origins: a comment', *History in Africa*, 1983, pp. 1–11. For a literal version, from a member of the Dalhousie school, see A. Nwauwa, 'Integrating Arochukwu into the regional chronological structure', *History in Africa*, 1991, pp. 297ff. As he recognises, there are difficulties with these data, not least the mutual inconsistency of the various genealogies. They were also collected in a politically charged context – ascertaining the putative 'chief' of Arochukwu.

80 Public Record Office, London (consulted when located in Chancery Lane, now at Kew): CO520/14, R. Moor, Memo concerning the Aro Expedition, f. 355. The context in which this document was written, of course, encouraged exaggeration.

81 S. Crowther and J. C. Taylor, *The Gospel on the Banks of the Niger* (London, 1859), pp. 199–200.

82 See p. 247 above.

83 O. Dapper, *Description de l'Afrique* (Fr. trans. 1786), p. 312. This identification is not certain, and some have suggested 'Ijebu'.

84 D. Northrup, *Trade without Rulers* (Oxford, 1978) pp. 26–7.

85 E. Isichei, *Igbo Worlds* (Philadelphia, 1978), pp. 57ff.

86 Duarte Pacheco Pereira, *Esmeraldo de situ orbis* (trans. G. H. T. Kimble, Hakluyt, 2nd series, LXXIX), p. 132. It should be noted that this source mentions salt, but not fish, of which there is much later evidence. It also mentions the importation of slaves from the interior to the Delta.

87 This is argued by E. J. Alagoa, 'Long distance trade and states in the Niger Delta', *Journal of African History*, 1970, pp. 319ff.

88 Ibid., p. 324; for evidence of canoe-making centres in and near the Delta, see E. Isichei, *A History of Nigeria* (Harlow, 1983), pp. 114–15

89 J. Pratt, 'African town or village life in the Niger Delta', *Western Equatorial Diocesan Magazine*, 1905, p. 147.

90 R. Horton, 'From fishing village to city-state: a social history of New Calabar', in M. Douglas and P. Kaberry (eds.), *Man in Africa* (London, 1969), pp. 53–4.

91 E. J. Alagoa, 'The development of institutions in the states of the eastern Niger Delta', *Journal of African History*, 1971, p. 274.

92 Fombo papers (University of Ibadan Library), fo. 34. For comparable cases elsewhere, see pp. 337–8 above.

93 K. K. Nair, *Politics and Society in South Eastern Nigeria, 1841–1906* (London, 1972) and A. J. H. Latham, *Old Calabar 1600–1891* (London, 1973).

94 According to the 1963 Census, there were 2,006,000 Ibibio and 166,000 Efik. Nineteenth-century figures for the Efik were much lower, according to a resident missionary; the population of Duke Town was 2,000 in 1805, and was between 5,000 and 6,000, in 1846, when that of Creek Town was about 4,000 (Nair, *Politics*, p. 110, n. 47; Latham, *Old Calabar*, p. 91). There were much greater numbers in the farming areas.

95 Latham, *Old Calabar*, p. 17.

96 D. Northrup, *Trade without Rulers* (Oxford, 1978). p. 38.

97 For a more detailed account, see Isichei, *A History of Nigeria*, pp. 167ff.

98 M. Ruel, *Leopards and Leaders* (London, 1974).

99 T. J. Hutchinson, *Impressions of Western Africa* (London, 1858), p. 143. Slaves were at first excluded but later allowed to join the lower grades.

100 P. A. Talbot, *In the Shadow of the Bush* (London, 1912), p. 39.

101 Ibid., p. 40.

102 D. Dalby, 'The indigenous scripts of West Africa and Surinam: their inspiration and design', *African Language Studies*, 1968, pp. 156ff.

103 R. Austen, 'The metamorphoses of middlemen: the Duala, Europeans, and the Cameroon hinterland, ca. 1800–ca. 1960', *International Journal of African Historical Studies*, 1983, p. 3; this article (pp. 1ff.) is the main source for this account. See also E. Ardener, 'Documentary and linguistic evidence for the rise of the trading polities between Rio del Rey and Cameroons, 1500–1650', in I. M. Lewis (ed.), *History and Social Anthropology* (London, 1968), pp. 81ff. The people are conventionally called Duala, the place Douala.

104 It is shown in Phil Agland's ethnographic film of the Baka (DJA Rivers Films, for Channel 4).

105 The original was destroyed during the Second World War; extracts are published in D. Forde (ed.), *Efik Traders of Old Calabar* (London, 1968).

106 E. Isichei, *A History of Christianity in Africa* (London, 1995), pp. 59–60.

107 Ibid., p. 55.

108 J. Adams, *Remarks on the Country extending from Cape Palmas to the River Congo* (London, 1823), pp. 124–5.

20   WEST AFRICA 1800 TO 1870

1 Quoted in M. Klein, *Islam and Imperialism in Senegal: Sine-Saloum 1847–1914* (Stanford, 1968), p. 80.

2 FO2/178, F. Bertie, memo, 25 March, 1898.

3 Quoted in I. Wilks, 'Land, labour, capital and the forest kingdom of Asante', in

J. Friedman and M. Rowlands (eds.), *The Evolution of Social Systems* (London, 1977), p. 526.

4 J. F. Schön and S. A. Crowther, *Journals* (London, 1842), Schön's journal, 26 Aug. 1841, p. 48.

5 This point was made by J. F. A. Ajayi, 'West Africa in the anti-slave trade era', *Cambridge History of Africa*, V: *From c. 1790 to c. 1870*, ed. J. Flint (1976), p. 201. But the organisation of this volume of the *Cambridge History of Africa* is a striking example of the distortions he repudiates – apart from a chapter on the jihads, West African history is dealt with in chapters entitled, respectively, 'Freed slave colonies in West Africa' and 'West Africa in the anti-slave trade era'.

6 Governor White, on the Fante, in 1814, cited in M. McCarthy, *Social Change and the Growth of British Power in the Gold Coast* (Lanham, 1983), p. 51.

7 Rhodes House, Oxford. MS Afr. r. 81, R. P. Nicholson, 'Northern Nigeria notes, 1900–1905'.

8 Some regard the expression 'merchant capitalism' as a contradiction in terms.

9 FO 84/1683, Draft, G[ranville] to Aberdare, 6 Feb. 1884.

10 E. Baines in 1835, cited in E. Wolf, *Europe and the People without History* (Berkeley, 1982), p. 271.

11 Ibid., p. 273.

12 R. Austen, 'The abolition of the overseas slave trade: a distorted theme in West African history', *Journal of the Historical Society of Nigeria*, 1970, p. 274.

13 S. Daget, 'France, suppression of the illegal trade, and England, 1817–1850', in D. Eltis and J. Walvin (eds.), *The Abolition of the Atlantic Slave Trade* (Madison, 1981), pp. 205–6.

14 *The African Times*, 23 Jan. 1863, p. 79.

15 For a much fuller account of missionary activity and new Christian communities, see E. Isichei, *A History of Christianity in Africa from Antiquity to the Present* (London, 1995), pp. 83ff. and pp. 153ff.

16 Gurney, quoted in G. Moorhouse, *The Missionaries* (Newton Abbot, 1975), p. 30.

17 Chichester to Sagbua *et. al.*, 1848, in E. Stock, *History of the Church Missionary Society* (London, 1899), II, p. 105.

18 David and Charles Livingstone, *Narrative of an Expedition to the Zambesi and Its Tributaries* (London, 1865), p. 77.

19 CMS Archives, G3/A3/1884/129, D. C. Crowther to Lang, 30 June 1884.

20 CMS G3/A3/1897, Bennett to Baylis, 27 March, 1897.

21 P. Lovejoy, 'The volume of the Atlantic slave trade: a aynthesis', *Journal of African History*, 1982, p. 490, Table 6.

22 McCarthy, *Social Change*, pp. 72–6. She argues that the impact of abolition was relatively minor. It was not perceived in this way in Asante, largely because of the difficulty of obtaining alternative exports. Reynolds suggests that the Fante were weakened by the loss of export revenue, and thus made vulnerable both to Asante invasions and to British encroachment (E. Reynolds, *Trade and Economic Change on the Gold Coast* (Harlow, 1974)).

23 McCarthy, *Social Change*, p. 76.

24 FO84/1030, Hutchinson to Clarendon, 20 Feb. 1857.

25 R. Law, 'Trade and politics behind the Slave Coast: the lagoon traffic and the rise of Lagos 1500–1800', *Journal of African History*, 1983, pp. 321ff.

26 A. Jones and M. Johnson, 'Slaves from the Windward Coast', *Journal of African History*, 1980, p. 33.

27 E. Reynolds, 'Abolition and economic change on the Gold Coast', in Eltis and Walvin, *The Abolition of the Atlantic Slave Trade*, pp 145–7.

28 Austen, 'The abolition of the overseas slave trade', p. 269.

29 T. De Gregori, *Technology and the Economic Development of the Tropical African Frontier* (Cleveland and London, 1969), pp. 176–7. The use of petroleum increased the demand for tin containers. Although this and other sources refer to palm oil as an industrial lubricant, Austen ('The abolition of the overseas slave trade', p. 274) questions this.

30 J. Adams, *Remarks on the Country extending from Cape Palmas to the River Congo* (London, 1823), p. 247.

31 Ibid., facing title page.

32 FO84/1001, Hutchinson to Bonny Court of Equity, 24 April 1856, encl 2 in Hutchinson to Clarendon, 30 April 1856.

33 C. Newbury, *The Western Slave Coast and Its Rulers* (Oxford, 1961), pp. 56–7; Lagos figures declined after this.

34 G. Brooks, 'Peanuts and colonialism: consequences of the commercialization of peanuts in West Africa, 1830–70', *Journal of African History*, 1975, pp. 29ff.

35 Quoted in C. Newbury, 'Prices and profitability in early nineteenth-century West African trade', in C. Meillassoux (ed.), *The Development of Indigenous Trade and Markets in West Africa* (London, 1971), p. 96.

36 M. Klein, 'Social and economic factors in the Muslim revolution in Senegambia', *Journal of African History*, 1972, p. 424.

37 P. Curtin, 'The abolition of the slave trade from Senegambia', in Eltis and Walvin, *The Abolition of the Atlantic Slave Trade*, p. 93.

38 Quoted in I. Wilks, *Asante in the Nineteenth Century* (2nd edn, Cambridge, 1989), p. 178; also p. 17.

39 M. Johnson, 'By ship or by camel: the struggle for the Cameroons ivory trade in the nineteenth century', *Journal of African History*, 1978, p. 539; this is the source for the account which follows.

40 C. A. Gordon, *Life on the Gold Coast* (London, 1847), extract in F. Wolfson, *Pageant of Ghana* (London, 1959), p. 128.

41 C. Dickens, *Bleak House*, Ch. 4, 'Telescopic philanthropy'.

42 A. Upward, 'The Province of Kabba', *Journal of the African Society*, 1903, p. 244.

43 D. Northrup, 'The compatibility of the slave and palm oil trades in the Bight of Biafra', *Journal of African History*, 1976, p. 361.

44 R. Law, 'Human sacrifice in pre-colonial West Africa', *African Affairs*, 1985, pp. 77–8.

45 A. Ryder, *Benin and the Europeans 1485–1897* (Harlow, 1969), pp. 247–50.

46 E. Isichei, 'Historical change in an Ibo polity: Asaba to 1885', *Journal of African History*, 1969, pp. 423–4.

47 W. B. Baikie, *Narrative of an Exploring Voyage up the Rivers Kwora and Binue* (London, 1856), p. 315.

48 H. M. Waddell, *Twenty Nine Years in the West Indies and Central Africa* (London, 1863), p. 297.

49 Latham interprets this differently, on the grounds that human sacrifice had already been abolished (A. J. H. Latham, *Old Calabar 1600–1891* (Oxford, 1973), p. 94). But Waddell's contemporary account says clearly, 'They knew of the law to abolish human sacrifices, and knew also that it was secretly violated' (Waddell, *Twenty Nine Years*, p. 467).

50 For this, and further examples, see E. Isichei, *A History of Nigeria* (Harlow, 1983), pp. 247–8.

51 R. and J. Lander, *Journal of an Expedition* (abridged and ed. R. Hallett, London, 1965), p. 64.

52 H. Tugwell, 'A visit to the Yoruba, Ondo, Ekiti and Kukuruku countries', *Western Equatorial Africa Diocesan Magazine*, 1907, p. 44. For the case of Dahomey, see pp. 373–4 below.

53 A. G. Hopkins, *An Economic History of West Africa* (London, 1973), p. 143.

54 Ibid., pp. 125–7.

55 J. Dupuis, *Journal of a Residence in Ashantee* (London, 1824; 2nd edn London, 1966), p. 167, quoting the Asantehene, Osei Bonsu.

56 Ibid., p. 164.

57 R. Burton, *A Mission to Gelele, King of Dahome* (1864, 2nd edn. London, 1966), p. 344. For similar views at an earlier period, see A. Dalzel, *The History of Dahomy* (London, 1793), p. 218.

58 A. G. Laing, *Travels in the Timannee, Koranko, and Soolima Countries* (London, 1825), extract in C. Fyfe, *Sierra Leone Inheritance* (London, 1964), p. 82.

59 FO 84/1001, letter from King Eyamba of Calabar, 1 Dec. 1842, encl in Hutchinson to Clarendon, 24 June 1856.

60 Text in Stock, *History of the Church Missionary Society*, II, p. 104.

61 Brodie Cruickshank, Report, 9 Nov. 1848, extract in C. Newbury, *The Western Slave Coast and its Rulers* (Oxford, 1961), p. 51.

62 E. Isichei, 'The quest for social reform in the context of traditional religion', *African Affairs*, 1978, p. 476.

63 J. Duncan, *Travels in Western Africa in 1845 and 1846* (London, 1847), II, p. 270.

64 R. Law, *The Oyo Empire c. 1600–c. 1836* (Oxford, 1977) p. 254.

65 I. A. Akinjogbin, *Dahomey and its Neighbours 1708–1818* (Cambridge, 1967), pp. 185–6. The context was his desire to increase trade with Portugal.

66 Dupuis, *Residence in Ashantee*, p. 245.

67 CMS G3/A3/1883, D. C. Crowther to CMS, London, 10 May 1883, re Bonny.

68 Wilks, *Asante in the Nineteenth Century*, p. 270.

69 R. Kea, 'Firearms and warfare on the Gold and Slave Coasts from the sixteenth to the nineteenth centuries', *Journal of African History*, 1971, p. 201.

70 Osei Bonsu, quoted in T. E. Bowdich, *Mission from Cape Coast Castle to Ashantee*, (1824, 3rd edn London, 1966), p. 72.

71 Dupuis, *Residence in Ashantee*, p. 45.

72 Quoted in A. Boahen, 'Politics in Ghana, 1800–1874', in J. F. A. Ajayi and M. Crowder (eds.), *History of West Africa* (London, 1974), II, p. 171.

73 Ibid., p. 178.

74 McCarthy, *Social Change*, p. 94.

75 Dupuis, *Residence in Ashantee*, pp. 97, 107–8.

76 D. Kimble, *A Political History of Ghana: The Rise of Gold Coast Nationalism* (Oxford, 1963), p. 6 n. 4.

77 Bowdich, *Mission from Cape Coast Castle*, p. 334.

78 Dupuis, *Residence in Ashantee*, p. xl.

79 Boahen, 'Politics in Ghana', p. 197.

80 Dupuis, *Residence in Ashantee*, p. 226.

81 T. McCaskie, 'Accumulation, wealth and belief in Asante history', *Africa*, 1983, p. 36.

82 Ibid., pp. 35ff.

83 Brodie Cruickshank, *Eighteen Years on the Gold Coast of Africa* (1853, 2nd edn, London, 1966), II, pp. 262–4.

84 Ibid., II, p. 33.

85 T. Laing in 1853, cited in Kimble, *A Political History of Ghana*, p. 153.

86 D. Headrick, *The Tools of Empire* (New York, 1981), p. 146.

87 J. E. Casely Hayford in 1903, quoted in Kimble, *A Political History of Ghana*, p. 6 n 2.

88 W. Bosman, *A New and Accurate Description of the Coast of Guinea* (1704, London, 1967 reprint), p. 59.

89 McCarthy, *Social Change*, p. 128.

90 Quoted in Kimble, *A Political History of Ghana*, pp. 203–4.

91 Boahen, 'Politics in Ghana', p. 221.

92 Resolution 3, text in Kimble, *A Political History of Ghana*, p. 208.

93 J. Africanus Horton, *West African Countries and People* (1868, Edinburgh, 1969 reprint), Chs. 10 and 11.

94 See p. 371 above.

95 A. Datta and R. Porter, 'The Asafo system in historical perspective', *Journal of African History*, 1971, pp. 279ff.

96 Ibid., p. 296.

97 J. Lombard, 'The kingdom of Dahomey', in D. Forde and P. Kaberry (eds.), *West African Kingdoms in the Nineteenth Century* (London, 1967), p. 83.

98 F. E. Forbes, *Dahomey and the Dahomans* (London, 1851) II, p. 108.

99 Quoted in J. Yoder, 'Fly and elephant parties: political polarisation in Dahomey, 1840–1870', *Journal of African History*, 1974, p. 428.

100 Forbes, *Dahomey and the Dahomans*, I, p. 115.

101 P. Manning, 'The slave trade in the Bight of Benin 1640–1890', in H. Gemery and J. Hogendorn (eds.), *The Uncommon Market* (New York, 1979) p. 124 and n. 68. Some slaves were exported much later to São Thomé and German Kamerun.

102 Forbes, *Dahomey and the Dahomans*, II, p. 175; also I, p. 115.

103 D. Ross, 'Dahomey', in M. Crowder (ed.), *West African Resistance* (London, 1971), p. 161.

104 See S. Barnes, *Africa's Ogun, Old World and New* (Bloomington, 1989); J. Murphy, 'Oshun the Dancer', in C. Olson (ed.), *The Book of the Goddess Past and Present* (New York, 1983), pp. 190ff.

105 R. Hallett (ed. and abridged), *The Niger Journal of Richard and John Lander* (London, 1965), p. 87.

106 J. F. A. Ajayi, 'The aftermath of the fall of Old Oyo', in Ajayi and Crowder, *History of West Africa*, II, pp. 144–5.

107 Law, *Oyo Empire*, p. 298.

108 S. Johnson, *The History of the Yorubas* (1921, Lagos, 1973 reprint), p. 288.

109 Law, *Oyo Empire*, pp. 274–5.

110 CMS CA2/085, Townsend, Journal, quarter ending 25 Dec. 1847.

111 Townsend, in *Church Missionary Intelligencer*, 1853, p. 42; Owande in *Niger and Yoruba Notes*, 1899, p. 30.

112 Horton, *West African Countries and People*, Chs. 12 and 13.

113 J. Herskovitz Kopytoff, *A Preface to Modern Nigeria: The Sierra Leonians in Yoruba* (Madison, 1965), pp. 178ff.

114 S. Akintoye, *Revolution and Power Politics in Yorubaland* (London, 1971), p. 47.

115 B. Awe, 'Militarism and economic development in nineteenth century Yoruba country: the Ibadan example', *Journal of African History*, 1973, p. 68.

116 Johnson, *The History of the Yorubas*, p. 321.

117 Ibid., pp. 400–1. Johnson also describes his draconian punishment of theft.

118 *Church Missionary Intelligencer*, 1853, p. 249.

119 FO84/1508, Hopkins to FO, 23 Nov. 1878.

120 FO 84/1031, Campbell to Clarendon, 4 April 1857.

121 FO403/32, Craigie to Salmon, 11 Aug. 1984.

122 *Bulletin de la Congregation* [Holy Ghost Fathers], IX, Report for May 1902–Oct. 1904, p. 800.

123 Johnson, 'By ship or by camel', p. 538.

124 CMS CA3/04, John to Crowther, 22 March 1879.

125 CMS G3A3/1884/20, Crowther to Lang, 14 Dec. 1883.

126 These sources are given *in extenso* in E. Isichei, *Igbo Worlds* (London, 1978), pp. 288 and 293.

127 An elder of Obeledu, in 1972, text in ibid., p. 48.

128 CMS CA 3/037/86A, J. C. Taylor, Journal, 23 Nov. 1864.

129 The classic study is C. Fyfe, *A History of Sierra Leone* (London, 1962), the main source for what follows; because of its size and arrangement (it lacks chapter headings and subheadings) it is not easy to use.

130 K. Wylie, *The Political Kingdoms of the Temne: Temne Government in Sierra Leone, 1825–1910* (New York, 1977), p. 172.

131 CO 879/25, J. C. E. Parkes and T. G. Laws, 'Particulars relating to the tribes and districts of Sierra Leone and its vicinity' (1886), fo. 38.

132 Wylie, *Political Kingdoms of the Temne*, pp. 39–40.

133 Ibid., p. 32.

134 CO 879/25, Parkes and Laws, 'Particulars', fo. 9.

135 M. Jackson, *The Kuranko: Dimensions of Social Reality in a West African Society* (London, 1977), pp. 2–3; the quotation (p. 2) is from A. G. Laing, *Travels in the Timanee, Kooranko and Soolima Countries* (London, 1825) p. 195.

136 Quoted in A. Abraham, *Mende Government and Politics under Colonial Rule* (Freetown, 1978), p. 1.

137 Ottobah Cugoano, *Thoughts and Sentiments on the Evil of Slavery* (1787, London, 1969; Olaudah Equiano, *Interesting Narrative* (1789, London, 1989). The modern editions are edited and introduced by Paul Edwards.

138 Extract in Fyfe, *Sierra Leone Inheritance*, p. 111.

139 A. M. Falconbridge, *Narrative of Two Voyages to the River Sierra Leone* (London, 1794), p. 201.

140 J. F. A. Ajayi, 'Henry Venn and the policy of development', *Journal of the Historical Society of Nigeria*, 1959, p. 338.

141 Quoted in J. Peterson, *Province of Freedom: A History of Sierra Leone 1787–1870* (London, 1969), p. 236.

142 Text in ibid., p. 287.

143 Ibid., p. 288.

144 Horton, *West African Countries and People*, p. 55.

145 M. Jackson, *The Kuranko* (New York, 1977), p. 4. Saralon, like Saro, is a form of 'Sierra Leone'.

146 Editorial in *Sierra Leone Weekly News*, 8 April 1916, quoted in L. Spitzer, 'The

Sierra Leone Creoles, 1870–1900', in P. Curtin (ed.), *Africa and the West* (Madison, 1972), p. 100.

147 Extract in Fyfe, *Sierra Leone Inheritance*, p. 220.

148 There is a lack of good monographic material on nineteenth-century Liberia, but see T. Shick, *Behold the Promised Land: A History of Afro-American Settler Society in Nineteenth Century Liberia* (Baltimore, 1977) and the two monographs on the Kru listed below. Much of the scholarly material on Liberia is by anthropologists and political scientists.

149 J. G. Liebenow, *Liberia: The Evolution of Privilege* (Ithaca and London, 1969), pp. 14–15.

150 Wynkoop in 1834, quoted in P. E. H. Hair, 'Notes on the discovery of the Vai script, with a bibliography', *Sierra Leone Language Review*, 1963, p. 40.

151 MacGregor Laird and R. A. K. Oldfield, *Narrative of an Expedition into the Interior of Africa* (London 1837), I, p. 35. See also G. E. Brooks Jr, *The Kru Mariner in the Nineteenth Century: An Historical Compendium* (Newark, N.J. 1972), and. R. W. Davis, *Ethnohistorical Studies on the Kru Coast* (Newark, N.J., 1976).

152 H. Clapperton, *Journal of a Second Expedition into the Interior of Africa* (London, 1829), p. 199; C. Ifemesia, 'British enterprise on the Niger 1830–1869' (University of London Ph.D. thesis, 1959), p. 480; FO 84/1117, Hutchinson to Russell, 12 Feb. 1860.

153 FO 84/775, Draft of Beecroft's appointment, 30 June 1849.

154 Salisbury to Lyons, 12 Nov. 1879, quoted in Kimble, *A Political History of Ghana*, p. 13; this seems to refer to ports east of the Volta. (See also, pp. 12–13 and 12 n.5).

155 FO 403/18, Wingfield (CO) to Pauncefort (FO), 15 April 1882.

156 M. T. Taussig, *The Devil and Commodity Fetishism in South America* (North Carolina, 1980).

157 C. Monteil, 'Fin de siècle à Médine', *Bulletin de l'IFAN*, series B, 1966, pp. 149–50. Monteil was in Medina from 1897 to 1899; Silman was his interpreter, Souleyman Goundiamou.

21 CENTRAL AFRICA

1 J. Vansina, *The Tio Kingdom of the Middle Congo 1880–1892* (London, 1973), p. 307.

2 J. Dias, 'Famine and disease in the history of Angola c. 1830–1930', *Journal of African History*, 1981, p. 352.

3 See p. 331 above.

4 J. Miller, *Way of Death: Merchant Capitalism and the Angolan Slave Trade 1730–1830* (London, 1988) p. 38. I am enormously indebted to this extraordinary book.

5 See p. 395 below.

6 R. Harms, *River of Wealth, River of Sorrow* (New Haven and London, 1981), p. 2; J. Miller, *Way of Death*, pp. 4–5.

7 O. Dapper, *Description de l'Afrique* (Amsterdam, 1686), p. 360.

8 Harms, *River of Wealth*, p. 6, citing H. M. Stanley, *Through the Dark Continent* (New York, 1879), II, p. 359.

9 A. Hilton, *The Kingdom of Kongo* (Oxford, 1985), pp. 54–5.

10 Miller, *Way of Death*, pp. 77, 89–90.

11 D. Birmingham, *The Portuguese Conquest of Angola* (London, 1965), p. 46.
12 Miller, *Way of Death,* title of Ch. 8.
13 Dapper, *Description de l'Afrique*, p. 360.
14 P. Martin, *The External Trade of the Loango Coast 1576–1870* (Oxford, 1972), p. 4. The Woyo live around Cabinda.
15 There is a very rich literature on Kongo history and ethnography. The most important sources for the account which follows are J. Thornton, *The Kingdom of Kongo: Civil War and Transition 1641–1718* (Madison, 1983); and Hilton, *The Kingdom of Kongo*, pp. 6–7.
16 B. Davidson, *Black Mother Africa: The Years of Trial* (London, 1968), pp. 119–25; also his *The African Past: Chronicles from Antiquity to Modern Times* (Harmondsworth, 1964), pp. 194–7.
17 Hilton, *The Kingdom of Kongo*, pp. 53–65.
18 See R. Gray, '*Come vero principe catolico:* the Capuchins and the rulers of Soyo in the late seventeenth century', *Africa*, 1983, pp. 39ff., reprinted in his *Black Christians and White Missionaries* (New Haven and London, 1990).
19 Duarte Pacheco Pereira, *Esmeraldo de situ orbis* (trans. G. H. T. Kimble, Hakluyt, 2nd series, LXXIX), p. 144.
20 J. Vansina, *Paths in the Rainforests* (Madison, 1990), p. 201.
21 A. Bastian, *San Salvador* (1859), cited in J. Vansina, *Kingdoms of the Savanna* (Madison, 1966), p. 68.
22 There is a large literature on the Jaga, who have been variously interpreted. An alternative view is that they were slave dealers seeking to bypass the middleman and trade directly with the Portuguese. The Portuguese also called the Imbangala 'Jaga' (Hilton, *The Kingdom of Kongo*, pp. 69–72; also her 'The Jaga reconsidered', *Journal of African History*, 1981, pp. 191–202). Cf. J. C. Miller, 'Requiem for the Jaga', *Cahiers d'études africaines*, 1973, pp. 121–49; J. Thornton, 'A resurrection for the Jaga', *Cahiers d'études africaines*, 1978, pp. 223–7; J. C. Miller, 'Thanatopsis', *Cahiers d'études africaines*, 1978, pp. 229–31.
23 Hilton, *The Kingdom of Kongo*, p. 70.
24 Ibid., p. 124; cf. Thornton, *The Kingdom of Kongo: Civil War and Transition* p. 19.
25 Hilton, *The Kingdom of Kongo*, pp. 120, 122–3.
26 Ibid., pp. 73, 78, 80, 82.
27 Thornton, *The Kingdom of Kongo: Civil War and Transition,* pp. 23–5.
28 Giovanni Cavazzi, quoted in J. Thornton, 'The state in African historiography: a reassessment', *Ufahamu*, 1973, p. 116.
29 G. da Roma, *Relation* (a mid-seventeenth-century Capuchin account), quoted in Thornton, *The Kingdom of Kongo: Civil War and Transition*, p. 41.
30 Girolamode Montessarchio (seventeenth-century Capuchin), quoted in Thornton, 'The state in African historiography', p. 119.
31 F. Pigafetta, *A Report of the Kingdom of Congo* (based on information from Duarte Lopez) (1591, London, 1981 reprint), p. 32.
32 For contrasting perspectives on Dona Beatrice, see Hilton, *The Kingdom of Kongo*, pp. 208–10; Thornton, *The Kingdom of Kongo: Civil War and Transition*, pp. 106–13; and S. Axelson, *Culture Confrontation in the Lower Congo* (Uppsala, 1970), pp. 136–41.
33 Quoted in Thornton, *The Kingdom of Kongo: Civil War and Transition*, p. 96.
34 Vansina, *Paths in the Rainforests*, pp. 158–9.

35 P. Martin, 'The trade of Loango in the seventeenth and eighteenth centuries', in R. Gray and D. Birmingham (eds.), *Pre-Colonial African Trade* (New York, 1970), pp. 139ff.

36 Vansina, *Paths in the Rainforests*, pp. 204–7.

37 Martin, *External Trade*, pp. 169–70.

38 J. Janzen, *Lemba: A Drum of Affliction in Africa and the New World* (New York and London, 1982); this fine monograph is the main source for what follows.

39 Dapper, *Description d l'Afrique*, p. 337.

40 Ibid., p. 336.

41 Janzen, *Lemba*, p. 53.

42 Dapper, *Description d l'Afrique*, p. 334.

43 Vansina, *The Tio Kingdom*, pp. 439ff. Chapter 16 of this study is the main source for the account which follows. In some respects, his thought has advanced since this book was written, and a more recent interpretation can be found in the relevant sections of his *Paths in the Rainforests*.

44 Pacheco Pereira, *Esmeraldo*, p. 144. The reference is to 'Anzica'; on its identification, see Vansina, *The Tio Kingdom*, p. 445.

45 Vansina, *Paths in the Rainforests*, p. 365 n. 55.

46 R. Harms, *River of Wealth, River of Sorrow: The Central Zaire Basin in the Era of the Slave and Ivory Trade, 1500–1891* (New Haven and London, 1981). This is the source for the account which follows.

47 Vansina, *The Tio Kingdom*, p. 311.

48 T. S. Eliot, *Four Quartets*, Burnt Norton, V (London, 1944), p. 12.

49 Harms, *River of Wealth*, pp. 199–204.

50 Hilton, *The Kingdom of Kongo*, p. 75; Thornton, *The Kingdom of Kongo: Civil War and Transition*, p. 33, interprets the devaluation of *nzimbu* differently.

51 B. Heitze, 'Historical notes on the Kisama of Angola', *Journal of African History*, 1972, pp. 407ff.

52 Birmingham, *The Portuguese Conquest of Angola*, p. 24.

53 Ibid., p. 8; D. Birmingham, 'Early African trade in Angola and its hinterland', in Gray and Birmingham, *Pre-Colonial African Trade*, pp. 164–6. This refers to coastal salt pans, not the rock salt of Kisama.

54 See for instance, Birmingham, *The Portuguese Conquest of Angola*, p. 17 and J. Vansina, *Kingdoms of the Savanna* (Madison, 1966), p. 84. Vansina has long since moved beyond the interpretations in this study.

55 J. Miller, *Kings and Kinsmen* (London, 1976).

56 J. Miller, 'The significance of drought, disease and famine in the agriculturally marginal zones of west-central Africa', *Journal of African History*, 1982, pp. 17ff.; 'Famine in the agriculturally marginal zones of west-central Africa', *Journal of African History*, 1982, pp. 23–33. The ban on marriage and procreation was not total, but meant that Imbangala infants were seen as illegitimate, and birth took place outside the encampment (Miller, *Kings and Kinsmen*, p. 226).

57 J. Miller, 'Slaves, slavers and social change in nineteenth century Kasanje', in F. Heimer (ed.), *Social Change in Angola* (Munich, 1973), pp. 10ff.

58 Miller, *Way of Death*, p. 33.

59 J. Thornton, 'Legitimacy and political power: Queen Njinga, 1624–1663', *Journal of African History*, 1991, p. 40; see J. Miller, 'Queen Nzinga of Matamba

in a new perspective', *Journal of African History*, 1975, pp. 201–16. Nzinga is the more familiar spelling; the consonant in question is prnoounced like the *j* in French 'jeune'.

60 Miller, *Way of Death*, p. 33.

61 Jan Vansina, *Art History in Africa* (Harlow, 1984), pp. 208–9.

62 Miller, 'The paradoxes of impoverishment' in D. Birmingham and P. Martin (eds.), *History of Central Africa*, I (Harlow, 1983), p. 134.

63 The language of the Mbundu, however, seems to be closer to that of the Kongo than to that of the Ovimbundu (Miller, *Kings and Kinsmen*, p. 38).

64 G. Childs, 'The kingdom of Wambu (Huambo): a tentative chronology', *Journal of African History*, 1964, p. 368 n. 4; archaeology in Angola was impossible for many years after this.

65 Ibid., p. 370.

66 J. D. Birmingham, 'Central Africa from Cameroun to the Zambezi', *Cambridge History of Africa*, IV: *From c. 1600 to c. 1790*, ed. R. Gray (1975), p. 362.

67 Dias, 'Famine and disease', pp. 362–3.

68 J.-L. Vellut, 'Notes sur le Lunda et la frontière luso-africaine', *Etudes d'histoire africaine*, 1972, pp. 70–1, 74.

69 Ibid., p. 110.

70 Birmingham, 'Central Africa', p. 372.

71 Vellut, 'Notes sur le Lunda', p. 83.

72 Birmingham, 'Central Africa', pp. 374–5.

73 Cadornega, cited in ibid., p. 355. The identification with the Lunda here is not certain.

74 Birmingham, *Trade and Conflict*, p. 161.

75 R. E. Schechter, 'A propos the Drunken King: cosmology and history', in J. Miller (ed.), *The African Past Speaks: Essays on Oral Tradition and History* (Folkestone, 1980), pp. 108–25.

76 Vellut, 'Notes sur le Lunda', p. 78; T. Q. Reefe, 'The societies of the eastern savanna', in Birmingham and Martin, *History of Central Africa*, I, pp. 189–93 (Reefe states that the Kazembe's court spoke Luba, acquired in an earlier sojourn in a Luba-speaking area). See A. Roberts, *A History of Zambia* (Nairobi, 1976), pp. 83–96.

77 Birmingham, *Trade and Conflict*, pp. 148–9.

78 Birmingham, 'Central Africa', p. 378.

79 As an appendix to another narrative, in R. F. Burton (trans.), *Lacerda's Journey to Cazembe in 1798* (London, 1873).

80 The major sources for Lozi history, on which the following account is based, are M. Mainga, *Bulozi under the Luyana Kings* (London, 1973), valuable as an account from within, and G. Prins, *The Hidden Hippopotamus* (Cambridge, 1980), an interesting essay in multidimensional history.

81 Mainga, *Bulozi*, p. 64.

82 Prins, *The Hidden Hippopotamus*, p. 19.

83 See Mainga, *Bulozi*, p. 215 for four alternative king lists.

84 Prins, *The Hidden Hippopotamus*, pp. 117–18.

85 D. Livingstone, *Missionary Travels and Researches in South Africa* (London, 1857), p. 215.

86 F. Coillard, *On the Threshold of Central Africa* (London, 1897), p. 271. The queen is the Mulena Mukwae, ruler of the court in the south.

87 Mainga, *Bulozi*, p. 61; see also W. G. Clarence-Smith, 'Slaves, commoners and landlords in Bulozi, c. 1875 to 1906', *Journal of African History*, 1979, pp. 219ff.

88 Mainga, *Bulozi*, pp. 36–40; Prins, *The Hidden Hippopotamus*, pp. 97–105.

89 Mainga, *Bulozi*, pp. 40, 54.

90 See p. 112 above.

91 A. Wilson, 'Long distance trade and the Luba Lomami empire', *Journal of African History*, 1972, pp. 582ff.

92 J. C. Yoder, 'The historical study of a Kanyok genesis myth', in Miller, *African Past Speaks*, pp. 82–107 (cf. p. 108 above). The phrase 'on the edge of empires' is part of the title of Yoder's doctoral thesis. He suggests that the myth was developed by the Mwena Kanyok in the eighteenth century, to assert his authority *vis-à-vis* Luba raids on the one hand, and local chiefs who also claimed Luba forebears.

93 A. Roberts, *A History of the Bemba* (University of Wisconsin, 1973), pp. 39ff.

94 R. Burton, *A Mission to Glele King of Dahomey* (1864, 2nd edn London, 1966), p. 344 n. 4.

95 Miller, *Way of Death*, p. 644.

96 D. Birmingham, 'The forest and the savanna of Central Africa', *Cambridge History of Africa*, V: *From c. 1790 to c. 1870*, ed. J. Flint (1976), p. 228.

97 Dias, 'Famine and disease', p. 360.

98 W. G. Clarence-Smith, *Slaves, Peasants and Capitalists in Southern Angola* (Cambridge, 1979), pp. 8, 21–2.

99 D. Birmingham, 'The coffee barons of Cazengo', *Journal of African History*, 1978, p. 523.

100 Clarence-Smith, *Slaves, Peasants and Capitalists*; Birmingham, 'The coffee barons of Cazengo', pp. 523ff.

101 Dias, 'Famine and disease', pp. 361–2.

102 Vansina, *The Tio Kingdom* pp. 282–7.

103 The account which follows is based on J. Miller, 'Chokwe trade and conquest in the nineteenth century', in Gray and Birmingham, *Pre-Colonial African Trade*, pp. 175ff.

104 Quoted in K. D. Patterson, *The Northern Gabon Coast to 1874* (Oxford, 1975), pp. 33–4.

105 Brun in 1611, quoted in ibid., p. 14.

106 Ibid., p. 90.

107 Ibid., pp. 33–5.

108 Ibid., pp. 49 and 127.

109 C. Chamberlin, 'The migration of the Fang into central Gabon during the nineteenth century: a new interpretation', *International Journal of African Historical Studies*, 1978, pp. 429ff.; he suggests that they came from rather closer at hand – one group came from the region between the Ntem and Woleu rivers (in Cameroon and Equatorial Guinea respectively) and one from the middle Ogowé.

110 Ibid., pp. 447, 452–3.

111 J. Binet, *Sociétés de danse chez les Fang du Gabon* (1972), p. 14, quoted in J. Guyer, 'Wealth in people and self-realization in Equatorial Africa', *Man*, 1993, p. 245.

112 Dias, 'Famine and disease', pp. 363–5.

113 Quoted in ibid., p. 368.

114 Ibid., pp. 368, 371–3, 374.

22 SOUTHERN AFRICA

1 Moshoeshoe to Governor Sir George Cathcart, the epigraph to L. Thompson, *Survival in Two Worlds: Moshoeshoe of Lesotho* (Oxford, 1975).

2 R. Ross, *Cape of Torments: Slavery and Resistance in South Africa* (London, 1983), p. 20.

3 J. Armstrong, 'The slaves, 1652–1795', in R. Elphick and H. Giliomee (eds.), *The Shaping of South African Society 1652–1820* (Cape Town, 1979), p. 75.

4 R. Moffat, *Missionary Labours and Scenes in Southern Africa* (first pub. 1842; New York, 1969 edition), p. 69.

5 J. Philip, *Researches in South Africa* (London, 1828), II, pp. 263, 272. The Settler commando system began in 1774.

6 L. Anthing's Report of 1862, quoted in J. S. Marais, *The Cape Coloured People 1652–1937* (1939, Johannesburg, 1962 reprint), p. 28.

7 J. A. Heese, cited in R. Elphick and R. Shell, 'Intergroup relations: Khoikhoi, settlers, slaves and free blacks, 1652–1795', in Elphick and Giliomee, *The Shaping of South African Society*, p. 134.

8 There were also to be separate African and Indian branches.

9 Moffat, *Missionary Labours*, p. 184.

10 Ibid., pp. 200–1.

11 J. Cobbing, 'The Mfecane as alibi: thought on Dithakong and Mbolompo', *Journal of African History*, 1988, pp. 496ff.; this is endorsed by E. Eldridge, 'Sources of conflict in southern Africa, ca. 1800–1830: the "Mfecane" Reconsidered', *Journal of African History*, 1992, pp. 15ff.

12 The phrase comes from Eldridge, 'Sources of conflict', p. 1.

13 Mfecane is generally thought to mean 'grinding' in 'Nguni' languages. According to Cobbing, it is a neologism, first used by a white historian in 1928, and 'has no root in any African language' while 'Difaqane' was invented by a white historian in 1912 (Cobbing, 'The Mfecane as Alibi', pp. 487, 490 n. 19).

14 Ibid., pp. 503–4, citing D. Hedges, 'Trade and politics in southern Mozambique in the eighteenth and nineteenth centuries' (University of London, Ph.D. thesis, 1978).

15 Expressions of this kind, which are conventional in the literature, in a sense perpetuate a Great Man view of events.

16 J. Omer-Cooper, *The Zulu Aftermath* (London, 1966), pp. 24ff. The point was made still earlier in studies by Max Gluckman.

17 Eldridge, 'Sources of conflict', pp. 26–7.

18 J. Guy, 'Ecological factors in the rise of Shaka and the Zulu kingdom', in S. Marks and A. Atmore (eds.), *Economy and Society in Pre-Industrial South Africa* (London, 1980), pp. 102ff.

19 M. Hall, *The Changing Past: Farmers, Kings and Traders in Southern Africa, 200–1860* (Claremont, 1987), p. 126. He has published a detailed dendroclimatic study of this subject.

20 Eldridge, 'Sources of conflict', p. 32.

21 M. Legassick, 'The Sotho-Tswana peoples before 1800', in L. Thompson (ed.), *African Societies in Southern Africa* (London, 1969), p. 96 n. 25.

22 Eldridge, 'Sources of conflict', pp. 29, 32.

23 A. Smith, 'The trade of Delagoa Bay as a factor in Nguni politics', in Thompson, (ed.), *African Societies in Southern Africa*, pp. 171ff.

24 Eldridge, 'Sources of conflict', pp. 7–15.

25 Ibid., p. 10; Hall, *The Changing Past*, p. 186. See p. 419 below.

26 P. Bonner, *Kings, Commoners and Concessionaires* (Cambridge, 1983), p. 21.

27 Thus, Wright has shown that the Zulu impact on Natal came later than had been previously thought. Cobbing ('Mfecane as alibi', pp. 492ff.) attributes the disturbances on the highveld to the activities of white traders (and missionaries) obtaining slave labour for the Cape. No other scholar accepts this interpretation of missionaries' role; there are serious difficulties with the postulate of widespread enslavement between 1807 and 1828 (see J. Omer-Cooper, 'Has the Mfecane a future? A response to the Cobbing critique', *Journal of Southern African Studies*, 1993, pp. 286–90). Eldridge ('Sources of conflict', pp. 15ff.) agrees that European settlers and Griqua, but not missionaries, caused much of the upheaval on the highveld.

28 See p. 14 above.

29 But see C. Hamilton, ' "The character and objects of Chaka": a reconsideration of the making of Shaka as Mfecane motor', *Journal of African History*, 1992, pp. 37ff.

30 Some of the events attributed to Shaka's life belong to international stereotypes of the hero. Illegitimacy is an example; details vary. The earliest accounts state that Shaka's mother conceived before his father was circumcised. A frequently cited version states that his mother, Nandi, was expelled for her violent temper (see D. Golan, 'The life story of King Shaka and gender tensions in the Zulu state', *History in Africa*, 1990, pp. 95ff.).

31 *The Colonist*, 19 Aug. 1928 [*sic* for 1828], quoted in Hamilton, ' "The character and objects of Chaka" ', p. 56.

32 T. Cope (ed.), *Izibongo: Zulu Praise Poems* (Oxford, 1968), p. 88. The reference is to his massacre of his mother's clan, in revenge for his treatment as a boy.

33 Ibid., pp. 74, 76.

34 Testimony of Baleka, in *James Stuart Archive*, quoted in Hamilton, ' "The character and objects of Chaka', p. 61.

35 Golan, 'The life story of King Shaka', p. 105. She interprets Shaka's hostility to pregnancy as a symbolic expression of gender antagonisms in the Zulu state. He may have had a pathological fear of an heir who would supplant him (but brothers were a much more common danger in southern Bantu history). The simplest and most likely explanation is that he was gay.

36 Ibid., p. 104. See p. 147 above.

37 It was, for instance, rejected in these terms by Cobbing in his paper, 'Telling it as it was: the lineages of the theory of the Mfecane' (Out of Africa Conference, Canberra, July 1995).

38 E. J. and J. D. Krige, *The Realm of a Rain Queen* (London, 1943), pp. 1–12.

39 A. Kuper, *Wives for Cattle: Bridewealth and Marriage in Southern Africa* (London, 1982), p. 65.

40 P. Delius, *The Land Belongs to Us* (London, 1984), pp. 17–19.

41 Bonner, *Kings, Commoners*, p. 24. In the Swazi case, however, these were classificatory cousins.

42 H. Kuper, *An African Aristocracy* (2nd edn, New York, 1980), p. 13.

43 Bonner, *Kings, Commoners*, p. 49.

44 Cobbing has questioned this sequence of events; but see Omer-Cooper, 'Has the Mfecane a future?', pp. 282–3.

45 R. Brown, 'The external relations of the Ndebele kingdom', in Thompson, *African Societies* , p. 261. Some estimates are much lower.

46 Quoted in N. Bhebe, 'The Ndebele and Mwari before 1893: a religious conquest of the conquerors by the vanquished', in J. Schoffeleers (ed.), *Guardians of the Land* (Salisbury, 1978), p. 293. For a more detailed study, see his *Christianity and Traditional Religion in Western Zimbabwe* (London, 1979).

47 Cobbing questions the generally accepted view that their departure was due to their defeat by the Zulu; on this, see Omer-Cooper, 'Has the Mfecane a future?', p. 282.

48 D. Beach, *The Shona and Zimbabwe* (London, 1980), p. 265.

49 Quoted in J. McCracken, *Politics and Christianity in Malawi 1875–1940* (Cambridge, 1977), p. 60.

50 P. Redmond, 'Some results of military contacts between the Ngoni and their neighbours in 19th century southern East Africa', *Transafrican Journal of History*, 1976, p. 86.

51 Quoted in ibid., p. 84; this is the main source for my account here.

52 W. Rau, 'Chewa religion and the Ngoni conquest', in Schoffeleers, *Guardians of the Land*, pp. 131ff.

53 Ibid., p. 137.

54 D. Kaspin, 'Chewa visions and revisions of power: transformations of the Nyau dance in central Malawi', in J. and J. Comaroff, *Modernity and Its Malcontents* (Chicago, 1993), pp. 34ff.

55 I. Schapera (ed.), *Livingstone's African Journal, 1853–1856* (London, 1963), p. 364.

56 Quoted in M. Mainga, *Bulozi under the Luyana Kings* (London, 1973), p. 83.

57 D. Livingstone, *Missionary Travels and Researches in South Africa* (London, 1857), p. 179.

58 K. D. Patterson and G. W. Hartwig, 'The disease factor: an introductory overview', in their *Disease in African History* (Durham, N.C., 1978), p. 9.

59 Mainga, *Bulozi*, p. 1.

60 Coillard's journal, 1886, quoted in G. Prins, *The Hidden Hippopotamus* (Cambridge 1980), p. 201.

61 Quoted in Mainga, *Bulozi*, p. 105.

62 An informant in 1840, quoted in L. Thompson, *Survival in Two Worlds: Moshoeshoe of Lesotho* (Oxford, 1975), p. 36.

63 Older studies emphasised depopulation. More recent work has modified this view. The debate has political implications, as the voortrekkers claimed to have settled in unoccupied lands.

64 Livingstone, *Missionary Travels and Researches in South Africa*, p. 30.

65 Thompson, *Moshoeshoe*, pp. 21–2. The account which follows is based on this study.

66 Moshoeshoe to Governor Sir George Cathcart, quoted as the epigraph in ibid.

67 Ibid., p. 25.

68 Ibid., p. 75.

69 Ibid., p. 80.

70 Cobbing, 'Mfecane as alibi', p. 519.

71 See Shakespeare, *Henry IV, Part 1*, II, 3.

72 J. Campbell in 1815, quoted in J. B. Peires, *The House of Phalo: A History of the Xhosa People in the Days of Their Independence* (Berkeley, 1982), p. 78.

73   Ibid., p. 58.
74   Ibid., p. 71.
75   Ibid., p. 91.
76   Ibid., p. 44.
77   Ibid., p. 73.
78   The roots of the cattle killing are complex and well explored by Peires; earlier
     land alienation had made it impossible to abandon the homestead of the
     deceased, and other mortuary rituals had been given up in the smallpox epidemic
     of 1770. When customary rites of separation were abandoned, ancestors
     impinged more closely on daily life. There are many parallels with Melanesian
     cargo cults.
79   J. B. Peires, '"Soft" believers and "hard" unbelievers in the Xhosa cattle-
     killing', *Journal of African History*, 1986, p. 453.
80   J. B. Peires, 'Suicide or genocide? Xhosa perceptions of the Nongqawuse
     catastrophe', *Radical History Review*, 1990, p. 55.
81   Quoted in ibid., p. 51.
82   Cobbing, 'The Mfecane as alibi', pp. 493–4.
83   P. Retief, 'Manifesto', in A. du Toit and H. Giliomee (eds.), *Afrikaner Political
     Thought, Analysis and Documents*, I: *1780–1850* (Berkeley, 1983), p. 214.
84   Bonner, *Kings, Commoners*, p. 41. This belongs to a large genre of comparable
     predictions and may well be apocryphal; but it embodies a basic Swazi statement
     of values.
85   Quoted in A. Ross, *John Philip 1775–1851* (Aberdeen, 1986), p. 95.
86   L. Switzer, 'The African community and its press in Victorian South Africa',
     Cahiers d'études africaines, 1984, p. 469.
87   Quoted in L. Thompson, *A History of South Africa* (New Haven and London,
     1990), p. 80.
88   D. Williams, 'Tiyo Soga 1829–71', in C. Saunders (ed.) *Black Leaders in
     Southern African History* (London, 1979), pp. 127ff.; D. Chanaiwa, 'African
     humanism in southern Africa: the utopian, traditionalist and colonialist worlds
     of mission educated elites', in A. Mugomba and M. Nyaggah (eds.), *Independence
     without Freedom: The Political Economy of Education in Southern Africa* (Santa
     Barbara, 1980), p. 13.
89   R. H. Davis, 'School vs. blanket and settler: Elijah Makiwane and the leadership
     of the Cape school community', *African Affairs*, 1979, pp. 12–13.
90   I. Schapera, *Tribal Innovators: Tswana Chiefs and Social Change* (London,
     1970).
91   I. Schapera (ed.), *David Livingstone: Family Letters 1841–56* (London, 1959), I,
     p. 132.
92   I. Schapera (ed.), *Livingstone's Missionary Correspondence 1841–56* (London,
     1961), pp. 14–15, 81.
93   M. Marable, 'John L. Dube and the politics of segregated education in South
     Africa', in Mugomba and Nyaggah, *Independence without Freedom*, pp. 113ff.
94   For which see C. Bundy, *The Rise and Fall of the South African Peasantry*
     (London, 1979).
95   Quoted in Chanaiwa, 'African humanism', p. 10.
96   Rev. Gwayi Tyamzashe (R. Turrell, 'Kimberley, labour and compounds, 1871–
     1888', in S. Marks and R. Rathbone (eds.), *Industrialisation and Social Change in
     South Africa* (Harlow, 1982), p. 69 n. 6.

23 EAST AND EAST CENTRAL AFRICA

1 Text in D. W. Cohen, *The Historical Tradition of Busoga* (Oxford, 1972), p. 53.

2 D. and C. Livingstone, *Narrative of an Expedition to the Zambesi and its Tributaries* (New York, 1866), p. 522.

3 J. Thomson, *To the Central Lakes and Back* (1881) quoted in A. Smith, 'The southern section of the interior 1840–1884', in R. Oliver and G. Mathew (eds.), *History of East Africa* (Oxford, 1963), I, p. 258.

4 See P. Manning, *Slavery and African Life* (Cambridge, 1990), p. 84.

5 Quoted in J. Iliffe, *A Modern History of Tanganyika* (Cambridge, 1979), p. 35.

6 Ibid., p 80.

7 A Roberts, 'Nyamwezi trade', in R. Gray and D. Birmingham, (eds.), *Pre-Colonial African Trade* (London, 1970), pp. 71–2, and his *History of Zambia* (London, 1976), p. 141.

8 R Austen, 'Patterns of development in nineteenth century East Africa', *African Historical Studies*, 1971, pp. 645ff.

9 Yohannah Abdallah, *The Yaos* (trans. M. Sanderson, Zomba, 1919), p. 33.

10 Ibid., p. 44.

11 The main source for this account is D. Beach, *The Shona and Zimbabwe 900–1850* (London, 1980).

12 This is now changing – see P. Sinclair, 'Archaeology in eastern Africa', *Journal of African History*, 1991, p. 209.

13 Beach, *The Shona*, pp. 355–6 n. 1.

14 A. Isaacman, *Mozambique: The Africanization of a European Institution: The Zambezi Prazos, 1750–1902* (Madison, 1972); M. D. Newitt, *Portuguese Settlement on the Zambezi* (New York, 1973).

15 I. Isaacman, 'The origin, formation and early history of the Chikunda of South Central Africa', *Journal of African History*, 1972, p. 450.

16 Ibid., p. 459.

17 Roberts, *History of Zambia*, p. 125.

18 Beach, *The Shona*, pp. 222–6.

19 M. Hall, *The Changing Past: Farmers, Kings and Traders in Southern Africa 200–1860* (Cape Town, 1987), p. 94.

20 Beach, *The Shona*, p. 316.

21 Monclaro, extract in G. S. P. Freeman-Grenville, *The East African Coast: Select Documents from the First to the Earlier Nineteenth Century* (Oxford, 1966 reprint), p. 138.

22 Abdullah, *The Yaos*, p. 26. The standard modern account is E. Alpers, *Ivory and Slaves in East Central Africa* (London, 1975).

23 Abdullah, *The Yaos*, p. 30. Guns became important in the mid-nineteenth century.

24 Alpers, *Ivory and Slaves*, pp. 20–1.

25 E. Alpers, 'The story of Swema: female vulnerability in nineteenth century East Africa', in C. C. Robertson and M Klein (eds.), *Women and Slavery in Africa* (Madison, 1983), pp. 185ff.

26 Livingstone, *Narrative*, p. 171; see J. McCracken, *Politics and Christianity in Malawi 1875–1940* (Cambridge, 1977), p. 6.

27 Livingstone, *Narrative*, p. 502; on the Bisa see also Roberts, *History of Zambia*, pp. 120–1.

28 But the Omani were Ibadi, the Swahili Sunni.
29 G. S. P. Freeman-Grenville, *The French at Kilwa Island* (Oxford, 1965), p. 127 n. 2.
30 See Morice to de Cossigny, 4 Nov. 1776, in Freeman-Grenville, *The French at Kilwa Island*, p. 82.
31 A Shorter, 'The Kimbu', in A. Roberts (ed.), *Tanzania before 1900* (Nairobi, 1968), p. 105.
32 João dos Santos, 'Ethiopia Oriental' (1609) in G. M. Theal, *Records of South-Eastern Africa* (1901, Cape Town, 1964 reprint), VII, pp. 321–2.
33 Alpers, *Ivory and Slaves*, pp. 86–7.
34 J. Thomson, *Central African Lakes*, quoted in A. Roberts, *A History of the Bemba* (Madison, 1973), p. 197.
35 Quoted in J. Lamphear, 'The Kamba and the northern Mrima coast', in Gray and Birmingham, *Pre-Colonial African Trade*, p. 84.
36 Livingstone, *Narrative*, p. 288.
37 W. G. Clarence-Smith, 'The economics of the eastern slave trade', in his *The Economics of the Indian Ocean Slave Trade in the Nineteenth Century* (London, 1989), pp. 5–7; the figure is based on the detailed study by R. Austen in the same volume, 'The 19th century Islamic slave trade from East Africa ... a tentative census', pp. 21ff.
38 G. Campbell, 'Madagascar and Mozambique in the slave trade of the western Indian Ocean 1800–1861', in Clarence-Smith, *Indian Ocean Slave Trade*, p. 166.
39 Clarence-Smith, 'The economics', p. 10.
40 M. Carter and H. Gerbeau, 'Covert slaves and coveted coolies in the early 19th century', in Clarence-Smith, *The Indian Ocean Slave Trade*, p. 205, n 11.
41 D. Eltis, *Economic Growth and the Ending of the Transatlantic Slave Trade* (New York, 1987), Table A. 9, p. 252, also pp. 177 ff.
42 F. Cooper, *Plantation Slavery on the East Coast of Africa* (New Haven, 1977), p. 50; a source written in 1819 attributed their introduction to two Frenchmen.
43 Ibid., pp. 81ff.
44 Clarence-Smith, 'The economics', p. 4. For orchilia, see p. 404 above.
45 Roberts, 'The Nyamwezi', p. 129. Caravans travelled in the dry season, when no farming was done. But there were dry-season tasks, and some porters remained on the coast for some time.
46 Abdullah, *The Yaos* p. 31.
47 M. Wright, 'Women in peril: a commentary on the life-stories of captives in nineteenth-century East-Central Africa', *African Social Research*, 1975, p. 810.
48 G. Hartwig, *The Art of Survival in East Africa* (New York, 1976), pp. 123–4.
49 This paragraph is based on S. Feierman, *The Shambaa Kingdom, a History* (Madison, 1974), pp. 175–9.
50 A Roberts, 'Political change in the nineteenth century', in I. N. Kimambo and A. J. Temu (eds.), *A History of Tanzania* (Nairobi, 1969), p. 67.
51 Ibid., p. 65.
52 Burton, *Lake Regions*, II, p. 7, quoted in Smith, 'Southern interior', p. 261.
53 Oral text in Roberts, 'The Nyamwezi', p. 126.
54 Iliffe, *A Modern History*, p. 44.
55 N. Bennett, *Mirambo of Tanzania (1840?–1884)*, (New York, 1971), p. 12.
56 Iliffe, *A Modern History*, p. 45, quoting estimates of over 100,000 Africans on the central caravan route in *c.* 1890. He points out that in 1874 Stanley paid his

porters 24 shillings a month, which remained standard among European employers; unskilled labourers in Tanga earned about 13 shillings a month in 1910, and little more in the 1930s.

57 D. Crawford, *Thinking Black* (London, 1913) is a valuable, though prejudiced, first-hand account of Msiri's state. See also D. Birmingham, 'The forest and the savanna of Central Africa', in J. Flint (ed.), *The Cambridge History of Africa*, V, pp. 246–7.

58 J. Lamphear, 'The Kamba and the northern Mrima coast', in Gray and Birmingham, *Pre-Colonial African Trade*, pp. 75ff., the main source for my account.

59 There are suggestions that they were earlier more widely dispersed; Nyamwezi traditions mention the Kamba, and they are said to have waged war in the area of modern Dar es Salaam (Lamphear, 'The Kamba', p. 78 n. 2). The meaning of these traditions is uncertain, and different peoples may be the 'Kamba' of these traditions.

60 Ibid., p. 83.

61 L. von Hoehnel, *Discovery of Lakes Rudolf and Stephanie* (1894), cited in ibid., p. 85.

62 Interview, undated but *c.* 1777, text in Freeman-Grenville, *French at Kilwa Island*, p. 106. Italics added for clarity.

63 Abdullah, *The Yaos*, p. 32.

64 L. M. Fotheringham, *Adventure in Nyasaland* (London, 1891), quoted in G. Shepperson, 'The Jumbe of Kota Kota and some aspects of the history of Islam in British Central Africa', in I. M. Lewis (ed.), *Islam in Tropical Africa* (London, 1966), p. 194. Similarly, 'Portuguese' is often used to refer to Goans and ethnic Africans with Portuguese names and varying degrees of Portuguese culture.

65 Burton, quoted in Roberts, 'The Nyamwezi', p. 132.

66 A Redmayne, 'Mkwawa and the Hehe wars', *Journal of African History*, 1968, p. 410.

67 M. Wright and P. Lary, 'Swahili settlements in northern Zambia and Malawi', *African Historical Studies*, 1971, p. 551. This article provides much data on Swahili traders in the interior.

68 A. Unomah and J. B. Webster, 'East Africa, the expansion of commerce', in J. Flint (ed.), *Cambridge History of Africa*, V: *From c. 1790 to c. 1870* (1976), p. 307.

69 J. Thomson in 1879, quoted in Smith, 'The southern section of the interior' in Oliver and Mathew, *History of East Africa*, I, p. 272. At the time he wrote, Ujiji was in decline.

70 Shepperson, 'Kota Kota', p. 195.

71 G. Hartwig, 'The Victoria Nyanza as a trade route', *Journal of African History*, 1970, p. 549.

72 A. Low, 'The northern interior', in Oliver and Mathew, *History of East Africa*, I, p. 301.

73 J. Bernsten, 'The Maasai and their neighbours, variables of interaction', *African Economic History*, 1976, pp. 1ff.

74 T. Beidelman, 'Myth, legend and oral history: a Kaguru traditional text', *Anthropos*, 1970, p. 84.

75 R. Waller, 'The Maasai and the British 1895–1905: the origins of an alliance', *Journal of African History*, 1976, pp. 529ff.

76 Ibid., p. 532.

77 On the identity of the protagonists, and the terminology, see J. Bernsten, 'The enemy is us: eponymy in the historiography of the Maasai', *History in Africa*, 1980, pp. 1ff.

78 Bernsten, 'The Maasai and their neighbours', p. 6.

79 A. Jacobs, 'Maasai pastoralism in historical perspective', in T. Monod (ed.), *Pastoralism in Tropical Africa* (London, 1975), p. 408.

80 Here, as elsewhere in this study, one must choose between the familiar (*laibon*, Samburu) and the more accurate (*il oibonok*, Sambur).

81 D. Ellis, 'The Nandi protest of 1923', *Journal of African History*, 1976, pp. 556–7.

82 L. Cassanelli, *The Shaping of Somali Society* (Philadelphia, 1982), pp. 147ff. is the source of this paragraph.

83 Hartwig, *The Art of Survival*, p. 68.

84 S. Feierman, 'The Shambaa', in Roberts, *Tanzania before 1900*, p. 6.

85 J. Vansina, *Paths in the Rainforests* (Madison, 1990), p. 74.

86 D. W. Cohen, 'Peoples and states of the Great Lakes region', J. F. Ade Ajayi (ed.), *Africa in the Nineteenth Century* (UNESCO General History of Africa, Paris, 1989), VI, p. 276.

87 D. W. Cohen, *The Historical Tradition of Busoga* (Oxford, 1972), p. 12.

88 See J. Tosh, 'The northern interlacustrine region', in Gray and Birmingham, *Precolonial Trade*, pp. 103ff.

89 D. W. Cohen, *Womunafu's Bunafu* (Princeton, 1977), p. 132.

90 Ibid., p. 76.

91 Quoted in I. Berger, *Religion and Resistance: East African Kingdoms in the Precolonial Period* (Tervuren, 1981), p. 20.

92 For late nineteenth-century Buganda, see especially M. Wright, *Buganda in the Heroic Age* (Nairobi, 1971) and D. A. Low, *Religion and Society in Buganda 1875–1900* (East African Studies 8, n. d. but 1957).

93 C. S. Nason, 'Proverbs of the Baganda', *Uganda Journal*, 1936, p. 250. See also p. 136 above.

94 J. A. Rowe, 'The purge of Christians at Mwanga's court', *Journal of African History*, 1964, p. 68. Some sources suggest forty Christians were martyred.

95 Quoted in A Moorehead, *The White Nile* (London, 1960), p. 172 (a Eurocentric but entertaining account of the white proconsuls).

96 Ali Mazrui, 'Religious strangers in Uganda: from Emin Pasha to Amin Dada', *African Affairs*, 1977, pp. 21ff.

97 G. Hartwig, 'Social consequences of epidemic diseases: the nineteenth century in eastern Africa', in G. Hartwig and K. D. Patterson, *Disease in African History* (Durham, N.C., 1978), p. 39.

98 J. Rennie, 'The precolonial kingdom of Rwanda: a reinterpretation', *Transafrican Journal of History* 1972, pp. 11–47, and sources cited there. For more recent work, see D. Newbury, 'Trick cyclists? Recontextualizing Rwandan dynastic chronology', *History in Africa*, 1994, pp. 191ff.

99 Berger, *Religion and Resistance*, p. 82.

100 Ibid., p. 82. For a different interpretation, cf. J. Freedman, 'Three Muraris, three Gahayas and the four phases of Nyabingi', in J. B. Webster (ed.), *Chronology, Migration and Drought in Interlacustrine Africa* (London, 1979), pp. 175ff.

101 Bennett, *Mirambo*, p 42.

102 J. Omer-Cooper, *The Zulu Aftermath* (London, 1966), p 64.

103 Shorter, 'The Kimbu', p. 112.

104 This transition is evident in Iliffe, *A Modern History*. See, for instance, p. 63, where he calls Nyungu 'a man of appalling cruelty'.

105 A nineteenth-century speech, preserved in oral tradition and quoted in Redmayne, 'Mkwawa', pp. 428–9.

106 Abdallah, *The Yaos*, pp. 50, 54. My account of Mataka is based on this source. For the wider context, see also E. Alpers, 'Trade, state, and society among the Yao in the nineteenth century', *Journal of African History*, 1969, pp. 415–16.

107 This account is based on Feierman, *The Shambaa Kingdom*.

108 Redmayne, 'Mkwawa', p. 414. This is the source of my account.

109 A government-appointed and salaried chief.

110 This account is based on Bennett, *Mirambo*.

111 A. Shorter, 'Nyungu-ya-Mawe and the "Empire of the Ruga-Rugas"', *Journal of African History*, 1968, pp. 235–9. This is the source for what follows.

112 Quoted in Moorehead, *The White Nile*, p. 147.

113 Low, 'The northern interior', p. 314.

114 Hartwig, *The Art of Survival*, p. 89.

115 C. St John, 'Kazembe and the Tanganika–Nyasa corridor', in Gray and Birmingham, *Pre-Colonial African Trade*, p. 213.

116 Unomah and Webster, 'East Africa', p. 304, citing I. Kimambo, *A Political History of the Pare*, pp. 189–90.

117 Berger, *Religion and Resistance*, p. 5.

118 Roberts, 'The Nyamwezi', p. 129; Hartwig, *The Art of Survival*, p. 71.

119 Hans Cory, quoted in T. O. Ranger, 'The movement of ideas 1850–1939', in Kimambo and Temu, *A History of Tanzania*, pp. 167–8.

120 D. W. Cohen and E. S. Atieno Odhiambo, *Siaya: The Historical Anthropology of an African Landscape* (London, 1989), p. 10.

121 Kerebe oral text, quoted in Hartwig, 'Social consequences of epidemic diseases', p. 32.

122 Hartwig, *The Art of Survival*, pp. 197ff.

123 Iliffe, *A Modern History*, p. 82; McCracken, *Politics and Christianity in Malawi*, pp. 13–14.

124 Roberts, 'Political change', p. 67.

125 Abdullah, *The Yaos*, pp. 43–4.

126 Ibid., p. 51.

127 J. L. Krapf, *Travels, Researches and Missionary Labours* (1860, London, 1968), p. 157.

128 See p. 402 above.

129 D. and C. Livingstone, *Narrative of an Expedition*; O. Chadwick, *MacKenzie's Grave* (London, 1959).

130 Hartwig, *Search for Security*, pp. 73–4.

131 Roberts, 'Nyamwezi trade', p. 63.

132 Wright, 'Women in peril', pp. 809–11. See Robertson and Klein, *Women and Slavery in Africa*; M. Wright, *Strategies of Slaves and Women* (1993) was not available to me.

133 L. Schiller, 'The royal women of Buganda', *The International Journal of African Historical Studies*, 1990, pp. 455ff.

134 Quoted in Berger, *Religion and Resistance*, p. 18.

135 Ibid., pp. 22–3.

136 M. Wright, *German Missions in Tanganyika* (Oxford, 1971), p. 89.

137 For Malagasy Christianity, see M Jarrett-Kerr, *Patterns of Christian Acceptance* (London, 1972), pp. 16–22.

138 Berger, *Religion and Resistance*, p. 19.

139 Burton, *The Lake Regions of Central Africa*, p. 485, cited in Hartwig, 'Social consequences of epidemic diseases,' p. 26, also p. 39.

140 Ibid., pp. 76–7, 122–3.

141 Cholera kills by dehydration; this was accelerated by techniques such as bleeding. K. Kiple and V. H. King, *Another Dimension to the Black Diaspora: Diet, Disease, and Racism* (Cambridge, 1981), pp. 147ff.

142 Hartwig, 'Social consequences of epidemic diseases', pp. 27–8, citing the work which is the precursor of modern studies of disease in Africa, James Christie, *Cholera Epidemics in East Africa* (1876).

143 Roberts, 'The Nyamwezi', p. 130; Shorter, 'The Kimbu', pp. 105, 108.

144 Quoted in H. Kjeshus, *Ecology, Control and Economic Development in East African History* (London, 1977), p. 162; see also the classic study by J. Ford, *The Role of the Trypanosomiases in African Ecology: A Study of the Tsetse Fly* (Oxford, 1971).

145 On the Kamba see J. L. Krapf, *Travels, Researches*, p. 142; on Ukerewe, see Hartwig, *The Art of Survival*, p. 162.

146 Kimbu song, quoted in St John, 'Kazembe and the Tanganika–Nyasa corridor', pp. 215–16. See also Shorter, 'The Kimbu', p. 107 in the same volume.

147 C. Brooke, 'The heritage of famine in central Tanzania', *Tanzania Notes and Records*, 1967, p. 20.

148 This account is based on C. Ambler, *Kenyan Communities in the Age of Imperialism* (New Haven and London, 1988), pp. 122ff. It is only just to add, as Ambler points out (p. 137), that it was also called the famine of rice, or of gunny sacks, in reference to European attempts to aid its victims.

149 Ibid., p. 144.

150 Quoted in T. Ranger, *The African Churches of Tanzania* (Historical Association of Tanzania, paper 5, n.d.), pp. 7–8.

151 R. G. Willis, 'Kaswa: oral tradition of a Fipa prophet,' *Africa*, 1970, p. 253.

Some suggestions for further reading

The detailed notes in this book provide guidance to the sources on particular issues – often in articles in learned journals. The guide which follows is intended to assist students locate the major books in a particular field. I have restricted it to works in English and, for the most part, excluded articles in periodicals. In each field, I have endeavoured to include very recent works, with detailed up-to-date bibliographies in each particular field.

THEMATIC STUDIES

The following deserve special note:

John Iliffe, *The African Poor: A History* (Cambridge, 1987). A work of great humanity and insight.

R. Austen, *African Economic History* (London, 1987). An outstanding book, with excellent bibliographies.

Jan Vansina, *Art History in Africa* (London, 1984).

D. Crummey (ed.), *Banditry, Rebellion and Social Protest in Africa* (London, 1986).

S. Miers and I. Kopytoff, *Slavery in Africa: Historical and Anthropological Perspectives* (Madison, 1977).

P. Lovejoy, *Transformations in Slavery: A History of Slavery in Africa* (Cambridge, 1983).

P. Lovejoy (ed.), *The Ideology of Slavery in Africa* (Beverly Hills, 1981).

P. Manning, *Slavery and African Life* (Cambridge, 1990).

J. Goody, *Technology, Tradition and the State in Africa* (London, 1971) – a famous and influential study; its conclusions have been modified by later work.

Elizabeth Isichei, *A History of Christianity in Africa from Antiquity to the Present* (London, 1985).

PRELUDE AND CHAPTER 6

On oral history and method in general

Jan Vansina, *Oral Tradition: A Study in Historical Methodology* (London, 1972 reprint) – enormously influential in its time.

Jan Vansina, *Oral Tradition as History* (Madison, 1985) – a more recent analysis.

David Henige, *The Chronology of Oral Tradition: Quest for a Chimera* (Oxford, 1974) – an extremely influential study which, as its title suggests, critiques the reliability of oral tradition.

Joseph Miller (ed.), *The African Past Speaks: Essays on Oral Tradition and History* (Folkestone, 1980).

K. Barber and P. de Moraes Farias (eds.), *Discourse and Its Disguises* (Birmingham, 1989) an important collection of essays on oral sources.

A number of important works by anthropologists have reinterpreted their discipline. Two outstanding examples by Africa specialists are:

Johannes Fabian, *Time and the Other: How Anthropology Makes Its Object* (New York, 1983).

Michael Jackson, *Paths towards a Clearing: Radical Empiricism and Ethnographic Inquiry* (Bloomington and Indianapolis, 1989) – a moving interpretation of the culture of the Kuranko of north-east Sierra Leone.

On historiography

C. Fyfe (ed.) *African Studies since 1945: A Tribute to Basil Davidson* (London, 1976). A pioneering collection, now rather out of date, as are the following two very influential examples of dependency theory applied to Africa:

W. Rodney, *How Europe Underdeveloped Africa* (London and Dar es Salaam, 1972), 1972).

Samir Amin, *Neo-Colonialism in West Africa* (English trans. Harmondsworth, 1973).

Caroline Neale, *Writing 'Independent' History: African Historiography 1960–1980* (Westport, 1985). A lively survey.

Igor Kopytoff (ed.), *The African Frontier: The Reproduction of Traditional African Societies* (Bloomington and Indianapolis, 1987). An attempt to apply the frontier model, so influential in studies of white settler societies, to black Africa.

A good introduction to the Mode of Production debate is:

A. Foster-Carter, 'The Modes of Production controversy', *New Left Review*, 1978, pp. 47–77; and particularly the issue of the *Canadian Journal of African Studies* devoted to the issue (1985, vol. 19, 1).

History in Africa is a journal which publishes much of the most innovative work on the methodology of African history.

The Africa Studies Review publishes major bibliographic surveys on particular themes (such as peasants, the growth of the state, or urbanisation) by leading scholars.

CHAPTER 2 (AFRICAN PREHISTORY)

This is an area where new discoveries continue to be made, often effecting considerable changes to the received wisdom on a given subject. The journal *Nature* is an excellent source for keeping up to date (there are references to specific articles in the notes to this chapter, but future issues will continue to update the subject), and major 'finds' are often reported in *Time* and *Newsweek*. The best introduction to the subject matter of Chapters 2 and 3 is:

D. W. Phillipson, *African Archaeology* (2nd edn, Cambridge, 1993). It contains a good bibliography.

CHAPTER 3 (AFRICAN PREHISTORY *c.* 10,000 TO *c.* 500 BE)

J. Mack and P. Robertshaw (eds.), *Culture History in the Southern Sudan* (Nairobi, 1982). The standard classification of African languages – the basis for all language maps of the continent and most later research is:

J. H. Greenberg, *The Languages of Africa* (3rd edn, Bloomington, 1970). Note also D. Dalby (ed.), *Language and History in Africa* (London, 1970).

For a more recent collection of essays, spanning archaeology and historical linguistics, see:

C. Ehret and M. Posnansky, *The Archaeological and Linguistic Reconstruction of African History* (Berkeley and Los Angeles, 1982).

J. Vansina, *Paths in the Rainforests: Towards a History of Political Tradition in Equatorial Africa* (Madison, 1990). The best account of early western Bantu history.

Much writing on the history of disease refers to a later period. This is true of:

G. Hartwig and K. D. Patterson (eds.), *Disease in African History* (Durham, N.C., 1978) and

K. F. Kiple and V. H. King, *Another Dimension to the Black Diaspora: Diet, Disease, and Racism* (Cambridge, 1981).

See also K. F. Kiple (ed.), *The Cambridge World History of Human Disease* (Cambridge, 1993).

Thurstan Shaw et al. (eds.), *The Archaeology of Africa: Food, Metal and Towns* (London and New York, 1993) is a vast compilation – 44 chapters and over 800 pages.

A number of older collections are still of value:

J. Harlan, J. de Wet and A. Stemler (eds.), *Origins of African Plant Domestication* (The Hague, 1976).

P. Ucko and G. W. Dimbleby (eds.), *The Domestication and Exploitation of Plants and Animals* (London, 1969).

Note also valuable studies on the history of pastoralism:

Andrew B. Smith, *Pastoralism in Africa: Origins and Development Ecology* (London, 1992) and

P. Bonte and J. Galaty, *Herders, Warriors and Traders: Pastoralism in Africa* (Boulder, 1991).

CHAPTER 5 (COPPER AND IRON)

Eugenia Herbert, *Red Gold of Africa: Copper in Precolonial History and Culture* (Madison, 1984).

Eugenia Herbert, *Iron, Gender and Power* (Bloomington 1993).

R. Haaland and P. Shinnie (eds.), *African Iron Working – Ancient and Traditional* (Oslo, 1985) and

T. A. Wertime and J. D. Muhly, *The Coming of the Age of Iron* (New Haven, 1980).

CHAPTERS 7 AND 21 (CENTRAL AFRICA)

J. Vansina, *Paths in the Rainforests: Towards a History of Political Tradition in Equatorial Africa* (Madison, 1990) is an indispensable starting point, as is:

D. Birmingham and P. M. Martin (eds.), *History of Central Africa* (Harlow, 1986 reprint) volume I.

There is a considerable body of important studies of particular states and peoples. Deservedly famous books include:

J. Vansina, *The Children of Woot: A History of the Kuba Peoples* (Madison, 1978);

R. Harms, *River of Wealth, River of Sorrow: The Central Zaire Basin in the Era of the Slave and Ivory Trade, 1500–1891* (New Haven and London, 1981). A study of the Bobangi, canoe traders on the Zaire and Ubangi;

J. Miller, *Kings and Kinsmen: Early Mbundu States in Angola* (London, 1976);

J. Miller, *Way of Death: Merchant Capitalism and the Angolan Slave Trade 1730–1830* (London, 1988) – a monumental study of the impact of Atlantic trade on Angola;

T. Q. Reefe, *The Rainbow and the Kings: A History of the Luba Empire to 1891* (Berkeley and Los Angeles, 1981).

Much has been written on the Kongo kingdom; the indispensable starting point is to be found in:

J. Thornton, *The Kingdom of Kongo Civil War and Transition 1641–1718* (Wisconsin, 1983) and

A. Hilton, *The Kingdom of Kongo* (Oxford, 1985).

K. D. Patterson, *The Northern Gabon Coast to 1874* (Oxford, 1975).

P. Martin, *The External Trade of the Loango Coast 1576–1870* (Oxford, 1972), pp. 52ff.

D. Birmingham, *Trade and Conflict in Angola* (Oxford, 1966).

W. G. Clarence-Smith, *Slaves, Peasants and Capitalists in Southern Angola* (Cambridge, 1979).

On East Central Africa note:

G. Prins, *The Hidden Hippopotamus* (Cambridge, 1980) on the Lozi, for whom see also:

M. Mainga, *Bulozi under the Luyana Kings* (London, 1973).

D. N. Beach, *The Shona and Zimbabwe 900–1850* (London, 1980).

A. D. Roberts, *A History of Zambia* (London, 1976).

Bridglal Pachai (ed.), *Malawi: The History of the Nation* (London, 1973).

Martin Hall, *The Changing Past: Farmers, Kings, and Traders in Southern Africa, 200–1860* (Cape Town, 1987) is an extremely clear and interesting account by an archaeologist. It includes ancient Zimbabwe.

Some excellent studies of religious change have appeared. For an outstanding study of a cult in the Zaire basin, see:

J. Janzen, *Lemba: A Drum of Affliction in Africa and the New World* (New York and London, 1982).

In East Central Africa, see:

J. M. Schoffeleers, *River of Blood* (Madison, 1992) and J. M. Schoffeleers (ed.), *Guardians of the Land* (Salisbury [Harare], 1979).

On long-distance trade, see:

R. Gray and D. Birmingham (eds.), *Pre-Colonial African Trade* (New York, 1970), and

E. Alpers, *Ivory and Slaves in East Central Africa* (London, 1975).

CHAPTERS 8 AND 23 (EAST AND EAST CENTRAL AFRICA)

T. Spear, *Kenya's Past: An Introduction to Historical Method in Africa* (Harlow, 1981), makes excellent use of language data. Note also:

D. Nurse and T. Spear, *The Swahili* (Philadelphia, 1985), a good starting point to a much-studied subject.

Two older collections, which are still of some value, are:

A. Roberts (ed.), *Tanzania before 1900* (Nairobi, 1966).

B. A. Ogot, (ed.), *Kenya before 1900: Eight Regional Studies* (Nairobi, 1986 reprint).

There are excellent monographs on particular states and peoples, often making extensive use of oral tradition. Note:

S. Feierman, *The Shambaa Kingdom: A History* (Madison, 1974).

G. Hartwig, *The Art of Survival in East Africa: The Kerebe and Long Distance Trade, 1800–1895* (New York, 1976).

D. W. Cohen, *The Historical Tradition of Busoga Mukama and Kintu* (Oxford, 1972).

B. Ogot, *History of the Southern Luo* (Nairobi, 1976).

S. Karugire, *A History of the Kingdom of Knore in Western Uganda to 1896*, (Oxford, 1971).

M. S. M. Kiwanuka, *A History of Buganda* (London, 1971).

G. Muriuki, *A History of Kikuyu 1500–1900* (Nairobi, 1974).

A recent and original collection, on East Africa and the region to its north, is to be found in:

D. Johnson and D. Anderson, *The Ecology of Survival: Case Studies from Northeast African History* (London, 1988).

J. Iliffe, *A Modern History of Tanzania* (Cambridge, 1979) – mainly on a later period, but the first chapter is relevant to the time span of this book.

On religious change, note:

I. Berger, *Religion and Resistance: East African Kingdoms in the Precolonial Period* (Tervuren, 1981).

On trade, note:

R. Gray and D. Birmingham (eds.), *Pre-Colonial African Trade* (New York, 1970) and

E. Alpers, *Ivory and Slaves in East Central Africa* (London, 1975).

A. Sheriff, *Slaves, Spices and Ivory in Zanzibar* (London, 1987).

C. H. Ambler, *Kenyan Communities in the Age of Imperialism* (New Haven, 1988), is an important book dealing with a slightly later period. Note also:

F. Cooper, *Plantation Slavery on the East Coast of Africa* (New Haven, 1977).

CHAPTERS 9 AND 22 (SOUTHERN AFRICA)

Good introductions:

Martin Hall, *The Changing Past: Farmers, Kings, and Traders in Southern Africa, 200–1860* (Cape Town, 1987) – an archaeologist's perspective.

Leonard Thompson, *A History of South Africa* (New Haven, 1990).

J. D. Omer-Cooper, *A History of Southern Africa* (London, 1987).

L. Thompson (ed.), *African Societies in Southern Africa* (London, 1969) (older, but some useful sections).

For contrasting views of the San, see:

R. Lee, *The !Kung San: Men, Women and Work in a Foraging Society* (Cambridge, 1979) and

E. Wilmsen, *Land Filled with Flies: A Political Economy of the Kalahari* (Chicago, 1989).

There are some fine studies of southern Africa's rock art:

P. Vinnicombe, *People of the Eland* (Pietermaritzburg, 1976) and

D. Lewis-Williams and T. Dowson, *Images of Power* (Johannesburg, 1985).

There is a very rich literature on South Africa from the seventeenth century on, in part reflecting the abundant source material:

E. Elphick and H. Gilomee (eds.), *The Shaping of South African Society 1652–1820* (2nd edn, Cape Town, 1979) is the best starting point.

Note also:

R. Elphick, *Kraal and Castle; Khoikhoi and the Peopling of White South Africa* (2nd edn, Johannesburg, 1985).

R. Ross, *Cape of Torments: Slavery and Resistance in South Africa* (London, 1983).

S. Marks and A. Atmore (eds.), *Economy and Society in Pre-Industrial South Africa* (London, 1980).

S. Marks and R. Rathbone (eds.), *Industrialisation and Social Change in South Africa* (Harlow, 1982) covers a later period.

J. D. Omer-Cooper, *The Zulu Aftermath* (London, 1966) – a pioneering study, now outdated.

Cf. J. B. Peires (ed.), *Before and after Shaka* (Grahamstown, 1983).

J. Cobbing, 'The Mfecane as alibi: thought on Dithakong and Mbolompo', *Journal of African History*, 1988, pp. 496ff. and

E. Eldridge, 'Sources of conflict in southern Africa, ca. 1800–1830: the 'Mfecane' reconsidered', *Journal of African History*, 1992, pp. 15ff.

Leonard Thompson, *Survival in Two Worlds: Moshoeshoe of Lesotho, 1786–1870* (Oxford, 1975).

A more recent study of the Sotho is E. A. Eldridge, *A South African Kingdom* (Cambridge, 1993).

B. Peires, *The House of Phalo: A History of the Xhosa People in the Days of Their Independence* (Berkeley, 1982).

P. Delius, *The Land Belongs to Us: The Pedi Polity, the Boers and the British in the Nineteenth Century Transvaal* (London, 1984).

P. Bonner, *Kings, Commoners and Concessionaires: the Evolution and Dissolution of the Nineteenth-Century Swazi State* (Cambridge, 1983).

I. Schapera, *Tribal Innovators: Tswana Chiefs and Social Change* (London, 1970).

C. Bundy, *The Rise and Fall of the South African Peasantry* (London, 1979).

CHAPTER 10 (NORTHERN AFRICA IN ANTIQUITY)

The best account of northern Africa in the ancient world is to be found in the relevant chapters of the first two volumes of *The Cambridge History of Africa*.

The chapters on Egypt in vol. I were reprinted as B. G. Trigger et al., *Ancient Egypt: A Social History* (Cambridge, 1983).

Those who require a straightforward overview of ancient Egypt should consult C. Aldred, *The Egyptians* (rev. edn, London, 1984). One of its strengths is its excellent line drawings.

A recent interpretation of the early period is A. J. Spencer, *Early Egypt: The Rise of Civilisation in the Nile Valley* (London, 1993).

A. K. Bowman, *Egypt after the Pharaohs* (Berkeley, 1986) is the standard account of this subject.

W. Y. Adams, *Nubia: Corridor to Africa* (Princeton, 1977) – a huge, definitive study ranging from the origins of human settlement to modern times.

P. L. Shinnie, *Meroe: A Civilisation of the Sudan* (London, 1967).

S. Munro-Hay, *Aksum* (Edinburgh, 1991).

For a recent introduction to the early church in northern Africa, see Chapter 1 of E. Isichei, *A History of Christianity in Africa from Antiquity to the Present* (London, 1995); see also:

W. H. C. Frend, 'The Christian period in Mediterranean Africa *c*. AD 200 to 700', *Cambridge History of Africa*, II, pp. 410ff. – a good overview.

W. H. C. Frend, *The Donatist Church* (2nd edn, Oxford, 1971). Its thesis has been much debated. Frend reflects on this in his 'The Donatist church – forty years on', in C. Landman and D. Whitelaw (eds.), *Windows on Origins* (Pretoria, 1985), pp. 71ff.

W. H. C. Frend, *The Rise of the Monophysite Movement* (Cambridge, 1972).

P. Brown, *Augustine of Hippo: A Biography* (London, 1967) – one of the best biographies of an African.

P. Brown, *Religion and Society in the Age of St Augustine* (London, 1972).

CHAPTER 11 (NORTHERN AFRICA *c*. 700 TO *c*. 1500: SOME OF THESE BOOKS ALSO COVER A LATER PERIOD)

Again, the relevant chapters in the *Cambridge History of Africa*, vols. II and III, are probably the best survey of the subject.

I. M. Lapidus, *A History of Islamic Societies* (Cambridge, 1993 reprint) – an authoritative introduction to Islamic history in general.

J. M. Abun-Nasr, *A History of the Maghrib in the Islamic Period* (revised edn, Cambridge, 1987).

M. Brett (ed.), *Northern Africa: Islam and Modernization* (London, 1973).

R. le Tourneau, *Fez in the Age of the Marinides* (Norman, Okla. 1961).

R. le Tourneau, *The Almohad Movement in North Africa in the Twelfth and Thirteenth Centuries* (Princeton, 1969).

C. Geertz, *Islam Observed: Religious Development in Morocco and Indonesia* (New Haven and London, 1968).

M. Brett and W. Forman, *The Moors: Islam in the West* (London, 1980) beautifully illustrated; also covers Muslim Spain).

R. Irwin, *The Middle East in the Middle Ages: The Early Mamluk Sultanate 1250–1382* (Cambridge, 1986).

Yusuf Fadl Hasan, *The Arabs and the Sudan: From the Seventh to the Early Sixteenth Century* (Edinburgh, 1967).

N. R. Keddie and B. Baron (eds.), *Women in Middle Eastern History: Shifting Boundaries in Sex and Gender* (New Haven and London, 1991). Includes good material on Egypt.

A. Ehrenkreuz, *Saladin* (Albany, 1972).

W. Y. Adams, *Nubia: Corridor to Africa* (Princeton, 1977).

CHAPTER 15 (NORTHERN AFRICA FROM *c.* 1500 TO *c.* 1870) AND CHAPTER
12 (THE NORTH-EAST)

Again, there is excellent material in the *Cambridge History of Africa*.

A. Laroui, *The History of the Maghrib: An Interpretive Essay* (Eng. trans. Princeton, 1977).

C. Issawi, *An Economic History of the Middle East and North Africa* (London, 1982).

P. M. Holt, *Egypt and the Fertile Crescent 1526–1922: A Political History* (London, 1966).

R. Hess, *The Forgotten Frontier: A History of the Sixteenth-Century Ibero-African Frontier* (Chicago and London, 1978).

R. Rabinow, *Symbolic Domination, Cultural Form and Historical Change in Morocco* (Chicago, 1975).

W. Spencer, *Algiers in the Age of the Corsairs* (Norman, Okla., 1976).

L. Valensi, *Tunisian Peasants in the Eighteenth and Nineteenth Centuries* (1977, Eng. trans. Cambridge, 1985).

On the nineteenth century in Egypt and the Maghrib

M. Morsy, *North Africa 1800–1900: A Survey from the Nile Valley to the Atlantic* (London and New York, 1984) – a clear and excellent introduction.

P. J. Vatikiotis, *The History of Egypt from Muhammad Ali to Sadat* (2nd edn, London, 1980).

A. Hourani, *Arabic Thought in the Liberal Age 1798–1939* (London, 1962).

Afaf Lutfi al-Sayyid Marsot, *Egypt in the Reign of Muhammad Ali* (Cambridge, 1984).

L. C. Brown, *The Tunisia of Ahmad Bey 1837–1855* (Princeton, 1974).

E. Burke, *Prelude to Protectorate in Morocco* (Chicago, 1976).

R. Gray, *A History of the Southern Sudan 1839–1899* (Oxford, 1961).

P. Holt, *The Mahdist State in the Sudan* (London, 1958).

On Ethiopia and Somalia note two important recent books:

D. Johnson and D. Anderson (eds.), *The Ecology of Survival: Case Studies from Northeast African History* (London and Colorado, 1988).

D. Donham and W. James, *The Southern Marches of Imperial Ethiopia: Essays in History and Social Anthropology* (Cambridge, 1986).

For an earlier period, note Taddesse Tamrat, *Church and State in Ethiopia 1270–1527* (Oxford, 1972).

L. Cassanelli, *The Shaping of Somali Society: Reconstructing the History of a Pastoral People 1600–1900* (Philadelphia, 1982).

J. Mack and P. Robertshaw (eds.), *Culture History in the Southern Sudan* (Nairobi, 1982).

D. Levine, *Greater Ethiopia: The Evolution of a Multiethnic Society* (Chicago, 1974).

A general book which pays detailed attention to Ethiopia is J. Iliffe, *The African Poor: A History* (Cambridge, 1987).

Mordechai Abir, *Ethiopia: The Era of the Princes: The Challenge of Islam and Re-Unification of the Christian Empire, 1769–1855* (New York, 1968).

S. Rubenson, *King of Kings: Tewodros of Ethiopia* (Addis Ababa, 1966).

CHAPTERS 13 AND 16 (THE WESTERN SUDAN)

J. F. A. Ajayi and M. Crowder (eds.), *History of West Africa* vol. I (3rd edn, Harlow, 1985) – a good introduction to the subject.

N. Levtzion and J. F. P. Hopkins (eds.) *Corpus of Early Arabic Sources for West African History* (Cambridge, 1981) – superb collection of source material.

The important archaeological research of S. K. and R. J. McIntosh on the Jenne area is most easily accessed through their journal articles, such as S. K. and R. J. McIntosh, 'West African prehistory', *American Scientist*, 1981, pp. 601–13 and S. K. McIntosh and R. J. McIntosh, 'Current directions in West African prehistory', *Annual Review of Anthropology*, 1983, pp. 245–9.

G. Connah, *Three Thousand Years in Africa* (Cambridge, 1981) describes research at Daimah, near Lake Chad.

N. Levtzion, *Ancient Ghana and Mali* (London, 1973).

N. Levtzion and J. Voll, *Eighteenth Century Renewal And Reform in Islam* (Syracuse, N.Y., 1987).

H. T. Norris, *Saharan Myth and Saga* (Oxford, 1972) – a classic, dealing with the mythical world of Saharan peoples.

M. Adamu, *The Hausa Factor in West African History* (Zaria, 1978).

R. L. Roberts, *Warriors Merchants and Slaves: The State and the Economy in the Middle Niger Valley, 1700–1914* (Stanford, 1987).

M. Klein, *Islam and Imperialism in Senegal: Sine-Saloum 1847–1914* (Stanford, 1968).

D. Robinson, *Chiefs and Clerics* (Oxford, 1975), p. 1.

P. D. Curtin, *Economic Change in Precolonial Africa: Senegambia in the Era of the Slave Trade* (Madison, 1975).

J. R. Willis (ed.), *Studies in West Africa Islamic History: The Cultivators of Islam* (London, 1979).

D. Robinson, *Chiefs and Clerics: The History of Abdul Bokar Kan and Futa Toro 1853–1891* (Oxford, 1975).

D. Robinson, *The Holy War of Umar Tal* (Oxford, 1985).

M. Hiskett, *Sword of Truth: The Life and Times of the Shehu Usuman dan Fodio* (New York, 1973).

S. Abubakar, *The Lamibe of Fombina: A Political History of Adamawa 1809–1901* (Zaria, 1977).

Y. B. Usman, *The Transformation of Katsina* (Zaria, 1981).

D. M. Last, *The Sokoto Caliphate* (London, 1967).

Y. Person is the leading authority on Samori; he is the author of a magisterial three-volume study, *Damori: une révolution Dyula* (3 vols., Dakar, 1968–75); for a more accessible and short version in English, see his 'Samori and resistance to the French', in R. Rotberg and A. Mazrui, *Protest and Power in Black Africa* (New York, 1970), pp. 80ff. and 'Guinea-Samori', in M. Crowder (ed.), *West African Resistance* (London, 1971).

P. Lovejoy, *Caravans of Kola: The Hausa Kola Trade 1700–1900* (Zaria, 1980).

CHAPTERS 14, 19 AND 20 (WEST AFRICA)

Useful general texts include:

J. F. A. Ajayi and M. Crowder (eds.), *History of West Africa*, vols. I (3rd edn, Harlow, 1985) and II (London, 1974).

E. Isichei, *History of West Africa since 1800* (London and Basingstoke, 1977).

A. Hopkins, *An Economic History of West Africa* (London, 1973).

Fine studies by archival historians.

R. Law, *The Oyo Empire 1600–1836: A West African Imperialism in the Era of the Atlantic Slave Trade* (Oxford, 1977).

R. Law, *The Slave Coast of West Africa 1550–1750* (Oxford, 1991).

A. F. C. Ryder, *Benin and the Europeans* (London, 1969).

Walter Rodney, *A History of the Upper Guinea Coast, 1550–1750* (Oxford, 1970).

There is a rich literature on West African visual arts; it includes:

F. Willett, *Ife in the History of West African Sculpture* (London, 1967).

Denis Williams, *Icon and Image: A Study of Sacred and Secular Forms of African Classical Art* (London, 1974).

Thurstan Shaw, *Nigeria: Its Archaeology and Early History* (London, 1978).

R. F. Thompson, *African Art in Motion* (Los Angeles, 1974).

P. Ben-Amos, *The Art of Benin* (London, 1980).

E. Isichei, *A History of Nigeria* (Harlow, 1983) – a major thematic history, which discusses art, religion, economic change and much more.

On small-scale societies, see:

E. Isichei (ed.), *Studies in the History of Plateau State, Nigeria* (London, 1982).

E. Isichei, *The Ibo People and the Europeans* (London, 1973) and *A History of the Igbo People* (London and Basingstoke, 1976).

R. Henderson, *The King in Every Man* (New Haven and London, 1972) – a superb story of a single Igbo town.

D. Northrup, *Trade without Rulers* (Oxford, 1978).

A. J. H. Latham, *Old Calabar 1600–1891* (London, 1973).

D. Forde and P. Kaberry (eds.), *West African Kingdoms in the Nineteenth Century* (London, 1969 reprint).

R. Kea, *Settlements, Trade and Politics in the Seventeenth-Century Gold Coast* (Baltimore and London, 1982).

For contrasting views of Asante, see:

I. Wilks, *Asante in the Nineteenth Century* (Cambridge, 2nd edn, 1989) and

T. C. McCaskie, *State and Society in Asante* (Cambridge, 1995).

M. McCarthy, *Social Change and the Growth of British Power in the Gold Coast* (Lanham, 1983).

D. Kimble, *A Political History of Ghana: The Rise of Gold Coast Nationalism* (Oxford, 1963) – a classic of enduring value.

On Sierra Leone and Liberia:

C. Fyfe, *A History of Sierra Leone* (London, 1962).

J. Peterson, *Province of Freedom: A History of Sierra Leone 1787–1870* (London, 1969).

K. Wylie, *The Political Kingdoms of the Temne: Temne Government in Sierra Leone, 1825–1910* (New York, 1977).

T. Shick, *Behold the Promised Land: A History of Afro-American Settler Society in Nineteenth Century Liberia* (Baltimore, 1977).

CHAPTER 18 (THE ATLANTIC SLAVE TRADE)

P. D. Curtin, *The Rise and Fall of the Plantation Complex* (Cambridge, 1990).

H. Gemery and J. Hogendorn, *The Uncommon Market: Essays in the Economic History of the Atlantic Slave Trade* (New York, 1979).

P. D. Curtin, *The Atlantic Slave Trade: A Census* (Madison, 1969). A Pioneering classic, which inspired much later research.

P. Lovejoy, *Transformations in Slavery* (Cambridge, 1983).

D. Eltis and J. Walvin (eds.), *The Abolition of the Atlantic Slave Trade* (Madison, 1981).

D. Eltis, *Economic Growth and the Ending of the Transatlantic Slave Trade* (New York, 1987).

P. Lovejoy, *Transformations in Slavery: A History of Slavery in Africa* (Cambridge, 1983).

P. Lovejoy (ed.), *The Ideology of Slavery in Africa* (Beverly Hills, 1981).

P. Manning, *Slavery and African Life* (Cambridge, 1990).

J. Inikori (ed.), *Forced Migrations* (London, 1982).

J. Thornton, *Africa and Africans in the Making of the Atlantic World, 1400–1680* (Cambridge, 1992).

A. W. Crosby, *The Columban Exchange: Biological and Cultural Consequences of 1492* (Westport, Conn., 1973 edition).

CHAPTER 17 (THE CENTRAL SUDAN)

D. Cordell, 'The Savanna belt of north-central Africa', in D. Birmingham and P. M. Martin (eds.), *History of Central Africa* (Harlow, 1983), I, pp. 30 ff.

H. Fisher, 'The central Sahara and Sudan', in *Cambridge History of Africa*, IV, pp. 58ff.

R. S. O'Fahey and J. L. Spaulding, *Kingdoms of the Sudan* (London, 1974) – on the Funj and Dar Fur.

L. Brenner, *The Shehus of Kukawa* (London, 1973).

A. Singer and B. Street (eds.), *Zande Themes* (Oxford, 1972).

D. Cordell, 'Eastern Libya, Wadi and the Sanusiya: a tariqa and a trade route', *Journal of African History*, 1977, pp. 21ff.

R. Collins, 'Sudanese factors in the history of the Congo', in Yusuf Fadl Hasan (ed.), *Sudan in Africa* (Khartoum, 1971), pp. 156ff.

Index